HTML

The Definitive Guide

HTML
The Definitive Guide

Second Edition

Chuck Musciano and Bill Kennedy

O'REILLY™

Cambridge · Köln · Paris · Sebastopol · Tokyo

HTML: The Definitive Guide, Second Edition
by Chuck Musciano and Bill Kennedy

Copyright © 1997, 1996 O'Reilly & Associates, Inc. All rights reserved.
Printed in the United States of America.

Editor: Mike Loukides

Production Editor: Nancy Wolfe Kotary

Printing History:

April 1996:	First Edition.
July 1996:	Minor corrections. Updated for HTML 3.2.
May 1997:	Second Edition.

This book is printed on acid-free paper with 85% recycled content, 15% post-consumer waste. O'Reilly & Associates is committed to using paper with the highest recycled content available consistent with high quality.

ISBN: 1-56592-235-2 [7/97]*

This book is dedicated to our wives and children,

Cindy, Courtney, and Cole, and

Jeanne, Eva, and Ethan.

Without their love and patience
we never would have had
the time or strength to write.

Table of Contents

Preface

Learning Hypertext Markup Language—most commonly known by its acronym, HTML—is like learning any new language, computer or human. Most students first immerse themselves in examples. Think how adept you'd become if Mom, Dad, your brothers, and sisters all spoke fluent HTML. Studying others is a natural way to learn, making learning easy and fun. Our advice to anyone wanting to learn HTML is to get out there on the World Wide Web with a suitable browser and see for yourself what looks good, what's effective, what works for you. Examine others' HTML source files and ponder the possibilities. Mimicry is how many of the current webmasters have learned the language.

Imitation can take you only so far, though. Examples can be both good and bad. Learning by example will help you talk the talk, but not walk the walk. To become truly conversant, you must learn how to use the language appropriately in many different situations. You could learn that by example, if you live long enough.

Remember, too, that computer-based languages are more explicit than human languages. You've got to get the HTML syntax correct, or it won't work. Then, too, there is the problem of "standards." Committees of academics and industry experts try to define the proper syntax and usage of a computer language like HTML. The problem is that HTML browser manufacturers like Netscape and Microsoft choose what parts of the standard they will use and which parts they will ignore. They even make up their own parts, which may eventually become standards.

To be safe, the better way to become fluent in HTML is through a comprehensive language reference: a resource that covers the language syntax, semantics, and variations in detail, and helps you distinguish between good and bad usage.

There's one more step leading to fluency in a language. To become a true master of HTML, you need to develop your own style. That means knowing not only what is appropriate, but what is effective. Layout matters. A lot. So does the order of presentation within a document, between documents, and between document collections.

Our goal in writing this book is to help you become fluent in HTML, fully versed in the language's syntax, semantics, and elements of style. We take the natural learning approach with examples: good ones, of course. We cover every element of the currently accepted version (3.2) of the language in detail, as well as all of the current "extensions" supported by the popular HTML browsers, explaining how each element works and how it interacts with all the other elements.

And, with all due respect to Strunk and White, throughout the book we give you suggestions for style and composition to help you decide how best to use the language and accomplish a variety of tasks, from simple online documentation to complex marketing and sales presentations. We'll show you what works and what doesn't; what makes sense to those who view your pages, and what might be confusing.

In short, this book is a complete guide to creating documents using HTML, starting with basic syntax and semantics, and finishing with broad style directions that should help you create beautiful, informative, accessible documents that you'll be proud to deliver to your browsers.

Our Audience

We wrote this book for anyone interested in learning and using HTML, from the most casual user to the full-time design professional. We don't expect you to have any experience in the language before picking up this book. In fact, we don't even expect that you've ever browsed the World Wide Web, although we'd be surprised if you haven't at least experimented with this technology. Being connected to the Internet is not necessary to use this book, but if you're not connected, this book becomes like a travel guide for the homebound.

The only things we ask you to have are a computer, a text editor that can create simple ASCII text files, and copies of the latest, leading World Wide Web browsers—Netscape and Internet Explorer. Because HTML is stored in a universally accepted format—ASCII text—and because the language is completely independent of any specific computer, we won't even make an assumption about the kind of computer you're using. However, browsers do vary by platform and operating system, which means your HTML documents can and often do look quite different depending on the computer and version of browser. We will explain how certain language features are used by various popular browsers as we go through the book, paying particular attention to how they are different.

If you are new to HTML, the World Wide Web, or hypertext documentation in general, you should start by reading Chapter 1, *HTML and the World Wide Web*. In it, we describe how all the World Wide Web technologies come together to create webs of interrelated documents.

If you are already familiar with the Web, but not HTML specifically, or if you are interested in the new features in HTML, start by reading Chapter 2, *HTML Quick Start*. This chapter is a brief overview of the most important features of the language and serves as a roadmap to how we approach the language in the remainder of the book.

Subsequent chapters deal with specific language features in a roughly top-down approach to HTML. Read them in order for a complete tour through the language, or jump around to find the exact feature you're interested in.

Text Conventions

Throughout the book, we use a `constant-width` typeface to highlight any literal element of the HTML standard, and tags and attributes. We always use lowercase letters for HTML tags. (Although the language standard is case-insensitive with regard to tag and attribute names, this isn't so for other elements like source filenames, so be careful.) We use *italic* to indicate new concepts when they are defined and those elements you need to supply when creating your own documents, such as tag attributes or user-defined strings.

We discuss elements of the language throughout the book, but you'll find each one covered in depth (some might say nauseating detail) in a shorthand, quick-reference definition box that looks like the box on the following page.

The first line of the box contains the element name, followed by a brief description of its function. Next, we list the various attributes, if any, of the element: those things that you may or must specify as part of the element.

We use the following symbols to identify tags and attributes that are not in the HTML 3.2 standard (the last official version), but are additions to the language:

N Netscape Navigator extension to the standard

O Internet Explorer extension to the standard

The description also includes the ending tag, if any, for the tag, along with a general indication if the end tag may be safely omitted in general use.

<*html*>

Function:
  Delimits a complete HTML document
Attributes:
  VERSION
End tag:
  </html>; may be omitted
Contains:
  head_tag, body_tag, frames
Used in:
  HTML documents

"Contains" names the rule in the HTML grammar that defines the elements to be placed within this tag. Similarly, "Used in" lists those rules that allow this tag as part of their content. These rules are defined in Appendix A, *HTML Grammar.*

Finally, HTML is a fairly "intertwined" language: You will occasionally use elements in different ways depending on context, and many elements share identical attributes. Wherever possible, we place a cross-reference in the text that leads you to a related discussion elsewhere in the book. These cross-references, like the one at the end of this paragraph, serve as a crude paper model of hypertext documentation, one that would be replaced with a true hypertext link should this book be delivered in an electronic format. [tag syntax, 3.3.1]

We encourage you to follow these references whenever possible. Often, we'll only cover an attribute briefly and expect you to jump to the cross-reference for a more detailed discussion. In other cases, following the link will take you to alternative uses of the element under discussion, or to style and usage suggestions that relate to the current element.

Is HTML 3.2 Really a Big Deal?

Depending on our mood, when people ask us about the "new" HTML 3.2 standard, we respond with a groan, a bemused smile, or uproarious laughter. Folks, HTML 3.2 doesn't shake any Web foundations. In fact, the new language standard simply confirms what most Web observers have known for some time now, that the browser manufacturers wag the tail of the HTML standards dog.

Until about mid-1995, people actually were serious about HTML standards. (Some of us still are.) Until then, standards guided the development of new browsers. After release of HTML 2.0, however, the elders of the World Wide Web Consortium (W3C) responsible for such language-standards matters lost control. The abortive HTML+ standard never got off the ground, and HTML 3.0 became so bogged down in debate that the W3C simply shelved the entire draft standard. HTML 3.0 never happened, despite what some opportunistic marketers claim in their literature.

What mired the development of new language standards was Netscape Navigator. Most Web analysts agree that Netscape's quick success in becoming the browser of choice for an overwhelming majority of users can be attributed directly to the company's implementation of useful and exciting additions to HTML. Today, all other browser manufacturers—in particular, the behemoth Microsoft Corp. who appreciates the meaning of "de facto standard" better than anyone in the business—have to implement Netscape's HTML extensions if they expect to have any chance of competing in the web browser marketplace. By pushing the W3C to officially release HTML standard version 3.2, which for all intents and purposes standardizes most of Netscape's language extensions, the other browser manufacturers gain legitimacy for their products without having to acknowledge the leading competitor. Internet Explorer can now be "HTML 3.2–compliant," rather than submissively "Netscape Navigator–compliant."

The paradox is that the HTML 3.2 standard is *not* the definitive resource. There are many more features of the language in popular use by both Netscape and/or Internet Explorer than are included in this latest language standard. We promise you, things can get downright confusing when trying to sort it all out.

We've managed to sort things out, so you don't have to sweat over what works with what browser and what doesn't work. This book, therefore, is the definitive guide to HTML. We give details for all the elements of the HTML 3.2 standard, plus the variety of interesting and useful extensions to the language—some proposed standards—that the popular browser manufacturers have chosen to include in their products, such as:

- Cascading Style Sheets
- Frames
- Layers
- Text font size and face controls
- Java and JavaScript
- Inline multimedia
- Spacers
- Multiple columns

And while we tell you about each and every feature of the language, standard or not, we also tell you which browsers or different versions of the same browser implement a particular extension and which don't. That's critical knowledge when you want to create web pages that take advantage of the latest version of Netscape Navigator versus pages that are accessible to the larger number of people using Internet Explorer, Mosaic, or even Lynx, a popular text-only browser for UNIX systems.

In addition, there are a few things that are closely related but not directly part of HTML. For example, we touch, but do not handle CGI and Java programming. CGI and Java programs work closely with HTML documents and run with or alongside browsers, but are not part of the language itself, so we don't delve into them. Besides, they are comprehensive topics that deserve their own books, such as *CGI Programming on the World Wide Web* and *Java in a Nutshell* from O'Reilly & Associates, for instance.

In short, this book is your definitive guide to HTML as it is and should be used, including every extension we could find. Many aren't documented anywhere, even in the plethora of online guides. But, if we've missed anything, certainly let us know and we'll put it in the next edition.

We'd Like to Hear From You

We have tested and verified all of the information in this book to the best of our ability, but you may find that features have changed (or even that we have made mistakes!). Please let us know about any errors you find, as well as your suggestions for future editions, by writing:

O'Reilly & Associates, Inc.
101 Morris Street
Sebastopol, CA 95472
1-800-998-9938 (in the U.S. or Canada)
1-707-829-0515 (international/local)
1-707-829-0104 (FAX)

Since the HTML standards and browser additions to the language are evolving so rapidly, some of the information in this book may be slightly out of date by the time you read it. Please check out updates and corrections at *http://www.ora.com/ info/html/*.

You can also send us messages electronically. To be put on the mailing list or request a catalog, send email to:

nuts@ora.com

To ask technical questions or comment on the book, send email to:

bookquestions@ora.com

Acknowledgments

We did not compose, and certainly could not have composed this book without generous contributions from many people. Our wives Jeanne and Cindy (with whom we've just become reacquainted) and our young children Eva, Ethan, Courtney, and Cole (they happened *before* we started writing) formed the front lines of support. And there are numerous neighbors, friends, and colleagues who helped by sharing ideas, testing browsers, and letting us use their equipment to explore HTML. You know who you are, and we thank you all. (Ed Bond, we'll be over soon to repair your Windows.)

We also thank our technical reviewers, Kane Scarlett, Eric Raymond, and Chris Tacy, for carefully scrutinizing our work. We took most of your keen suggestions. And we especially thank Mike Loukides, our editor, who had to bring to bear his vast experience in book publishing to keep us two mavericks corralled.

And, finally, we thank the many people at O'Reilly & Associates who poked our words into sensibility and put them onto these pages. These folks include: Nancy Wolfe Kotary, project manager and copyeditor for the book; Mike Sierra, FrameMaker specialist; Chris Reilley, technical illustrator; Edie Freedman, cover designer; Nancy Priest, interior layout designer; Seth Maislin, indexer; Madeleine Newell, for production assistance; and John Files and Sheryl Avruch, for overall quality control. Also, thanks to all the many people at O'Reilly who worked on the first edition.

1

HTML and the World Wide Web

Though it began as a military experiment and spent its adolescence as a sandbox for academics and eccentrics, recent events have transformed the worldwide network of computer networks—also known as the *Internet*—into a rapidly growing and wildly diversified community of computer users and information vendors. Today, you can bump into Internet users of nearly any and all nationalities, of any and all persuasions, from serious to frivolous individuals, from businesses to nonprofit organizations, and from born-again evangelists to pornographers.

In many ways, the World Wide Web—the open community of hypertext-enabled document servers and readers on the Internet—is responsible for the meteoric rise in the network's popularity. You, too, can become a valued member by contributing: writing HTML documents and making them available to web "surfers" worldwide.

Let's climb up the Internet family tree to gain some deeper insight into its magnificence, not only as an exercise of curiosity, but to help us better understand just who and what it is we are dealing with when we go online.

1.1 The Internet

Although popular media accounts often are confused and confusing, the concept of the Internet really is rather simple. It's a collection of networks—a network of networks—computers sharing digital information via a common set of networking and software protocols. Nearly anyone can connect their computer to the Internet and immediately communicate with other computers and users on the Net.

What is confusing about the Internet is that it can be like an oriental bazaar: it's not well organized, there are few content guides, and it can take a lot of time and technical expertise to tap its full potential.

That's because...

1.1.1 In the Beginning

The Internet began in the late 1960s as an experiment in the design of robust computer networks. The goal was to construct a network of computers that could withstand the loss of several machines without compromising the ability of the remaining ones to communicate. Funding came from the U.S. Department of Defense, which had a vested interest in building information networks that could withstand nuclear attack.

The resulting network was a marvelous technical success, but was limited in size and scope. For the most part, only defense contractors and academic institutions could gain access to what was then known as the ARPAnet (Advanced Research Projects Agency network of the Department of Defense).

With the advent of high-speed modems for digital communication over common phone lines, some individuals and organizations not directly tied to the main digital pipelines began connecting and taking advantage of the network's advanced and global communications. Nonetheless, it wasn't until these last few years (around 1993, actually) that the Internet really took off.

Several crucial events led to the meteoric rise in popularity of the Internet. First, in the early 1990s, businesses and individuals eager to take advantage of the ease and power of global digital communications finally pressured the largest computer networks on the mostly U.S. government-funded Internet to open their systems for nearly unrestricted traffic. (Remember, the network wasn't designed to route information based on content—meaning that commercial messages went through university computers that at the time forbade such activity.)

True to their academic traditions of free exchange and sharing, many of the orig-inal Internet members continued to make substantial portions of their electronic collections of documents and software available to the newcomers—free for the taking! Global communications, a wealth of free software and information: who could resist?

Well, frankly, the Internet was a tough row to hoe back then. Getting connected and using the various software tools, if they were even available for their computers, presented an insurmountable technology barrier for most people. And most available information was plain-vanilla ASCII about academic subjects, not the neatly packaged fare that attracts users to the online services, such as America

Online, Prodigy, or CompuServe. The Internet was just too disorganized and, outside of the government and academia, few people had the knowledge or interest to learn how to use the arcane software or had the time to spend rummaging through documents looking for ones of interest.

1.1.2 HTML and the World Wide Web

It took another spark to light the Internet rocket. At about the same time the Internet opened up for business, some physicists at CERN, the European Particle Physics Laboratory, released an authoring language and distribution system they developed for creating and sharing multimedia-enabled, integrated electronic documents over the Internet. And so was born *Hypertext Markup Language* (HTML), browser software, and the World Wide Web. No longer did authors have to distribute their work as fragmented collections of pictures, sounds, and text. HTML unified those elements. Moreover, the World Wide Web's systems enabled *hypertext linking*, whereby documents automatically reference other documents, located anywhere around the world: less rummaging, more productive time online.

Lift-off happened when some bright students and faculty at the National Center for Supercomputing Applications (NCSA) at the University of Illinois, Urbana-Champaign wrote a web browser called Mosaic. Although designed primarily for viewing HTML documents, the software also had built-in tools to access the much more prolific resources on the Internet, such as FTP archives of software and Gopher-organized collections of documents.

With versions based on easy-to-use graphical-user interfaces familiar to most computer owners, Mosaic became an instant success. It, like most Internet software, was available on the Net for free.* Millions of users snatched up a copy and began surfing the Internet for "cool web pages."

1.1.3 Golden Threads

There you have the history of the Internet and the World Wide Web in a nutshell: from rags to riches in just two short years. The Internet has spawned an entirely new medium for worldwide information exchange and commerce, and its pioneers are profiting well. For instance, when the marketers caught on to the fact that they could cheaply produce and deliver eye-catching, wow-and-whizbang commercials

---

* Not all browsers are free, nor are all browsers free to everyone. Various client browser and server software is commercially available, including documentation and support. Internet "bundled" software sold through mail order or retail often contains a licensed copy of one of the popular browsers like Netscape or Internet Explorer, possibly customized for the package. Moreover, the browsers available for download over the Internet typically contain licensing agreements which stipulate that the software is free only for use by non-profit organizations.

and product catalogs to those millions of Web surfers around the world, there was no stopping the stampede of blue suede shoes. Even the key developers of Mosaic and related web server technologies sensed potential riches. They left NCSA and formed Netscape Communications to produce the Netscape Navigator browser and web server software that is useful for Internet commercial activity.

Business users and marketing opportunities have helped invigorate the Internet and fuel its phenomenal growth, particularly on the World Wide Web. According to a recent marketing survey by *Activ*Media, Inc. (Peterborough, NH), over half of Internet enterprises become profitable within a year of launch! But do not forget that the Internet is first and foremost a place for social interaction and information sharing, not a strip mall or direct advertising medium. Internet users, particularly the old-timers, adhere to commonly held, but not formally codified, rules of *netiquette* that prohibit such things as "spamming" special-interest newsgroups with messages unrelated to the topic at hand or sending unsolicited email. And there are millions of users ready to remind you of those rules should you inadvertently or intentionally ignore them.

And, certainly, the power of HTML and network distribution of information go well beyond marketing and monetary rewards: serious informational pursuits also benefit. Publications, complete with images and other media like executable software, can get to their intended audience in a blink of an eye, instead of the months traditionally required for printing and mail delivery. Education takes a great leap forward when students gain access to the great libraries of the world. And at times of leisure, the interactive capabilities of HTML links can reinvigorate our otherwise television-numbed minds.

1.2 *Talking the Internet Talk*

Every computer connected to the Internet (even a beat-up old Apple II) has a unique address: a number whose format is defined by the *Internet Protocol (IP)*, the standard that defines how messages are passed from one machine to another on the Net. An *IP address* is made up of four numbers, each less than 255, joined together by periods, such as 192.12.248.73 or 131.58.97.254.

While computers deal only with numbers, people prefer names. For this reason, each computer on the Internet also has a name bestowed upon it by its owner. There are several million machines on the Net, so it would be very difficult to come up with that many unique names, let alone keep track of them all. Recall, though, that the Internet is a network of networks. It is divided into groups known as *domains*, which are further divided into one or more *subdomains*. So, while you might choose a very common name for your computer, it becomes unique when you append, like surnames, all of the machine's domain names as a period-separated suffix, creating a *fully qualified* domain name.

This naming stuff is easier than it sounds. For example, the fully qualified domain name *www.ora.com* translates to a machine named "www" that's part of the domain known as "ora," which, in turn, is part of the commercial (com) branch of the Internet. Other branches of the Internet include educational (edu) institutions, nonprofit organizations (org), U.S. government (gov), and Internet service providers (net). Computers and networks outside the United States have a two-letter abbreviation at the end of their names: for example, "ca" for Canada, "jp" for Japan, and "uk" for the United Kingdom.

Special computers, known as *name servers*, keep tables of machine names and their associated unique IP numerical addresses, and translate one into the other for us and for our machines. Domain names must be registered with the nonprofit organization InterNIC. Once registered, the owner of the domain name broadcasts it and its address to other domain name servers around the world. Each domain and subdomain has an associated name server, so ultimately every machine is known uniquely by both a name and an IP address.

1.2.1 Clients, Servers, and Browsers

The Internet connects two kinds of computers: *servers*, which serve up documents, and *clients*, which retrieve and display documents for us humans. Things that happen on the server machine are said to be on the *server side*, while activities on the client machine occur on the *client side*.

To access and display HTML documents, we run programs called *browsers* on our client computers. These browser clients talk to special *web servers* over the Internet to access and retrieve electronic documents.

Several Web browsers are available—most are free—each offering a different set of features. For example, browsers like Lynx run on character-based clients and display documents only as text. Others run on clients with graphical displays and render documents using proportional fonts and color graphics on a 1024×768, 24-bit-per-pixel display. Others still—Netscape Navigator, Microsoft's Internet Explorer, NCSA Mosaic, Netcom's WebCruiser, and InterCon's NetShark, to name a few—have special features that allow you to retrieve and display a variety of electronic documents over the Internet, including audio and video multimedia.

1.2.2 The Flow of Information

All web activity begins on the client side, when a user starts their browser. The browser begins by loading a *home page* HTML document from either local storage or from a server over some network, such as the Internet. In the latter case, the client browser first consults a domain name server to translate the home page document server's name, such as *www.ora.com*, into an IP address, before sending a request to that server over the Internet. This request (and the server's reply) is formatted according to the dictates of the *HyperText Transfer Protocol* (HTTP) standard.

A server spends most of its time listening to the Internet, waiting for document requests with the server's unique address stamped on it. Upon receipt, the server verifies that the requesting browser is allowed to retrieve documents from the server and, if so, checks for the requested document. If found, the server sends (downloads) the document to the browser. The server usually logs the request, the client computer's name, document requested, and the time.

Back on the browser, the document arrives. If it's a plain-vanilla ASCII text file, most browsers display it in a common, plain-vanilla way. Document directories, too, are treated like plain documents, although most graphical browsers will display folder icons, which the user can select with the mouse to download the contents of subdirectories.

Browsers also retrieve binary files from a server. Unless assisted by a *helper* program or specially enabled by *plug-in* software or *applets*, which display an image or video file or play an audio file, the browser usually stores downloaded binary files directly on a local disk for later attention by the user.

For the most part, however, the browser retrieves a special document that appears to be a plain text file, but contains both text and special markup codes called *tags*. The browser processes these HTML documents, formatting the text based upon the tags and downloading special accessory files, such as images.

The user reads the document, selects a hyperlink to another document, and the entire process starts over.

1.2.3 Beneath the World Wide Web

We should point out at this juncture that browsers and HTTP servers need not be part of the Internet's World Wide Web to function. In fact, you never need to be connected to the Internet, or to any network for that matter, to write HTML documents and operate a browser. You can load up and display on your client browser locally stored HTML documents and accessory files directly. This isolation is good: it gives you the opportunity to finish, in the editorial sense of the word, a document collection for later distribution. Diligent HTML authors work locally to write and proof their documents before releasing them for general distribution, thereby sparing readers the agonies of broken image files and bogus hyperlinks.*

---

* Vigorous testing of the HTML documents once they are made available on the Web is, of course, also highly recommended and necessary to rid them of various linking bugs.

Organizations, too, can be connected to the Internet and the World Wide Web, but also maintain private webs and HTML document collections for distribution to clients on their local network, or *intranet*. In fact, private webs are fast becoming the technology of choice for the paperless offices we've heard so much about these last few years. With HTML document collections, businesses and other enterprises can maintain personnel databases, complete with employee photographs and online handbooks, collections of blueprints, parts, and assembly manuals, and so on—all readily and easily accessed electronically by authorized users and displayed on a local computer.

1.3   HTML: What It Is

HTML is a document-layout and hyperlink-specification language. It defines the syntax and placement of special, embedded directions that aren't displayed by the browser, but tell it how to display the contents of the document, including text, images, and other support media. The language also tells you how to make a document interactive through special hypertext links, which connect your document with other documents—on either your computer or someone else's, as well as with other Internet resources, like FTP and Gopher.

1.3.1   HTML Standards and Extensions

The basic syntax and semantics of HTML are defined in the HTML standard, currently Version 3.2. HTML is a young language, barely five years old, but already in its third iteration. Don't be too surprised if another version appears before you finish reading this book. Given the pace of these standards matters, one never knows when or if a new standard version will come to fruition.

Browser developers rely upon the HTML standard to program the software that formats and displays common HTML documents. Authors use the standard to make sure they are writing effective, correct HTML documents. Nonetheless, commercial forces have pushed developers to add into their browsers—Netscape Navigator and Internet Explorer, in particular—nonstandard extensions meant to improve the language. Many times, these extensions are implementations of future standards still under debate. Extensions can foretell future standards because so many people use them.

In this book, we explore in detail the syntax, semantics, and idioms of HTML 3.2, along with the many important extensions that are supported in the latest versions of the most popular browsers, so that any aspiring HTML author can create fabulous documents with a minimum of effort.

1.3.2 Standards Organizations

Like many popular technologies, HTML started out as an informal specification used by only a few people. As more and more authors began to use the language, it became obvious that more formal means were needed to define and manage—to standardize—HTML's features, making it easier for everyone to create and share documents.

1.3.2.1 The World Wide Web Consortium

The World Wide Web Consortium (W3C) was formed with the charter to define the standard versions of HTML. Members are responsible for drafting, circulating for review, and modifying the standard based on cross-Internet feedback to best meet the needs of the many.

Beyond HTML, the W3C has the broader responsibility of standardizing any technology related to the World Wide Web; they manage the HTTP standard, as well as related standards for document addressing on the Web. And they solicit draft standards for extensions to existing Web technologies, such as internationalization of the HTML standard.

If you want to track HTML development and related technologies, contact the W3C at *http://www.w3.org/*. Several Internet newsgroups are devoted to the Web, each a part of the *comp.infosystems.www* hierarchy. These include *comp.infosystems.www.authoring.html* and *comp.infosystems.www.authoring.images.*

1.3.2.2 The Internet Engineering Task Force

Even broader in reach than W3C, the Internet Engineering Task Force (IETF) is responsible for defining and managing every aspect of Internet technology. The World Wide Web is just one small part under the purview of the IETF.

The IETF defines all of the technology of the Internet via official documents known as Requests For Comment, or RFCs. Individually numbered for easy reference, each RFC addresses a specific Internet technology—everything from the syntax of domain names and the allocation of IP addresses to the format of electronic mail messages.

To learn more about the IETF and follow the progress of various RFCs as they are circulated for review and revision, visit the IETF home page, *http://www.ietf.org/*.

1.4 HTML: What It Isn't

With all its multimedia-enabling, new page layout features, and the hot technologies that give life to HTML documents over the Internet, it is also important to understand the language's limitations: HTML is not a word processing tool, a desktop publishing solution, or even a programming language, for that matter. That's because its fundamental purpose is to define the structure and appearance of documents and document families so that they might be delivered quickly and easily to a user over a network for rendering on a variety of display devices. Jack of all trades, but master of none, so to speak.

1.4.1 Content Versus Appearance

Before you can fully appreciate the power of the language and begin creating effective HTML documents, you must yield to its one fundamental rule: HTML is designed to structure documents and make their content more accessible, not to format documents for display purposes.

HTML does provide many different ways to let you define the appearance of your documents: font specifications, line breaks, and preformatted text are all features of the language. And, of course, appearance is important, since it can have either detrimental or beneficial effects on how users access and use the information in your HTML documents.

But with HTML, content is paramount; appearance is secondary, particularly since it is less predictable given the variety of browser graphics and text-formatting capabilities. Besides, HTML contains many more ways for structuring your document content without regard to the final appearance: section headers, structured lists, paragraphs, rules, titles, and embedded images are all defined by HTML without regard for how these elements might be rendered by a browser.

If you treat HTML as a document-generation tool, you will be sorely disappointed in your ability to format your document in a specific way. There is simply not enough capability built into HTML to allow you to create the kind of documents you might whip up with tools like FrameMaker or Microsoft Word. Attempts to subvert the supplied structuring elements to achieve specific formatting tricks seldom work across all browsers. In short, don't waste your time trying to force HTML to do things it was never designed to do.

Instead, use HTML in the manner for which it was designed: indicating the structure of a document so that the browser can then render its content appropriately. HTML is rife with tags that let you indicate the semantics of your document content, something that is missing from tools like Frame or Word. Create your documents using these tags and you'll be happier, your documents will look better, and your readers will benefit immensely.

1.4.2 Specific Limitations of HTML

There are limits to the kinds of formatting and document structuring HTML can provide. Extensions to the language remove some of the restrictions imposed by HTML 3.2; other limitations linger.

Specifically, the features that do not exist in the HTML 3.2 standard, but are made possible by extensions implemented by the various browser manufacturers and are generally considered part of HTML 3.2, include:

- Framed document layout

- Scripted dynamic documents

- Moving and layered text

- Absolute text and image positioning

Those niceties that just aren't available in any standard version of HTML are:

- Footnotes, end notes, automatic tables of contents, or indexes

- Headers and footers

- Tabs and other automatic character spacing

- Nested numbered lists

- Mathematical typesetting

1.4.3 Yielding to the Browser

Many novice HTML authors try to get around these limitations by taking careful note of how their browser displays the contents of certain tags and then misusing those tags to achieve formatting tricks. For example, some authors nest certain kinds of lists several levels deep, not because they are actually creating deeply nested lists, but because they want their text specially indented.

There are many different browsers running on many different computers and they all do things differently. Even two different users using the same browser version on their machines can reconfigure the software so that the same HTML document will look completely different. What looks fabulous on your personal browser can and often does look terrible on other browsers.

Yield to the browser. Let it format your document in whatever way it deems best. Recognize that the browser's job is to present your documents to the user in a consistent, usable way. Your job, in turn, is to use HTML effectively to mark up your documents so that the browser can do its job effectively. Spend less time trying to achieve format-oriented goals. Instead, focus your efforts on creating the actual document content and adding the HTML tags to structure that content effectively.

1.5 Nonstandard Extensions

You don't have to write in HTML 3.2 for long before you realize its limitations. That's why Netscape Navigator quickly became the most popular browser less than a year after it was released. While others were content to implement HTML standards, the developers at Netscape were hard at work extending the language and their browser to capture the potentially lucrative and certainly exciting commercial markets on the Web.

With a market presence like that, Netscape leads not only the market, but the standards drive as well. Those browser features that Netscape provides and that aren't part of HTML 3.2 quickly become de facto standards because so many people use them. Consequently, Netscape is the browser other developers must emulate. For instance, Internet Explorer, developed in collaboration with Spyglass (the purveyor of NCSA technologies) and bundled with Windows 95, adopts most of Netscape's enhancements to HTML and has some embellishments of its own.

1.5.1 Extensions: Pro and Con

Every software vendor adheres to the technological standards; it's embarrassing to be incompatible and your competitors will take every opportunity to remind buyers of your product's failure to comply, no matter how arcane or useless that standard might be. At the same time, vendors seek to make their products different and better than the competition's offerings. Netscape's and Internet Explorer's extensions to standard HTML are perfect examples of these market pressures at work.

Many HTML document authors feel safe using these extended browsers' nonstandard extensions, because of their combined and commanding share of users. For better or worse, extensions to HTML made by the folks at Netscape or Microsoft instantly become part of the street version of HTML, much like English slang creeping into the vocabulary of most Frenchmen despite the best efforts of the Académie Française.

The reality, however, is that browsers are becoming less and less standard—de facto or not. The W3C isn't keeping up. And other browser developers are not about to remain quiescent for long. Increasingly, browser competitors are implementing the many extensions to HTML and adding a few of their own for good measure.

1.5.2 Avoiding Extensions

In general, we urge you to resist using an HTML extension unless you have a compelling and overriding reason to do so. By using them, particularly in key portions of your documents, you run the risk of losing a substantial portion of your potential readership. Sure, the Netscape community is large enough to make this point moot now, but even so, you are excluding several million people without Netscape from your pages.

Of course, there are varying degrees of dependency on HTML extensions. If you use some of the horizontal rule extensions, for example, most other browsers will ignore the extended attributes and render a conventional horizontal rule. On the other hand, reliance upon a number of font size changes and text alignment extensions to control your document appearance will make your document look terrible on many alternative browsers. It might not even display at all on browsers that don't support the extensions.

We admit that it is a bit disingenuous of us to decry the use of HTML extensions while presenting complete descriptions of their use. In keeping with the general philosophy of the Internet, we'll err on the side of handing out rope and guns to all interested parties while hoping you have enough smarts to keep from hanging yourself or shooting yourself in the foot.

Our advice still holds, though: only use an extension where it is necessary or very advantageous, and do so with the understanding that you are disenfranchising a portion of your audience. To that end, you might even consider providing separate, standards-based versions of your documents to accommodate users of other browsers.

1.5.3 Beyond Extensions: Exploiting Bugs

It is one thing to take advantage of an extension to HTML, and quite another to exploit known bugs in a particular version of a browser to achieve some unusual document effect.

A good example is the multiple-body bug in Version 1.1 of Netscape Navigator. The HTML standard insists that an HTML document have exactly one `<body>` tag, containing the body of the document. The now-obsolete browser allowed any number of `<body>` tags, processing and rendering each `<body>` in turn. By placing several `<body>` tags in an HTML document, an author could achieve crude animation effects when the document was first loaded into the browser. The most popular trick used several `<body>` tags, each with a slightly different background color. This trick results in a document fade-in effect.

The party ended when Version 1.2 of Netscape fixed the bug. Suddenly, thousands of documents lost their fancy fade-in effect. Although faced with some rather fierce complaints, to their credit, the people at Netscape stood by their decision to adhere to the standard, placing compliance higher on their list of priorities than nifty rendering hacks.

In that light, we can unequivocally offer this advice: *never* exploit a bug in a browser to achieve a particular effect in your documents.

1.6 Tools for the HTML Designer

While you can use the barest of barebones text editors to create HTML documents, most HTML authors have a bit more elaborate toolbox of software utilities than a simple word processor. You also need, at least, a browser so you can test and refine your work. Beyond the essentials are some software tools specialized for HTML document preparation and editing, and others for developing and preparing accessory multimedia files.

1.6.1 Essentials

At the very least, you'll need an editor, a browser to check your work, and ideally, a connection to the Internet.

1.6.1.1 Word processor or HTML editor?

Some authors use the word-processing capabilities of their specialized HTML editing software. Others, such as ourselves, prefer to compose their work on a general word processor and later insert the HTML tags and their attributes. Still others embed HTML tags as they compose.

We think the stepwise approach—compose, then mark up—is the better way. Word processors typically have more and better writing tools, such as an outliner, spell-checker, and thesaurus, so you can craft the document's flow and content well, disregarding for the moment its look. We find that once we've defined and written the document's content, it's much easier to make a second pass to judiciously and effectively add the HTML tags to format the text. Note, too, that, unless specially trained (if they can be), spell-checkers and thesauruses typically choke on HTML markup tags and their various parameters. You can spend what seems to be a lifetime clicking the ignore button on all those otherwise valid markup tags when syntax- or spell-checking an HTML document.

When and how you embed HTML tags into your document dictates the tools you need. Some word processors, such as WordPerfect or Word, come with automated tools, and there are third-party ones, too, that automatically translate your word-processed documents into HTML. Don't expect miracles, though. Except for boilerplate documents, you probably will need to nurse those automated HTML documents to full health.

Another word of caution about HTML editors: not all adhere to the HTML 3.2 standard, so examine their specifications before using one, and certainly before purchasing one. Moreover, some of the WYSIWYG (what-you-see-is-what-you-get) HTML editors don't have up-to-date built-in browsers, so they may erroneously decode the HTML tags and give you misleading displays.

1.6.1.2 Browser software

Obviously, you should view your newly composed HTML documents and test their functionality before you release them for use by others. For serious HTML authors, particularly those looking to push their documents beyond the HTML standards, we recommend that you have several browser products, perhaps with versions running on different computers, just to be sure one's delightful display isn't another's nightmare.

The currently popular, and so most important, browsers are Netscape Navigator and Internet Explorer. Obtain evaluation copies of the software via anonymous FTP from their respective servers (*ftp.netscape.com* and *ftp.microsoft.com*), or contact your local computer software dealer for a commercial version (about $50).

1.6.1.3 Internet connection

We think you should have bona fide access to the Internet if you are really serious about learning and honing your HTML writing skills. Okay, it's not absolutely essential since you can compose and view HTML documents locally. And for some, a connection is perhaps not even possible or practical, but make the effort: there's sometimes no better way to learn than by example. HTML examples abound on the Internet, both good and bad, whose source HTML you can download and examine.

Moreover, an Internet connection *is* essential for development and testing if you include hypertext links to Internet services in your HTML documents. But, most of all, an Internet connection gives you access to a wealth of tips and ongoing updates to the language through special-interest newsgroups, as well as much of the essential and accessory software you can use to prepare HTML document collections.

1.6.2 An Extended Toolkit

If you're serious about creating documents, you'll soon find there are all sorts of nifty tools that make life easier. The list of freeware, shareware, and commercial products grows daily, so it's not very useful to provide a list here. This is, in fact, another good reason why you should get an Internet connection; various groups keep updated lists of HTML resources on the Web. If you are really dedicated to writing in HTML, you will visit those sites, and you will visit them regularly to keep abreast of the language, tools, and trends.

We think the following three web sites are the most useful for HTML authors. Each contains dozens, sometimes hundreds, of hyperlinks to detailed descriptions of products and other important information for the HTML author. Go at it.

> *http://www.stars.com*
> *http://union.ncsa.uiuc.edu/HyperNews/get/www.html*
> *http://www.yahoo.com*

2

HTML Quick Start

We didn't spend hours studiously poring over some reference book before we wrote our first HTML document. You probably shouldn't, either. HTML is simple to read and understand, and it's simple to write, too. So let's get started without first learning a lot of arcane rules.

To help you get that quick, satisfying start, we've included this chapter as a brief summary of the many elements of HTML. Of course, we've left out a lot of details and some tricks you should know. Read the upcoming chapters to get the essentials for becoming fluent in HTML.

Even if you are familiar with HTML, we recommend you work your way through this chapter before tackling the rest of the book. It not only gives you a working grasp of basic HTML and its jargon, you'll also be more productive later, flush with the confidence that comes from creating attractive documents in such a short time.

2.1 Writing Tools

Use any text editor to create HTML documents, as long as it can save your work on disk in ASCII text file format. That's because even though HTML documents include elaborate text layout and pictures, they're all just plain old ASCII documents themselves. A fancier WYSIWYG editor or an HTML translator for your favorite word processor are fine, too—although they may not support the many nonstandard HTML features we discuss later in this book. You'll probably end up touching up the HTML source text they produce, as well.

While not needed to compose HTML, you should have at least one version of a popular World Wide Web browser installed on your computer to view your work, preferably Netscape Navigator or Microsoft's Internet Explorer. That's because the HTML source document you compose on your text editor doesn't look anything like what gets displayed by a browser, even though it's the same document. Make sure what your readers actually see is what you intended by viewing the HTML document yourself with a browser. Besides, the popular ones are free over the Internet. If you can't retrieve a browser copy yourself, get a friend to give you a copy.

Also note that you don't need a connection to the Internet or the World Wide Web to write and view your HTML documents. You may compose and view your documents stored on a hard drive or floppy disk that's attached to your computer. You can even navigate among your local documents with HTML's hyperlinking capabilities without ever being connected to the Internet, or any other network, for that matter. In fact, we recommend that you work locally to develop and thoroughly test your HTML documents before you share them with others.

We strongly recommend, however, that you *do* get a connection to the Internet and to the World Wide Web if you are serious about composing your own HTML documents. You may download and view others' interesting web pages and see how they accomplished some interesting feature—good or bad. Learning by example is fun, too. (Reusing others' work, on the other hand, is often questionable, if not downright illegal.) An Internet connection is essential if you include in your work hyperlinks to other documents on the Internet.

2.2 A First HTML Document

It seems every programming language book ever written starts off with a simple example on how to display the message, "Hello, World!" Well, you won't see a "Hello, World!" example in this book. After all, this is a style guide for the next millennium. Instead, ours sends greetings to the World Wide Web:

```
<html>
<head>
<title>My first HTML document</title>
</head>
<body>
<h2>My first HTML document</h2>
Hello, <i>World Wide Web!</i>
```

```
<!-- No "Hello, World" for us -->
<p>
              Greetings from<br>
<a href="http://www.ora.com">O'Reilly & Associates</a>
<p>
Composed with care by:
<cite>(insert your name here)</cite>
<br>&copy;2000 and beyond
</body>
</html>
```

Go ahead: Type in the example HTML source on a fresh word-processing page and save it on your local disk as *myfirst.html.* Make sure you select to save it in ASCII format; word processor–specific file formats like Microsoft Word's *.doc* files save hidden characters that can confuse the browser software and disrupt your HTML document's display.

After saving *myfirst.html* (or *myfirst.htm* if you are using a DOS- or Windows 3.11-based computer) onto disk, start up your browser, locate, and then open the document from the program's File menu. Your screen should look like Figure 2-1.

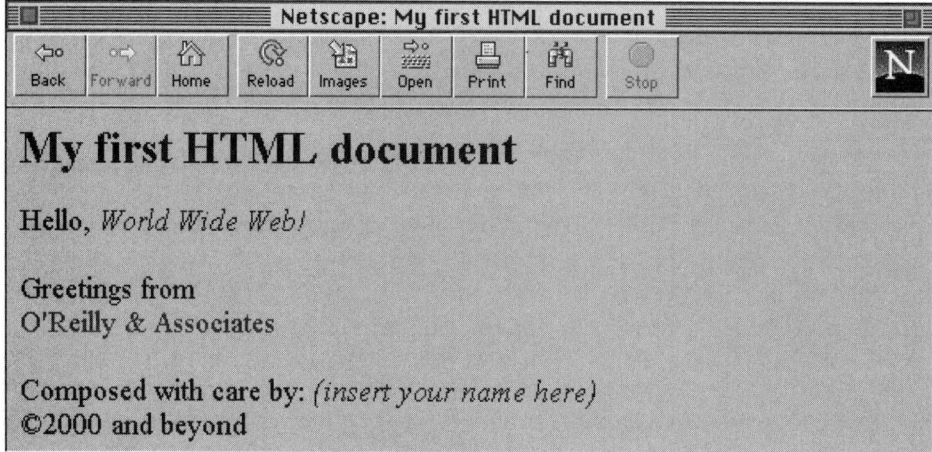

Figure 2-1. A very simple HTML document

2.3 HTML Embedded Tags

You probably have noticed right away, perhaps in surprise, that the browser displays less than half of the example source text. Closer inspection of the source reveals that what's missing is everything that's bracketed inside a pair of less-than (<) and greater-than (>) characters. [tag syntax, 3.3]

HTML is an embedded language: you insert the language's directions or *tags* into the same document that you and your readers load into a browser to view. The browser uses the information inside the HTML tags to decide how to display or otherwise treat the subsequent contents of your HTML document.

For instance, the `<i>` tag that precedes the word "Hello" in the simple example tells the browser to display the following text in italic.* [physical styles, 4.5]

The first word in a tag is its formal name, which usually is fairly descriptive of its function, too. Any additional words in a tag are special *attributes*, sometimes with an associated value after an equal sign (=), which further define or modify the tag's actions.

2.3.1 Start and End Tags

Most tags define and affect a discrete region of your HTML document. The region begins where the tag and its attributes first appear in the source document (also called the *start tag*) and continues until a corresponding *end tag*. An end tag is the start tag's name preceded by a forward slash (/). For example, the end tag that matches the "start italicizing" `<i>` tag is `</i>`.

End tags never include attributes. Most, but not all, tags have an end tag. And, to make life a bit easier for HTML authors, the browser software often infers an end tag from surrounding and obvious context, so you needn't explicitly include some end tags in your source HTML document. (We tell you which are optional and which are never omitted when we describe each tag in later chapters.) Our simple example is missing an end tag that is so commonly inferred and hence not included in the source that many veteran HTML authors don't even know that it exists. Which one?

2.4 HTML Skeleton

Notice, too, in our simple example source that precedes Figure 2-1, the HTML document starts and ends with `<html>` and `</html>` tags. Of course, these tags tell the browser that the entire document is composed in HTML. The HTML standard requires an `<html>` tag for every HTML document, but most browsers can detect and properly display HTML encoding in a text document that's missing this outermost structural tag. [`<html>`, 3.5.1]

Like our example, all HTML documents have two main structures: a *head* and a *body,* each bounded in the source by respectively named start and end tags. You

---

* Italicized text is a very simple example and one that most browsers, except the text-only variety like Lynx, can handle. In general, the browser tries to do as it is told, but as we demonstrate in upcoming chapters, browsers vary from computer to computer and from user to user, as do the fonts that are available and selected by the user for viewing HTML documents. Assume that not all are capable or willing to display your HTML document exactly as it appears on your screen.

put information about the document in the head and the contents you want displayed in the browser's window inside the body. Except in rare cases, you'll spend most of your time working on your HTML document's body content. [<head>, 3.6.1] [<body>, 3.7.1]

There are several different document header tags you may use to define how a particular document fits into a document collection and into the larger scheme of the Web. Some nonstandard header tags even animate your document.

For most documents, however, the important header element is the title. Every HTML document is required by the HTML standard to have a title. Choose a meaningful one; the title should instantly tell the reader what the document is about. Enclose yours, as we do for the title of our example, between the <title> and </title> tags in your document's header. The popular browsers typically display the title at the top of the document's window onscreen. [<title>, 3.6.2]

2.5 The Flesh on an HTML Document

Except for the <html>, <head>, <body>, and <title> tags, the HTML standard has few other required structural elements. You're free to include pretty much anything else in the contents of your document. (The Web surfers among you know that HTML authors have taken full advantage of that freedom, too.) Perhaps surprisingly, though, there are only three main types of HTML content: tags (which we describe above), comments, and text.

2.5.1 Comments

Like computer-programming source code, a raw HTML document, with all its embedded tags, can quickly become nearly unreadable. We strongly encourage that you use HTML comments to guide your composing eye.

Although it's part of your document, nothing in a comment, including the body of your comment that goes between the special starting tag "<!--" and ending tag delimiters "-->" gets included in the browser display of your document. Now you see a comment in the source, like in our simple HTML example, and now you don't on the display, as evidenced by our comment's absence in Figure 2-1. Anyone can download the source text of the HTML document and read the comments, though, so be careful what you write. [comments, 3.4.3]

2.5.2 Text

If it isn't a tag or a comment, it's text. The bulk of content in most of your HTML documents—the part readers see on their browser displays—is text. Special tags give the text structure, such as headings, lists, and tables. Others advise the browser how the content should be formatted and displayed.

2.5.3 Multimedia

What about images and other multimedia elements we see and hear as part of our web browser displays? Aren't they part of the HTML document? No. The data that comprise digital images, movies, sounds, and other multimedia elements that may be included in the browser display are in documents separate from the HTML document. You include references to those multimedia elements via special tags in the HTML document. The browser uses the references to load and integrate other types of documents with your HTML text.

We didn't include any special multimedia references in the previous example simply because they are separate, nontext documents you can't just type into a text processor. We do, however, talk about and give examples on how to integrate images and other multimedia in your HTML documents later in this chapter, as well as in extensive detail in subsequent chapters.

2.6 HTML and Text

Text-related HTML tags comprise the richest set of all in the standard language. That's because HTML emerged as a way to enrich the structure and organization of text.

HTML came out of academia. What was and still is important to those early developers was the ability of their mostly academic, text-oriented documents to be scanned and read without sacrificing their ability to distribute documents over the Internet to a wide diversity of computer display platforms. (ASCII text is the only universal format on the global Internet.) Multimedia integration is something of an appendage to HTML, albeit an important one.

And page layout is secondary to structure in HTML. We humans visually scan and decide textual relationships and structure based on how it looks; machines can only read encoded markings. Because HTML documents have encoded tags that relate meaning, they lend themselves very well to computer-automated searches and recompilation of content—features very important to researchers. It's not so much *how* something is said in HTML as *what* is being said.

Accordingly, HTML is not a page-layout language. In fact, given the diversity of user-customizable browsers as well as the diversity of computer platforms for retrieval and display of electronic documents, all HTML strives to accomplish is to *advise,* not dictate, how the document might look when rendered by the browser.

You cannot force the browser to display your document in any certain way. You'll hurt your brain if you insist otherwise.

2.6.1 *Appearance of Text*

For instance, you cannot predict what font and what absolute size—8- or 40-point Helvetica, Geneva, Subway, or whatever—will be used for a particular user's text display. Okay, so the latest browsers now support HTML style sheets and other desktop publishing-like features that let you control the layout and appearance of your documents. But users may change their browser's display characteristics and override your carefully laid plans at will; the majority of browsers out there don't support these new layout features, and some browsers are text-only with no nice fonts at all. What to do? Concentrate on content. Cool pages are a flash in the pan. Deep content will bring people back for more and more.

Nonetheless, style does matter for readability, and it is good to include it where you can, as long as it doesn't interfere with content presentation. You can attach common style attributes to your text with *physical style* tags like the italic `<i>` tag in the simple example. More importantly and truer to the language's original purpose, HTML has *content-based* style tags that attach *meaning* to various text passages. And you can alter text display characteristics, such as font style and size, color, and so on, with Cascading Style Sheets and JavaScript-based Style Sheets.

All of today's graphical browsers recognize the physical and content-related text style tags and change the appearance of their related text passage to visually convey meaning or structure. You just can't predict exactly what that change will look like.

2.6.1.1 *Content-based text styles*

Content-based style tags indicate to the browser that a specific portion of your HTML text has a specific usage or meaning. The `<cite>` tag in our simple example, for instance, means the enclosed text is some sort of citation—the document's author, in this case. Browsers commonly, although not universally, display the citation text in italic, not as regular text. [content-based styles, 4.4]

While it may or may not be obvious to the current reader that the text is a citation, someday, someone might create a computer program that searches a vast collection of HTML documents for embedded `<cite>` tags and compiles a special list of citations from the enclosed text. Similar software agents already scour the Internet for HTML-embedded information to compile listings, such as the infamous Webcrawler and the Lycos Home Page databases of web sites.

The most common content-based style used today is that of emphasis, indicated with the `<em>` tag. And if you're feeling really emphatic, you might use the `<strong>` content style. Other content-based styles include `<code>`, for snippets of programming code; <kbd>, to denote text entered by the user via a keyboard; <samp>, to mark sample text; <dfn>, for definitions; and <var>, to delimit variable names within programming code samples. All of these tags have corresponding end tags.

2.6.1.2 Physical styles

Even the barest of barebones text processors conform to a few traditional text styles, such as italic and bold characters. While HTML is not a word-processing tool in the traditional sense, it does provide tags that tell the browser explicitly to display (if it can) a character, word, or phrase in a particular physical style.

Although you should use related content-based tags for the reasons we argue above, sometimes form is more important than function. So use the <i> tag to italicize text, without imposing any specific meaning; the <b> tag to display text in boldface; or the <tt> tag so that the browser, if it can, displays the text in a teletype-style monospaced typeface. [physical styles, 4.5]

It's easy to fall into the trap of using physical styles when you should really be using a content-based style instead. Discipline yourself now to use the content-based styles, because, as we argue above, they convey meaning as well as style, thereby making your documents easier to automate and manage.

2.6.1.3 Special text characters

Not all text characters available to you for display by a browser can be typed from the keyboard. And some characters have special meanings in HTML, such as the brackets around tags, which if not somehow differentiated when used for plain text—the less-than sign (<) in a math equation, for example—will confuse the browser and trash your document. HTML gives you a way to include any of the many different characters that comprise the ASCII character set anywhere in your text through a special encoding of its *character entity*.

Like the copyright symbol in our simple example, a character entity starts with an ampersand followed by its name, and terminated with a semicolon. (Alternatively, you may also use the character's position number in the ASCII table of characters preceded by the pound or sharp sign (#) in lieu of its name in the character entity sequence.) When rendering the document, the browser displays the proper character, if it exists in the user's font. [character entities, 3.4.2]

For obvious reasons, the most commonly used character entities are the greater-than (>), less-than (<), and ampersand (&) characters. Check Appendix E, *Character Entities*, to find what symbol the character entity ¦ represents.

2.6.2 Text Structures

It's not obvious in our simple example, but the common carriage returns we use to separate paragraphs in our source document have no meaning in HTML, except in special circumstances. You could have typed the document onto a single line in your text editor and it would still appear the same in Figure 2-1.*

You'd soon discover, too, if you hadn't read it here first, that except in special cases, browsers typically ignore leading and trailing spaces, and sometimes more than a few in between. (If you look closely at the source example, the line "Greetings from" looks like it should be indented by leading spaces, but it isn't in Figure 2-1.)

2.6.2.1 Paragraphs and line breaks

A browser takes the text in the body of your document and "flows" it onto the computer screen, disregarding any common carriage-return or line-feed characters in the source. The browser fills as much of each line of the display window as possible, beginning flush against the left margin, before stopping after the rightmost word and moving on to the next line. Resize the browser window, and the text reflows to fill the new space; indicating HTML's inherent flexibility.

Of course, readers would rebel if your text just ran on and on, so HTML does provide both explicit and implicit ways to control the basic structure of your document. The most rudimentary and common ways are with the paragraph (<p>) and the line-break (<br>) tags. Both break the text flow, which consequently restarts on a new line. The only apparent difference is that with most browsers, the paragraph tag adds more vertical space after the line break. [<p>, 4.1.2] [
, 4.7.1]

By the way, the HTML standard includes an end tag for the paragraph tag, but not for the line break tag. Few authors ever include the paragraph end tag in their documents; the browser usually can figure out where one paragraph ends and another begins.† Give yourself a star if you knew that </p> even exists.

---

* We use a computer programming-like style of indentation so our source HTML documents are more readable. It's not obligatory, nor are there any formal style guidelines for source HTML document text formats. We do, however, highly recommend you adopt your own consistent style, so that you and others can easily follow your source documents.

† The paragraph end tag is being used more commonly now that the popular browsers support the paragraph-alignment attribute.

2.6.2.2 Headings

Besides breaking your text into paragraphs, you also can organize your documents into sections with headings. Just as they do on this and other pages in this printed book, HTML headings not only divide and entitle discrete passages of text: they also convey meaning visually. With HTML, however, headings also lend themselves to machine-automated analyses.

There are six HTML heading tags, `<h1>` through `<h6>`, with corresponding end tags. Typically, the browser displays their contents in, respectively, very large to very small font sizes, and sometimes in boldface. The text inside the `<h4>` tag is usually the same size as the regular text. [headings, 4.2.1]

The heading tags also typically break the current text flow, standing alone on lines and separated from surrounding text, even though there aren't any explicit paragraph or line-break tags before or after a heading.

2.6.2.3 Horizontal rules

Besides headings, HTML also provides horizontal rule lines that help delineate and separate the sections of your document.

When the browser encounters an `<hr>` tag in your document, it breaks the flow of text and draws a line completely across the display window on a new line. The flow of text resumes immediately below the rule. [`<hr>`, 5.1.1]

2.6.2.4 Preformatted text

Occasionally, you'll want the browser to display a block of text as-is: for example, with indented lines and vertically aligned letters or numbers that don't change even though the browser window might get resized. The HTML `<pre>` tag rises to those occasions. All text up to the closing `</pre>` end tag appears in the browser window exactly as you type it, including carriage returns and line feeds, leading, trailing, and intervening spaces. Although very useful for tables and forms, `<pre>` text turns out pretty dull; the popular browsers render the block in a monospace typeface. [`<pre>`, 4.7.5]

2.7 Hyperlinks

While text may be the meat and bones of an HTML document, its heart is hypertext. Hypertext gives users the ability to retrieve and display a different document in your own or someone else's collection simply by a click of the mouse on an associated word or phrase (*hyperlink*) in your HTML document. Use these interactive hyperlinks to help readers easily navigate and find information—in your own, or others' collections—of otherwise separate documents in a variety of formats, including multimedia, HTML, and plain ASCII text. Hyperlinks literally bring the wealth of knowledge on the whole Internet to the tip of the mouse pointer.

To include a hyperlink to some other document in your own collection or on a server in Timbuktu, all you need to know is the document's unique address and how to drop an *anchor* into your HTML document.

2.7.1 URLs

While it is hard to believe, given the millions, perhaps billions, of them out there, every document and resource on the Internet has a unique address known as its *uniform resource locator* (URL; commonly pronounced "you-are-ell"). A URL is comprised of the document's name preceded by the hierarchy of directory names in which the file is stored (*pathname*), the Internet *domain name* of the server that hosts the file, and the software and manner by which the browser and the document's host server communicate to exchange the document (*protocol*):

>   *protocol://server_domain_name/pathname*

Here are some sample URLs:

>   *http://www.kumquat.com/docs/catalog/price_list.html*
>   *http:price_list.html*
>   *http://www.kumquat.com/*
>   *ftp://ftp.netcom.com/pub/*

The first example is what's known as an *absolute* or complete URL. It includes every part of the URL format—protocol, server, and the pathname of the document.

While absolute URLs leave nothing to the imagination, they can lead to big head-aches when you move documents to another directory or server. Fortunately, browsers also let you use *relative* URLs and automatically fill in any missing portions with respective parts from the current document's *base* URL. The second example is the simplest relative URL of all; it assumes that the *price_list.html* docu-ment is located on the same server and in the same directory as the current document.

Relative URLs are also useful if you don't know a directory or document's name. The third URL example, for instance, points to *kumquat.com*'s web home page.

Although appearances may deceive, the last FTP example URL actually is abso-lute; it points directly at the contents of the */pub* directory.

2.7.2 Anchors

The anchor (`<a>`) tag is the HTML feature for defining both the source and the destination of a hyperlink.* You'll most often see and use the `<a>` tag with its `href` attribute to define a source hyperlink. The value of the attribute is the URL of the destination.

The contents of the source `<a>` tag—the words and/or images between it and its `</a>` end tag—is the portion of the HTML document that is specially activated in the browser display and that users select to take a hyperlink. These *anchor* contents usually look different from the surrounding content (text in a different color or underlined, images with specially colored borders), and the mouse pointer icon changes when passed over them. The `<a>` tag contents, therefore, should be text or an image (icons are great) that explicitly or intuitively tells users where the hyperlink will take them. [`<a>`, 7.3.1]

For instance, the browser will specially display and change the mouse pointer when it passes over the "Kumquat Archive" text in the following example:

```
For more information on kumquats, visit our
<a href="http://www.kumquat.com/archive.html">
Kumquat Archive</a>
```

If the user clicks the mouse button on that text, the browser automatically retrieves from the server *www.kumquat.com* a web *(http:)* page named *archive.html*, and then displays it for the user.

2.7.3 Hyperlink Names and Navigation

Pointing to another document in some collection somewhere on the other side of the world is not only cool, but it also supports your own HTML documents. Yet the hyperlinks' chief duty is to help users navigate your collection in their search for valuable information. Hence, the concept of the home page and supporting HTML documents has arisen.

None of your HTML documents should run on and on. First, there's the performance issue: the value of your work suffers, no matter how rich it is, if the document takes forever to download, and if once retrieved, users must endlessly scroll up and down through the display to find a particular section.

---

* The nomenclature here is a bit unfortunate: the "anchor" tag should mark just a destination, not the jumping off point of a hyperlink, too. You "drop anchor"; you don't jump off one. We won't even mention the atrociously confusing terminology the HTML standard uses for the various parts of a hyperlink except to say that someone got things all "bass ackwards."

Rather, design your work as a collection of several compact and succinct pages, like chapters in a book, each focused to a particular topic for quick selection and browsing by the user. Then use hyperlinks to organize that collection.

For instance, use your home page—the leading document of the collection—as a master index full of brief descriptions and respective hyperlinks to the rest of your collection.

You should also use the special attribute of the `<a>` tag called `name`. Anchors with the `name` attribute serve as internal hyperlink targets in your HTML documents. Normally, the browser displays a freshly downloaded document at the beginning. Name anchors let you begin the display at the section of interest further down. Simply include them anywhere that they make sense as a hyperlink target. They do not change the appearance of enclosed or surrounding content.

Thereafter, you may append the name, after a separating pound sign (#), as a suffix in the URL of a hyperlink that references that specific place in your document. For instance, to reference a specific topic in an archive, such as "Kumquat Stew Recipes" in our example Kumquat Archive, you mark that section with a name anchor:

```
... preceding content...
<a name="Stews">
<h3>Kumquat Stew Recipes</h3>
</a>
```

In the same or another document, you prepare a source hyperlink that points directly to those recipes by including the section's anchor name as a suffix to the document's URL, separated by a pound sign:

```
For more information on kumquats, visit our
<a href="http://www.kumquat.com/archive.html">
  Kumquat Archive</a>,
and perhaps try one or two of our
<a href="http://www.kumquat.com/archive.html#Stews">
  Kumquat Stew Recipes</a>.
```

If selected by the user, the latter hyperlink causes the browser to download the *archive.html* document and start the display at our "Stews" anchor.

2.7.4 Anchors Beyond HTML

HTML hyperlinks are not limited to other HTML documents. Anchors let you point to nearly any type of document available over the Internet, including other Internet services.

However, "let" and "enable" are two different things. Browsers can manage the various Internet services, like FTP and Gopher, so that users can download non-HTML documents. They don't yet fully or gracefully handle multimedia.

Today, there are few standards for the many types and formats of multimedia. Computer systems connected to the Web vary wildly in their abilities to display those sound and video formats. Except for some graphics images, standard HTML gives you no specific provision for display of multimedia documents except the ability to reference one in an anchor. The browser, which retrieves the multimedia document, must activate a special *helper* application, download and execute an associated *applet*, or have a *plugin* accessory installed to decode and display it for the user.

Although HTML and most web browsers currently avoid the confusion by side-stepping it, that doesn't mean you can't or shouldn't exploit multimedia in your HTML documents: just be aware of the limitations.

2.8   *Images Are Special*

Image files are multimedia elements you may reference with anchors in your HTML document for separate download and display by the browser. But, unlike other multimedia, standard HTML has a provision for image display "in line" with the text,* and images can serve as intricate maps of hyperlinks. That's because there is some consensus in the industry concerning image file formats—specifically, GIF and JPEG—and the graphical browsers have built in decoders that integrate those image types into your document.

2.8.1   *Inline Images*

The HTML tag for inline images is `<img>`; its required `src` attribute is the URL of the GIF or JPEG image you want to insert in the document. [`<img>`, 5.2.6]

The browser separately loads images and places them into the text flow as if the image were some special, albeit sometimes very large, character. Normally, that means the browser aligns the bottom of the image to the bottom of the current line of text. You can change that with the special `<img>` `align` attribute whose value you set to put the image at the `top`, `middle`, or `bottom` of adjacent text. Examine Figure 2-2 through Figure 2-4 for the image alignment you prefer. Of course, wide images may take up the whole line, and hence break the text flow. Or you may place an image by itself, by including preceding and following paragraph or line-break tags.

Experienced HTML authors use images not only as supporting illustrations, but also as quite small inline characters or glyphs, added to aid browsing readers'

---

* Browser developers are integrating other multimedia besides GIF and JPEG graphics for inline display. Internet Explorer, for instance, supports a tag that plays background audio.

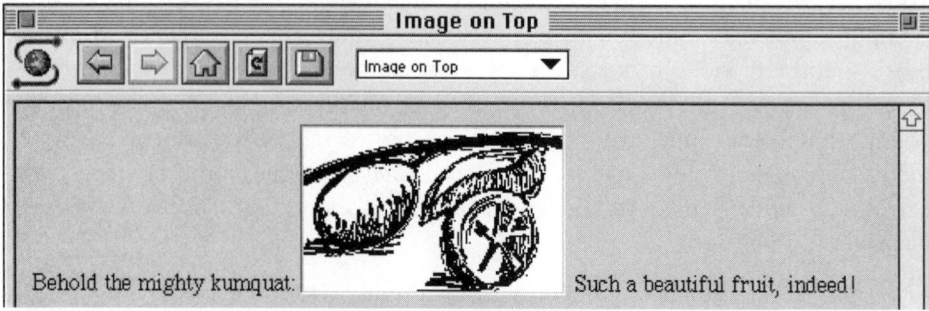

Figure 2-2. An inline image aligned with the bottom of the text (default)

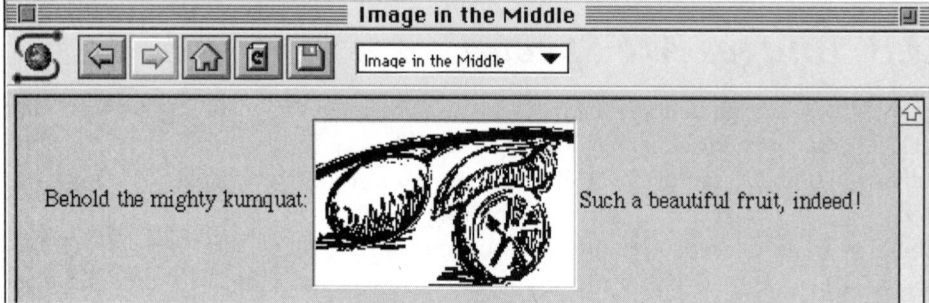

Figure 2-3. An inline image specially aligned with the middle of the text

Figure 2-4. An inline image specially aligned with the top of the text

eyes and to highlight sections of the documents. Veteran HTML authors commonly add custom list bullets or more distinctive section dividers than the conventional horizontal rules. Images, too, may be included in a hyperlink, so that users may select an inline thumbnail sketch to download a full-screen image. The possibilities with inline images are endless.

2.8.2 Image Maps

Image maps are images within an anchor with a special attribute: they may contain more than one hyperlink.

One way to enable an image map is by adding the `ismap` attribute to an `<img>` tag placed inside an anchor tag (`<a>`). When the user clicks somewhere in the image, the graphical browser sends the relative x,y coordinates of the mouse position to the server that is also designated in the anchor. A special server program then translates the image coordinates into some special action, such as downloading another HTML document. [`ismap`, 7.5.1]

A good example of the use of an image map might be to locate a hotel while traveling. The user clicks on a map of the region they intend to visit, for instance, and your image map's server program might return the names, addresses, and phone numbers of local accommodations.

While very powerful and visually appealing, these standard so-called *server-side* image maps mean that HTML authors must have some access to the map's coordinate-processing program on the server. Many authors don't even have access to the server. Recent innovations in browser software remove those barriers by enabling *client-side* image maps.

Rather than depending on a web server, the `usemap` attribute for the `<img>` tag and the `<map>` and `<area>` tags let HTML authors embed all the information the browser needs to process an image map in the same document as the image. Because of their reduced network bandwidth and server independence, client-side image maps are becoming increasingly popular among HTML authors. [`usemap`, 7.5.2]

2.9 Lists, Searchable Documents, and Forms

Thought we'd exhausted HTML text elements? Headers, paragraphs, and line breaks are just the rudimentary text-organizational elements of an HTML document. The language also provides several advanced text-based structures, including three types of lists, "searchable" documents, and forms. Searchable documents and forms go beyond text formatting, too; they are a way to interact with your readers. Forms let users enter text and click checkboxes and radio buttons to select particular items and then send that information back to the server. Once received, a special server application processes the form's information and responds accordingly, e.g., filling a product order or collecting data for a user survey.*

---

* The server-side programming required for processing forms is beyond the scope of this book. We give some basic guidelines in the appropriate chapters, but please consult the server documentation and your server administrator for details.

The HTML syntax for these special features and their various attributes can get rather complicated; they're not quick-start grist. So we mention them here and urge you to read on for details in later chapters.

2.9.1 Unordered, Ordered, and Definition Lists

The three types of HTML lists match those we are most familiar with: unordered, ordered, and definition lists. An unordered list—one in which the order of items is not important, such as a laundry or grocery list—gets bounded by `<ul>` and `</ul>` tags. Each item in the list, usually a word or short phrase, is marked by the `<li>` (list-item) tag and, when rendered, appears indented from the left margin. The browser also typically precedes each item with a leading bullet symbol. [`<ul>`, 8.1.1] [`<li>`, 8.3]

Ordered lists, bounded by the `<ol>` and `</ol>` tags, are identical in format to unordered ones, including the `<li>` tag for marking list items. However, the order of items is important—equipment assembly steps, for instance. The browser accordingly displays each item in the list preceded by an ascending number. [`<ol>`, 8.2.1]

Definition lists are slightly more complicated than unordered and ordered lists. Within a definition list's enclosing `<dl>` and `</dl>` tags, each list item has two parts, each with a special tag: a short name or title, contained within a `<dt>` tag, followed by its corresponding value or definition, denoted by the `<dd>` tag. When rendered, the browser usually puts the item name on a separate line (although not indented), and the definition, which may include several paragraphs, indented below it. [`<dl>`, 8.7.1]

The various types of lists may contain nearly any type of content normally allowed in the body of the HTML document. So, you can organize your collection of digitized family photographs into an ordered list, for example, or put them into a definition list complete with text annotations. HTML even lets you put lists inside of lists (nesting), opening up a wealth of interesting combinations.

2.9.2 Searchable Documents

The simplest type of user interaction provided by HTML is the *searchable* document. You create a searchable HTML document by including an `<isindex>` tag in its header or body. The browser automatically provides some way for the user to type one or more words into a text input box, and to pass those keywords to a related processing application on the server. [`<isindex>`, 7.6.1]

The processing application on the server uses those keywords to do some special task, such as perform a database search or match the keywords against an authentication list to allow the user special access to some other part of your document collection.

2.9.3 Forms

Obviously, searchable documents are very limited—one per document and only one user input element. Fortunately, HTML provides better, more extensive support for collecting user input though *forms.*

You create one or more special form sections in your HTML document, bounded with the `<form>` and `</form>` tags. Inside the form, you may put predefined as well as customized text-input boxes allowing for both single and multiline input. You may also insert checkboxes and radio buttons for single- and multiple-choice selections, and special buttons that work to reset the form or send its contents to the server. Users fill out the form at their leisure, perhaps after reading the rest of the document, and then click a special send button that makes the browser send the form's data to the server. A special server-side program you provide then processes the form and responds accordingly, perhaps by requesting more information from the user, modifying subsequent HTML documents the server sends to the user, and so on. [`<form>`, 10.1.1]

HTML forms provide everything you might expect of an automated form, including input area labels, integrated contents for instructions, default input values, and so on—except automatic input verification; your server-side program has to perform that function.

2.10 *Tables*

For a language that emerged from academia—a place steeped in data—it's not surprising to find that HTML supports a set of tags for data tables that not only align your numbers, but can specially format your text, too.

Five tags enable tables, including the `<table>` tag itself and a `<caption>` tag for including a description of the table. Special tag attributes let you change the look and dimensions of the table. You create a table row by row, putting between the table row (`<tr>`) tag and its end tag (`</tr>`) either table header (`<th>`) or table data (`<td>`) tags and their respective contents for each cell in the table. Headers and data may contain nearly any regular HTML content, including text, images, forms, and even another table. As a result, you can also use HTML tables for advanced text formatting, such as for multicolumn text and sidebar headers (see Figure 2-5). For more information, see Chapter 11, *Tables.*

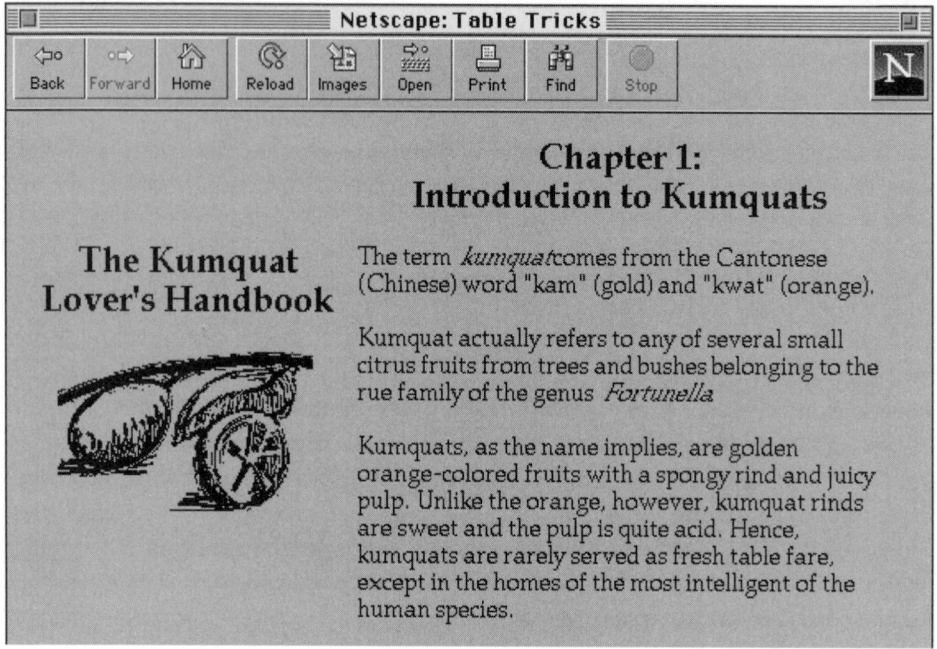

Figure 2-5. HTML tables let you perform page layout tricks, too

2.11 Frames

Anyone who has had more than one application window open on their graphical desktop at a time can immediately appreciate the special, nonstandard feature of HTML offered by Netscape Navigator and Internet Explorer: frames. For more information on frames, see Chapter 12, *Frames*.

Figure 2-6 is an example of a frame display. It shows how the document window may be divided into many individual windows separated by rule lines and scroll bars. What is not immediately apparent in the example, though, is that each frame may display an independent document, and not necessarily HTML ones, at that. A frame may contain any valid content that the browser is capable of displaying, including multimedia. If the frame's contents include a hypertext link the user selects, the new document's contents, even another frame document, may replace that same frame, another frame's content, or the entire browser window.

Frames are defined in a special HTML document in which you replace the `<body>` tag with one or more `<frameset>` tags that tell the browser how to divide its main window into discrete frames. Special `<frame>` tags go inside the `<frameset>` tag and point to the documents that go inside the frames.

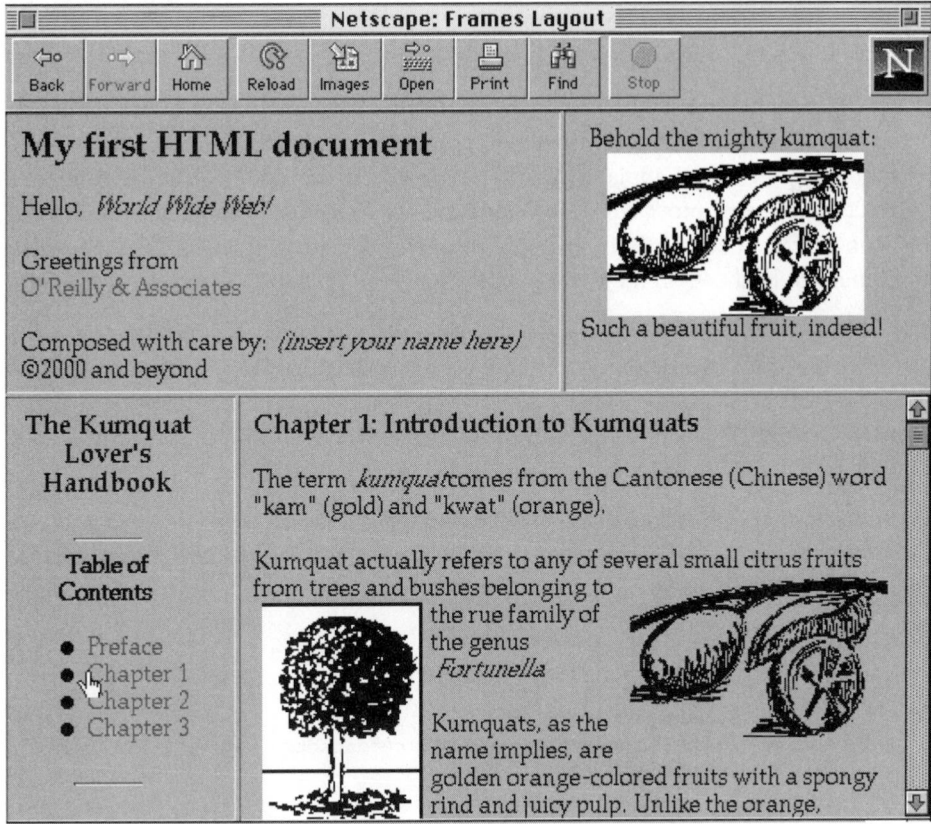

Figure 2-6. Frames divide the window into many document displays

The individual documents referenced and displayed in the frame document window act independently, to a degree; the frame document controls the entire window. You can, however, direct one frame's document to load new content into another frame. Selecting an item from a table of contents, for example, might cause the browser to load and display the referenced document into an adjacent frame for viewing. That way, the table of contents always is available to the user as he or she browses the collection.

2.12 *Style Sheets and JavaScript*

The very latest browsers also have support for two powerful innovations to HTML: style sheets and JavaScript. Like their desktop-publishing cousins, style sheets allow you to control how your HTML pages look—text font styles and sizes, colors, backgrounds, alignments, and so on. More importantly, style sheets give you a way to impose display characteristics uniformly over the entire document and over an entire collection of documents.

JavaScript is a programming language with functions and commands that let you control how the browser behaves for the user. Now, this is not a programming book, but there are two reasons we mention JavaScript here and cover the language in fair detail in later chapters: First, you embed JavaScript programs ("applets") directly into your HTML documents to achieve some very powerful and fun effects. Second, it is through JavaScript that the folks at Netscape also implement style sheets in their latest browser.

The World Wide Web Consortium—the putative standards organization—prefers that you use the Cascading Style Sheets (CSS) model for HTML document design. Both the latest versions of Netscape (Version 4) and Internet Explorer (Version 3) support CSS and JavaScript, but only Netscape currently supports JavaScript-based Style Sheets (JSS).

To illustrate the differences between CSS and JSS, here are the two ways you can make all the top-level (H1) header text in your HTML document appear in the color red. First, using CSS:

```
<html>
<head>
<title>CSS Example</title>
<!-- Hide CSS properties within comments so old browsers
don't choke on or display the unfamiliar contents. -->
  <style type="text/CSS1">
    <!--
    H1 {color: red}
    -->
  </style>
</head>
<body>
<H1>I'll be red if your browser supports CSS</H1>
Something in between.
<H1>I should be red, too!</H1>
</body>
</html>
```

Using JSS:

```
<html>
<head>
<title>JSS Example</title>
  <style type="text/javascript">
  <!--
    tags.H1.color = "red"
  //-->
  </style>
</head>
<body>
```

```
<H1> I'll be red if your browser supports JSS</H1>
Something in between.
<H1>I should be red, too!</H1>
</body>
</html>
```

The examples are nearly identical, but the devil is in the details. Both have their own peculiar syntax that is unfamiliar to most everyone except programmers. The nastiest detail, however, and one that will drive many an HTML author batty, is that JSS, like its parent JavaScript language, is case-sensitive—type "h1" instead of "H1" in the style description and you ain't gonna see red. Type "h1" in the CSS style description (or in the tag, for that matter) and it still works.

Frankly, we prefer the CSS way for the very reason of its forgiving nature, as we explain in Chapter 9, *Cascading Style Sheets*, even though JSS is a more powerful and comprehensive accessory. And you may otherwise become quite familiar with JavaScript by using the language to extend the capabilities of your HTML documents. In that case, adopting JSS with its case-sensitive warts may not be all that daunting, maybe even an easy transition (that's perhaps what Netscape is hoping).

You get a taste of the JavaScript language in the above JSS example. It is an object-oriented language. It views your document and the browser that displays your documents as a collection of parts ("objects") that have certain properties that you may change or compute. This is some very powerful stuff, but not something that most HTML authors will want to handle. Rather, most of us probably will snatch the quick and easy, yet powerful JavaScript applets that proliferate across the Web and embed them in our own HTML documents. We tell you how (JSS too) in Chapter 13, *Executable Content*.

2.13 Forging Ahead

Clearly, this chapter represents the tip of the iceberg. If you've read this far, hopefully your appetite has been whetted for more. By now you've got a basic understanding of the scope and features of HTML; proceed through subsequent chapters to expand your knowledge and learn more about each feature of HTML.

3

Anatomy of an HTML Document

HTML documents are very simple, and writing one shouldn't intimidate even the most timid of computer users. First, although you might use a fancy WYSIWYG editor to help you compose it, an HTML document is ultimately stored, distributed, and read by a browser as a simple ASCII text file.* That's why even the poorest user with a barebones text editor can compose the most elaborate of HTML pages. (Accomplished webmasters often elicit the admiration of HTML "newbies" by composing astonishingly cool pages using the crudest text editor on a cheap laptop computer and performing in odd places like on a bus or in the bathroom.) HTML writers should, however, keep several of the popular browsers on hand and alternate among them to view new documents under construction. Remember, browsers differ in how they display a page; not all browsers implement all of the HTML standards; and some have their own special extensions to the language.

3.1 Appearances Can Deceive

HTML documents never look alike when displayed by a text editor and when displayed by an HTML browser. Simply take a look at any source HTML document off the World Wide Web. At the very least, return characters, tabs, and leading spaces, although important for readability of the source text document, are ignored for the most part in HTML. There also is a lot of extra text in an HTML source document, mostly from the display tags and interactivity markers

---

* Informally, both the text and the markup tags in an HTML document are ASCII characters. Technically, unless you specify otherwise, text and tags are made up of eight-bit characters as defined in the standard ISO-8859-1 Latin character set. The HTML standard does support alternative character encoding, including Arabic and Cyrillic. See Appendix E, *Character Entities*, for details.

and their parameters that affect portions of the document, but don't themselves appear in the display.

Accordingly, new HTML authors are confronted with having to develop not only a presentation style for their HTML pages, but a different style for their HTML source text. The source document's layout should highlight the programming-like markup aspects of HTML, not its display aspects. And it should be readable not only by you, the author, but by others, as well.

Experienced HTML document writers typically adopt a programming-like style, albeit very relaxed, for their source HTML text. We do the same throughout this book, and that style will become apparent as you compare our source HTML examples with the actual display of the document by a browser.

Our formatting style is simple, but serves to create readable, easily maintained documents:

- Except for the document structural tags like `<html>`, `<head>`, and `<body>`, any HTML element we used to structure the content of a document is placed on a separate line and indented to show its nesting level within the document. Such elements include lists, forms, tables, and similar tags.

- Any HTML element used to control the appearance or style of text is inserted in the current line of text. This includes basic font style tags like `<b>` (bold text) and document linkages like `<a>` (hypertext anchor).

- Avoid, where possible, the breaking of a URL onto two lines.

- Add extraneous newline characters to set apart special sections of the HTML document, for instance around paragraphs or tables.

The task of maintaining the indentation of your source HTML ranges from trivial to onerous. Some text editors, like Emacs, manage the indentation automatically; others, like common word processors, couldn't care less about indentation and leave the task completely up to you. If your editor makes your life difficult, you might consider striking a compromise, perhaps by indenting the tags to show structure, but leaving the actual text without indentation to make modifications easier.

No matter what compromises or stands you make on source code style, however, it's important that you adopt one. You'll be very glad you did when you go back to that HTML document you wrote three months ago searching for that really cool trick you did with. . . . Now, where was that?

3.2 Structure of an HTML Document

An HTML document consists of text, which defines the content of the document, and tags, which define the structure and appearance of the document. The structure of an HTML document is simple, too, consisting of an outer `<html>` tag enclosing the document header and body:

```
<html>
<head>
<title>Barebones HTML Document</title>
</head>
<body>
This illustrates, in a very <i>simp</i>le way,
the basic structure of an HTML document.
</body>
</html>
```

Each document has a *head* and a *body*, delimited by the `<head>` and `<body>` tags. The head is where you give your HTML document a title and where you indicate other parameters the browser may use when displaying the document. The body is where you put the actual contents of the HTML document. This includes the text for display and document control markers (tags) that advise the browser how to display the text. Tags also reference special-effects files including graphics and sound, and indicate the hot spots (*hyperlinks* and *anchors*) that link your document to other documents.

3.3 HTML Tags

For the most part, HTML document tags are simple to understand and use, since they are made up of common words, abbreviations, and notations. For instance, the `<i>` and `</i>` tags tell the browser to respectively start and stop italicizing the text characters that come between them. Accordingly, the syllable "simp" in our barebones HTML example would appear italicized on a browser display.

The HTML standard and its various extensions define how and where you place tags within a document. Let's take a closer look at that syntactic sugar that holds together all HTML documents.

3.3.1 The Syntax of a Tag

Every HTML tag consists of a tag *name*, sometimes followed by an optional list of tag *attributes*, all placed between opening and closing brackets (< and >). The simplest tag is nothing more than a name appropriately enclosed in brackets, such as `<head>` and `<i>`. More complicated tags contain one or more attributes, which specify or modify the behavior of the tag.

Tag and attribute names are not case-sensitive. There's no difference in effect between <head>, <Head>, <HEAD>, or even <HeaD>; they are all equivalent. The values that you assign to a particular attribute may be case-sensitive, however, depending on your browser and server. In particular, file location and name references—universal resource locators (URLs)—are case-sensitive. [URLs, 7.2]

Tag attributes, if any, belong after the tag name, each separated by one or more tab, space, or return characters. Their order of appearance is not important.

A tag attribute's value, if any, follows an equal sign (=) after the attribute name. You may include spaces around the equal sign, so that `width=6`, `width = 6`, `width =6`, and `width= 6` all mean the same. For readability, however, we prefer not to include spaces. That way, it's easier to pick out an attribute/value pair from a crowd of pairs in a lengthy tag.

If an attribute's value is a single word or number (no spaces), you may simply add it after the equal sign. All other values should be enclosed in single or double quotation marks, especially those values that contain several words separated by spaces. The length of the value is limited to 1024 characters.

Most browsers are tolerant of how tags are punctuated and broken across lines. Nonetheless, avoid breaking tags across lines in your source document whenever possible. This rule promotes readability and reduces potential errors in your HTML documents.

3.3.2 Sample Tags

Here are some tags with attributes:

```
<a href="http://www.ora.com/catalog.html">
<ul compact>
<input name=filename size=24 maxlength=80>
<link title="Table of Contents">
```

The first example is the `<a>` tag for a hyperlink to O'Reilly & Associates' World Wide Web–based catalog of products. It has a single attribute, `href`, followed by the catalog's address in cyberspace—its URL.

The second example shows a tag that formats text into an unordered list of items. Its single attribute—`compact`, which limits the space between list items—does not require a value.

The third example shows a tag with multiple attributes, each with a value that does not require enclosing quotation marks.

The last example shows proper use of enclosing quotation marks when the attribute value is more than one word long.

Finally, what is not immediately evident in these examples is that while attribute names are not case-sensitive (`href` works the same as `HREF` and `HreF`), most attribute values are case-sensitive. The value `filename` for the `name` attribute in the `<input>` tag example is not the same as the value `Filename`, for instance.

3.3.3 Starting and Ending Tags

We alluded earlier to the fact that most HTML tags have a beginning and an end and affect the portion of text between them. That enclosed text segment may be large or small, from a single text character, syllable, or word, such as the italicized "simp" syllable in our barebones example, to the `<html>` tag that bounds the entire document. The starting component of any tag is the tag name and its attributes, if any. The corresponding ending tag is the tag name alone, preceded by a slash. Ending tags have no attributes.

3.3.4 Proper and Improper Nesting

Tags can be put inside the affected segment of another tag (nested) for multiple tag effects on a single segment of the HTML document. For example, a portion of the following text is both bold and included as part of an anchor defined by the `<a>` tag:

```
<body>
This is some text in the body, with a
<a href="another_doc.html">link, a portion of which
is <b>set in bold</b></a>
</body>
```

According to the HTML standard, you must end nested tags starting with the most recent one and work your way back out. For instance in the example, we end the bold tag (`</b>`) before ending the link tag (`</a>`) since we started in the reverse order: `<a>` tag first, then `<b>` tag. It's a good idea to follow that standard, even though most browsers don't absolutely insist you do so. You may get away with violating this nesting rule for one browser, sometimes even with all current browsers. But eventually a new browser version won't allow the violation and you'll be hard pressed to straighten out your source HTML document.

3.3.5 Tags Without Ends

According to the HTML standard, only a few tags do not have an ending tag. For example, the `<br>` tag causes a line break; it has no effect otherwise on the subsequent portion of the document and, hence, does not need an ending tag.

The standard HTML tags that do not have corresponding ending tags are:

```
<area>
<base>
<basefont>
<br>
<hr>
<img>
<input>
<isindex>
<link>
<meta>
<nextid>
<option>
<param>
```

3.3.6 Omitting Tags

You often see documents in which the author seemingly has forgotten to include many ending tags in apparent violation of the HTML standard. But your browser doesn't complain, and the documents displays just fine. What gives? The HTML standard lets you omit certain tags or their endings for clarity and ease of preparation. The HTML standard writers didn't intend the language to be tedious.

For example, the `<p>` tag that defines the start of a paragraph has a corresponding end tag `</p>`, but the `</p>` ending tag rarely is used. In fact, many HTML authors don't even know it exists! [`<p>`, 4.1.2]

Rather, the HTML standard lets you omit a starting tag or ending tag whenever it can be unambiguously inferred by the surrounding context. Many browsers make good guesses when confronted with missing tags, leading the document author to assume that a valid omission was made. When in doubt, add the ending tag: it'll make life easier for yourself, the browser, and anyone else who might need to modify your document in the future.

3.3.7 Ignored or Redundant Tags

Browsers sometimes ignore tags. This usually happens with redundant tags whose effects merely cancel or substitute for themselves. The best example is a series of `<p>` tags, one after the other with no intervening text. Unlike the similar series of repeating return characters in a text-processing document, most browsers skip to a new line only once. The extra `<p>` tags are redundant and usually ignored by the browser.

In addition, most browsers ignore any tag that they don't understand or that was incorrectly specified by the document author. Browsers habitually forge ahead and make some sense of a document, no matter how badly formed and error-ridden it may be. This isn't just a tactic to overcome errors, it's also an important strategy for extensibility. Imagine how much harder it would be to add new features to the language if the existing base of browsers choked on them.

The thing to watch out for with nonstandard tags that aren't supported by most browsers is their enclosed contents, if any. Browsers that recognize the new tag may process those contents differently than those that don't support the new tag. For example, Internet Explorer supports a `<comment>` tag whose contents serve to document the source HTML and are not intended to be viewed by the user. However, none of the other browsers recognizes the `<comment>` tag and render its contents on the user's screen, effectively defeating the tag's purpose in addition to ruining the document's appearance. [comments, 3.4.2]

3.4 Document Content

Nearly everything else you put into your HTML document that isn't a tag is by definition content, and the majority of that, in most HTML documents, is text. Like tags, document content is encoded using a specific character set, the ISO-8859-1 Latin character set, by default. This character set is a superset of conventional ASCII, adding the necessary characters to support the Western European languages. If your keyboard does not allow you to directly enter the characters you need, you can use character entities to insert the desired characters.

3.4.1 Advice Versus Control

Perhaps the hardest rule to remember when marking up an HTML document is that all the tags you insert regarding text display and formatting are only advice for the browser: they do not explicitly control how the browser will display the document. In fact, the browser can choose to ignore all of your tags and do what it pleases with the document content. What's worse, the user (of all people!) has control over text-display characteristics of his or her own browser.

Get used to this lack of control. The best way to use HTML markup to control the appearance of your documents is to concentrate on the content of the document, not on its final appearance. If you find yourself worrying excessively about spacing, alignment, text breaks, and character positioning, you'll surely end up with ulcers. You will have gone beyond the intent of HTML. If you focus on delivering information to users in an attractive manner, using the tags to advise the browser as to how best to display that information, you are using HTML effectively, and your documents will render well on a wide range of browsers.

3.4.2 Character Entities

Besides common text, HTML gives you a way to display special text characters you might not normally be able to include in your source document or which have other purposes in HTML. A good example is the less-than or opening bracket (<) symbol. In HTML, it normally signifies the start of a tag, so if you insert it simply as part of your text, the browser will get confused and probably misinterpret your document.

In HTML, the ampersand character instructs the browser to insert a special character, formally known as a *character entity*. For example, the command < inserts that pesky less-than symbol into the rendered text. Similarly, > inserts the greater-than symbol, and & inserts an ampersand. There can be no spaces between the ampersand, the entity name, and the required, trailing semicolon. (Semicolons aren't special characters; you don't need to use an ampersand sequence to display a semicolon normally.)

You also may replace the entity name after the ampersand with a decimal value between 0 and 255 corresponding to the entity's position in the character set. Hence, the sequence < does the same thing as < and represents the less-than symbol. In fact, you could substitute all the normal characters within an HTML document with ampersand-special characters, such as A for a capital "A" or a for its lowercase version, but that would be silly. A complete listing of all characters, their names, and numerical equivalents can be found in Appendix E, *Character Entities*.

Keep in mind that not all special characters can be rendered by all browsers. Some browsers just ignore many of the special characters; with others, the characters aren't available in the character sets on a specific platform. Be sure to test your documents on a range of browsers before electing to use some of the more obscure character entities.

3.4.3 Comments

Comments are another type of textual content that appear in the source HTML document, but are not rendered by the user's browser. Comments fall between the special <!-- and --> markup elements. Browsers ignore the text between the comment character sequences.

Here's a sample comment:

```
<!-- This is a comment -->
<!-- This is a
multiple line comment
that ends on this line -->
```

There must be a space after the initial `<!--` and preceding the final `-->`, but otherwise you can put nearly anything inside the comment. The biggest exception to this rule is that the HTML standard doesn't let you nest comments.[*]

As we mentioned above, Internet Explorer also lets you place comments within a special `<comment>` tag. Everything between the `<comment>` and `</comment>` tag is ignored by Internet Explorer, but all other browsers will display the comment to the user. Because of this undesirable behavior, we do not recommend using the `<comment>` tag for comments. Instead, always use the `<!--` and `-->` sequences to delimit comments.

Besides the obvious use of comments for HTML source documentation, many World Wide Web servers use comments to take advantage of features specific to the document server software. These servers scan the document for specific character sequences within conventional HTML comments and then perform some action based upon the commands embedded in the comments. The action might be as simple as including text from another file (known as a *server-side include*) or as complex as executing other commands on the server to dynamically generate the document contents.

3.5 *HTML Document Elements*

Every HTML document should conform to the HTML SGML DTD, the formal Document Type Definition that defines the HTML standard. The DTD defines the tags and syntax that are used to create an HTML document. You can inform the browser which DTD your document complies with by placing a special SGML (Standard Generalized Markup Language) command in the first line of the document:

```
<!DOCTYPE HTML PUBLIC "-//W3C//DTD HTML 3.2 Final//EN">
```

This cryptic message indicates that your document is intended to be compliant with the HTML 3.2 final DTD defined by the World Wide Web Consortium (W3C). Other versions of the DTD define more restricted versions of the HTML standard, and not all browsers support all versions of the HTML DTD. In fact, specifying any other doctype may cause the browser to misinterpret your document when displaying it for the user. It's also unclear what doctype to use when including in the HTML document the various tags that are not standards, but are very popular features of a popular browser—the Netscape extensions, for instance, or even the deprecated HTML 3.0 standard, for which a DTD was never released.

---

[*] Netscape does let you nest comments, but the practice is tricky; you cannot always predict how other browsers will react to nested comments.

Almost no one precedes their HTML documents with the SGML doctype command. Because of the confusion of versions and standards, we don't recommend that you include the prefix with your HTML documents either. There are other mechanisms to better define your document contents, such as the `version` attribute for the `<html>` tag.

3.5.1 The *<html>* Tag

As we saw earlier, the `<html>` and `</html>` tags serve to delimit the beginning and end of an HTML document. Since the typical browser can easily infer from the enclosed source that it is an HTML document, you don't really need to include the tag in your source document.

<html>

Function:
    Delimits a complete HTML document

Attributes:
    VERSION

End tag:
    </html>; may be omitted

Contains:
    head_tag, body_tag, frames

That said, it's considered good form to include this tag so that other tools, particularly more mundane text-processing ones, can recognize your document as an HTML document. At the very least, the presence of the beginning and ending `<html>` tags ensures that the beginning or the end of the document haven't been inadvertently deleted.

Inside the `<html>` tag and its end tag are the document's head and body. Within the head, you'll find tags that identify the document and define its place within a document collection. Within the body is the actual document content, defined by tags that determine the layout and appearance of the document text. As you might expect, the document head is contained within a `<head>` tag and the body is within a `<body>` tag, both of which are defined below.

Netscape Navigator and Internet Explorer extend the `<html>` tag so that the `<body>` tag may be replaced by a `<frameset>` tag, defining one or more display frames that, in turn, contain actual document content. See Chapter 12, *Frames*, for more information.

By far, the most common form of the `<html>` tag is simply:

```
<html>
...document head and body content
</html>
```

When the `<html>` tag appears without the **version** attribute, the HTML document server and browser assume the version of HTML used in this document is supplied to the browser by the server.

3.5.1.1 The version attribute

The `<html>` **version** attribute defines the HTML standard version used to compose the document. If included, the value of the **version** attribute should read exactly:

```
version="-//W3C//DTD HTML 3.2 Final//EN"
```

This attribute better identifies an HTML document's origins and contents than the SGML doctype command. However, some browsers may alter their processing of the document based upon the HTML version specified by this attribute, so be careful. Again, the confusion of extensions and versions and the lack of standards guidance makes us uneasy, and we do not recommend you include version information in your document, except perhaps as part of a leading comment.

3.6 The Document Header

The HTML document header describes the various properties of the document, including its title, position within the Web, and relationship with other documents. Most of the data contained within the document header are never actually rendered as content visible to the user.

3.6.1 The <head> Tag

The `<head>` tag has no attributes and serves only to encapsulate the other header tags. Since it always occurs near the beginning of a document, just after the `<html>` tag and before the `<body>` or `<frameset>` tag, both the `<head>` tag and its corresponding ending `</head>` can be unambiguously inferred by the browser and so can be safely omitted from the document. Nonetheless, we do encourage you to include them in your documents, since it promotes readability and better supports document automation.

The `<head>` tag may contain a number of other tags that help define and manage the document's content. These include, in any order of appearance: `<base>`, `<isindex>`, `<link>`, `<meta>`, `<nextid>`, `<title>`, and `<style>`.

<head>

Function:
> Defines the document header

Attributes:
> None

End tag:
> </head>; rarely omitted

Contains:
> *head_content*

Used in:
> *html_tag*

For more information, see Chapter 7, *Links and Webs* and Chapter 9, *Cascading Style Sheets.*

3.6.2 The <title> Tag

The `<title>` tag does exactly what you might expect: the words you place inside its start and end tags define the title for your document. (We told you this stuff is pretty much self-explanatory and easier than you might think at first glance.) The title is used by the browser in some special manner, most often placed in the browser window's title bar or on a status line. Usually, too, the title becomes the default name for a link to the document if the document is added to a link collection or to a user's "hot list."

<title>

Function:
> Defines the document title

Attributes:
> None

End tag:
> </title>; never omitted

Contains:
> *plain_text*

Used in:
> *head_content*

The <title> tag is the only thing required within the <head> tag. Since the <head> tag itself and even the <html> tag may be safely omitted, the <title> tag could be the first line within a valid HTML document. Beyond that, most browsers will even supply a generic title for documents lacking a <title> tag, such as the document's filename, so you don't even have to supply a title. That goes a bit too far even for our down-and-dirty tastes. No respectable author of an HTML document should serve up a document missing the <title> tag and a title.

Browsers do not specially format title text and ignore anything other than text inside the title start and end tags, such as images or links to other documents.

Here's an even barer barebones example of a valid HTML document to highlight the header and title tags:

```
<html>
<head>
<title>HTML: The Definitive Guide</title>
</head>
</html>
```

3.6.2.1 What's in a title?

Selecting the right title is crucial to defining a document and ensuring that it can be effectively used within the World Wide Web.

Keep in mind that users can access each of your documents in a collection in nearly any order and independently of one another. Each document's title should therefore define the document both within the context of your other documents as well as on its own merits.

Titles that include references to document sequencing are usually inappropriate. Simple titles, like "Chapter 2" or "Part VI" do little to help a user understand what the document might contain. More descriptive titles, such as "Chapter 2: Advanced Square Dancing" or "Part VI: Churchill's Youth and Adulthood," convey both a sense of place within a larger set of documents and specific content that invites the reader to read on.

Self-referential titles also aren't very useful. A title like "My Home Page" is completely content-free, as are titles like "Feedback Page" or "Popular Links." You want a title to convey a sense of content and purpose so that users can decide, based upon the title alone, whether to visit that page or not. "The Kumquat Lover's Home Page" is descriptive and likely to draw in lovers of the bitter fruit, as are "Kumquat Lover's Feedback Page" and "Popular Links Frequented by Kumquat Lovers."

People spend a great deal of time creating documents for the Web, often only to squander that effort with an uninviting, ineffective title. As special software that automatically collects links for users becomes more prevalent on the Web, the only descriptive phrase associated with your pages when they are inserted into some vast link database will be the title you choose for them. We can't emphasize this enough: take care to select descriptive, useful, context-independent titles for each of your HTML documents.

3.6.3 Related Header Tags

Other tags you may include within the `<head>` tag deal with specific aspects of document creation, management, linking, automation, or layout. That's why we only mention them here, and describe them in greater detail in other, more appropriate sections and chapters of this book.

Briefly, the special header tags are:

`<link>` *and* `<base>`
> Define the current document's base location and relationship to other documents. [`<link>`, 7.7.2] [`<base>`, 7.7.1]

`<isindex>`
> Creates automatic document indexing forms, allowing users to search databases of information using the current document as a querying tool. [`<isindex>`, 7.6.1]

`<nextid>`
> Makes creation of unique document labels easier when using document automation tools. [`<nextid>`, 7.8.2]

`<meta>`
> Provides additional document data not supplied by any of the other `<head>` tags. [`<meta>`, 7.8.1]

`<style>`
> Lets you create Cascading Style Sheet properties to control body-content display characteristics for the entire document. [`<style>`, 9.1.2]

3.7 The Document Body

The document body is the meat of the matter; it's where you put the contents of your document. The `<body>` tag delimits the document body.

C. M. Buche
3S321 Blackthorn Ln.
Warrenville, IL 60555-2614

3.7.1 The <body> Tag

Within HTML 3.2, the <body> tag has a number of attributes that control the color and background of your document. Various browsers, as we'll see, have extended the tag to give even greater control over your document's appearance.

<body>

Function:
    Defines the document body

Attributes:
    ALINK
    BACKGROUND
    BGCOLOR
    BGPROPERTIES **O**
    CLASS **N** **O**
    LEFTMARGIN **O**
    LINK
    ONBLUR **N** **O**
    ONFOCUS **N** **O**
    ONLOAD **N** **O**
    ONUNLOAD **N** **O**
    STYLE **N** **O**
    TEXT
    TOPMARGIN **O**
    VLINK

End tag:
    </body>; may be omitted

Contains:
    body_content

Used in:
    html_tag

Anything inside the <body> tag and its ending counterpart </body> is called *body content*. The simplest HTML document might have only a sequence of text paragraphs within the <body> tag. More complex documents will include heavily formatted text, graphical figures, tables, and a variety of special effects.

Since the position of the <body> and </body> tags can be inferred by the browser, they can safely be omitted from the document. However, like the <html> and <head> tags, we recommend that you include the <body> tags in your document to make them more easily readable and maintainable.

The various attributes for the `<body>` tag can be loosely grouped into two sets: those that give you some control over the document's appearance, such as its background, text, and hyperlink display colors, and those that associate programmable functions with the document itself. We address the appearance attributes (`alink`, `background`, `bgcolor`, `bgproperties`, `leftmargin`, `link`, `text`, `topmargin`, and `vlink`) in 5.3, along with the `class` and `style` attributes for cascading and JavaScript style sheets, described in Chapter 9, *Cascading Style Sheets*. The programmatic attributes (`onBlur`, `onFocus`, `onLoad`, and `onUnload`) are covered in 13.3.3.

Netscape and Internet Explorer also implement a special type of HTML document in which you replace the `<body>` tag with one or more `<frameset>` tags. This so-called *frame* document divides the display window into one or more independent windows, each displaying a different document. We describe this innovation in Chapter 12, *Frames*.

4

Text Basics

In this day and age of hoopla and hype, *how* has become almost as important as *what*—and in some cases, more important. Any successful presentation, even a thoughtful tome, should have its text organized into an attractive, effective document. Organizing text into attractive documents is HTML's forte. The language gives you a number of tools that help you mold your text and get your message across. HTML also helps structure your document so your target audience has easy access to your words.

Always keep in mind while designing your documents (here we go again!), that HTML tags, particularly in regard to text, only advise—they do not dictate—how a browser will ultimately render the document. Rendering varies from browser to browser. Don't get too entangled with trying to get just the right look and layout. Your attempts may and probably will be thwarted by the browser.

4.1 Divisions and Paragraphs

Like most text processors, a browser wraps the words it finds in the HTML text to fit the horizontal width of its viewing window. Widen the browser's window and words automatically flow up to fill the wider lines. Squeeze the window and words wrap downwards.

Unlike most text processors, however, HTML uses explicit division (`<div>`), paragraph (`<p>`), and line-break (`<br>`) tags to control the alignment and flow of text. Return characters, although quite useful for readability of the source HTML document, typically are ignored by the browser—HTML authors must use the `<br>` to explicitly force a text line break. The `<p>` tag, while also performing the task, carries with it meaning and effects beyond a simple line break.

The `<div>` tag is a little different. Codified in the HTML 3.2 standard, `<div>` was included in the language to be a simple organizational tool—divide the document into discrete sections—whose somewhat obtuse meaning meant few authors used it. But recent browser innovations—the align and style-related style and class attributes—now let you more distinctly label and thereby define individual sections of your HTML documents, as well as control the alignment and appearance of those sections. These features breathe real life and meaning into the `<div>` tag.

By associating a class name with the various sections of your HTML document, each delimited by a `<div class=`*name*`>` tag and attribute (you can do the same with other tags like `<p>`, too), you not only label those divisions for automated processing and management (collect all the bibliography divisions, for instance), but you may also define different, distinct display styles for those portions of your document. For instance, you might define one divisional class for your document's abstract (`<div class=abstract>`, for example), another for the body, a third for the conclusion, and a fourth divisional class for the bibliography (`<div class=biblio>`, for example).

Each class, then, might be given a different display definition in a document-level or externally related style sheet: the abstract indented and in an italic face (`div.abstract {left-margin: +0.5in; font-style: italic}`, for example); the body in a left-justified roman face; the conclusion similar to the abstract; and the bibliography automatically numbered and formatted appropriately.

We provide a detailed description of style sheets, classes, and their applications in Chapter 9, *Cascading Style Sheets*.

4.1.1 The <div> Tag

As defined in the HTML 3.2 standard, the `<div>` tag divides your document into separate, distinct sections. It may be used strictly as an organizational tool, without any sort of formatting associated with it; it becomes more effective in this regard if you add the class attribute to label the division. The `<div>` tag may also be combined with the align attribute to control the alignment of whole sections of your document's content in the display.

<div>

Function:
> Defines a block of text

Attributes:
> ALIGN
> CLASS **N** **O**
> LANG **O**
> NOWRAP **O**
> STYLE **N** **O**

End tag:
> </div>; usually omitted

Contains:
> *body_content*

Used in:
> *block*

4.1.1.1 The align attribute

The align attribute for `<div>` justifies the enclosed content to either the `left` (default), `center`, or `right` of the browser display. The `<div>` tag may be nested, and the alignment of the nested `<div>` tag takes precedence over the containing `<div>` tag. Further, other nested alignment tags, such as `<center>`, aligned paragraphs (see `<p>` in 4.1.2), or specially aligned table rows and cells, override the effect of `<div>`.

4.1.1.2 The nowrap attribute

Supported only by Internet Explorer, this attribute suppresses automatic word wrapping of the text within the division. Line breaks will occur where you have placed carriage returns in your HTML source document.

While the `nowrap` attribute probably doesn't make much sense for large sections of text that would otherwise be flowed together on the page, it can make things a bit easier when creating blocks of text with many explicit line breaks: poetry, for example, or addresses. You don't have to insert all those explicit `<br>` tags in a text flow within a `<div nowrap>` tag. On the other hand, all other browsers ignore the `nowrap` attribute and merrily flow your text together anyway. If you are targeting only Internet Explorer with your documents, consider using `nowrap` where needed, but otherwise, we can't recommend this attribute for general use.

4.1.1.3   The lang attribute

The `lang` attribute lets you specify the language used within the division. The value of the attribute is any of the ISO standard two-character language abbreviations. For example, adding `lang=en` tells the browser that the division is written in English. Presumably, the browser may make layout or typographic decisions based upon your language choice.

This attribute is only supported by Internet Explorer; all other browsers ignore it. Even within Internet Explorer, there are no behaviors defined for any specific language.

4.1.1.4   The style and class attributes

Use the `style` attribute with the `<div>` tag to create an inline style for the content enclosed by the tag. The `class` attribute lets you apply the style of a predefined class of the `<div>` tag to the contents of this division. The value of the `class` attribute is the name of a style defined in some document-level or externally defined style sheet. In addition, class-identified divisions also lend themselves well for computer processing of your documents, such as extraction of all divisions whose class name is "biblio," for example, for the automated assembly of a master bibliography. [`style` attribute, 9.1.1] [`class` attribute, 9.2.4]

4.1.2   The <p> Tag

The `<p>` tag signals the start of a paragraph. That's not well known even by some veteran webmasters because it runs counterintuitive to what we've come to expect from experience. Most word processors we're familiar with use just one special character, typically the return character, to signal the *end* of a paragraph.

In the recommended HTML way, each paragraph starts with `<p>` and ends with the corresponding `</p>` tag. And while a sequence of newline characters in a text processor-displayed document creates an empty paragraph for each one, HTML browsers typically ignore all but the first paragraph tag.

In practice, you also can ignore the starting `<p>` tag at the beginning of the first paragraph, as well as the `</p>` tag at the end of all paragraphs, since they can be implied from other tags that occur in the document, and hence safely omitted. For example:

```
<body>
This is the first paragraph, at the very beginning of the
body of this document.
<p>
The tag above signals the start of this second paragraph.
When rendered by a browser, it will begin slightly below the
end of the first paragraph, with a bit of extra whitespace
```

<p>

Function:
　　Defines a paragraph of text

Attributes:
　　ALIGN
　　CLASS Ⓝ Ⓞ
　　STYLE Ⓝ Ⓞ

End tag:
　　</p>; usually omitted

Contains:
　　text

Used in:
　　block

```
between the two paragraphs.
<p>
This is the last paragraph in the example.
</body>
```

Notice that we haven't included the paragraph start tag (<p>) for the first paragraph or any end paragraph tags at all in the example; they can be unambiguously inferred by the browser and are therefore unnecessary.

In general, you'll find that human document authors tend to omit postulated tags whenever possible, while automatic document generators tend to insert them. That may be because the software designers didn't want to run the risk of having their product chided by competitors as not adhering to the HTML standard, even though we're splitting letter-of-the-law hairs here. Go ahead and be defiant: omit that first paragraph's <p> tag and don't give a second thought to paragraph ending </p> tags, provided, of course, that your document's structure and clarity are not compromised.

4.1.2.1 Paragraph rendering

When encountering a new paragraph (<p>) tag, a browser typically inserts one blank line plus some extra vertical space into the document before starting the new paragraph. The browser then collects all the words and, if present, inline images into the new paragraph, ignoring leading and trailing spaces (not spaces between words, of course) and return characters in the HTML text. The browser software then flows the resulting sequence of words and images into a paragraph that fits within the margins of its display window, automatically generating line breaks as needed to wrap the text within the window. For example, compare how a browser arranges the text into lines and paragraphs (Figure 4-1) to how the preceding HTML example is printed on the page. The browser may also automatically hyphenate long words, and the paragraph may be full-justified to stretch the line of words out towards both margins.

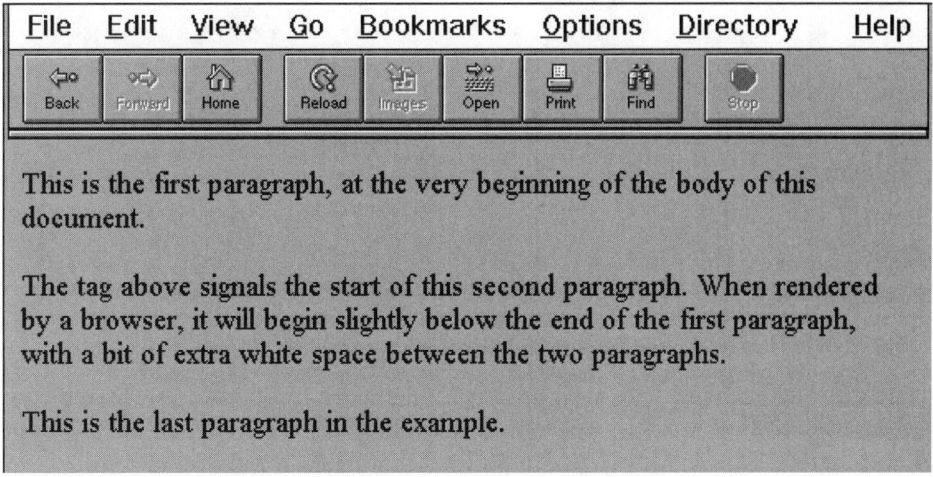

Figure 4-1. Browsers ignore common return characters in the source HTML document

The net result is that you do not have to worry about line length, word wrap, and line breaks when composing your HTML documents. The browser will take any arbitrary sequence of words and images and display a nicely formatted paragraph.

If you want to control line length and breaks explicitly, consider using a preformatted text block with the **<pre>** tag. If you need to force a line break, use the **
** tag. [<pre>, 4.7.5] [
, 4.7.1]

4.1.2.2 The align attribute

Most browsers automatically left-justify a new paragraph. To change this behavior, HTML 3.2 gives you the align attribute for the **<p>** tag and provides three kinds of content justification: left, right, or center.

Figure 4-2 shows you the effect of each alignment, as rendered from the following source:

```
<p align=right>
Right over here!
<br>
This is too.
<p align=left>
Slide back left.
<p align=center>
Smack in the middle.
</p>
Left's the default.
```

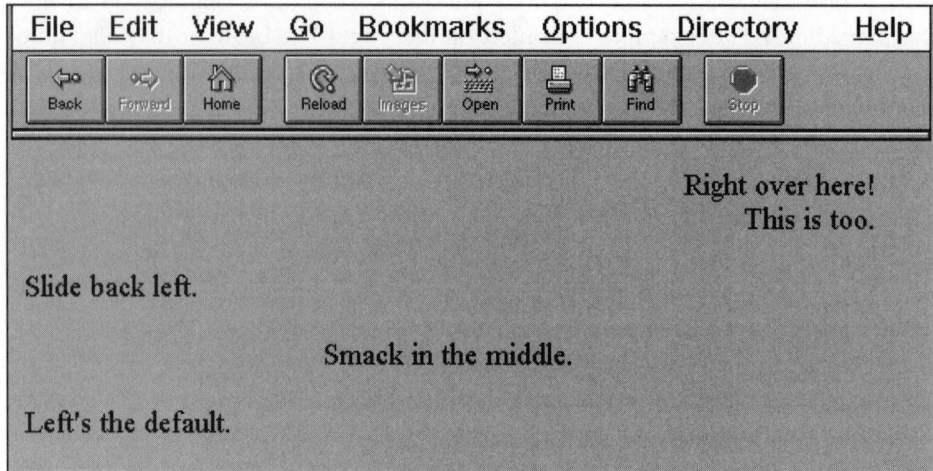

Figure 4-2. Effect of the align attribute on paragraph justification (Netscape 2.0)

Notice in the example that the paragraph alignment remains in effect until the browser encounters another `<p>` tag or an ending `</p>` tag (we deliberately left out a final `<p>` tag in the example to illustrate the effects of the `</p>` end tag on paragraph justification). Other body elements may also disrupt the current paragraph alignment and cause subsequent paragraphs to revert to the default left alignment, including forms, headers, tables, and most other body content-related tags.

4.1.2.3 *The style and class attributes*

Use the `style` attribute with the `<p>` tag to create an inline style for the paragraph's contents. The `class` attribute lets you label the paragraph with a name that refers to a predefined class of the `<p>` tag declared in some document-level or externally defined style sheet. And, class-identified paragraphs lend themselves well for computer processing of your documents, such as extraction of all paragraphs whose class name is "citation," for example, for automated assembly of a master list of citations. [`style` attribute, 9.1.1] [`class` attribute, 9.2.4]

4.1.2.4 *Allowed paragraph content*

An HTML paragraph may contain any element allowed in a text flow, including conventional words and punctuation, links (`<a>`), images (`<img>`), line breaks (`<br>`), font changes (`<b>`, `<i>`, `<tt>`, `<u>`, `<strike>`, `<big>`, `<small>`, `<sup>`, `<sub>`, and `<font>`), and content-based style changes (`<cite>`, `<code>`, `<dfn>`, `<em>`, `<kbd>`, `<samp>`, `<strong>`, and `<var>`). If any other element occurs within the paragraph, it implies the paragraph has ended, and the browser assumes the closing `</p>` tag was not specified.

4.1.2.5 Allowed paragraph usage

You may specify a paragraph only within a *block*, along with other paragraphs, lists, forms, and preformatted text. In general, this means that paragraphs can appear where a flow of text is appropriate, such as in the body of a document, an element in a list, and so on. Technically, paragraphs cannot appear within a header, anchor, or other element whose content is strictly text-only. In practice, most browsers ignore this restriction and format the paragraph as a part of the containing element.

4.2 Headings

Users have a hard enough time reading what's displayed on a screen. A long flow of text, unbroken by title, subtitles, and other headers, crosses the eyes and numbs the mind, not to mention the fact that it makes it nearly impossible to scan the text for a specific topic.

You should always break a flow of text into several smaller sections within one or more headings (like this book!). HTML defines six levels of headings that can be used to structure a text flow into a more readable, more manageable document. And, as we discuss in Chapter 5, *Rules, Images, and Multimedia*, and in Chapter 9, *Cascading Style Sheets*, there are a variety of graphical and text-style tricks that help divide your HTML document and make its contents more accessible as well as more readable to users.

4.2.1 Heading Tags

The six heading tags, written as `<h1>`, `<h2>`, `<h3>`, `<h4>`, `<h5>`, and `<h6>`, indicate the highest (`<h1>`) to the lowest (`<h6>`) precedence a heading may have in the document.

The enclosed text within a heading typically is uniquely rendered by the browser, depending upon the display technology available to it. The browser may choose to center, embolden, enlarge, italicize, underline, or change the color of headings to make each stand out within the document. And to thwart the most tedious HTML writers, users, too, often can alter how a browser will render the different headings.

Fortunately, in practice most browsers use a diminishing character point size for the sequence of headers, so that `<h1>` text is quite large and `<h6>` text is quite minuscule (see Figure 4-3, for example).

By tradition, HTML authors have come to use `<h1>` headers for document titles, `<h2>` headers for section titles, and so on, often matching the way many of us were taught to outline our work with heads, subheads, and sub-subheads.

<h1>, <h2>, <h3>, <h4>, <h5>, <h6>

Function:

Define one of six levels of headers

Attributes:

ALIGN
CLASS **N** **O**
STYLE **N** **O**

End tag:

</h1>, </h2>, </h3>, </h4>, </h5>, </h6>; never omitted

Contains:

text

Used in:

body_content

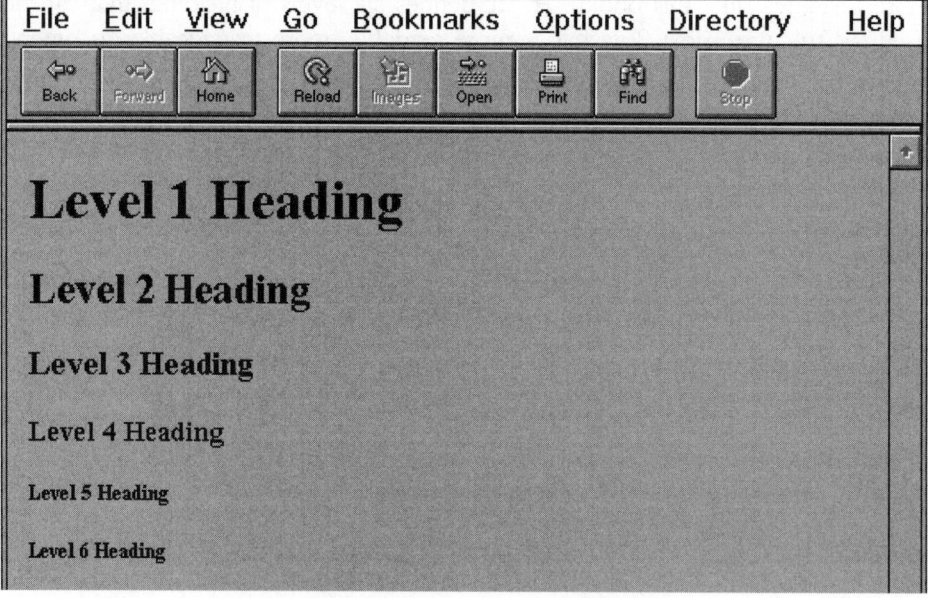

Figure 4-3. Browsers typically use diminishing text sizes for rendering headings

Finally, don't forget to include the appropriate heading end tags in your document. The browser won't insert one automatically for you, and omitting the ending tag for a heading can have disastrous consequences for your document.

4.2.1.1 The align attribute

The default heading alignment for most browsers is left. Like the `<div>` and `<p>` tags, you can alter this alignment with the `align` attribute and one of the values: `left`, `center`, or `right`. Figure 4-4 shows these alternative alignments as rendered from the following source:

```
<h1 align=right>Right over here!</h1>
<h2 align=left>Slide back left.</h2>
<h3 align=center>Smack in the middle.</h3>
```

Figure 4-4. The headings align attribute in action

4.2.1.2 The style and class attributes

The `style` and `class` attributes for the heading tags let you define an inline style for the content enclosed by the header tag, and format the content according to a predefined style sheet class. [`style` attribute, 9.1.1] [`class` attribute, 9.2.4]

4.2.2 Appropriate Use of Headings

It's good form to repeat your document title in the first heading tag, since the title you specify at the beginning of your HTML document doesn't appear in the user's main display window. It should match the title in the document header. The following HTML segment is a good example of repeating the document's title in the header and in the body of the document:

```
<html>
<head>
<title>Kumquat Farming in North America</title>
</head>
<body>
<h3>Kumquat Farming in North America</h3>
<p>
Perhaps one of the most enticing of all fruits is the...
```

While the browser may place the title somewhere in the document window and may also use it to create bookmarks or hotlist entries, all of which vaguely are somewhere on the user's desktop, the level three title heading in the example will always appear at the very beginning of the document. It serves as a visible title to the document regardless of how the browser handles the `<title>` tag contents. And, unlike the `<title>` text, the heading title will appear at the beginning of the first page should the user elect to print the document. [`<title>`, 3.6.2]

In the example, we chose to use a level three header (`<h3>`) whose rendered font typically is just a bit larger than the regular document text. Levels one and two are larger still and often a bit overbearing. You should choose a level of heading that you find useful and attractive and use that level consistently throughout your documents.

Once you have established the top-level heading for your document, use additional headings at the same or lower level throughout to add structure and "scanability" to the document. If you use a level three heading for the document title, break your document into several sections using level four headings. If you have the urge to subdivide your text further, consider using a level two heading for the title, level three for the section dividers, and level four for the subsections.

4.2.3 Using Headings for Smaller Text

For most graphical browsers, the fonts used to display `<h1>`, `<h2>`, and `<h3>` headers are larger, `<h4>` is the same, and `<h5>` and `<h6>` are smaller than the regular text size. HTML writers typically use the latter two sizes for boilerplate text, like a disclaimer or a copyright notice. Experiment with `<h5>` and `<h6>` to get the effect you want. See how a typical browser renders the copyright reference in the following sample HTML segment (see Figure 4-5):

```
resulting in years of successful kumquat production
throughout North America.
</p>
<h6>This document copyright 1995 by the Kumquat Growers of
America. All rights reserved. </h6>
</body>
</html>
```

4.2.4 Allowed Heading Content

A heading may contain any element allowed in *text*, including conventional text, link anchors (`<a>`), images (`<img>`), line breaks (`<br>`), font embellishments (`<b>`, `<i>`, `<tt>`, `<u>`, `<strike>`, `<big>`, `<small>`, `<sup>`, `<sub>`, and

Figure 4-5. HTML authors typically use header level six for boilerplate text

<font>), and content-based style changes (<cite>, <code>, <dfn>, <em>, <kbd>, <samp>, <strong>, and <var>).

In practice, however, font or style changes may not take effect within a heading, since the heading itself prescribes a font change within the browser.

There is widespread abuse of the heading tags as a mechanism for changing the font of an entire document. Technically, paragraphs, lists, and other block elements are not allowed within a heading and may be mistaken by the browser to indicate the implied end of the heading. In practice, most browsers apply the style of the heading to all contained paragraphs. We discourage this practice since it is not only a violation of the HTML standard, but usually ugly to look at. Imagine if your local paper printed all the copy in headline type!

If you really want to change the entire font or type size of your document, consider instead defining a unique style for the <body> tag of your document. This style will be applied to all the content within the <body> and will make later modification of your document style much easier. See Chapter 9, *Cascading Style Sheets* for details.

4.2.5 Allowed Heading Usage

Formally, the HTML standard allows headings only within *body content.* In practice, most browsers recognize headings almost anywhere, formatting the rendered text to fit within the current element. In all cases, the occurrence of a heading signifies the end of any preceding paragraph or other text element, so you can't use the heading tags to change font sizes in the same line. HTML 3.2, however, defines the <font> tag for inline font size adjustments; see 4.6 for details.

4.2.6 Adding Images to Headings

It is possible to insert one or more images within your headings, from small bullets or icons to full-sized logos. Combining a consistent set of headings with corresponding icons across a family of documents is not only visually attractive, but an effective way of aiding users' perusal of your document collection. [<img>, 5.2.6]

Adding an image to a heading is easy. For example, the following text puts an "information" icon inside the "For More Information" heading, as you can see in Figure 4-6.

```
<h2>
<img src="info.gif">
For More Information</h2>
```

In general, images within headings look best at the beginning of the heading, aligned with the bottom or middle of the heading text.

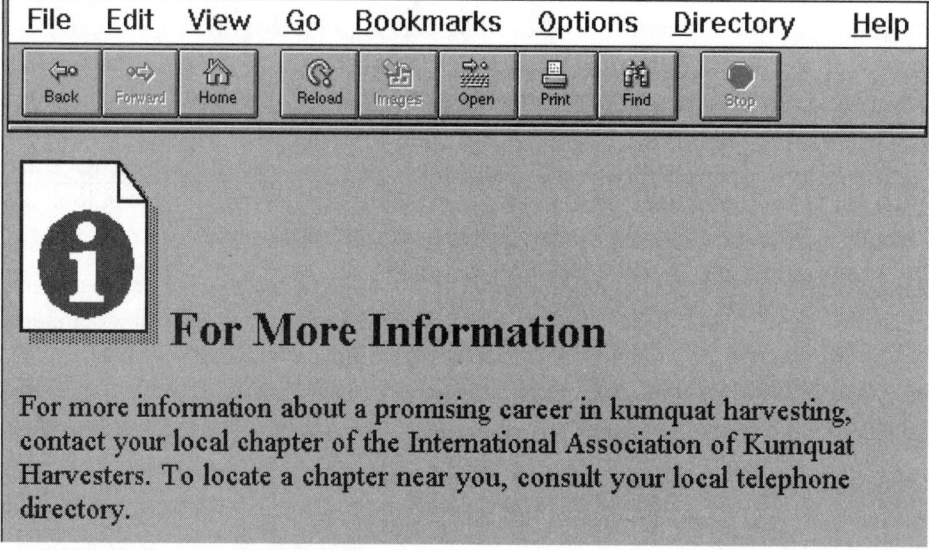

Figure 4-6. An image within a heading

4.3 Changing Text Appearance

HTML offers a number of tags that change the appearance of text. In general, these tags can be grouped into two flavors: content-based styles and physical styles.

In addition, the W3C has put forth a draft for a new standard way in which HTML authors may control the look and layout of their document text through Cascading Style Sheets. Netscape, too, in their latest browser has implemented style sheets through JavaScript. We describe the HTML tag-based text styles in this chapter. See Chapter 9, *Cascading Style Sheets*, for details about cascading and JavaScript-based style sheets.

4.3.1   Content-Based Styles

Content-based style tags inform the browser that the enclosed text has a specific meaning, context, or usage. The browser then formats the text in a manner consistent with that meaning, context, or usage.

Because font style is specified via semantic clues, the browser can choose a display style that is appropriate for the user. Since such styles vary by locale, using content-based styles helps ensure that your documents will have meaning to a broader range of readers. This is particularly important when a browser is targeted at blind or handicapped readers whose display options are radically different from conventional text or are extremely limited in some way.

The HTML standard does not define a format for each of the content-based styles except that they must be rendered in a manner different from the regular text in a document. The standard doesn't even insist that the content-based styles be rendered differently from one another. In practice, you'll find that many of these tags have fairly obvious relationships with conventional print, having similar meanings and rendered styles, and are rendered in the same style and fonts by most browsers.

4.3.2   Physical Styles

We use the word "intent" a lot when we talk about content-based style tags. That's because the meaning conveyed by the tag is more important than the way a browser displays the text. In some cases, however, you might want the text to appear explicitly in italic or bold, perhaps for legal or copyright reasons. In those cases, use a physical style for the text.

While the tendency with other text-processing systems is to control style and appearance explicitly, with HTML you should avoid explicit, physical tags except on rare occasions. Rather, provide the browser with as much contextual information as possible. Use the content-based styles. Even though current browsers may do nothing more than display their text in italic or bold, future browsers and various document-generation tools may use the content-based styles in any number of creative ways.

4.4 Content-Based Style Tags

It takes discipline to use the content-based styles, since it is easier to simply think of how your text should look, not necessarily what it may also mean. Once you get started using content-based styles, your documents will be more consistent and better lend themselves to automated searching and content compilation.

Content-Based Style Tags

Function:
> Alter the appearance of text based upon the meaning, context, or usage of the text

Attributes:
> CLASS 🅽 🄾
> STYLE 🅽 🄾

End tag:
> Never omitted

Contains:
> *text*

Used in:
> *text*

4.4.1 The <cite> Tag

The `<cite>` tag usually indicates that the enclosed text is a bibliographic citation like a book or magazine title. By convention, the citation text is rendered in italic. For example, see Figure 4-7 for the NCSA Mosaic rendering of this source text:

```
While kumquats are not mentioned in Melville's
<cite>Moby Dick</cite>, it is nonetheless apparent
that the mighty cetacean represents the bitter
"kumquat-ness" within every man. Indeed, when Ahab
spears the beast, its flesh is tough, much like the noble fruit.
```

Use the `<cite>` tag to set apart any reference to another document, especially those in the traditional media, such as books, magazines, journal articles, and the like. If an online version of the referenced work exists, you also should enclose the citation within the `<a>` tag and make it a hyperlink to that online version.

The `<cite>` tag also has a hidden feature: it enables you or someone else to automatically extract a bibliography from your documents. It is easy to envision a browser that compiles tables of citations automatically, displaying them as foot-

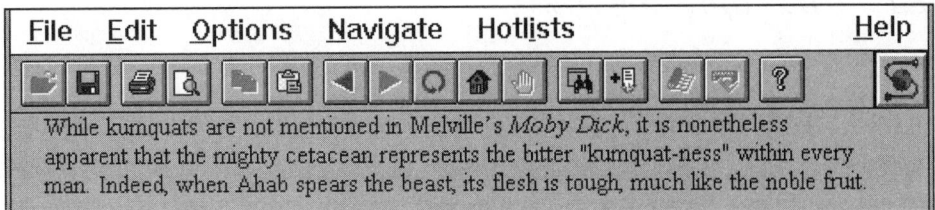

Figure 4-7. Mosaic renders <cite> in italic

notes or as a separate document entirely. The semantics of the `<cite>` tag go far beyond changing the appearance of the enclosed text; they enable the browser to present the content to the user in a variety of useful ways.

4.4.2 The <code> Tag

Software code warriors have become accustomed to a special style of text presentation for their source programs. The `<code>` tag is for them. It renders the enclosed text in a monospaced, teletype-style font like Courier familiar to most programmers and readers of O'Reilly's series of books, including this one.

This following bit of en`<code>`ed text is rendered in monospaced font style by Netscape as shown in Figure 4-8.

```
The array reference <code>a[i]</code> is identical to
the pointer reference <code>*(a+i)</code>.
```

Figure 4-8. Use <code> to present computer-speak

You should use the `<code>` tag only for text that represents computer source code or other machine-readable content. While the `<code>` tag usually just makes text appear in a monospaced font, the implication is that it is source code and future browsers may add other display effects. For example, a programmer's browser might look for `<code>` segments and perform some additional text formatting like special indentation of loops and conditional clauses. If the only effect you desire is a monospaced font, use the `<tt>` tag instead.

4.4.3 The <dfn> Tag

Use `<dfn>` to tag those defining instances of special terms or phrases. It may not result in any formatting changes by the browser. Instead, `<dfn>` might assist in creating a document index or glossary.

For example, use the `<dfn>` tag to introduce a new phrase to the reader:

```
When analyzing annual crop yields, <dfn>rind spectroscopy</dfn> may
prove useful. By comparing the relative levels of saturated
hydrocarbons in fruit from adjacent trees, rind spectroscopy has been
shown to be 87% effective in predicting an outbreak of trunk dropsy in
trees under four years old.
```

Notice that we delimit only the first occurrence of "rind spectroscopy" with a `<dfn>` tag in the example. Good style tells us not to clutter the text with high-lighted text. As with the many other content-related and physical style tags, the fewer the better.* As a general style, especially in technical documentation, set off new terms when they are first introduced to help your readers better understand the topic at hand, but resist tagging the terms thereafter.

4.4.4 The <em> Tag

The `<em>` tag tells the client browser to present the enclosed text with emphasis. For nearly all browsers, this means the text is rendered in italic. For example, Netscape will emphasize by italicizing the words "always" and "never" in the following sample:

```
Kumquat growers must <em>always</em> refer to kumquats
as "the noble fruit," <em>never</em> as just a "fruit."
```

Adding emphasis to your text is a tricky business. Too little, and the emphatic phrases may be lost. Too much, and you lose the urgency. Like any seasoning, emphasis is best used sparingly.

Although invariably displayed in italic, the `<em>` tag has broader implications as well and someday browsers may render emphasized text with a different special effect. The `<i>` tag explicitly italicizes text; use it if all you want is italic. Besides emphasis, also consider using `<em>` when presenting new terms or as a fixed style when referring to a specific type of term or concept. For instance, one of O'Reilly's book styles is to specially format file and device names. In the HTML version, `<em>` might be used to differentiate those terms from simple italic for emphasis.

---

* If you need convincing that less is better when applying the content-based and physical style tags, try reading a college textbook in which someone has highlighted what they considered important words and phrases with a yellow pen.

4.4.5 The <kbd> Tag

Speaking of special style for technical concepts, there is the <kbd> tag. As you probably already suspect, it is used to indicate text that is typed on a keyboard. Its enclosed text typically is rendered by the browser in monospaced font style.

The <kbd> tag is most often used in computer-related documentation and manuals, such as in this example:

```
Type <kbd>quit</kbd> to exit the utility, or type
<kbd>menu</kbd> to return to the main menu.
```

4.4.6 The <samp> Tag

The <samp> tag indicates a sequence of literal characters that should have no other interpretation by the user. This tag is most often used when a sequence of characters is taken out of its normal context. For example, the following source:

```
The <samp>ae</samp> character sequence may be converted
to the &aelig; ligature if desired.
```

is rendered by Netscape as shown in Figure 4-9.

Figure 4-9. Setting off sample text using the <samp> tag

(The special HTML reference for the "ae" ligature entity is æ and is converted to its appropriate æ ligature character by most browsers.) For more information, see Appendix E, *Character Entities*.

In general, the <samp> tag is not used very often. It should be used in those few cases where special emphasis needs to be placed on small character sequences taken out of their normal context.

4.4.7 The <strong> Tag

Like the <em> tag, the <strong> tag is for emphasizing text, except with more gusto. Browsers typically display the <strong> tag differently than the <em> tag, usually by making the text bold (versus italic), so that users can distinguish between the two. For example, in the following text, the emphasized "never" appears in italic with Mosaic, while the `<strong>` "forbidden" is rendered in bold characters (see Figure 4-10).

```
One should <em>never</em> make a disparaging remark
about the noble fruit. In particular, mentioning
kumquats in conjunction with vulgar phrases is
expressly <strong>forbidden</strong> by the Association
bylaws.
```

If common sense tells us that the `<em>` tag should be used sparingly, the `<strong>` tag should appear in documents even more infrequently. `<em>` text is like shouting. `<strong>` text is nothing short of a scream. Like a well-chosen epithet voiced by an otherwise taciturn person, restraint in the use of `<strong>` makes its use that much more noticeable and effective.

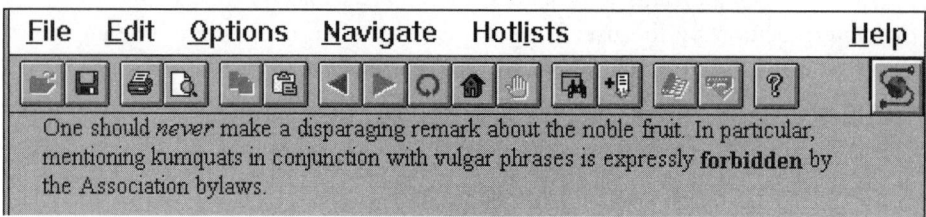

Figure 4-10. Strong and emphasized text are rendered differently by Mosaic

4.4.8 The `<var>` Tag

The `<var>` tag, another computer-documentation trick, indicates a variable name or a user-supplied value. The tag is most often used in conjunction with the `<code>` and `<pre>` tags for displaying particular elements of computer programming code samples and the like. `<var>`-tagged text typically is rendered in monospace font, as shown in Figure 4-11, which displays Netscape's rendering of the following example:

```
The user should type
<pre>
  cp <var>source-file</var>   <var>dest-file</var>
</pre>
replacing the <var>source-file</var> with the name of
the source file, and <var>dest-file</var> with the name
of the destination file.
```

Like the other computer programming and documentation-related tags, the `<var>` tag not only makes it easy for users to understand and browse your documentation, but automated systems might someday use the appropriately tagged text to extract information and useful parameters mentioned in your document. Once again, the more semantic information you provide to your browser, the better it can present that information to the user.

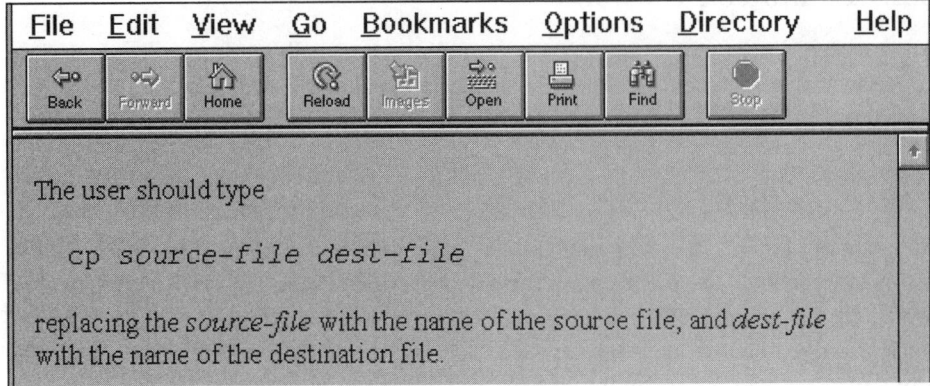

Figure 4-11. The <var> tag typically appears in preformatted (<pre>) computer code

4.4.9 The style and class Attributes

Although each content-based tag has a defined style, you can override that style by defining your own look for each tag. This new look can be applied to the content-based tags using either the `style` or `class` attributes. [`style` attribute, 9.1.1] [`class` attribute, 9.2.4]

4.4.10 Summary of Content-Based Tags

The various graphical browsers render text inside content-based tags in similar fashion; text-only browsers like Lynx have consistent styles for the tags. Table 4-1 summarizes these browsers' display styles for the native tags. However, style sheet definitions may override these native display styles.

Table 4-1. Content-based tags

Tag	Netscape	Internet Explorer	Lynx
`<cite>`	*italic*	*italic*	monospace
`<code>`	monospace	monospace	monospace
`<dfn>`	n/a	*italic*	n/a
`<em>`	*italic*	*italic*	monospace
`<kbd>`	monospace	**monospace bold**	monospace
`<samp>`	monospace	monospace	monospace
`<strong>`	**bold**	**bold**	monospace
`<var>`	*italic*	monospace	monospace

4.4.11 Allowed Content

Any content-based style tag may contain any item allowed in *text*, including conventional text, anchors, images, and line breaks. In addition, other content-based and physical style tags can be embedded within the content.

4.4.12 Allowed Usage

Any content-based style tag may be used anywhere an item allowed in *text* is used. In practice, this means you can use the `<em>`, `<code>`, or other like tags anywhere in your HTML document except inside `<title>`, `<listing>`, or `<xmp>` tagged segments. You can use text style tags in headings, too, but their effect may be overridden by the effects of the heading tag itself.

4.4.13 Combining Content-Based Styles

It may have occurred to you to combine two or more of the various content-based styles to create interesting and perhaps even useful hybrids. Thus, an emphatic citation might be achieved with:

```
<cite><em>Moby Dick</em></cite>
```

In practice, Dr. Frankenstein, the browser usually ignores the monster; as you can test by typing and viewing the example yourself, Moby Dick gets the citation without emphasis.

The HTML standard does not require the browser to support every possible combination of content-based styles and does not define how the browser should handle such combinations. Someday, maybe. For now, it's best to choose one tag and be satisfied.

4.5 Physical Style Tags

There are ten physical styles provided by the current HTML standard, including bold, italic, monospaced, underlined, and strike-through text. In addition, the modern browsers support blinking, larger, smaller, superscript, and subscript text. All physical style tags require an ending tag.

4.5.1 The `<b>` Tag

The `<b>` tag is the physical equivalent of the `<strong>` content-based style tag, but without the latter's extended meaning. The `<b>` tag explicitly boldfaces a character or segment of text that is enclosed between it and its corresponding (`</b>`) end tag. If a boldface font is not available, the browser may use some other representation, such as reverse video or underlining.

Physical Style Tags

Function:
   Specify a physical style for text

Attributes:
   CLASS **N** **O**
   STYLE **N** **O**

End tag:
   Never omitted

Contains:
   text

Used in:
   text

4.5.2 *The <big> Tag*

The `<big>` tag makes it easy to increase the size of text without worrying about all of the details of virtual font sizes available with the `<font>` tag described later in this chapter. It couldn't be simpler: The browser renders the text between the `<big>` tag and its matching `</big>` ending tag one font size larger than the surrounding text. If that text is already at the largest size, `<big>` has no effect. [`<font>`, 4.6.3]

Even better, you can nest `<big>` tags to enlarge the text. Each `<big>` tag makes the text one size larger, up to a limit of size seven, as defined by the font model.

Be careful with your use of the `<big>` tag, though. Because browsers are quite forgiving and try hard to understand a tag, those that don't support `<big>` often interpret it to mean bold.

4.5.3 *The <blink> Tag*

Text contained between the `<blink>` tag and its end tag `</blink>` does just that: blink on and off. Netscape for Macintosh, for example, simply and reiteratively reverses the background and foreground colors for the `<blink>` enclosed text. The HTML standard does not include `<blink>`; it is supported as an extension by Netscape.

We cannot effectively reproduce the animated effect here in these static pages, but it is easy to imagine and probably best left to the imagination, too. That's because blinking text has two primary effects: it gets your reader's attention, and then promptly annoys them to no end. Blinking text should be used sparingly in any context.

4.5.4 The <i> Tag

The <i> tag is like the <em> content-based style tag. It and its necessary (</i>) end tag tell the browser to render the enclosed text in an italic or oblique type-face. If the typeface is not available to the browser, highlighting, reverse video, or underlining might be used.

4.5.5 The <small> Tag

The <small> tag works just like its <big> counterpart (see previous descrip-tion), except it decreases the size of text instead of increasing it. If the enclosed text is already at the smallest size supported by the font model, <small> has no effect.

Like <big>, you may also nest <small> tags to sequentially shrink text. Each <small> tag makes the text one size smaller than the containing <small> tag, down to a limit of size one.

4.5.6 The <s> Tag

The <s> tag is an abbreviated form of the <strike> tag supported by both Internet Explorer and Netscape.

4.5.7 The <strike> Tag

Most browsers will put a line through ("strike through") text that appears inside the <strike> tag and its </strike> end tag. Presumably, it is an editing markup that tells the reader to ignore the text passage, reminiscent of the days before typewriter correction tape. You'll rarely, if ever, see the tag in use today, but expect it to become more commonplace as marketers of consumer items hawked on the Web slash prices on their slow-moving products.

4.5.8 The <sub> Tag

The text contained between the _{tag and its} end tag gets displayed half a character's height lower, but in the same font and size as the current text flow. Both <sub> and its <sup> counterpart are useful for math equations and in scientific notation, as well as with chemical formulæ.

4.5.9 *The <sup> Tag*

The ^{tag and its} end tag superscripts the enclosed text; it gets displayed half a character's height higher, but in the same font and size as the current text flow. This tag is useful for adding footnotes to your documents, along with exponential values in equations. In combination with the <a> tag, you can create nice, hyperlinked footnotes:

```
The larval quat
weevil<a href="footnotes.html#note74"><sup><small>74</small></sup></a>
is a
```

This example assumes that *footnotes.html* contains all your footnotes, appropriately delimited as named document fragments.

4.5.10 *The <tt> Tag*

In a manner like the <code> and <kbd> tags, the <tt> tag and necessary </tt> end tag direct the browser to display the enclosed text in a monospaced typeface. For those browsers that already use a monospaced typeface, this tag may make no discernible change in the presentation of the text.

4.5.11 *The <u> Tag*

This tag tells the browser to underline the text contained between the <u> and the corresponding </u> tag. The underlining technique is simplistic, drawing the line under spaces and punctuation as well as the text.

4.5.12 *The style and class Attributes*

Although each physical tag has a defined style, you can override that style by defining your own look for each tag. This new look can be applied to the physical tags using either the **style** or **class** attributes. [style attribute, 9.1.1] [class attribute, 9.2.4]

4.5.13 *Summary of Physical Style Tags*

The various graphical browsers render text inside the physical style tags in similar fashion. Table 4-2 summarizes these browser's display styles for the native tags. Style sheet definitions may override these native display styles.

The following HTML source example illustrates some of the various physical tags as rendered by Netscape for Figure 4-12:

```
Explicitly <b>boldfaced</b>, <i>italicized</i>, or
<tt>teletype-style</tt> text should be used
<big><big>sparingly</big></big>.
```

```
Otherwise, drink <strike>lots</strike> 1x10<sup>6</sup>
drops of H<sub><small><small>2</small></small></sub>O.
```

Table 4-2. Physical style tags

Tag	Meaning	Display Style
<b>	Bold contents	**bold**
<big>	Increased font size	bigger text
<blink>	Alternating fore and background colors	blinking text
<i>	Italic contents	*italic*
<small>	Decreased font size	smaller text
<s>, <strike>	Strike-through text	~~strike~~
<sub>	Subscripted text	subscript
<sup>	Superscripted text	superscript
<tt>	Teletypewriter style	monospaced
<u>	Underlined contents	underlined

Figure 4-12. Use physical text tags with caution

4.5.14 Allowed Content

Any physical style tag may contain any item allowed in *text*, including conventional text, anchors, images, and line breaks. You also can combine physical style tags with other content-based ones.

4.5.15 Allowed Usage

Any physical style tag may be used anywhere an item allowed in *text* can be used. In general, this means anywhere within a document except in the <title>, <listing>, and <xmp> tags. You could use a physical style tag in a heading, but the browser will probably override and ignore its effect in lieu of the heading tag.

4.5.16 Combining Physical Styles

You probably will have better luck, Dr. Frankenstein, combining physical tags than you might have combining content-based tags to achieve multiple effects. For instance, Netscape renders the following in bold and italic typeface:

```
<b><i>Thar she blows!</i></b>
```

In practice, other browsers may elect to ignore such nesting. The HTML 3.2 standard does require the browser to "do their best" to support every possible combination of styles, but does not define how the browser should handle such combinations. Although most browsers make a good attempt at doing so, do not assume that all combinations will be available to you.

4.6 Expanded Font Handling

HTML 3.2 defines tags that give you more explicit control over the colors and sizes of the font characters that form your HTML text. Internet Explorer and Netscape go even further, providing a way for you to specify the display font itself.

4.6.1 The Extended Font Size Model

Instead of absolute point values, HTML 3.2 uses a relative model for sizing fonts. Ranging in size from 1, the smallest, to 7, the largest, the default (*basefont*) font size is 3.

It is almost impossible to reliably state the actual font sizes used for the various virtual sizes. Most browsers let the user change the physical font size, and the default sizes vary from browser to browser. It may be helpful to know, however, that each virtual size is successively 20 percent larger or smaller than the default font size 3. Thus, font size 4 is 20 percent larger, font size 5 is 40 percent larger, and so on, while font size 2 is 20 percent smaller and font size 1 is 40 percent smaller than font size 3.

4.6.2 The <basefont> Tag

The <basefont> tag lets you define the basic size for the font that the browser will use to render normal document text.

The <basefont> tag has a single attribute recognized by all browsers, `size`, whose value determines the document's base font size. It may be specified as an absolute value from 1 to 7, or as a relative value by placing a plus or minus sign before the value. In the latter case, the base font size is increased or decreased by that relative amount. The default base font size is 3.

<basefont>

Function:
  Define base font size for relative font size changes

Attributes:
  COLOR ❶
  NAME ❶
  SIZE

End Tag:
  </basefont>, optionally used

Contains:
  Nothing

Used in:
  block, head_content

Internet Explorer supports two additional attributes for the `<basefont>` tag: `color` and `name`. These attributes control the color and typeface used for the text in a document and are used just like the analogous color and face attributes for the `<font>` tag, described below.

Authors typically include the `<basefont>` tag in the head of an HTML document, if at all, to set the base font size for the entire document. Nonetheless, the tag may appear nearly anywhere in the document, and it may appear several times throughout the document, each with a new size attribute. With each occurrence, the `<basefont>` tag's effects are immediate and hold for all subsequent text.

In an egregious deviation from the HTML and SGML standards, the browsers interpret the ending `</basefont>` tag *not* to terminate the effects of the most recent `<basefont>` tag. Instead, the `</basefont>` end tag resets the base font size to the default value of 3, which is the same as writing `<basefont size=3>`.

The following example source and Figure 4-13 illustrate how Netscape responds to the `<basefont>` tag and `</basefont>` end tag, including fixed and relative attribute values:

```
Unless the base font size was reset above,
Netscape renders this part in font size 3.
<basefont size=7>
This text should be rather large (size 7).
<basefont size=-1> Oh,
<basefont size=-1> no!
<basefont size=-1> I'm
<basefont size=-1> shrinking!
</basefont>
Ah, back to normal.
```

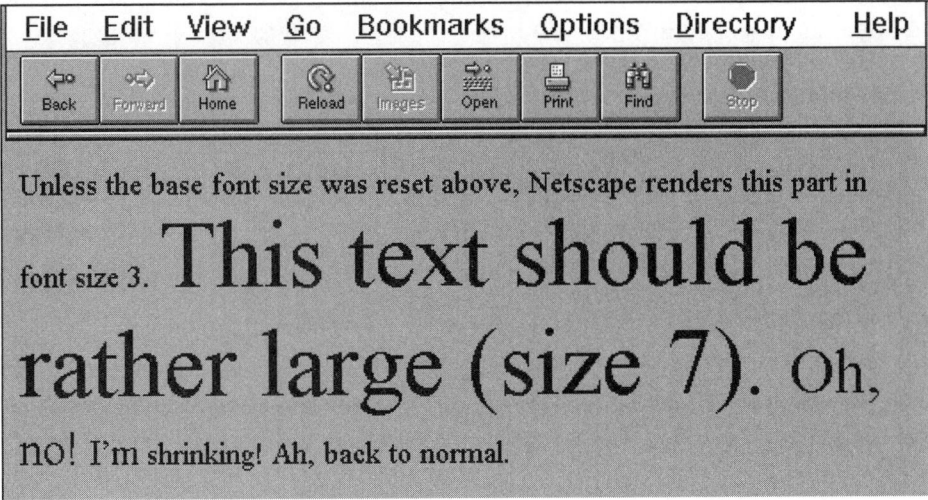

Figure 4-13. Playing with <basefont>

We recommend against ever using </basefont>; use <basefont size=3> instead.

4.6.3 The <font> Tag

The <font> tag lets you change the size, style, and color of text. It should be used like any other physical or content-based style tag for changing the appearance of a short segment of text.

<font>

Function:
   Set the font size for text

Attributes:
   COLOR
   FACE N O
   SIZE

End Tag:
   </font>, always used

Contains:
   text

Used in:
   text

To control the color of text for the entire document, see the attributes for the `<body>` tag described in 5.3.1.

4.6.3.1 The size attribute

The value of the `size` attribute must be one of the virtual font sizes (1–7) described earlier, defined as an absolute size for the enclosed text or preceded by a plus or minus sign (+ or –) to define a relative font size that the browser adds to or subtracts from the base font size (see the `<basefont>` tag above). The browsers automatically round the size to 1 or 7 if the calculated value exceeds either boundary.

In general, use absolute size values when you want the rendered text to be an extreme size, either very large or very small, or when you want an entire paragraph of text to be a specific size.

For example, using the largest font for the first character of a paragraph makes for a crude form of illustrated manuscript (see Figure 4-14):

```
<p>
<font size=7>C</font>all me Ishmael.
```

Figure 4-14. Exaggerating the first character of a sentence

Also, use an absolute font when inserting a delightfully unreadable bit of "fine" print—boilerplate or legalese—at the bottom of your documents (see Figure 4-15):

```
<p>
<font size=1>
All rights reserved. Unauthorized redistribution of this document is
prohibited. Opinions expressed herein are those of the authors, not the
Internet Service Provider.
```

Except for the extremes, use relative font sizes to render text in a size different than the surrounding text, to emphasize a word or phrase, for example (see Figure 4-16):

```
<p>
Make sure you <font size=+1>always</font> sign and date the form!
```

Figure 4-15. Use the tiniest font for boilerplate text

Figure 4-16. Use relative sizes for most Netscape text embellishments

If your relative size change results in a size greater than seven, the browser uses font 7. Similarly, font sizes less than one are rendered with font 1.

Notice that specifying `size=+1` or `size=-1` is identical in effect to the `<big>` and `<small>` respectively. However, nested relative changes to the font size are not cumulative as they are for the alternate tags. Each `<font>` tag is relative to the base font size, not the current font size. [`<big>`, 4.5.2] For example (see Figure 4-17):

```
<p>
The ghost moaned, "oo<font size=+1>oo<font size=+2>oo<font
size=+3>oo</font>oo</font>oo</font>oo."
```

Contrast this with the `<big>` tag, which increases the size one level as you nest the tags.

Figure 4-17. Relative font sizes accumulate

4.6.3.2 The color attribute

The `color` attribute for the `<font>` tag sets the color of the enclosed text. The value of the attribute may be expressed in either of two ways: as the red, green, and blue (RGB) components of the desired color or as a standard color name. Enclosing quotes are recommended, but not required.

The RGB color value, denoted by a preceding pound sign, is a six-digit hexadecimal number. The first two digits are the red component, from 00 (no red) to FF (bright red). Similarly, the next two digits are the green component and the last two digits are the blue component. Black is the absence of color, #000000; white is all colors, #FFFFFF.

For example, to create basic yellow text, you might use:

```
Here comes the <font color="#FFFF00">sun</font>!
```

Alternatively, you may set the enclosed font color using any one of the many standard color names. See Appendix F, *Color Names and Values*, for a list of common ones. For instance, you could also have made the above sample text yellow with the following source:

```
Here comes the <font color=yellow>sun</font>!
```

4.6.3.3 The face attribute

Internet Explorer and Netscape let you change the font style in a text passage with the `face` attribute for the `<font>` tag.*

The quote-enclosed value of `face` is one or more display font names separated with commas.

The font face displayed by the browser depends on which fonts are available on the individual user's system. The browser parses the list of font names, one after the other, until it matches one with a font name supported by the user's system. If none match, the text display defaults to the font style set by the user in their browser's preferences. For example:

```
This text is in the default font. But,
<font face="Braggadocio, Machine, Zapf Dingbats">
heaven only knows</font>
what font face is this one?
```

If the Internet Explorer user has the Braggadocio, Machine, or none of the listed font typefaces installed in their system, they will be able to read the "heaven only knows" message in the respective or default font style. Otherwise, the message

---

* For the HTML purist, for the once-powerful user, who had ultimate control over their browser, this is egregious, indeed. Form over function; look over content—what next? Embedded video commercials you can't stop?

will be garbled because the Zapf Dingbats font contains symbols, not letters. Of course, the alternative is true, too; you may intend that the message be a symbol-encoded secret.

4.7 Precise Spacing and Layout

HTML style sheets notwithstanding, the original concept of the language is for specifying document content without indicating format; to delineate the structure and semantics of a document, not how that document is to be presented to the user. Normally, you should leave word wrapping, character and line spacing, and other presentation details up to the browser. That way, the document's content—its rich information, not good looks—are what matter. When looks matter more, such as for commercial presentations, look to style sheets for layout control (see Chapter 9, *Cascading Style Sheets*).

That said, there are certain occasions when explicitly interrupting normal HTML text formatting makes sense. Besides, HTML currently is the *only* language of the World Wide Web. And, clearly, commercial advertising and other forms of style-over-content, short-lived HTML documents do need to have some control over format. We're adamant, not fanatic.

*4.7.1 The
 Tag*

The <br> tag interrupts the normal line filling and word wrapping of paragraphs within an HTML document. It has no ending tag, but simply marks the point in the flow where a new line should begin. Most browsers simply stop adding words and images to the current line, move down and over to the left margin, and resume filling and wrapping.

**
**

Function:
   Insert a line break into a text flow

Attributes:
   CLEAR

End tag:
   None

Contains:
   Nothing

Used in:
   text

This effect is handy when formatting conventional text with fixed line breaks, such as addresses, song lyrics, or poetry. Notice, for example, the lyrical breaks when the following source is rendered by Netscape:

```
<h3>
Heartbreak Hotel</h3>
<p>
Ever since my baby left me<br>
I've found a new place to dwell.<br>
It's down at the end of lonely street<br>
Called <cite>Heartbreak Hotel</cite>.
</p>
```

The results are shown in Figure 4-18.

Figure 4-18. Give lyrics their breaks (<br>)

Also notice how the `<br>` tag causes text to simply start a new line, while the browser, when encountering the `<p>` tag, typically inserts some vertical space between adjacent paragraphs. [`<p>`, 4.1.2]

4.7.1.1 The clear attribute

Normally, the `<br>` tag tells the browser to immediately stop the current flow of text and resume at the left margin of the next line or against the right border of a left-justified inline graphic or table. Sometimes you'd rather the current text flow resume below any tables or images currently blocking the left or right margins.

HTML 3.2 provides that capability with the `clear` attribute for the `<br>` tag. It can have one of three values: `left`, `right`, or `all`, each related to one or both of the margins. When the specified margin or both margins are clear of images, the browser resumes the text flow.

Figure 4-19 illustrates the effects of the `clear` attribute when Netscape renders the following HTML fragment:

```
<img src="http:kumquat.gif" align=left>
This text should wrap around the image, flowing between the
image and the right margin of the document.
<br clear=left>
This text will flow as well, but will be below the image,
extending across the full width of the page. There will
be white space above this text and to the right of the
image.
```

Figure 4-19. Clearing images before resuming text flow after the <br> tag

Inline HTML images are just that—normally in line with text, but usually only a single line of text. Additional lines of text flow below the image unless that image is specially aligned by `right` or `left` attribute values for the `<img>` tag (similarly for `<table>`). Hence, the `clear` attribute for the `<br>` tag only works in combination with left- or right-aligned images or tables. [image alignment, 5.2.6.4] [table alignment, 11.2.1.1]

The following HTML code fragment illustrates how to use the `<br>` tag and its `clear` attribute as well as the `<img>` tag's alignment attributes to place captions directly above, centered on the right, and below an image that is aligned against the left margin of the browser window:

```
Paragraph tags separate leading and following
text flow from the captions.
<p>
I'm the caption on top of the image.
<br>
<img src="kumquat.gif" align=absmiddle>
This one's centered on the right.
<br clear=left>
This caption should be directly below the image.
<p>
And the text just keeps flowing along....
```

Figure 4-20 illustrates the results of this example code.

You might also include a `<br clear=all>` tag just after an `<img>` tag or table that is at the very end of a section of your document. That way, you ensure that the subsequent section's text doesn't flow up and against that image and confuse the reader. [`<img>`, 5.2.6]

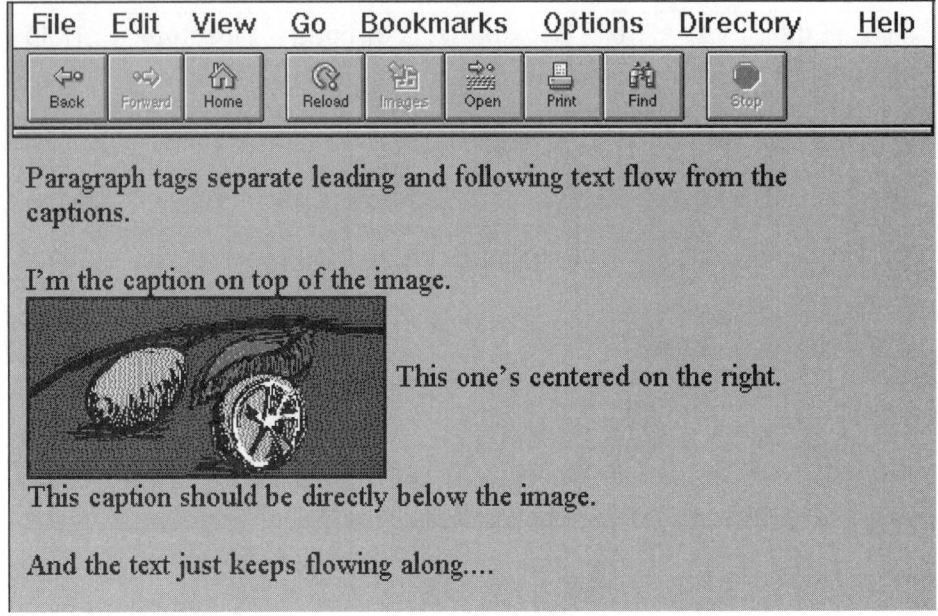

Figure 4-20. Captions placed on top, center-right, and below an image

4.7.2 The <nobr> Tag

Occasionally, you may have a phrase you want to appear unbroken on a single line in the user's browser window, even if that means the text extends beyond the visible region of the window. Computer commands are good examples. Typically, one types in a computer command—even a multiword one—on a single line. Because you cannot predict exactly how many words will fit inside an individual's browser window, the HTML-based sequence of computer-command words may end up broken into two or more lines of text. Command syntax is confusing enough; it doesn't need the extra cross-eyed effect of being wrapped onto two lines.

With standard HTML, the way to make sure text phrases stay intact across the browser display is to enclose those segments in a `<pre>` tag and format it by hand. That's acceptable and nearly universal for all browsers. However, `<pre>`

alters the display font from the regular text, and manual line breaks inside the `<pre>` tag are not always rendered correctly. [`<pre>`, 4.7.5]

<nobr> Ⓝ ❶

Function:
> Create a region of non-breaking text

Attributes:
> None

End Tag:
> </nobr>; always used

Contains:
> *text*

Used in:
> *block*

The modern browsers offer the `<nobr>` tag alternative to `<pre>` so you can be sure enclosed text stays intact on a single line while retaining normal text style. The effect is to make the browser treat the tag's contents as though they were a single, unbroken word. The tag contents retain the current font style, and you can change to another style within the tag.

Here's the `<nobr>` tag in action with our computer-command example:

```
When prompted by the computer, enter
<nobr>
<tt>find . -name \*.html -exec rm \{\}\;</tt>.
</nobr>
After a few moments, the load on your server will begin
to diminish and will eventually drop to zero.
```

Notice in the example source and its display (Figure 4-21) that we've included the special `<tt>` tag inside the `<nobr>` tag. If the `<nobr>`-tagged text cannot fit on a partially filled line of text, the extended browser precedes it with a line break, as shown in the figure. The `<nobr>` segment may then extend beyond the right window boundary. [`<tt>`, 4.5.10]

The `<nobr>` tag does not suspend the browser's normal line-filling process; it still collects and inserts images and—believe it, or not—asserts forced line breaks caused by the `<br>` or `<p>` tags, for example. The `<nobr>` tag's only action is to suppress an automatic line break when the current line reaches the right margin.

Also, you might think this tag is needed only to suppress line breaks for phrases, not a sequence of characters without spaces that can exceed the browser

Figure 4-21. The <nobr> extension suppresses text wrapping

window's display boundaries. Today's browsers do not hyphenate words automatically, but someday soon they probably will. It makes sense to protect any break-sensitive sequence of characters with the <nobr> tag.

4.7.3 The <wbr> Tag

The <wbr> tag is the height of HTML text-layout finesse. Used with the <nobr> tag, <wbr> advises the extended browser when it may insert a line break in an otherwise nonbreakable sequence of text. Unlike the <br> tag, which always causes a line break even within a <nobr> tagged segment, the <wbr> tag works only when placed inside a <nobr>-tagged content segment and causes a line break only if the current line already had extended beyond the browser's display window margins.

<wbr> N O

Function:
  Define potential line break point if needed

Attributes:
  None

End Tag:
  None

Contains:
  Nothing

Used in:
  text

Now, `<wbr>` may seem incredibly esoteric to you, but scowl not. There may come a time when you want to make sure portions of your document appear on a single line, but you don't want to overrun the browser window margins so far that readers will have to camp on the horizontal scroll bar just to read your fine prose. By inserting the `<wbr>` tag at appropriate points in the nonbreaking sequence, you let the browser gently break the text into more manageable lines:

```
<p>
<nobr>
This is a very long sequence of text that is
forced to be on a single line, even if doing so causes
<wbr>
the browser to extend the document window beyond the
size of the viewing pane and the poor user must scroll right
<wbr>
to read the entire line.
</nobr>
```

You'll notice in our rendered version (Figure 4-22) that both `<wbr>` tags take effect. By increasing the horizontal window size or by reducing the font size, you may fit all of the segment before the first `<wbr>` tag within the browser window. In that case, only the second `<wbr>` would have an effect; all the text leading up to it would extend beyond the window's margins.

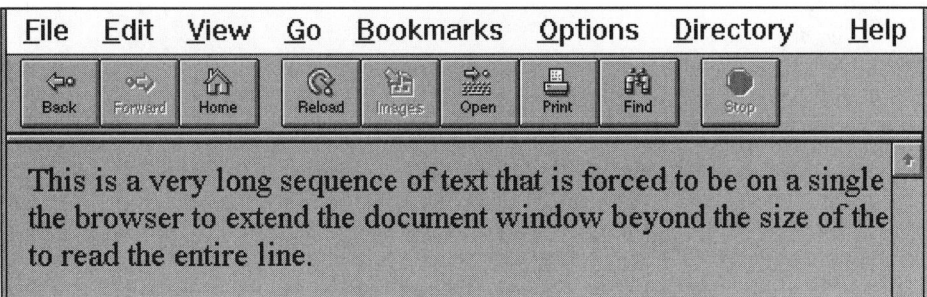

Figure 4-22. Gentle line breaks with <wbr>

4.7.4 Better Line-Breaking Rules

Unlike most browsers, and to their credit, Netscape and Internet Explorer do not consider tags to be a line-break opportunity. Consider the unfortunate consequences to your document's display if, while rendering the example segment below, the browser puts the comma adjacent to the "du" or the period adjacent to the word "df" on a separate line. Netscape and Internet Explorer will not:

```
Make sure you type <tt>du</tt>, not <tt>df</tt>.
```

4.7.5 The `<pre>` Tag

The `<pre>` tag and its required end tag (`</pre>`) define a segment inside which the browser renders text in exactly the character and line spacing defined in the source HTML document. Normal word wrapping and paragraph filling are disabled, and extraneous leading and trailing spaces are honored. The browser displays all text between the `<pre>` and `</pre>` tags in a monospaced font.

<pre>

Function:
    Render a block of text without any formatting

Attributes:
    CLASS ☒ ❶
    STYLE ☒ ❶
    WIDTH

End tag:
    `</pre>`; never omitted

Contains:
    pre_content

Used in:
    block

HTML authors most often use the `<pre>` formatting tag when the integrity of columns and rows of characters must be retained; for instance, in tables of numbers that must line up correctly. Another application for `<pre>` is to set aside a blank segment—a series of blank lines—in the document display, perhaps to clearly separate one content section from another, or to temporarily hide a portion of the document when it first loads and is rendered by the user's browser.

Tab characters have their desired effect within the `<pre>` block, with tab stops defined at every eight character positions. We discourage their use, however, since tabs aren't consistently implemented among the various browsers. Use spaces to ensure correct horizontal positioning of text within `<pre>`-formatted text segments.

A common use of the `<pre>` tag is to present computer source code, as in the following example:

```
<p>
The processing program is:
<pre>
main(int argc, char **argv)
```

```
{   FILE *f;
    int i;

    if (argc != 2)
      fprintf(stderr, "usage: %s &lt;file&gt;\n",
        argv[0]);
    <a href="http:process.c">process</a>(argv[1]);
    exit(0);
}
</pre>
```

The result is displayed by Mosaic as shown in Figure 4-23.

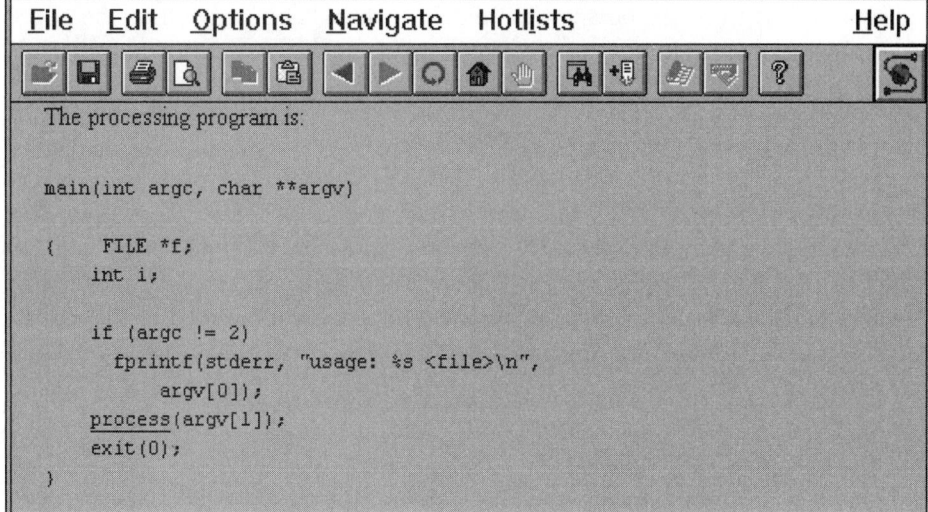

Figure 4-23. Use the <pre> tag to preserve the integrity of columns and rows

4.7.5.1 Allowable content

The text within a `<pre>` segment may contain physical and content-based style changes, along with anchors, images, and horizontal rules. When possible, the browser should honor style changes, within the constraint of using a monospaced font for the entire `<pre>` block.

Tags that cause a paragraph break (headings, `<p>`, and `<address>` tags, for example), must not be used within the `<pre>` block. Some browsers will interpret paragraph-ending tags as simple line breaks, but this behavior is not consistent across all browsers.

Since style markup and other tags are allowed in a `<pre>` block, you must use entity equivalents for the literal characters: `&lt;` for <, `&gt;` for >, and `&amp;` for the ampersand.

You place tags into the `<pre>` block as you would in any other portion of the HTML document. For instance, study the reference to the "process" function in the previous example. It contains a hyperlink (using the `<a>` tag) to its source file named *process.c.*

4.7.5.2 The width attribute

The `<pre>` tag has a single optional attribute, `width`, that determines the number of characters to fit on a single line within the `<pre>` block. The browser may use this value to select a font or font size that fits the specified number of characters on each line in the `<pre>` block. It does not mean that the browser will wrap and fill text to the specified width. Rather, lines longer than the specified width simply extend beyond the visible region of the browser's window.

The `width` attribute is only advice for the user's browser; it may or may not be able to adjust the view font to the specified width.

4.7.5.3 The style and class attributes

Although the browsers usually display `<pre>` content in a defined style, you can override that style and add special effects, such as a background picture, by defining your own style for the tag. This new look can be applied to the `<pre>` tags using either the `style` or `class` attributes. [style attribute, 9.1.1] [class attribute, 9.2.4].

4.7.6 The <center> Tag

The `<center>` tag's effects are obvious: content, including text, graphics, tables, and so on, are each centered inside the browser's window. For text, this means that each line, individually, gets centered after the text flow is filled and wrapped. The `<center>` alignment remains in effect until canceled with its `</center>` end tag.

Line-by-line is a common, albeit primitive, way to center text, and it should be used judiciously. That's because the browsers do not attempt to balance a centered paragraph or other block-related elements, such as elements in a list. So, keep your centered text short and sweet. Titles make good centering candidates; a centered list usually is difficult to follow.

Beyond that, you'll rarely see conventional text centered, except for some lyrical prose, so readers may react badly to large segments of centered prose in your documents. Rather, HTML authors more commonly use `<center>` to center a table or image in the display window (there is no explicit center alignment option for inline images or tables).

<center>

Function:
   Center a section of text

Attributes:
   None

End tag:
   </center>; never omitted

Contains:
   body_content

Used in:
   block

Because users will have varying window widths, display resolutions, and so on, you may also want to employ the <nobr> and <wbr> extension tags (see previous descriptions) to keep your centered text intact and looking good. For example:

```
<center>
<nobr>
Copyright 1995 by QuatCo Enterprises.<wbr>
All rights reserved.
</nobr>
</center>
```

The <nobr> tags in the sample source help ensure that the text remains on a single line, and the <wbr> tag controls where the line may be broken if it exceeds the browser's display window width.

Centering also is useful for creating distinctive section headers, although you may now achieve the same effect with an explicit align=center attribute in the respective heading tag. You might also center text using align=center in conjunction with the <div> or <p> tags. In general, the <center> tag can be replaced by an equivalent <div align=center> or similar tag and its use should be discouraged. It is only retained in HTML 3.2 for historical purposes and may be removed from later versions of the standard.

4.7.7 *The <listing> Tag*

The <listing> tag is a deprecated element of HTML 3.2, meaning that its use is discouraged and that it may disappear entirely in subsequent versions of the language. We include it here for historical reasons, since it has the same effect on text formatting as the <pre> tag with a specified width of 132 characters.

\<listing\>

Function:
   Render a block of text without any formatting

Attributes:
   CLASS 🅽 🅞
   STYLE 🅽 🅞

End tag:
   \</listing\>; never omitted

Contains:
   literal_text

Used in:
   block

The only difference between `<pre>` and `<listing>` is that no other markup is allowed within the `<listing>` tag. So you don't have to replace the literal <, >, and & characters with their entity equivalents in a `<listing>` block as you must inside a `<pre>` block.

Since the `<listing>` tag is the same as a `<pre width=132>` tag, and because it might not be supported in later version of the language, we recommend you stay away from using `<listing>`.

4.7.8 The \<xmp\> Tag

Like the `<listing>` tag, the `<xmp>` tag is a deprecated element of HTML 3.2 included here mostly for historical reasons.

The `<xmp>` tag formats text just like the `<pre>` tag with a specified width of 80 characters. However, unlike the `<pre>` tag, you don't have to replace the literal <, >, and & characters with their entity equivalents within an `<xmp>` block. The name `<xmp>` is short for "example"; the language's designers intended the tag be used to format examples of text originally displayed on 80-column wide displays. Because the 80-column display has mostly gone the way of green screens and teletypes, and since the effect of a `<xmp>` tag is basically the same as `<pre width=80>`, don't use `<xmp>`; it may disappear entirely in subsequent versions of HTML.

4.7.9 The \<plaintext\> Tag

Tired of tags? Insert a `<plaintext>` tag into your document and browsers will treat the rest of your text just as written with no markup allowed. The text will be

---

\<xmp\>

Function:

   Render a block of text without any formatting

Attributes:

   CLASS **N** **O**
   STYLE **N** **O**

End tag:

   \</xmp\>, never omitted

Contains:

   literal_text

Used in:

   block

---

displayed in a monospaced font with no other formatting, unless you specially change that with the style or class attribute. There is no ending tag for `<plaintext>` (of course, no markup!).

\<plaintext\>

Function:

   Render a block of text without any formatting

Attributes:

   None

End tag:

   None

Contains:

   literal_text

Used in:

   block

The main mission for `<plaintext>` is to make existing ASCII documents palatable to browsers. In the early days of the Web, this may have been necessary, but today's browsers, which handle exceptional documents gracefully thanks to embedded MIME-type encoding, have made this tag obsolete. It is included here for completeness, but we strongly discourage its use.

4.8 Block Quotes

A common element in conventional documents is the block quote, a lengthy copy of text from another document. Traditionally, short quotes are set off with quotation marks, while block quotes are made entirely of separate paragraphs within the main document, typically with special indentation and sometimes italicized— features that you may change through style or class definitions (see Chapter 9, *Cascading Style Sheets*).

4.8.1 The <blockquote> Tag

All of the text within the `<blockquote>` and `</blockquote>` tags is set off from the regular document text, usually with indented left and right margins, and sometimes in italicized typeface. Actual rendering varies from browser to browser, of course.

<blockquote>

Function:
Define a block quotation

Attributes:
CLASS **N** **O**
STYLE **N** **O**

End tag:
</blockquote>, never omitted

Contains:
body_content

Used in:
block

The HTML standard allows any and all markup within the `<blockquote>`, although some physical and content-based styles may conflict with the font used by the browser for the block quote. Experimentation will reveal those little warts.

The `<blockquote>` tag is often used to set off long quotations from other sources:

```
We acted incorrectly in arbitrarily changing the Kumquat
Festival date. Quoting from the Kumquat Growers' Bylaws:
<blockquote>
  The date of the Kumquat Festival may only be changed by
  a two-thirds vote of the General Membership, provided
  that a <strong>60 percent quorum</strong> of the Membership
```

```
       is present.
     </blockquote>
     (Emphasis mine) Since such a quorum was not present, the
     vote is invalid.
```

4.8.1.1 The style and class attributes

Although the browsers usually display `<blockquote>` content in a defined style, you can override that style and add special effects, such as a background picture, by defining your own style for the tag. This new look can be applied to the `<blockquote>` tags using either the `style` or `class` attributes. [`style` attribute, 9.1.1] [`class` attribute, 9.2.4].

4.9 Addresses

Addresses are a very common element in text documents, and HTML provides a special tag that sets addresses apart from the rest of a document's text. While this may seem a bit extravagant—addresses have few formatting peculiarities that would require a special tag—it is an example of content, not format, that is the intent and purpose of HTML markup.

By defining text that comprises an address, the author lets the browser format that text in a different manner, as well as process that text in ways helpful to users. It also makes the content readily accessible to automated readers and extractors. For instance, an online directory might include addresses the browser collects into a separate document or table, or automated tools might extract addresses from a collection of documents to build a separate database of addresses.

4.9.1 The <address> Tag

The `<address>` and its required end (`</address>`) tag tell a browser that the enclosed text is an address. The browser may format the text in a different manner than the rest of the document text, or use the address in some special way. You also have control over the display properties through the style and class attributes for the tag (see Chapter 9, *Cascading Style Sheets*).

The text within the `<address>` tag may contain any element normally found in the body of an HTML document, excluding another `<address>` tag. Style changes are allowed, but may conflict with the style chosen by the browser to render the address element.

We think most, if not all, HTML documents should have their authors' addresses included somewhere convenient to the user, usually at the end. At the very least, the address should be the author's or webmaster's email address, along with a link to their home page. Street addresses and phone numbers are optional; personal ones are usually not included for reasons of privacy.

<address>

Function:
   Define an address

Attributes:
   CLASS 🅽 🅞
   STYLE 🅽 🅞

End tag:
   </address>, never omitted

Contains:
   body_content

Used in:
   address_content

For example, the address for the webmaster responsible for a collection of commercial web documents often appears in source documents as follows, including the special `mailto:` URL protocol that lets users activate the browser's email tool:

```
<address>
  <a href="mailto:webmaster@ora.com">Webmaster</a><br>
  O'Reilly & Associates, Inc.<br>
  Cambridge, Massachusetts<br>
</address>
```

Figure 4-24 displays the results.

Figure 4-24. The <address> tag in action

Whether it is short and sweet or long and complete, make sure every document you create has an address attached to it. If something is worth creating and putting on the Web, it is worth comment and query by your readership. Anonymous documents carry little credibility on the Web.

4.9.1.1 The style and class attributes

Although the browsers usually display `<address>` content in a defined style, you can override that style and add special effects, such as a background picture, by defining your own style for the tag. This new look can be applied to the `<address>` tags using either the `style` or `class` attributes. [`style` attribute, 9.1.1] [`class` attribute, 9.2.4].

4.10 Special Character Encoding

For the most part, characters within HTML documents that are not part of a tag are rendered as-is by the browser. However, some characters have special meaning and are not directly rendered, while other characters can't be typed into the source document from a conventional keyboard. Special characters need either a special name or a numeric character encoding for inclusion in an HTML document.

4.10.1 Special HTML Characters

As has become obvious in the discussion and examples leading up to this section of the book, three special characters in HTML source documents have very special meaning: the less-than sign (<), the greater-than sign (>), and the ampersand (&). These characters delimit tags and special character references. They'll confuse a browser if left dangling alone or with improper tag syntax. So you've got to go out of your way to include their actual, literal characters in your HTML documents. The only exception to this is that these characters may appear literally within the `<listing>` and `<xmp>` tags.

Similarly, you've got to use a special encoding to include double quotation mark characters within a quoted string, or when you want to include a special character that doesn't appear on your keyboard but is part of the ISO Latin-1 character set implemented and supported by most browsers.

4.10.2 Inserting Special Characters

To include a special character in your HTML document, you enclose either its standard entity name or a pound sign (#) and its numeric position in the Latin-1 standard character set* inside a leading ampersand and an ending semicolon,

---

* The popular ASCII character set is a subset of the more comprehensive Latin-1 character set. Composed by the well-respected International Organization for Standardization (ISO), the Latin-1 set is a list of all letters, numbers, punctuation marks, and so on, commonly used by Western language writers, organized by number and encoded with special names. Appendix E, *Character Entities* contains the complete Latin-1 character set and encoding.

without any spaces in-between. Whew. That's a long explanation for what is really a simple thing to do, as the following example illustrates. The example23 shows how to include a greater-than sign in a snippet of code by using the character's entity name. It also demonstrates how to include a greater-than sign in your HTML text by referencing its Latin-1 numeric value:

```
if a &gt; b, then t = 0
if a &#62; b, then t = 0
```

Both examples cause the text to be rendered as:

```
if a > b, then t = 0
```

The complete set of character entity values and names are in Appendix E, *Character Entities*. You could write an entire HTML document using character encoding, but that would be silly.

5

Rules, Images, and Multimedia

While the body of most HTML documents is text, an appropriate seasoning of horizontal rules, images, and other multimedia elements make for a much more inviting and attractive document. These features of HTML are not simply gratuitous geegaws that make your documents look pretty, mind you. Multimedia elements bring HTML documents alive, providing a dimension of valuable information often unavailable in other media, such as print. In this chapter, we describe in detail how you can insert special multimedia elements into your documents, when their use is appropriate, and how to avoid overdoing it.

5.1 Horizontal Rules

Horizontal rules give you a way to separate sections of your document visually. That way, you give readers a clean, consistent, visual indication that one portion of your document has ended and another portion is beginning. Horizontal rules effectively set off small sections of text, delimit document headers and footers, and provide extra visual punch to headings within your document.

5.1.1 The <hr> Tag

The <hr> tag tells the browser to insert a horizontal rule across the display window. Like the <br> tag, <hr> forces a simple line break, although unlike <br>, <hr> causes the paragraph alignment to revert to the default (left-justified). The browser places the rule immediately below the current line, and content flow resumes below the rule. [
, 4.7.1]

The rendering of a horizontal rule is at the discretion of the browser. Typically, it extends across the entire document. Graphical browsers may render the rule with a chiseled or embossed effect; character-based browsers most likely use dashes or underscores to create the rule.

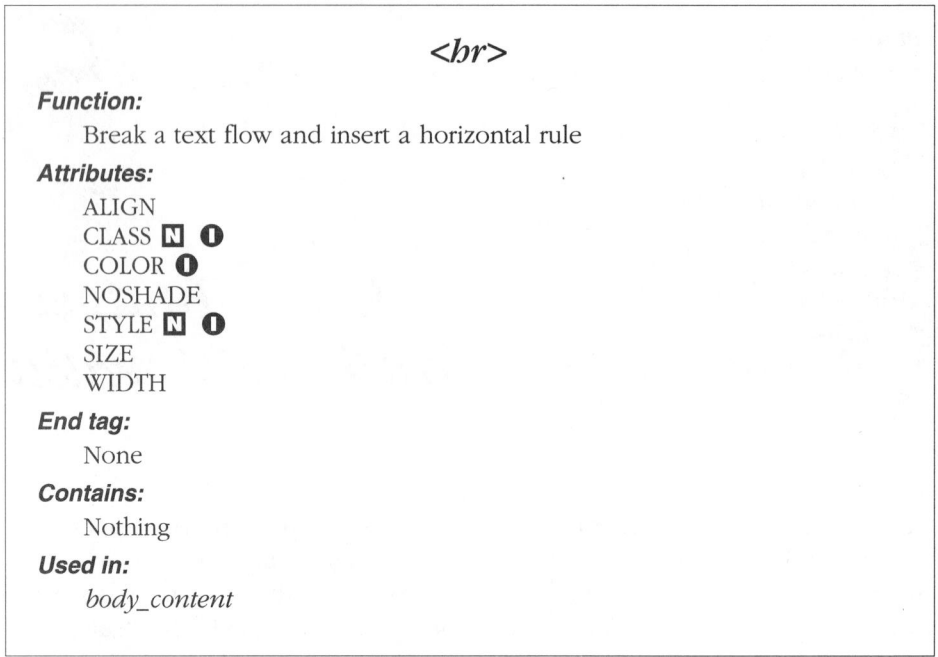

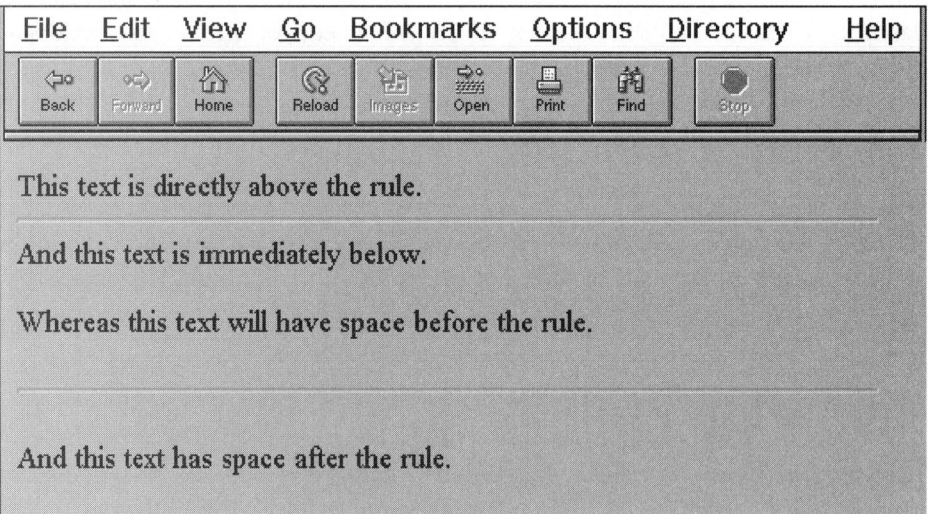

Figure 5-1. Paragraph tags give your text extra elbow room

There is no additional space above or below a horizontal rule. If you wish to set it off from the surrounding text, you must explicitly place the rule in a new paragraph, followed by another paragraph containing the subsequent text. For example, note the spacing around the horizontal rules in the following source and in Figure 5-1:

```
This text is directly above the rule.
<hr>
And this text is immediately below.
<p>
Whereas this text will have space before the rule.
<p>
<hr>
<p>
And this text has space after the rule.
```

A paragraph tag following the rule tag is necessary if you want the content beneath the rule line aligned in any style other than the default left.

5.1.1.1 The size attribute

Normally, browsers render horizontal rules three pixels[*] thick with a chiseled, 3D appearance, making the rule look incised into the page. You may thicken the rules with the `size` attribute. The required value is the thickness, in pixels. You can see the effects of this attribute in Figure 5-2 as constructed from the following source:

```
<p>
This is conventional document text,
followed by a normal, 3-pixel tall rule line.
<hr>
The next three rule lines are 12, 36, and 72 pixels tall.
<hr size=12>
<hr size=36>
<hr size=72>
```

5.1.1.2 The noshade attribute

You may not want a 3D rule line, preferring a flat, 2D rule. Just add the `noshade` attribute (no value required) to the `<hr>` tag to eliminate the effect. Note the difference in appearance of a "normal" 3D rule versus the `noshade` 2D one in Figure 5-3. (We've also exaggerated the rule's thickness for obvious effect, as evident in the source HTML fragment.)

```
<hr size=32>
<hr size=32 noshade>
```

5.1.1.3 The width attribute

The default rule is drawn across the full width of the view window. You can shorten or lengthen rules with the `width` attribute, creating rule lines that are either an absolute number of pixels wide or extend across a certain percentage of

---

[*] A pixel is one of the many tiny dots that make up the display on your computer. While display sizes vary, a good rule of thumb is that one pixel equals one point on a common 75 dot-per-inch display monitor. A point is a unit of measure used in printing and is roughly equal to 1/72 of an inch (there are 72.27 points in an inch, to be exact). Typical typefaces used by various browsers are usually 12 points tall, yielding six lines of text per inch.

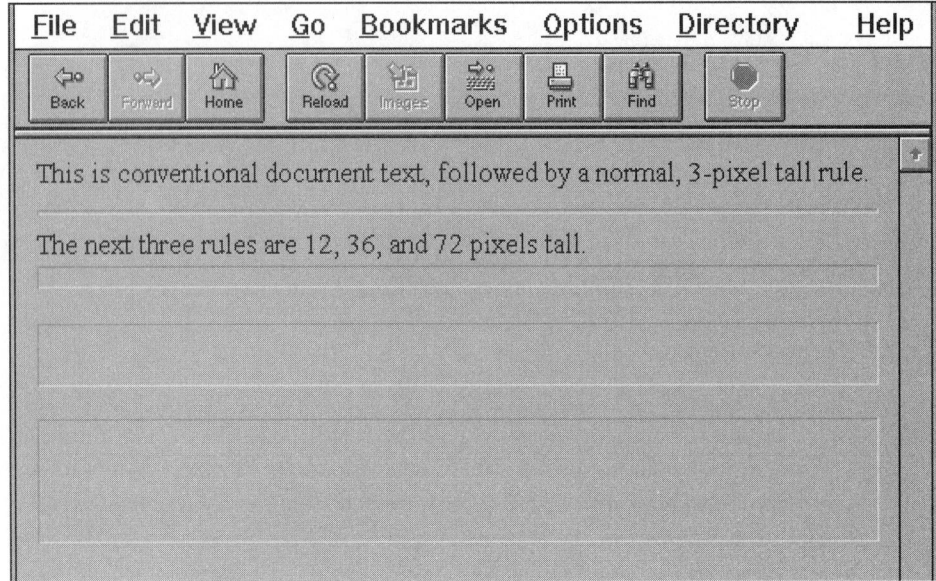

Figure 5-2. Netscape lets you vary the horizontal rule size

Figure 5-3. Netscape's 3D rule versus the noshade 2D option

the current text flow. Most browsers automatically center partial-width rules; see the `align` attribute (below) to left- or right-justify horizontal rules.

Here are some examples of `width`-specified horizontal rules (see Figure 5-4):

```
The following rules are 40 and 320 pixels wide
no matter the actual width of the browser window
<hr width=40>
<hr width=320>
Whereas these next two rules will always extend across
10 and 75 percent of the window, regardless of its width:
<hr width="10%">
<hr width="75%">
```

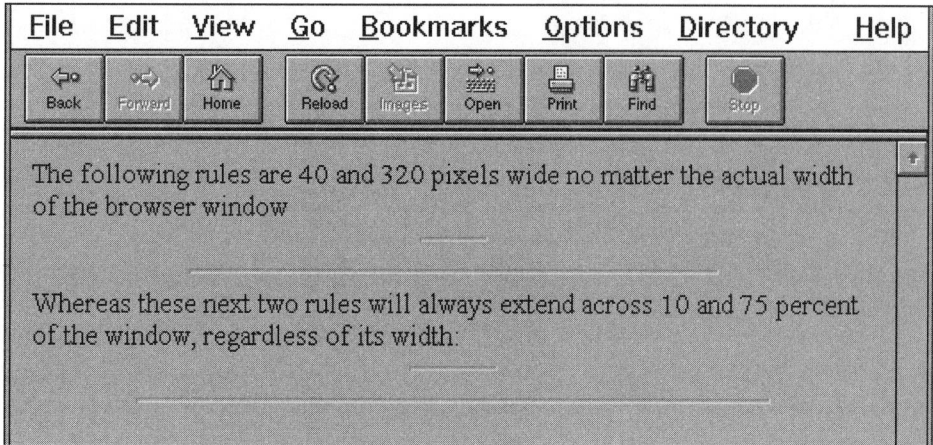

Figure 5-4. Absolute versus relative rule widths

Notice, too, that the relative (percentage) value for the `width` attribute is enclosed in quotation marks; the absolute (integer) pixel value is not. In fact, the quotation marks aren't absolutely necessary, but since the percent symbol normally means that an encoded character follows, failure to enclose the percent width value in quotation marks may confuse other browsers and trash a portion of your rendered document.

In general, it isn't a good idea to specify the width of a rule as an exact number of pixels. Browser windows vary greatly in their width, and what might be a small rule on one browser might be annoyingly large on another. For this reason, we recommend specifying rule width as a percentage of the window width. That way, when the width of the browser window changes, the rules retain their same relative size.

5.1.1.4 The align attribute

The `align` attribute for a horizontal rule can have one of three values: `left`, `center`, or `right`. For those rules whose width is less than the current text flow, the rule will be positioned relative to the window margins accordingly. The default alignment is `center`.

A varied rule alignment makes for nice section dividers. For example, the source shown below alternates a 35 percent-wide rule from right to center to the left margin (see Figure 5-5).

```
<hr width="35%" align=right>
<h3>Fruit Packing Advice</h3>
...
```

```
<hr width="35%" align=center>
<h3>Shipping Kumquats</h3>
...
<hr width="35%" align=left>
<h3>Juice Processing</h3>
...
```

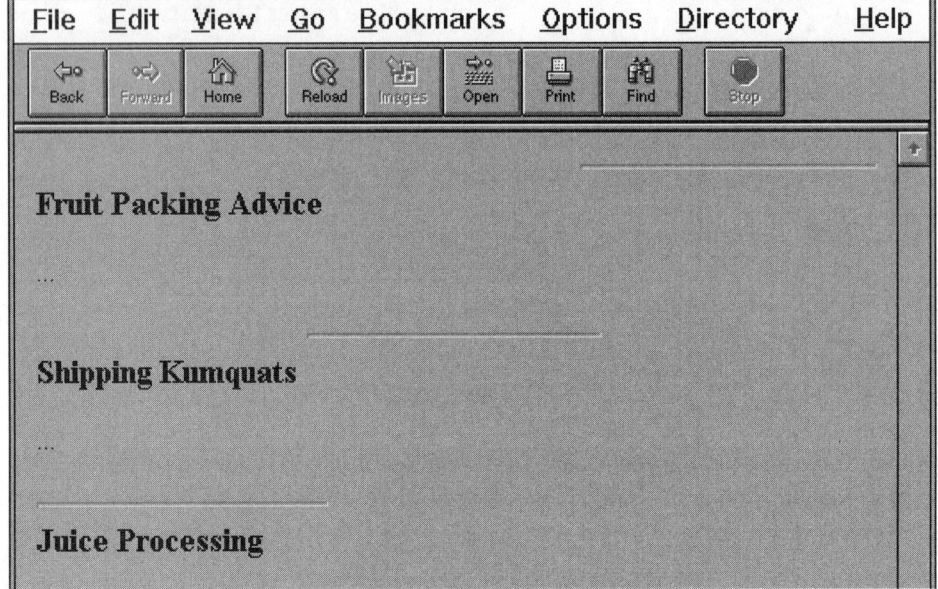

Figure 5-5. Varying horizontal rule alignment makes for subtle section dividers

5.1.1.5 The color attribute

Supported only by Internet Explorer, the `color` attribute lets you set the color of the rule. The value of this attribute is either the name of a color or a hexadecimal triple defining a specific color. For a complete list of color names and values, see Appendix F, *Color Names and Values*.

By default, a rule is set to the same color as the document background, with the chiseled edges slightly darker and lighter than the background color. You lose the 3D effect when you specify another color, either in a style sheet or with the `color` attribute.

5.1.1.6 The style and class attributes

The `style` attribute for the `<hr>` tag creates an inline style for the tag, over-riding any other style rule in effect. The `class` attribute lets you apply a predefined set of properties for this particular `<hr>` tag; its value is the name of that class. [`style` attribute, 9.1.1] [`class` attribute, 9.2.4]

5.1.1.7 Combining rule attributes

You may combine the various rule attribute extensions and their order isn't important. To create big squares, for example, combine the `size` and `width` attributes
(see Figure 5-6):

```
<hr size=32 width="50%" align=center>
```

Figure 5-6. Combining rule attributes for special effects

In fact, some combinations of rule attributes are necessary—`align` and `width`,
for example. `Align` alone appears to do nothing because the default rule width
stretches all the way across the display window.

5.1.2 Using Rules to Divide Your Document

Horizontal rules provide a handy visual navigation device for your readers. To use
`<hr>` effectively as a section divider, first determine how many levels of headings
your document has and how long you expect each section of the document to
be. Then decide which of your headings warrant being set apart by a rule.

A horizontal rule can also delimit the front matter of a document, separating the
table of contents from the document body, for example. Use a rule also to separate the document body from a trailing index, bibliography, or list of figures.

Experienced HTML authors also use horizontal rules to mark the beginning and
end of a form. This is especially handy for long forms that make users scroll up
and down the page to view all the fields. By consistently marking the beginning
and end of a form with a rule, you help users stay within the form, better
ensuring they won't inadvertently miss a portion when filling out its contents.

5.1.3 Using Rules in Headers and Footers

A fundamental style approach to HTML document families is to have a consistent
look and feel, including a standard header and footer for each document. Typically, the header contains navigational tools that help users easily jump to internal
sections as well as related documents in the family, while the footer contains

author and document information as well as feedback mechanisms like an email link to the webmaster.

To ensure these headers and footers don't infringe on the main document contents, consider using rules directly below the header and above the footer. For example (see also Figure 5-7):

```
<body>
Kumquat Growers Handbook - Growing Season Guidelines
<hr>
<h1>Growing Season Guidelines</h1>
Growing season for the noble fruit varies throughout the
United States, as shown in the following map:
<p>
<img src="pics/growing-season.gif">
<p>
<hr>
<i>Provided as a public service by the
<a href="feedback.html">Kumquat Lovers of America</a></i>
```

By consistently setting apart your headers and footers using rules, you help users locate and focus upon the main body of your document.

5.2 Inserting Images in Your Documents

One of the most compelling features of HTML is its ability to include images with your document text, either as an intrinsic component of the document (inline images), as separate documents specially selected for download via hyperlinks, or as a background for your document. When judiciously added to the body content, images—static and animated icons, pictures, illustrations, drawings, and so on—can make your documents more attractive, inviting, and professional looking, as well as informative and easier to browse. You may also specially enable an image so that it becomes a visual map of hyperlinks. When used to excess, however, images make your document cluttered, confusing, and inaccessible, as well as unnecessarily lengthening the time it takes for users to download and view your pages.

5.2.1 Understanding Image Formats

The HTML standard does not prescribe an official format for images. However, the popular browsers specifically accommodate only certain image formats: GIF and JPEG, in particular (see following sections for explanations). Most other multimedia formats require special accessory applications that each browser owner must obtain, install, and successfully operate to view the special files. So it's not too surprising that GIF and JPEG are the de facto image standards on the Web.

Both image formats were already in widespread use before the Web came into being, so there's lots of supporting software out there to help you prepare your

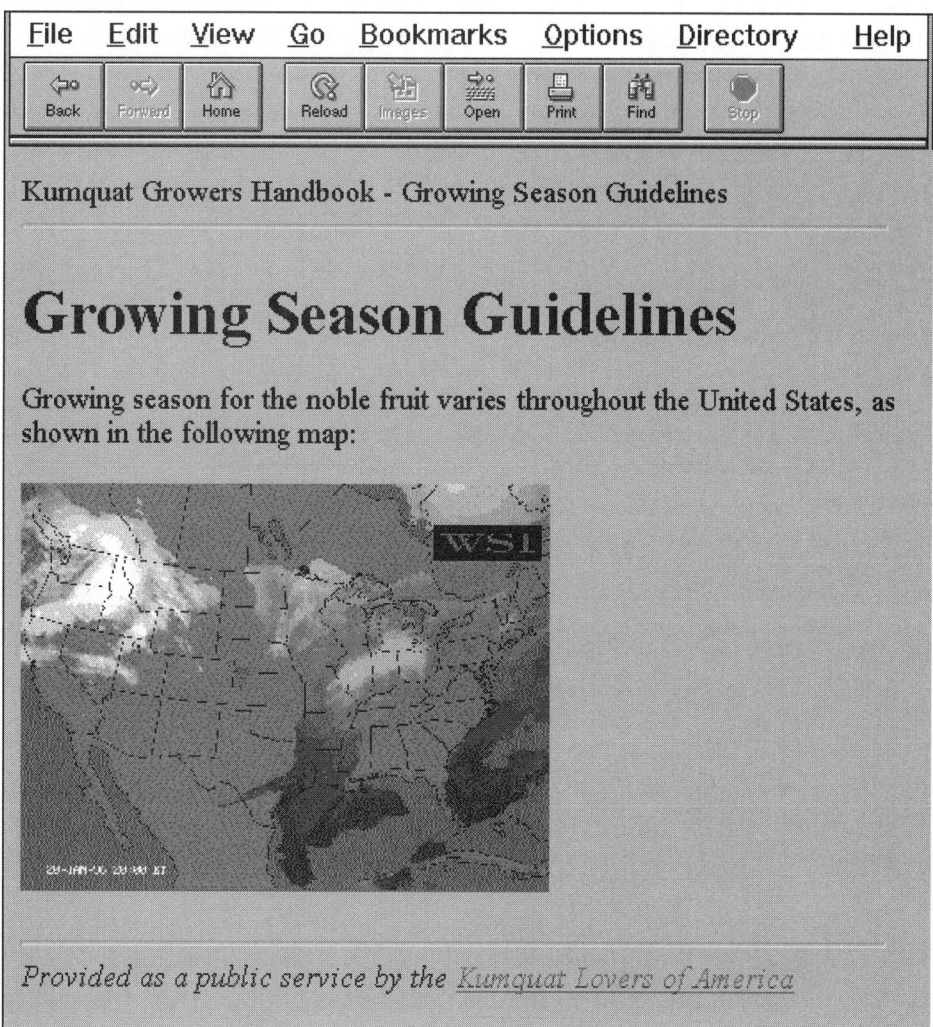

Figure 5-7. Clearly delineate headers and footers with horizontal rules

graphics for either format. However, each has its own advantages and drawbacks, including features that some browsers exploit for special display effects.

5.2.1.1   GIF

The Graphics Interchange Format (GIF) was first developed for image transfer among users of the CompuServe online service. The format has several features that make it popular for use in HTML documents. Its encoding is cross-platform, so that with appropriate GIF decoding software (included with most browsers), the graphics you create and make into a GIF file on a Macintosh, for example, can be loaded into a Windows-based PC, decoded, and viewed without a lot of fuss. The second main feature is that GIF uses special compression technology that can significantly reduce the size of the image file for faster transfer over a network. GIF compression is "lossless," too; none of an image's original data is altered or deleted, so the uncompressed and decoded image exactly matches its original. And GIF images can be easily animated.

Even though GIF image files invariably have the *.gif* (or *.GIF*) filename suffix, there actually are two GIF versions: the original GIF87 and an expanded GIF89a, which supports several new features, including transparent backgrounds, interlaced storage, and animation, that are popular with HTML authors (see 5.2.1.2). The currently popular browsers support both GIF versions, which use the same encoding scheme that maps 8-bit pixel values to a color table, for a maximum of 256 colors per image. Most GIF images have even fewer colors and there are special tools to simplify the colors in more elaborate graphics. By simplifying the GIF images, you create a smaller color map and enhance pixel redundancy for better file compression and consequent faster downloading.

However, because of the limited number of colors, a GIF-encoded image is not always appropriate, particularly for photorealistic pictures (see JPEG discussion later in this chapter). Rather, GIFs make excellent icons, reduced color images, and drawings.

Because most graphical browsers explicitly support the GIF format, it is currently the most widely accepted image-encoding format on the Web. It is acceptable for both inline images and externally linked ones. When in doubt as to which image format to use, choose GIF.* It will work in almost any situation.

5.2.1.2 Interlacing, transparency, and animation

GIF images can be made to perform three special tricks: interlacing, transparency, and animation. With interlacing, a GIF image seemingly materializes on the display, rather than progressively flowing onto it from top to bottom. Normally, a GIF encoded image is a sequence of pixel data, in order row-by-row, from top to bottom of the image. While the common GIF image renders onscreen like pulling down a window shade, interlaced GIFs open like a venetian blind. That's because interlacing sequences every fourth row of the image. Users get to see a full image—top to bottom, albeit fuzzy—in a quarter of the time it takes to download and display the remainder of the image. The resulting quarter-done image usually is clear enough so that users with slow network connections can evaluate whether to take the time to download the remainder of the image file.

---

* We cannot resist the temptation to point out that choosy authors choose GIF.

Not all graphical browsers, although able to display an interlaced GIF, are actually able to display the materializing effects of interlacing. With those that do, users still can defeat the effect by choosing to delay image display until after download and decoding. Older browsers, on the other hand, always download and decode images before display, and don't support the effect at all.

Another popular effect available with GIF images—GIF89a-formatted images, actually—is the ability to make a portion of them transparent so that what's underneath—usually the browser window's background—shows through. The transparent GIF image has one color in its color map designated as the background color. The browser simply ignores any pixel in the image that uses that background color, thereby letting the display window's background show through. By carefully cropping its dimensions and by using a solid, contiguous background color, a transparent image can be made to seamlessly meld into a page's surrounding content or float above it.

Transparent GIF images are great for any graphic you want to meld into the document and not stand out as a rectangular block. Transparent GIF logos are very popular, as are transparent icons and dingbats—any graphic that should appear to have an arbitrary, natural shape. You may also insert a transparent image inline with conventional text to act as a special character glyph within conventional text.

The downside to transparency is that the GIF image will look lousy if you don't remove its border when included in a hyperlink anchor (`<a>` tag), or is otherwise specially framed. And content flow happens around the image's rectangular dimensions, not adjacent to its apparent shape. That can lead to unnecessarily isolated images or odd-looking sections in your HTML pages.

The third unique trick available to the HTML author with GIF89a-formatted images is the ability to do simple frame-by-frame animation. Using special GIF animation software utilities, you may prepare a single GIF89a file to contain a series of GIF images. The browser displays each image in the file, one after the other, something like the page-flipping animation booklets we had (even drew!) as kids. Special control segments between each image in the GIF file let you set the number of times the browser runs through the complete sequence (looping), how long to pause between each image, whether or not the image space gets wiped to background before the browser displays the next image, and so on. By combining these control features with those normally available for GIF images, including individual color tables, transparency, and interlacing, you can create some very appealing and elaborate animations.[*]

---

[*] Songline Studios has published an entire book dedicated to GIF animation: *GIF Animation Studio*, by Richard Koman (1996).

Although simple, GIF animation is powerful for one other important reason: You don't need to specially program your HTML documents to achieve animation. But there is one major downside that limits their use except for small, icon-sized, or thin bands of space in the browser window: GIF animation files get large fast, even if you are careful not to repeat static portions of the image in successive animation cells. And if you have several animations in one document, download delays may—and usually will—annoy the user. If there is any feature on your HTML that deserves close scrutiny for excess, it's GIF animation.

Any and all GIF tricks—interlacing, transparency, and animation—don't just happen; you need special software to prepare the GIF file. Many image tools now save your creations or acquired images in GIF format, and most now let you enable transparency, as well as let you make interlaced GIF files. There also are a slew of shareware and freeware programs specialized for these tasks, as well as for creating GIF animation. Look into your favorite Internet software archives for GIF graphics and conversion tools and also see Chapter 15, *Tips, Tricks, and Hacks*, for details on creating transparent images.

5.2.1.3 JPEG

The Joint Photographic Experts Group (JPEG) is a standards body that developed what is now known as the JPEG image-encoding format. Like GIFs, JPEG images are platform-independent and specially compressed for high-speed transfer via digital communication technologies. Unlike GIF, JPEG supports tens of thousands of colors for more detailed, photorealistic digital images. And JPEG uses special algorithms that yield much higher data-compression ratios. It is not uncommon, for example, for a 200-kilobyte GIF image to be reduced to a 30-kilobyte JPEG image. To achieve that amazing compression, JPEG does lose some image data. However, you can adjust the degree of "lossiness" with special JPEG tools, so that although the uncompressed image may not exactly match the original, it will be close enough that most people cannot tell the difference.

Although JPEG is an excellent choice for photographs, it's not a particularly good choice for illustrations. The algorithms used for compressing and uncompressing the image leave noticeable artifacts when dealing with large areas of one color. Therefore, if you're trying to display a drawing, the GIF format may be preferable.

The JPEG format, usually designated by the *.jpg* (or *.JPG*) filename suffix, is nearly universally understood by today's graphical browsers. On rare occasions, you'll come across an older browser that cannot directly display JPEG images.

5.2.2 When to Use Images

Most pictures are worth a thousand words. But don't forget that no one pays attention to a blabbermouth. First and foremost, think of your HTML document images as visual tools, not gratuitous trappings. They should support your text content and help readers navigate your documents. Use images to clarify, illustrate, or exemplify the contents. Content supporting photographs, charts, graphs, maps, and drawings are all natural candidates for appropriate HTML images. Product photographs are essential components in online catalogs and shopping guides, for example. And link-enabled icons and dingbats, including animated images, can be effective visual guides to internal and external resources. If an image doesn't do any of these valuable services for your document, throw it out already!

One of the most important considerations when adding images to a document is the additional delay they add to the retrieval time for a document over the network, particularly for modem connections. While a simple text document might run, at most, 10 or 15 thousand bytes, images can easily extend to hundreds of thousands of bytes each. And the total retrieval time for a document is not only equal to the sum of all its component parts, but also to compounded networking overhead delays since each image requires a separate connection and download request between the client browser and the web server. Depending on the speed of the connection (*bandwidth*, usually expressed as bits or bytes per second) as well as network congestion that can delay connections, a single document containing one 100-kilobyte image may take anywhere from around 30 seconds through a 28.8 kilobit-per-second modem connection in the wee hours of the morning when most everyone else is asleep, to well over *ten minutes* with a 9600 bit-per-second modem at noontime. You get the picture?

5.2.3 *When to Use Text*

Text hasn't gone out of style. For some users, it is the only portion of your document they can access. We argue that, in most circumstances, your documents should be usable by readers who cannot view images or have disabled their automatic download in their browser to improve their low-speed connection. While the urge to add images to all of your documents may be strong, there are times when pure text documents make more sense.

Documents being converted to the Web from other formats rarely have embedded images. Reference materials and other serious content often is completely usable in a text-only form.

You should create text-only documents when access speed is critical and potentially slow. If you know that many users will have only low-speed connections to your pages, you should accommodate them by avoiding the use of images within your documents. Better yet, provide a home (leading) page that lets readers decide between duplicate collections of your work: one containing the images, and another stripped of them. (The popular browsers include special picture icons as place holders for yet-to-be downloaded images, which can trash and muddle your document's layout into an unreadable mess.)

Text is most appropriate—supporting images only, without frills or nonessential graphics—if your documents are to be readily searchable by any of the many Web indexing services. Images are almost always ignored by these search engines. If the major content of your pages is provided with images, very little information about your documents will find its way into the online web directories.

5.2.4 Speeding Image Downloads

There are several ways to ameliorate the overhead and delays inherent with images, besides being very choosy about which to include in your documents.

Keep it simple.

> A full-screen, 24-bit color graphic, even when reduced in size by digital compression with one of the standard formats like GIF or JPEG, is still going to be a network bandwidth hog. Acquire and use the various image management tools to optimize image dimensions and number of colors into the fewest number of pixels. Simplify your drawings. Stay away from panoramic photographs. Avoid large empty backgrounds in your images, as well as gratuitous borders and other space-consuming elements. Also avoid dithering (blending two colors among adjacent pixels to achieve a third color); the technique can significantly reduce the compressibility of your images. Strive for large areas of uniform colors, which compress readily in both GIF and JPEG format.

Reuse images.

> This is particularly true for icons and GIF animations. Most browsers cache incoming document components in local storage for the very purpose of quick, network connection–less retrieval of data. For smaller GIF animation files, try to prepare each successive image to only update portions that change in the animation, rather than redraw the entire image (this speeds up the animation, too).

Divide up large documents.

> This is a general rule that includes images. Many small document segments, organized through hyperlinks (of course!) and effective tables of contents tend to be better accepted by users than a few large documents. In general, people would rather "flip" several pages than dawdle waiting for a large one to download. (It's related to the TV channel-surfing syndrome.) One accepted rule of thumb is to keep your documents under 50 kilobytes each, so even the slowest connections won't overly frustrate your readers.

Isolate necessarily large graphics.

Provide a special link to large images, perhaps one that includes a thumbnail of the graphic, thereby letting readers decide if and when they want to spend the time downloading the full image. And since the downloaded image isn't mixed with other document components like inline images, it's much easier for the reader to identify and save the image on their system's local storage for later study. (For details on non-inline image downloads, see 4.7.)

Specify image dimensions.

Finally, another way to improve performance is by including the image's rectangular height and width information in its tag. By supplying those dimensions, you eliminate the extra steps the extended browsers must take to download, examine, and calculate an image's space in the document. There is a downside to this approach, however, that we explore in 5.2.6.11.

5.2.5   JPEG or GIF?

You may choose to use only JPEG or GIF images in your HTML documents if your sources for images or your software toolset prefers one over the other format. Both are nearly universally supported by today's browsers, so there shouldn't be any user-viewing problems.

Nevertheless, we recommend that you acquire the facilities to create and convert to both formats, to take advantage of their unique capabilities. For instance, use GIF's transparency feature for icons and dingbats. Alternatively, use JPEG for large and colorful images for faster downloading.

5.2.6   The `<img>` Tag

The `<img>` tag lets you reference and insert a graphic image into the current text flow of your HTML document. There is no implied line or paragraph break before or after the `<img>` tag, so images can be truly "inline" with text and other content.

The format of the image itself is not defined by the HTML standard, although the popular graphical browsers support GIF and JPEG images. The HTML standard doesn't specify or restrict the size or dimensions of the image, either. Images may have any number of colors, but how those colors are rendered is highly browser-dependent.

Image presentation in general is very browser-specific. Images may be ignored by nongraphical browsers. Browsers operating in a constrained environment may modify the image size or complexity. And users, particularly those with slow network connections, may choose to defer image loading altogether. Accordingly,

<img>

Function:

Inserts an image into a document

Attributes:

ALIGN
ALT
BORDER
CONTROLS **O**
DYNSRC **O**
HEIGHT
HSPACE
ISMAP
LOOP **O**
LOWSRC **N**
NAME **N**
ONABORT **N**
ONERROR **N**
ONLOAD **N**
SRC
START **O**
USEMAP
VSPACE
WIDTH

End tag:

None

Contains:

Nothing

Used in:

text

you should make sure your documents make sense and are useful, even if the images are completely removed.

5.2.6.1 The src attribute

The `src` attribute for the `<img>` tag is required (unless you use `dynsrc` with Internet Explorer-based movies; see 5.2.7.1). Its value is the image file's URL, either absolute or relative to the HTML document referencing the image. To unclutter their document storage, HTML authors typically collect image files into a separate folder they often name something like "pics" or "images." [URLs, 7.2]

For example, this HTML fragment places an image of a famous kumquat packing plant into the narrative text (see Figure 5-8):

```
Here we are, on day 17 of the tour, in front of the kumquat
packing plant:
<p>
<img src="pics/packing_plant.gif">
<p>
What an exciting moment, to see the boxes of fruit moving
```

In the example, the paragraph (`<p>`) tags surrounding the `<img>` tag cause the browser to render the image by itself with some vertical space after the preceding text and before the trailing text. Text may also abut the image, as we describe in 5.2.6.4.

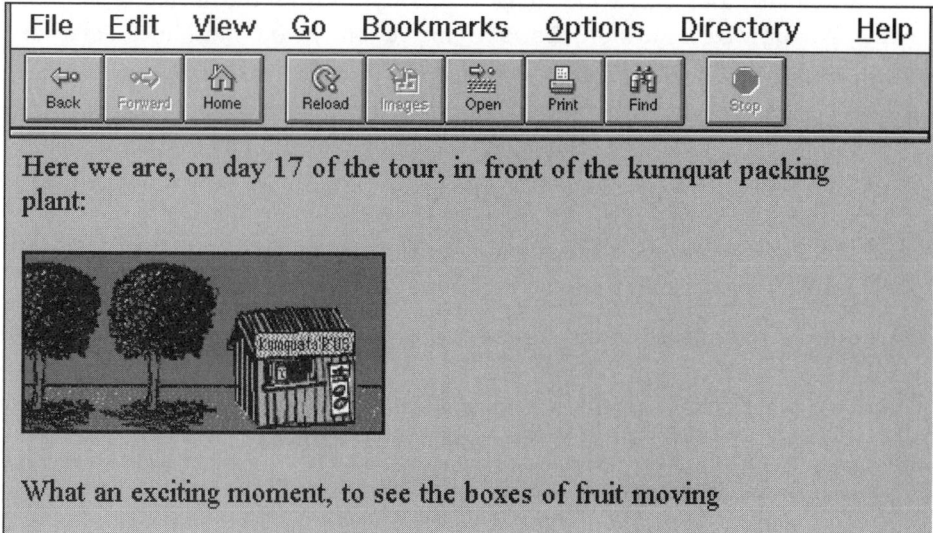

Figure 5-8. Image integrated with text

5.2.6.2 *The lowsrc attribute*

To the benefit of users, particularly those with slow Internet connections, Netscape provides the `lowsrc` companion to the `src` attribute in the `<img>` tag as a way to speed up document rendering. The `lowsrc` attribute's value, like `src`, is the URL of an image file that the browser loads and displays when it first encounters the `<img>` tag. Then, when the document has been completely loaded and can be read by the user, Netscape goes back and retrieves the image specified by the `src` attribute.

Ostensibly, the `lowsrc` image is a low-resolution, abbreviated version of the final `src` image that loads faster by comparison to quickly give the reader an idea of its content until the final, higher-resolution image eventually replaces it onscreen. But the `lowsrc` attribute can also be used for some very special effects.

Netscape uses the `lowsrc` image's dimensions to reserve space in the document for both the `lowsrc` and `src` images, unless you explicitly allocate that space with the `height` and `width` attributes described later in this chapter. Hence, if the dimensions of the image specified in the `src` attribute are different than those for the `lowsrc` image or your explicitly included height and width values, the `src` image will be reduced, enlarged, stretched, and/or compressed to fit in the allotted space. Moreover, the `lowsrc` and `src` images needn't be identical, so you might take advantage of the delayed rendering of the `src` image for simple animation.

The `lowsrc` attribute is for Netscape only. Other browsers ignore it and only load the image specified by the `src` attribute. Netscape won't load either image if the user chooses not to auto-load images. In that case, both images will load in order when the user clicks the images button or clicks the image icon placeholder. No browser loads the `lowsrc` image only; you must include a `src` image, otherwise nothing will appear except the missing image icon.

5.2.6.3 *The alt attribute*

The `alt` attribute specifies alternative text the browser may show if image display is not possible or disabled by the user. It's an option, but one we highly recommend you exercise for most images in your document. This way, if the image is not available, the user still has some indication of what it is that's missing.

The value for the `alt` attribute is a text string of up to 1024 characters, enclosed in quotation marks if you include spaces or other punctuation. The alternative text may contain entity references to special characters, but it may not contain any other sort of markup; in particular, no style tags are allowed.

Graphical browsers ignore the `alt` attribute if the image is available and downloading is enabled by the user. Otherwise, they insert the `alt` attribute's text as a label next to an image placeholder icon. Well-chosen `alt` labels thereby additionally support those users with a graphical browser who have disabled their automatic image download because of a slow connection to the Web.

Nongraphical, text-only browsers like Lynx put the `alt` text directly into the content flow just like any other text element. So, when used effectively, the `alt` tag sometimes can transparently substitute for missing images. (Your text-only browser users will appreciate not being constantly reminded of their second-class Web citizenship.) For example, consider using an asterisk as the `alt` attribute alternative to a special bullet icon:

```
<h3><img src="pics/fancy_bullet.gif" alt="*">Introduction</h3>
```

A graphical browser displays the bullet image, while in a nongraphical browser the `alt` asterisk takes the place of the missing bullet. Similarly, use `alt` text to replace special image bullets for list items. For example, the following code:

```
<ul>
  <li> Kumquat recipes <img src="pics/new.gif" alt="(New!)">
  <li> Annual harvest dates
</ul>
```

displays the `new.gif` image with graphical browsers, and the text "(New!)" with text-only browsers.

The `alt` attribute lets you use even more complex text (see Figure 5-9):

```
Here we are, on day 17 of the tour, in front of the kumquat
packing plant:
<p>
<img src="pics/packing_plant.gif"
  alt="[Image of our tour group outside the main packing plant]">
<p>
What an exciting moment, to see the boxes of fruit moving
```

```
Here we are, on day 17 of the tour, in front of the kumquat packing
plant:

[Image of our tour group outside the main packing plant]

What an exciting moment, to see the boxes of fruit moving
```

`Commands: Use arrow keys to move, '?' for help, 'q' to quit, '<-' to go back`

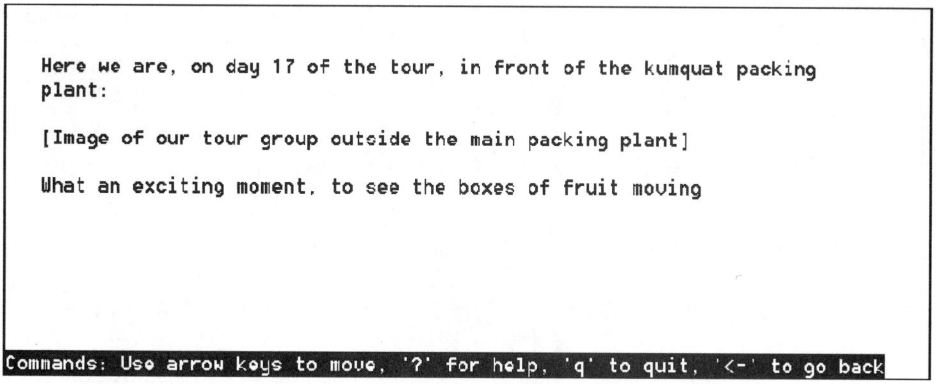

Figure 5-9. Text-only browsers like Lynx display an image's alt attribute text

5.2.6.4 The align attribute

The HTML standard does not define a default alignment for images with respect to other text and images in the same line of text, so you cannot absolutely predict how the mixture of text and images will look.* HTML images normally appear in line with a single line of text. Our common media like magazines typically wrap text around images, with several lines next to and abutting the image, not just a single line.

Fortunately, HTML document designers can exert some control over the alignment of images with the surrounding text through the `align` attribute for the `<img>` tag. The HTML standard specifies five image-alignment attribute values: `left`, `right`, `top`, `middle`, and `bottom`. The `left` and `right` values flow any subsequent text around the image, which is moved to the corresponding margin; the remaining three align the image vertically with respect to the surrounding text. Netscape adds four more vertical alignment attributes to that list: `texttop`, `absmiddle`, `baseline`, and `absbottom`, while Internet Explorer adds `center`.

---

* Most of the popular graphical browsers normally insert an image so that its base aligns with the baseline of the text—the same alignment as that specified by the attribute value of `bottom`. Nonetheless, HTML document designers should assume that alignment varies between browsers and always include the desired type of image alignment.

The following list contains descriptions for the inline HTML image alignments; see
Figure 5-10 for examples.

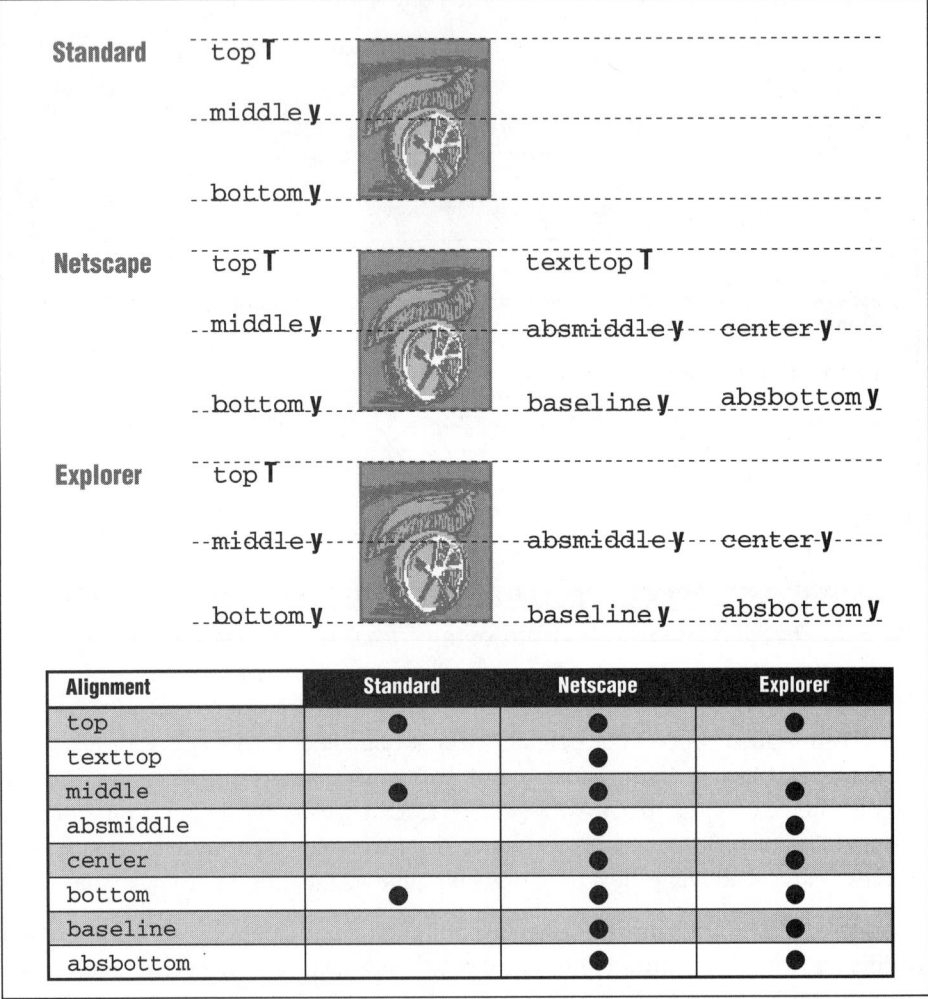

Figure 5-10. HTML standard and browser-extended inline image alignments with text

Alignment	Standard	Netscape	Explorer
top	●	●	●
texttop		●	
middle	●	●	●
absmiddle		●	●
center		●	●
bottom	●	●	●
baseline		●	●
absbottom		●	●

`top`

> The top of the image is aligned with the top edge of the tallest item in the
> current line of text. If there are no other images in the current line, the top of
> the image is aligned with the top of the text.

`texttop` ▉

> The `align=texttop` attribute and value tells Netscape to align the top of
> the image with the top of the tallest text item in the current line. This is

slightly different from the standard HTML `top` option, which aligns the top of the image with the top of the tallest item, image or text, in the current line. If the line contains no other images that extend above the top of the text, `texttop` and `top` have the same effect.

`middle`

Netscape and Internet Explorer treat the `middle` image alignment value differently: Netscape always aligns the middle of the image to the baseline of the text, regardless of other inline elements, such as another inline image (see Figure 5-11). Internet Explorer, on the other hand, aligns the middle of the image to the middle of the tallest item in the current line, text or image (see Figure 5-12). Notice the alignments and differences in Figures 5-11 and 5-12, particularly when only one image contains the `align` attribute. Both figures display the HTML fragment:

```
Line of text
<img src="pics/horiz.gif" align=middle>
<img src="pics/vert.gif">
goes on ...
<br clear=left>
<p>
Line of text
<img src="pics/horiz.gif" align=middle>
<img src="pics/vert.gif" align=middle>
goes on ...
```

Also note that Internet Explorer Version 3 treats `middle`, `absmiddle`, and `center` the same, whereas earlier Internet Explorer versions and the current Netscape (Version 4) distinguishes between `middle` and `absmiddle` alignments. (If you are confused as to exactly what each alignment value means, please raise your hand.)

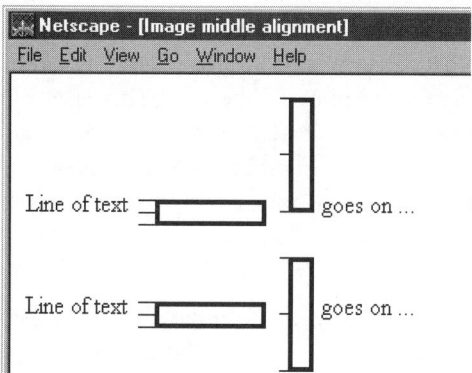

Figure 5-11. Netscape aligns middle of image to baseline of text

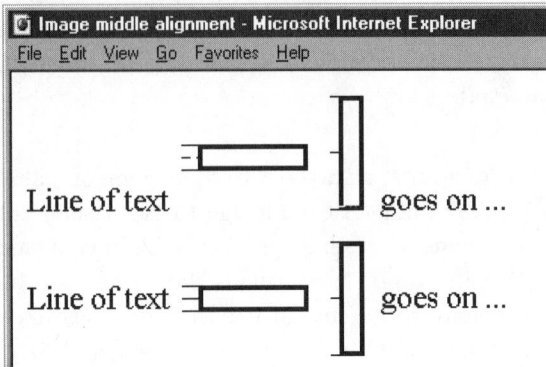

Figure 5-12. Internet Explorer aligns middle of image to middle of tallest line element

absmiddle

If you set the `align` attribute of the `<img>` tag to `absmiddle`, the browser will fit the absolute middle of the image to the absolute middle of the current line. For Netscape and earlier versions of Internet Explorer, this is different from the common `middle` option, which aligns the middle of the image with the baseline of the current line of text (the bottom of the characters). Version 3 of Internet Explorer, on the other hand, treats `absmiddle` the same as `middle` and `center`.

center

The `center` image alignment value gets treated the same as `absmiddle` by both Internet Explorer and Netscape, but note that the browsers treat `absmiddle` and `middle` differently.

bottom *and* baseline *(default)*

With Netscape and earlier versions of Internet Explorer, the `bottom` and `baseline` image alignment values have the same effect as if you didn't include any alignment attribute at all: the browsers align the bottom of the image in the same horizontal plane as the baseline of the text. This is not to be confused with the `absbottom`, which takes into account letter "descenders" like the tail on the lowercase "y." Internet Explorer Version 3, on the other hand, treats `bottom` the same as `absbottom`. (Did we see a hand up in the audience?)

absbottom

The `align=absbottom` attribute tells the browsers to align the bottom of the image with the true bottom of the current line of text. The true bottom is the lowest point in the text taking into account descenders, even if there are no descenders in the line. A descender is the tail on a "y," for example; the baseline of the text is the bottom of the "v" in the "y" character.

Use the `top` or `middle` alignment values for best integration of icons, dingbats, or other special inline effects with the text content. Otherwise, `align=bottom` (the default) usually gives the best appearance. When aligning one or more images on a single line, select the alignment that gives the best overall appearance to your document.

5.2.6.5 Wrapping text around images

The `left` and `right` image alignment values tell the browser to place an image against the left or right margin, respectively, of the current text flow. The browser then renders subsequent document content in the remaining portion of the flow adjacent to the image. The net result is that the document content following the image gets wrapped around the image.

```
<img src="pics/kumquat.gif" align=left>
The kumquat is the smallest of the citrus fruits, similar in
appearance to a tiny orange. The similarity ends with its appearance,
however. While oranges are generally sweet, kumquats are extremely
bitter. Theirs is an acquired taste, to be sure.
```

Figure 5-13 shows text flow around a left-aligned image.

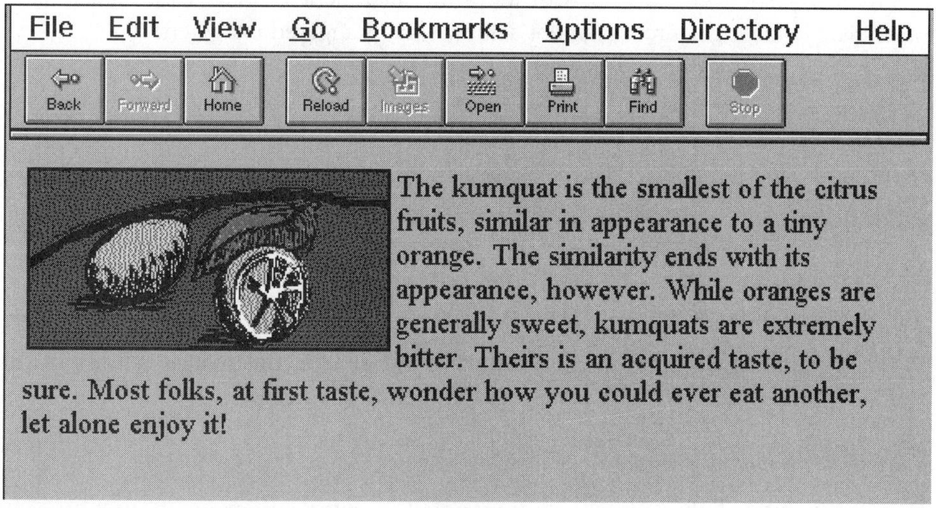

Figure 5-13. Text flow around a left-aligned image

You can place images against both margins simultaneously (Figure 5-14) and the text will run down the middle of the page between them:

```
<img src="pics/kumquat.gif" align=left>
<img src="pics/tree.gif" align=right>
The kumquat is the smallest of the citrus fruits, similar in
appearance to a tiny orange. The similarity ends with its appearance,
however. While oranges are generally sweet, kumquats are extremely
bitter. Theirs is an acquired taste, to be sure.
```

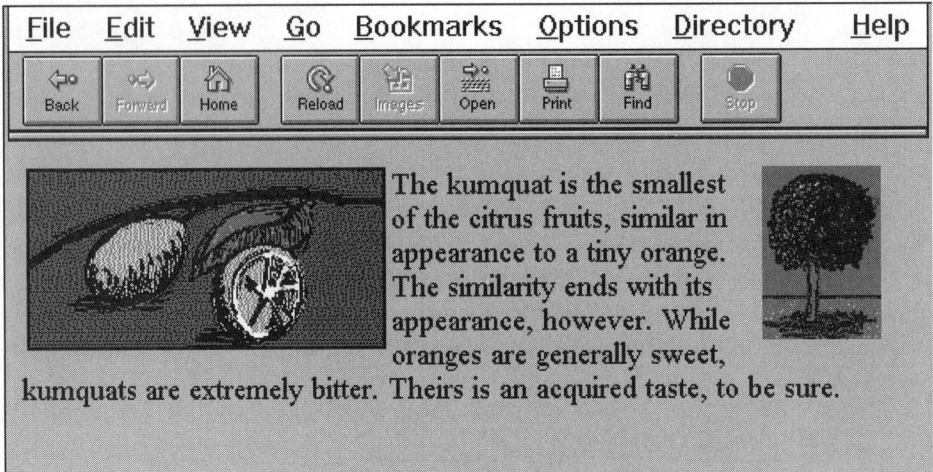

Figure 5-14. Running text between left- and right-aligned images

While text is flowing around an image, the left (or right) margin of the page is temporarily redefined to be adjacent to the image as opposed to the edge of the page. This means that subsequent images with the same alignment will stack up against each other. The following source fragment achieves that staggered image effect:

```
<img src="pics/marcia.gif" align=left>
Marcia!
<br>
<img src="pics/jan.gif" align=left>
Jan!
<br>
<img src="pics/cindy.gif" align=left>
Cindy!
```

The results of this example are shown in Figure 5-15.

When the text flows beyond the bottom of the image, the margin returns to its former position, typically at the edge of the browser window.

5.2.6.6 Centering an image

Have you noticed that you can't horizontally center an image in the browser window with the `align` attribute? The `middle` and `absmiddle` values center the image vertically with the current line, but the image is horizontally justified depending on what content comes before it in the current flow and the dimensions of the browser window.

You can horizontally center an inline image in the browser window, but only if it's isolated from surrounding content, such as by paragraph, division, or line break tags. Then, either use the `<center>` tag, or use the `align=center`

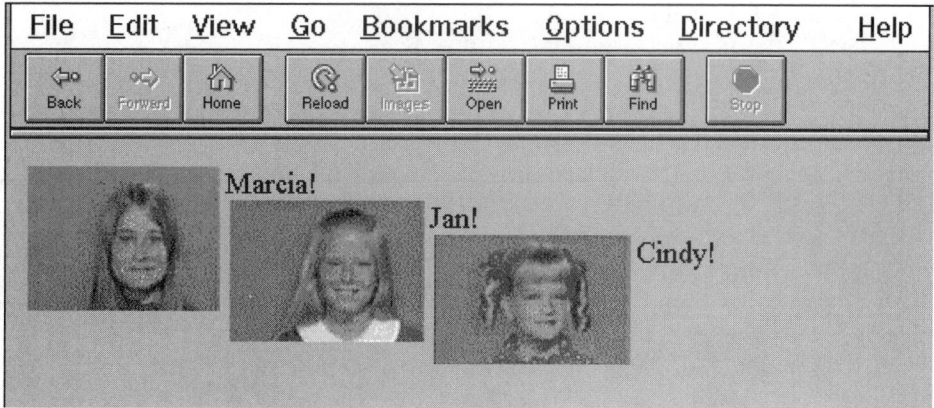

Figure 5-15. Three very lovely girls

attribute or center-justified style in the paragraph or division tag to center the image. For example:

```
Kumquats are tasty treats
<br>
<center>
<img src="pics/kumquat.gif">
</center>
that everyone should strive to eat!
```

Use the paragraph tag with its `align=center` attribute if you want some extra space above and below the centered image:

```
Kumquats are tasty treats
<p align=center>
<img src="pics/kumquat.gif">
</p>
that everyone should strive to eat!
```

5.2.6.7 *The border attribute*

Browsers normally render images that also are hyperlinks (included in an `<a>` tag) with a two-pixel-wide colored border, indicating to the reader that the image can be selected to visit the associated document. You can change the thickness of that border with the `border` attribute to the `<img>` tag. The value of the `border` attribute is an integer equal to the border thickness in pixels.

Figure 5-16 shows you the thick and thin of image borders, as rendered from the following HTML source:

```
<a href="test.html">
 <img src="pics/kumquat.gif" border=1>
</a>
<a href="test.html">
  <img src="pics/kumquat.gif" border=2>
```

```
</a>
<a href="test.html">
  <img src="pics/kumquat.gif" border=4>
</a>
<a href="test.html">
  <img src="pics/kumquat.gif" border=8>
</a>
```

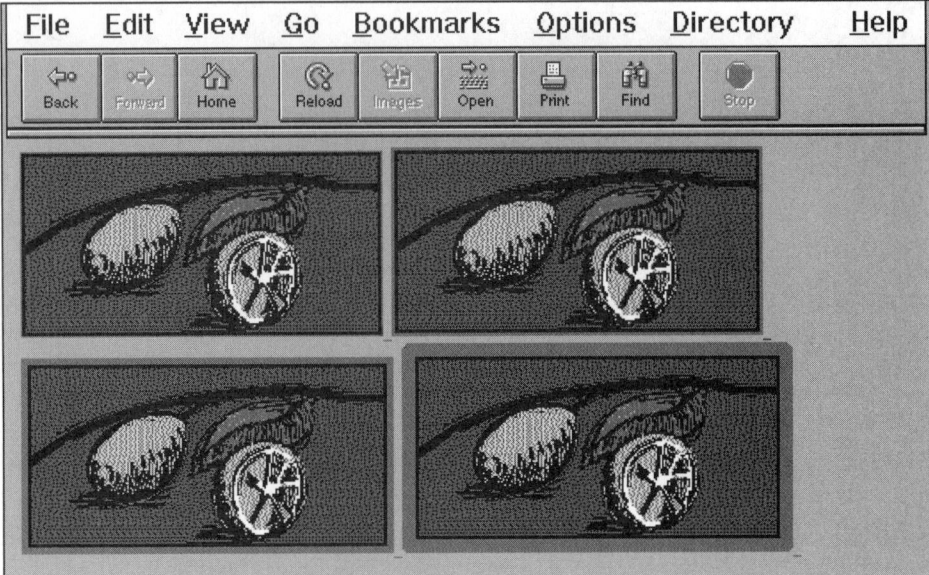

Figure 5-16. The thick and thin of image borders

5.2.6.8 Removing the image border

You can eliminate the border around an image hyperlink altogether with the `border=0` attribute within the `<img>` tag. For some images, particularly image maps, the absence of a border can greatly improve the appearance of your pages. Images that are clearly link buttons to other pages may also look best without a border.

Be careful, though, that by removing the border, you don't diminish your page's usability. No border means you've removed a common visual indicator of a link, making it less easy for your readers to find the links on the page. Browsers will change the mouse cursor as readers pass it over an image that is a hyperlink, but you should not assume they will, nor should you make readers test your border-less images to find hidden links.

We strongly recommend that you use some additional way with borderless images to let your readers know to click the images. Even including simple text instructions will go a long way to making your pages more accessible to readers.

5.2.6.9 *The height and width attributes*

Normally, a graphical browser determines the size of an image and, hence, the rectangular space to reserve for it in the display window, by retrieving the image file and extracting its embedded height and width specifications. This is not the most efficient way to render a document since the browser must sequentially examine each image file and calculate its screen space before rendering adjacent and subsequent document content. That can significantly increase the amount of time it takes to render the document and delay scanning by the user.

A more efficient way for HTML authors to specify an image's dimensions is with the `height` and `width` `<img>` attributes. That way, the browser can calculate and reserve space before actually downloading an image, speeding document rendering. Both attributes require an integer value that indicates the image size in pixels; the order in which they appear in the `<img>` tag is not important.

5.2.6.10 *Resizing and flood-filling images*

A hidden feature of the `height` and `width` attributes is that you don't need to specify the actual image dimensions; the attribute values can be larger or smaller than the actual size of the image. The browser automatically scales the image to fit the predefined space. This gives you a down-and-dirty way of creating thumbnail versions of large images and a way to enlarge very small pictures. Be careful, though: the browser still must download the entire file, no matter what its final rendered size is, and you will distort an image if you don't retain its original height versus width proportions.

Another trick with `height` and `width` provides an easy way to flood-fill areas of your page and can also improve document performance. Suppose you want to insert a colored bar across your document.* Rather than create an image to the full dimensions, create one that is just one pixel high and wide and set it to the desired color. Then use the `height` and `width` attributes to scale it to the larger size:

```
<img src="pics/one-pixel.gif" width=640 height=20>
```

The smaller image downloads much faster than a full-scale image, and the `width` and `height` attributes create the desired bar after the tiny image arrives at the browser (see Figure 5-17).

One last trick with the `width` attribute is to use a percentage value instead of an absolute pixel value. This causes the browser to scale the image to a percentage

---

* This is one way to create colored horizontal rules in Netscape 3 or earlier, which don't support the `col-or` attribute of the `<hr>` tag.

Figure 5-17. This bar was made from a one-pixel image

of the document window width. Thus, to create a colored bar 20 pixels high and the width of the window, you could use:

```
<img src="pics/one-pixel.gif" width="100%" height=20>
```

As the document window changes size, the image will change size as well.

If you provide a percentage `width` and omit the `height`, the browser will retain the image's aspect ratio as it grows and shrinks. This means that the height will always be in the correct proportion to the width and the image will display without distortion.

5.2.6.11 Problems with height and width

Although the `height` and `width` attributes for the `<img>` tag can improve performance and let you perform some neat tricks, there is a particularly knotty downside to using them. The browser sets aside the specified rectangle of space to the prescribed dimensions in the display window even if the user has turned off automatic download of images. What the user often is left with is a page full of semi-empty frames with meaningless picture placeholder icons inside. The page looks terribly unfinished and is mostly useless. Without accompanying dimensions, on the other hand, the browser simply inserts a placeholder icon inline with the surrounding text, so at least there's something there to read in the display.

We don't have an answer to this dilemma, other than to insist that you use the `alt` attribute with some descriptive text so that users at least know what they are missing (see 5.2.6.3). We do recommend that you include these size attributes because we encourage any practice that improves network performance.

5.2.6.12 The hspace and vspace attributes

Graphical browsers usually don't give you much space between an image and the text around it. And unless you create a transparent image border that expands the space between them, the typical two-pixel buffer between an image and adjacent text is just too close for most designers' comfort. Add the image into a hyperlink, and the special colored border will negate any transparent buffer space you labored to create, as well as draw even more attention to how close the adjacent text butts up against the image.

The `hspace` and `vspace` attributes can give your images breathing room. With `hspace`, you specify the number of pixels of extra space to leave between the image and text on the left and right sides of the image; the `vspace` value is the number of pixels on the top and bottom. Figure 5-18 shows the difference between two wrapped images.

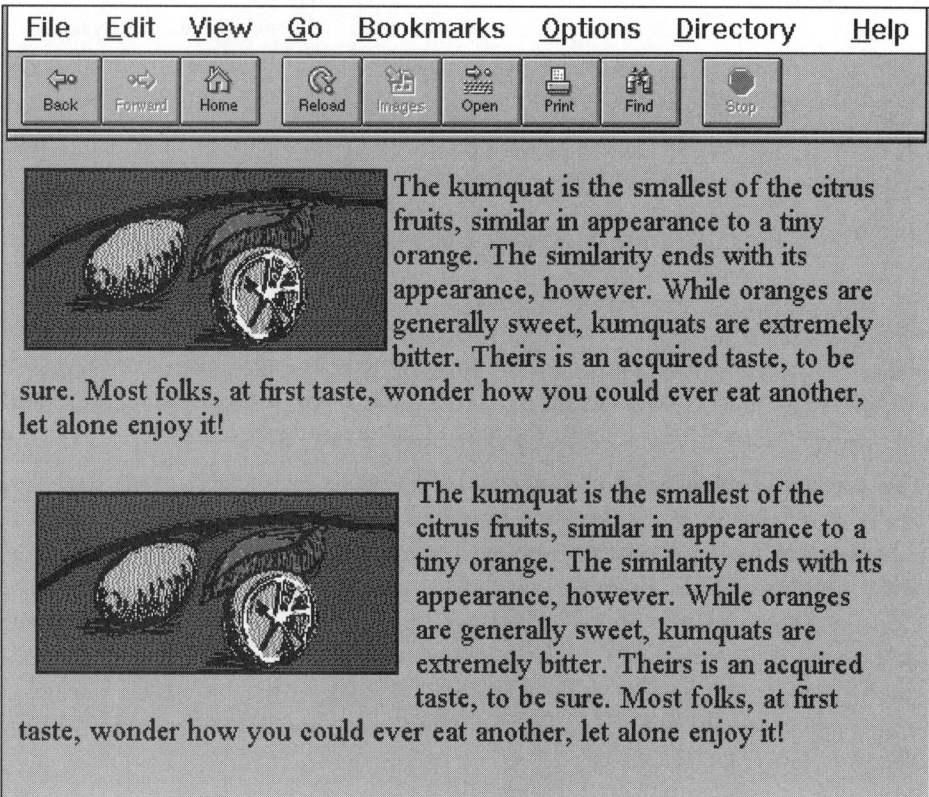

Figure 5-18. Improve image/text interfaces with vspace and hspace extensions

```
<img src="pics/kumquat.gif" align=left>
The kumquat is the smallest of the citrus fruits, similar
in appearance to a tiny orange. The similarity ends with its
appearance, however. While oranges are generally sweet,
kumquats are extremely bitter. Theirs is an acquired taste,
to be sure. Most folks, at first taste, wonder how you could
ever eat another, let alone enjoy it!
<p>
<img src="pics/kumquat.gif" align=left hspace=10 vspace=10>
The kumquat is the smallest of the citrus fruits, similar
```

```
in appearance to a tiny orange. The similarity ends with its
appearance, however. While oranges are generally sweet,
kumquats are extremely bitter. Theirs is an acquired taste,
to be sure. Most folks, at first taste, wonder how you could
ever eat another, let alone enjoy it!
```

We're sure you'll agree that the additional space around the image makes the text easier to read and the overall page more attractive.

5.2.6.13 The ismap and usemap attributes

The `ismap` and `usemap` attributes for the `<img>` tag tell the browser that the image is a special mouse-selectable visual map of one or more hyperlinks, commonly known as an *image map*. The `ismap` style of image maps, known as a *server-side* image map, may only be specified within an `<a>` tag hyperlink. [`<a>`, 7.3.1]

For example:

```
<a href="/cgi-bin/images/map2">
  <img src="pics/map2.gif" ismap>
</a>
```

The browser automatically sends the x,y position of the mouse (relative to the upper-left corner of the image) to the server when the user clicks somewhere on the `ismap` image. Special server software (the */cgi-bin/images/map2* program in the example) may then use those coordinates to determine a response.

The `usemap` attribute provides a *client-side* image map mechanism that effectively eliminates server-side processing of the mouse coordinates and its incumbent network delays and problems. Using special `<map>` and `<area>` tags, HTML authors provide a map of coordinates for the hyperlink-sensitive regions in the `usemap` image along with related hyperlink URLs. The value of the `usemap` attribute is a URL that points to that special `<map>` section. The browser on the user's computer translates the coordinates of a click of the mouse on the image into some action, including loading and displaying another document. [`<map>`, 7.5.3] [`<area>`, 7.5.4]

For example, the following source specially encodes the 100-pixel wide by 100-pixel tall `map2.gif` image into four segments, each of which, if clicked by the user, links to a different document. Also notice that we've included, validly, the `ismap` image map processing capability in the example `<img>` tag so that users of other, `usemap`-incapable browsers have access to the alternative, server-side mechanism to process the image map:

```
<a href="/cgi-bin/images/map2">
  <img src="pics/map2.gif" ismap usemap="#map2">
</a>
...
```

```
<map name="map2">
  <area coords="0,0,49,49" href="link1.html">
  <area coords="50,0,99,49" href="link2.html">
  <area coords="0,50,49,99" href="link3.html">
  <area coords="50,50,99,99" href="link4.html">
</map>
```

Geographical maps make excellent `ismap` and `usemap` examples: browsing a nationwide company's pages, for instance, the user might click on their home town on a map to get the addresses and phone numbers for nearby retail outlets. The advantage of the `usemap` client-side image map processing is that it does not require a server or special server software and so, unlike the `ismap` mechanism, can be used in non-web (networkless) environments, such as local files or CD-ROM.

Please read our more complete discussion of anchors and links, including image maps within links, in 7.5.

5.2.6.14 The name, onAbort, onError, and onLoad attributes

There are four `<img>` attributes currently supported by Netscape that let you use JavaScript to manipulate the image. The first is the `name` attribute, which lets you label the image so that it can be referenced by a JavaScript applet. For example,

```
<img src="pics/kumquat.gif" name="kumquat">
```

lets you later refer to that picture of a kumquat as simply "kumquat" in a Java-Script applet perhaps to erase or otherwise modify it. You cannot individually manipulate an image with JavaScript if it is not named.

The other three attributes let you provide JavaScript event handlers. The value of the attribute is a chunk of JavaScript code, enclosed in quotation marks; it may consist of one or more JavaScript expressions, separated by semicolons.

Netscape invokes the `onAbort` event handler if the user stops loading an image, usually by clicking the browser's "stop" button. You might, for instance, use an `onAbort` message to warn users if they stop loading some essential image, such as an image map (see 6.5):

```
<img src="pics/kumquat.gif" usemap="#map1"
onAbort="window.alert"('Caution: This image contains important
   hyperlinks. Please load the entire image.')">
```

The `onError` attribute is invoked if some error occurs during the loading of the image, but not for a missing image or one that the user chose to stop loading. Presumably, the applet could attempt to recover from the error or load a different image in its place.

Netscape executes the JavaScript code associated with the `<img>` tag's `onLoad` attribute right after the browser successfully loads and displays the image.

See 13.3.3 for more information about JavaScript and event handlers.

5.2.6.15 Combining <img> attributes

You may combine any of the various standard and extension attributes for images where and when they make sense. The order for inclusion of multiple attributes in the <img> tag is not important, either. Just be careful not to use redundant attributes or you won't be able to predict the outcome.

5.2.7 Video Extensions

The special `controls`, `dynsrc`, `loop`, and `start` attribute extensions for the <img> tag are unique to Internet Explorer and are extensions to the HTML 3.2 standard. They let you embed an inline movie into the body content, just like an image.

Equivalent behavior is available in Netscape via an extension program known as a plug-in. Plug-ins place an additional burden on the user, in that each user must find and install the appropriate plug-in before being able to view the inline video. The Internet Explorer <img> tag extensions, on the other hand, make video display an intrinsic part of the browser. [plug-ins, 13.2]

However, the Internet Explorer movie extensions currently are very limited. They are not supported by any other browser and can only be used with Audio Video Interleave (AVI) formatted movie files, since that's the player format built into Internet Explorer and enabled through Windows 95. Moreover, recent innovations in browser technology, *applets* in particular, may make Internet Explorer's approach of extending the already overloaded <img> tag obsolete.

5.2.7.1 The dynsrc attribute

Use the `dynsrc` attribute extension in the <img> tag to reference an AVI movie for inline display by Internet Explorer. Its required value is the URL of the movie file enclosed in quotation marks. For example, this text displays the tag and attribute for an AVI movie file entitled *intro.avi*:

```
<img dynsrc="movies/intro.avi">
```

The browser sets aside a video viewport in the HTML display window and plays the movie, with audio if it's included in the clip and if your computer is able to play audio. Internet Explorer treats `dynsrc` movies similar to inline images: in line with current body content and according to the dimension of the video frame. And, like common images, the `dynsrc` referenced movie file gets displayed immediately after download from the server. You may change those defaults and add some user controls with other attributes, as described below.

Because all other browsers currently ignore the special Internet Explorer attributes for movies, they may become confused by an <img> tag that does not contain the otherwise required `src` attribute and an image URL. We recommend that you include the `src` attribute and a valid image file URL in all `<img>` tags, including those that reference a movie for Internet Explorer users. The other browsers display the still image in place of the movie; Internet Explorer does the reverse and plays the movie, but does not display the image. Note that the order of attributes does not matter. For example:

```
<img dynsrc="movies/intro.avi" src="pics/mvstill.gif">
```

Internet Explorer loads and plays the AVI movie *intro.avi*; other graphical browsers will load and display the *mvstill.gif* image instead.

5.2.7.2 *The controls attribute*

Normally, Internet Explorer plays a movie inside a framed viewport once, without any visible user controls. The user may restart, stop, and continue the movie by clicking inside that viewport with the mouse. Use the `controls` attribute (no value) to add visible controls to the movie viewport so that the user may, with the mouse, play, fast-forward, reverse, stop, and pause the movie, like on a VCR. If the movie clip includes a sound track, Internet Explorer provides an audio volume control as well. For example:

```
<img dynsrc="movies/intro.avi" controls src="pics/mvstill.gif">
```

adds the various playback controls to the video window of the *intro.avi* movie clip, as shown in Figure 5-19.

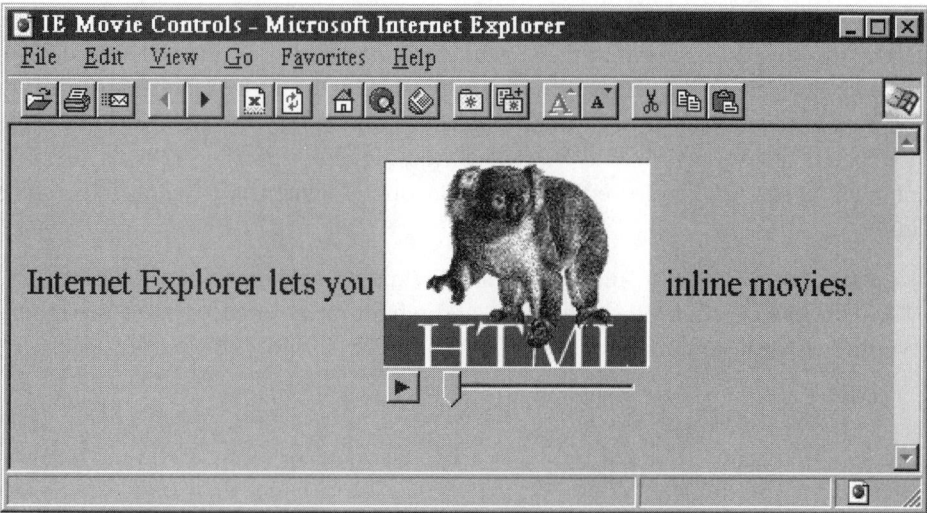

Figure 5-19. The controls attribute adds movie playback controls to the video playback frame

5.2.7.3 The loop attribute

Internet Explorer normally plays a movie clip from beginning to end once after download. The `loop` attribute for the movie `<img>` tag lets you have the clip play repeatedly for an integer number of times set by the attribute's value, or forever if the value is `infinite`. The user may still cut the loop short by clicking on the movie image, by pressing the stop button, if given controls (see previous), or by moving on to another document.

The following *intro.avi* movie clip will play from beginning to end, then restart at the beginning and play through to the end nine more times:

```
<img dynsrc="movies/intro.avi" loop=10 src="pics/mvstill.gif">
```

Whereas the following movie will play over and over again, incessantly:

```
<img dynsrc="movies/intro.avi" loop=infinite src="pics/mvstill.gif">
```

Looping movies aren't necessarily meant to annoy. Some special effects animations, for instance, are a sequence of repeated frames or segments. Rather than string the redundant segments into one, long movie that extends its download time, simply loop the single, compact frame or segment.

5.2.7.4 The start attribute

Normally, an Internet Explorer movie clip starts playing as soon as it's downloaded. You can modify that behavior with the **start** attribute in the movie's `<img>` tag. By setting its value to **mouseover**, you delay playback until the user passes the mouse pointer over the movie viewport. The other valid **start** attribute value, **fileopen**, is the default: start playback just after download. It is included because both values may be combined in the **start** attribute to cause the movie to automatically playback once after download, and then whenever the user passes the mouse over its viewport. Add a value-separating comma, with no intervening spaces, or else enclose them in quotes, when combining the **start** attribute values.

For example, our by-now-infamous *intro.avi* movie will play once when its host HTML document is loaded by the user, and whenever he or she passes the mouse over the movie's viewport:

```
<img dynsrc="movies/intro.avi" start="fileopen,mouseover"
     src="pics/mvstill.gif">
```

5.2.7.5 Combining movie <img> attributes

Treat Internet Explorer inline movies as you would any image, mixing and matching the various movie-specific, as well as the standard and extended `<img>` tag attributes and values supported by the browser. For example, you might align the movie (or its image alternate, if displayed by another browser) to the right of the browser window:

```
<img dynsrc="movies/intro.avi" src="pics/mvstill.gif" align=right>
```

Combining attributes to achieve a special effect is good. We also recommend you combine attributes to give control to the user, when appropriate. For instance, if you set up a movie to loop incessantly, you should also include the `controls` attribute so the user can stop the movie without having to leave the HTML document.

As we stated in 5.2.7.4, by combining attributes you can also delay playback until the user passes the mouse over its viewport. Magically, the movie comes alive and plays continuously:

```
<img dynsrc="movies/magic.avi" start=mouseover
    loop=infinite src="pics/magic.gif">
```

5.3 Document Colors and Background Images

The HTML 3.2 standard provides a number of attributes for the **<body>** tag that allow the HTML author to define text, link, and document background colors, in addition to defining an image to be used as the document background. Internet Explorer extends these attributes to include document margins and better background image control. And, of course, the latest style sheet technologies integrated into the current browsers let you manipulate all these various display parameters.

5.3.1 Extensions to the <body> Tag

The attributes that control the document background, text color, and document margins are used with the **<body>** tag. [<body>, 3.7.1]

5.3.1.1 The bgcolor attribute

You can change the default background color in the browser window to another hue with the `bgcolor` attribute for the **<body>** tag. Like the `color` attribute for the **<font>** tag, the required value of the `bgcolor` attribute may be expressed in either of two ways: as the red, green, and blue (RGB) components of the desired color or as a standard color name. Appendix F, *Color Names and Values*, provides a complete discussion of RGB color encoding along with a table of acceptable color names you can use with the `bgcolor` attribute.

Setting the background color is easy. To get a pure red background using RGB encoding, try:

```
<body bgcolor="#FF0000">
```

For a more subtle background, try:

```
<body bgcolor=peach>
```

5.3.1.2 The background attribute

If a splash of color isn't enough, you may also place an image into the background of a document with the `background` attribute in its `<body>` tag.

The required value of the `background` attribute is the URL of an image. The browser automatically repeats (tiles) the image both horizontally and vertically to fill the entire window.

You normally should choose a small, somewhat dim image to create an interesting but unobtrusive background pattern. Besides, a small, simple image traverses the network much faster than an intricate, full-screen image.

Figure 5-20 shows you how the extended browsers repeatedly render a single brick to create a wall of bricks for the document background:

```
<body background="pics/onebrick.gif">
```

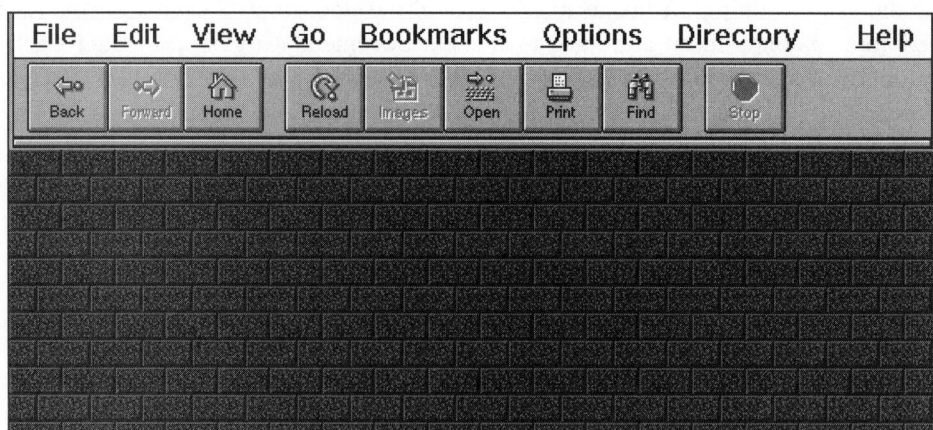

Figure 5-20. One brick becomes many in a Netscape background

Background images of various dimensions and sizes create interesting vertical and horizontal effects on the page. For instance, a tall skinny image might set off your document heading:

```
<body background="pics/vertical_fountain.gif">
<h3>Kumquat Lore</h3>
For centuries, many myths and legends have arisen around the kumquat.
```

If the *vertical_fountain.gif* is a narrow, tall image whose color grows lighter towards its base and whose length exceeds the length of the document body, the resulting document might look like the one shown in Figure 5-21.

Figure 5-21. A tall and skinny background

You can achieve a similar effect horizontally with an image that is much wider than it is long (see Figure 5-22).

Figure 5-22. A long and skinny background

5.3.1.3 The bgproperties attribute

The `bgproperties` attribute extension for the `<body>` tag is exclusive to Internet Explorer and only works in conjunction with the `background` attribute extension. The `bgproperties` attribute has a single value, `fixed`. It freezes the background image to the browser window, so it does not scroll with the other window contents. Hence, the example *H2Omark.gif* background image servers as a watermark for the document:

```
<body background="pics/H2Omark.gif" bgproperties="fixed">
```

5.3.1.4 The text attribute

Once you alter a document's background color or add a background image, you also might need to adjust the text color to ensure that users can read the text. The `text` attribute for the `<body>` tag does just that: it sets the color of all nonanchor text in the entire document.

Give the `text` attribute a color value in the same format as you use to specify a background color (see `bgcolor` above)—an RGB triplet or color name, as described in Appendix F, *Color Names and Values*. For example, to produce a document with blue text on a pale yellow background, use:

```
<body bgcolor="#777700" text="blue">
```

Of course, it's best to select a text color that contrasts well with your background color or image.

5.3.1.5 The link, vlink, and alink attributes

The `link`, `vlink`, and `alink` attributes of the `<body>` tag control the color of hypertext (`<a>` tag) in your documents. All three accept values that specify a color as an RGB triplet or color name, just like the `text` and `bgcolor` attributes.

The `link` attribute determines the color of all hyperlinks the user has not yet followed. The `vlink` attribute sets the color of all links the extended browser user had followed at one time or another. The `alink` attribute defines a color for active link text—one that is currently selected by the user and is under the mouse cursor with the mouse button depressed.

Like text color, you should be careful to select link colors that can be read against the document background. Moreover, the link colors should be different from the regular text as well as from each other.

5.3.1.6 The leftmargin attribute

Peculiar to Internet Explorer, the `leftmargin` attribute extension for the `<body>` tag lets you indent the left margin relative to the left edge of the browser's window, much like a margin on a sheet of paper. Other browsers ignore this attribute and normally left-justified body content abuts the left edge of the document window.

The value of the `leftmargin` attribute is the integer number of pixels for that left-margin indent; a value of 0 is the default. The margin is filled with the background color or image.

For example, Internet Explorer renders the following text justified against a margin 50 pixels away from the left edge of the browser window (see Figure 5-23):

```
<body leftmargin=50>
Internet Explorer lets you indent the<br>
&lt;--left margin<br>
away from the left edge of the window.
</body>
```

Figure 5-23. Internet Explorer's leftmargin attribute for indenting body content

5.3.1.7 The topmargin attribute

Like `leftmargin`, the `topmargin` attribute extension currently is exclusive to Internet Explorer. It may be included in the `<body>` tag to set a margin of space at the top of the document. The margin space is filled with the document's background color or image.

Body content begins flowing below the integer number of pixels you specify as the value for `topmargin`; a value of 0 is the default.

For example, Internet Explorer renders the following text at least 50 pixels down from the top edge of the browser window (see Figure 5-24):

```
<body topmargin=50>
<center>
^^^^^^^^^^^^^^^^^^^^^^^^^^^^^^^^^^^^^^^^^^^^^
</center>
Internet Explorer can give your documents
a little extra headroom.
</body>
```

Figure 5-24. Internet Explorer's topmargin attribute for lowering body content

5.3.1.8 The style and class attributes

You also can set all the various style-related `<body>` features and then some with HTML style sheets. But, although you may include the `style` attribute with the `<body>` tag to create an inline style for the entire body content, we recommend that you set the styles for the entire document body at the document level (`<style>` tag inside the document head) or via a collection-level (imported) style sheet. Use the `class` attribute and name value to apply the appropriate style of a predefined class of the `<body>` tag to the contents. (Since there can only be one body per document, what is the point of setting a class name otherwise?) We cover the use of `style` and class definitions in Chapter 9, *Cascading Style Sheets*.

5.3.1.9 Mixing and matching body attributes

Although `background` and `bgcolor` attributes can appear in the same `<body>` tag, a background image will effectively hide the selected background color unless the image contains substantial portions of transparent areas, as we described earlier in this chapter. But even if the image does hide the background color, go ahead and include the `bgcolor` attribute and some appropriate color value. That's because users can turn off image downloading, which includes background images, and so they may find your page otherwise left naked and unappealing. Moreover, without a `bgcolor` attribute or a downloaded (for whatever reason) background image, the browsers merrily ignore your text and link color attributes, too, reverting instead to its own default values, or the ones chosen by the user.

5.3.2 Extending a Warning

The various color and image extensions work wonderfully, particularly the colorful ones, assuming that all users have a 256-color display, lots of available memory, unlimited network bandwidth, and good visual acuity. In reality, many users have monochrome or limited color displays, limited memory for caching images, extremely restricted network bandwidth, and poor vision.

Because of these limitations, you should seriously consider not using any of these extensions in your documents. Much like early users of the Macintosh felt compelled to create documents using ransom-note typography ("I've got 40 fonts on this thing, and I'm going to use them all!"), many authors cannot avoid adding some sort of textured background to every document they create ("I've got 13 wood grains and 22 kinds of marbling, and I'm going to use them all!").

In reality, except for the very clever ones, texture-mapped backgrounds add no information to your documents. The value of your document ultimately lies in its text and imagery, not the cheesy blue swirly pattern in the background. No matter how cool it looks, your readers are not benefiting and could be losing readability.

We advise you not to use the color extensions except for comparatively frivolous endeavors or unless the extension really adds to the document's value, such as for business advertising and marketing pages.

5.3.2.1 Problems with background images

Here are some of the things that can go wrong with background images:

- The time to load the document is increased by the amount of time needed to load the image. Until the background image is completely downloaded, no further document rendering is possible.

- The background image takes up room in the browser's local cache, displacing other images that might actually contain useful information. This makes other documents, which might not even have backgrounds, take that much longer to load.

- The colors in the image may not be available on the user's display, forcing the browser to dither the image. This replaces large areas of a single color with repeating patterns of several other closer, but not cleaner, colors and can make the text more difficult to read.

- Because the browser must actually display an image in the background, as opposed to filling an area with a single color, scrolling through the document can take much longer.

- Even if it's clear onscreen, text printed on top of an image invariably is more difficult, if not impossible, to read.

- Fonts vary widely between machines; the ones you use with your browser that work fine with a background pattern often end up jagged and difficult to read on another machine.

5.3.2.2 Problems with background, text, and link colors

There also are a slew of problems you will encounter if you play with background colors, including:

- The color you choose, while just lovely in your eyes, may look terrible to the user. Why annoy them by changing what users most likely have already set as their own default background color?

- While you may be a member of the "light text on a dark background" school of document design, many people also favor the "dark text on a light background" style that has been consistently popular for over three thousand years. Instead of bucking the trend, assume that the user has already set their browser to a comfortable color scheme.

- Some users are color-blind. What may be a nifty-looking combination of colors to you may be completely unreadable to others. One combination in particular to avoid is green for unvisited links and red for visited links. Millions of men are afflicted with red/green color blindness.

- Your brilliant hue may not be available on the user's display, and the browser may be forced to choose one that's close instead. For displays with very few colors (like those of several million 16-color VGA Windows-based machines currently in use) the close colors for the text and the background might be the same color!

- For the same reasons above, active, unvisited, and visited links may all wind up as the same color on limited-color displays.

- By changing text colors, particularly those for visited and unvisited links, you may completely confuse the user. By changing those colors, you effectively force them to experiment with your page, clicking a few links here and there to learn your color scheme.

- Most page designers have no formal training in cognitive psychology, fine arts, graphic arts, or industrial design, yet feel fully capable of selecting appropriate colors for their documents. If you must fiddle with the colors, ask a professional to pick them for you.

5.3.2.3 And then again

There is no denying the fact that these extensions result in some very stunning HTML documents. And they are fun to explore and play with. So, rather than leave this section on a sour note of caution, we encourage you to go ahead and play—just play carefully.

5.4 Background Audio

There is one other form of inline multimedia generally available to web surfers— audio. Most browsers treat audio multimedia as separate documents, downloaded and displayed by special helper applications, applets, or plug-ins. Internet Explorer, on the other hand, contains a built-in sound decoder and supports a special HTML tag that lets you integrate an audio file with your document that plays in the background as a soundtrack for your page. [applets, 13.1] [plug-ins, 13.2]

We applaud the developers of Internet Explorer for providing a mechanism that more cleanly integrates audio into HTML documents. And the possibilities with audio are very enticing. But at the same time, we caution authors that the special tags and attributes for audio don't work with other browsers, and whether this is the method that the majority of browsers will eventually support is not at all assured. So, beware.

5.4.1 The <bgsound> Tag

Use the <bgsound> tag to play a soundtrack in the background. This tag is for Internet Explorer documents only. All other browsers ignore the tag. It downloads and plays an audio file when the host HTML document is first downloaded by the user and displayed in their browser. The background sound file also will replay whenever the user refreshes the browser display.

<bgsound> ❶

Function:
  Plays a soundtrack in the document background

Attributes:
  LOOP
  SRC

End tag:
  None

Contains:
  Nothing

Used in:
  body_content

5.4.1.1 The src attribute

The `src` attribute is required for the <bgsound> tag. Its value references the URL for the related sound file. For example, when the Internet Explorer user first downloads an HTML document containing the tag:

```
<bgsound src="audio/welcome.wav">
```

they will hear the *welcome.wav* audio file—perhaps an inviting message—play once through their computer's sound system.

Currently, Internet Explorer can handle three different sound format files: `wav`, the native format for PCs; `au`, the native format for most UNIX workstations; and MIDI, a universal music-encoding scheme (see also Table 5-1).

Table 5-1. Common multimedia formats and respective filename extensions

Format	Type	Extension	Platform of Origin
GIF	Image	*gif*	Any
JPEG	Image	*jpg, jpeg, jpe*	Any
XBM	Image	*xbm*	UNIX
TIFF	Image	*tif, tiff*	Any
PICT	Image	*pic, pict*	Any
Rasterfile	Image	*ras*	Sun
MPEG	Movie	*mpg, mpeg*	Any
AVI	Movie	*avi*	Microsoft
QuickTime	Movie	*qt, mov*	Apple
AU	Audio	*au, snd*	Sun
WAV	Audio	*wav*	Microsoft
AIFF	Audio	*aif, aiff*	Apple
MIDI	Audio	*midi, mid*	Any
PostScript	Document	*ps, eps, ai*	Any
Acrobat	Document	*pdf*	Any

5.4.1.2 The loop attribute

Like Internet inline movies, the `loop` attribute for the browser's `<bgsound>` tag lets you replay a background soundtrack for a certain number of times (or over and over again forever), at least until the user moves on to another page or quits the browser.

The value of the `loop` attribute is the integer number of times to replay the audio file, or `infinite`, which makes the soundtrack repeat endlessly.

For example:

```
<bgsound src="audio/tadum.wav" loop=10>
```

repeats the ta-dum soundtrack ten times, whereas:

```
<bgsound src="audio/noise.wav" loop=infinite>
```

continuously plays the noise soundtrack.

5.4.2 *Alternative Audio Support*

There are other ways to include audio in your documents, using more general mechanisms that support other embedded media as well. The most common alternative to the `<bgsound>` tag is the `<embed>` tag, originally implemented by Netscape. Because of its more general nature, we cover the `<embed>` tag in 13.2.

5.5 *Animated Text*

In what appears to be an effort to woo advertisers, Internet Explorer has added a form of animated text to HTML. The animation is simple—text scrolling horizontally across the display—but effective for moving banners and other elements that readily and easily animate an otherwise static document. On the other hand, like the `<blink>` tag, animated text can easily become intrusive and abusive for the reader. Use with caution, please, if at all.

5.5.1 *The <marquee> Tag*

The `<marquee>` tag defines the text that scrolls across the Internet Explorer user's display.

The `<marquee>` tag is for Internet Explorer only, and it is an extension to the HTML 3.2 standard. The text between the `<marquee>` tag and its required `</marquee>` end tag scrolls horizontally across the display. The various tag attributes control the size of the display area, its appearance, its alignment with the surrounding text, and the scrolling speed.

The `<marquee>` tag and attributes are ignored by other browsers, but its contents are not. They are displayed as static text, sans any alignment or special treatments afforded by the `<marquee>` tag attributes.

5.5.1.1 *The align attribute*

Internet Explorer places `<marquee>` text into the surrounding body content just as if it were an embedded image. As a result, you can align the marquee within the surrounding text.

The `align` attribute accepts a value of `top`, `middle`, or `bottom`, meaning that the specified point of the marquee will be aligned with the corresponding point in the surrounding text. Thus:

```
<marquee align=top>
```

aligns the top of the marquee area with the top of the surrounding text. Also see the `height` and `width`, `hspace` and `vspace` attributes later in this chapter that control the dimensions of the marquee.

<marquee> ❶

Function:

Create a scrolling text marquee

Attributes:

ALIGN
BEHAVIOR
BGCOLOR
CLASS
DIRECTION
HEIGHT
HSPACE
LOOP
STYLE
SCROLLAMOUNT
SCROLLDELAY
VSPACE
WIDTH

End tag:

</marquee>; never omitted

Contains:

plain_text

Used in:

body_content

5.5.1.2 The behavior, direction, and loop attributes

Together, these three attributes control the style, direction, and duration of the scrolling in your marquee.

The `behavior` attribute accepts three values:

`scroll` *(default)*

The value of `scroll` causes the marquee to act like the grand marquee in Times Square: the marquee area is empty initially; the text then scrolls in from one side (controlled by the `direction` attribute), continues across until it reaches the other side of the marquee, and then scrolls off until the marquee is once again empty.

`slide`

This value causes the marquee to start empty. Text then scrolls in from one side (controlled by the `direction` attribute), stops when it reaches the other side, and remains onscreen.

```
alternate
```
Specifying `alternate` as the value for the `behavior` attribute causes the marquee to start with the text fully visible at one end of the marquee area. The text then scrolls until it reaches the other end, whereupon it reverses direction and scrolls back to its starting point.

If you do not specify a marquee `behavior`, the default `behavior` is `scroll`.

The `direction` attribute sets the direction for marquee text scrolling. Acceptable values are either `left` (the default) or `right`. Note that the starting end for the scrolling is opposite to the direction: `left` means that the text starts at the right of the marquee and scrolls to the left. Remember also that rightward-scrolling text is counter-intuitive to anyone who reads left to right.

The `loop` attribute determines how many times the marquee text scrolls. If an integer value is provided, the scrolling action is repeated that many times. If the value is `infinite`, the scrolling repeats until the user moves on to another document within the browser.

Putting some of these attributes together:

```
<marquee align=center loop=infinite>
  Kumquats aren't filling
  ..........          Taste great, too!
</marquee>
```

The example message starts at the right side of the display window (default direction), scrolls leftward all the way across and off the Internet Explorer display, and then starts over again until the user moves on to another page. Notice the intervening periods and spaces for the "trailer"; you cannot append one marquee to another.

Also, the `slide`-style of scrolling looks jerky when repeated and should only be scrolled once. Other scrolling behaviors work well with repeated scrolling.

5.5.1.3 The bgcolor attribute

The `bgcolor` attribute lets you change the background color of the marquee area. It accepts either an RGB color value or one of the standard color names. See Appendix F, *Color Names and Values* for a full discussion of both color-specification methods.

To create a marquee area whose color is yellow, you would write:

```
<marquee bgcolor=yellow>
```

5.5.1.4 The height and width attributes

The `height` and `width` attributes determine the size of the marquee area. If not specified, the marquee area extends all the way across the Internet Explorer display and will be just high enough to enclose the marquee text.

Both attributes accept either a numeric value, indicating an absolute size in pixels, or a percentage, indicating the size as a percentage of the browser window height and width.

For example, to create a marquee that is 50 pixels tall and occupies one-third of the display window width, use:

```
<marquee height=50 width="33%">
```

While it is generally a good idea to ensure the `height` attribute is large enough to contain the enclosed text, it is not uncommon to specify a width that is smaller than the enclosed text. In this case, the text scrolls the smaller marquee area, resulting in a kind of "viewport" marquee familiar to most people.

5.5.1.5 The hspace and vspace attributes

The `hspace` and `vspace` attributes let you create some space between the marquee and the surrounding text. This usually makes the marquee stand out from the text around it.

Both attributes require an integer value specifying the space needed in pixels. The `hspace` attribute creates space to the left and right of the marquee; the `vspace` attribute creates space above and below the marquee. To create 10 pixels of space all the way around your marquee, for example, use:

```
<marquee vspace=10 hspace=10>
```

5.5.1.6 The scrollamount and scrolldelay attributes

These attributes control the speed and smoothness of the scrolling marquee.

The `scrollamount` attribute value is the number of pixels needed to move text each successive movement during the scrolling process. Lower values mean smoother, but slower scrolling; higher numbers create faster, but jerkier text motion.

The `scrolldelay` attribute lets you set the number of milliseconds to wait between successive movements during the scrolling process. The smaller this value, the faster the scrolling.

You can use a low `scrolldelay` to mitigate the slowness of a small, smooth `scrollamount`. For example,

```
<marquee scrollamount=1 scrolldelay=1>
```

scrolls the text one pixel for each movement, but does so as fast as possible. In this case, the scrolling speed is limited by the capabilities of the browser's computer.

5.5.1.7 *The style and class attributes*

The `style` attribute for the `<marquee>` tag creates an inline style for the text enclosed by the tag, overriding any other style rule in effect. The `class` attribute lets you format the content according to a predefined class of the `<marquee>` tag; its value is the name of that class. [`style` attribute, 9.1.1] [`class` attribute, 9.2.4].

5.6 Other Multimedia Content

The Web is completely open-minded about the types of content that can be exchanged by servers and browsers. In this section, we look at a different way to reference images, along with audio, video, and other document formats.

5.6.1 Embedded Versus Referenced Content

Images currently enjoy a special status among the various media that can be included within an HTML document and displayed inline with other content by all but a few browsers. Sometimes, however, as we discussed earlier in this chapter, you may also reference images externally, particularly large ones in which details are important, but not immediately necessary to the document content. Other multimedia elements, including digital audio and video, can be referenced as separate documents external to the current one.

You normally use the anchor tag (`<a>`) to link external multimedia elements to the current document. Just like other link elements selected by the user, the browser downloads the multimedia object and presents it to the user, possibly with the assistance of an external application or plug-in. Referenced content is always a two-step process: present the document that links to the desired multimedia object, then present the object if the user selects the link. [`<a>`, 7.3.1]

In the case of images, you can choose how to present images to the user: inline and immediately available via the `<img>` tag, or referenced and subsequently available via the `<a>` tag. If your images are small and critical to the current document, you should provide them inline. If they are large or are only a secondary element of the current document, make them available as referenced content via the `<a>` tag.

If you choose to provide images via the `<a>` tag, it is sometimes a courtesy to your readers to indicate the size of the referenced image in the referencing document and perhaps provide a thumbnail sketch. Users can then determine whether it is worth their time and expense to retrieve it.

5.6.2 Referencing Audio, Video, and Images

You reference any external document, regardless of type or format, in an HTML document via a conventional anchor (`<a>`) link:

```
The <a href="sounds/anthem.au">Kumquat Grower's Anthem</a> is a
rousing tribute to the thousands of 'quat growers around the world.
```

Just like any referenced document, the server delivers the desired multimedia object to the browser when the user selects the link. If the browser finds the document is not HTML, but some other format, it automatically invokes an appropriate rendering tool to display or otherwise convey the contents of the object to the user.

You can configure your browser with special helper applications that handle different document formats in different ways. Audio files, for example, might be passed to an audio-processing tool, while video files are given to a video-playing tool. If a browser has not been configured to handle a particular document format, the browser will inform you and offer to simply save the document to disk. You can later use an appropriate viewing tool to examine the document.

Browsers identify and specially handle multimedia files from one of two different hints: either from the file's Multipurpose Internet Mail Extension (MIME) type provided by the server or from a special suffix in the file's name. The browser prefers MIME because of its richer description of the file and its contents, but will infer the file's contents (type and format) of the object by the file suffix; *.gif* or *.jpg*, for GIF and JPEG encoded images, for example, or *.au* for a special sound file.

Since not all browsers look for a MIME type, nor will they all be correctly configured with helper applications by their users, you should always use the correct file suffix in the names of multimedia objects. See Table 5-1 for examples.

5.6.3 Appropriate Linking Styles

Creating effective links to external multimedia documents is critical. The user needs some indication of what the object is and perhaps the kind of application the linked object needs to execute. Moreover, most multimedia objects are quite large, so common courtesy tells us to provide users with some indication of the time and expense involved in downloading it.

In lieu of, or in addition to, the anchor and surrounding text, a small thumbnail of large images or a familiar icon that indicates the referenced object's format may be useful.

5.6.4 Embedding Other Document Types

The Web can deliver nearly any type of electronic document, not just graphics, sound, and video files. To display them, however, the client browser needs a helper application installed and referenced. Recent browsers also support *plug-in* accessory software and, as described in Chapter 13, *Executable Content,* which may extend the browser for some special function, including inline display of multimedia objects.

For example, consider a company whose extensive product documentation was prepared and stored in some popular layout application like FrameMaker, Quark XPress, or PageMaker. The Web offers an excellent way for distributing that documentation over a worldwide network, but converting to HTML would be too costly at this time.

The solution is to prepare a few HTML documents that catalog and link the alternative files and invoke the appropriate display applet. Or, make sure the users' browsers have the plug-in software or are configured to invoke the appropriate helper application—FrameMaker, for example, if the document is in FrameMaker format. Then, if a link to a FrameMaker document is chosen, the tool is started and accordingly displays the document.

5.7 *Beyond HTML*

Ever since the publication of Vernor Vinge's ground-breaking science fiction novelette *True Names* in 1978, many computer programmers and users have been fascinated by the ideas of "virtual reality" and "cyberspace"—computer interfaces using 3D surround graphics with which a user could interact in something like the way our physical bodies interact with the real world.

In 1994, two Silicon Valley programmers with backgrounds in computer graphics went public with the provocative idea that the distributed-hypertext model of HTML might be used as a foundation for building cyberspace. A working group began adapting and enhancing a graphics-description language previously developed at Silicon Graphics Inc. to be used with HTML and Web software.

The result was Virtual Reality Markup Language (VRML). VRML follows the HTML model in several important respects. Like HTML, VRML is a content-based, plain-ASCII markup language that describes its universe at a high level, and leaves it up to the browser or client program to make detailed presentation decisions. VRML technology has since evolved even more rapidly than the Web itself. As of April 1997, Microsoft was in the process of extending the VRML standard, and support for an earlier version of VRML was available as an add-on for the popular Netscape browser for PCs.

VRML documents describe worlds populated with 3D shapes. Developers build objects from basic shapes, such as cubes, cones, and spheres, with a variety of surface effects, including texture maps and lighting, available for composing realistic objects. It's possible to associate URLs with objects in a VRML world in such a way that when a user touches the object, they are transported to another VRML world, an HTML document, or a CGI (Common Gateway Interface) script (which itself may generate a VRML world).

Some intriguing demonstration interfaces to large databases have already been built and suggest the beginnings of true cyberspace architecture. So far, however, these demonstrations fall short of the strong virtual-reality experience depicted in science-fiction books and movies. Three related problems bar the way. The design problem is that VRML currently has no capacity to do animation. VRML worlds are static. While it's easy to move the user's viewpoint in a VRML world, the only way to actually move or alter a VRML object is to generate an entirely new document and render it. Proposals to support animation description are in the works, but none have yet been adopted as of April 1997. This may well have changed by the time this book arrives in bookstores.

The second, practical problem is that reasonably priced desktop machines in 1997 simply don't have the capacity to do realistic animation of general scenes. The computational cost of point-plotting, hidden-line elimination, texture-mapping, and lighting calculations gets very large, very quickly. Companies that care about animation, like Pixar and Industrial Light and Magic, use multimillion-dollar special-purpose supercomputers for this job because they have to. Current VRML browsers, for example, frequently have to drop back from full-surface rendering to wireframe mode when moving the viewer's eyepoint. Even without animation, rendering of static images including texture-mapping, spheres and sculpted surfaces, can take many seconds, which is unacceptably slow.

The third problem is that VRML worlds are not yet shared spaces. For virtual reality to begin to approach the interactive richness of the real world, it must be possible to interact in a VRML world not merely with objects but with the "avatar" or cyberspatial manifestations of other users. This is an area of very active interest to the VRML developers (many of whom have been directly inspired by the Black Sun environment depicted in Neil Stephenson's immensely popular science fiction novel, *Snow Crash*), but no single solution has yet emerged. (There are other, comparatively minor problems: VRML has no sound capability, for example. But it's easy to imagine a solution for this one within current technology.)

Thus, VRML is still currently more a promise and a technology direction than a complete answer to the virtual-reality question. But the trend-curves of desktop hardware performance and the amount of money being poured into better multi-media graphics accelerators make it one worth watching carefully. With another few years' hardware evolution and a few foreseeable VRML language enhance-ments, a true distributed cyberspace, built around and using WWW servers, may well be within our reach.

6

Document Layout

HTML was conceived in academia, not on Madison Avenue. It was originally intended to be an easy-to-use markup language to help people make their documents more readable through text embellishments like headers as well as more extensible to their own and others' work through hyperlinks; and include other media besides text—not for pizzazz, but to better explain and illustrate their work. HTML is not a page layout tool. Well, at least not yet.

As we discussed in Chapter 1, *HTML and the World Wide Web*, the language has evolved with the Internet itself. In particular, chances are probably a hundred to one that the web user is now not a college professor doing research, but a youngster surfing for a cool site or a buyer shopping for product information and the best deal. Commercial interests—the driving force of the Web today—demand increasingly complex page formats and visual displays to attract the ever-growing population of users, emphasizing look and feel over content.

From the start of their enterprise, the developers at Netscape have been at the forefront of browser design that addresses the needs of commercial interests. Their newest venture extends HTML to provide authors with far more sophisticated page layout capabilities than previous versions.

In this chapter, we cover three new features that are unique to Netscape Navigator: spacers, multiple columns, and layers. Like tables and frames, these new tags are seductive in the extreme, luring the designer away from the HTML standard with the promise of exciting new page layout capabilities. As always, we admonish you to use these extensions only where absolutely necessary, since you alienate a portion of your audience each time you elect to include these tags in your documents.

6.1 Creating Whitespace

One of the simplest elements in any page design is the empty space surrounding content. Empty space is often just as important to the look and feel of a page as the areas filled with text and images. Commonly known as *whitespace*, these empty areas shape and contain the content of your page.

Native HTML has no way to create empty space on your page, short of using a `<pre>` tag filled with blank lines or an empty image. In fact, browsers—acting according to the HTML standard—remove leading, trailing, and any other extra spaces in text and ignore extra linefeeds. Netscape fills this void with the `<spacer>` tag. [`<pre>`, 4.7.5]

6.1.1 The *<spacer>* Tag

Use the `<spacer>` tag to create horizontal, vertical, and rectangular whitespace in your documents.

<spacer> Ⓝ

Function:
    Define a blank area in a document

Attributes:
    ALIGN
    HEIGHT
    SIZE
    TYPE
    WIDTH

End tag:
    None

Contains:
    Nothing

Used in:
    text

6.1.1.1 Creating horizontal space

The most common use of the `<spacer>` tag is to create horizontal whitespace within a line of text. To achieve this effect, set the value of the `type` attribute to `horizontal` and use the `size` attribute to define the width, in pixels (not text characters), of the horizontal area. For example,

```
<spacer type=horizontal size=100>
```

inserts 100 pixels of space in line with the current line of text. Netscape appends subsequent content at the end of the spacer if sufficient space remains on the current line. Otherwise, it places the next element onto the next line, following the normal word-wrap behavior used by Netscape.

If there is not enough room to place the entire `<spacer>` tag's whitespace on the current line, the browser shortens the space to fit on the current line. In a sense, the size of the spacer is soft, telling the browser to insert up to the specified number of pixels until the end of the current line is reached.

For example, if a spacer is 100 pixels wide, and there are only 75 pixels of space remaining on the current line within the browser's display window, Netscape will insert 75 pixels of space into the line and place the next element at the beginning of the next line in the display. Accordingly, a horizontal spacer will never be broken across a line, creating space at the end of one line and the beginning of the next.

By far, the most common application of the horizontal spacer is to indent the first line of a paragraph. Simply place a horizontal spacer at the start of a paragraph to get the desired result:

```
<spacer type=horizontal size=50>
The effects of cooler weather on the kumquat's ripening process
vary based upon the temperature.  Temperatures above 28&deg;
sweeten the fruit, while four or more hours below 28&deg; will
damage the tree.
```

The results can be seen in Figure 6-1.

Figure 6-1. Indenting a paragraph with a horizontal <spacer>

Of course, you also can use horizontal spacers to insert additional space between letters or words in a line of text. This might be useful for displaying poetry or specialized ad copy. But don't use a spacer to create an indented block of text—you cannot predict the size of the user's browser window, font sizes, and so forth, and, hence, where it will break a particular line of text. Instead, use the `<block-quote>` tag or adjust the paragraph's left margin with an appropriate style.

6.1.1.2 Creating vertical space

You may insert extra whitespace between lines of text and paragraphs in your documents by setting the `type` attribute in the `<spacer>` tag to `vertical`. The `size` attribute must also be included. Make its value a positive integer equal to the amount of whitespace, in pixels.

The vertical spacer acts just like the `<br>` tag. Both tags cause an immediate line break. The difference is, of course, that with the vertical spacer you control how far below the current line of text Netscape should start the subsequent line. The white space is added to—and therefore is never less than—the normal amount of space that would appear below the current line of text as a result of the paragraph's line spacing.

Since HTML pages are infinitely tall, the vertical space may be any number of pixels high. Of course, it'd be sophomoric to be excessive (oh, okay, try `size=100000000`). Most of today's monitors have a vertical scan of no more than 1,024 lines. So a vertical pixel size value of 1025 ensures that the next line of text will be placed off the user's screen, if that is the effect you desire.

Vertical spacers aren't quite as common as horizontal spacers, but they can still be useful. In the following text, we've used a vertical spacer to provide a bit more separation between the document's header and the regular text:

```
<h1 align=right>Temperature Effects</h1>
<spacer type=vertical size=50>
The effects of cooler weather on the kumquat's ripening process
vary based upon the temperature.  Temperatures above 28&deg;
sweeten the fruit, while four or more hours below 28&deg; will
damage the tree.
```

The results can be seen in Figure 6-2.

Figure 6-2. Using a vertical <spacer> to separate a header from the text

6.1.1.3 Creating blocks of space

The third spacer type creates a rectangular block of blank space, much like a blank image. Set the `type` attribute to `block` and include three other attributes to fully define the space: `width`, `height`, and `align`.

The `width` and `height` attributes specify the size of the spacer in pixels. These attributes are used only when the `type` attribute is set to `block` and are otherwise ignored. Similarly, the `size` attribute is ignored when the `<spacer>` type is `block`. You must give a positive integer value to both the `width` and `height` attributes; their default value is zero.

The third required spacer block attribute, `align`, controls how Netscape places the empty block relative to the surrounding text. The values for this attribute are identical to those for the `align` attribute in the `<img>` tag. Use the `top`, `texttop`, `middle`, `absmiddle`, `baseline`, `bottom`, and `absbottom` values to obtain the desired vertical alignment of the block spacer. Use the `left` and `right` values to force the block spacer to the indicated margin and cause the following text to flow up and around the spacer. The default value is `bottom`. For a complete description of the `align` attribute and its values, see 5.2.6.4.

As an example, this HTML fragment places the compass points around an empty area:

```
<center>
North
<br>
West
<spacer type=block width=50 height=50 align=absmiddle>
East
<br>
South
</center>
```

The resulting document is shown in Figure 6-3.

Figure 6-3. Using a block spacer to create space in a document

6.1.2 Mimicking the <spacer> Tag

Since only Netscape supports the `<spacer>` tag, other browsers ignore it, ruining your carefully contrived layout. It is possible to completely emulate the `<spacer>` tag using the `<img>` tag and a special, small image. And, as we mentioned earlier, new HTML style sheet properties also let you do much of what `<spacer>` does, in a more orderly and comprehensive fashion, too.

For an image to emulate `<spacer>`, you'll need a GIF image that is completely transparent. Since no part of the image will ever be seen, you can make it as small as you'd like; we recommend a 1×1 pixel GIF image. In the following examples, our tiny 1×1 pixel transparent image is named *small.gif.*

To emulate a horizontal spacer of the form:

```
<spacer type=horizontal size=n>
```

use this `<img>` tag:

```
<img src=small.gif width=n height=1>
```

Replace *n* with the desired pixel width, of course. Keep in mind, however, that the width of the `<img>` tag is fixed and may not integrate into the text flow exactly like the `<spacer>` tag would, especially if the `<img>` tag falls at or near the end of a line of text.

To emulate a vertical spacer of the form:

```
<spacer type=vertical size=n>
```

use this HTML fragment:

```
<br>
<img src=small.gif width=1 height=n>
<br>
```

The `<br>` tags are needed to emulate the line-breaking behavior of the vertical spacer. Again, replace *n* with the desired height.

To emulate a block spacer of the form:

```
<spacer type=block width=w height=h align=a>
```

use this `<img>` tag:

```
<img src=small.gif width=w height=h align=a>
```

Replace *w, h,* and *a* with the desired width, height, and alignment values.

Given that simple replacements exist for all the variants of the `<spacer>` tag, you might wonder why it is needed at all. If nothing else, the `<spacer>` tag will render faster, since the equivalent `<img>` tag will require that an image be retrieved from a server and scaled before it is inserted into your text. While this is a small issue for most users, there may be cases where using the `<spacer>` tag in lieu of an `<img>` tag makes sense.

6.2 Multicolumn Layout

Multicolumn text formatting is one of the most commonly used features of desktop publishing. In addition to creating attractive pages in a variety of formats, multiple columns let you present your text using shorter, easier-to-read lines. HTML page designers have longed for the ability to easily create multiple text columns in a single page, but have been forced to use various tricks, such as multicolumn tables (see Chapter 15, *Tips, Tricks, and Hacks*).

Netscape has neatly solved this problem by supporting the unique `<multicol>` tag. While fancy unbalanced columns and straddling are not possible with this tag, as they are with tables, conventionally balanced text columns are easy to create with `<multicol>`. And while this capability is available only with Netscape, the `<multicol>` tag degrades nicely in other browsers.

6.2.1 The <multicol> Tag

The `<multicol>` tag creates multiple columns of text and lets you control the size and number of columns.

<multicol> 🅽

Function:
Format text with multiple columns

Attributes:
CLASS
COLS
GUTTER
STYLE
WIDTH

End tag:
</multicol>; always used

Contains:
body_content

Used in:
block

The <multicol> tag can contain any other HTML content, much like the <div> tag. All of the content within the <multicol> tag is displayed just like conventional content, except that Netscape places the contents into multiple columns instead of just one.

The <multicol> tag creates a break in the text flow and inserts a blank line before rendering its content into multiple columns. After the tag, another blank line is added and the text flow resumes using the previous layout and formatting.

Netscape automatically balances the columns, making each approximately the same length. Where possible, the browser moves text between columns to accomplish the balancing. In some cases, the columns cannot be perfectly balanced because of embedded images, tables, or other large elements.

You can nest <multicol> tags, embedding one set of columns within another set of columns. While infinite nesting is supported, more than two levels of nesting is generally impractical and results in unattractive text flows.

6.2.1.1 The cols attribute

The cols attribute is required by the <multicol> tag to define the number of columns. If omitted, Netscape creates just one column, as if the <multicol> tag isn't there at all. You may create any number of columns, but in practice, more than three or four columns make text unreadable on most displays.

The following example creates a three-column layout:

```
<h1 align=right>Temperature Effects</h1>
<multicol cols=3>
The effects of cooler weather on the kumquat's ripening process
vary based upon the temperature.  Temperatures above 28&deg;
sweeten the fruit, while four or more hours below 28&deg; will
damage the tree.  The savvy quat farmer will carefully monitor
the temperature, especially in the predawn hours when the
mercury dips to its lowest point.  Smudge pots and grove heaters
may be required to keep the trees warm; many growers will spray
the trees with water to create an insulating layer of ice over
the fruit and leaves.
<p>
If a disastrous frost is predicted, below 20&deg;, the only
recourse may be to harvest the fruit early to save it from an
assured disaster.  Kumquats may subsequently be ripened using
any of the popular methane and cyanoacrylate injection systems
used for other citrus fruits.  Used correctly, these systems will
produce fruit whose taste is indistinguishable from tree-ripened
kumquats.
</multicol>
```

The results are shown in Figure 6-4.

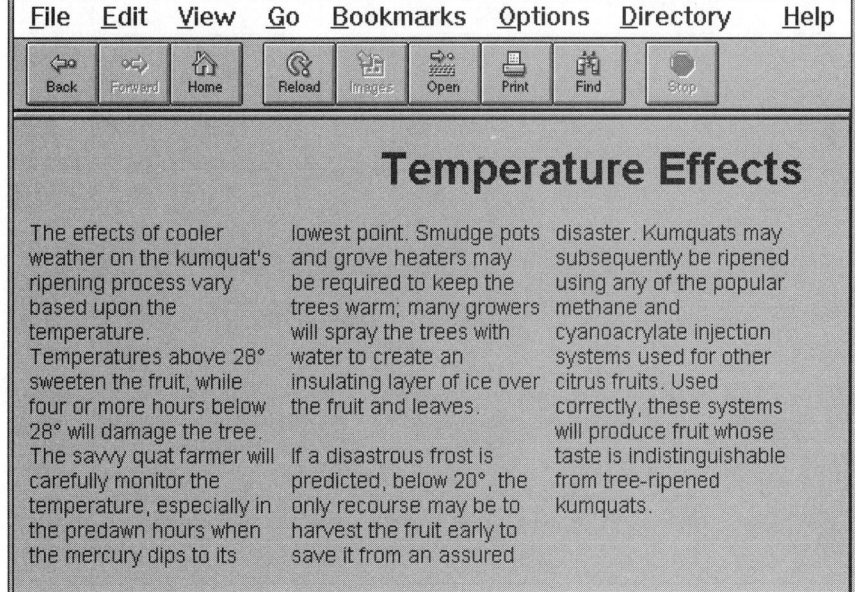

Figure 6-4. A three-column <multicol> document segment

You can see in Figure 6-4 how Netscape has balanced the columns to approximately equal lengths. You also can see how several lines within the columns appear shorter, since longer words were wrapped to the next line of text. These overly ragged right margins within the columns are unavoidable and serve to emphasize that you shouldn't create more than four or five columns in a flow. Our example is still barely readable if displayed as five columns; it breaks down completely and even induces rendering errors if `cols` is set to 7, as shown in Figure 6-5.

6.2.1.2 The gutter attribute

The space between columns is known as the *gutter*. By default, Netscape creates a gutter 10 pixels wide between each of your columns. To change this, set the `gutter` attribute's value to the desired width in pixels. Netscape will reserve this much space between your columns; the remaining space will be used for the columns themselves.

Figure 6-6 shows the effect this can have on your columns. In this figure, we've reformatted our sample text using `<multicol cols=3 gutter=50>`. Contrast this with Figure 6-4, which uses the default 10 pixel gutters.

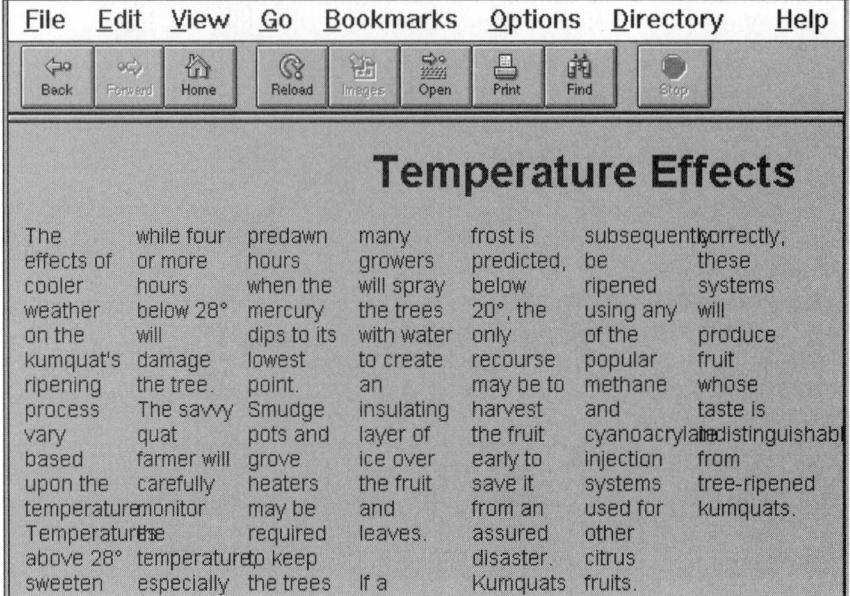

Figure 6-5. Too many columns create unreadable pages

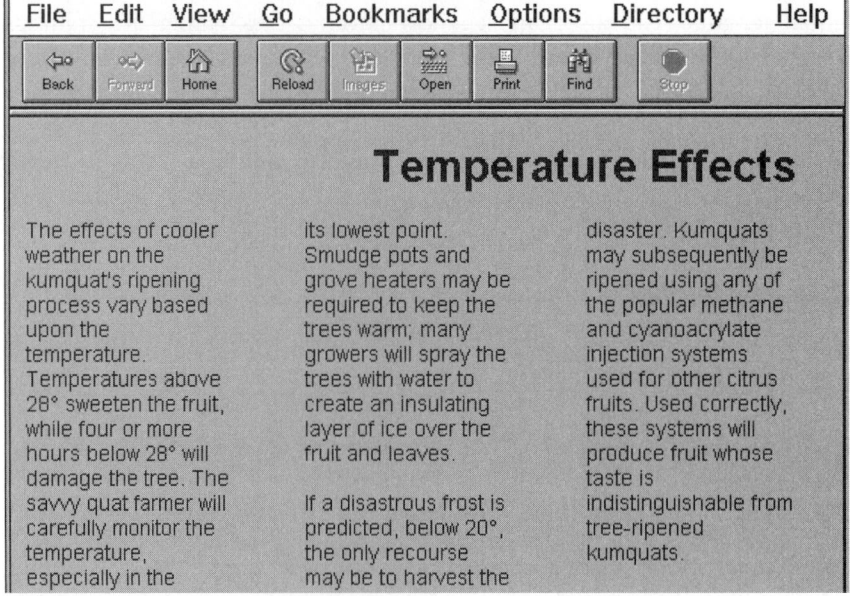

Figure 6-6. Gutter widths can be changed with the gutter attribute

6.2.1.3 The width attribute

Normally, the `<multicol>` tag fills the current width of the current text flow. To
have your multiple columns occupy a thinner space, or to extend them beyond

the visible window, use the `width` attribute to specify the overall width of the `<multicol>` tag. The columns will be resized so that the columns plus the gutters fill the width you've specified.* The width may be specified as an absolute number of pixels or as a percentage of the width of the current text flow.

Figure 6-7 shows the effects of adding `width="75%"` to our column example, retaining the default gutter width of 10 pixels.

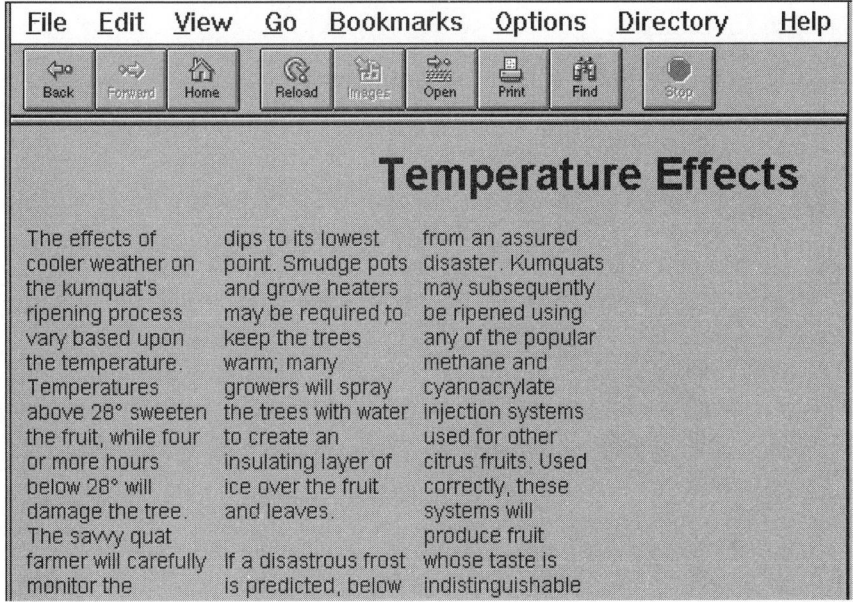

Figure 6-7. Changing the width of the <multicol> tag

Be careful when you reduce the size of your columns if they include images or other fixed-width elements. Netscape will not wrap text around images that extend beyond the boundaries of a column. Instead, the image simply covers the adjacent columns, ruining your document. Always make sure that embedded elements in columns are small enough to fit within your columns, even on fairly small browser displays.

6.2.1.4 The style and class attributes

Use the `style` attribute with the `<multicol>` tag to create an inline style for all the content inside the tag. The `class` attribute lets you label the section with a name that refers to a predefined class of the `<muticol>` tag declared in some

---

* To be exact, each column will be $(w–g(n–1))/n$ pixels wide, where w is the width of the `<multicol>` tag, g is the width of a gutter, and n is the number of columns. Thus, using `<multicol cols=3 gutter=10 width=500>` creates columns that are 160 pixels wide.

document-level or externally defined style sheet. [style attribute, 9.1.1] [class attribute, 9.2.4].

6.2.2 Multiple Columns and Other Browsers

As we've noted, the <multicol> tag is supported only by Netscape. Fortunately, when other browsers encounter the <multicol> tag, they ignore it and render the enclosed text as part of the normal text flow, usually with little consequent disruption to the document.

The only problem may be that the contents of the <multicol> tag flow up into the previous flow, without an intervening break. For that reason, you might consider preceding every <multicol> tag with a <p> tag. Netscape won't mind, and other browsers will at least perform a paragraph break before rendering your multicolumn text in a single column.

It is possible emulate the <multicol> tag using tables, but the results are crude and difficult to manage across multiple browsers. To do so, create a single row table with a cell for each column. Place an appropriate amount of the text flow in each cell to achieve balanced columns. The difficulty, of course, is that the "appropriate amount" varies wildly between browsers, making it almost impossible to create multiple columns that are attractive on several different browsers.

If you must have multiple columns, and can tolerate your columns reverting to a single column on incompatible browsers, we recommend you use the <multicol> tag.

6.2.3 Effective Multicolumn Layouts

We've offered advice on columns throughout these sections. Here is a quick recap of our tips for creating effective column layouts:

- Use a small number of columns.

- Don't use excessively wide gutters.

- Ensure that embedded elements like images and tables fit in your columns on most displays.

- Precede each <multicol> tag with a <p> tag to improve your document's appearance on other browsers.

- Avoid nesting <multicol> tags more than two deep.

6.3 Layers

Spacers and multiple columns are natural extensions to conventional HTML, existing within a document's normal flow. The latest version of Netscape (4.0) takes HTML into an entirely new dimension with layers. It transforms the single-element document model into one containing many layered elements that are combined to form the final document.

Layers supply the layout artist with a most critical element missing in standard HTML: absolute positioning of content within the browser window. In a nutshell, layers let you define a self-contained unit of HTML content that can be positioned anywhere in the browser window, placed above or below other layers, and made to appear and disappear as you desire. Document layouts that were impossible with conventional HTML are trivial with layers.

If you think of your document as a sheet of paper, layers are like sheets of clear plastic laid atop your document. For each layer, you define the content of the layer, its position relative to the base document, and the order in which it is placed on the document. Layers can be transparent or opaque, visible or hidden, providing an endless combination of layout options.

6.3.1 The <layer> Tag

HTML document content layers are each defined with the <layer> tag. A layer can be thought of as a miniature HTML document whose content is defined between the <layer> and </layer> tags. Alternatively, the content of the layer can be retrieved from another HTML document by using the src attribute with the <layer> tag.

Regardless of its origin, Netscape formats a layer's content exactly like a conventional document, except that the result is contained within that separate layer, apart from the rest of your document. You control the position and visibility of this layer using the attributes of the <layer> tag.

Layers may be nested, too. Nested layers move with the containing layer and are visible only if the containing layer itself is visible.

6.3.1.1 The name attribute

If you plan on creating a layer and never referring to it, you needn't give it a name. However, if you plan to stack other layers relative to the current layer, as we demonstrate later in this chapter, or modify your layer using JavaScript, you'll need to name your layers using the **name** attribute. The value you give **name** is a text string, whose first character must be a letter, not a number or symbol.

Once named, you can refer to the layer elsewhere in the document, and change it while the user interacts with your page. For example, this bit of HTML:

```
<layer name="warning" visibility=hide>
Warning!  Your input parameters were not valid!
</layer>
```

<layer> N

Function:

Define a layer of content within a document

Attributes:

ABOVE
BACKGROUND
BELOW
BGCOLOR
CLASS
CLIP
LEFT
NAME
SRC
STYLE
TOP
VISIBILITY
WIDTH
Z-INDEX

End tag:

</layer>; always used

Contains:

body_content

Used in:

block

---

creates a layer named `warning` that is initially hidden. If in the course of validating a form using a JavaScript routine, you find an error and want to display the
warning, you would use the command:

```
warning.visibility = show;
```

Netscape then makes the layer visible to the user.

6.3.1.2 The left and top attributes

Without attributes, a layer gets placed in the document window as if it were part
of the normal document flow. Layers at the very beginning of a document get put
at the top of the Netscape window; layers that are between conventional document content get placed in line with that content.

The power of layers, however, is that you can place them anywhere in the document. Use the `top` and `left` attributes for the `<layer>` tag to specify its absolute position in the document display.

Both attributes accept an integer value equal to the number of pixels offset from the top left (0,0) edge of the document's display space or, if nested inside another layer, the containing layer's display space. As with other document elements whose size or position extends past the edge of the browser's window, Netscape gives the user scrollbars so that they can access layered elements outside the current viewing area.

Here is a simple layer example that staggers three words diagonally down the display—not something you can do easily, and certainly not with the same precision, in conventional HTML:

```
<layer left=10 top=10>
  Upper left!
</layer>
<layer left=50 top=50>
  Middle!
</layer>
<layer left=90 top=90>
  Lower right!
</layer>
```

The result is shown in Figure 6-8.

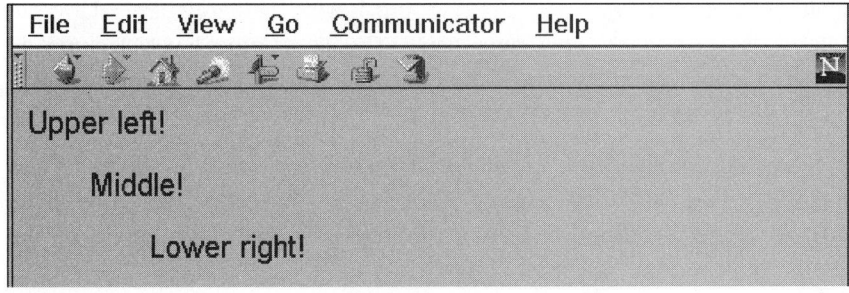

Figure 6-8. Simple text positioning with the <layer> tag

Admittedly, this example is a bit dull. Here's a better one that creates a drop shadow behind a heading:

```
<layer>
  <layer left=2 top=2>
    <h1><font color=gray>Introduction to Kumquat Lore</font></h1>
  </layer>
  <layer left=0 top=0>
    <h1>Introduction to Kumquat Lore</h1>
  </layer>
</layer>
```

```
<h1> </h1>
Early in the history of man, the kumquat played a vital role in the
formation of religious beliefs.  Central to annual harvest
celebrations was the day upon which kumquats ripened.  Likened to the
sun (<i>sol</i>), the golden fruit was taken (<i>stisus</i>) from the
trees on the day the sun stood highest in the sky.  We carry this day
forward even today, as our summer <i>solstice</i>.
```

Figure 6-9 shows the result.

Figure 6-9. Creating drop shadow effects with multiple layers

We used a few tricks to create the drop shadow effect for the example header. First, Netscape covers layers created earlier in the document by later layers. Hence, we create the gray shadow first, followed by the actual heading, so that it appears on top, above the shadow. We also enclosed these two layers in a separate containing layer. This way, the shadow and header positions are relative to the containing layer, not the document itself. The containing layer, lacking an explicit position, gets placed into the document flow as if it were normal content and winds up where a conventional heading would appear in the document.

Normal document content, however, still starts at the top of the document, and would end up behind the fancy heading. To push it below the layered heading, we include an empty heading (save for a nonbreaking space—` `) before including our conventional document text.

This is important enough to repeat: normal document content following a `<layer>` tag is positioned directly under the layer it follows. This effect can be circumvented using an inline layer, described in 6.3.2.

6.3.1.3 The above, below, and z-index attributes

Layers exist in three dimensions, occupying space on the page and stacked atop one another and the conventional document content. As we mentioned above, layers normally get stacked in order of their appearance in the document—layers at the beginning get covered by later layers in the same display area.

You can control the stacking order of the layers with the **above**, **below**, and **z-index** attributes for the **<layer>** tag. These attributes are mutually exclusive; use only one per layer.

The value for the **above** or **below** attribute is the name of another layer in the current document. Of course, that referenced layer must have a **name** attribute whose value is the same name you use with the **above** or **below** attribute in the referring **<layer>** tag. You also must have created the referenced layer earlier in the document; you cannot refer to a layer that comes later in your document.

In direct contradiction with what you might expect, Netscape puts the current layer below the **above** named layer, and above the **below** named layer.[*] Oh, well. Note that the layers must occupy the same display space for you to see any effects.

Let's use our drop shadow layer example again to illustrate the **above** attribute:

```
<layer>
  <layer name=text left=0 top=0>
    <h1>Introduction to Kumquat Lore</h1>
  </layer>
  <layer name=shadow above=text left=2 top=2>
    <h1><font color=gray>Introduction to Kumquat Lore</font></h1>
  </layer>
</layer>
```

The **above** attribute in the layer named **shadow** tells Netscape to position the shadow layer so that the layer named **text** is above it.

The **above** and **below** attributes can get confusing when you stack several layers. We find it somewhat easier to use the **z-index** attribute for keeping track of which layers go over which. With **z-index**, you specify the order in which Netscape stacks the layers: higher z-index value layers get put on top of lower z-index value layers.

For example, to create our drop shadow using the **z-index** attribute:

```
<layer>
  <layer left=0 top=0 z-index=2>
    <h1>Introduction to Kumquat Lore</h1>
  </layer>
  <layer left=2 top=2 z-index=1>
    <h1><font color=gray>Introduction to Kumquat Lore</font></h1>
  </layer>
</layer>
```

---

[*] One cannot help but wonder if the **above** and **below** attributes were implemented in the wee hours of the morning.

Normally, Netscape would display the second layer—the gray one in this case—on top of the first layer. But since we've given the gray layer a lower `z-index` value, it is placed behind the first layer.

The `z-index` values need not be sequential, although they must be integers, so we could've used the values 99 and 2, respectively, and gotten the same result in the previous example. And you need not specify a `z-index` for all the layers that occupy the same display space—only those you want to raise or lower in relation to other layers. However, be aware that the order of precedence may get confusing if you don't `z-index` all related layers.

For instance, what order of precedence by color would you predict when Netscape renders the following sequence of layers?

```
<layer left=0 top=0 z-index=3>
  <h1><font color=red>Introduction to Kumquat Lore</font></h1>
</layer>
<layer left=4 top=4>
  <h1><font color=green>Introduction to Kumquat Lore</font></h1>
</layer>
<layer left=8 top=8 z-index=2>
  <h1><font color=blue>Introduction to Kumquat Lore</font></h1>
</layer>
```

Give yourself a star if you said that the green header goes on top of the red header which goes on top of the blue header. Why? Because the red header is of lower priority than the green header based on order of appearance, and we forced the blue layer below the red one by giving it a lower `z-index` value. Netscape displays `z-index`ed layers according to their given order and non-`z-index`ed layers according to their order of appearance in the document. Precedence based on order of appearance also applies for layers that have the same `z-index` value. If you nest layers, all the layers at the same nesting level get ordered according to their `z-index` attributes. This group is then ordered as a single layer among all the layers at the containing level. In short, layers nested within a layer cannot be interleaved among layers at a different level.

For example, consider these nested layers, with their content and end tags omitted for clarity (indentation indicates nest level):

```
<layer name=a z-index=20>
  <layer name=a1 z-index=5>
  <layer name=a2 z-index=15>
<layer name=b z-index=30>
  <layer name=b1 z-index=10>
  <layer name=b2 z-index=25>
  <layer name=b3 z-index=20>
<layer name=c z-index=10>
```

Layers a, b, and c are at the same level, with layers a1 and a2 nested with a, and b1, b2, and b3 nested within b. Although the z-index numbers might at first glance appear to cause Netscape to interleave the various nested layers, the actual ordering of the layers, from bottom to top, is c, a, a1, a2, b, b1, b3, and b2.

If two layers are nested within the same layer and have the same z-index value, the layer defined later in the document is placed on top of the previously defined layer.*

6.3.1.4 The background and bgcolor attributes

Like the corresponding attributes for the `<body>` tag, you may define the background color and an image for the layer with the `bgcolor` and `background` attributes, respectively.† By default, the background of a layer is transparent, allowing lower layers to show through.

The `bgcolor` attribute accepts a color name or RGB triple as its value, as defined in Appendix F, *Color Names and Values*. If specified, Netscape sets the entire background of the layer to this color, rendering the layer opaque. This attribute is handy for creating a colored box behind text, as a highlighting or attention-getting mechanism. It will, however, hide any layers below it, including conventional HTML content.

The `background` attribute accepts the URL of an image as its value. The image is tiled to fill the area occupied by the layer. If portions of the image are transparent, those portions of the layer will be transparent and underlying layers will show through.

If you include both attributes, the background color will show through the transparent spots in the background image. The whole layer will be opaque.

The `background` attribute is useful for placing a texture behind text, but it fails miserably when the goal is to render text in front of a fixed image. Since the size of a layer is dictated by its contents, not the background image, using the image as the background will cause it to be clipped or tiled, depending on the size of the text. To place text reliably atop an image, use one layer nested within another:

```
<layer>
  <img src="sunset.gif">
  <p>
  <layer top=75>
    <h2 align=center>And they lived happily ever after...</h2>
  </layer>
</layer>
```

---

* This, of course, applies to layers inside the same containing nest only.

† Note that you may also control the background color, as well as many other display features of not just a single, but all `<layer>` tags within your document using style sheets. See 6.3.1.9.

Netscape sets aside space for the entire image in the outer layer. The inner layer occupies the same space, except that we shift it down 75 pixels to align the text better over the image. The result is shown in Figure 6-10.

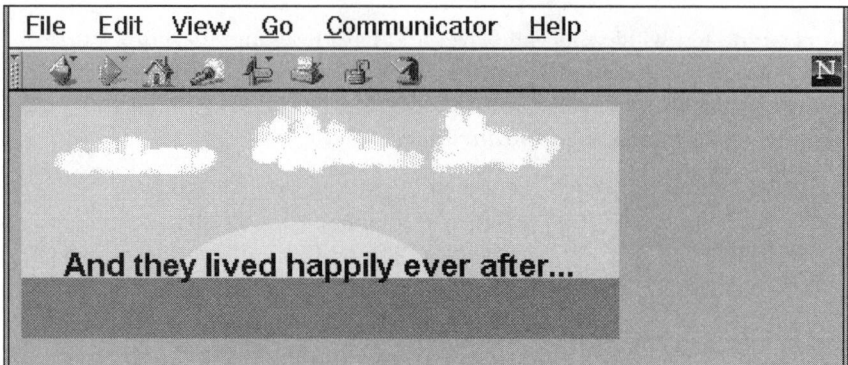

Figure 6-10. Placing text over an image using layers

6.3.1.5 The visibility attribute

Layers, by default, are usually seen (but most often not heard). You can change that by setting the `visibility` attribute to `show`, `hide`, or `inherit`. As expected, `show` forces the layer to be seen, `hide` hides it from view, and `inherit` explicitly declares that you want the layer to inherit its parent's visibility. The default value for this attribute is `inherit`. Layers that are not nested are considered to be children of the main document, which is always visible. Thus, non-nested layers lacking the `visibility` attribute are initially visible.

It makes little sense to hide layers unless you plan to reveal them later. In general, this attribute is only used when you include some JavaScript routines with your document that will reveal the hidden layers as a result of some user interaction. [JavaScript, 13.3]

Layers that are hidden do not block layers below them from view. Instead, a hidden layer can best be thought of as being transparent. One way to hide content in the main document is to place an opaque layer over the content. To display the hidden context, hide the opaque layer, revealing the content underneath.

6.3.1.6 The width attribute

Layers are only as big as necessary to contain their content. The initial width of a layer is defined to be the distance from the point at which the layer is created in the current text flow to the right margin. Netscape then formats the layer's contents to that width and makes the height of the layer tall enough to contain all of the layer's contents. If the contents of the layer wind up smaller than the initial width, the layer's width is then reduced to this smaller amount.

You can explicitly set the width of a layer using the `width` attribute. The value of this attribute defines the width of the layer in pixels. As expected, Netscape then sets the height based upon the size of the layer's contents, wrapped to the specified width. If elements in the layer—such as images—cannot be wrapped and instead extend past the right margin of the layer, only a portion of the element will be shown. The remainder will be clipped by the edge of the layer and not shown. This is similar to the behavior of an image in the main document window. If the image extends beyond the edge of the browser window, only a portion of the image is displayed. Unlike the browser window, however, layers cannot sport scrollbars allowing the user to scroll around in the layer's contents.

6.3.1.7 *The src attribute*

The contents of a layer are not restricted to what you type between its `<layer>` and `</layer>` tags; you can also refer to and automatically load the contents of another document into the layer with the `src` attribute. The value of the `src` attribute is the URL of the document containing the layer's content.

This document is not a full-fledged HTML document and in particular, should not contain `<body>` or `<head>` tags. Any other HTML content is allowed.

You can combine conventional layer content with content taken from another file by using both the `src` attribute and placing content within the `<layer>` tag. In this case, the content from the file is placed in the layer first, followed by any inline content within the tag itself. If you choose to use the `src` attribute without supplying additional inline content, you still must supply the closing `</layer>` tag to end the definition of the layer.

The `src` attribute provides, for the first time, a source inclusion capability in HTML. Previously, to insert content from one HTML document within another, you had to rely on a server-based capability to read the other file and insert it into your document at the correct location. Since layers are positioned, by default, at their defining point within the current flow, including another file in your document is simple:

```
...other content
<layer src="boilerplate"></layer>
...more content
```

Since a layer is rendered as a separate HTML entity, the contents of the included file will not be flowed into the containing text. Instead, it is as if the inserted text were contained within a `<div>` tag or other block-level HTML element.

6.3.1.8 The clip attribute

Normally, users see the entire layer unless it is obscured by a covering layer. With the clip attribute, you can mask off portions of a layer, revealing only a rectangular portion within the layer.

The value of the clip attribute is two or four integer values, separated by commas, defining pixel offsets into the layer corresponding to the left, top, right, and bottom edges of the clip area. If only two values are supplied, they correspond to the right and bottom edges of the visible area, and Netscape then assumes that the top and left values are zero. Therefore, `clip="75,100"` is equivalent to `clip="0,0,75,100"`.

The area of the layer outside the visible area is made transparent, allowing whatever is under the layer to show through.

The `clip` attribute is handy for hiding portions of a layer, or for creating fade and wipe effects using JavaScript functions to change the clipping window over time.

6.3.1.9 The style and class attributes

Use the `style` attribute with the `<layer>` tag to create an inline style for all the content inside a layer. The `class` attribute lets you label the layer with a name that refers to a predefined class of the `<layer>` tag declared in some document-level or externally defined stylesheet. Accordingly, you may choose to use a style sheet instead of individual and redundant `bgcolor` tag attributes to define a background color for all your document layers or for a particular class of layers. [`style` attribute, 9.1.1] [`class` attribute, 9.2.4].

6.3.2 The <ilayer> Tag

While you control the position of a `<layer>` using `top` and `left` attribute coordinates relative to the document's entire display space, Netscape provides a separate tag—`<ilayer>`—that lets you position individual layers with respect to the current flow of content, much like an inline image.

An `<ilayer>` tag creates a layer that occupies space in the containing text flow. Subsequent content is placed after the space occupied by the `<ilayer>`. This is in contrast to the `<layer>` tag, which creates a layer above the containing text flow, allowing subsequent content to be placed under the layer just created.

The `<ilayer>` tag removes the need for an enclosing, attribute-free `<layer>` that serves to put a nest of specially positioned layers inline with the content flow, much like we did in most of the examples in the previous sections of this chapter. The attributes of the `<ilayer>` are the same as those for the `<layer>` tag.

<ilayer> N

Function:

Define an inline layer of content within a text flow

Attributes:

ABOVE
BACKGROUND
BELOW
BGCOLOR
CLASS
CLIP
LEFT
NAME
SRC
STYLE
TOP
VISIBILITY
WIDTH
Z-INDEX

End tag:

</ilayer>; always used

Contains:

body_content

Used in:

text

6.3.2.1 The top and left attributes

The only attributes that distinguish the actions of the `<ilayer>` tag from its `<layer>` sibling are the `top` and `left` attributes: Netscape renders `<ilayer>` content directly in the containing text flow, offset by the `top` and `left` attribute values from the upper-left corner of that inline position—not the document's upper-left display corner, as with `<layer>`. Netscape will also accept negative values for the `top` and `left` attributes of the `<ilayer>` tag, letting you shift the contents above and to the left of the current flow.

For example, to subscript, superscript, or shift words within the current line, you could use:

```
This <ilayer top=4>word</ilayer> is shifted down, while
this <ilayer left=10>one</ilayer> is shifted over.  With a negative
value, words can be moved <ilayer top=-4>up</ilayer> and to
the <ilayer left=-10>left</ilayer>.
```

The resulting effects are shown in Figure 6-11. Notice how the shifted words overlap and obscure the surrounding text. Netscape makes no effort to make room for the shifted elements; they are simply placed in a different spot on the page.

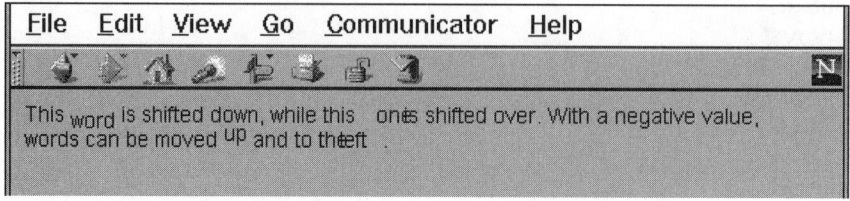

Figure 6-11. Moving inline layers with respect to the adjacent text

6.3.2.2 Combining <layer> and <ilayer>

Anything you can create with a regular layer can be used within an inline layer. However, do bear in mind always that the `top` and `left` attribute offsets are indeed from the `<ilayer>` content's allotted position, not from the document display space. Accordingly, use `<ilayer>` to position content inline with the conventional HTML document flow, and `<layer>` to position elements and content precisely in the document display space.

Also (and fortunately), Netscape does not distinguish between `<ilayer>` and `<layer>` tags when it comes to order of appearance. You may declare that an `<ilayer>` appear below some `<layer>` by using the `name` and `above` attributes:

```
<layer name=me>I'm on top</layer>
<ilayer above=me>I'm on the bottom</ilayer>
```

Similarly, you may reorder the appearance of both absolute and inline layers where they overlap by assigning `z-index` attribute values to the various elements. Nesting rules apply, as well.

7

Links and Webs

Until this point, we've dealt with HTML documents as standalone entities, concentrating on the language elements you use for structure and to format your work. The true power of HTML, however, lies in its ability to join collections of documents together into a full library of information, and to link documents with other collections around the world. Just as readers have considerable control over how the document looks onscreen, with hyperlinks they also have control over the order of presentation as they navigate through your information. It's the "HT" in HTML—hypertext—and it's the twist that spins the Web.

7.1 Hypertext Basics

A fundamental feature of hypertext is that you can hyperlink documents; you can point to another place inside the current document, inside another document in the local collection, or inside a document anywhere on the Internet. The documents thereby become an intricately woven web of information. Get the name analogy now? The target document is usually somehow related to and enriches the source; the linking element in the source should convey that relationship to the reader.

Hyperlinks can be used for all kinds of effects. They can be used inside tables of contents and lists of topics. With a click of the mouse on their browser screen, readers select and automatically jump to a topic of interest in the same document or to another document located in an entirely different collection somewhere around the world.

Hyperlinks also point readers to more information about a mentioned topic. "For more information, see 'Kumquats on Parade,'" for example. HTML authors use hyperlinks to reduce repetitive information. For instance, we recommend you sign your name to each of your documents. Rather than include full contact information in each document, a hyperlink connects your name to a single place that contains your address, phone number, and so forth.

A hyperlink, or *anchor* in HTML standard parlance, is marked by the `<a>` tag and comes in two flavors. As we detail below, one type of anchor creates a hot spot in the document that, when activated and selected (usually with a mouse) by the user, causes the browser to link. It automatically loads and displays another portion of the same or another document altogether, or triggers some Internet service-related action, such as sending email or downloading a special file. The other type of anchor creates a label, a place in an HTML document that can be referenced as a hyperlink.*

There also are some mouse-related events associated with hyperlinks that, through the new JavaScript technologies, let you perform some new and exciting effects.

7.2 Referencing Documents: The URL

As we discussed earlier, every document on the World Wide Web has a unique address. (Imagine the chaos if they didn't.) The document's address is known as its *uniform resource locator* (URL).†

Several HTML tags include a URL attribute value, including hyperlinks, inline images, and forms. All use the same URL syntax to specify the location of a Web resource, regardless of the type or content of that resource. That's why it's known as a *uniform* resource locator.

Since they can be used to represent almost any resource on the Internet, URLs come in a variety of flavors. All URLs, however, have the same top-level syntax:

```
scheme:scheme_specific_part
```

---

* Both types of HTML anchors use the same tag; perhaps that's why they have the same name. Nonetheless, we find it's easier if you differentiate them and think of the one type that provides the hotspot and address of a hyperlink as the "link," and the other type that marks the target portion of a document as the "anchor."

† "URL" usually is pronounced "you are ell," not "earl."

The *scheme* describes the kind of object the URL references; the *scheme_specific_ part* is, well, the part that is peculiar to the specific scheme. The important thing to note is that the *scheme* is always separated from the *scheme_specific_part* by a colon with no intervening spaces.

7.2.1   Writing a URL

URLs are written using the displayable characters in the US-ASCII character set. If you need to use a character in a URL that is not part of this character set, you must encode the character using a special notation. The encoding notation replaces the desired character with three characters: a percent sign and two hexadecimal digits whose value corresponds to the position of the character in the ASCII character set.

This is easier than it sounds. One of the most common encoded special characters is the space character, whose position in the character set is 20 hexadecimal. To encode a space in a URL, replace it with %20:

    http://www.kumquat.com/new%20pricing.html

This URL actually retrieves a document named *new pricing.html* from the server.

7.2.1.1   Handling reserved and unsafe characters

In addition to the nonprinting characters, you'll need to encode reserved and unsafe characters in your URLs as well.

Reserved characters are those characters that have a specific meaning within the URL itself. For example, many URLs use the slash character to separate elements of a pathname within the URL. If you need to include a slash in a URL that is not intended to be an element separator, you'll need to encode it as %2F:

    http://www.calculator.com/compute?3%2f4

This URL actually references the resource named *compute* on the *www.calculator.com* server and passes the string 3/4 to it, as delineated by the question mark (?). Presumably, the resource is actually a server-side program that performs some arithmetic function on the passed value and returns a result.

Unsafe characters are those that have no special meaning within the URL, but may have a special meaning in the context in which the URL is written. For example, the double quotation mark character (") is used to delimit URLs in many HTML tags. If you were to include a double quotation mark directly in a URL, you would probably confuse the HTML browser. Instead, encode the double quotation mark as %22 to avoid any possible conflict.

Other reserved and unsafe characters that should always be encoded are shown in Table 7-1.

Table 7-1. Reserved and unsafe characters and their URL encodings

Character	Description	Usage	Encoding
;	Semicolon	Reserved	%3B
/	Slash	Reserved	%2F
?	Question mark	Reserved	%3F
:	Colon	Reserved	%3A
@	At sign	Reserved	%40
=	Equal sign	Reserved	%3D
&	Ampersand	Reserved	%26
<	Less than sign	Unsafe	%3C
>	Greater than sign	Unsafe	%3E
"	Double quotation mark	Unsafe	%22
#	Hash symbol	Unsafe	%23
%	Percent	Unsafe	%25
{	Left curly brace	Unsafe	%7B
}	Right curly brace	Unsafe	%7D
|	Vertical bar	Unsafe	%7C
\	Backslash	Unsafe	%5C
^	Caret	Unsafe	%5E
~	Tilde	Unsafe	%7E
[	Left square bracket	Unsafe	%5B
]	Right square bracket	Unsafe	%5D
`	Back single quotation mark	Unsafe	%60

In general, you should always encode a character if there is some doubt as to whether it can be placed as-is in a URL. As a rule of thumb, any character other than a letter, number, or any of the characters $-_.+!*'()$, should be encoded.

It is never an error to encode a character, unless that character has a specific meaning in the URL. For example, encoding the slashes in an http URL will cause them to be used as regular characters, not as pathname delimiters, breaking the URL.

7.2.2 The http URL

The http URL is, by far, the most common within the World Wide Web. It is used to access documents stored on an http server, and it has two formats:

```
http://server:port/path#fragment
http://server:port/path?search
```

Some of the parts are optional. In fact, the most common form of the http URL simply is:

```
http://server/path
```

designating the unique server and the directory path and name of a document.

7.2.2.1 The http server

The *server* is the unique Internet name or Internet Protocol (IP) numerical address of the computer system that stores the Web resource. Like us, we suspect you'll mostly use more easily remembered Internet names for the servers in your URLs.[*] The name consists of several parts, including the server's actual name and the successive names of its network domain, each part separated by a period. Typical Internet names look like *www.ora.com* or *hoohoo.ncsa.uiuc.edu.*[†]

It has become something of a convention that webmasters name their servers *www* for quick and easy identification on the Web. For instance, O'Reilly & Associates' web server's name is *www*, which, along with the publisher's acronym-based domain name, becomes the very easily remembered web site *www.ora.com.* Similarly, Sun Microsystems's web server is named *www.sun.com*; Apple Computer's is *www.apple.com*, and even Microsoft makes their web server easily memorable as *www.microsoft.com.* The naming convention has very obvious benefits, which you, too, should take advantage of if you are called upon to create a web server for your organization.

You may also specify the address of a server using its numerical IP address. The address is a sequence of four numbers, zero to 255, separated by periods. Valid IP addresses look like 137.237.1.87 or 192.249.1.33.

It'd be a dull diversion to tell you now what the numbers mean or how to derive an IP address from a domain name, particularly since you'll rarely if ever use one in a URL. Rather, this is a good place to hyperlink: pick up any good Internet networking treatise for rigorous detail on IP addressing, such as Ed Krol's *The Whole Internet User's Guide and Catalog*, published by O'Reilly & Associates (1994, Second Edition).

---

[*] Each Internet-connected computer has a unique address; a numeric (IP) address, of course, because computers deal only in numbers. Humans prefer names, so the Internet folks provide us with a collection of special servers and software (Domain Name System or DNS) that automatically resolve Internet names into IP addresses. InterNIC, a nonprofit agency, registers domain names mostly on a first-come, first-serve basis, and distributes new names to DNS servers worldwide.

[†] In the United States and for some Canadian establishments, the three-letter suffix of the domain name identifies the type of organization or business that operates that portion of the Internet. For instance, "com" is a commercial enterprise; "edu" is an academic institution; and "gov" identifies a government-based domain. Outside the United States, a less-descriptive suffix is assigned; typically a two-letter abbreviation of the country name: "jp" for Japan and "de" for Deutschland, for instance. That convention indicates the traditional distribution of the Internet and presumably will change dramatically as the network proliferates in the rest of the world.

7.2.2.2 The http port

The *port* is the number of the communication port to which the client browser connects to the server. It's a networking thing: servers do many things besides serve up web documents and resources to client browsers: electronic mail, FTP document fetches, filesystem sharing, and so on. Although all that network activity may come into the server on a single wire, it's typically divided into software-managed "ports" for service-specific communications—something analogous to boxes at your local post office.

The default URL port for web servers is 80. Special secure web servers (Secure HTTP, SHTTP or Secure Socket Layer, SSL) run on port 443. Most web servers today use port 80; you need only to include a port number along with an immediately preceding colon in your URL if the target server does *not* use port 80 for web communication.

When the Web was in its infancy many months ago, pioneer webmasters ran their Wild Wild Web connections on all sorts of port numbers. For technical and security reasons, system-administrator privileges are required to install a server on port 80. Lacking such privileges, these webmasters chose other, more easily accessible, port numbers.

Now that web servers have become acceptable and are under the care and feeding of responsible administrators, documents being served on some port other than 80 or 443 should make you wonder if that server is really on the up and up. Most likely, the maverick server is being run by a clever user unbeknownst to the server's bona fide system administrators.

7.2.2.3 The http path

The document *path* is the UNIX-style hierarchical location of the file in the server's storage system. The pathname consists of one or more names separated by slashes. All but the last name represent directories leading down to the document; the last name is usually that of the document itself.

It has become a convention that for easy identification, HTML document names end with the suffix *.html* (they're otherwise plain ASCII text files, remember?). You can easily identify a PC-based server: their restrictions on filenames mean you can have only the three-letter *.htm* name suffix for HTML documents.

Although the server name in a URL is not case-sensitive, the document pathname may be. Since most web servers are run on UNIX-based systems and UNIX file names are case-sensitive, the document pathname will be case-sensitive, too. Web servers running on DOS machines are not case-sensitive, so the document pathname is not, but since it is impossible to know the operating system of the server you are accessing, always assume that the server has case-sensitive pathnames and take care to get the case correct when typing your URLs.

Certain conventions regarding the document pathname have arisen. If the last element of the document path is a directory, not a single document, the server usually will send back either a listing of the directory contents or the HTML index document in that directory. You should end the document name for a directory with a trailing slash character, but in practice, most servers will honor the request even if the character is omitted.

If the directory name is just a slash alone or sometimes nothing at all, you will retrieve the first (top-level) HTML document or so-called *home page* in the upper-most root directory of the server. Every well-designed http server should have an attractive, well-designed "home page"; it's a shorthand way for users to access your web collection since they don't need to remember the document's actual file-name, just your server's name. That's why, for example, you can type *http://www.ora.com* into Netscape's "Open" dialog box and get O'Reilly's home page.

Another twist: if the first component of the document path starts with the tilde character (~), it means that the rest of the pathname begins from the personal HTML directory in the home directory of the specified user on the server machine. For instance, the URL *http://www.kumquat.com/~chuck/* would retrieve the top-level page from Chuck's document collection.

Different servers have different ways of locating documents within a user's home directory. Many search for the documents in a directory named *public_html*. UNIX-based servers are fond of the name *index.html* for home pages.

7.2.2.4 The http document fragment

The *fragment* is an identifier that points to a specific section of a document. In URL specifications, it follows the server and pathname and is separated by the pound sign (#). A fragment identifier indicates to the browser that it should begin displaying the target document at the indicated fragment name. As we describe in more detail below, you insert fragment names into a document with the `<a>` tag and the `name` attribute. Like pathnames, a fragment name may be any sequence of characters.

The fragment name and the preceding hash symbol are optional; omit them when referencing a document without defined fragments.

Formally, the fragment element only applies to target files that are HTML docu-ments. If the target of the URL is some other document type, the fragment name may be misinterpreted by the browser.

Fragments are useful for long documents. By identifying key sections of your document with a fragment name, you make it easy for readers to link directly to that portion of the document, avoiding the tedium of scrolling or searching through the document to get to the section that interests them.

As a rule of thumb, we recommend that every section header in your documents be accompanied by an equivalent fragment name. By consistently following this rule, you'll make it possible for readers to jump to any section in any of your documents. Fragments also make it easier to build tables of contents for your document families.

7.2.2.5 The http search parameter

The *search* component of the http URL, along with its preceding question mark, is optional. It indicates that the path is a searchable or executable resource on the server. The content of the search component is passed to the server as parameters that control the search or execution function.

The actual encoding of parameters in the search component is dependent upon the server and the resource being referenced. The parameters for searchable resources are covered later in this chapter, when we discuss searchable documents. Parameters for executable resources are discussed in Chapter 10, *Forms*.

Although our initial presentation of http URLs indicated that a URL can have either a fragment identifier or a search component, some browsers let you use both in a single URL. If you so desire, you can follow the search parameter with a fragment identifier, telling the browser to begin displaying the results of the search at the indicated fragment. Netscape, for example, supports this usage.

We don't recommend this kind of URL, though. First and foremost, it doesn't work on a lot of browsers. Just as important, using a fragment implies that you are sure that the results of the search will have a fragment of that name defined within the document. For large document collections, this is hardly likely. You are better off omitting the fragment, showing the search results from the beginning of the document, and avoiding potential confusion among your readers.

7.2.2.6 Sample http URLs

Here are some sample http URLs:

```
http://www.ora.com/catalog.html
http://www.ora.com/
http://www.kumquat.com:8080/
http://www.kumquat.com/planting/guide.html#soil_prep
http://www.kumquat.com/find_a_quat?state=Florida
```

The first example is an explicit reference to a bona fide HTML document named *catalog.html* that is stored in the root directory of the *www.ora.com* server. The second references the top-level home page on that same server. That home page may or may not be *catalog.html.* Sample three, too, assumes there is a home page in the root directory of the *www.kumquat.com* server, and that the web connection is to the nonstandard port 8080.

The fourth example is the URL for retrieving the web document named *guide.html* from the *planting* directory on the *www.kumquat.com* server. Once retrieved, the browser should display the document beginning at the fragment named *soil_prep.*

The last example invokes an executable resource named *find_a_quat* with the parameter named *state* set to the value *Florida.* Presumably, this resource generates an HTML response that is subsequently displayed by the browser.

7.2.3 The javascript URL

The javascript URL actually is a pseudo-protocol, not usually included in discussions of URLs. Yet, with advanced browsers like Netscape and Internet Explorer, the javascript URL can be associated with a hyperlink and used to execute JavaScript commands when the user selects the link. Expect to see many examples of link-related JavaScript effects in HTML documents on the Web. [JavaScript URLs, 13.3.4]

7.2.3.1 The javascript URL arguments

What follows the javascript pseudo-protocol is one or more semicolon-separated JavaScript expressions and methods, including references to multi-expression JavaScript functions that you embed within the `<script>` tag in your HTML documents (see Chapter 13, *Executable Content,* for details). For example:

```
javascript:window.alert('Hello, world!')
javascript:doFlash('red', 'blue'); window.alert('Do not press me!')
```

are valid URLs that you may include as the value for a link reference (see 4.1.2 and 6.4.3). The first example contains a single JavaScript method that activates an alert dialog with the simple message.

The second javascript URL example contains two arguments: the first calls a JavaScript function, `doFlash`, which presumably you have located elsewhere in the document within the `<script>` tag and which perhaps flashes the background color of the document window between the red and blue. The second expression is the same alert method as in the first example, but with a slightly different message.

The javascript URL may appear in a hyperlink sans arguments, too. In that case, the Netscape browser alone—not Internet Explorer—opens a special JavaScript editor wherein the user may type in and test the various expressions and methods.

7.2.4 The ftp URL

The ftp URL is used to retrieve documents from an FTP (File Transfer Protocol) server.* It has the format:

```
ftp://user:password@server:port/path;type=typecode
```

7.2.4.1 The ftp user and password

FTP is an authenticated service, meaning that you must have a valid username and password in order to retrieve documents from a server. However, most FTP servers also support restricted, nonauthenticated access known as *anonymous FTP*. In this mode, anyone can supply the username "anonymous" and be granted access to a limited portion of the server's documents. Most FTP servers also assume (but may not grant, of course) anonymous access if the username and password are omitted.

If you are using an ftp URL to access a site that requires a username and password, include the *user* and *password* components in the URL, along with the colon (:) and "at" sign (@). More commonly, you'll be accessing an anonymous FTP server, and the user and password components can be omitted.

If you keep the user component along with the "at" sign, but omit the password and the preceding colon, most browsers will prompt you for a password after connecting to the FTP server. This is the recommended way of accessing authenticated resources on an FTP server, since it prevents others from seeing your password.

We recommend you *never* place an ftp URL with a user name and password in any HTML document. The reasoning is simple: anyone can retrieve the document, extract the user name and password from the URL, log into the FTP server, and tamper with its documents.

7.2.4.2 The ftp server and port

The ftp *server* and *port* are bound by the same rules as the server and port in an http URL, as described above. The server must be a valid Internet domain name

---

* FTP is an ancient Internet protocol that dates back to the Dark Ages, around 1975 or so. It was designed as a simple way to move files between machines and remains popular and useful to this day. Some people who are unable to run a true web server will place their documents on a server that speaks FTP instead.

or IP address of an FTP server. The port specifies the port on which the server is listening for requests.

If the port and its preceding colon are omitted, the default port of 21 is used. It is necessary to specify the port only if the FTP server is running on some port other than 21.

7.2.4.3 *The ftp path and transfer type*

The *path* component represents a series of directories, separated by slashes leading to the file to be retrieved. By default, the file is retrieved as a binary file; this can be changed by adding the *typecode* (and the preceding `;type=`) to the URL.

If the typecode is set to `d`, the path is assumed to be a directory. The browser will request a listing of the directory contents from the server and display this listing to the user. If the typecode is any other letter, it is used as a parameter to the FTP type command before retrieving the file referenced by the path. While some FTP servers may implement other codes, most servers accept `i` to initiate a binary transfer and `a` to treat the file as a stream of ASCII text.

7.2.4.4 *Sample ftp URLs*

Here are some sample ftp URLs:

```
ftp://www.kumquat.com/sales/pricing
ftp://bob@bobs-box.com/results;type=d
ftp://bob:secret@bobs-box.com/listing;type=a
```

The first example retrieves the file named *pricing* from the *sales* directory on the anonymous FTP server at *www.kumquat.com*. The second logs into the FTP server on *bobs-box.com* as user `bob`, prompting for a password before retrieving the contents of the directory named *results* and displaying them to the user. The last example logs into *bobs-box.com* as `bob` with the password `secret` and retrieves the file named *listing*, treating its contents as ASCII characters.

7.2.5 *The file URL*

The file URL specifies a file stored on a machine without indicating the protocol used to retrieve the file. As such, it has limited use in a networked environment. Its real benefit, however, is that it can reference a file on the user's machine, and is particularly useful for referencing personal HTML document collections, such as those "under construction" and not yet ready for general distribution, or HTML document collections on CD-ROM. It has the format:

```
file://server/path
```

7.2.5.1 The file server

The file *server*, like the http server described above, must be the Internet domain name or IP address of the machine containing the file to be retrieved. No assumptions are made as to how the browser might contact the machine to obtain the file; presumably the browser can make some connection, perhaps via a Network File System or FTP, to obtain the file.

If the server is omitted, or the special name `localhost` is used, the file is assumed to reside on the same machine upon which the browser is running. In this case, the browser simply accesses the file using the normal facilities of the local operating system. In fact, this is the most common usage of the file URL. By creating document families on a diskette or CD-ROM and referencing your hyperlinks using the *file://localhost/* URL, you create a distributable, standalone document collection that does not require a network connection to use.

7.2.5.2 The file path

This is the path of the file to be retrieved on the desired server. The syntax of the *path* may differ based upon the operating system of the server; be sure to encode any potentially dangerous characters in the path.

7.2.5.3 Sample file URLs

The file URL is easy:

```
file://localhost/home/chuck/document.html
file:///home/chuck/document.html
file://marketing.kumquat.com/monthly_sales.html
```

The first URL retrieves */home/chuck/document.html* from the user's local machine. The second is identical to the first, except we've omitted the *localhost* reference to the server; the server name defaults to the local server. Do notice, however, the extra forward slash is required for this alternate form.

The third example uses some protocol to retrieve *monthly_sales.html* from the *marketing.kumquat.com* server.

7.2.6 The news URL

The news URL accesses either a single message or an entire newsgroup within the Usenet news system. It has two forms:

```
news:newsgroup
news:message_id
```

An unfortunate limitation in news URLs is that they don't allow you to specify a server for the *newsgroup*. Rather, users specify their news-server resource in their browser preferences. At one time, not long ago, Internet newsgroups were nearly universally distributed; all news servers carried all the same newsgroups and their respective articles, so one news server was as good as any. Today, the sheer bulk of disk space needed to store the daily volume of newsgroup activity is often prohibitive for any single news server, and there's also local censorship of newsgroups. Hence, you cannot expect that all newsgroups, and certainly not all articles for a particular newsgroup, will be available on the user's news server.

Moreover, many users' browsers may not be correctly configured to read news. We recommend you avoid placing news URLs in your documents except in rare cases.

7.2.6.1 Accessing entire newsgroups

There are several thousand newsgroups devoted to nearly every conceivable topic under the sun and beyond. Each group has a unique name, composed of hierarchical elements separated by periods. For example,

```
comp.infosys.www.announce
```

is the World Wide Web announcements newsgroup. To access this group, use the URL:

```
news:comp.infosys.www.announce
```

7.2.6.2 Accessing single messages

Every message on a news server has a unique message identifier (ID) associated with it. This ID has the form:

```
unique_string@server
```

The *unique_string* is a sequence of ASCII characters; the server is usually the name of the machine from which the message originated. The *unique_string* must be unique among all the messages that originated from the server. A sample URL to access a single message might be:

```
news:12A7789B@news.kumquat.com
```

In general, message IDs are cryptic sequences of characters not readily understood by humans. Moreover, the lifespan of a message on a server is usually measured in days, after which the message is deleted and the message ID is no longer valid. The bottom line: single message news URLs are difficult to create, become invalid quickly, and are generally not used.

7.2.7 The nntp URL

The nntp URL goes beyond the news URL to provide a complete mechanism for accessing articles in the Usenet news system. It has the form:

```
nntp://server:port/newsgroup/article
```

7.2.7.1 The nntp server and port

The nntp *server* and *port* are defined similarly to the http server and port, described earlier. The server must be the Internet domain name or IP address of a nntp server; the port is the port on which that server is listening for requests.

If the port and its preceding colon are omitted, the default port of 119 is used.

7.2.7.2 The nntp newsgroup and article

The *newsgroup* is the name of the group from which an article is to be retrieved, as defined in 6.2.6.

The *article* is the numeric id of the desired article within that newsgroup. Although the article number is easier to determine than a message id, it falls prey to the same limitations of single message references using the news URL, above. Specifically, articles do not last long on most nntp servers, and nntp URLs quickly become invalid as a result.

7.2.7.3 Sample nntp URLs

A sample nntp URL might be:

```
nntp://news.kumquat.com/alt.fan.kumquats/417
```

This URL retrieves article 417 from the *alt.fan.kumquats* newsgroup on *news.kumquat.com*. Keep in mind that the article will only be served to machines that are allowed to retrieve articles from this server. In general, most nntp servers restrict access to those machines on that same local area network.

7.2.8 The mailto URL

The mailto URL causes an electronic mail message to be transmitted to a named recipient. It has the format:

```
mailto:address
```

The *address* is any valid email address, usually of the form:

```
user@server
```

Thus, a typical mailto URL might look like:

```
mailto:cmusciano@aol.com
```

Browsers like Netscape honor multiple recipients in the mailto URL, separated by a comma. For example,

```
mailto:cmusciano@aol.com,booktech@ora.com,archive@myserver.com
```

will address the message to all three recipients. There should be no spaces before or after the commas in the URL.

7.2.8.1 Defining mail header fields

Most browsers open an email composition window when the user selects a mailto URL. The recipient's address is filled in, taken from the URL, but the message subject and various other header fields are left blank. Many webmasters would like to fill in these fields as a courtesy to their readers, but the URL standard provides no way to do this.

The modern browsers extend the mailto URL to fill this gap. By adding CGI-like parameters to the mailto header, you can set the value of the subject with Netscape and Internet Explorer, and also cc (carbon copy) and bcc (blind carbon copy) fields for the mail message with Netscape. All of these URLs work with Netscape; only the first one works correctly with Internet Explorer. [CGI parameters, 10.1.1.7]

```
mailto:cmusciano@aol.com?subject=Loved your book!
mailto:cmusciano@aol.com?cc=booktech@ora.com
mailto:cmusciano@aol.com?bcc=archive@myserver.com
```

As you can probably guess, the first URL sets the subject of the message. Note that spaces are allowed; you don't have to replace them with the hexadecimal equivalent %20. The second URL places the address booktech@ora.com in the cc field of a Netscape message. Similarly, the last example sets the bcc field of the message. You may also set several fields in one URL by separating the field definitions with ampersands. For example,

```
mailto:cmusciano@aol.com?subject=Loved your book!&cc=booktech@ora.com&
bcc=archive@myserver.com
```

sets the subject and carbon-copy address. (This line would normally appear as a single line but is broken here due to the width of the page.)

Internet Explorer Version 3 does not recognize the bcc and cc fields in the mailto URL and will either complain about them if they appear alone, or will append them to a preceding subject.

7.2.9 The telnet URL

The telnet URL opens an interactive session with a desired server, allowing the user to log in and use the machine. Often, the connection to the machine automatically starts a specific service for the user; in other cases, the user must know the commands to type to use the system. The telnet URL has the form:

```
telnet://user:password@server:port/
```

7.2.9.1 The telnet user and password

The telnet *user* and *password* are used exactly like the user and password components of the ftp URL, described previously. In particular, the same caveats apply regarding protecting your password and never placing it within a URL.

Just like the ftp URL, if you omit the password from the URL, the browser should prompt you for a password just before contacting the telnet server.

If you omit both the user and password, the telnet occurs without supplying a user name. For some servers, telnet automatically connects to a default service when no user name is supplied. For others, the browser may prompt for a user-name and password when making the connection to the telnet server.

7.2.9.2 The telnet server and port

The telnet *server* and *port* are defined similarly to the http server and port, described above. The server must be the Internet domain name or IP address of a telnet server; the port is the port on which that server is listening for requests.

If the port and its preceding colon are omitted, the default port of 23 is used.

7.2.10 The gopher URL

Gopher is a web-like document retrieval system that achieved some popularity on the Internet just before the World Wide Web took off, completely replacing Gopher. Some Gopher servers still exist, though, and the gopher URL lets you access Gopher documents. The gopher URL has the form:

```
gopher://server:port/path
```

7.2.10.1 The gopher server and port

The gopher *server* and *port* are defined similarly to the http server and port, described previously. The server must be the Internet domain name or IP address of a gopher server; the port is the port on which that server is listening for requests.

If the port and its preceding colon are omitted, the default port of 70 is used.

7.2.10.2 The gopher path

The path can take one of three forms:

```
type/selector
type/selector%09search
type/selector%09search%09gopherplus
```

The *type* is a single character value denoting the type of the gopher resource. If the entire path is omitted from the gopher URL, the type defaults to 1.

The *selector* corresponds to the path of a resource on the Gopher server. It may be omitted, in which case the top-level index of the Gopher server is retrieved.

If the Gopher resource is actually a Gopher search engine, the *search* component provides the string for which to search. The search string must be preceded by an encoded horizontal tab (%09).

If the Gopher server supports Gopher+ resources, the *gopherplus* component supplies the necessary information to locate that resource. The exact content of this component varies based upon the resources on the gopher server. This component is preceded by an encoded horizontal tab (%09). If you want to include the *gopherplus* component but omit the search component, you must still supply both encoded tabs within the URL.

7.2.11 Absolute and Relative URLs

URLs come in two flavors: absolute and relative. An absolute URL is the complete address of a resource and has everything your system needs to find a document and its server on the Web. At the very least, an absolute URL contains the scheme and all required elements of the *scheme_specific_part* of the URL. It may also contain any of the optional portions of the *scheme_specific_part*.

With a relative URL you provide an abbreviated document address that, when automatically combined with a "base address" by the system, becomes a complete address for the document. Within the relative URL, any component of the URL may be omitted. The browser automatically fills in the missing pieces of the relative URL using corresponding elements of a base URL. This base URL is usually the URL of the document containing the relative URL, but may be another document specified with the **<base>** tag. [<base>, 7.7.1]

7.2.11.1 Relative schemes and servers

A common form of a relative URL is missing the scheme and server name. Since many related documents are on the same server, it makes sense to omit the scheme and server name from the relative URL. For instance, assume the base document was last retrieved from the server *www.kumquat.com*. The relative URL, then:

```
another-doc.html
```

is equivalent to the absolute URL:

```
http://www.kumquat.com/another-doc.html
```

Table 7-2 shows how the base and relative URLs in the example are combined to form an absolute URL.

Table 7-2. Forming an absolute URL

	Protocol	Server	Directory	File
Base URL	http	www.kumquat.com	/	
Relative URL	↓	↓	↓	another-doc.html
↓	↓	↓	↓	↓
Absolute URL	http	www.kumquat.com	/	another-doc.html

7.2.11.2 Relative document directories

Another common form of a relative URL omits the leading slash and one or more directory names from the beginning of the document pathname. The directory of the base URL is automatically assumed to replace these missing components. It's the most common abbreviation because most HTML authors place their collection of documents and subdirectories of support resources in the same directory path as the home page. For example, you might have a *special/* subdirectory containing FTP files referenced in your HTML document. Let's say that the absolute URL for that HTML document is:

```
http://www.kumquat.com/planting/guide.html
```

A relative URL for the file *README.txt* in the *special/* subdirectory, then, looks like this:

```
ftp:special/README.txt
```

You'll actually be retrieving:

```
ftp://www.kumquat.com/planting/special/README.txt
```

Visually, the operation looks like that in Table 7-3.

Table 7-3. Forming an absolute FTP URL

	Protocol	Server	Directory	File
Base URL	http	www.kumquat.com	/planting	guide.html
Relative URL	ftp	↓	special	README.txt
↓	↓	↓	↓	↓
Absolute URL	ftp	www.kumquat.com	/planting/special	README.txt

7.2.11.3 Using relative URLs

Relative URLs are more than just a typing convenience. Because they are relative to the current server and directory, you can move the entire set of documents to another directory or even another server and never have to change a single relative link. Imagine the difficulties if you had to go into every source HTML document and change the URL for every link every time you move it. We'd loathe using hyperlinks! Use relative URLs wherever possible.

7.3 Creating Hyperlinks

Use the HTML `<a>` tag to create links to other documents and to name anchors for fragment indentifiers within documents.

7.3.1 The `<a>` Tag

HTML authors use the `<a>` tag most commonly with its `href` attribute to create a hypertext link, or *hyperlink*, for short, to another place in the same document or to another document. In these cases, the current document is the source of the link; the value of the `href` attribute, a URL, is the target.[*]

The other way you can use the `<a>` tag is with the `name` attribute to mark a hyperlink target, or fragment identifier, in an HTML document.

It is possible to use both the `name` and `href` attributes within a single `<a>` tag, defining a link to another document and a fragment identifier within the current document. We recommend against this, since it overloads a single tag with multiple functions, and some browsers may not be able to handle it.

Instead, use two `<a>` tags when such a need arises. Your HTML source will be easier to understand and modify, and will work better across a wider range of browsers.

7.3.1.1 Allowed content

Between the `<a>` tag and its required end tag, you may put only regular text, line breaks, images, and headings. The browser renders all of these elements normally, but with the addition of some special effects to indicate that it is a hyperlink to another document. For instance, the popular graphical browsers typically underline and color the text and draw a colored border around images that are enclosed by `<a>` tags.

While the allowed content may seem restricted (the inability to place style markup within an `<a>` tag is a bit onerous, for instance), most browsers let you put just about anything within an `<a>` tag that makes sense. To be compliant with

---

[*] You may run across the terms "head" and "tail," which reference the target and source of a hyperlink. This naming scheme assumes that the referenced document (the head) has many tails that are embedded in many referencing documents throughout the Web. We find this naming convention confusing and stick to the concept of source and target documents throughout this book.

<a>

Function:

> Define anchors within a text flow

Attributes:

> CLASS ◼ ⑴
> HREF
> NAME
> ONCLICK ◼ ⑴
> ONMOUSEOUT ◼ ⑴
> ONMOUSEOVER ◼ ⑴
> REL
> REV
> STYLE ◼ ⑴
> TARGET ◼ ⑴
> TITLE

End Tag:

> </a>, always present

Contains:

> *a_content*

Used in:

> *text*

---

the HTML standard, place the `<a>` tag inside other markup tags, not the opposite. For example, while most browsers make sense of either variation on this anchor theme:

```
To subscribe to
<cite><a href="ko.html">Kumquat Online</a></cite>,
```

```
To subscribe to
<a href="ko.html"><cite>Kumquat Online</cite></a>,
```

only the first example is technically correct.

7.3.1.2 The href attribute

Use the `href` attribute to specify the URL of the target of the link. Its value is any valid document URL, absolute or relative, including a fragment identifier or a Java-Script code fragment. If the user selects the contents of the `<a>` tag, the browser will retrieve and display the document indicated by the URL specified by the `href` attribute or execute the list of JavaScript expressions, methods, and functions. [URLs, 7.2]

A simple `<a>` tag that references another document might be:

```
The <a href="http:growing_season.html">growing
season</a> for kumquats in the Northeast.
```

which appears in the Netscape display as shown in Figure 7-1.

Figure 7-1. Hyperlink to another HTML document

Notice that the phrase "growing season" is specially rendered by the browser, letting the user know that it is a link to another document. Users also typically have the option to specially set the text color of the link and have the color change when a link is taken; blue initially and then red after it has been selected at least once, for instance.

More complex anchors might include images:

```
<ul>
  <li><a href="pruning_tips.html">
      <img src="pics/new.gif">New pruning tips!</a>
  <li><a href="xhistory.html">
      <img src="pics/new2.gif">Kumquats throughout history</a>
</ul>
```

Mosaic, like most graphical browsers like Netscape and Internet Explorer, places a special border around images that are part of an anchor, as shown in Figure 7-2.

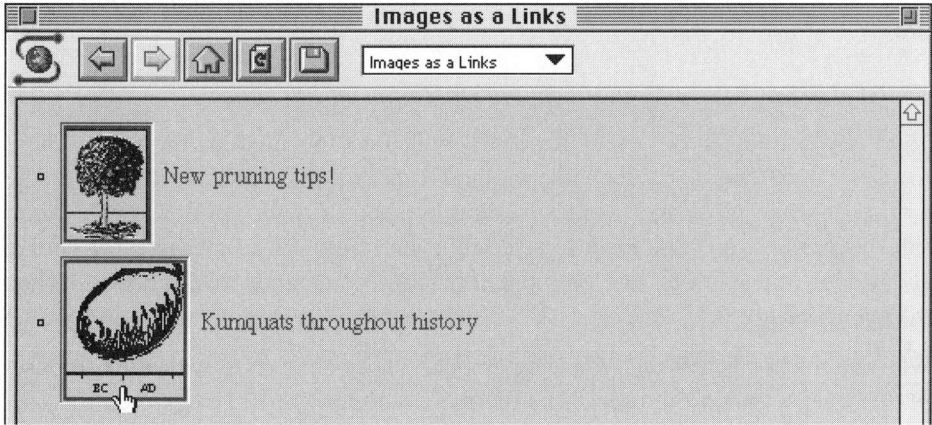

Figure 7-2. Mosaic puts a special border around an image that is inside an anchor

7.3.1.3 The name attribute

Use the `name` attribute to place a fragment identifier within an HTML document. Once created, the fragment identifier becomes a potential target of a link.

An easy way to think of a fragment identifier is as the HTML analog of the `goto` statement label common in many programming languages. The `name` attribute within the `<a>` tag places a label within a document. When that label is used in a link to that document, it is the equivalent of telling the browser to `goto` that label.

The value of the `name` attribute is any character string, enclosed in quotation marks; for example:

```
<h2><a name="Pruning">Pruning Your Kumquat Tree</a></h2>
```

Notice that we set the anchor in a section header of presumably a large document. It's a practice we encourage you use for all major sections of your work for easier reference and future smart processing, such as automated extraction of topics.

The following link, when taken by the user:

```
<a href="growing_guide.html#Pruning">
```

jumps directly to the section of the document we named above.

The contents of the `<a>` tag are not displayed in any special way with the `name` attribute.

Technically, you do not have to put any document content within the `<a>` tag with the `name` attribute since it simply marks a location in the document. In practice, some browsers ignore the tag unless some document content—a word or phrase, even an image—is between the `<a>` and `</a>` tags. For this reason, it's probably a good idea to have at least one displayable element in the body of any `<a>` tag.

7.3.1.4 The onClick, onMouseOver, and OnMouseOut attributes

There are a number of "event handlers" built into the modern browsers. These handlers watch for certain conditions and user actions, such as a click of the mouse or when an image finishes loading into the browser window. With client-side JavaScript, you may include selected event handlers as attributes of certain HTML tags and execute one or more JavaScript commands and functions when the event occurs.

With the anchor (`<a>`) tag, you may associate JavaScript code with three mouse-related events: when the user clicks the mouse button (`onClick`), when the user moves the mouse pointer onto the tag's contents (`onMouseOver`), and when the user moves the mouse pointer off the hyperlink (`onMouseOut`). The value of the event handler is—enclosed in quotation marks—one or a sequence of semicolon-separated JavaScript expressions, methods, and function references that the browser executes when the event occurs. [JavaScript event handlers, 13.3.3]

For example, a popular, albeit simple, use of the **onMouseOver** event with a hyperlink is to print an expanded description of the tag's destination in the JavaScript-aware browser's status box (Figure 7-3). Normally, the browser displays the frequently cryptic destination URL there whenever the user passes the mouse pointer over an **<a>** tag's contents:

```
<a href="http://www.ora.com/kumquats/homecooking/recipes.html#quat5"
  onMouseOver="window.status='A recipe for kumquat soup.';return true">
  <img src="pics/bowl.gif" border=0>
</a>
```

We argue that the contents of the tag itself should explain the link, but there are times when window space is tight and an expanded explanation is helpful, such as when the link is in a table of contents.

Figure 7-3. Use JavaScript to display a message in the browser's status box

See Chapter 13, *Executable Content*, for more about JavaScript.

7.3.1.5 The rel and rev attributes

The **rel** and **rev** attributes express a formal relationship and direction between source and target documents. The **rel** attribute specifies the relationship from the source document to the target; the **rev** attribute specifies the relationship from the target to the source. Both attributes can be placed in a single **<a>** tag, and the browser may use them to specially alter the appearance of the anchor content or to automatically construct document navigation menus. Other tools also may use these attributes to build special link collections, tables of contents, and indexes.

The value of either the **rel** or **rev** attribute is a space-separated list of relationships. The actual relationship names and their meanings are up to you: they are not formally addressed by the HTML standard. For example, a document that is part of a sequence of documents might include its relationship in a link:

```
<a href="part-14.html" rel=next rev=prev>
```

The relationship from the source to the target is that of moving to the next document; the reverse relationship is that of moving to the previous document.

These document relationships are also used in the `<link>` tag in the document `<head>`. The `<link>` tag establishes the relationship without actually creating a link to the target document; the `<a>` tag creates the link and imbues it with the relationship attributes. [`<link>`, 7.7.2]

Commonly used document relationships appear in the list below.

`next`
    Links to the next document in a collection

`prev`
    Links to the previous document in a collection

`head`
    Links to the top-level document in a collection

`toc`
    Links to a collection's table of contents

`parent`
    Links to the document above the source

`child`
    Links to a document below the source

`index`
    Links to the index for this document

`glossary`
    Links to the glossary for this document

In general, few browsers take advantage of these attributes to modify the link appearance. However, these attributes are a great way to document links you create, and we recommend you take the time to insert them whenever possible.

7.3.1.6 *The style and class attributes*

Use the `style` and `class` attributes for the `<a>` tag to control the display style for the content enclosed by the tag, and to format the content according to a predefined class of the `<a>` tag. [`style` attribute, 9.1.1] [`class` attribute, 9.2.4]

7.3.1.7 *The target attribute*

The `target` attribute lets you specify where to display the contents of a selected hyperlink. Commonly used in conjunction with frames or multiple browser windows, the value of this attribute is the name of the frame or window in which the referenced document should be loaded. If the named frame or window exists, the document is loaded in that frame or window. If not, a new window is created, given the specified name, and the document is loaded in that new window. For more information, including a list of special target names, see 12.7.

7.3.1.8 The title attribute

The `title` attribute lets you specify a title for the document to which you are linking. The value of the attribute is any string, enclosed in quotation marks. The browser might use it when displaying the link, perhaps flashing the title when the mouse passes over the link. The browser might also use the `title` attribute when adding this link to a user's hotlist.

The `title` attribute is especially useful for referencing an otherwise unlabeled resource, such as an image or a non-HTML document. For example, the browser might include the following title on this otherwise wordless image display page:

```
<a href="pics/kumquat.gif"
   title="A photograph of the Noble Fruit">
```

Ideally, the value specified should match the title of the referenced document, but it's not required.

7.3.1.9 The urn attribute

The `urn` attribute defines the more general *universal resource name* (URN) for a referenced document. The value of this attribute is a string enclosed in quotes. The actual syntax and semantics of the URN have not yet been defined, making this attribute little more than a place keeper for future versions of HTML.

7.3.2 Linking to Other Documents

You make a hyperlink to another document with the `<a>` tag and its `href` attribute, which defines the URL of the target document. The contents of the `<a>` tag are presented to the user in some distinctive manner to indicate the link is available.

When creating a link to another document, you should consider adding the `title`, `rel`, and `rev` attributes to the `<a>` tag. They help document the link you are creating and allow the browser to further embellish the display anchor contents.

7.3.3 Linking Within a Document

Creating a link within the same HTML document or to a specific fragment of another document is a two-step process. The first step is to make the target fragment; the second is to create the link to the fragment.

Use the `<a>` tag with its `name` attribute to identify a fragment. The value of the `name` attribute is used in hyperlinks that point to the fragment. Here's a sample fragment identifier:

```
<h3><a name="Section_7">Section 7</a></h3>
```

A hyperlink to the fragment is an `<a>` tag with the `href` attribute, in which the attribute's value—the target URL—ends with the fragment's name, preceded by the pound sign (#). A reference to the previous example's fragment identifier, then, might look like:

```
See <a href="index.html#Section_7">Section 7</a>
for further details.
```

By far the most common use of fragment identifiers is in creating a table of contents for a lengthy document. Begin by dividing your document into several logical sections, using appropriate headers and consistent formatting. At the start of each section, add a fragment identifier for that section, typically as part of the section title as a header. Finally, make a list of links to those fragment identifiers at the beginning of your document.

Our sample document extolling the life and wonders of the mighty kumquat, for example, is quite long and involved, including many sections and subsections of interest. It is a document to be read and read again. To make it easy for kumquat lovers everywhere to quickly find their section of interest, we've included fragment identifiers for each major section, and placed an ordered list of links—a hotlinked table of contents, as it were—at the beginning of each of the Kumquat Lover's documents, a sample of which appears below along with sample fragment identifiers that appear in the same document. The ellipsis symbol (...) means there are intervening segments of content, of course.

```
    . . .
  <h3>Table of Contents</h3>
  <ol>
    <li><a href="#soil_prep">Soil Preparation</a>
    <li><a href="#dig_hole">Digging the Hole</a>
    <li><a href="#planting">Planting the Tree</a>
  </ol>
    . . .
  <h3><a name=soil_prep>Soil Preparation</a></h3>
    . . .
  <h3><a name=dig_hole>Digging the Hole</a></h3>
    . . .
  <h3><a name=planting>Planting the Tree</a></h3>
    . . .
```

The kumquat lover can thereby click the desired link in the table of contents and jump directly to the section of interest, without lots of tedious scrolling.

Notice also that this example uses relative URLs—a good idea if you ever intend to move or rename the document without breaking all the hyperlinks.

7.4 Creating Effective Links

A document becomes hypertext by tossing in a few links in the same way that water becomes soup when you throw in a few vegetables. Technically, you've met the goal, but the outcome may not be very palatable.

Inserting anchors into your documents is something of an art, requiring good writing skills, HTML prowess, and an architectural sense of your documents and their relationships to others on the Web. Effective links flow seamlessly into a document, quietly supplying additional browsing opportunities to the reader without disturbing the current document. Poorly designed links scream out, interrupt the flow of the source document, and generally annoy the reader.

While there are as many linking styles as there are authors, here are a few of the more popular ways to link your documents. All do two things: they give the reader quick access to related information, and they tell the reader how the link is related to the current contents.

7.4.1 Lists of Links

Perhaps the most common way to present hyperlinks in HTML documents is in ordered or unordered lists in the style of a table of contents or list of resources.

Two schools of style exist. One puts the entire list item into the source anchor; the other abbreviates the item and puts a shorthand phrase in the source anchor. In the former, make sure you keep the anchor content short and sweet; in the latter, use a direct writing style that makes it easy to embed the link.

If your list of links becomes overly long, consider organizing it into several sublists grouped by topic. Readers can then scan the topics (set off, perhaps, as `<h3>` headers) for the appropriate list and then scan that list for the desired document.

The alternative list style is much more descriptive, but also more wordy, so you have to be careful it doesn't end up cluttered:

```
<p>
Kumquat-related documents include:
<ul>
  <li>A concise guide to <a href="kumquat_farming.html">
      profitable kumquat farming</a>,
      including a variety of business plans, lists of fruit
      packing companies, and farming supply companies.
  <li>101 different ways to <a href="kumquat_uses">
```

```
        use a kumquat</a>, including stewed kumquats and kumquat pie!
    <li>The kumquat is a hardy tree, but even the greenest of
        thumbs can use a few <a href="news:alt.kumquat_growers">
        growing tips</a> to increase
        their yield.
    <li>The business of kumquats is an expanding one, as
        shown by this 10 year overview of the
        <a href="http://www.ora.com/kumquat_report/">
        kumquat industry</a>.
</ul>
```

It sometimes gets hard to read a source HTML document. Imagine the clutter if we'd used anchors with fragment identifiers for each of the subtopics in the list item explanations. Nonetheless, it all looks pristine and easily navigable when displayed by the browser, such as with Mosaic as shown in Figure 7-4.

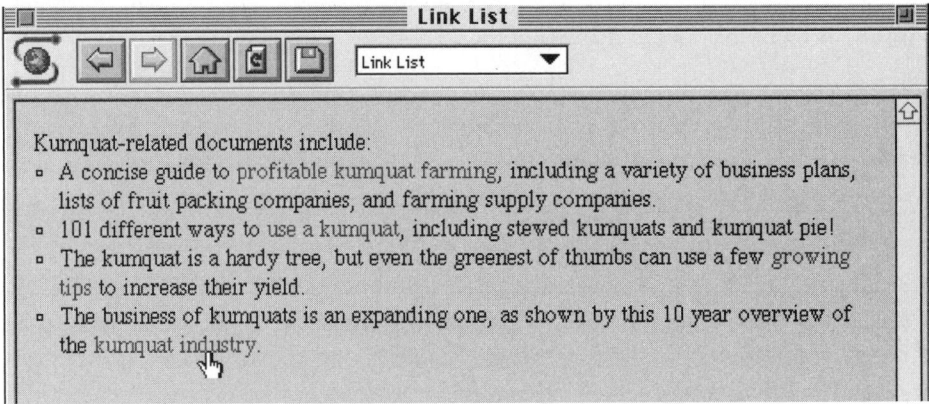

Figure 7-4. Wordy but effectively descriptive link list

This more descriptive style of presenting a link list tries hard to draw readers into the linked document by giving a fuller taste of what they can expect to find. Because each list element is longer and requires more scanning by the reader, you should use this style sparingly and dramatically limit the number of links.

In general, use the brief list style when presenting large numbers of links to a well-informed audience. The second, more descriptive style is better suited to a smaller number of links for which your readership is less well-versed in the topic at hand.

7.4.2 Inline References

If you aren't collecting links into lists, you're probably sprinkling them throughout your document. So-called inline links are more in keeping with the true spirit of hypertext since they enable the reader to mark their current place in the document, visit the related topic in more depth or find a better explanation, and then come back to the original and continue reading. That's very personalized information processing.

The biggest mistake made by novice HTML authors, however, is to overload their documents with links and treat them as if they are panic buttons demanding to be pressed. You may have seen this style of linking; HTML pages with the word "here" all over the place, like the panic-ridden example in Figure 7-5 (we can't bring ourselves to show you the source HTML for this travesty).

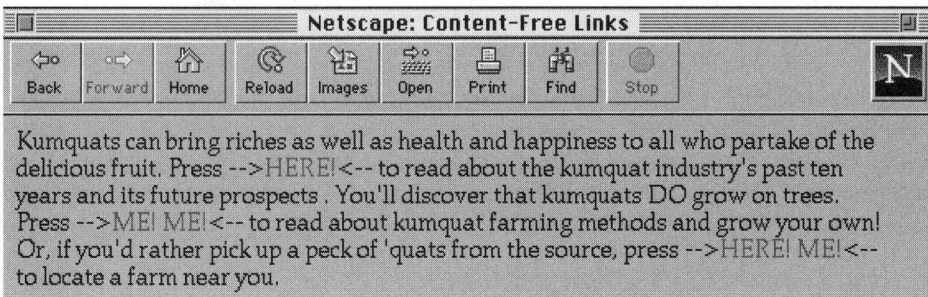

Figure 7-5. Links should not wave and yell like first-graders, "Here! Me! Me!"

As links, phrases like "click here" and "also available" are content-free and annoying. They make the person who is scanning the page for an important link read all the surrounding text to actually find the reference.

The better, more refined style for an inline link is to make every one contain a noun or noun/verb phrase relating to the topic at hand. Compare how kumquat farming and industry news references are treated in the Figure 7-6 to the "Here! Me! Me!" example in Figure 7-5.

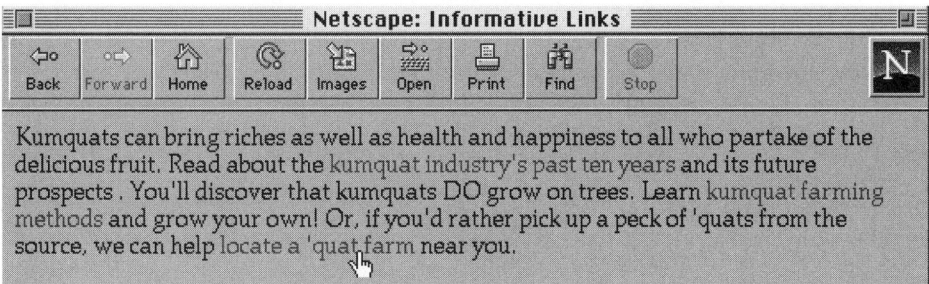

Figure 7-6. Kinder, gentler inline links work best

A quick scan of Figure 7-6 immediately yields useful links to "kumquat farming methods" and "kumquat industry's past ten years." There is no need to read the surrounding text to understand where the link will take you. Indeed, the immediately surrounding content in our example, as for most inline links, serves only as syntactic sugar in support of the embedded links.

Embedding links into the general discourse of a document takes more effort to create than link lists. You've got to actually understand the content of the current as well as the target documents, be able to express that relationship in just a few words, and then intelligently incorporate that link at some key place in the source document. Hopefully this key place is where you might expect the user is ready to interrupt their reading and ask a question or request more information. To make matters even more difficult, particularly for the traditional tech writer, this form of author-reader conversation is most effective when presented in active voice (he, she, or it does something to an object versus the object having something done to it). The effort expended is worthwhile, though, resulting in more informative, easily read documents. Remember, you'll write the document once, but it will be read thousands, if not millions, of times. Please your readers, please.

7.4.3 Linking Do's and Don'ts

Here are some hints for creating links:

- Keep the link content as concise as possible. Long links or huge inline graphic icons for links are visually disruptive and potentially confusing.

- Never place two links immediately adjacent to one another. Most browsers make it difficult to tell where one link stops and the next link starts. Separate them with regular text or line breaks.

- Be consistent. If you are using inline references, make all of your links inline references. If you choose to use lists of links, stick to either the short or long form; don't mix styles in a single document.

- Try reading your document with all the nonanchor text removed. If some links suddenly make no sense, rewrite them so that they stand on their own. (Many people scan documents looking only for links; the surrounding text becomes little more than a gray background to the visually more compelling links.)

7.4.4 Using Images and Links

It has become fashionable to use images and icons instead of words for link contents. For instance, instead of the word "next," some HTML authors might use an icon of a little pointing hand. A link to the home page is not complete without a picture of a little house. Links to searching tools must now contain a picture of a magnifying glass, question mark, or binoculars.

Resist falling prey to the "Mount Everest syndrome" of inserting images simply because you can. Again, it's a matter of context. If you or your document's readers can't tell at a glance what relationship a link has with the current document, you've failed. Use cute images for links sparingly, consistently, and only in ways that help readers scan your document for important information and leads. Also be ever mindful that your pages may be read by someone from nearly anywhere on Earth (perhaps beyond, even), and that images do not translate consistently across cultural boundaries. (Ever hear what the "okay" hand sign common in the United States means to a Japanese person?)

Creating consistent iconography for a collection of pages is a daunting task, one that really should be done with the assistance of someone formally schooled in visual design. Trust us, the kind of mind that produces nifty code and does good HTML is rarely suited to creating beautiful, compelling imagery. Find a good visual designer; your pages and readers will benefit immeasurably.

7.5 Mouse-Sensitive Images

Normally, an image placed within an anchor simply becomes part of the anchor content. The browser may alter the image in some special way (usually with a special border) to clue the reader that it is a link, but the user clicks the image in the same way they click a textual link.

The HTML standard provides a feature that lets you embed many different links inside the same image. Clicking different areas of the image causes the browser to link to different target documents. Such mouse-sensitive images, known as *image maps*, open up a variety of creative linking styles.

There are two ways to create image maps, known as server-side and client-side image maps. The former, enabled by the `ismap` attribute for the `<img>` tag, requires access to a server and related image map processing applications. The latter is created with the `usemap` attribute for the `<img>` tag, along with corresponding `<map>` and `<area>` tags. Since translation of the mouse position in the image to a link to another document happens on the user's machine, client-side image maps don't require a special server connection, and even can be implemented in non-web environments, such as on a local hard drive or on a CD-ROM-based document collection. [`<map>`, 7.5.3] [`<area>`, 7.5.4] [`<img>`, 5.2.6]

7.5.1 Server-Side Image Maps

You add an image to an anchor simply by placing an `<img>` tag within the body of the `<a>` tag. Make that embedded image into a mouse-sensitive one by adding the `ismap` attribute to the `<img>` tag. This special `<img>` attribute tells the browser that the image is a special map containing more than one link. (The `ismap` attribute is ignored by the browser if the `<img>` tag is not within an `<a>` tag.) [`<img>`, 5.2.6]

When the user clicks some place within the image, the browser passes the coordinates of the mouse pointer along with the URL specified in the `<a>` tag to the document server. The server uses the mouse pointer coordinates to determine which document to deliver back to the browser.

When `ismap` is used, the `href` attribute of the containing `<a>` tag must contain the URL of a server application or, for some HTTP servers, a related map file that contains the coordinate and linking information. If the URL is simply that of a conventional document, errors may result and the desired document will most likely not be retrieved.

The coordinates of the mouse position are screen pixels counted from the upper-left corner of the image beginning with (0,0). The coordinates are added to the end of the URL, preceded by a question mark.

For example, if a user clicks 43 pixels over and 15 pixels down from the upper-left corner of the image displayed from the following link:

```
<a href="/cgi-bin/imagemap/toolbar.map">
<img ismap src="pics/toolbar.gif">
</a>
```

the browser sends the following search parameters to the HTTP server:

```
/cgi-bin/imagemap/toolbar.map?43,15
```

In the example, *toolbar.map* is a special image map file inside the *cgi-bin/imagemap* directory and containing coordinates and links. A special image map process uses that file to match the passed coordinates (43,15 in the example) and return with the selected hyperlink document.

7.5.1.1 Server-side considerations

With mouse-sensitive `ismap`-enabled image maps, the browser is only required to pass along the URL and mouse coordinates to the server. Converting these coordinates into a specific document is handled by the document server. The conversion process differs between servers and is not defined by the HTML standard.

You need to consult with your web server administrators and perhaps even read your server's documentation to determine how to create and program an image map. Most servers come with some software utility, typically located in a *cgi-bin/imagemap* directory, to handle image maps. And most of these use a text file containing the image map regions and related hyperlinks that is referenced by your image map URL to process the image map query.

Here's an example image map file that describes the sensitive regions in our example image:

```
# Imagemap file=toolbar.map

default                    dflt.html
circle 100,30,50           link1.html
rectangle 180,120,290,500  link2.html
polygon 80,80,90,72,160,90 link3.html
```

Each sensitive region of the image map is described by a geometric shape and defining coordinates in pixels, such as the circle with its center point and radius, the rectangle's upper-left and lower-right edge coordinates, and the loci of a polygon. All coordinates are relative to the upper-left corner of the image (0,0). Each shape has a related URL.

An image map processing application typically tests each shape in the order it appears in the image file and returns the document specified by the corresponding URL to the browser if the user's mouse x,y coordinates fall within the boundaries of that shape. That means it's okay to overlap shapes; just be aware which takes precedence. Also, the entire image need not be covered with sensitive regions: if the passed coordinates don't fall within a specified shape, the default document gets sent back to the browser.

This is just one example for how an image map may be processed and the accessory files required for that process. Please huddle with your webmaster and server manuals to discover how to implement a server-side image map for your HTML documents and system.

7.5.2 Client-Side Image Maps

The obvious downside to server-side image maps is that they require a server. That means you need access to the required HTTP server or its */cgi-bin/* directory, which isn't always available. And server-side image maps limit portability, since not all image map processing applications are the same.

Server-side image maps also mean delays for the user while browsing, since the browser must get the server's attention to process the image coordinates. That's even if there's no action to take, such as a section of the image that isn't hyperlinked and doesn't lead anywhere.

Client-side image maps suffer from none of these difficulties. Enabled by the `usemap` attribute for the `<img>` tag, and defined by special `<map>` and `<area>` extension tags, client-side image maps let HTML authors include in their documents a map of coordinates and links that describe the sensitive regions of an image. The browser on the client computer translates the coordinates of the mouse position within the image into an action, such as loading and displaying another document. And special JavaScript-enabled attributes provide a wealth of special effects for client-side image maps. [JavaScript event handlers, 13.3.3]

To create a client-side image map, include the `usemap` attribute as part of the `<img>` tag. Its value is the URL of a `<map>` segment in an HTML document that contains the map coordinates and related link URLs. The document in the URL identifies the HTML document containing the map; the fragment identifier in the URL identifies the map to be used. Most often, the map is in the same document as the image itself, and the URL can be reduced to the fragment identifier: a pound sign (#) followed by the map name.

For example, the following source fragment tells the Netscape or Internet Explorer browser that the *map.gif* image is a client-side image map and that its mouse-sensitive coordinates and related link URLs are found in the `map` section of the document named *map*:

```
<img src="pics/map.gif" usemap="#map">
```

7.5.3 *The <map> Tag*

For client-side image maps to work, you must include somewhere in the HTML document a set of coordinates and URLs that define the mouse-sensitive regions of a client-side image map and the hyperlink to take for each region that is clicked by the user. You include those coordinates and links as values of attributes in special `<area>` tags; the collection of `<area>` specifications are enclosed within the `<map>` tag and its end tag `</map>`.

<map>

Function:
    Encloses client-side image map (usemap) specifications

Attributes:
    NAME

End Tag:
    </map>, always present

Contains:
    map_content

Used in:
    body_content

The <map> segment may appear anywhere in the body of any HTML document. Browsers that do not support client-side image maps will ignore the contents of the <map> tag. The <map> contents never get displayed in the browser window.

The value of the name attribute in the <map> tag is the name used by the usemap attribute in an <img> tag to locate the image map specification. The name must be unique and not used by another <map> in the document, but more than one image map may reference the same <map> specifications. [usemap, 5.2.6.13]

7.5.4 The <area> Tag

The guts of a client-side image map are the <area> tags within the map segment. These <area> tags define each mouse-sensitive region and the action the browser should take if that region is selected by the user in an associated client-side image map.

<area>

Function:
  Defines coordinates and links for a region on a client-side image map

Attributes:
  ALT
  COORDS
  HREF
  NOHREF
  NOTAB **❶**
  ONMOUSEOUT **Ⓝ** **❶**
  ONMOUSEOVER **Ⓝ** **❶**
  SHAPE
  TABORDER **❶**
  TARGET **Ⓝ** **❶**
  TITLE **❶**

End Tag:
  None

Contains:
  Nothing

Used in:
  map_content

The region defined by an <area> tag acts just like any other hyperlink: when the user moves the mouse pointer over the region of the image, the pointer icon will change and the browser displays the URL of the related hyperlink in the status box at the bottom of the browser window.[*] Regions of the client-side image map not defined in at least one <area> tag are not mouse-sensitive.

7.5.4.1 The alt attribute

Like its cousin for the <img> tag, the alt attribute for the <area> tag lets you attach a text label to the image, except in this case the label is associated with a particular area of the image. The browser may present this label to the user when the mouse passes over the area, and it may also be used by a nongraphical browser to present the client-side image map as a list of links identified by the alt labels.

7.5.4.2 The coords attribute

The required coords attribute of the <area> tag defines coordinates of a mouse-sensitive region in a client-side image map. The number of coordinates and their meaning depend upon the region's shape as determined by the shape attribute, later in this chapter. You may define hyperlink regions as rectangles, circles, and polygons within a client-side image map. The appropriate values for each shape are:

circle

> coords="x,y,r" where x and y define the position of the center of the circle (0,0 is the upper-left corner of the image) and r is its radius in pixels.

polygon

> coords="x1,y1,x2,y2,x3,y3,..." where each pair of x,y coordinates define a vertex of the polygon, with 0,0 being the upper-left corner of the image. At least three pairs of coordinates are required to define a triangle, higher order polygons require a larger number of vertices. The polygon is automatically closed, so it is not necessary to repeat the first coordinate at the end of the list to close the region.

rectangle

> coords="x1,y1,x2,y2" where the first coordinate pair is one corner of the rectangle and the other pair is the corner diagonally opposite, with "0,0" being the upper-left corner of the image. Note that a rectangle is just a shortened way of specifying a polygon with four vertices.

For example, the following fragment defines a single mouse-sensitive region in the lower-right quarter of a 100×100 image and another circular region smack in the middle:

---

[*] That is, unless you activate a JavaScript event handler that writes the contents of the status box. See the onMouse event handlers in 7.5.4.6.

```
<map name="map1">
  <area shape=rectangle coords="75,75,99,99">
  <area shape=circle coords="50,50,25">
</map>
```

If the coordinates in one `<area>` tag overlap with another region, the first `<area>` tag takes precedence. The browsers ignore coordinates that extend beyond the boundaries of the image.

7.5.4.3 The href attribute

Like the `href` attribute for the anchor (`<a>`) tag, the `href` attribute for the `<area>` tag defines the URL of the desired link if its region in the associated image map is clicked. The value of the `href` attribute is any valid URL, relative or absolute, including JavaScript code.

For example, the browser will load and display the *link4.html* document if the user clicks in the lower-left quarter of a 100×100-pixel image, as defined by the first image map `<area>` tag in the following example:

```
<map name="map">
  <area coords="75,75,99,99" href="link4.html">
  <area coords="0,0,25,25" href="javascript:window.alert('Oooh, tickles!')"
</map>
```

The second `<area>` tag in the example uses a JavaScript URL, which, when the user clicks in the upper-left quadrant of the image map, executes a JavaScript alert method that displays the silly message in a dialog.

7.5.4.4 The nohref attribute

The `nohref` attribute for the `<area>` tag lets you define a mouse-sensitive region in a client-side image map for which no action is taken even though the user may select it. You must include either an `href` or a `nohref` attribute for each `<area>` tag.

7.5.4.5 The notab and taborder attributes

Supported only by Internet Explorer, the `notab` and `taborder` attributes control how the areas in your client-side image maps are integrated with the tabbing sequence of the document.

The browser skips over `notab` areas as the user presses the tab key to move the cursor around the document. Otherwise, this area will be part of the tabbing sequence.

Also with Internet Explorer, imagemap areas get inserted into the tabbing sequence in the order in which they are encountered in the document, along with other tab-sensitive elements like form fields. Use the `taborder` attribute to change that default order. The value of the attribute is an integer indicating the position of this area in the overall tab sequence for the document.

7.5.4.6 The onMouseOver and OnMouseOut attributes

Two of the same mouse-related JavaScript event handlers that work for the anchor (`<a>`) tag also work with client-side image map hyperlinks: `onMouse-Over` for when the user moves the mouse pointer over the `<area>` defined region of the map, and `onMouseOut` for when the user moves the mouse pointer off that area. The value of the event handler is—enclosed in quotation marks—one or a sequence of semicolon-separated JavaScript expressions, methods, and function references that the browser executes when the event occurs. [`<a>` event handler, 7.3.1.4]

For example, a popular, albeit simple, use of the `onMouseOver` event is to print a more descriptive explanation in the browser's status box whenever the user passes the mouse pointer over a region of the image map:

```
<area href="http://www.ora.com/kumquats/homecooking/recipes.html#quat5"
    onMouseOver="self.status='A recipe for kumquat soup.';return true">
```

In context with a text-based hyperlink, we argue that the contents of the tag itself should explain the link. But images can be deceptive, so we urge you to use the event handlers to provide text descriptions with your image maps.

The `onClick` mouse-related event isn't included as one of the `<area>` link-related events, but it can be simulated: simply use a JavaScript URL as the tag's `href` value. This approach is particularly useful to direct users away from default areas of an image map and onto those areas with real hyperlinks. See the client-side image map in 7.5.5 for an example.

7.5.4.7 The shape attribute

According to the HTML standard, use this attribute to define the shape of an image map's mouse-sensitive region: a circle (`circ` or `circle`), polygon (`poly` or `polygon`), or rectangle (`rect` or `rectangle`).

The value of the `shape` attribute affects how the browser interprets the value of the `coords` attribute. If you don't include a `shape` attribute, the value `default` is assumed. According to the standard, default means that the area covers the entire image. In practice, the browsers default to a rectangular area and expect to find four `coords` values. And if you don't specify a shape and don't include four coordinates with the tag, the browser ignores the area altogether.

In fact, Netscape is the only browser that even recognizes the `shape` value `default` to provide a catch-all area for clicks that fall outside all the other defined hotspots. Since areas are in a "first-come, first-served" order in the `<map>`

tag, you should place the default area last. Otherwise, it covers up any and all areas that follow in your image map.

7.5.4.8 The target attribute

The `target` attribute gives you a way to control where the contents of the selected hyperlink in the image map get displayed. Commonly used in conjunction with frames or multiple browser windows, the value of this attribute is the name of the frame or window in which the referenced document should be loaded. If the named frame or window exists, the document is loaded in that frame or window. If not, a new window is created, given the specified name, and the document is loaded in that new window. For more information, including a list of special target names, see 12.7.

7.5.4.9 The title attribute

The `title` attribute lets you specify a title for the document to which the image map's area links. The value of the attribute is any string, enclosed in quotes. The browser might use the title when displaying the link, perhaps flashing the title when the mouse passes over the area. The browser might also use the `title` attribute when adding this link to a user's hotlist.

The `title` attribute is especially useful for referencing an otherwise unlabeled resource, such as an image or a non-HTML document. Ideally, the value specified should match the title of the referenced document, but it's not required.

7.5.5 A Client-Side Image Map Example

The following example fragment draws together the various components of a client-side image map we discussed earlier in this section. It includes the `<img>` tag with the image reference and `usemap` attribute with a `name` that points to a `<map>` that defines four mouse-sensitive regions (three plus a default) and related links:

```
<body>
...
<img src="pics/map.gif" usemap="#map1" border=0>
...
<map name="map1">
  <area shape=rect coords="0,20,40,100"
      href="k_juice.html"
      onMouseOver="self.status='How to prepare kumquat juice.'
        ;return true">
  <area shape=rect coords="50,50,80,100"
      href="k_soup.html"
      onMouseOver="self.status='A recipe for hearty kumquat soup.'
        ;return true">
  <area shape=rect coords="90,50,140,100"
```

```
        href="k_fruit.html"
        onMouseOver="self.status='Care and handling of the native
                    kumquat.'
        ;return true">
  <area shape=default
        href="javascript:window.alert('Choose the cup or one of the
            bowls.')"
        onMouseOver="self.status='Select the cup or a bowl for more
                    information.'
        ;return true">
</map>
```

See Figure 7-7 for the results.

Figure 7-7. A simple client-side image map with JavaScript-enabled mouse event

7.5.6 Handling Other Browsers

Unlike its server-side `ismap` counterpart, the client-side image map tag (`<img usemap>`) doesn't need to be included in an `<a>` tag. But it may be, so that you can gracefully handle browsers that are unable to process client-side image maps.

For example, Mosaic or early versions of Netscape simply load a document named *main.html* if the user clicks the *map.gif* image referenced in the following source fragment. The extended browsers, on the other hand, will divide the image into mouse-sensitive regions, as defined in the associated `<map>`, and link to a particular name anchor within the same *main.html* document if the image map region is selected by the user:

```
<a href="main.html">
  <img src="pics/map.gif" ismap usemap="map1">
</a>
...
<map name="map1">
  <area coords="0,0,49,49" href="main.html#link1">
  <area coords="50,0,99,49" href="main.html#link2">
  <area coords="0,50,49,99" href="main.html#link3">
  <area coords="50,50,99,99" href="main.html#link4">
</map>
```

To make an image map fully backward-compatible with all image map-capable browsers, you may also include both client-side and server-side processing for the same image map. Capable browsers will honor the faster client-side processing; all other browsers will ignore the `usemap` attribute in the `<img>` tag and rely upon the referenced server process to handle user selections in the traditional way. For example:

```
<a href="/cgi-bin/images/map.proc">
  <img src="pics/map2.gif" usemap="#map2" ismap>
</a>
...
<map name="map2">
  <area coords="0,0,49,49" href="link1.html">
  <area coords="50,0,99,49" href="link2.html">
  <area coords="0,50,49,99" href="link3.html">
  <area coords="50,50,99,99" href="link4.html">
</map>
```

7.5.7 *Effective Use of Mouse-Sensitive Images*

Some of the most visually compelling pages we've seen on the Web have mouse-sensitive images: maps with regions that when clicked, for example, lead to more information about a country or town, or result in more detail about the location and who to contact at a regional branch of a business. We've even seen a mouse-sensitive image of a fashion model whose various clothing parts lead to their respective catalog entries, complete with detailed description and price tag for ordering.

The visual nature of mouse-sensitive images coupled with the need for an effective interface means that you should strongly consider having an artist, a user-interface designer, and even a human-factors expert evaluate your mouse-sensitive imagery. At the very least, engage in a bit of user testing to make sure people know where to click to move to the desired document. Make sure the "mouseable" areas of the image indicate this to the user using a consistent visual mechanism. Consider using borders, drop shadows, or color changes to indicate those areas that can be selected by the user.

Finally, always remember that the decision to use mouse-sensitive images is an explicit decision to exclude text-based and image-restricted browsers from your pages. This includes the many millions of browsers connecting to the Internet via slow modem connections. For these people, downloading your beautiful images is simply too expensive. To keep from disenfranchising a growing population, make sure any page that has a mouse-sensitive image has a text-only equivalent easily accessible from a link on the image-enabled version. Some thoughtful webmasters even provide separate pages for users preferring full graphics versus mostly text.

7.6 Creating Searchable Documents

Another extensible form of an HTML link that does not use the <a> tag is one that causes the server to search a database for a document that contains a user-specified keyword or words. An HTML document that contains such a link is known as a *searchable* document.

7.6.1 The <isindex> Tag

For a searchable document designated by the <isindex> tag, the browser provides a way for the user to enter one or more search terms and passes those key words along with a search-engine's URL to the server. The server matches the keywords against a database of terms to select the next document for display.

<isindex>

Function:
  Indicates that a document can be searched

Attributes:
  ACTION ❶
  PROMPT

End tag:
  None

Contains:
  Nothing

Used in:
  head_content

When a browser encounters the <isindex> tag, it adds a standard search inter-face to the document (rendered by Netscape in Figure 7-8).

```
<html>
<head>
<title>Kumquat Advice Database</title>
<base href="cgi-bin/quat-query">
<isindex>
</head>
<body>
<h3>Kumquat Advice Database</h3>
<p>
Search this database to learn more about kumquats!
</body>
</html>
```

Figure 7-8. A searchable document

The user types a list of space-separated keywords into the field provided. When the user presses the return key, the browser automatically appends the query list to the end of a URL and passes the information along to the server for further processing.

While the HTML standard only allows the `<isindex>` tag to be placed in the document header, most browsers let the tag appear anywhere in the document and inserts the search field in the content flow where the `<isindex>` tag appears. This convenient extension lets you add instructions and other useful elements before presenting the user with the actual search field.

7.6.1.1 The prompt attribute

The browser provides a leading prompt just above or to the left of the user-entry field. Netscape's default prompt, for example, is, "This is a searchable index. Enter search keywords:" (Figure 7-8). That default prompt is not the best for all occasions, so it is possible to change it with the `prompt` attribute.

When added to the `<isindex>` tag, the value of the `prompt` attribute is the string of text that precedes the keyword entry field placed in the document by the browser.

For example, compare Figure 7-8 with Figure 7-9, in which we added the following prompt to the previous source example:

```
<isindex prompt="To learn more about kumquats, enter a keyword:">
```

Older browsers will ignore the `prompt` attribute, but there is little reason not to include a better prompt string for your more up-to-date readership.

7.6.1.2 The query URL

Besides the `<isindex>` tag in the header of a searchable document, the other important element of this special HTML tag is the query URL. By default, it is the

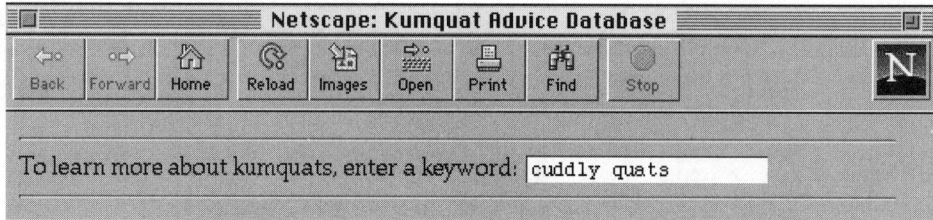

Figure 7-9. The prompt attribute creates custom prompts in searchable documents

URL of the source document itself—not good if your document can't handle the query. Rather, most authors use the **<base>** attribute to point to a different URL for the search. [<base>, 7.7.1]

The browser appends a question mark to the query URL, followed by the specified search parameters. Nonprintable characters are appropriately encoded; multiple parameters are separated by a plus sign (+).

In the previous example, if a user types "insect control" in the search field, the browser would retrieve the URL:

```
cgi-bin/quat-query?insect+control
```

7.6.1.3 The action attribute

For Internet Explorer only, you can specify the query URL for the index with the **action** attribute. The effect is exactly as if you had used the **href** attribute with the **<base>** tag: the browser links to the specified URL with the search parameters appended to the URL.

While the **action** attribute provides the desirable feature of divorcing the document's base URL from the search index URL, it will cause your searches to fail if the user is not using Internet Explorer. For this reason, we do not recommend that you use the **action** attribute to specify the query URL for the search.

7.6.1.4 Server dependencies

Like image maps, searchable documents require support from the server to make things work. How the server interprets the query URL and its parameters is not defined by the HTML standard.

You should consult your server's documentation to determine how you can receive and use the search parameters to locate the desired document. Typically, the server breaks the parameters out of the query URL and passes them to a program designated by the URL.

7.7 *Establishing Document Relationships*

Very few HTML documents stand alone. Instead, a document is usually part of a collection of documents, each connected by the one or several of the hypertext strands we describe in this chapter. One document may be a part of several collections, linking to some documents and being linked to by others. Readers move between the document families as they follow the links that interest them.

You establish an explicit relationship between two documents when you link them. Conscientious authors use the `rel` attribute of the `<a>` tag to indicate the nature of the link. In addition, two other tags may be used within a document to further clarify the location and relationship of a document within a document family. These tags, `<base>` and `<link>`, are placed within the body of the `<head>` tag. [`<head>`, 3.6.1]

7.7.1 *The <base> Header Element*

As we previously explained, URLs within a document can be either absolute (with every element of the URL explicitly provided by the author) or relative (with certain elements of the URL omitted and supplied by the browser). Normally, the browser fills in the blanks of a relative URL by drawing the missing pieces from the URL of the current document. You can change that with the `<base>` tag.

<base>

Function:
  Define the base URL for other anchors in the document
Attributes:
  HREF
  TARGET **N** **O**
End tag:
  None
Contains:
  Nothing
Used in:
  head_content

The `<base>` tag must appear only in the document header, not its body contents. The browser thereafter uses the specified base URL, not the current document's URL, to resolve all relative URLs, including those found in `<a>`, `<img>`, `<link>`, and `<form>` tags. It also defines the URL that will be used to resolve queries in searchable documents containing the `<isindex>` tag. [URLs, 7.2]

7.7.1.1 The href attribute

The `href` attribute must have a valid URL as its value, which the browser then uses to define the absolute URL against which relative URLs are based within the document. For example, the `<base>` tag in this document head,

```
<html>
<head>
<base href="http://www.kumquat.com/">
</head>
...
```

tells the browser that any relative URLs within this document are relative to the top-level document directory on *www.kumquat.com*, regardless of the address and directory of the machine from which the user had retrieved the current document.

Contrary to what you may expect, you can make the base URL relative, not absolute. The browser actually forms an absolute base URL out of this relative URL by filling in the missing pieces with the URL of the document itself. This property can be used to good advantage. For instance, in this next example,

```
<html>
<head>
<base href="/info/">
</head>
...
```

the browser will make the `<base>` URL into one that is relative to the server's */info/* directory, which probably is not the same directory of the current document. Imagine if you had to re-address every link in your document with that common directory. Not only does the `<base>` tag help you shorten those URLs in your document that have a common root, it also lets you constrain the directory from which relative references are retrieved without binding the document to a specific server.

7.7.1.2 The target attribute

When working with documents inside frames, the target attribute with the `<a>` tag ensures that a referenced URL gets loaded into the correct frame. Similarly, the `target` attribute for the `<base>` tag lets you establish the default name of one of the frames or windows in which the browser is to display redirected hyperlinked documents. [frames, 12.1]

If you have no other default target for your hyperlinks within your frames, you may want to consider using `<base target=_top>`. This will ensure that links that are not specifically targeted to a frame or window will thereby load in the top-level browser window. This eliminates the embarrassing and common error of having references to pages on other sites appear within a frame on your pages, instead of within their own pages. A minor bit of HTML, to be sure, but it makes life much easier for your readership.

7.7.1.3 Using <base>

The most important reason for using <base> is to ensure that any relative URLs within the document will resolve into a correct document address, even if the document itself is moved or renamed. This is particularly important when creating a document collection. By placing the correct <base> tag in each document, you can move the entire collection between directories and even servers without breaking all of the links within the documents.

You also need to use the <base> tag for a searchable document (<isindex>) if you want user queries posed to a URL different from the host document.

Note that a document that contains both the <isindex> tag and other relative URLs may have problems if the relative URLs are not relative to the desired index processing URL. Since this is usually the case, do not use relative URLs in searchable documents that use the <base> tag to specify the query URL for the document.

7.7.2 The <link> Header Element

Use the <link> tag to define the relationship between the current document and another in a Web collection.

The <link> tags belongs in the <head> content, nowhere else. The attributes of the <link> tag are used like those of the <a> tag, but their effects serve only to document the relationship between documents. The <link> tag has no content and no closing </link> element.

7.7.2.1 The href attribute

As with its other tag applications, the href attribute specifies the URL of the target <link> tag. It is a required attribute, too, and its value is any valid document URL. The specified document is assumed to have a relationship to the current document.

7.7.2.2 The rel and rev attributes

The rel and rev attributes express the relationship between the source and target documents. The rel attribute specifies the relationship from the source document to the target; the rev attribute specifies the relationship from the target document to the source document. Both attributes can be included in a single <link> tag.

<link>

Function:
  Define a relationship between this document and another document

Attributes:
  HREF
  REL
  REV
  TITLE
  TYPE ▣ ➊

End tag:
  None

Contains:
  Nothing

Used in:
  head_content

The value of either attribute is a space-separated list of relationships. The actual relationship names are not specified by the HTML standard, although some have come into common usage as listed in 7.3.1.5. For example, a document that is part of a sequence of documents might use:

```
<link href="part-14.html" rel=next rev=prev>
```

when referencing the next document in the series. The relationship from the source to the target is that of moving to the next document; the reverse relationship is that of moving to the previous document.

7.7.2.3 *The title attribute*

The `title` attribute lets you specify the title of the document to which you are linking. This attribute is useful when referencing a resource that does not have a title, such as an image or a non-HTML document. In this case, the browser might use the `<link>` title when displaying the referenced document. For example,

```
<link href="pics/kumquat.gif"
   title="A photograph of the Noble Fruit">
```

tells the browser to use the indicated title when displaying the referenced image.

The value of the attribute is an arbitrary character string, enclosed in quotation marks.

7.7.2.4 *The type attribute*

The `type` attribute provides the MIME content type of the linked document. Supported by both Internet Explorer and Netscape, the type attribute can be used with any linked document. It is often used to define the type of linked style sheets. In this context, the value of the `type` attribute is usually `text/css`. For example,

```
<link href="styles/classic.css" rel=stylesheet type="text/css">
```

creates a link to an external style sheet within the `<head>` of a document. See Chapter 9, *Cascading Style Sheets*, for details.

7.7.2.5 *How browsers might use <link>*

Although the HTML standard does not require browsers to do anything with the information provided by the `<link>` tag, it's not hard to envision how this information might be used to enhance the presentation of a document.

As a simple example, suppose you consistently provide `<link>` tags for each of your documents that define `next`, `prev`, and `parent` links. A browser could use this information to place a standard toolbar at the top or bottom of each document containing buttons that would jump to the appropriate related document. By relegating the task of providing simple navigational links to the browser, you are free to concentrate on the more important content of your document.

As a more complex example, suppose a browser expects to find a `<link>` tag defining a glossary for the current document, and that this glossary document is itself a searchable document. Whenever a reader clicked on a word or phrase in the document, the browser could automatically search the glossary for the definition of the selected phrase, presenting the result in a small pop-up window.

As the Web and HTML evolve, expect to see more and more uses of the `<link>` tag to explicitly define document relationships on the Web.

7.8 Supporting Document Automation

There are two additional header tags whose primary function is to support document automation, interacting with the Web server itself and document-generation tools.

7.8.1 *The <meta> Header Element*

Given the rich set of HTML header tags for defining a document and its relationship with others that go unused by most HTML authors, you'd think we'd all be satisfied.

<meta>

Function:
   Supply additional information about a document

Attributes:
   CHARSET ❶
   CONTENT
   HTTP_EQUIV
   NAME

End tag:
   None

Contains:
   Nothing

Used in:
   head_content

But, no. There's always someone with special needs. They want to be able to give even more information about their precious document, information that might be used by browsers, readers of the HTML source, or by document-indexing tools. The <meta> tag is for you who need to go beyond the beyond.

The <meta> tag belongs in the document header and has no content. Instead, attributes of the tag define name/value pairs that associate the document. In certain cases, these values are used by the web server serving the document to further define the document content type to the browser.

7.8.1.1 The name attribute

The name attribute supplies the name of the name/value pair defined by the <meta> tag. The HTML standard does not define any predefined <meta> names. In general, you are free to use any name that makes sense to you and other readers of your HTML source.

One common name used is keywords, which defines a set of keywords for the document. When encountered by any of the popular search engines on the Web, these keywords will be used to categorize the document. If you want your documents to be indexed by a search engine, consider putting this kind of tag in the <head> of each document:

```
<meta name="keywords" content="kumquats, cooking, peeling, eating">
```

If the name attribute is not provided, the name of the name/value pair is taken from the http-equiv attribute.

7.8.1.2 The content attribute

The `content` attribute provides the value of the name/value pair. It can be any valid string, enclosed in quotes, if necessary. It should always be specified in conjunction with either a `name` or `http`-equiv attribute.

As an example, you might place the author's name in a document with:

```
<meta name="Authors" content="Chuck Musciano & Bill Kennedy">
```

7.8.1.3 The http-equiv attribute

The `http-equiv` attribute supplies a name for the name/value pair and instructs the server to include the name/value pair in the MIME document header that is passed to the browser before sending the actual document.

When a server sends a document to a browser, it first sends a number of name/value pairs. While some servers might send a number of these pairs, all servers send at least one:

```
content-type: text/html
```

This tells the browser to expect to receive an HTML document.

When you use the `<meta>` tag with the `http-equiv` attribute, the server will add your name/value pairs to the content header it sends to the browser. For example, adding:

```
<meta http-equiv="charset" content="iso-8859-1">
<meta http-equiv="expires" content="31 Dec 99">
```

causes the header sent to the browser to contain:

```
content-type: text/html
charset: iso-8859-1
expires: 31 Dec 99
```

Of course, adding these additional header fields makes sense only if your browser accepts the fields and uses them in some appropriate manner.

7.8.1.4 The charset attribute

Internet Explorer provides explicit support for a `charset` attribute in the `<meta>` tag. Set the value of the attribute to the name of the character set to be used for the document. This is not the recommended way to define a document's character set. Rather, we recommend always using the `http-equiv` and `content` attributes to define the character set.

7.8.2 The *<nextid>* Header Element

This tag is not defined in the HTML 3.2 standard and should not be used. We describe it here for historical reasons.

<nextid>

Function:
   Define the next valid document entity identifier

Attributes:
   n

End tag:
   None

Contains:
   Nothing

Used in:
   head_content

The idea behind the `<nextid>` tag is to provide some way of automatically indexing fragment identifiers.

7.8.2.1 The n attribute

The `n` attribute specifies the name of the next generated fragment identifier. Although the HTML standard does not define the format of this name, it is typically an alphabetic string followed by a two-digit number. A typical `<nextid>` tag might look like this:

```
<html>
<head>
<nextid n=DOC54>
</head>
...
```

An automatic-document generator might use the `nextid` information, then, to successively name fragment identifiers `DOC54`, `DOC55`, and so forth within this document.

8

Formatted Lists

Making information more accessible is the single most important quality of HTML. The language's excellent collection of text style and formatting tools helps you organize your information into documents readers quickly understand, scan, and extract, possibly with automated browser agents.

Beyond embellishing your text with specialized text tags, HTML also provides a rich set of tools that help you organize content into formatted lists. There's nothing magical or mysterious about HTML lists. In fact, the beauty of HTML lists is their simplicity. They're based on common list paradigms we encounter every day, such as an unordered laundry list, ordered instruction lists, and dictionary-like definition lists. All are familiar, comfortable ways of organizing content. All provide powerful means for quickly understanding, scanning, and extracting pertinent information from your HTML documents.

8.1 Unordered Lists

Like a laundry or shopping list, an unordered list in HTML is a collection of related items that have no special order or sequence. The most common unordered list you'll find on the Web is a collection of hyperlinks to other documents. Some common topic, like "Related Kumquat Lovers' Sites," allies the items in an unordered list, but they have no order among themselves.

8.1.1 The <ul> Tag

The <ul> tag signals the browser that the following content, ending with the </ul> tag, is an unordered list of items. Inside, each item in the unordered list is identified by a leading `<li>` tag. Otherwise, nearly anything HTML-wise goes, including other lists, text, and multimedia elements. [`<li>`, 8.3]

<ul>

Function:
> Define an unordered list

Attributes:
> CLASS **N** **O**
> COMPACT
> STYLE **N** **O**
> TYPE

End tag:
> </ul>, never omitted

Contains:
> *list_content*

Used in:
> *block*

Typically, the browser adds a leading bullet character and formats each item on a new line, indented somewhat from the left margin of the document. The actual rendering of unordered lists, however, varies widely between browsers, so you shouldn't get bent out of shape trying to attain exact positioning of the elements. For instance, some browsers treat the start of an unordered list as a new paragraph and, like the `<p>` tag, leave a blank line above the list. Other browsers simply start the list item after a simple line break. Browsers vary, too, in how much space they use between list items. For example, the following source:

```
Popular Kumquat recipes:
<ul>
  <li>Pickled Kumquats
  <li>'Quats and 'Kraut (a holiday favorite!)
  <li>'Quatshakes
</ul>
There are so many more to please every palate!
```

appears to the Mosaic user as shown in Figure 8-1.

Tricky HTML authors sometimes use nested unordered lists, with and without `<li>`-tagged items, to take advantage of the automatic, successive indenting. You can produce some fairly slick text segments that way. Just don't depend on it for

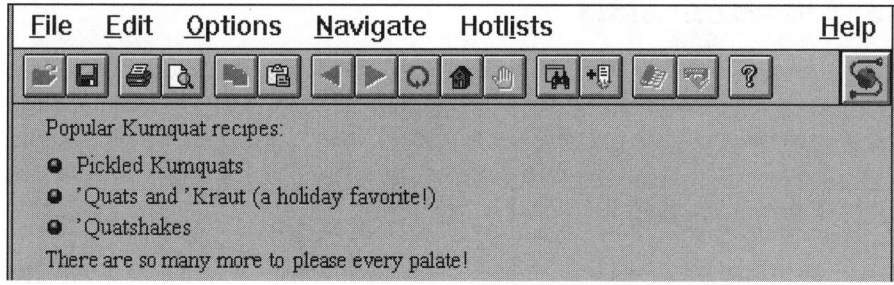

Figure 8-1. A simple unordered list

all browsers, including future ones. Rather, it's best to use the **border** property with a style definition in the paragraph (**<p>**) or division (**<div>**) tag to indent nonlist sections of your document (see Chapter 9, *Cascading Style Sheets*).

8.1.1.1 *The type attribute*

The graphical browsers automatically bullet each **<li>**-tagged item in an unordered list. Netscape and Internet Explorer use a solid circle, for example; Mosaic precedes unordered list items with a hollow square (on the Mac) or a round ball (PC and UNIX). Browsers that support HTML 3.2 let you use the **type** attribute to specify which bullet symbol you'd rather have precede items in an unordered list. This attribute may have a value of either **disc**, **circle**, or **square**. All the items within that list will thereafter use the specified bullet symbol, unless an individual item overrides the list bullet type, as described later in this chapter.

8.1.1.2 *Compact unordered lists*

If you like wide open spaces, you'll hate the optional **compact** attribute for the **<ul>** tag. It tells the browser to squeeze the unordered list into an even smaller, more compact text block. Typically, the browser reduces the line spacing between list items. And it may reduce the indentation between list items, if it does anything at all (usually it doesn't).

Some browsers ignore the **compact** attribute, so you should not overly depend on its formatting attributes.

8.1.1.3 *The style and class attributes*

The **style** attribute for the **<ul>** tag creates an inline style for the elements enclosed by the tag, overriding any other style rule in effect. The **class** attribute lets you format the content according to a predefined class of the **<ul>** tag; its value is the name of that class. [style attribute, 9.1.1] [class attribute, 9.2.4].

8.2 Ordered Lists

Use an ordered list when the sequence of the list items is important. A list of instructions is a good example, as are tables of content and lists of document footnotes or endnotes.

8.2.1 The <ol> Tag

The typical browser formats the contents of an ordered list just like an unordered list, except that the items are numbered instead of bulleted. The numbering starts at one and is incremented by one for each successive ordered list element tagged with <li>. [<li>, 8.3]

<ol>

Function:
  Define an ordered list

Attributes:
  CLASS N O
  COMPACT
  START
  STYLE N O
  TYPE

End tag:
  </ol>, never omitted

Contains:
  list_content

Used in:
  block

HTML 3.2 has a number of features that provide a wide variety of ordered lists. You can change the start value of the list and select any of five different numbering styles. Here is a sample ordered list:

```
<h3>Pickled Kumquats</h3>
Here's an easy way to make a delicious batch of pickled 'quats:
<ol>
   <li>Rinse 50 pounds of fresh kumquats
   <li>Bring eight gallons white vinegar to rolling boil
   <li>Add kumquats gradually, keeping vinegar boiling
   <li>Boil for one hour, or until kumquats are tender
   <li>Place in sealed jars and enjoy!
</ol>
```

This is rendered by Netscape as shown in Figure 8-2.

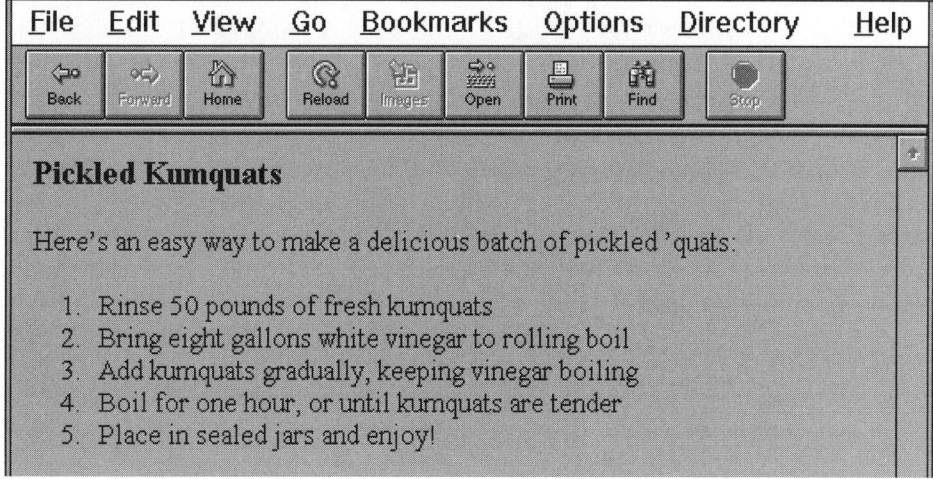

Figure 8-2. An ordered list

8.2.1.1 The start attribute

Normally, browsers automatically number ordered list items beginning with the Arabic numeral 1. The `start` attribute for the `<ol>` tag lets you change that beginning value. To start numbering a list at 5, for example:

```
<ol start=5>
  <li> This is item number 5.
  <li> This is number six!
  <li> And so forth...
</ol>
```

8.2.1.2 The type attribute

By default, browsers number ordered list items with a sequence of Arabic numerals. Besides being able to start the sequence at some number other than 1, you can use the `type` attribute with the `<ol>` tag to change the numbering style itself. With the `<ol>` tag, the `type` attribute may have a value of "A" for numbering with capital letters, "a" for numbering with lowercase letters, "I" for capital Roman numerals, "i" for lowercase Roman numerals, or "1" for common Arabic numerals. (See Table 8-1).

The `start` and `type` attribute extensions work in tandem. The `start` attribute sets the starting value of the item integer counter at the beginning of an ordered list. The `type` attribute sets the actual numbering style. For example, the following ordered list starts numbering items at 8, but because the style of

Table 8-1. HTML 3.2 type values for numbering ordered lists

Type Value	Generated Style	Sample Sequence
A	Capital letters	A, B, C, D
a	Lowercase letters	a, b, c, d
I	Capital Roman numerals	I, II, III, IV
i	Lowercase Roman numerals	i, ii, iii, iv
1	Arabic numerals	1, 2, 3, 4

numbering is set to i, the first number is the lowercase Roman numeral, "viii." Subsequent items are numbered with the same style, each value incremented by 1 as shown in this example:

```
<ol start=8 type="i">
  <li> This is the Roman number 8.
  <li> The numerals increment by 1.
  <li> And so forth...
</ol>
```

The results are shown in Figure 8-3.

Figure 8-3. The start and type attributes work in tandem

The type and value of individual items in a list can be different from the list as a whole, as described in 3.1.

8.2.1.3 Compact ordered lists

Like the unordered list, the ordered list in HTML has an optional `compact` attribute. When instructed to compact the ordered list, the browser may reduce the indentation, reduce the amount of space between the sequence numbers and the list items, or both. Some browsers cannot compact and so do nothing.

8.2.1.4 The style and class attributes

The `style` attribute for the `<ol>` tag creates an inline style for the elements enclosed by the tag, overriding any other style rule in effect. The `class` attribute lets you format the content according to a predefined class of the `<ol>` tag; its value is the name of that class. [`style` attribute, 9.1.1] [`class` attribute, 9.2.4].

8.3 *The <li> Tag*

It should be quite obvious to you by now that the `<li>` tag defines an item in a list. It's the universal tag for HTML list items in ordered (`<ol>`) and unordered (`<ul>`) lists, as we discuss above, and for directories (`<dir>`) and menus (`<menu>`), which we discuss in detail later in this chapter.

<li>

Function:
> Define an item within an ordered, unordered, directory, or menu list

Attributes:
> CLASS **N** **O**
> STYLE **N** **O**
> TYPE
> VALUE

End tag:
> </li>, usually omitted

Contains:
> *flow*

Used in:
> *list_content*

Because the end of a list element can always be inferred by the surrounding document structure, most authors omit the ending `</li>` tags for their list elements. That makes sense because it becomes easier to add, delete, and move elements around within a list. We recommend not using the `</li>` end tag.

Although universal in meaning, there are some differences and restrictions to the use of the `<li>` tag for each HTML list type. In unordered and ordered lists, what follows the `<li>` tag may be nearly anything, including other lists and multiple paragraphs. Typically, if it handles indentation at all, the browser successively indents nested list items, and the content in those items is justified to the innermost indented margin.

Directory and menu lists are another matter. They are lists of short items like a single word or simple text blurb and nothing else. Consequently, `<li>` items within `<dir>` and `<menu>` tags may not contain other lists or other block elements, including paragraphs, preformatted blocks, or forms.

Clean documents, fully compliant with the HTML standard, should not contain any text or other document item inside the unordered, ordered, directory, or menu lists that is not contained within an `<li>` tag. Most browsers are tolerant of violations to this rule, but then you can't hold the browser responsible for compliant rendering for exceptional cases, either.

8.3.1 Changing the Style and Sequence of Individual List Items

Just as you can change the bullet or numbering style for all of the items in an unordered or ordered list, you also can change the style for individual items within those lists. With ordered lists, you also can change the value of the item number. As you'll see, the combinations of changing style and numbering can lead to a variety of useful list structures, particularly when included with nested lists.

8.3.1.1 The type attribute

Acceptable values for the `type` attribute in the `<li>` tag are the same as the values for the appropriate list type: items within unordered lists may have their type set to `circle`, `square`, or `disc`, while items in an ordered list may have their type set to any of the values shown previously in Table 8-1. The change affects the current item and any subsequent items in the list.

There is no way to revert back to the list's default type once you have changed the type for a single item; you'll need to explicitly reset the type on the next item. Thus, to make a single item in a list different from the rest, you'll need to change two items: the actual item you want changed, and the next item, which must be changed back to the general list format.

Figure 8-4 shows the effect that changing the `type` for an individual item in an ordered list has on subsequent items, as rendered by Netscape from the following source:

```
<ol>
  <li type=A>Changing the numbering style
  <li type=a>Doesn't alter the order!
  <li> &lt;-- See? It's a "c"!
  <li type=I>Uppercase Roman numerals!
  <li type=i>Lowercase Roman numerals!
  <li type=1>Plain ol' numbers!
</ol>
```

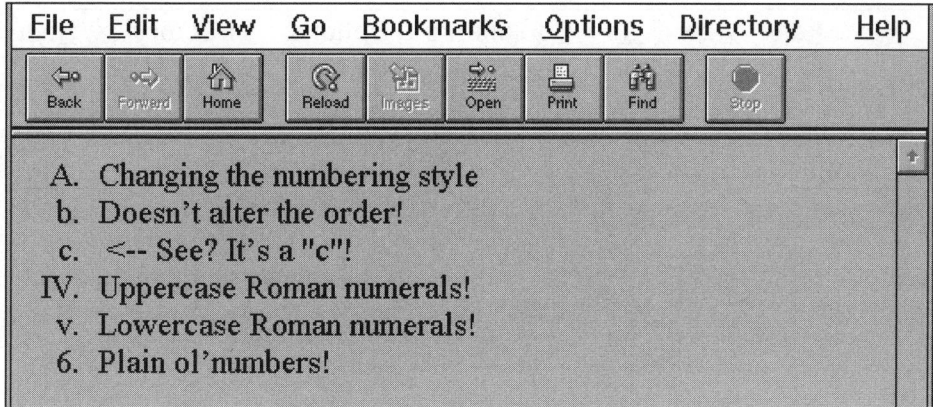

Figure 8-4. Changing the numbering style for each item in an ordered list

Notice how the `type` attribute changes the display style of the number, but not the value of the number itself.

8.3.1.2 The value attribute

The `value` attribute lets you change the number of a specific list item and the ones that follow it. Since the ordered list is the only HTML list with sequentially numbered items, the `value` attribute is only valid when used within an `<li>` tag inside an ordered list.

To change the current and subsequent numbers attached to each item in an ordered list, simply set the `value` attribute to any integer. For example, the following source uses the `value` attribute to jump the numbering on items in an ordered list:

```
<ol>
  <li>Item number 1
  <li>And the second
  <li value=9> Jump to number 9
  <li>And continue with 10...
</ol>
```

The results are shown as rendered by Netscape in Figure 8-5.

8.3.1.3 The style and class attributes

The `style` attribute for the `<li>` tag creates an inline style for the elements enclosed by the tag, overriding any other style rule in effect. The `class` attribute lets you format the content according to a predefined class of the `<li>` tag; its value is the name of that class. [`style` attribute, 9.1.1] [`class` attribute, 9.2.4]

Figure 8-5. The value attribute lets you change individual item numbers in an ordered list

8.4 Nesting Lists

Except inside directories or menus, lists nested inside other lists are fine. Menu and directory lists can be embedded within other lists.

Indents for each nested list are cumulative, so take care not to nest lists too much; the list contents could quickly turn into a thin ribbon of text flush against the right edge of the browser document window.

8.4.1 Nested Unordered Lists

The items in each nested unordered list may be preceded by a different bullet character at the discretion of the browser. For example, Internet Explorer Version 2 for the Macintosh uses an alternating series of hollow, solid circular, and square bullets for the various nests in the following source HTML text as shown in Figure 8-6:

```
<ul>
  <li>Morning Kumquat Delicacies
  <ul>
    <li>Hot Dishes
    <ul>
      <li>Kumquat omelet
      <li>Kumquat waffles
      <ul>
        <li>Country style
        <li>Belgian
      </ul>
      <li>Kumquats and toast
    </ul>
    <li>Cold Dishes
    <ul>
      <li>Kumquats and cornflakes
```

```
      <li>Pickled Kumquats
      <li>Diced Kumquats
    </ul>
  </ul>
</ul>
```

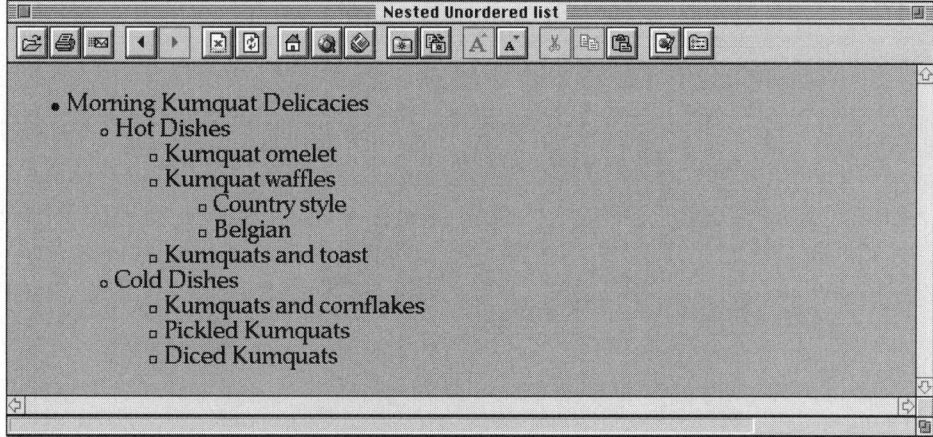

Figure 8-6. Bullets change for nested unordered list items

You can change the bullet style for each unordered list and even individual list items (see the `type` attribute discussion earlier in this chapter), but the repertoire of bullets is limited. For example, Internet Explorer for Windows 95 uses a solid disc regardless of the nesting level.

8.4.2 Nested Ordered Lists

By default, browsers number the items in ordered lists beginning with the Arabic numeral 1, nested or not. It would be great if the HTML standard numbered nested ordered lists in some rational, consecutive manner. For example, the items in the second nest of the third main ordered list might be successively numbered "3.2.1," "3.2.2," "3.2.3," and so on.

With the `type` and `value` attributes, however, you do have a lot more latitude in how you create nested ordered lists. An excellent example is the traditional style for outlining, which uses the many different ways of numbering items offered by the `type` attribute (see Figure 8-7):

```
<ol type=A>
  <li>A History of Kumquats
  <ol type=1>
    <li>Early History
    <ol type=a>
      <li>The Fossil Record
      <li>Kumquats: The Missing Link?
    </ol>
```

```
    <li>Mayan Use of Kumquats
    <li>Kumquats in the New World
  </ol>
  <li>Future Use of Kumquats
</ol>
```

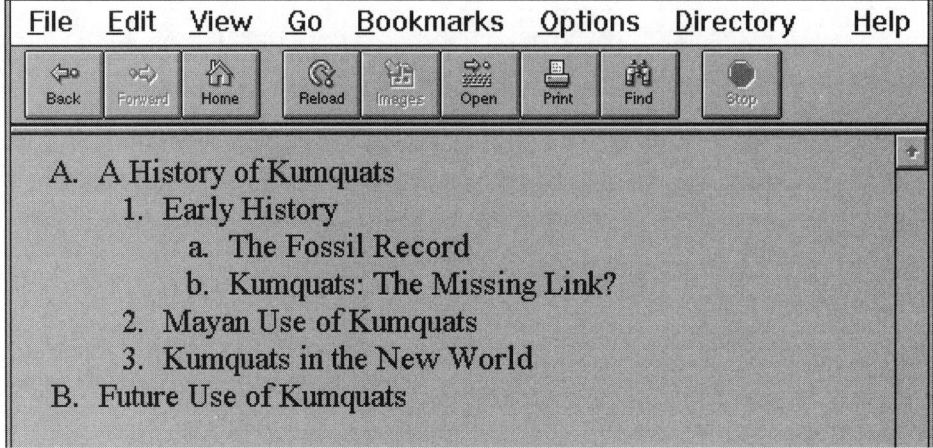

Figure 8-7. The type attribute lets you do traditional outlining with ordered lists

8.5 Directory Lists

The directory list is a specialized form of the unordered list. [`<ul>`, 8.1.1]

8.5.1 The <dir> Tag

The designers of HTML originally dedicated the `<dir>` tag for displaying lists of files. As such, the browser, if it treats `<dir>` and `<ul>` differently at all (most don't), expects the various list elements to be quite short, possibly no longer than 20 characters or so. Some browsers display the elements in a multicolumn format and may not use a leading bullet.

As with the unordered list, define directory list items with the `<li>` tag. When used within a directory list, however, the `<li>` tag may not contain any block element, including paragraphs, other lists, preformatted text, or forms.

The following example puts the directory tag to its traditional task of presenting a list of filenames:

```
The distribution tape has the following files on it:
<dir>
  <li><code>README</code>
  <li><code>Makefile</code>
```

<dir>

Function:

Define a directory list

Attributes:

CLASS 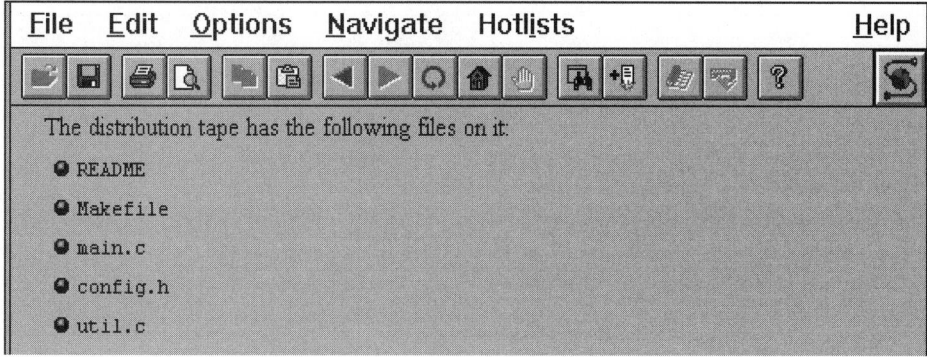 🅝 🅞
COMPACT
STYLE 🅝 🅞

End tag:

</dir>, never omitted

Contains:

list_content

Used in:

block

```
    <li><code>main.c</code>
    <li><code>config.h</code>
    <li><code>util.c</code>
  </dir>
```

Notice that we use the `<code>` tag to ensure that the filenames would be rendered in an appropriate manner (see Figure 8-8).

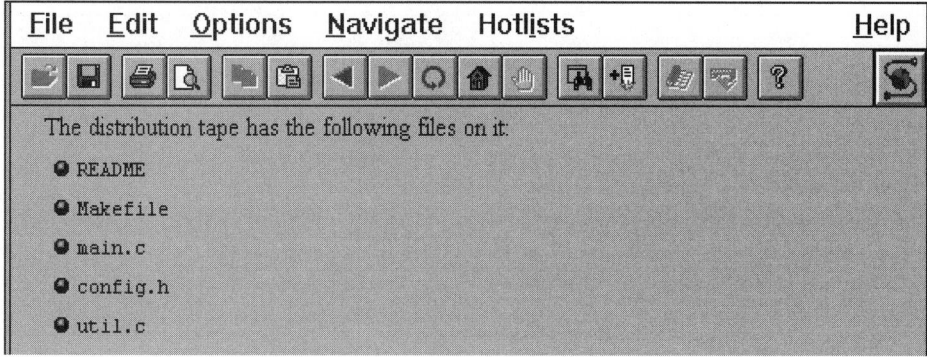

Figure 8-8. An example <dir> list

Like the other formatting tags we've seen so far, the `<dir>` tag has an optional `compact` attribute for producing an even more reduced list display, even though virtually none of the browsers is either willing or capable of compacting directory lists.

You can change the style used to bullet the `<dir>` list items with the `type` attribute extension and the values `circle`, `square`, or `disc`. This behavior is identical to the `type` attribute in an unordered list.

8.5.1.1 *The style and class attributes*

The `style` attribute for the `<dir>` tag creates an inline style for the elements enclosed by the tag, overriding any other style rule in effect. The `class` attribute lets you format the content according to a predefined class of the `<dir>` tag; its value is the name of that class. [`style` attribute, 9.1.1] [`class` attribute, 9.2.4]

8.6 Menu Lists

The HTML menu list is yet another specialized form of the unordered list.

8.6.1 The <menu> Tag

The `<menu>` tag displays a list of short choices to the reader, such as a menu of links to other documents. The browser may use a special (typically more compact) representation of items in a menu list compared with the general unordered list, or even use some sort of graphical pull-down menu to implement the menu list. If the list items are short enough, the browser may even display them in a multicolumn format, and may not append a leading bullet with each list item.

<menu>

Function:
    Define a menu list
Attributes:
    CLASS **N** **O**
    COMPACT
    STYLE **N** **O**
    TYPE
End tag:
    </menu>, never omitted
Contains:
    list_content
Used in:
    block

Like an unordered list, define the menu list items with the `<li>` tag. When used within a menu list, however, the `<li>` tag may not contain any block element, including paragraphs, other lists, preformatted text, or forms.

Compare the source text below and the Mosaic display (Figure 8-9) with the directory (Figure 8-8) and unordered (Figure 8-1) list displays we presented earlier in this chapter.

```
<p>
Some popular kumquat recipes include:
<menu>
  <li>Pickled Kumquats
  <li>'Quats and 'Kraut (a holiday favorite!)
  <li>'Quatshakes
</menu>
There are many more to please every palate!
```

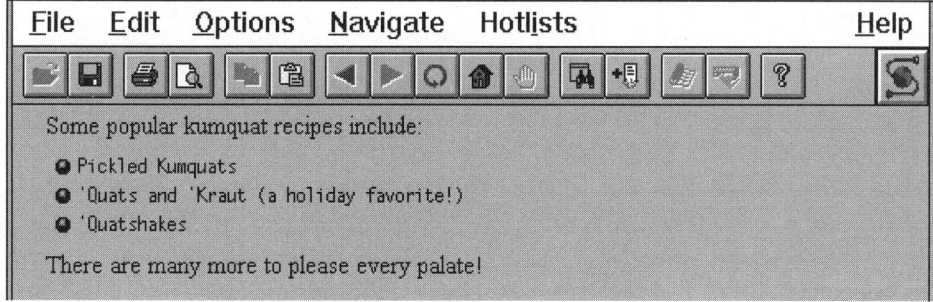

Figure 8-9. Sample <menu> list

The <menu> tag also has the `compact` attribute to produce an even more reduced list presentation, although in practice, few browsers are willing or able to implement the compacted menu list display. Netscape, in fact, doesn't distinguish between a menu and an unordered list.

You can change the style of the bullet that precedes the <menu> list items with the `type` attribute extension and the values `circle`, `square`, or `disc`. This behavior is identical to that of the `type` attribute in an unordered list.

8.6.1.1 The style and class attributes

The `style` attribute for the <menu> tag creates an inline style for the elements enclosed by the tag, overriding any other style rule in effect. The `class` attribute lets you format the content according to a predefined class of the <menu> tag; its value is the name of that class. [`style` attribute, 9.1.1] [`class` attribute, 9.2.4].

8.7 Definition Lists

HTML also supports a list style entirely different from the ordered, unordered, menu, and directory lists we've discussed so far: definition lists. Like the entries you find in a dictionary or encyclopedia, complete with text, pictures, and other multimedia elements, the definition list is the ideal way to present a glossary, list of terms, or other name/value lists in HTML.

8.7.1 The <dl> Tag

The definition list is enclosed by the <dl> and </dl> tags. Within those tags, each item in a definition list is composed of two parts: a term followed by its definition or explanation. Instead of <li>, each item name in a <dl> list is marked with the <dt> tag, followed by the item's definition or explanation as marked by the <dd> tag.

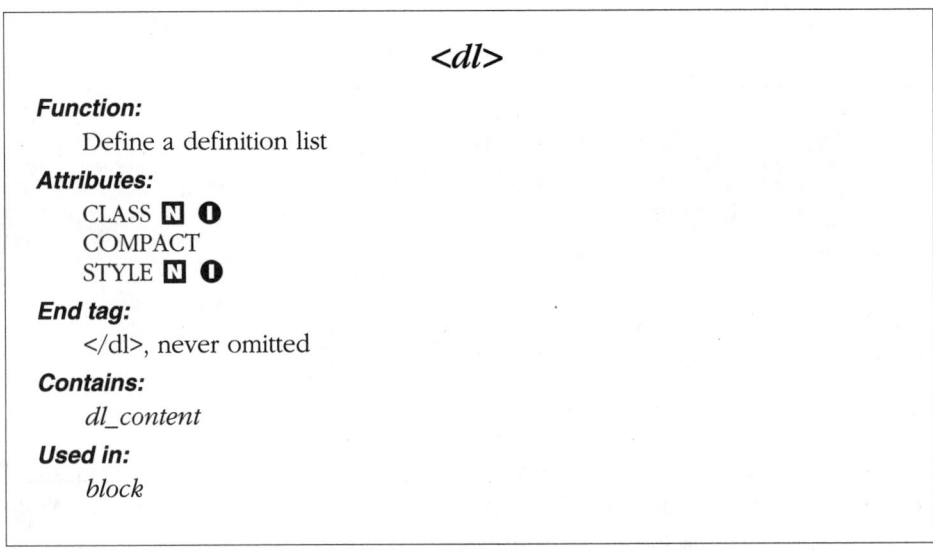

Browsers typically render the item or term name at the left margin and render the definition or explanation below it and indented. If the definition terms are very short (typically less than three characters), the browser may choose to place the first portion of the definition on the same line as the term. See how the source HTML definition list below gets displayed by Netscape in Figure 8-10.

```
<h3>Common Kumquat Parasites</h3>
<dl>
  <dt>Leaf mites
  <dd>The leaf mite will ravage the Kumquat tree, stripping it
      of any and all vegetation.
  <dt>Trunk dropsy
  <dd>This microscopic larvae of the common opossum
      chigger will consume the structural elements of the
      tree trunk, causing it to collapse inward.
</dl>
```

As with other list types, you can add more space between the list items by inserting paragraph <p> tags between them or by defining a spacious style for the <li> tag.

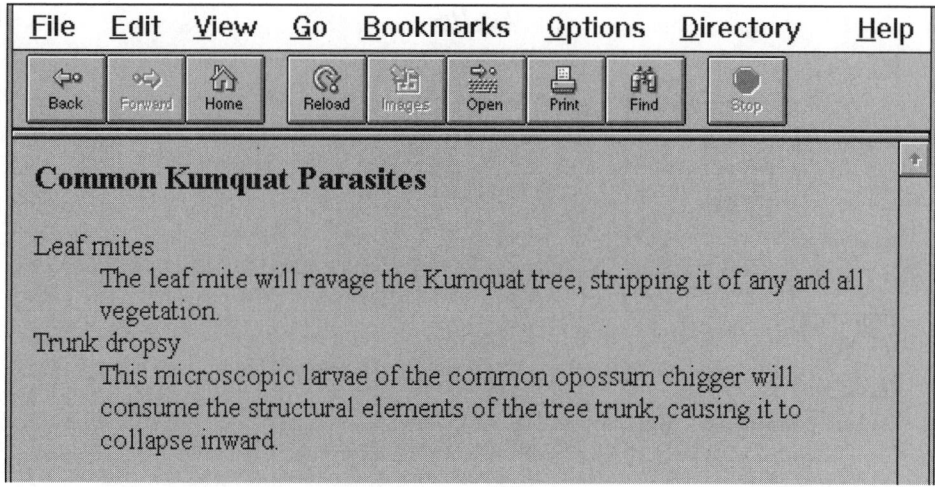

Figure 8-10. A definition list as presented by Netscape

8.7.1.1 More compact definition lists

The `<dl>` tag also has the `compact` attribute, advising the browser to make the list presentation as small as possible. The browser may choose to reduce the inter-item spacing, shift the definition to the left margin instead of indenting, or reduce the size of the type used to present the list. Whether or not a browser actually does any of these things is up to its manufacturer. Few do.

8.7.1.2 The style and class attributes

The `style` attribute for the `<dl>` tag creates an inline style for the elements enclosed by the tag, overriding any other style rule in effect. The `class` attribute lets you format the content according to a predefined class of the `<dl>` tag; its value is the name of that class. [`style` attribute, 9.1.1] [`class` attribute, 9.2.4].

8.7.2 The <dt> Tag

This `<dt>` tag defines the term component of a definition list. It is only valid when used within a definition `<dl>` list preceding the term or item, before the `<dd>` tag and the term's definition or explanation.

Traditionally, the definition term that follows the `<dt>` tag is short and sweet—a word or few. Technically, it can be any length. If long, the browser may exercise the option of extending the item beyond the display window, or wrap it onto the next line where the definition begins.

Since the end of the `<dt>` tag immediately precedes the start of the matching `<dd>` tag, it is unambiguous and so not required.

\<dt>

Function:
Define a definition list term

Attributes:
CLASS **N** **O**
STYLE **N** **O**

End tag:
\</dt>, always omitted

Contains:
text

Used in:
dl_content

8.7.2.1 Formatting text with \<dt>

In practice, browsers are either too lenient or too dumb to enforce the HTML rules, so some tricky HTML authors misuse the `<dt>` tag to shift the left margin right and left, respectively, for fancy text displays. (Remember, tab characters and leading spaces don't usually work with regular text.) We don't condone violating the HTML standard and caution you once again about tricked-up documents. Use style sheets instead.

8.7.2.2 The style and class attributes

The `style` attribute for the `<dt>` tag creates an inline style for the elements enclosed by the tag, overriding any other style rule in effect. The `class` attribute lets you format the content according to a predefined class of the `<dt>` tag; its value is the name of that class. [`style` attribute, 9.1.1] [`class` attribute, 9.2.4]

8.7.3 The \<dd> Tag

The `<dd>` tag marks the start of the definition portion of an item in a definition list. According to the HTML standard, `<dd>` belongs only inside a definition `<dl>` list, immediately following the `<dt>` tag and term and preceding the definition or explanation.

The content that follows the `<dd>` tag may be any HTML construct, including other lists, block text, and multimedia elements. Although treating it otherwise identically as conventional content, browsers typically indent definition list `<dd>` definitions. And since the start of another term and definition (`<dt>`) or the

---

<dd>

Function:
Define a definition list term

Attributes:
CLASS **N O**
STYLE **N O**

End tag:
</dd>, always omitted

Contains:
flow

Used in:
dl_content

---

required end tag of the definition (</dl>) unambiguously terminates the preceding definition, the </dd> tag is not needed and its absence makes your source text more readable.

8.7.3.1 The style and class attributes

The style attribute for the <dd> tag creates an inline style for the elements enclosed by the tag, overriding any other style rule in effect. The class attribute lets you format the content according to a predefined class of the <dd> tag; its value is the name of that class. [style attribute, 9.1.1] [class attribute, 9.2.4].

8.8 Appropriate List Usage

In general, use unordered lists for:

- Hotlists and other link collections
- Short, nonsequenced groups of text
- Emphasizing the high points of a presentation

In general, use ordered lists for:

- Tables of content
- Instruction sequences
- Sets of sequential sections of text
- Assigning numbers to short phrases that can be referenced elsewhere

In general, use definition lists for:

- Glossaries

- Custom bullets (make the item after the `<dt>` tag an icon-sized bullet image)

- Any list of name/value pairs

9

Cascading
Style Sheets

Style sheets are the way publishing professionals manage the overall "look" of their publications—backgrounds, fonts, colors, and so on—from a single page to huge collections of documents. Most desktop publishing software supports style sheets, as do the popular word processors. All desktop publishers and graphic designers worth their salt are out there making web pages. So the cry-to-arms was inevitable: "Whaddaya mean HTML has no style sheets?!"

From its earliest origins, HTML focused on content over style. Authors are encouraged to worry about providing high quality information, and leave it to the browser to worry about presentation. We strongly urge you, too—as we do throughout this book—to adopt that philosophy in your HTML documents, especially those destined for the World Wide Web. Don't mistake style for substance.

However, while use of the HTML `<font>` tag and related attributes like `color` produce acute presentation effects, style sheets, when judiciously applied, bring consistency and order to whole document collections, as well as to individual documents. Remember, too, that presentation is for the benefit of the reader. Even the original designers of HTML understood the interplay between style and readability. For instance, readers can quickly identify section heads in a document when they are enclosed in header tags like `<h2>`, which the modern browsers present in large and often bold type. Style sheets extend that presentation with several additional effects, including colors and a wider selection of fonts, so that readers can even better distinguish elements of your document. But most importantly, style sheets let the HTML author control the presentation attributes for all the tags in a document—for a single document or a whole collection of many documents, and from a single master style sheet.

In early 1996, the World Wide Web Consortium put together a draft proposal defining Cascading Style Sheets (CSS) for HTML. This draft proposal quickly matured into a recommended standard, which the commercial browser manufacturers were quick to exploit. Internet Explorer 3.0, introduced in the summer of 1996, implements a subset of the W3C standard. Netscape Navigator has broader support for style sheets in Version 4.0, which was introduced in 1997. Style is fast achieving parity with content on the World Wide Web.

In keeping with our philosophy of favoring real implementations over standards, we'll start by documenting style sheets as they currently work in the real world. At this writing, style sheets were partially supported by Internet Explorer 3.0 and the third pre-release of Netscape 4.0. We know that browser support of style sheets will change faster than we can reprint this book, so we have created a separate "compliance document" that you can use to determine how style sheets are implemented by the latest releases of the browsers. You can find this document at *http://www.ora.com/info/html/*. The information in this document should always be considered more timely and accurate than the information in this book.

Since we realize that eventual compliance with the W3C standard is likely, we'll cover all the components of the standard in this chapter, even if they are not yet supported by any browser. As always, we'll denote clearly what is real, what is proposed, and what is actually supported.

9.1 The Elements of Styles

At the simplest level, a style is nothing more than a rule that tells the browser how to display a particular HTML tag. Each tag has a number of properties associated with it, whose values define how that tag is rendered by the browser. A rule defines a specific value for one or more properties of a tag. For example, most tags have a `color` property, the value of which defines the color used to display that tag. Other properties include font attributes, line spacing, margins, borders, and the like, which we describe in detail later in this chapter.

There are three ways to attach a style to a tag: inline styles, document-level styles, and external style sheets. You may use one or more style types in your documents. The browser either merges the style definitions from each style or redefines the style characteristic for a tag's contents. Styles from these various sources are applied to your document, combining and defining style properties that cascade from external style sheets through local document styles, ending with inline styles. This cascade of properties and style rules gives rise to the standard's name: Cascading Style Sheets.

We cover the syntactic basics of the three style sheet techniques here. We delve more deeply into the appropriate use of inline, document-level, and external style sheets at the end of this chapter.

9.1.1 Inline Styles: The style Attribute

The inline style is the simplest way to attach a style to a tag—just include a `style` attribute with the tag along with a list of properties and their values. The browser uses those style properties to render the contents of just this instance of the tag.

For instance, the following style tells the browser to display the level-one header text, "I'm so bluuuuoooo!", not only in the `<h1>` tag style characteristic of the browser, but also in the color blue and italicized (if the browser is capable):

```
<h1 style="color: blue; font-style: italic">I'm so bluuuuoooo!</h1>
```

This type of style definition is called "inline" because it occurs with the tag as it appears in the document. The scope of the style covers the contents of that tag only. Since inline styles are sprinkled throughout your document, they can be difficult to maintain. Use the `style` attribute sparingly and only in those rare circumstances when you cannot achieve the same effects otherwise.

9.1.2 Document-Level Style Sheets

The real power of style sheets dawns when you place a list of presentation rules within the head of an HTML document. Enclosed within their own `<style>` and `</style>` end tags, so-called "document-level" style sheets affect all the same tags within that document, except for tags that contain an overriding inline `style` attribute.

\<style\>

Function:
> Defines a document-level style sheet

Attributes:
> TYPE

End tag:
> </style>; rarely omitted

Contains:
> *styles*

Used in:
> *head_content*

The `<style>` tag must appear within the `<head>` of a document. Everything between the `<style>` and `</style>` tags is considered part of the style rules to be applied to the document. To be perfectly correct, the content of the `<style>` tag is not HTML and is not bound by the normal rules for HTML content. The `<style>` tag, in effect, lets you insert foreign content into your HTML document that the browser uses to format your tags.

The `<style>` tag has just one attribute, `type`. It defines the types of styles you are including within the tag. Cascading style sheets always carry the type `text/css`; JavaScript style sheets use the type `text/javascript`. You may omit the `type` attribute and hope the browser will figure out the kind of styles you are using. We prefer to include the `type` attribute so that there is no opportunity for confusion. [JavaScript style sheets, 13.4]

For example, a style-conscious browser will display the contents of all `<h1>` tags as blue, italic text in a document that has the following document-level style sheet definition in its head:

```
<head>
<title>All True Blue</title>
<style type="text/css">
  <!--
  /* make all H1 headers blue */
  H1: {color: blue; font-style: italic}
  -->
</style>
</head>
<body>
<h1>I'm so bluuuuoooo!</h1>
...
<h1>I am ba-loooooo, tooooo!<h1>
```

9.1.3 External Style Sheets

You may also place style definitions, like our document-level style sheet example for `<h1>` tags, in a text file with the MIME type of `text/css` and import this "external" style sheet into your HTML documents. Because an external style sheet is a file separate from the HTML document and is loaded by the browser over the network, you can store it anywhere, reuse it often, and even use others' style sheets. But most importantly, external style sheets give you the power to influence the display styles not only of all related tags in a single documents, but for an entire collection of documents.

For example, suppose we create a file named **gen_styles.css** containing the style rule:

```
H1 {color: blue; font-style: italic}
```

For each and every one of our HTML documents in our collections, we can tell the browser to read the contents of the **gen_styles.css** file, which in turn will color all the **<h1>** tag contents blue and render the text in italic. Of course, that will be true only if the user's machine is capable of these style tricks, they are using a style-conscious browser, and the style isn't overridden by a document-level or inline style definition.

You can load external style sheets into your HTML document in two different ways: linked or imported.

9.1.3.1 Linked external style sheets

One way to load an external style sheet is to use the **<link>** tag:

```
<head>
<title>Style linked</title>
<link rel=stylesheet type="text/css"
      href="http://www.kumquats.com/styles/gen_styles.css"
      title="The blues">
</head>
<body>
<h1>I'm so bluuuuoooo!</h1>
...
<h1> I am ba-loooooo, tooooo!<h1>
```

Recall that the **<link>** tag creates a relationship between the current document and some other document on the Web. In the example, we tell the browser that the document named in the **href** attribute is a **stylesheet**, and that its contents conform to the CSS standard, as indicated by the **type** attribute. We also provide a **title** for the style sheet, making it available for later reference by the browser. [<link>, 7.7.2]

The **<link>** tag must appear in the **<head>** of a document. The URL of the style sheet may be absolute or relative to the document's base URL. The type may also be **text/javascript**, indicating (for Netscape only) that the style rules are written in JavaScript instead of the CSS syntax. [JavaScript style sheets, 13.4]

9.1.3.2 Imported external style sheets

The second technique for loading an external style sheet imports the files with a special command within the **<style>** tag:

```
<head>
<title>Imported style sheet</title>
<style>
  <!--
    @import url(http://www.kumquats.com/styles/gen_styles.css);
    @import url(http://www.kumquats.com/styles/spec_styles.css);
```

```
    BODY: {background: url(backgrounds/marble.gif)}
  -->
</style>
</head>
```

The `@import` command expects a single URL parameter that names the network path to the external style sheet. The `url` keyword, parentheses, and trailing semicolon are all required elements of the `@import` command. The URL may be absolute or relative to the document's base URL. The `@import` command must appear before any conventional style rules, either in the `<style>` tag or in an external style sheet. Otherwise, the browser ignores the preceding style definitions. This ordering also means that subsequent style rules can override rules in the imported sheet, and indeed they do. [URL property values, 9.3.1.4]

The `@import` command can appear in a document-level style definition or even in another external style sheet, letting you create nested style sheets.

9.1.4 Linked Versus Imported Style Sheets

At first glance, it may appear that linked and imported style sheets are equivalent, using different syntax for the same functionality. This is true if you use just one `<link>` tag in your document. However, special rules come into play if you include two or more `<link>` tags within a single document.

With one `<link>` tag, the browser loads the styles in the referenced style sheet and formats the document accordingly, with any document-level and inline styles overriding the external definitions. With two or more `<link>` tags, the browser presents the user with a list of all the `<link>`ed style sheets. The user can then select one of the sheets, which is used to format the document. The other `<link>`ed style sheets are ignored.

On the other hand, the style-conscious browser merges, as opposed to separating, multiple `@import`ed style sheets to form a single set of style rules for your document. The last imported style sheet takes precedence if there are duplicate definitions among the style sheets.

Hence, if `gen_styles.css` in our example (9.1.3.2) tells the browser to make `<h1>` contents blue and italic, and then `spec_styles.css` tells the browser to make `<h1>` text red, then the `<h1>` tag contents will appear red and italic. And if we later define another color, say yellow, for `<h1>` tags in a document-level style definition, the `<h1>` tags will all be yellow, and italic. Cascading effects. See?

Imported styles override linked external styles, just as document-level and inline styles override external style definitions. To bring this all together, consider the example:

```
<html>
<head>
<link rel=stylesheet href=sheet1.css type=text/css>
<link rel=stylesheet href=sheet2.css type=text/css>
<style>
<!--
  @import url(sheet3.css);
  @import url(sheet4.css);
-->
</style>
</head>
```

Using the CSS model, the browser will prompt the user to choose between `sheet1.css` and `sheet2.css`. It will then load the selected sheet, followed by `sheet3.css` and `sheet4.css`. Duplicate styles defined in `sheet3.css` or `sheet4.css` and in any inline styles will override styles defined in the selected sheet.

9.1.5 Limitations of Current Browsers

Referencing a style sheet with the `<link>` tag currently is the only way to apply an external style sheet to a document. Netscape 4.0 ignores the `@import` command but continues to process other style rules within the `<style>` tag. Internet Explorer 3 treats `@import` as an error. This means that not only does an `@import`ed external style sheet not take effect, but none of the styles following the `@import` command take effect, either. And, worse, Internet Explorer 3 ignores any and all document-level style rules if you `<link>` an external one, regardless of whether any of the external rules relate to the same tags or not.

Neither Netscape or Internet Explorer support multiple `<link>`ed style sheets as proposed by the CSS standard. Instead, Netscape loads all the `<link>`ed style sheets, with rules in later sheets possibly overriding rules in earlier sheets. Internet Explorer only loads the first `<link>`ed sheet and ignores the remaining sheets.

We hope the standard will someday prevail so that style sheets, already mystifying to most, will become that much less confusing.

9.1.6 Style Comments

Comments are welcome inside the `<style>` tag and in external style sheets, but don't use a standard HTML comment. Rather, enclose style comments beginning with the sequence `/*` and ending with `*/`, as we did in the example above. (Those of you who are familiar with the C programming language will recognize these comment markings.) Use this comment syntax for both document-level and external style sheets. Comments may not be nested.

We recommend documenting your styles whenever possible, especially in external style sheets. Whenever the possibility exists that your styles may be used by other authors, comments make it much easier to understand your styles.

9.1.7 Handling Style-Less Browsers

In our document-level style examples above, you've probably noticed that we placed the style definition inside an HTML comment tag (`<!--` and `-->`). That's because although the older, style-less browsers will ignore the `<style>` tag itself, they will display the style definitions. Needless to say, your documents will not go over well when the first half of the display contains all your style rules.

The newer, style-conscious browsers ignore HTML comments within a `<style>` tag. Since style-less browsers will be with us for some time to come, make sure you always place your document-level style rules inside HTML comments. HTML comments should not be used in external style sheets.

9.1.8 Style Precedence

You may import more than one external style sheet and combine them with document-level and inline style effects in many different ways. Their effects cascade (hence, the name, of course). You may specify the font type for our example `<h1>` tag, for instance, in an external style definition, whereas its color may come from a document-level style sheet.

Style sheet effects are not cumulative, however: of the many styles which may define different values for the same property—colors for the contents of our example tag, for instance—the one that takes precedence can be found by following these rules, in order:

- Sort by origin. A style defined "closer" to a tag takes precedence over a more "distant" style. So an inline style takes precedence over a document-level style, which takes precedence over the effects of an external style.

- If more than one applicable style exists, sort by class. Properties defined as a class of a tag (see 9.2.4) take precedence over a property defined for the tag in general.

- If multiple styles still exist, sort by specificity. The properties for a more specific contextual style (see 9.2.3) take precedence over properties defined for a less specific context.

- If multiple styles still exist, sort by order. The property specified later takes precedence. Internet Explorer defies this rule, honoring only the first definition of a rule and ignoring any subsequent ones.

This bug in Internet Explorer will drive authors to distraction. In the following example, Netscape will set the color of the `<h1>` tag contents green, while Internet Explorer 3 will use red:

```
<head>
<style>
<!--
  H1 {color: blue; color: red}
  H1 {color: green}
-->
</style>
```

Our advice: write styles that conform to the CSS standard. Eventually, Internet Explorer will get fixed, and in the meantime, your documents will look good in Netscape, which is in use by more users anyway.

The relationship between style properties and conventional tag attributes is almost impossible to predict. Style sheet–dictated background and foreground colors— whether defined externally, at the document level, or inline—override the various `color` attributes that may appear within a tag. But the `align` attribute of an inline image usually takes precedence over a style-dictated alignment.

There is an overwhelming myriad of style and tag presentation-attribute combinations. You need a crystal ball to predict which combination wins and which loses the precedence battle. The rules of redundancy and style vs. attribute precedence are not clearly elucidated in the W3C CSS standard, nor is there a clear pattern of precedence implemented in the style-conscious browsers. This is particularly unfortunate since there will be an extended period, perhaps several years long, in which users may or may not use a styles-conscious browser. HTML authors will have to implement both styles and non-style presentation controls to achieve the same effects.

Nonetheless, our recommendation is to run—as fast as you can—away from one-shot, inline, localized kinds of presentation effects like those afforded by the `<font>` tag and `color` attribute. They have served their temporary purpose; it's now time to bring consistency (without the pain!) back into your document presentation. Use styles. It's the HTML way.

9.2 Style Syntax

The syntax of a style, as you may have gleaned from our previous examples, is fairly straightforward.

9.2.1 The Basics

A style rule is made up of at least three basic parts: a tag *selector*, which identifies the name of the tag that the style rule affects, followed by a curly brace ({}) enclosed, semicolon-separated list of one or more style `property:value` declaration pairs:

```
tag-selector {property1:value1; property2:value1 value2 value3; ...}
```

Properties require at least one value, but may include two or more values. Separate multiple values with a space, as is done for the three values that define `property2` in the example. Some properties require that multiple values be separated with commas.

Style-conscious browsers ignore letter case in any element of a rule. Hence, `H1` and `h1` are the same selector, and `COLOR`, `color`, `ColOR`, and `cOLor` are equivalent properties. Convention dictates, however, that tag names be in all capitals, and that you write properties and values in lowercase. We'll abide by those conventions throughout this book.

Any valid HTML tag name (a tag minus its enclosing "<" and ">" characters and attributes) can be a selector. You may include more than one tag name in the list of selectors, as we explain in the following sections.

9.2.2 Multiple Selectors

When separated by commas, all the tags named in the selector list get affected by the property values in the style rule. This can make life very easy for the HTML author. For instance:

```
H1, H2, H3, H4, H5, H6 {text-align: center}
```

does exactly the same thing as:

```
H1 {text-align: center}
H2 {text-align: center}
H3 {text-align: center}
H4 {text-align: center}
H5 {text-align: center}
H6 {text-align: center}
```

Both styles tell the browser to center the contents of the header tag levels 1–6. Clearly, the first version is easier to type, understand, and modify. And it takes less time and fewer resources to transmit across a network, as well.

9.2.3 Contextual Selectors

Normally, the style-conscious browser applies styles to the tags wherever they appear in your document, without regard to context. However, the CSS standard does define a way to have a style applied only when a tag occurs within a certain context within a document, such as when it is nested within other tags.

To create a contextual selector, list the tags in the order in which they should be nested in your document, outermost tag first. When that nesting order is encountered by the browser, the style properties will be applied to the last tag in the list.

For example, here's how you might use contextual styles to define the classic numbering sequence used for outlines: capital letters for the outer level, uppercase Roman numerals for the next level, lowercase letters for the next, and Arabic numerals for the innermost level:

```
OL LI {list-style: upper-alpha}
OL OL LI {list-style: upper-roman}
OL OL OL LI {list-style: lower-alpha}
OL OL OL OL LI {list-style: decimal}
```

According to the example style sheet, when the style-conscious browser encounters the `<li>` tag nested within one `<ol>` tag, it uses the **upper-alpha** value for the `list-style` property of the `<li>` tag. When it sees an `<li>` tag nested within two `<ol>` tags, the same browser will use the **upper-roman list-style**. Nest an `<li>` tag within three and four `<ol>` tags, and you'll see the **lower-alpha** and **decimal list-style** used, respectively.

Similarly, you may impose a specific style on tags related only by context. For instance, this contextual style definition will color the emphasis tag's (`<em>`) contents red only when it appears inside a level-one header tag (`<h1>`), not elsewhere in the document:

```
H1 EM {color: red}
```

If there is a potential ambiguity between two contextual styles, the more specific context prevails. Like individual tags, you may also have several contextual selectors mixed with individual selectors, each and all separated by commas, sharing the same list of style declarations. For example,

```
H1 EM, P STRONG, ADDRESS {color: red}
```

means that you'll see red whenever the `<em>` tag appears within an `<h1>` tag, or when the `<strong>` tag appears within a `<p>` tag, and for the contents of the `<address>` tag.

The nesting need not be exact to match the rule. For example, if you nest the `<strong>` tag within a `<ul>` tag within a `<p>` tag, you'll still match the rule for P STRONG that we defined above. If a particular nesting matches several style rules, the most specific rule is used. For example, if you defined two contextual selectors:

```
P STRONG {color: red}
P UL STRONG {color: blue}
```

and use the sequence `<p><ul><strong>` in your document, the second, more specific rule applies, coloring the contents of the `<strong>` tag blue.

Contextual selectors are supported by Netscape 4.0, but not by Internet Explorer 3.0. In fact, Internet Explorer 3.0 considers contextual selectors an error and ignores any subsequent style definitions.

9.2.4 Style Classes

There is one more feature of style sheets that we haven't mentioned yet: classes. Classes let you create, at the document level or in an external style sheet, several different styles for a single tag, each distinguished by a class name. To apply the style class, you name it as the value of the `class` attribute in the tag.

9.2.4.1 Regular classes

In a technical paper you might want to define one paragraph style for the abstract, another for equations, and a third for centered quotations. None of the paragraph tags may have an explicit context in the HTML document so you could distinguish it from the others. Rather, you may define each as a different style class:

```
<style>
<!--
P.abstract {font-style: italic;
            left-margin: 0.5cm;
            right-margin: 0.5cm}
P.equation {font-family: Symbol;
            text-align: center}
H1, P.centered {text-align: center;
               left-margin: 0.5cm;
               right-margin: 0.5cm}
-->
<style>
```

Notice first in the example that defining a class is simply a matter of appending a period-separated class name as a suffix to the tag name as the selector in a style rule. The class name can be any sequence of letters, numbers, and hyphens, but must begin with a letter.[*] And classes, like all selectors, may be included with other selectors, separated by commas, as in the third example. The only restriction on classes is that they cannot be nested: `P.equation.centered` is not allowed, for example.

Accordingly, the first rule in the example creates a class of paragraph styles named "abstract" whose text will be italic and indented from the left and right

---

[*] Due to its support of JavaScript style sheets, Netscape cannot handle class names that happen to match JavaScript keywords. The class "abstract," for instance, generates an error in Netscape.

margins by a half-centimeter. Similarly, the second paragraph style class "equation," instructs the browser to center the text and to use the Symbol typeface to display the text. The last style rule creates a style with centered text and half-centimeter margins, applying this style to all level-one headers as well as creating a class of the `<p>` tag named `centered` with that style.

To use a particular class of a tag, you add the `class` attribute to the tag, as in this example:

```
<p class=abstract>
This is the abstract paragraph.  See how the margins are indented?
</p>
<h3>The equation paragraph follows</h3>
<p class=equation>
a = b + 1
</p>
<p class=centered>
This paragraph's text should be centered.
</p>
```

For each paragraph, the value of the `class` attribute is the name of the class to be used for that tag.

9.2.4.2 Generic classes

You may also define a class without associating it with a particular tag, and then apply that class selectively through your documents for a variety of tags. For example,

```
.italic {font-style: italic}
```

creates a generic class named `italic`. To use it, simply include its name with the `class` attribute. So, for instance, use `<p class=italic>` or `<pre class=italic>` to create an italic paragraph or preformatted text block.

Generic classes are quite handy and make it easy to apply a particular style to a broad range of tags. Generic classes are currently supported only by Netscape 4.0.

9.2.4.3 Style pseudo-classes

In addition to conventional style classes, the CSS standard defines pseudo-classes, although no browser yet uses them. They are the way you define the display style for certain tag states. Pseudo-classes are like regular classes, with two notable differences: they are attached to the tag name with a colon instead of a period, and they have predefined names, not arbitrary ones you may give them.

There are five pseudo-classes, three of which are associated with the `<a>` tag. The other two go with the `<p>` tag.

The browsers distinguish three special states for the hyperlinks created by the
`<a>` tag: not visited, being visited, and visited. The browser may change the
appearance of the tag's contents to indicate its state, such as underlining or
changing the colors. Through pseudo-classes, the HTML author can control how
these states get displayed by defining styles for `A:link`, `A:active`, and
`A:visited`. The `link` pseudo-class controls the appearance of links that are not
selected by the user and have not yet been visited. The `active` pseudo-class
defines the appearance of links that are currently selected by the user and are
being processed by the browser. The `visited` pseudo-class defines those links
that have already been visited by the user.

To completely define all three states of the `<a>` tag, you might write

```
A:link {color: blue}
A:active {color: red; font-weight: bold}
A:visited {color: green}
```

Unvisited links will be shown in blue. When the user clicks a link, the browser
will change its text color to red and make it bold. Once visited, the link will revert
to conventional green text.

The two other pseudo-classes go with the `<p>` tag, and are named `first-
letter` and `first-line`. As you might expect, these pseudo-classes control
the appearance of the first letter and first line, respectively, of a paragraph and
create effects commonly found in printed media, such as initial drop-caps and
bold first lines. For example:

```
P:first-line {font-style: small-caps}
```

converts the first line of a paragraph to small capital letters. Similarly,

```
P:first-letter {font-size: 200%; float: left}
```

tells the browser to make the first letter of a paragraph twice as large as the
remaining text and float the letter to the left, allowing the first two lines of the
paragraph to float around the larger initial letter.[*]

9.2.4.4 *Mixing classes*

You may mix pseudo-classes with regular classes by appending the pseudo-class
name to the selector's class name. For example, here are some rules that define
plain, normal, and fancy anchors:

---

[*] The properties that can be specified for the `first-letter` and `first-line` pseudo-classes are the
font properties, color and background properties, `text-decoration`, `vertical-align`, `text-
transform`, `line-height`, and `clear`. In addition, the `first-letter` pseudo-class accepts the
margin properties, padding properties, border properties, and `float`. The `first-line` pseudo-class
also accepts the `word-spacing` and `letter-spacing` properties.

```
A.plain:link, A.plain:active, A.plain:visited {color: blue}
A:link {color: blue}
A:visited {color: green}
A:active {color: red}
A.fancy:link {text-style: italic}
A.fancy:visited {text-style: normal}
A.fancy:active {text-weight: bold; font-size: 150%}
```

The `plain` version of <a> is always blue, no matter the state of the link. Normal links start out blue, turn red when active, and convert to green when visited. The `fancy` link inherits the color scheme of the normal <a> tag, but adds italic text for unvisited links, converts back to normal text after being visited, and actually grows 50 percent in size and becomes bold when active.

A word of warning about that last property of the `fancy` class: specifying a font size change for a transient display property will result in lots of browser redisplay activity when the user clicks on the link. Given that some browsers run on slow machines, this redisplay may be annoying to your readers. Given also that implementing that sort of display change is something of a pain, it is unlikely that most browsers will support radical appearance changes in <a> tag pseudo-classes.

9.2.4.5 Class inheritance

Classes inherit the style properties of their generic base tag. For instance, all the properties of the plain <p> tag apply to a specially defined paragraph class, except where the class overrides a particular property.

Classes cannot inherit from other classes, only from the unclassed version of the tag they represent. In general, therefore, you should put as many common styles into the rule for the basic version of a tag, and only create classes for those properties which are unique to that class. This makes maintenance and sharing of your style classes easier, especially for large document collections.

9.3 Style Properties

At the heart of the Cascading Style Sheet specification are 53 properties that let you control how the style-conscious browser presents your documents to the user. The standard collects these properties into six groups: fonts, colors and backgrounds, text, boxes and layout, lists, and tag classification. We'll stick with that taxonomy, and preface the whole shebang with a discussion of property values and inheritance before diving into the properties themselves.

You'll find a summary of the style properties in Appendix C, *Cascading Style Sheet Properties Quick Reference.*

9.3.1 Property Values

There are five distinct kinds of property values: keywords, length values, percentage values, URLs, and colors.

9.3.1.1 Keyword property values

A property may have a `keyword` value that expresses action or dimension. For instance, the effects of `underline` and `line-through` are obvious property values. And you can express property dimensions with keywords like `small` and `xx-large`. Some keywords are even relational: `bolder`, for instance, is an acceptable value for the `font-weight` property. Keyword values are not case sensitive: `Underline`, `UNDERLINE`, and `underline` are all acceptable keyword values.

9.3.1.2 Length property values

So-called `length` values (a term taken from the CSS standard) explicitly state the size of a property. They are numbers, some with decimals, too. Length values may have a leading "+" or "–" sign to indicate the value is to be added to or subtracted from the immediate value of the property. Length values must be followed immediately by a two-letter unit abbreviation—with no intervening spaces.

There are three kinds of length-value units: relative, pixels, and absolute. Relative units specify a size that is relative to the size of some other property of the content. Currently, there are only two relative units: em, which is the height of the current font (written as `em`), and x-height, which is the height of the letter "x" in the current font (abbreviated `ex`). The pixels unit, abbreviated `px`, is equal to the size of a pixel on the browser's display. Absolute property value units are more familiar to us all. They include inches (abbreviated `in`), centimeters (`cm`), millimeters (`mm`), points (`pt`, 1/72 of an inch), and picas (`pc`, twelve points).

All of the following are valid length values, although not all units are recognized by the style-conscious browsers:

```
1in
1.5cm
+0.25mm
-3pt
-2.5pc
+100em
-2.75ex
250px
```

9.3.1.3 Percentage property values

Similar to the relative length-value type, a percentage value describes a proportion relative to some other aspect of the content. It has an optional sign and decimal portion to its numeric value, and must have the percent sign (%) suffix. For example,

```
line-height: 120%
```

computes the separation between lines to be 120 percent of the current line height (usually relative to the text font height). Note that this value is not dynamic, though: changes made to the font height after the rule has been processed by the browser will not affect the computed line height.

9.3.1.4 URL property values

Some properties also accept, if not expect, a URL as a value. The syntax for using a URL in a style property is different from conventional HTML:

```
url(service://server.com/pathname)
```

The keyword `url` is required, as are the opening and closing parentheses. Do not leave any spaces between `url` and the opening parenthesis. The `url` value may contain either an absolute or a relative URL. However, note that the URL is relative to the immediate style sheet's URL, the one in which it is declared. This means that if you use a `url` value in a document-level or inline style, the URL is relative to the HTML document containing the style document. Otherwise, the URL is relative to the `@imported` or `<link>`ed external style sheet's URL.

9.3.1.5 Color property values

Color values specify colors in a property (surprised?). You can specify a color as a color name or a hexadecimal RGB triple, as is done for common HTML attributes, or as a decimal RGB triple unique to style properties. Both color names and hexadecimal RGB triple notation are described in Appendix F, *Color Names and Values*; we describe decimal triples below.

Unlike regular HTML, style sheets will accept three-digit hexadecimal color values. The single digit is doubled to create a conventional six-digit triple. Thus, the color `#78C` is equivalent to `#7788CC`. In general, three-digit color values are handy only for simple colors.

The decimal RGB triple notation is a bit different:

```
rgb(red, green, blue)
```

The `red`, `green`, and `blue` intensity value are integers in the range zero to 255 or integer percentages. As with a URL value, do not leave any spaces between `rgb` and the opening parenthesis.

For example, in decimal RGB convention, the color white is `rgb(255, 255, 255)` or `rgb(100%, 100%, 100%)`, and a medium yellow is `rgb(127, 127, 0)` or `rgb(50%, 50%, 0%)`.

Currently, no browser supports the `rgb` notation for color values. You must use either a hexadecimal triple or a color name in your style sheets instead.

9.3.2 Property Inheritance

In lieu of a specific rule for a particular tag, properties and their values for tags within tags are inherited from the parent tag. Thus, setting a property for the `<body>` tag effectively applies that property to every tag in the body of your document, except for those that specifically override it. So, to make all the text in your document blue, you need only say:

```
BODY {color: blue}
```

rather than create a rule for every tag you use in your document.

This inheritance extends to any level. If you later created a `<div>` tag with text of a different color, the style-conscious browser will display all the text contents of the `<div>` tag and all its enclosed tags in that new color. When the `<div>` tag ends, the color reverts to the that of the containing `<body>` tag.

In many of the following property descriptions, we refer to the tag containing the current tag as the "parent element" of that tag.

9.3.3 Font Properties

The loudest complaint we hear about HTML is that the language lacks font styles and characteristics that even the simplest of text editors implement. The various `<font>` attributes supported by the extended browsers address part of the problem, but they are tedious to use since each text font change requires a different `<font>` tag.

Style sheets change all that, of course. The CSS standard provides six font properties that modify the appearance of text contained within the affected tag: `font-family`, `font-height`, `font-size`, `font-style`, `font-variant`, and `font-weight`. In addition, there is a universal `font` property that lets you declare all of the font changes with a single property.

Please, be aware that style sheets cannot overcome limitations of the client system nor can the browser conjure effects if the fonts it uses do not provide the means.

9.3.3.1 The font-family property

The `font-family` property accepts a comma-separated list of font names, one of which will be selected by the style-conscious browser for display of the tag's text. The browser uses the first font named in the list that also is installed and available for display on the client machine.

Font name values are for specific font styles, such as Helvetica or Courier, or a generic font style as defined by the CSS standard: `serif`, `sans-serif`, `cursive`, `fantasy`, and `monospace`. Each browser defines which actual font name is to be used for each generic font. For instance, Courier is the most popular choice for a monospace font.

Since fonts vary wildly among browsers, when specifying a font style, you should always provide several choices, ending with a suitable generic font. For example,

```
H1 {font-family: Helvetica, Univers, sans-serif}
```

causes the browser to look for and use Helvetica, and then Univers. If neither font is available for the client display, the browser will use the generic sans serif typeface.

For font names that contain spaces—New Century Schoolbook, for example—enclose them in quotation marks. For example:

```
P {font-family: Times, "New Century Schoolbook", Palatino, serif}
```

That extra set of double quotation marks in an inline style rule will cause problems. Accordingly, use single quotation marks in an inline style:

```
<p style="font-family: Times, 'New Century Schoolbook', Palatino,
serif">
```

In practice, you need not use quotation marks: the browser will ignore spaces before and after the font name, and convert multiple internal spaces to a single space. Thus,

```
P {font-family: Times, New Century Schoolbook, Palatino, serif}
<p style="font-family: Times, New Century Schoolbook, Palatino, serif">
```

are both legal, but we recommend that you use quotation marks anyway, just in case things change.

9.3.3.2 The font-size property

The `font-size` property lets you prescribe absolute or relative length values, percentages, and keywords to define the font size. For example:

```
P {font-size: 12pt}
P {font-size: 120%}
P {font-size: +2pt}
P {font-size: medium}
P {font-size: larger}
```

The first rule is probably the most used because it is the most familiar: it sets the font size to a specific number of points (12 in this example). The second example rule sets the font size to be 20 percent larger than the parent element's font size. The third increases the font size by two points.

The fourth example selects a predefined size set by the browser, identified by the `medium` keyword. Valid absolute-size keywords are `xx-small`, `x-small`, `small`, `medium`, `large`, `x-large`, and `xx-large`, and usually correspond to the seven font sizes used with the `size` attribute of the `<font>` tag.

The last `font-size` rule selects the next size larger than the font associated with the parent element. Thus, if the size were normally `medium`, it would be changed to `large`. You can also specify `smaller`, with the expected results.

The relative and absolute size keywords are not currently supported by any browser.

9.3.3.3 The font-style property

Use the `font-style` property to slant text. The default style is `normal`, and may be changed to `italic` or `oblique`. For example,

```
H2 {font-style: italic}
```

makes all level-two header text italic. As of this writing, Netscape 4 and Internet Explorer 3 support only the `italic` value for `font-style`.

9.3.3.4 The font-variant property

The `font-variant` property lets you select a variant of the desired font. The default value for this property is `normal`, indicating the conventional version of the font. You may also specify `small-caps` to select a version of the font in which the lowercase letters have been replaced with small capital letters.

This property is not supported by any browser.

9.3.3.5 The font-weight property

The `font-weight` property controls the weight or boldness of the font. The default value of this property is `normal`. You may specify `bold` to obtain a bold version of a font, or use the relative `bolder` and `lighter` values to obtain a version of the font that is bolder or lighter than the parent element's font.

To specify varying levels of lightness or boldness, set the value to a multiple of 100, between the values 100 (lightest) and 900 (boldest). The value `400` is equal to the `normal` version of the font, and `700` is the same as specifying `bold`.

Internet Explorer 3 and Netscape 4 support the `normal` and `bold` values. Neither support the `lighter` and `bolder` values. Netscape supports the numeric boldness values; Internet Explorer does not.

Internet Explorer 3 does support a series of "traditional" boldness names taken from old-style typography. These names are `extra-light`, `light`, `demi-light`, `medium`, `demi-bold`, `bold`, and `extra-bold`. These names were used in an early draft of the CSS standard and then dropped from the final recommended standard. We don't recommend using these names; expect Internet Explorer to drop support for them at some point. (Too bad, actually.)

9.3.3.6 The font property

More often than not you'll find yourself specifying more than one font-related property at a time for a tag's text content display. A complete font specification can get somewhat unwieldy; for example:

```
P {font-family: Times, Garamond, serif;
   font-weight: bold;
   font-size: 12pt;
   line-height: 14pt}
```

To mitigate this troublesome and potentially unreadable collection, use the comprehensive `font` property and group all of these attributes into one set of declarations:

```
P {font: bold 12pt/14pt Times, Garamond, serif}
```

The grouping and ordering of font attributes is important within the `font` property. The font style, weight, and variant attributes must be specified first, followed by the font size and the line height separated by a slash character, and ending with the list of font families. Of all the properties, the size and family are required; the others may be omitted. [`line-height` property, 9.3.5.2]

Here are some more sample `font` properties:

```
EM {font: italic 14pt Times}
H1 {font: 900 24pt/48pt sans-serif}
CODE {font: 12pt Courier, monospace}
```

The first example tells the style-conscious browser to emphasize `<em>` text using a 14-point italic Times face. The second rule has `<h1>` text displayed in the boldest 24-point sans-serif font available, with an extra 24 points of space between the lines of text. Finally, text within a `<code>` tag is set in 12-point Courier, or the browser-defined monospace font.

We leave it to your imagination to conjure up examples of the abuses you could foster with the font styles. Perhaps a recent issue of *Wired* magazine, notorious for their avant-garde font and other print-related abuses, would be helpful in that regard?

9.3.4 Color and Background Properties

Every element in your document has a foreground and a background color that the browser uses to render the element. In some cases, the background is not a color, but an image. The color and background style properties control these colors and images.

The children of an HTML element normally inherit the foreground color of their parent. For instance, if you make `<body>` text red, the style-conscious browser also will display header and paragraph text in red.

Background properties behave differently, however—they are not inherited. Instead, each element has a default background that is transparent, allowing the parent's background to show through. Thus, setting the background image of the `<body>` tag does not cause that image to be reloaded for every element within the body tag. Instead, the browser loads the image once and displays it behind the rest of the document, serving as the background for all elements which do not themselves have an explicit background color or image.

9.3.4.1 The background-attachment property

If you specify a background image for an element, use the `background-attachment` property to control how that image is attached to the browser's display window. With the default value `scroll`, the browser moves the background image with the element as the user scrolls through the document. A value of `fixed` prevents the image from moving.

Internet Explorer 3 does not support this style property explicitly, but emulates it for the `<body>` tag with the `bgproperties=fixed` attribute. [bgproperties attribute, 5.3.1.3]

9.3.4.2 The background-color property

The `background-color` property controls the (you guessed it!) background color of an element. Set it to a color value or to the keyword `transparent`. The default value is `transparent`. The effects should be obvious.

While you may have become accustomed to setting the background color of an entire document through the special attributes for the `<body>` tag, the `background-color` style property can be applied to any HTML element. For example, to set the background color of one item in a bulleted list, you could use:

```
<li style="background-color: blue">
```

Similarly, all the table header cells in a document could be given a reverse video effect with:

```
TH {background-color: black; color: white}
```

If you really want your emphasized text to stand out, paint its background red:

```
EM {background-color: red}
```

Internet Explorer 3 does not support this CSS property explicitly, but you may achieve the same effects through its support of the general `background` property, as discussed in 9.3.4.6.

9.3.4.3 The background-image property

The `background-image` property puts an image behind the contents of an HTML element. Its value is either a URL or the keyword `none`. The default value is `none`.

As with background colors, you can place a background image behind the entire document, or behind selected elements of a document. With this style property, effects like placing an image behind a table or selected text are now simple:

```
<table style="background-image: url(backgrounds/woodgrain.gif)">
LI.marble {background-image: url(backgrounds/marble.gif)}
```

The first example uses an inline style to place a woodgrain finish behind a table. The second defines a list item class that places a marble background behind `<li>` tag that use the `class=marble` attribute. For example:

```
<h2>Here's what's for dinner tonight:</h2>
<ul>
<li class=marble>Liver with Onions
<li class=marble>Mashed Potatoes and Gravy
<li class=marble>Green Beans
<li class=marble>Choice of Milk, Tea, or Coffee
</ul>
<h2>And for dessert:</h2>
<ul>
<li>Creamed Quats in Milk  (YUM! YUM!)
</ul>
```

will produce a result like that in Figure 9-1.

If the image is larger than the containing element, it will be clipped to the area occupied by the element. If smaller, the image will be repeated to tile the area occupied by the element, as dictated by the value of the `background-repeat` attribute.

You control the position of the image within the element with the `background-position` property. The scrolling behavior of the image is managed by the `background-attachment` property.

While it may seem that a background color and a background image are mutually exclusive, you should usually define a background color even if you are using a background image. That way, if the image is unavailable, such as when the user

Figure 9-1. Placing a background image behind an element

doesn't automatically download images, the browser will display the background color instead. In addition, if the background image has transparent areas, the background color will be used to fill in those areas.

Internet Explorer 3 does not support the `background-image` property explicitly, but you may achieve the same effects through its support of the general `background` property, as discussed in 9.3.4.6.

9.3.4.4 The background-position property

By default, the style-conscious browser renders a background image starting in the upper-left corner of the allotted display area and tiled (if necessary) down and over to the lower-right corner of that same area. With the `background-position` property, you can offset the starting position of the background image down and to the right of that default point by an absolute (length) or relative (percentage or keyword) offset. The resulting image fills the area from that offset starting point to the lower-right corner of the display space.

You may specify one or two values for the `background-position` property. If you use a single value, it applies to both the vertical and horizontal positions. With two values, the first is the horizontal offset, and the second is the vertical offset.

Length values (with their appropriate units; see 9.3.1.2) indicate an absolute distance from the upper-left corner of the element behind which you display the background image. For instance,

```
TABLE {background-image: url(backgrounds/marble.gif);
       background-position: 10px 20px}
```

offsets the marble background 10 pixels to the right and 20 pixels down from the upper-left corner of any `<table>` element in your document.

Percentage values are a bit trickier, but somewhat easier to use. Measured from 0 to 100 percent from left to right and top to bottom, the center of the HTML element's content display space is at 50%, 50%. Similarly, the position one-third of the way across the area and two-thirds of the way down is at 33%, 66%. So, to offset the background for our example dinner menu to the center of the element's content display space, we use:

```
background-position: 50% 50%
```

You'll notice that the browser places the first *marble.gif* tile at the center of the content display area and tiles to the right and down the window, as shown in Figure 9-2.

Figure 9-2. Marbled background offset to the center of the display

So, why use a number when a single word will do? You can use the keywords `left`, `center`, and `right`, as well as `top`, `center`, and `bottom`, for `0%`, `50%`, and `100%`, respectively. To center an image in the tag's content area, then, you need only write:

```
background-position: center center
```

You can mix and match length and percentage values,* so that

```
background-position: 1cm center
```

places the image one centimeter to the right of the tag's left edge, centered vertically in the tag's area.

Internet Explorer 3 does not support this CSS property explicitly, but you may achieve similar effects with the general `background` property. See 9.3.4.6.

---

* That is, if the browser supports the value units. So far, Internet Explorer and Netscape support only a meager repertoire of length units—pixels and percents.

9.3.4.5 The background-repeat property

Normally, the browser tiles a background image to fill the allotted space, repeating the image both down and to the right. Use the `background-repeat` property to alter this "repeat" (default value) behavior. To have the image repeat horizontally but not vertically, use the value `repeat-x`. For only vertical repetition, use `repeat-y`. To suppress tiling altogether, use `no-repeat`.

A common use of this property is to place a watermark or logo in the background of a page without repeating the image over and over. For instance:

```
BODY {background-image: url(backgrounds/watermark.gif);
      background-position: center middle;
      background-repeat: no-repeat
     }
```

will place the watermark image in the background at the center of the page.

Another popular trick is to create a vertical ribbon down the right-hand side of the page:

```
BODY {background-image: url(backgrounds/ribbon.gif);
      background-position: top right;
      background-repeat: repeat-y
     }
```

Internet Explorer 3 does not support this CSS property explicitly, but you may achieve similar effects with the general `background` property, described in the next section.

9.3.4.6 The background property

Like the various font properties, the many background CSS properties can get cumbersome to write and hard to read later. So, like the `font` property, there also is a general `background` property.

The background property accepts values from any and all of the `background-color`, `background-image`, `background-attachment`, `background-repeat`, and `background-position` properties, in any order. If you do not specify values for some of the properties, that property is explicitly set to its default value. Thus,

```
background: red
```

sets the `background-color` property to red and resets the other background properties to their default values. A more complex example:

```
background: url(backgrounds/marble.gif) blue repeat-y fixed center
```

sets all the background image and color properties at once, resulting in a marble image on top of a blue background (blue showing through any transparent areas). The image repeats vertically, starting from the center of the content display area, and does not scroll when the user scrolls the display. Notice that we included just a single position value (`center`) and the browser used it for both the vertical and horizontal positions.

Internet Explorer 3 supports only the `background` property and does not honor any of the individual background properties. For this reason, you may want to use the `background` property to achieve the broadest acceptance of your background image and color properties.

9.3.4.7 The color property

The `color` property sets the foreground color for a tag's contents—the color of the text lettering, for instance. Its value is either the name of a color, a hexadecimal RGB triple, or a decimal rgb triple, as outlined in 9.3.1.5. Thus, the following are all valid property declarations:

```
color: mauve
color: #ff7bd5
color: rgb(255, 125, 213)
color: rgb(100%, 49%, 84%)
```

Generally, you'll use the `color` property with text, but you may also modify non-textual content of a tag. For example, the following example produces a green horizontal rule:

```
HR {color: green}
```

If you do not specify a color for an element, it inherits the color of its parent element.

9.3.5 Text Properties

Cascading style sheets make a distinction between font properties, which control the size, style, and appearance of text, and text properties, which control how text is aligned and presented to the user.

9.3.5.1 The letter-spacing property

The `letter-spacing` property puts additional space between text letters as they are displayed by the browser. Set the property with either a length value or the default keyword `normal`, indicating that the browser should use normal letter spacing. For example:

```
BLOCKQUOTE {letter-spacing: 2px}
```

puts an additional two pixels between adjacent letters within the `<blockquote>` tag.

This property currently is not supported by any browser.

9.3.5.2 The line-height property

Use the `line-height` property to define the spacing between lines of a tag's text content. Normally, browsers single-space text lines—the top of the next line is just a few points below the last line. By adding to that line height (more commonly known as *leading* among typographers), you increase the amount of space between lines.

The `line-height` value can be an absolute or relative length, a percentage, a scaling factor, or the keyword `normal`. For example:

```
P {line-height: 14pt}
P {line-height: 120%}
P {line-height: 2.0}
```

The first example sets the line height to exactly 14 points between baselines of adjacent lines of text. The second computes the line height to 120 percent of the font size. The last example uses a scaling factor to set the line height to twice as large as the font size, creating double-spaced text. The value `normal`, the default, is usually equal to a scaling factor of 1.0 to 1.2.

Keep in mind that absolute and percentage values for `line-height` compute the line height based upon the value of the `font-size` property when the `line-height` property is defined. The computed property value will be inherited by children of the element. Subsequent changes to `font-size` by either the parent or child elements will not change the computed `line-height`.

Scaling factors, on the other hand, defer the line-height computation until the text is actually displayed. Hence, varying `font-sizes` affect `line-height` locally. In general, it is best to use a scaling factor for the `line-height` property so that the line height will automatically change when the font size is changed.

Although usually considered separate from font properties, you may include this text-related `line-height` property's value as part of the shorthand notation of the `font` property. [font property, 9.3.3.6]

Internet Explorer 3 does not support scaling factors and may compute relative line heights incorrectly for text containing multiple font sizes.

9.3.5.3 The text-align property

Text justified with respect to the page margins is a rudimentary feature of nearly all text processors. The `text-align` property brings that capability to HTML for any block-level tag. Use one of four values: `left`, `right`, `center`, or `justify`. The default value is, of course, `left`. For example,

```
DIV {text-align: right}
```

tells the style-conscious browser to align all the text inside `<div>` tags against the right margin. The `justify` value tells the browser to align the text to both the left and right margins, spreading the letters and words in the middle to fit.

Internet Explorer 3 does not support the `justify` value for this property.

9.3.5.4 The text-decoration property

The `text-decoration` property produces all sorts of text embellishments, some of which also are available with the original physical style tags. Its value is one or more of the keywords `underline`, `overline`, `line-through`, and `blink`. The value `none` is the default and tells the style-conscious browser to present text normally.

The `text-decoration` property is handy for defining different link appearances. For example,

```
A:visited A:link A:active {text-decoration: underline overline}
```

puts lines above and below the links in your document.

This text property is not inherited, and non-textual elements are not affected by the `text-decoration` property.

Internet Explorer supports only the `underline` and `line-through` values for text-decoration; Netscape does not support the `overline` value.

9.3.5.5 The text-indent property

Although less common today, it still is standard practice to indent the first line of a paragraph of text.* And some text blocks, such as definitions, typically "outdent" the first line, creating what is called a *hanging indent.*

The CSS `text-indent` property lets you apply these features to any block tag and thereby control the amount of indentation of the first line of the block. Use length and percentage values; negative values create the hanging indent. Percentage values compute the indentation as a percentage of the parent element's width. The default value is zero.

To indent all the paragraphs in your document, for example:

```
P {text-indent: 3em}
```

The length unit `em` scales the indent as the font of the paragraph changes in size on different browsers.

---

* But not, obviously, in this book.

Hanging indents are a bit trickier because you have to watch out for the element borders. Negative indentation does not shift the left margin of the text; it simply shifts the first line of the element left, possibly into the margin, border, or padding of the parent element. For this reason, hanging indents only work as expected if you also shift the left margin of the element to the right by an amount equal to or greater than the size of the hanging indent. For example,

```
P.wrong {text-indent: -3em}
P.hang  {text-indent: -3em; margin-left: 3em}
P.large {text-indent: -3em; margin-left: 6em}
```

creates three paragraph styles. The first creates a hanging indent that extends into the left margin. The second creates a conventional hanging indent. The third creates a paragraph whose body is indented more than the hanging indent. All three styles are shown in use in Figure 9-3.

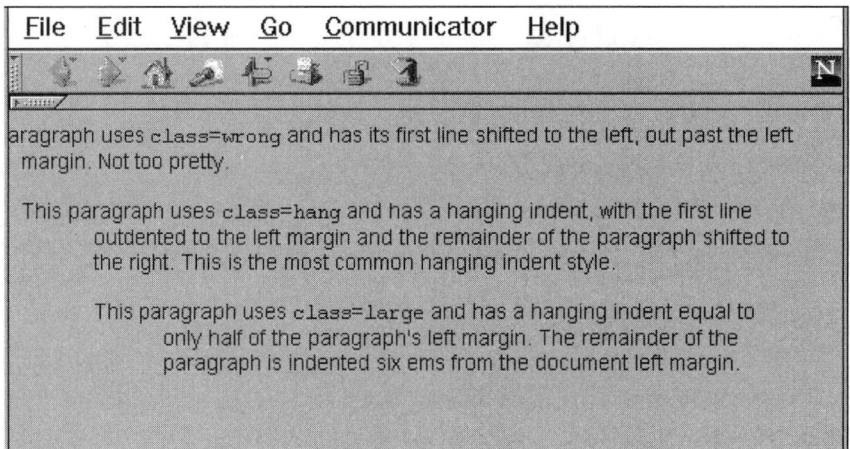

Figure 9-3. The effects of text-indent and margin-left on a paragraph

9.3.5.6 The text-transform property

The `text-transform` property changes the case for all the text within a tag. Valid values for this property are `capitalize`, `uppercase`, `lowercase`, and `none`, which is the default. The value `capitalize` ensures that the first letter of every word gets capitalized, while `uppercase` and `lowercase` affect every letter in the text.

The actual capitalization rules used by the browser depend upon the character encoding and language used by the browser.

This property is not supported by Internet Explorer 3. While supported by Netscape, this property is not inherited by child elements, as prescribed by the CSS standard.

9.3.5.7 The vertical-align property

The `vertical-align` property controls the relative position of an element with respect to the line containing the element. Valid values for this property include:

`baseline`
>   align the baseline of the element with the baseline of the containing element

`middle`
>   align the middle of the element with the middle (usually the x-height) of the containing element

`sub`
>   subscript the element

`super`
>   superscript the element

`text-top`
>   align the top of the element with the top of the font of the parent element

`text-bottom`
>   align the bottom of the element with the bottom of the font of the parent element

`top`
>   align the top of the element with the top of the tallest element in the current line

`bottom`
>   align the bottom of the element with the bottom of the lowest element in the current line

In addition, a percentage value indicates a position relative to the current baseline, so that a position of `50%` puts the element halfway up the line height above the baseline. A position value of `-100%` puts the element an entire line-height below the baseline of the current line.

This property is not supported by any browser.

9.3.5.8 The word-spacing property

Use the `word-spacing` property to add additional space between words within a tag. You can specify a length value or the keyword `normal` to revert to normal word spacing. For example,

```
H3 {word-spacing: 25px}
```

places an additional 25 pixels of space between words in the `<h3>` tag.

This property is currently not supported by any browser.

9.3.6 Box Properties

The CSS model assumes that HTML elements always fit within a rectangular box. Using the properties defined in this section, you can control the size, appearance, and position of the boxes containing the elements in your documents.

9.3.6.1 The CSS formatting model

Each element in an HTML document can fit in a rectangular box. The CSS authors call this box the "core content area" and surround it with three more boxes: the padding, the border, and the margin. Figure 9-4 shows these boxes and defines some useful terminology.

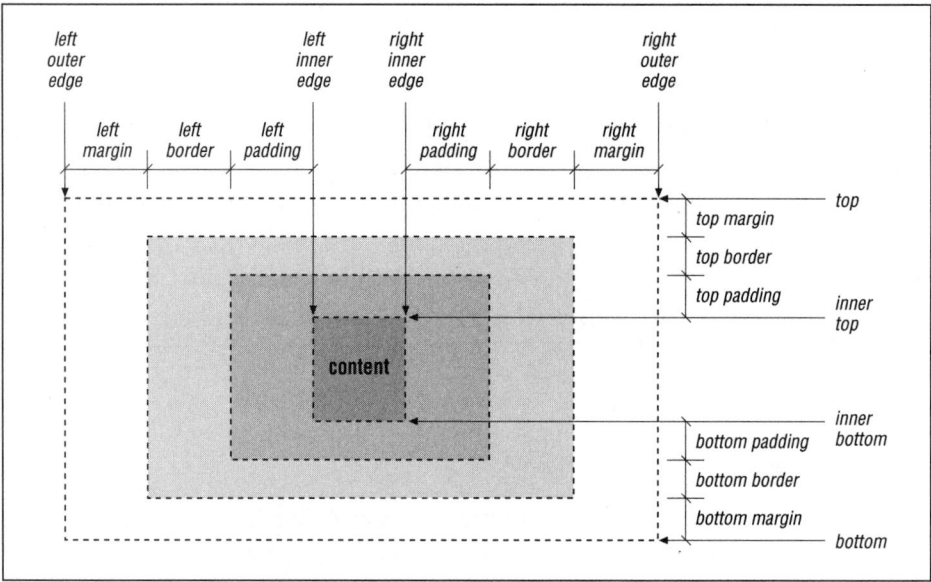

Figure 9-4. The CSS formatting model and terminology

The top, bottom, left-outer, and right-outer edges bound the content area of an element and all of its padding, border, and margin spaces. The inner-top, inner-bottom, left-inner, and right-inner edges define the sides of the core content area. The extra space around the element is the area between the inner and outer edges, including the padding, border, and margin. A browser may omit any and all of these extra spaces for any HTML element, and for many, the inner and outer edges are the same.

When elements are vertically adjacent, the bottom margin of the upper elements and the top margin of the lower elements overlap, so that the total space between the elements is the greater of the adjacent margins. For example, if one paragraph has a bottom margin of one inch, and the next paragraph has a top margin of one-half inch, the greater of the two margins, one inch, will be placed between the two paragraphs. These practice is known as *margin collapsing* and generally results in better document appearance.

Horizontally adjacent elements do not have overlapping margins. Instead, the CSS model adds together adjacent horizontal margins. For example, if a paragraph has a left margin of one inch, and is adjacent to an image with a right margin of one-half inch, the total space between the two will be 1.5 inches. This rule also applies for nested elements, so that a paragraph within a division will have a left margin equal to the sum of the division's left margin and the paragraph's left margin.

As shown in Figure 9-4, the total width of an element is equal to the sum of seven items: the left and right margins, the left and right borders, the left and right padding, and the element's content itself. The sum of these seven items must equal the width of the containing element. Of these seven items, only three (the element's width, and its left and right margins) can be given the value `auto`, indicating that the browser can compute a value for that property. When this becomes necessary, the browser follows these rules:

- If none of these properties are set to `auto`, and the total width is less than the width of the parent element, the `margin-right` property will be set to `auto` and made large enough to make the total width equal to the width of the parent element.

- If exactly one property is set to `auto`, that property will be made large enough to make the total width equal to the width of the parent element.

- If more than two properties are set to `auto`, and one of them is `width`, `margin-left` and `margin-right` will be set to zero and `width` will be made large enough to make the total width equal to the width of the parent element.

- If both the left and right margins are set to `auto`, they will always be set to equal values, centering the element within its parent.

There are special rules for floating elements. A floating element (such as an image with `align=left` specified) will not have its margins collapsed with the margins of containing or preceding elements, unless the floating element has negative margins. This is easy to see in Figure 9-5, which shows how this bit of HTML might be rendered:

```
<body>
<p>
<img align=left src="pics/img.gif">
Some sample text...
</body>
```

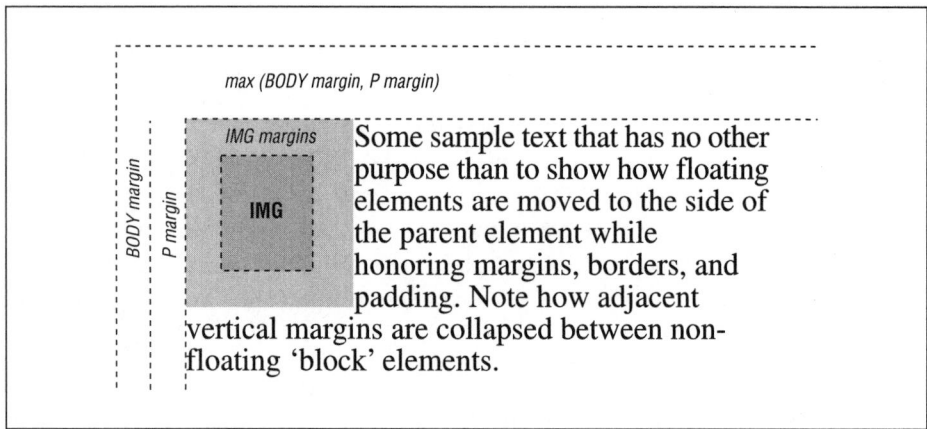

Figure 9-5. Handling the margins of floating elements

The browser moves the image, including its margins, as far as possible to the left and towards the top of the paragraph without overlapping the left and top margins of the paragraph or the document body. The left margins of the paragraph and the containing body are added, while their top margins are collapsed.

9.3.6.2 The border properties

The border surrounding an element has a color, a thickness, and a style. You use various properties to control these three aspects of the border on each of the four sides of an element. Shorthand properties make it easy to define the same color, thickness, and style for the entire border, if desired. Border properties are not inherited; you must explicitly set them for each element that has a border.

Unfortunately, none of the border properties are currently implemented by either Netscape or Internet Explorer.

9.3.6.3 The border-color property

Use the `border-color` property to set the border color. If not specified, the browser draws the border using the value of the element's `color` property.

The `border-color` property accepts from one to four color values. The number of values determines how they are applied to the borders (summarized in Table 9-1). If you include just one property value, all four sides of the border are set to the specified color. Two values set the top and bottom borders to the first value and the left and right borders to the second value. With three values, the first is the top border, the second sets the right and left borders, and the third color value is for the bottom border. Four values specify colors for each side, clockwise from the top, then right, bottom, and left borders, in that order.

Table 9-1. Order of effects for multiple border, margin, and padding property values

Number of values	Affected border(s), margin(s), or padding
1	All same.
2	First value sets *top* and *bottom*; second value sets *left* and *right*.
3	First value sets *top*; second sets both *left* and *right*; third value sets *bottom*.
4	First value sets *top*; second sets *right*; third sets *bottom*; and fourth value sets *left*.

9.3.6.4 The border-width property

The `border-width` property lets you change the width of the border. Like the `border-color` property, it accepts from one to four values that are applied to the various borders in a similar manner (Table 9-1).

Besides a specific length value, you may also specify the width of a border as one of the keywords `thin`, `medium`, or `thick`. The default value, if the width is not explicitly set, is `medium`. Some typical border widths are:

```
border: 1px
border: thin thick medium
border: thick 2mm
```

The first example sets all four borders to exactly one pixel. The second makes the top border `thin`, the right and left borders `thick`, and the bottom border `medium`. The last example makes the top and bottom borders `thick`, while the right and left borders will be 2 mm wide.

If you are uncomfortable defining all four borders with one property, you can use the individual `border-top-width`, `border-bottom-width`, `border-left-width`, and `border-right-width` properties to define the thickness of each border. Each property accepts just one value; the default is `medium`.

9.3.6.5 The border-style property

According to the CSS model, you have a number of embellishments you may apply to your HTML element borders.

The `border-style` property values include `none` (default), `dotted`, `dashed`, `solid`, `double`, `groove`, `ridge`, `inset`, and `outset`. The border-style-conscious browser applies one to four values for the property to each of the borders in the same order as for the border colors and widths, as described in Table 9-1.

The browser draws `dotted`, `dashed`, `solid`, and `double` borders as flat lines atop the tag's background. The `groove`, `ridge`, `inset`, and `outset` values create three-dimensional borders: The `groove` is an incised line; the `ridge` is an embossed line; the `inset` border makes the entire tag area appear set into the document; and the `outset` border makes the entire tag area appear raised above the document. The effect of the three-dimensional nature of these last four styles upon the tag's background image is undefined and left up to the browser. We'd like to show you examples, but none are supported by any current browser.

9.3.6.6 Borders in shorthand

Since specifying a complex border can get tedious, the CSS standard provides five shorthand properties that accept any or all of the width, color, and style values for one or all of the border edges. The `border-top`, `border-bottom`, `border-left`, and `border-right` properties affect their respective borders sides; the comprehensive `border` property controls all four sides of the border simultaneously. For example:

```
border-top: thick solid blue
border-left: 1ex inset
border-bottom: blue dashed
border: red double 2px
```

The first property makes the top border a thick, solid, blue line. The second sets the left border to use an inset effect that is as thick as the x-height of the element's font, while leaving the color the same as the element's color. The third property creates a blue dashed line at the bottom of the element, using the default medium thickness. Finally, the last property makes all four borders a red double line two pixels thick.

That last property raises two issues. First, you cannot supply multiple values to the `border` property to selectively affect certain borders like you can with the individual `border-color`, `border-width`, and `border-style` properties. The `border` property always affects all four borders around an element.

Secondly, a bit of reflection should reveal that it is not possible to create a double-line border just two pixels thick. In cases like this, the browser is free to adjust the thickness to render the border properly.

While we usually think of borders surrounding block elements like images, tables, and text flows, borders can also be applied to inline tags. This lets you put a box around a word or phrase within a text flow. The implementation of borders on inline tags that span multiple lines is undefined and left to the browser.

9.3.6.7 *The clear property*

Like its cousin attribute for the `<br>` tag, the `clear` property tells the browser whether to place a tag's contents adjacent to a "floating" element, or on the first line below. Text flows around floating elements like images and tables with an `align=left` or `align=right` attribute, or any HTML element with its `float` property set to anything but `none`. [
, 4.7.1] [float property, 9.3.6.8]

The value of the `clear` property can be `none`, `left`, `right`, or `both`. A value of `none`, the default, means that the browser acts normally and places the tag's contents adjacent to floating elements on either side if there is room to do so. The value `left` prevents contents from being placed adjacent to a floating element on its left; `right` prevents placement against a floating element on the right; and `both` prevents the tag's contents from appearing adjacent to any floating element.

The effect of this style is the same as having preceded the tag with a `<br>` tag with its `clear` attribute. Hence,

```
H1 {clear: left}
```

has the same effect as preceding every `<h1>` tag with `<br clear=left>`.

The `clear` property currently is not supported by Internet Explorer.

9.3.6.8 *The float property*

The `float` property designates a tag's display space as a floating element and causes text to flow around it in a specified manner. It is generally analogous to the `align` attribute for images and tables, but can be applied to any element, including text, images, and tables. [image alignment, 5.2.6.4] [table alignment, 11.2.1.1]

The `float` property accepts one of three values: `left`, `right`, or `none`, the default. Using `none` disables the `float` property; the others work like their `align` attribute-value counterparts, telling the browser to place the content to either side of the flow and allow other content to be rendered next to it.

Accordingly, the style-conscious browser will place a tag's contents specified with `float: left` against the left margin of the current text flow, and subsequent content will flow to its right, down and below the tag's contents. The `float: right` pair puts the tag contents against the right edge of the flow and flows other content on its left, down and below the tag's contents.

Although most commonly used with tables and images, it is perfectly acceptable to apply the `float` property to a text element. For example, the following would create a "run-in" header, with the text flowing around the header text.

```
H1 {float: left}
```

This property is not yet supported by Internet Explorer.

9.3.6.9 *The height property*

As you might suspect, the `height` property controls the height of the associated tag's display region. You'll find it most often used with images and tables, but it can be used to control the height of other HTML document elements as well.

The value of the `height` property is either a length value or the keyword `auto`, the default. Using `auto` implies that the affected tag has an initial height that should be used when displaying the tag. Otherwise, the height of the tag is set to the desired height. If an absolute value is used, the height is set to that length value. For example,

```
IMG {height: 100px}
```

tells the browser to display the image referenced by the `<img>` tag scaled so that it is 100 pixels tall. If you use a relative value, the base size to which it is relative is browser and tag dependent.

When scaling elements to a specific height, the aspect ratio of the object can be preserved by also setting the `width` property of the tag to `auto`. Thus,

```
IMG {height: 100px; width: auto}
```

ensures that the images are always 100 pixels tall, with an appropriately scaled width. [width property, 9.3.6.12]

This property is not yet supported by Internet Explorer; Netscape honors it only when used with the `<img>` tag.

9.3.6.10 *The margin properties*

Like the border properties, the various margin properties let you control the margin space around an element, just outside of its border (Figure 9-4). Margins are always transparent, allowing the background color or image of the containing element to show through. As a result, you can only specify the size of a margin; it has no color or rendered style.

The `margin-left`, `margin-right`, `margin-top`, and `margin-bottom` properties all accept a length or percentage value indicating the amount of space to reserve around the element. In addition, the keyword `auto` tells the style-conscious browser to revert to the margins it normally would place around an element. Percentage values are computed as a percentage of the containing element's width. The default margin, if not specified, is zero.

These are all valid margin settings:

```
BODY {margin-left: 1in; margin-top: 0.5in; margin-right: 1in}
P {margin-left: -0.5cm}
IMG {margin-left: 10%}
```

The first example creates one-inch margins down the right and left edges of the entire document, and a half-inch margin across the top of the document. The second example shifts the <p> tag one-half centimeter left into the left margin. The last example creates a margin to the left of the <img> tag equal to ten percent of the parent element's width.

Like the shorthand **border** property, you can use the shorthand **margin** property to define all four margins, using from one to four values which affect the margins in the order described in Table 9-1. Using this notation, our <body> margins in the above example also could have been specified as:

```
BODY {margin: 0.5in 1in}
```

The **margin-left** and **margin-right** properties interact with the **width** property to determine the total width of an element, as described in 9.3.6.1.

Internet Explorer 3 only supports the **margin-left**, **margin-right**, and **margin-top** properties. Accordingly, it only accepts up to three **margin** property values, and in an order different than the CSS standard: top, left, then right (no bottom).

9.3.6.11 The padding properties

Like the margin properties, the various padding properties let you control the padding space around an element, between the element's content area and its border (Figure 9-4). Padding is always rendered using the background color or image of the element. As a result, you can specify only the size of the padding; it has no color or rendered style.

The **padding-left**, **padding-right**, **padding-top**, and **padding-bottom** properties all accept a length or percentage value indicating the amount of space the style-conscious browser should reserve around the element. Percentage values are computed as a percentage of the containing element's width. The default padding is zero.

These are valid padding settings:

```
P {padding-left: 0.5cm}
IMG {padding-left: 10%}
```

The first example creates half a centimeter of padding between the contents of the <p> tag and its left border. The last example creates padding to the left of the <img> tag equal to 10 percent of the parent element's width.

Like the shorthand **margin** and **border** properties, you can use the shorthand **padding** property to define all four padding amounts, using one to four values to effect the padding sides as described in Table 9-1.

Internet Explorer 3 does not support any padding properties. Netscape supports only the four individual padding properties, not the shorthand `padding` property.

9.3.6.12 The width property

The `width` property is the companion to the `height` property and controls the width of an associated tag. Specifically, it defines the width of the element's content area, as shown in Figure 9-4. You'll see it most often used with images and tables, but you could conceivably use it to control the width of other elements as well.

The value for `width` property is either a length or percentage value or the keyword `auto`. The value `auto` is the default and implies that the affected tag has an initial width that should be used when displaying the tag. If a length value is used, the width is set to that value; percentage values compute the width to be a percentage of the width of the containing element. For example,

```
IMG {width: 100px}
```

displays the image referenced by the `<img>` tag scaled to 100 pixels wide.

When scaling elements to a specific width, the aspect ratio of the object is preserved if the `height` property of the tag is set to `auto`. Thus,

```
IMG {width: 100px; height: auto}
```

makes the images all 100 pixels wide, and scales their heights appropriately. [height property, 9.3.6.9]

The `width` property interacts with the `margin-left` and `margin-right` properties to determine the total width of an element, as described in 9.3.6.1.

This property is not supported by Internet Explorer; Netscape honors it only when associated with the `<img>` tag.

9.3.7 List Properties

The CSS standard lets you also control the appearance of HTML list elements: specifically, ordered and unordered lists.

Browsers format list items just like any other HTML block item, except that the block has some sort of marker preceding the contents. For unordered lists, the marker is a bullet of some sort; for numbered lists, the marker is a numeric or alphabetic character or symbol. The CSS list properties let you control the appearance and position of the marker associated with a list item.

9.3.7.1 The list-style-image property

The `list-style-image` property defines the image that the browser uses to mark a list item. The value of this property is the URL of an image file, or the keyword `none`. The default value is `none`.

The image is the preferred list marker. If it is available, the browser will display it in place of any other defined marker. If the image is unavailable, or if the user has disabled image loading, the marker defined by the `list-style-type` property (see 9.3.7.3) will be used.

Authors can use this property to define custom bullets for their unordered lists. While any image could conceivably be used as a bullet, we recommend that you keep your marker GIF or JPEG images small to ensure attractively rendered lists.

For example, by placing the desired bullet image in the file *mybullet.gif* on your server, you could use that image:

```
LI {list-style-image: url(pics/mybullet.gif); list-style-type: square}
```

In this case, the image will be used if the browser successfully downloads *mybullet.gif*. Otherwise, the browser will use a conventional square bullet.

This property is not supported by any browser.

9.3.7.2 The list-style-position property

There are two ways to position the marker associated with a list item: inside the block associated with the item, or outside the block. Accordingly, the `list-style-position` property accepts one of two values: `inside` or `outside`.

The default value is `outside`, meaning that the item marker will hang to the left of the item like this:

- This is a bulleted list
  with an "outside" marker

The value `inside` causes the marker to be drawn with the list item flowing around it, much like a floating image:

- This is a bulleted list
with an "inside" marker

Notice how the second line of text is not indented, but instead lines up with the left edge of the marker.

This property is not currently supported by any browser.

9.3.7.3 The list-style-type property

The `list-style-type` property serves double-duty in a sense, determining how both ordered and unordered list items are rendered by a style-conscious browser. This property has the same effect on a list item as its `type` attribute does. [`<li>` type, 8.3.1.1]

When used with items within an unordered list, the `list-style-type` property accepts one of four values: `disc`, `circle`, `square`, or `none`. The browser marks the unordered list items with the corresponding specified dingbat. The default value is `disc`; browsers change that default depending on the nesting level of the list.

When used with items within an ordered list, the `list-style-type` property accepts one of six values: `decimal`, `lower-roman`, `upper-roman`, `lower-alpha`, `upper-alpha`, or `none`. These values format the item numbers as decimal values, lowercase Roman numerals, uppercase Roman numerals, lowercase letters, or uppercase letters, respectively. Most browsers will use decimal numbering schemes if you don't set this property.

This property is not supported by any browser.

9.3.7.4 The list-style property

The `list-style` property is the shorthand version for all the other list-style properties. It accepts any or all of the values allowed for the `list-style-type`, `list-style-position`, and `list-style-image` properties, in any order and with values appropriate for the type of list it is to affect. These are valid `list-style` properties:

```
LI {list-style: disc}
LI {list-style: lower-roman inside}
LI {list-style: url(http://www.kumquat.com/images/tiny-quat.gif)
                square}
```

The first example creates list items that use a disc as the bullet image. The second causes numbered list items to use lowercase Roman numerals, drawn inside the list item's block. In the last example, a square will be used as the bullet image if the referenced image is unavailable.

This property is not currently supported by any browser.

9.3.7.5 Using list properties effectively

Although you may apply list properties to any HTML element, they will affect only the appearance of elements whose `display` property is set to `list-item`.

Normally, the only tag with this property is the `<li>` tag. [`display` property, 9.3.8.1]

This shouldn't deter you from using these properties elsewhere, particularly with the `<ul>` and `<ol>` tags. Since these properties are inherited by elements whose parents have them set, modifying a list property for the `<ul>` and `<ol>` tags will subsequently modify it for all the `<li>` tags contained within that list. This makes it much easier to define lists with a particular appearance.

For example, suppose you want to create a list style that uses lowercase Roman numerals. One way is to define a class of the `<li>` tag with the appropriate `list-style-type` defined:

```
LI.roman {list-style-type: lower-roman}
```

Within your list, you'll need to specify each list element using that class:

```
<ol>
  <li class=roman>Item one
  <li class=roman>Item two
  <li class=roman>And so forth
</ol>
```

Having to repeat the class name is tedious and error-prone. A better solution is to define a class of the `<ol>` tag:

```
OL.roman {list-style-type: lower-roman}
```

Any `<li>` tag within the list will inherit the property and use lowercase Roman numerals:

```
<ol class=roman>
  <li>Item one
  <li>Item two
  <li>And so forth
</ol>
```

This is much easier to understand and manage. If, at a later date, you want to change the numbering style, you need only change the `<ol>` tag properties, rather than have to find and change each instance of the `<li>` tag in the list.

You can use these properties in a much more global sense as well. Setting a list property on the `<body>` tag will change the appearance of all lists in the document; setting it on a `<div>` tag will change all the lists within that division.

9.3.8 *Classification Properties*

Classification properties are the most esoteric of the CSS style properties. They do not directly control how a style-conscious browser will render HTML elements. Instead, they tell the browser how to classify and handle various tags and their contents as they are encountered.

For the most part, you should not set these properties on an element unless you are trying to achieve a specific special effect. Even then, it is unlikely that the property will be supported by most browsers.

9.3.8.1 The display property

Every element in an HTML document can be classified, for display purposes, as a block item, an inline item, or a list item. Block elements, like headings, paragraphs, tables, and lists, are formatted as a separate block of text, separated from the previous and next block items. Inline items, like the physical and content-based style tags and hyperlink anchors, are rendered within the current line of text within a containing block. List items, specifically the <li> tag, are rendered like a block item, along with a bullet or number known as the *marker*.

The `display` property lets you change an element's display type to `block`, `inline`, `list-item`, or `none`. The first three values change the element's classification accordingly; the value `none` turns off the element, preventing it or its children from being displayed in the document.

Conceivably, you could wreak all sorts of havoc by switching element classifications, forcing paragraphs to be displayed as list items and converting hyperlinks to block elements. In practice, this is just puerile monkey business, and we don't recommend that you change element classifications without having a very good reason to do so.

Besides, this property currently is not supported by any browser.

9.3.8.2 The white-space property

The `white-space` property defines how the style-conscious browser treats whitespace (tabs, spaces, and carriage returns) within a block tag. The keyword value `normal`—the default—collapses whitespace, so that one or more spaces, tabs, and carriage returns are treated as a single space between words. The value `pre` emulates the <pre> tag, in that the browser retains and displays all spaces, tabs, and carriage returns. And, finally, the `nowrap` value tells the browser to ignore carriage returns and not insert automatic line breaks; all line-breaking must be done with explicit <br> tags.

Like the `display` property, the `white-space` property is rarely used for good instead of evil. Don't change how elements handle whitespace without having a compelling reason for doing so.

This property is not supported by any browser.

9.4 Tag-Less Styles: The <span> Tag

Up to now, we have used Cascading Style Sheets to change the appearance of content that is within a designated HTML tag. In some cases, however, you may want to alter the appearance of only a portion of a tag's contents—usually text. Designate these special segments with the `<span>` tag.

<span> Ⓝ ❶

Function:
>   Delimit arbitrary amount of text to which to apply a style rule

Attributes:
>   CLASS
>   STYLE

End tag:
>   </span>; never omitted

Contains:
>   *html_content*

Used in:
>   *body_content*

The `<span>` tag simply delimits a portion of HTML content (constrained by normal tag nesting rules, of course). Browsers treat the `<span>` tag as another physical- or content-based style tag. The only difference, of course, is that the default meaning of the `<span>` tag is to leave the text alone.

Although it may serve some other function in a future version of HTML, the `<span>` tag was introduced so that you can apply a style to an arbitrary section of document content, via a direct style, various style classes, or locally with an inline style. To define a style for the `<span>` tag, treat it like any other HTML tag:

```
SPAN {color: purple}
SPAN.bigger {font-size: larger}
```

and use it like any other style tag:

```
Quat harvest projections are <span class=bigger>bigger than ever</span>!
```

In a similar manner, the appearance of a `<span>` tag can be changed using an inline style:

```
Quat harvest projections are <span style="font-size: larger">bigger
than ever</span>!
```

Like any other physical or content-based style tag, `<span>` tags can be nested and may contain other tags. The `<span>` tag exists only to provide style management down to the phrase level in HTML.

9.5 Applying Styles to Documents

There are several issues you should consider before, during, and after you use styles in your HTML documents and document collections. The first, overarching issue is whether to use them at all. Frankly, few of the style effects are unique; most can be achieved, albeit less easily and with much less consistency, via the physical- and content-based style tags like `<i>` and `<em>` and the various tag attributes like `color` and `background`.

9.5.1 To Style or Not to Style

Effects aside, the biggest question looming in the minds of HTML developers as we write this chapter in early 1997 is whether Cascading Style Sheets, particularly external ones, ever will be fully supported by the major browsers, or whether some other style-sheet delivery mechanism will prevail. Both Netscape Navigator and Internet Explorer have support for Cascading Style Sheets in their most recent versions, but Microsoft's support is out of date and buggy while Netscape's is currently incomplete. Moreover, Netscape has put its development weight behind not CSS, but JavaScript-based styles (see 13.4).

So, currently, CSS style sheets are a bittersweet solution; they can create more work than they are worth. The majority of browsers in use today do not support styles. That means that to achieve the special effects for most users, you have to prepare redundant collections—mixed or separate—containing both styles and style-related tags and attributes, if you use styles at all. We're right back in the same boat we were in a year or so ago when deciding whether to use the many new Netscape extensions to HTML. We believe that this too will pass: Netscape promises complete support of the entire CSS standard, and Microsoft surely will update its support to keep pace with Netscape. While styles may be spotty at best in the first half of 1997, expect them to be pervasive by the end of the year.

9.5.2 Which Type of Style Sheet and When

Once you have decided to use HTML cascading style sheets (for pain or pleasure), the next question is which type of style sheet—inline, document-level, or external—should you apply and when? Each has its pros and cons; each is best applied under certain circumstances.

9.5.2.1 The pros and cons of external styles

Since style sheets ostensibly provide consistency in the presentation of your documents, external style sheets are the best and the easiest way to manage styles for your entire document collection. Simply place the desired style rules in a style sheet and apply those styles to the desired documents. Since all the documents are affected by a single style sheet, conversion of the entire collection to a new style is as simple as changing a single rule in the corresponding external style sheet.

Even in cases where documents may differ in style, it is often possible to collect a few basic style rules in a single sheet that can be shared among several otherwise different documents, including:

- Background color
- Background image
- Font sizes and faces
- Margins
- Text alignment

Another benefit of external style sheets is that other web authors who want to copy your style can easily access that sheet and make their pages look like yours. Imitation being the sincerest form of flattery, you should not be troubled when someone elects to emulate the look and feel of your pages. More to the point, you can't stop them from linking to your style sheets, so you might as well learn to like it. Like conventional HTML documents, it is not possible to encrypt or otherwise hide your style sheets so that others cannot view and use them.

The biggest problem with external style sheets is that they increase the amount of time needed to access a given web page. Not only must the browser download the page itself, it must also download the style sheet before the page can be displayed to the user. While most style sheets are relatively small, their existence can definitely be felt when accessing the Web over a slow connection.

Without appropriate discipline, external style sheets can become large and unwieldy. When creating style sheets, remember to include only those styles that are common to the pages using the sheet. If a set of styles is needed only for one or two sheets, you are better off isolating them in a separate sheet or adding them to a document using document-level styles. Otherwise, you may find yourself expending an exorbitant amount of effort counteracting the effects of external styles in many individual documents.

9.5.2.2 The pros and cons of document-level styles

Document-level styles are most useful when creating a custom document. They let you easily override one or more rules in your externally defined style to create a slightly different document.

You might also want to use document-level styles to experiment with new style rules before moving them to your style sheets. By adding and changing rules using document-level styles, you eliminate the risk of adding a broken style to your style sheets, breaking the appearance of all the documents that use that sheet.

The biggest problem with document styles is that you may succumb to using them in lieu of creating a formal, external style sheet to manage your document collection. It is easy to simply add rules to each document, cutting and pasting as you create new documents. Unfortunately, managing a collection of documents with document-level styles is tedious and error-prone. Even a simple change can result in hours of editing and potential mistakes.

As a rule of thumb, any style rule that impacts three or more documents should be moved to a style sheet and applied to those documents using the `<link>` tag or `@import` command. Adhering to this rule as you create your document families will pay off in the long run when it is time to change your styles.

9.5.2.3 *The pros and cons of inline styles*

And at the end of the cascade, inline styles override the more general styles. Get into the habit now of using inline styles rarely and just for that purpose, too. Inline styles cannot be reused, making style management difficult. Moreover, such changes are spread throughout your documents, making finding and altering inline styles error-prone. (That's why we might eschew tag- and attribute-based styles in the first place, no?)

Anytime you use an inline style, think long and hard as to whether the same effect might be accomplished using a style class definition. For instance, you are better off defining:

```
<style type="text/css">
<!--
  P.centered {text-align: center}
  EM.blue {color: blue}
-->
</style>
```

and later using:

```
<p class=centered>
<em class=blue>
```

instead of:

```
<p style="text-align: center">
<em style="color: blue">
```

Your styles are easier to find and manage and can be easily reused throughout your documents.

10

Forms

Forms, forms, forms, forms: we fill 'em out for nearly everything, from the moment we're born, 'til the moment we die. So what's to explain all the hoopla and excitement over HTML forms? Simply this: they make HTML truly interactive.

When you think about it, except for the limited input from users available through the <isindex> tag, HTML's interactivity is basically a lot of button pushing: click here, click there, go here, go there—there's no real user feedback, and it's certainly not personalized. Applets provide extensive user-interaction capability, but they can be difficult to write and are still not standardized for all browsers. Forms, on the other hand, are supported by almost every browser and make it possible to create documents that collect and process user input, and formulate personalized replies.

This powerful mechanism has far-reaching implications, particularly for electronic commerce. It finishes an online catalog by giving buyers a way to immediately order products and services. It gives nonprofit organizations a way to sign up new members. It gives market researchers a way to collect user data. It gives you an automated way to interact with your HTML document readers.

Mull over the ways you might want to interact with your readers while we take a look at both the client- and server-side details of creating forms.

10.1 Form Fundamentals

Unlike the <isindex> tag, you can put one or more forms in a single document. And unlike an <isindex> document, users can ignore the embedded forms, reading content and interacting with the document's links just as with a form-less document. [<isindex>, 7.6.1]

Forms are comprised of one or more text input boxes, clickable buttons, multiple-choice checkboxes, and even pull-down menus and clickable images, all placed inside the <form> tag. Within a form, you may also put regular body content, including text and images. The text is particularly useful for providing instructions to the users on how to fill out the form and for form element labels and prompts. And, within the various form elements, you can use JavaScript event handlers for a variety of effects like testing and verifying form contents and calculating a running sum.

Once a user fills out the various fields in the form, they click a special "Submit" button (or, sometimes, press the Return key) to submit the form to a server. The browser packages up the user-supplied values and choices and sends them to a server or to an email address.* The server passes the information along to a supporting program or application that processes the information and creates a reply, usually in HTML. The reply may be simply a thank you or it might prompt the user how to fill out the form correctly or to supply missing fields. The server sends the reply to the browser client who then presents it to the user. With emailed forms, the information is simply put into someone's mailbox; there is no notification of the form being sent.

The server-side data-processing aspects of forms are not part of the HTML standard; they are defined by the server's software. While a complete discussion of server-side forms programming is beyond the scope of this book, we'd be remiss if we did not include at least a simple example to get you started. To that end, we've included at the end of this chapter a few skeletal programs that illustrate the common styles of server-side forms programming.

10.1.1 *The <form> Tag*

You place a form anywhere inside the body of an HTML document with its elements enclosed by the <form> tag and its respective end tag </form>. You may, and we recommend you often do, include regular body content inside a form to specially label user-input fields and to provide directions, for example.

Browsers flow the special form elements into the containing paragraphs as if they were small images embedded into the text. There aren't any special layout rules for form elements, so you need to use other HTML elements, like the <br> and <p> tags, to control the placement of elements within the text flow. [<p>, 4.1.2] [
, 4.7.1]

---

* Some browsers, Netscape in particular, may also encrypt the information, securing it from credit-card thieves, for example. However, the encryption facility must also be supported on the server-side as well: contact the browser manufacturer for details.

<form>

Function:
   Defines a form

Attributes:
   ACTION
   CLASS ⬛ ❶
   ENCTYPE
   METHOD
   NAME ⬛
   ONRESET ⬛
   ONSUBMIT ⬛ ❶
   STYLE ⬛ ❶
   TARGET ⬛ ❶

End tag:
   </form>; never omitted

Contains:
   form_content

Used in:
   block

All of the form elements within a `<form>` tag comprise a single form. The browser sends all of the values of these elements—blank, default, or user-modified—when the user submits the form to the server.

You must define at least two special form attributes, which provide the name of the form's processing server and the method by which the parameters are to be sent to the server. A third, optional attribute lets you change how the parameters get encoded for secure transmission over the network.

10.1.1.1 The action attribute

The required `action` attribute for the `<form>` tag gives the URL of the application that is to receive and process the form's data.

Most webmasters keep their forms-processing applications in a special directory on their web server, usually named *cgi-bin*, which stands for Common Gateway Interface binaries.[*] Keeping these special forms-processing programs and applications in one directory makes it easier to manage and secure the server.

---

[*] The Common Gateway Interface (CGI) defines the protocol by which servers interact with programs that process form data.

A typical `<form>` tag with the `action` attribute looks like this:

```
<form action="http://www.kumquat.com/cgi-bin/update">
...
</form>
```

The example URL tells the browser to contact the server named *www.kumquat.com* and pass along the user's form values to the application named *update* located in the *cgi-bin* directory.

In general, if you see a URL that references a document in a directory named *cgi-bin*, you can be pretty sure that the document is actually an application that creates the desired page dynamically each time it's invoked.

10.1.1.2 The enctype attribute

The browser specially encodes the form's data before it passes that data to the server so it does not become scrambled or corrupted during the transmission. It is up to the server to either decode the parameters or to pass them, still encoded, to the application.

The standard encoding format is the Internet Media Type named "application/x-www-form-urlencoded." You can change that encoding with the optional `enctype` attribute in the `<form>` tag. The only optional encoding formats currently supported are "multipart/form-data" and "text/plain."

The multipart/form-data alternative is required for those forms that contain file-selection fields for upload by the user. The text/plain format should be used in conjunction with a `mailto` URL in the `action` attribute for sending forms to an email address instead of a server. Unless your forms need file-selection fields or you must use a `mailto` URL in the `action` attribute, you probably should ignore this attribute and simply rely upon the browser and your processing server to use the default encoding type. [file selection fields, 10.2.2.3]

10.1.1.3 The application/x-www-form-urlencoded encoding

The standard encoding—application/x-www-form-urlencoded—converts any spaces in the form values to a plus sign (+), nonalphanumeric characters into a percent sign (%) followed by two hexadecimal digits that are the ASCII code of the character, and the line breaks in multiline form data into %0D%0A.

The standard encoding also includes a name for each field in the form. (A "field" is a discrete element in the form, whose value can be nearly anything, from a single number to several lines of text—the user's address, for example.) If there is more than one value in the field, the values are separated by ampersands.

For example, here's what the browser sends to the server after the user fills out a form with two input fields labeled **name** and **address**; the former field has just one line of text, while the latter field has several lines of input:

```
name=O'Reilly+and+Associates&address=103+Morris+Street%0D%0A
Sebastopol,%0D%0ACA+95472
```

We've broken the value into two lines for clarity in this book, but in reality, the browser sends the data in an unbroken string. The **name** field is "O'Reilly and Associates" and the value of the **address** field, complete with embedded newline characters, is:

```
103 Morris Street
Sebastopol,
CA 95472
```

10.1.1.4 The multipart/form-data encoding

The multipart/form-data encoding encapsulates the fields in the form as several parts of a single MIME-compatible compound document. Each field has its own section in the resulting file, set off by a standard delimiter. Within each section, one or more header lines define the name of the field, followed by one or more lines containing the value of the field. Since the value part of each section can contain binary data or otherwise unprintable characters, no character conversion or encoding occurs within the transmitted data.

This encoding format is by nature more verbose and longer than the application/x-www-form-urlencoded format. As such, it can only be used when the **method** attribute of the **<form>** tag is set to **post**, as described below.

A simple example makes it easy to understand this format. Here's our previous example, when transmitted as multipart/form-data:

```
----------------------------146931364513459
Content-Disposition: form-data; name="name"

O'Reilly and Associates
----------------------------146931364513459
Content-Disposition: form-data; name="address"

103 Morris Street
Sebastopol,
CA 95472
----------------------------146931364513459--
```

The first line of the transmission defines the delimiter that will appear before each section of the document. It always consists of thirty dashes and a long random number that distinguishes it from other text that might appear in actual field values.

The next lines contain the header fields for the first section. There will always be a `Content-Disposition` field indicating that this section contains form data and providing the name of the form element whose value is in this section. You may see other header fields; in particular, some file-selection fields include a `Content-Type` header field that indicates the type of data contained in the file being transmitted.

After the headers, there is a single blank line followed by the actual value of the field on one or more lines. The section concludes with a repeat of the delimiter line that started the transmission. Another section follows immediately, and the pattern repeats until all of the form parameters have been transmitted. The end of the transmission is indicated by an extra two dashes at the end of the last delimiter line.

As we pointed out earlier, use multipart/form-data encoding only when your form contains a file-selection field. Here's an example of how the transmission of a file-selection field might look:

```
-----------------------------146931364513459
Content-Disposition: form-data; name="thefile"; filename="test"
Content-Type: text/plain

First line of the file
...
Last line of the file
-----------------------------146931364513459--
```

The only notable difference is that the `Content-Disposition` field contains an extra element, filename, that defines the name of the file being transmitted. There might also be a `Content-Type` field to further describe the file's contents.

10.1.1.5 *The text/plain encoding*

Use this encoding only when you don't have access to a form-processing server and need to send the form information by email (the form's `action` attribute is a `mailto` URL; see 10.1.1.13). The conventional encodings are designed for computer consumption; text/plain was designed with people in mind.

In this encoding, each element in the form is placed on a single line, with the name and value separated by an equal sign. Returning to our name and address example, the form data would be returned as:

```
name=O'Reilly and Associates
address=103 Morris Street%0D%0ASebastopol,%0D%0ACA 95472
```

As you can see, the only characters still encoded in this form are the carriage return and line feed characters in multiline text input areas. Otherwise, the result is easily readable and generally parsable by simple tools.

10.1.1.6 The method attribute

The other required attribute for the `<form>` tag sets the method by which the browser sends the form's data to the server for processing. There are two ways: the POST method and the GET method.

With the POST method, the browser sends the data in two steps: the browser first contacts the form-processing server specified in the `action` attribute, and once contact is made, sends the data to the server in a separate transmission.

On the server side, POST-style applications are expected to read the parameters from a standard location once they begin execution. Once read, the parameters must be decoded before the application can use the form values. Your particular server will define exactly how your POST-style applications can expect to receive their parameters.

The GET method, on the other hand, contacts the form-processing server and sends the form data in a single transmission step: the browser appends the data to the form's `action` URL, separated by the question mark character.

The common browsers transmit the form information by either method; some servers receive the form data by only one or the other method. You indicate which of the two methods—POST or GET—your forms-processing server handles with the `method` attribute in the `<form>` tag. Here's the complete tag including the GET transmission `method` attribute for the previous form example:

```
<form method=GET
   action="http://www.kumquat.com/cgi-bin/update">
   ...
</form>
```

Which one to use if your form-processing server supports both the POST and GET methods? Here are some rules of thumb:

- For best form-transmission performance, send small forms with a few short fields via the GET method.

- Because some server operating systems limit the number and length of command-line arguments that can be passed to an application at once, use the POST method to send forms that have many fields, or ones that have long text fields.

- If you are inexperienced in writing server-side form-processing applications, choose GET. The extra steps involved in reading and decoding POST-style transmitted parameters, while not too difficult, may be more work than you are willing to tackle.

- If security is an issue, choose POST. GET places the form parameters directly in the application URL where they easily can be captured by network sniffers or extracted from a server log file. If the parameters contain sensitive information like credit card numbers, you may be compromising your users without their knowledge. While POST applications are not without their security holes, they can at least take advantage of encryption when transmitting the parameters as a separate transaction with the server.

If you want to invoke the server-side application outside the realm of a form, including passing it parameters, use GET because it lets you include form-like parameters as part of a URL. POST-style applications, on the other hand, expect an extra transmission from the browser after the URL, something you can't do as part of a conventional <a> tag.

10.1.1.7 *Passing parameters explicitly*

The foregoing bit of advice warrants some explanation. Suppose you had a simple form with two elements named x and y. When the values of these elements are encoded, they look like this:

    x=27&y=33

If the form uses method=GET, the URL used to reference the server-side application looks something like this:

    http://www.kumquat.com/cgi-bin/update?x=27&y=33

There is nothing to keep you from creating a conventional <a> tag that invokes the form with any parameter value you desire, like so:

    <a href="http://www.kumquat.com/cgi-bin/update?x=19&y=104">

The only hitch is that the ampersand that separates the parameters is also the character-entity insertion character. When placed within the href attribute of the <a> tag, the ampersand will cause the browser to replace the characters following it with a corresponding character entity.

To keep this from happening, you must replace the literal ampersand with its entity equivalent, either & or &. With this substitution, our example of the nonform reference to the server-side application looks like this:

    <a href="http://www.kumquat.com/cgi-bin/update?x=19&y=104">

Because of the potential confusion that arises from having to escape the ampersands in the URL, server implementors are encouraged to also accept the semicolon as a parameter separator. You might want to check your server's documentation to see if they honor this convention. See Appendix E, *Character Entities*.

10.1.1.8 The name attribute

The `name` attribute is used to associate a name with the form. This name can subsequently be used in JavaScript code to reference and manipulate the form and its input elements. Unless you plan to control elements of your form with JavaScript, it is not necessary to include the `name` attribute. This attribute is supported only by Netscape.

10.1.1.9 The onsubmit and onreset attributes

The `onSubmit` attribute for the `<form>` tag is a special JavaScript event handler built into the modern browsers. The value of the event handler is—enclosed in quotation marks—one or a sequence of semicolon-separated JavaScript expressions, methods, and function references that the browser executes just before it actually submits the data to the form-processing server or sends it to an email address. [JavaScript event handlers, 13.3.3]

You may use the `onSubmit` event for a variety of effects. The most popular is for a client-side form-verification program that scans the form data and prompts the user to complete one or more missing elements. Another popular and much simpler use is to inform users when a `mailto` URL form is being processed via email (see 10.1.1.13).

The `onreset` attribute is used just like the `onsubmit` attribute, except that the associated JavaScript code is only executed if the user presses a "Reset" button in the form. This attribute is supported only by Netscape.

10.1.1.10 The style and class attributes

The `style` attribute for the `<form>` tag creates an inline style for the elements enclosed by the tag, overriding any other style rule in effect. The `class` attribute lets you format the content according to a predefined class of the `<form>` tag; its value is the name of that class. [`style` attribute, 9.1.1] [`class` attribute, 9.2.4]

The actual effects of `style` with `<form>` are hard to predict, however. In general, style properties affect the body content—text, in particular—that you may include as part of the form's contents, but `<form>` styles do affect the display characteristics of the form elements.

For instance, you may create a special font face and background color style for the form. The form's text labels, but not the text inside a text input form element, will appear in the specified font face and background color. Similarly, the text labels you put beside a set of radio buttons will be in the form-specified style, but not radio buttons themselves.

10.1.1.11 The target attribute

With the advent of frames, it is possible to redirect the results of a form to another window or frame. Simply add the `target` attribute to your `<form>` tag and provide the name of the window or frame to receive the results.

Like the `target` attribute used in conjunction with the `<a>` tag, you can use a number of special names with the `target` attribute in the `<form>` tag to create a new window or to replace the contents of existing windows and frames. [`<a>` target, 12.7.1]

10.1.1.12 A simple form example

In a moment we'll examine each element of a form in detail. Let's first take a quick look at a simple example to see how forms are put together. This one (shown in Figure 10-1) gathers basic demographic information about a user:

```
<form method=POST action="http://www.kumquat.com/demo">
  Name:
    <input type=text name=name size=32 maxlength=80>
  <p>
  Sex:
    <input type=radio name=sex value="M"> Male
    <input type=radio name=sex value="F"> Female
  <p>
  Income:
    <select name=income size=1>
      <option>Under $25,000
      <option>$25,001 to $50,000
      <option>$50,001 and higher
    </select>
  <p>
  <input type=submit>
</form>
```

The first line of the example starts the form and indicates we'll be using the POST method for data transmission to the form-processing server. The form's user-input elements follow, each defined by an `<input>` tag and `type` attribute. There are three elements in the simple example, each contained within its own paragraph.

The first element is a conventional text entry field, letting the user type up to 80 characters, but displaying only 32 of them at a time. The next element is a multiple-choice option, which lets the user select only one of two radio buttons. This is followed by a pull-down menu for choosing one of three options. The final element is a simple submission button, which, when clicked by the user, sets the form's processing in motion.

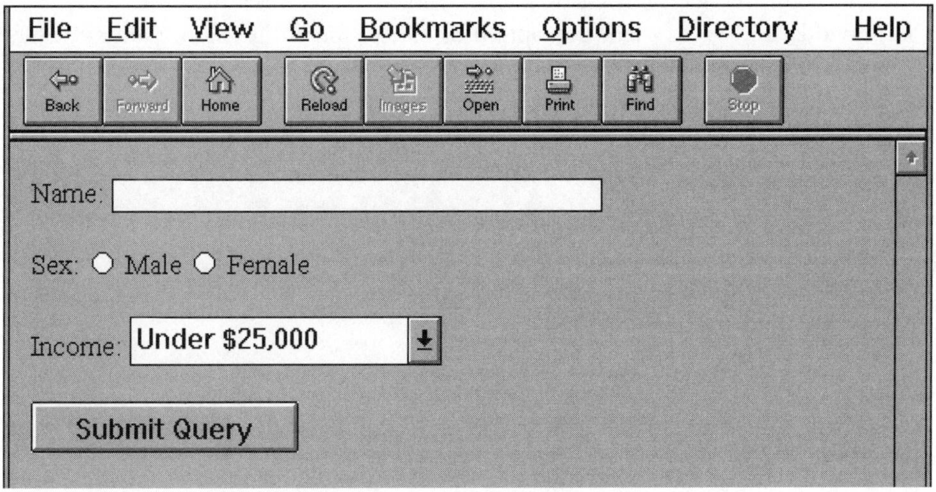

Figure 10-1. A simple form

10.1.1.13 Using mailto to collect form data ▣

It is becoming increasingly common to find authors who have no access to a web server other than to upload their HTML documents. Consequently, they have no ability to create or manage CGI programs. In fact, some providers, particularly those hosting space for hundreds or even thousands of sites, typically disable CGI services to limit their server's processing load or as a security precaution. If you are working with one of these sites, forms become a difficult, if not impossible, proposition.

All is not lost: You can use a mailto URL as the value of the form's `action` attribute. The Netscape browser will automatically email the various form parameters and values to the address supplied in the URL. The recipient of the mail can then process the form and take action accordingly.

For example, by substituting the following for the `<form>` tag in our previous example:

```
<form method=POST action="mailto:chuckandbill@ora.com"
enctype="text/plain"
    onSubmit="window.alert('This form is being sent by email, even
    though it may not appear that anything has happened...')">
```

the form data gets emailed to `chuckandbill` when submitted by the user, not otherwise processed by a server. Notice, too, that we have a simple JavaScript alert message that appears when the browser gets ready to send out the form data. The alert tells the user not to expect confirmation that the form data was sent (see Figure 10-2). Also, unless disabled by the user or if you omit the `method=POST` attribute, the browser typically will warn the user that they are about to send unencrypted ("text/plain") and thereby unsecure information over the network, and gives them the option to cancel the submission. Otherwise, the form is sent via email without incident or notification.

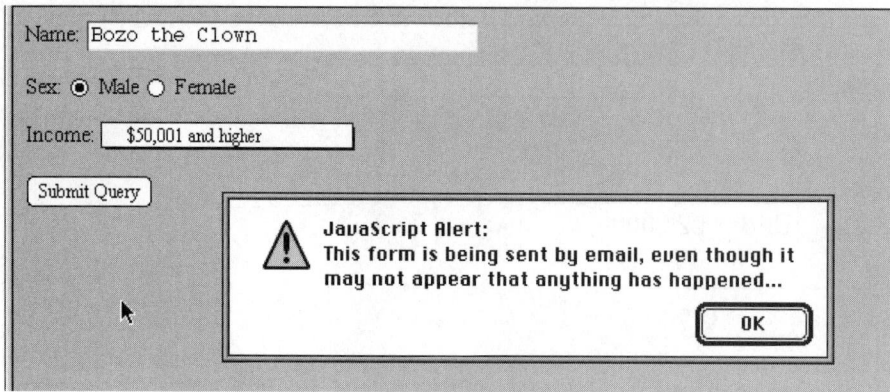

Figure 10-2. A warning about a mailto form submission

The body of the resulting emailed form message looks something like this:

```
name=Bozo the Clown
sex=M
 income=$50,001 and higher
```

If you choose to use the mailto form capability, there are several problems you may have to deal with:

- Your forms won't work on browsers that don't support a mailto URL as a form action.

- Some browsers, such as Internet Explorer, do not properly place the form data into the email message body and may even open an email dialog, confusing the user.

- Unlike with most form CGI scripts, a mailto doesn't present the user with a confirmation page to assure them that their form has been processed. After executing the mailto form, the user is left looking at the form, as if nothing had happened. (Use JavaScript to overcome this dilemma with an `onSubmit` or `onClick` event handler.) [JavaScript event handlers, 13.3.3]

- Your data may arrive in a form that is difficult, if not impossible, to read, unless you use a readable `enctype`, such as `text/plain`.

In spite of all this, mailto forms present an attractive alternative to the web author constrained by a restricted server. Our advice: use CGI scripts if at all possible, and fall back to mailto URLs if all else fails.

10.2 Form Input Elements

You create most form elements with the `<input>` tag.

10.2.1 The `<input>` Tag

Use the `<input>` tag to define any one of a number of common form elements, including text fields, multiple-choice lists, clickable images, and submission buttons. Although there are many attributes for this tag, only the `type` and `name` attributes are required for each element (only `type` for a submission or reset button; see following explanation), and as we describe in detail later, each type of input element uses only a subset of the allowed attributes. Additional `<input>` attributes may be required based upon which type of form element you specify. Table 10-1 summarizes the various form `<input>` types and attributes, required and optional.

Table 10-1. Required and optional form element attributes

Form Tag or `<input>` Type	\multicolumn Attributes (•=Required; o=Optional; blank=Not Supported)																			
	accept	align	border	cols	checked	maxlength	multiple	name	notab	onBlur	onChange	onClick	onFocus	onSelect	rows	size	src	taborder	value	wrap
button								•	o			o						o	•	
checkbox					o			•	o			o						o	•	
file	o						o	•	o	o	o	o	o				o	o	o	
hidden								•											•	
image		o	o					o	o			o					•	o		
password						o		•	o	o	o		o	o		o		o	•	
radio					o			•	o			o						o	•	
reset									o			o						o	o	
submit								o	o			o						o	o	
text						o		•	o	o	o		o	o		o		o	o	
`<select>`				o			o	•		o	o		o			o				
`<textarea>`				o				•		o	o		o	o	o				o	o

You select the type of element to include in the form with the `<input>` tag's required `type` attribute, and you name the field (used during the form-submission process to the server; see above) with the `name` attribute. Although the value of the `name` attribute is technically an arbitrary string, we recommend you use a name without embedded spaces or punctuation. If you stick to just

---

<input>

Function:

Create an input element within a form

Attributes:

ACCEPT
ALIGN
BORDER **N**
CLASS **N** **O**
CHECKED
MAXLENGTH
NAME
ONBLUR **N** **O**
ONCHANGE **N** **O**
ONCLICK **N** **O**
ONFOCUS **N** **O**
ONSELECT **N** **O**
SIZE
SRC
STYLE **N** **O**
TYPE
VALUE

End tag:

None

Contains:

Nothing

Used in:

form_content

---

letters and numbers (but no leading digits) and represent spaces with the under-score (_) character, you'll have fewer problems. For example, "cost_in_dollars" and "overhead_percentage" are good choices for element names; "$cost" and "overhead %" might cause problems.

10.2.2 Text Fields in Forms

The HTML standard lets you include three types of text entry fields in your forms: a conventional text entry field, a masked field for secure data entry, and a field that names a file to be transmitted as part of your form data. The first two are available with all browsers and accept `size`, `maxlength`, and `value` attributes. The file-selection field accepts only the `size` and `maxlength` attributes.

10.2.2.1 Conventional text fields

The most useful as well as the most common form input element is the text entry field. A text entry field appears in the browser window as an empty box on one line and accepts a single line of user input that becomes the value of the element when the user submits the form to the server. To create a text entry field inside a form in your HTML document, set the `type` of the `<input>` form element to `text`. Include a `name` attribute as well; it's required.

What constitutes a line of text differs among the various browsers. Fortunately, HTML gives us a way, with `size` and `maxlength` attributes, to dictate the width, in characters, of the text input display box, and how many total characters to accept from the user, respectively. The value for either attribute is an integer equal to the maximum number of characters you'll allow the user to see and type in the field. If `maxlength` exceeds `size`, then text scrolls back and forth within the text entry box. If `maxlength` is smaller than `size`, there will be extra blank space in the text entry box to make up the difference between the two attributes.

The default value for `size` is dependent upon the browser; the default value for `maxlength` is unlimited. We recommend you set them yourself. Adjust the `size` attribute so that the text entry box does not extend beyond the right margin of a typical browser window (about 60 characters with a very short prompt). Set `maxlength` to a reasonable number of characters; for example, 2 for state abbreviations, 12 for phone numbers, and so on.

A text entry field is usually blank at first until the user types something into it. You may, however, specify an initial default value for the field with the `value` attribute. The user may modify the default, of course. If the user presses a form's reset button, the value of the field is reset to this default value. [reset buttons, 10.2.5.2]

These are all valid text entry fields:

```
<input type=text name=comments>
<input type=text name=zipcode size=10 maxlength=10>
<input type=text name=address size=30 maxlength=256>
<input type=text name=rate size=3 maxlength=3 value="100">
```

The first example creates a text entry field set to the browser's default width and maximum length. As we argue above, this is not a good idea because defaults vary widely among browsers, and your form layout is sure to look bad with some of them. Rather, fix the width and maximum number of acceptable input characters as we do in the second example: it lets the user type in up to ten characters inside an input box ten characters wide. Its value will be sent to the server with the name "zipcode" when the user submits the form.

The third example field tells the browser to display a 30-character-wide text input box into which the user may type up to 256 characters. The browser automatically scrolls text inside the input box to expose the extra characters.

The last text input field is three characters wide, lets the user type in only three characters, and sets its initial value to 100.

Notice in the second and fourth example fields, it is implied that certain kinds of data are to be entered by the user—a postal code or a numeric rate, respectively. Except for limiting *how many*, HTML provides no way for you to dictate *what* characters may be typed into a text input field. For instance, in the last example field, the user may type "ABC" even though you intend it to be a number less than 1,000. Your server-side application must trap erroneous or mistaken input, as well as check for incomplete forms, and send the appropriate error message to the user when things aren't right. That can be a tedious process, so we emphasize again, provide clear and precise instructions and prompts. Make sure your forms tell users what kinds of input you expect from them, thereby reducing the number of mistakes they may make when filling it out.

10.2.2.2 Masked text fields

Like the Lone Ranger, the mask is on the good guys in a masked text field. It behaves just like a conventional text field in a form, except that the user-typed characters don't appear onscreen. Rather, the browser obscures the characters in a masked text to keep such things as passwords and other sensitive codes from prying eyes.

To create a masked text field, set the value of the `type` attribute to `password`. All other attributes and semantics of the conventional text field apply to the masked field. Hence, you must provide a name, and you may (we recommend it) specify a `size` and `maxlength` for the field, as well as an initial `value`.

Don't be misled: a masked text field is not all that secure. The typed-in value is only obscured onscreen; the browser transmits it unencrypted when the form is submitted to the server. So, while prying eyes may not see them onscreen, devious bad guys may steal the information electronically.

10.2.2.3 File selection fields

As its name implies, the field lets users select a file stored on their computer and send it to the server when they submit the form. Although part of the HTML 3.2 standard and documented by Microsoft as being supported, file-selection fields do not work in Internet Explorer 3.0. They do work in Netscape.

The browser presents the file-selection form field to the user like other text fields. With Netscape, it's accompanied by a button labeled "Browse" to its right. Users either type the pathname directly as text into the field or, with the Browse option, select the name of a locally stored file from a system-specific dialog box.

Create a file-selection field in a form by setting the value of the `type` attribute to `file`. Like other text fields, the `size` and `maxlength` of a file-selection field should be set to appropriate values, with the browser creating a field 20 characters wide, if not otherwise directed. Since file and directory names differ widely among systems, it makes no sense to provide a default value for this field. As such, the value attribute should not be used with this kind of text field.

The Browse button associated with Netscape's file-selection field opens a platform-specific file-selection dialog that allows users to select a value for the field. In this case, the entire pathname of the selected file is placed into the field, even if the length of that pathname exceeds the field's specified `maxlength`.

Use the `accept` attribute to constrain the types of files that the browser lets the user select. It's value is a comma-separated list of MIME encodings; users can only select files whose type matches one of those in the list. For example, to restrict the selection to images, you might add `accept="image/*"` to the file selection `<input>` tag.

Unlike other form input elements, the file-selection field only works correctly with a specific form data encoding and transmission method. If you include one or more file-selection fields in your form, you must set the `enctype` attribute of the `<form>` tag to `multipart/form-data` and the `<form>` tag's `method` attribute to `post`. Otherwise, the file-selection field behaves like a regular text field, transmitting its value (that is, the file's pathname) to the server instead of the contents of the file itself.

This is all easier than it may sound. For example, here is a form that collects a person's name and favorite file:

```
<form enctype="multipart/form-data" method=post
    action="cgi-bin/save_file">
Your name: <input type=text size=20 name=the_name>
<p>
Your favorite file: <input type=file size=20 name=fav_file>
</form>
```

The data transmitted from the browser to the server for this example form has two parts. The first contains the value for the name field, and the second contains the name and contents of the specified file:

```
---------------------------6099238414674
Content-Disposition: form-data; name="the_name"

One line of text field contents
---------------------------6099238414674
Content-Disposition: form-data; name="fav_file"; filename="abc"

First line of file
...
Last line of file
---------------------------6099238414674--
```

The browsers don't check that a valid file has been specified by the user. If no file is specified, the filename portion of the `Content-Disposition` header will be empty. If the file doesn't exist, its name appears in the filename subheader, but there will be no `Content-Type` header or subsequent lines of file content. Valid files may contain nonprintable or binary data; there is no way to restrict user-selectable file types. In light of these potential problems, the form-processing application on the server should be robust enough to handle missing files, erroneous files, extremely large files, and files with unusual or unexpected formats.

10.2.3 Checkboxes

The checkbox element gives users a way to quickly and easily select or deselect an item in your form. Checkboxes may also be grouped to create a set of choices, any of which may be selected or deselected by the user.

Create individual checkboxes by setting the `type` attribute for each `<input>` tag to `checkbox`. Include the required `name` and `value` attributes. If the item is selected, it will contribute a value when the form is submitted. If it is not selected, that element will not contribute a value. The optional `checked` attribute (no value) tells the browser to display a checked checkbox and include the value when submitting the form to the server unless the user specifically clicks the mouse to deselect (uncheck) the box.

The browsers include the value of selected (checked) checkboxes with other form parameters when they are submitted to the server. The value of the checked checkbox is the text string you specify in the required `value` attribute. For example:

```
<form>
  What pets do you own?
  <p>
    <input type=checkbox name=pets value="dog"> Dog
  <br>
    <input type=checkbox checked name=pets value="cat"> Cat
  <br>
    <input type=checkbox name=pets value="bird"> Bird
  <br>
    <input type=checkbox name=pets value="fish"> Fish
</form>
```

creates a checkbox group as shown in Figure 10-3.

Although part of the group, each checkbox element appears as a separate choice onscreen. Notice too, with all due respect to dog, bird, and fish lovers, that we've preselected the cat checkbox with the `checked` attribute in its tag. We've also provided text labels; the similar value attributes don't appear in the browser's

Figure 10-3. A checkbox group

window, but are the values included in the form's parameter list if the checkbox is selected and the form is submitted to the server by the user. Also, you need to use paragraph or line-break tags to control the layout of your checkbox group, as you do for other form elements.

In the example, if "Cat" and "Fish" are checked when the form is submitted, the values included in the parameter list sent to the server would be:

```
pets=cat
pets=fish
```

10.2.4 Radio Buttons

Radio-button form elements are similar in behavior to checkboxes, except that only one in the group may be selected by the user.* Create a radio button by setting the `type` attribute of the `<input>` element to `radio`. Like checkbox elements, radio buttons each require a `name` and `value` attribute. Radio buttons with the same name are members of a group. One of them may be initially checked by including the `checked` attribute with that element. If no element in the group is checked, the browser automatically checks the first element in the group.

You should give each radio button element a different value, so the server can sort them out after submission of the form.

Here's the previous example reworked so that now you get to choose only one animal as a favorite pet (see Figure 10-4):

---

* Some of us are old enough, while not yet senile, to recall when automobile radios had mechanical push-buttons for selecting a station. Pushing in one button popped out the previously depressed one, implementing a mechanical one-of-many choice mechanism.

```
<form>
  Which type of animal is your favorite pet?
  <p>
    <input type=radio name=favorite value="dog"> Dog
  <br>
    <input type=radio checked name=favorite value="cat"> Cat
  <br>
    <input type=radio name=favorite value="bird"> Bird
  <br>
    <input type=radio name=favorite value="fish"> Fish
</form>
```

Figure 10-4. Radio buttons allow only one selection per group

Again, like the previous example with checkboxes, we've tipped our hat toward felines, making the "Cat" radio button the default choice. If you select an alternative—"Bird," for instance—the browser automatically deselects "Cat." When the form is submitted to the server, the browser includes only one value with the name "favorite" in the list of form parameters; `favorite=bird`, if that was your choice.

Since one of the elements in a group of radio buttons is always selected, it makes no sense to create a single radio button; they should appear in your documents as groups of two or more. (Use checkboxes for on/off, yes/no types of form elements.)

10.2.5 Action Buttons

Although the terminology is potentially confusing, there is another class of buttons for HTML forms. Unlike the radio buttons and checkboxes described above, these special types of `<input>` form elements act immediately, their effects cannot be reversed, and they affect the entire contents of the form, not just the value of a single field. These "action" buttons (for lack of a better term) include submit, reset, regular, and clickable image buttons. When selected by the user, both the submit and image buttons cause the browser to submit all of the form's parameters to the form-processing server. A regular button does not submit the form, but can be used to invoke JavaScript code to manipulate or validate the form. The reset button acts locally to return a partially filled-out form to its original (default) state. [JavaScript event handlers, 13.3.3]

10.2.5.1 Submission buttons

The submit button (`<input type=submit>`) does what its name implies, setting in motion the form's submission to the server from the browser. You may have more than one submit button in a form. You may also include **name** and **value** attributes with the submit type of input form button.

With the simplest submit button (that without a **name** or **value** attribute), the browser displays a small rectangle or oval with the default label "Submit" (see Figure 10-1). Otherwise, the browser will label the button with the text you include with the tag's **value** attribute. If you provide a **name** attribute, the **value** attribute for the submit button will be added to the parameter list the browser sends along to the server. That's good, because it gives you a way to identify which button in a form was pressed, letting you process any one of several different forms with a single form-processing application.

The following are all valid submission buttons:

```
<input type=submit>
<input type=submit value="Order Kumquats">
<input type=submit value="Ship Overnight" name="ship_style">
```

The first one is also the simplest: the browser displays a button, labeled "Submit," which activates the form-processing sequence when clicked by the user. It does not add an element to the parameter list that the browser passes to the form-processing server and application.

The second example button has the **value** attribute that makes the displayed button label "Order Kumquats," but like the first example, does not include the button's value in the form's parameter list.

The last example sets the button label and makes it part of the form's parameter list. When clicked by the user, that last example of the submission button adds the parameter **ship_style="Ship Overnight"** to the form's parameter list.

10.2.5.2 Reset buttons

The reset type of form `<input>` button is nearly self-explanatory: it lets the user reset—erase or set to some default value—all elements in the form. Unlike the other buttons, a reset button does not initiate form processing. Instead, the browser does the work of resetting the form elements. The server never knows (or cares, for that matter) if or when the user might have pressed a reset button.

By default, the browser displays a reset button with the label "Reset." You can change that by specifying a `value` attribute with your own button label.

Here are two sample reset buttons:

```
<input type=reset>
<input type=reset value="Use Defaults">
```

The first one creates a reset button labeled "Reset"; the browser labels the second example reset button with "Use Defaults." They both initiate the same reset response in the browser.

10.2.5.3 Custom image buttons

The `image` type of `<input>` form element creates a custom button that is a "clickable" image. It's a special button made out of your specified image that, when clicked by the user, tells the browser to submit the form to the server, and includes the x,y coordinates of the mouse pointer in the form's parameter list, much like the mouse-sensitive image maps we discuss in Chapter 7, *Links and Webs*. Image buttons require a `src` attribute with the URL of the image file, and you can include a `name` attribute. You may also use `align` and `border` (Netscape only) attributes to control image alignment within the current line of text and the width of the frame that Netscape places around the image, respectively, much like the `align` and `border` attributes for the `<img>` tag (Internet Explorer doesn't border form `<input>` images). Interestingly, none of the Java-Script event handlers work with this type of form element, despite what the manufacturer's documentation says—not even `onClick`, which you might expect, since the image acts like the submit input type.

Here are a couple of valid image buttons:

```
<input type=image src="pics/map.gif" name=map>
<input type=image src="pics/xmap.gif" align=top name=map>
```

The browser displays the designated image within the form's content flow. The second button's image will be aligned with the top of the adjacent text, as specified by the `align` attribute. Some browsers (Netscape, for instance) also add a border, as it does when an image is part of an anchor (`<a>` tag), to signal that the image is a form button.

When the user clicks the image, the browser sends the horizontal offset, in pixels, of the mouse from the left edge of the image and the vertical offset from the top edge of the image to the server. These values are assigned the name of the image as specified with the name attribute, followed by ".x" and ".y," respectively. Thus, if someone clicked the image specified above, the browser would send parameters named `map.x` and `map.y` to the server.

Image buttons behave much like mouse-sensitive image maps, and, like the programs that process image maps, your form-processing application may use the x,y mouse-pointer parameters to choose a special course of action. You should use an image button when you need additional form information to process the user's request. If an image map of links is all you need, use a mouse-sensitive image map. Mouse-sensitive images also have the added benefit of providing server-side support for automatic detection of shape selection within the image, letting you deal with the image as a selectable collection of shapes. Buttons with images require you to write code that determines where the user clicked on the image and how this position can be translated to an appropriate action by the server.

10.2.5.4 Regular buttons

Using the `<input type=button>` tag, you can create a button that can be clicked by the user but that does not submit or reset the form. The **value** attribute can be used to set the label on the button; the **name** attribute, if specified, will cause the supplied value to be passed to the form processing script.

You might wonder what value such buttons provide. Little or none, unless you supply the `onClick` attribute, along with a snippet of JavaScript to be executed when the user clicks the button. Thus empowered, regular buttons can be used to validate form contents, update fields, manipulate the document, and initiate all sorts of client-side activity. [JavaScript event handlers, 13.3.3]

10.2.5.5 Multiple buttons in a single form

You can have several buttons of the same or different types in a single form. Even simple forms have both reset and submit buttons, for example. To distinguish between them, make sure each has a different **value** attribute, which the browser uses for the button label. Depending on the way you program the form-processing application, you might also make the **name** of each button different, but it is usually easier to name all similarly acting buttons the same and let the button handling subroutine sort them out by value. For instance:

```
<input type=submit name=action value="Add">
<input type=submit name=action value="Delete">
<input type=submit name=action value="Change">
<input type=submit name=action value="Cancel">
```

When the user selects one of these example buttons, a form parameter named `action` will be sent to the server. The value of this parameter will be one of the button names. The server-side application gets the value and behaves accordingly.

Since an image button doesn't have a `value` attribute, the only way to distinguish between several image buttons on a single form is to ensure they all have different names.

10.2.6 Hidden Fields

The last type of form input element we describe in this chapter is hidden from view. No, we're not trying to conceal anything. It's a way to embed information into your forms that cannot be ignored or altered by the browser or user. Rather, the `<input type=hidden>` tag's required `name` and `value` attributes automatically get included in the submitted form's parameter list. These serve to label the form and can be invaluable when sorting out different forms or form versions from a collection of submitted and saved forms.

Another use for hidden fields is to manage user/server interactions. For instance, it helps the server to know that the current form has come from a person who made a similar request a few moments ago. Normally, the server does not retain this information and each transaction between the server and client is completely independent from all other transactions.

For example, the first form submitted by the user might have asked for some basic information, such as the user's name and where they live. Based on that initial contact, the server might create a second form asking more specific questions of the user. Since it is tedious for users to re-enter the same basic information from the first form, the server can be programmed to put those values in the second form in hidden fields. When the second form comes back, all the important information from both forms is there, and the second form can be matched to the first one, if necessary.

Hidden fields may also direct the server towards some specific action. For example, you might embed the hidden field:

```
<input type=hidden name=action value=change>
```

Therefore, if you have one server-side application that handles the processing of several forms, each form might contain a different action code to help that server application sort things out.

10.2.7 The style and class Attributes

The `style` attribute for the `<input>` tag creates an inline style for the elements enclosed by the tag, overriding any other style rule in effect. The `class` attribute lets you format the content according to a predefined class of the `<input>` tag; its value is the name of that class. The style-conscious browsers cannot distinguish between the various input types, so we recommend that if you use style classes at all, use them with the various form input types. However, be aware that the style properties usually don't affect the appearance of the form element itself.

For instance, you may specify that a text input element should have a blue background and use the Arial typeface:

```
<input type=text name=name style="background: blue; font-family:
Arial">
```

That doesn't mean it will work. A thin border around the text input area will be blue, but the text input box itself will have a white background, and the input text will appear in the default typeface, not in Arial. [`style` attribute, 9.1.1] [`class` attribute, 9.2.4]

10.2.8 The notab and taborder Attributes

By default, every element (except hidden elements) is part of the form's tab order. As the user presses the tab key, the browser shifts the input focus from element to element in the form. For most browsers, the order of the elements in the tab order matches the order of the elements within the `<form>` tag. With Internet Explorer, you can explicitly control which elements are part of the form's tab order, and the position of those elements within the tab order.

To exclude an element from the tab order, add the `notab` attribute to the `<input>` tag. The element will be skipped when the user tabs around the form.

To reposition an element within the tab order, use the `taborder` attribute. The value of the attribute is the element's desired position in the tab order. If you really want to change a form's tab order, we suggest you include the `taborder` attribute with every element in the form, with an appropriate value for each element. In this way, you'll be sure to place every element explicitly in the tab order, and there will be no surprises when the user tabs through the form.

10.2.9 Form <input> Event Handlers

JavaScript browsers support five event handlers for the various `<input>` tag types. The `onClick` attribute is for when the user clicks a checkbox, radio, reset, or submit button.[*] Use the `onSelect`, `onFocus`, `onBlur`, and `onChange` event handlers for form text input-related types (text, password, and file) for when the user selects a form input text area to type in some information, moves the mouse into the text input box, moves away from the text input box, and has changed the value of the text, respectively.

---

[*] Interestingly, the image type of input button does not support any of the JavaScript event handlers; not even `onClick`, which is supported by the related submit and reset types, nor any of the event handlers that can be used with the `<img>` tag.

The value of the `<input>` event handler attribute is—enclosed in quotation marks—one or a sequence of semicolon-separated JavaScript expressions, methods, and function references that the browser executes when the event occurs. For example, you might include an `onClick` event with the Submit button; it calls a JavaScript routine that verifies the form is completely filled out before it is submitted over the network to a processing server. Other handlers might compute a running total for items checked on a shopping list, for example. See 13.3.3 for more information about JavaScript and event handlers.

10.3 Multiline Text Areas

The conventional and hidden-text types for forms restrict user input to a single line of characters. The `<textarea>` form tag sets users free.

10.3.1 The *<textarea> Tag*

The `<textarea>` tag creates a multiline text entry area in the user's browser display. In it, the user may type a nearly unlimited number of lines of text. Upon submission of the form, the browser collects all the lines of text, each separated by `"%0D%0A"` (carriage return/line feed), and sends them to the server as the value of this form element, using the name specified by the required `name` attribute.

You may include plain text inside the `<textarea>` tag and its end tag. That default text must be plain text—no tags or other special HTML elements. The contents may be modified by the user, and the browser uses that text as the default value if the user presses a reset button for the form. Hence, the text content is most often included for instructions and examples:

```
Tell us about yourself:
<textarea name=address cols=40 rows=4>
  Your Name Here
  1234 My Street
  Anytown, State Zipcode
</textarea>
```

10.3.1.1 The rows and cols attributes

A multiline text input area stands alone onscreen: body content flows above and below, but not around it. You can control its dimensions, however, by defining the `cols` and `rows` attributes for the visible rectangular area set aside by the browser for multiline input. We suggest you do set these attributes. The common browsers have a habit of setting aside the smallest, least readable region possible for `<textarea>` input, and the user can't resize it. Both attributes require integer

---

<textarea>

Function:

Create a multiline text input area

Attributes:

CLASS **N** **O**
COLS
NAME
ONBLUR **N** **O**
ONCHANGE **N** **O**
ONFOCUS **N** **O**
ONSELECT **N** **O**
ROWS
STYLE **N** **O**
WRAP **N**

End tag:

</textarea>; never omitted

Contains:

plain_text

Used in:

form_content

---

values for the respective dimension's size in characters. The browser automatically scrolls text that exceeds either dimension.

10.3.1.2 *The wrap attribute*

Normally, text typed in the text area by the user is transmitted to the server exactly as typed, with lines broken only where the user pressed the Enter key. Since this is often not the desired action by the user, you can enable word wrapping within the text area. When the user types a line that is longer than the width of the text area, the browser automatically moves the extra text down to the next line, breaking the line at the nearest point between words in the line.

With the `wrap` attribute set to `virtual`, the text is wrapped within the text area for presentation to the user, but the text is transmitted to the server as if no wrapping had occurred, except where the user pressed the Enter key.

With the `wrap` attribute set to `physical`, the text is wrapped within the text area and is transmitted to the server as if the user had actually typed it that way. This the most useful way to use word wrap, since the text is transmitted exactly as the user sees it in the text area.

To obtain the default action, set the `wrap` attribute to `off`.

As an example, consider the following 60 characters of text being typed into a 40-character-wide text area:

```
Word wrapping is a feature that makes life easier for users.
```

With `wrap=off`, the text area will contain one line and the user will have to scroll to the right to see all of the text. One line of text will be transmitted to the server.

With `wrap=virtual`, the text area will contain two lines of text, broken after the word "makes." Only one line of text will be transmitted to the server: the entire line with no embedded newline characters.

With `wrap=physical`, the text area will contain two lines of text, broken after the word "makes." Two lines of text will be sent to the server, separated by a newline character after the word "makes."

10.3.2 The style and class Attributes

The `style` attribute for the `<textarea>` tag creates an inline style for the text enclosed by the tag, overriding any other style rule in effect. The `class` attribute lets you format the content according to a predefined class of the `<textarea>` tag; its value is the name of that class. Be aware that the same disclaimer for applying styles with text-type form elements also apply to the `<textarea>` (see 2.7). [`style` attribute, 9.1.1] [`class` attribute, 9.2.4]

10.3.3 Form <textarea> Event Handlers

JavaScript browsers support four event handlers for the `<textarea>` tag type. Use the `onFocus`, `onBlur`, `onChange`, and `onSelect` event handlers to respectively execute a JavaScript program when the user moves the mouse into the text area, when the user moves away from the text input box, when the user has changed the value of the text, and when the user selects the text area to type in some information.

The value of the event handler attribute is—enclosed in quotation marks—one or a sequence of semicolon-separated JavaScript expressions, methods, and function references that the browser executes when the event occurs. For example, you might associate a window alert via the `onFocus` event with the text area to relay some instructions to the user on what information they should type into that area. See 13.3.3 for more information about JavaScripting and event handlers.

10.4 Multiple Choice Elements

Checkboxes and radio buttons give you powerful means for creating multiple-choice questions and answers, but they can lead to long forms that are tedious to write and put a fair amount of clutter onscreen. The `<select>` tag gives you two compact alternatives: pull-down menus and scrolling lists.

10.4.1 The <select> Tag

By placing a list of `<option>`-tagged items inside the `<select>` tag of a form, you magically create a pull-down menu of choices.

<select>

Function:
   Create single- and multiple-choice menus

Attributes:
   CLASS **N** **O**
   MULTIPLE
   NAME
   ONBLUR **N** **O**
   ONCHANGE **N** **O**
   ONCLICK **N** **O**
   ONFOCUS **N** **O**
   SIZE
   STYLE **N** **O**

End tag:
   </select>; never omitted

Contains:
   select_content

Used in:
   form_content

As with other form tags, the **name** attribute is required and used by the browser when submitting the `<select>` choices to the server. Unlike radio buttons, however, no item is preselected, so if none is selected, no values are sent to the server when the form is submitted. Otherwise, the browser submits the selected item or collects multiple selections, each separated with commas, into a single parameter list and includes the **name** attribute when submitting `<select>` form data to the server.

10.4.1.1 The multiple attribute

To allow more than one option selection at a time, add the `multiple` attribute to the `<select>` tag. This causes the `<select>` to behave like an `<input type=checkbox>` element. If `multiple` is not specified, exactly one option can be selected at a time, just like a group of radio buttons.

10.4.1.2 The size attribute

The `size` attribute determines how many options are visible to the user at one time. The value of `size` should be a positive integer. The default value is 1 when `size` isn't specified. At `size=1`, if `multiple` is not specified, the browser typically displays the `<select>` list as a pop-up menu. Size values greater than one or by specifying the `multiple` attribute causes the `<select>` to be displayed as a scrolling list.

In the following example, we've converted our previous checkbox example into a scrolling, multiple-choice menu. Notice also that the `size` attribute tells the browser to display three options at a time:

```
What pets do you own?
  <select name=pets size=3 multiple>
    <option>Dog
    <option>Cat
    <option>Bird
    <option>Fish
  </select>
```

The result is shown in Figure 10-5, along with the change in appearance when the `size` attribute is set to 1 and `multiple` is not specified.

Figure 10-5. A <select> element, formatted with size=1 (left) and size=3 (right)

10.4.1.3 Form <select> event handlers

JavaScript browsers support four event handlers for the <select> tag type. Use the onFocus, onBlur, onChange, and onSelect event handlers, respectively, to execute a JavaScript program when the user moves the mouse into the <select> element, when the user moves away from the element, when the user has changed the value of the element, and when the user selects the element.

The value of the event handler attribute is—enclosed in quotation marks—one or a sequence of semicolon-separated JavaScript expressions, methods, and function references that the browser executes when the event occurs. For example, you might associate a window alert via the onFocus event with the text area to relay some instructions to the user on what information they should type into that area. See 13.3.3 for more information about JavaScripting and event handlers.

10.4.1.4 The style and class attributes

The style attribute for the <select> tag creates an inline style for the text enclosed by the tag, overriding any other style rule in effect. The class attribute lets you format the content according to a predefined class of the <select> tag; its value is the name of that class. Be aware that few style properties affect the form element itself, and none affect its internal contents. [style attribute, 9.1.1] [class attribute, 9.2.4].

10.4.2 The <option> Tag

Use the <option> tag to define each item within a <select> form element.

The browser displays the <option> tag's contents as an element within the <select> tag's menu or scrolling list, so the content must be plain text only, without any other sort of markup.

10.4.2.1 The value attribute

Use the value attribute to set a value for each option the browser sends to the server if that option is selected by the user. If the value attribute has not been specified, the value of the option is set to the content of the <option> tag.

As an example, consider these options:

```
<option value=Dog>Dog
<option>Dog
```

Both have the same value. The first is explicitly set within the <option> tag; the second defaults to the content of the <option> tag itself.

<option>

Function:
   Define available options within a <select> menu

Attributes:
   CLASS 🅽 🅞
   SELECTED
   STYLE 🅽 🅞
   VALUE

End tag:
   </option>; always omitted

Contains:
   plain_text

Used in:
   select_content

10.4.2.2 *The selected attribute*

By default, all options within a multiple-choice <select> tag are unselected. Include the selected attribute (no value) inside the <option> tag to preselect one or more options, which the user may then deselect. Single-choice <select> tags will preselect the first option if no option is explicitly preselected.

10.4.2.3 *The style and class attributes*

The style attribute for the <option> tag creates an inline style for the text enclosed by the tag, overriding any other style rule in effect. The class attribute lets you format the content according to a predefined class of the <option> tag; its value is the name of that class. Be aware that few style properties affect the form element itself, and none affect its internal contents. [style attribute, 9.1.1] [class attribute, 9.2.4].

10.5 *Creating Effective Forms*

Properly done, a form can provide an effective user interface for your readers. With some server-side programming tricks, you can use forms to personalize the HTML documents you present to readers, and thereby significantly increase the value of your pages on the Web.

10.5.1 Browser Constraints

As with other HTML elements, browsers have varying abilities to display and manage forms.

10.5.1.1 Browser limitations

Unlike other graphical-user interfaces, browser displays are static. They have little or no capability for real-time data validation, for example, or to update the values in a form based upon user input, giving users help and guidance.* Hence, poorly designed web forms can be difficult to fill out.

Make sure your forms assist the user as much as possible in getting their input correct. Adjust the size of text input fields to give clues on acceptable input; five- (or the new nine-) character-wide zipcode fields, for instance. Use checkboxes, radio buttons, and selection lists whenever possible to narrow the list of choices the user must make.

Make sure you also adequately document your forms. Explain how to fill them out, supplying examples for each field. Provide appropriate hyperlinks to documentation that describes each field, if necessary.

When the form is submitted, make sure the server-side application exhaustively validates the user's data. If an error is discovered, present the user with intelligent error messages and possible corrections. One of the most frustrating aspects of filling out forms is having to start over from scratch whenever the server discovers an error. To alleviate this ugly redundancy and burden on your readers, consider spending extra time and resources on the server side that returns the user's completed form with the erroneous fields flagged for changes.

While all of these suggestions require significant effort on your part, they will pay off many times over by making life easier for your users. Remember, you'll write the HTML for the form just once, but it may be used thousands or even millions of times by users.

10.5.1.2 Handling limited displays

The most common client on the Web is a PC running Windows on a 640×480 pixel display. The actual document-viewing window typically is around 600×400 4pixels; roughly 75 readable characters wide and 30 to 50 lines tall. You should design your forms (and all your documents) so they are effective when viewed through a window of this size.

---

* This is not entirely true. While HTML does not provide for data validation and user guidance, it is possible to attach Java or JavaScript applets to your form elements that do a very nice job of validating form data, updating form fields based upon user input, and guiding users through your forms.

You should structure your form to naturally scroll into two or three logical sections. The user can fill out the first section, page down; fill out the second section, page down; and so forth.

You should also avoid wide input elements. It is difficult enough to deal with a scrolling-text field or text area without having to scroll the document itself horizontally to see additional portions of the input element.

10.5.2 User Interface Considerations

When you elect to create a form, you immediately assume another role: that of a user-interface designer. While a complete discussion of user interface design is beyond the scope of this book, it helps to understand a few basic design rules to create effective, attractive forms.

10.5.2.1 Basic user-interface design

Any user interface is perceived at several levels simultaneously. Forms are no different. At the lowest level, your brain recognizes shapes within the document, attempting to categorize the elements of the form. At a higher level, you are reading the text guides and prompts, trying to determine what input is required of you. At the highest level, you are seeking to accomplish a goal with the interface as your tool.

A good form accommodates all three of these perceptive needs. Input elements should be organized in logical groups so that your brain can process the form layout in chunks of related fields. Consistent, well-written prompts and supporting text assist and lead the user to enter the correct information. Text prompts also remind users of the task at hand and reinforce the form's goal.

10.5.2.2 Creating forms that flow

Users process forms in a predictable order, one element after another, seeking to find the next element as they finish the previous one. To accommodate this searching process, you should design your forms so that one field leads naturally to another, and related fields are grouped together. Similarly, groups should lead naturally to one another and should be formatted in a consistent manner.

Simply stringing a number of fields together does not constitute an effective form. You must put yourself in the place of your users, who are using the form for the first time. Test your form on unsuspecting friends and colleagues before you release it on the general public. Is it easy to determine the purpose of the form? Where do you start filling things out? Can the user find a button to push to submit the form? Is there an opportunity to confirm decisions? Do readers understand what is expected of them for each field?

Your forms should lead the user naturally through the process of supplying the necessary data for the application. You wouldn't ask for a street address before asking for the user's name; other rules may dictate the ordering of other groups of input elements. To see if your form really works, make sure you view it on several browsers and have several people fill it out and comment on its effectiveness.

10.5.3 Good Form, Old Chap

At first glance, the basic rule of HTML—content, not style—seems in direct opposition to the basic rule of good interface design—precise, consistent layout. Even so, it is possible to use some HTML elements to greatly improve the layout and readability of most forms.

Traditional page layout uses a grid of columns to align common elements within a page. The resulting implied vertical and horizontal "edges" of adjacent elements give a sense of order and organization to the page, and makes it easy for the eye to scan and follow.

HTML makes it hard, but you can accomplish the same sort of layout for your forms. For example, you can group related elements and separate groups with empty paragraphs or horizontal rules.

Vertical alignment is more difficult but not impossible. In general, forms are easier to use if you arrange the input elements vertically and aligned to a common margin. One popular form layout keeps the left edge of the input elements aligned, with the element labels immediately to the left of the elements. This is done by using tables to place and align each form element and its label. Here is our previous form example, with the labels placed in the first column and the corresponding elements in the second:

```
<form method=POST action="http://www.kumquat.com/demo">
  <table border=0>
    <tr valign=top>
      <td align=right>Name:</td>
      <td align=left><input type=text name=name size=32 maxlength=80>
      </td>
    </tr>
    <tr valign=top >
      <td align=right>Sex:</td>
      <td align=left>
        <input type=radio name=sex value="M"> Male <br>
        <input type=radio name=sex value="F"> Female
      </td>
    </tr>
    <tr valign=top >
      <td align=right>Income:</td>
      <td align=left>
```

```
        <select name=income size=1>
          <option>Under $25,000
          <option>$25,001 to $50,000
          <option>$50,001 and higher
        </select>
      </td>
    </tr>
    <tr valign=top>
      <td colspan=2 align=center>
        <input type=submit value="Submit Query">
      </td>
    </tr>
  </table>
</form>
```

Notice in the resulting rendered form shown in Figure 10-6 that the table has placed each input element in its own row. The `align` attributes in the table cells force the labels to the right and the elements to the left, creating a vertical margin through the form. By spanning the cell in the last row, the submission button is centered with respect to the entire form. In general, using tables in this manner makes form layout much easier and consistent throughout your documents.

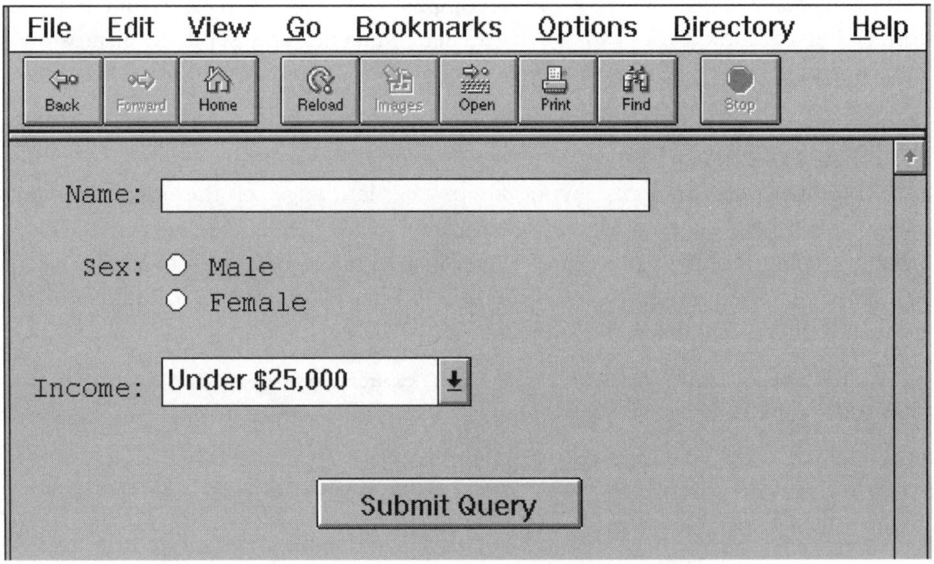

Figure 10-6. Using a consistent vertical margin to align form elements

You may find other consistent ways to lay out your forms. The key is to find a useful layout style that works well across most browsers and stick with it. Even though HTML has limited tools to control layout and positioning, take advantage of what is available to make your forms more attractive and easier to use.

10.6 Forms Programming

If you create forms, sooner or later you'll need to create the server-side application that processes your form. Don't panic. There is nothing magic about server-side programming, nor is it overly difficult. With a little practice and some perseverance, you'll be cranking out forms applications.

The most important advice we can give about forms programming is easy to remember: copy others' work. Writing a forms application from scratch is fairly hard; copying a functioning forms application and modifying it to support your form is far easier.

Fortunately, server vendors know this, and they usually supply sample forms applications with their server. Rummage about for a directory named *cgi-src*, and you'll discover a number of useful examples you can easily copy and reuse.

We can't hope to replicate all the useful stuff that came with your server, nor can we provide a complete treatise on forms programming. What we can do is offer a simple example of both GET and POST applications, giving you a feel for the work involved and hopefully getting you moving you in the right direction.

Before we begin, keep in mind that not all servers invoke these applications in the same manner. Our examples cover the broad class of servers derived from the original NCSA HTTP server. They also should work with the Netscape Communications family of server products and the public-domain Apache server. In all cases, consult your server documentation for complete details. You will find more detailed information in *CGI Programming for the World Wide Web* and *WebMaster in a Nutshell*, both published by O'Reilly & Associates.

10.6.1 Returning Results

Before we begin, we need to discuss how server-side applications end. All server-side applications pass their results back to the server (and on to the user) by writing that result to the application's standard output as a MIME-encoded file. Hence, the first line of the application's output must be a MIME content-type descriptor. If your application returns an HTML document, the first line is:

```
Content-type: text/html
```

The second line must be completely empty. Your application can return some other content type, too—just include the correct MIME type. A GIF image, for example, is preceded with:

```
Content-type: image/gif
```

Generic text that is not to be interpreted as HTML can be returned with:

```
Content-type: text/plain
```

This is often useful for returning the output of other commands that generate plain text instead of HTML.

10.6.2 Handling GET Forms

One of two methods for passing form parameters from client to server is the GET method. In that way, parameters are passed as part of the URL that invokes the server-side forms application. A typical invocation of a GET-style application might use a URL like this:

```
http://www.kumquat.com/cgi-bin/dump_get?name=bob&phone=555-1212
```

When the server processes this URL, it invokes the application named *dump_get* stored in the directory named *cgi-bin*. Everything after the question mark is passed to the application as parameters.

Things diverge a bit at this point, due to the nature of the GET-style URL. While forms place name/value pairs in the URL, it is possible to invoke a GET-style application with only values in the URL. Thus,

```
http://www.kumquat.com/cgi-bin/dump_get?bob+555-1212
```

is a valid invocation as well, with parameters separated by a plus sign (+). This is a common invocation when the application is referenced by a searchable document with the `<isindex>` tag. The parameters typed by the user into the document's text entry field are passed to the server-side application as unnamed parameters separated by plus signs.

If you invoke your GET application with named parameters, your server will pass those parameters to the application in one way; unnamed parameters are passed differently.

10.6.2.1 Using named parameters with GET applications

Named parameters are passed to GET applications by creating an environment variable named `QUERY_STRING` and setting its value to the entire portion of the URL following the question mark. Using our previous example, the value of `QUERY_STRING` would be set to:

```
name=bob&phone=555-1212
```

Your application must retrieve this variable and extract from it the parameter name/value pairs. Fortunately, most servers come with a set of utility routines that performs this task for you, so a simple C program that just dumps the parameters might look like:

```
#include <stdio.h>
#include <stdlib.h>

#define MAX_ENTRIES 10000

typedef struct {char *name;
                char *val;
                }entry;

char *makeword(char *line, char stop);
char x2c(char *what);
void unescape_url(char *url);
void plustospace(char *str);

main(int argc, char *argv[])

{   entry entries[MAX_ENTRIES];
    int num_entries, i;
    char *query_string;

/* Get the value of the QUERY_STRING environment variable */
    query_string = getenv("QUERY_STRING");

/* Extract the parameters, building a table of entries */
    for (num_entries = 0; query_string[0]; num_entries++) {
        entries[num_entries].val = makeword(query_string, '&'.;

        plustospace(entries[num_entries].val);
        unescape_url(entries[num_entries].val);
        entries[num_entries].name =
            makeword(entries[num_entries].val, '='.;
        }

/* Spit out the HTML boilerplate */
    printf("Content-type: text/html\n");
    printf("\n");

    printf("<html>");
    printf("<head>");
    printf("<title>Named Parameter Echo</title>\n");
    printf("</head>");
    printf("<body>");
    printf("You entered the following parameters:\n");
    printf("<ul>\n");

/* Echo the parameters back to the user */
    for(i = 0; i < num_entries; i++)
        printf("<li> %s = %s\n", entries[i].name,
                entries[i].val);
```

```
/* And close out with more boilerplate */
    printf("</ul>\n");
    printf("</body>\n");
    printf("</html>\n");
}
```

The example program begins with a few declarations that define the utility routines that scan through a character string and extract the parameter names and values.* The body of the program obtains the value of the QUERY_STRING environment variable using the getenv() system call, uses the utility routines to extract the parameters from that value, and then generates a simple HTML document that echoes back those values to the user.

For real applications, you'll want to insert your actual processing code after the parameter extraction and before the HTML generation. Of course, you'll also need to change the HTML generation to match your application's functionality.

10.6.2.2 Using unnamed parameters with GET applications

Unnamed parameters are passed to the application as command-line parameters. This makes writing the server-side application almost trivial. Here is a simple shell script that dumps the parameter values back to the user:

```
#!/bin/csh -f
#
# Dump unnamed GET parameters back to the user

echo "Content-type: text/html"
echo
echo '<html>'
echo '<head>'
echo '<title>Unnamed Parameter Echo</title>'
echo '</head>'
echo '<body>'
echo 'You entered the following parameters:'
echo '<ul>'

foreach i ($*)
    echo '<li>' $i
end

echo '</ul>'
echo '</body>'

exit 0
```

Again, we follow the same general style: output a generic document header, including the MIME content type, followed by the parameters and some closing

---

* These routines are usually supplied by the server vendor. They are not part of the standard C or UNIX libraries.

boilerplate. To convert this to a real application, replace the `foreach` loop with commands that actually do something.

10.6.3 Handling POST Forms

Applications that use POST-style parameters expect to read encoded parameters from their standard input. Like GET-style applications with named parameters, they can take advantage of the server's utility routines to parse these parameters.

Here is a program that echoes the POST-style parameters back to the user:

```
#include <stdio.h>
#include <stdlib.h>

#define MAX_ENTRIES 10000

typedef struct {char *name;
                char *val;
                } entry;

char *makeword(char *line, char stop);
char *fmakeword(FILE *f, char stop, int *len);
char x2c(char *what);
void unescape_url(char *url);
void plustospace(char *str);

main(int argc, char *argv[])

{   entry entries[MAX_ENTRIES];
    int num_entries, i;

/* Parse parameters from stdin, building a table of entries */
    for (num_entries = 0; !feof(stdin); num_entries++) {
        entries[num_entries].val = fmakeword(stdin, '&'. &cl);
        plustospace(entries[num_entries].val);
        unescape_url(entries[num_entries].val);
        entries[num_entries].name =
           makeword(entries[num_entries].val, '='.;
        }

/* Spit out the HTML boilerplate */
    printf("Content-type: text/html\n");
    printf("\n");
    printf("<html>");
    printf("<head>");
    printf("<title>Named Parameter Echo</title>\n");
    printf("</head>");
    printf("<body>");
    printf("You entered the following parameters:\n");
    printf("<ul>\n");
```

```
    /* Echo the parameters back to the user */
        for(i = 0; i < num_entries; i++)
            printf("<li> %s = %s\n", entries[i].name,
                        entries[i].val);

    /* And close out with more boilerplate */
        printf("</ul>\n");
        printf("</body>\n");
        printf("</html>\n");
    }
```

Again, we follow the same general form. The program starts by declaring the various utility routines needed to parse the parameters, along with a data structure to hold the parameter list. The actual code begins by reading the parameter list from the standard input and building a list of parameter names and values in the array named **entries**. Once this is complete, a boilerplate document header is written to the standard output, followed by the parameters and some closing boilerplate.

Like the other examples, this program is handy for checking the parameters being passed to the server application while you are early in the forms and application debugging process. You can also use it as a skeleton for other applications by inserting appropriate processing code after the parameter list is built up and altering the output section to send back the appropriate results.

11

Tables

Of all the extensions that found their way into the HTML 3.2 standard, none is more welcome than tables. While HTML tables are useful for the general display of tabular data, they also serve an important role in managing document layout. Creative use of tables, as we'll show in this chapter, can go a long way to enliven an otherwise dull document layout. And you may apply all the HTML styles to the various elements of a table to achieve a desktop-published look and feel.

11.1 The HTML Table Model

The standard HTML model for tables is fairly straightforward: a table is a collection of numbers and words arranged and related in rows and columns of *cells*. Most cells contain the data values; others contain row and column headers that describe the data.

You define a table and include all of its elements between the `<table>` tag and its corresponding `</table>` end tag. Table elements, including data items, row and column headers, and captions, each have their own markup tag. Working from top to bottom and left to right, you define, in sequence, the header and data for each column cell across the table, and progress down row by row.

The latest browsers also support an extended collection of tag attributes that make your tables look good, including special alignment of the table values and headers, borders, and table rule lines, and automatic sizing of the data cells to accommodate their content. The various popular browsers have slightly different sets of table attributes; we'll point out those variations as we go.

11.1.1 Table Contents

You may put nearly anything you might have within the body of an HTML document inside a table cell, including images, forms, rules, headings, and even another table. The browser treats each cell as a window unto itself, flowing the cell's content to fill the space, but with some special formatting provisions and extensions.

11.1.2 An Example Table

Here's a quick example that should satisfy your itching curiosity to see what an HTML table looks like in source code and when finally rendered as in Figure 11-1. More importantly, it shows you the basic structure of a table from which you can infer many of the elements, tag syntax and order, attributes, and so on, and to which you may refer as you read the following various detailed descriptions:

```
<table border cellspacing=0 cellpadding=5>
  <caption align=bottom>
    Kumquat versus a poked eye, by gender</caption>
  <tr>
    <td colspan=2 rowspan=2></td>
    <th colspan=2 align=center>Preference</th>
  </tr>
  <tr>
    <th>Eating Kumquats</th>
    <th>Poke In The Eye</th>
  </tr>
  <tr align=center>
    <th rowspan=2>Gender</th>
    <th>Male</th>
    <td>73%</td>
    <td>27%</td>
  </tr>
  <tr align=center>
    <th>Female</th>
    <td>16%</td>
    <td>84%</td>
  </tr>
</table>
```

11.1.3 Missing Features

HTML tables currently don't have all the features of a full-fledged table-generation tool you might find in a popular word processor. Rather than leave you in

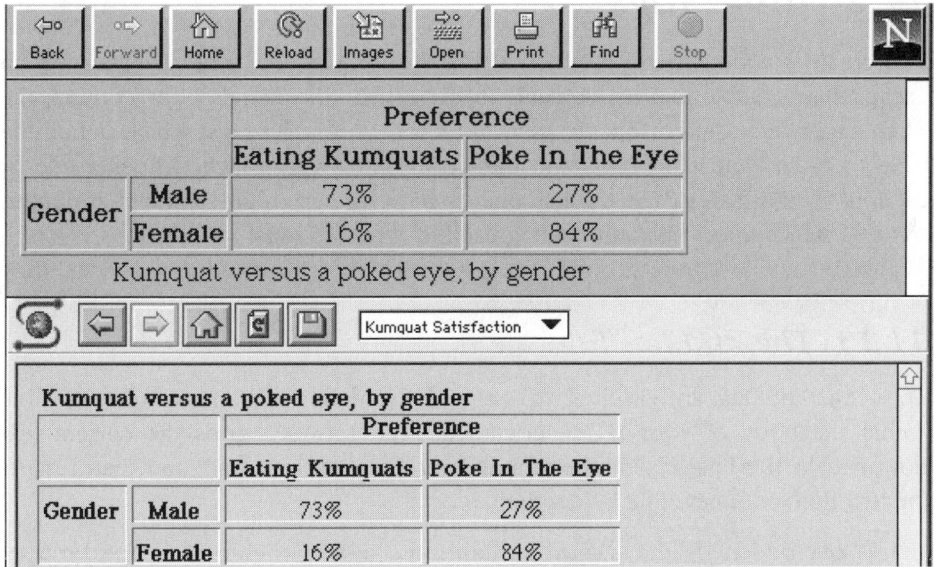

Figure 11-1. HTML table example rendered by Netscape (top) and by Mosaic (bottom)

suspense, we'll list those things up front so you don't beat your head against the wall later trying to do something that just can't be done (at least, not yet):

- The general problem of text alignment in HTML carries over into tables. You may align values inside their individual cells, but you cannot align them between cells. For instance, you cannot vertically align the decimal points in a column of numbers, even though they all might have the same number of digits, unless you use one of the monospace font styles.

- Netscape and Internet Explorer give you the ability to set the thickness of table and cell borders. Netscape allows only one line size for the table's borders and rules; Internet Explorer has limited provisions for varying rule widths between the header, body, and footer of a table.

- Except in Internet Explorer, HTML tables don't have running headers or footers. Of course, such things don't matter with an HTML browser where everything is on a single, infinitely long page. Running headers and footers are nice to have, though, when you print out a long table onto separate sheets of paper.

11.2 Table Tags

You create a wide variety of tables with only five tags: the `<table>` tag, which encapsulates a table and its elements in the HTML document's body content; the `<tr>` tag, which defines a table row; the `<th>` and `<td>` tags, which define the table's headers and data cells; and the `<caption>` tag, which defines a title or caption for the table. Each tag has one or more required and optional attributes, some of which affect not only the tag itself, but related tags. [`<tr>`, 11.2.2] [`<th>` and `<td>`, 11.2.3] [`<caption>`, 11.2.4]

11.2.1 The <table> Tag

The `<table>` tag and its `</table>` end tag define and encapsulate a table within the body of your HTML document. The browser stops the current text flow, breaks the line, inserts the table beginning on a new line, and then restarts the text flow on a new line below the table.

Unless overridden by the `align` attribute, the table's alignment in the browser window matches that of the containing text flow. Normally, this means that tables are aligned against the left margin of the current text flow. However, the table may be centered in the browser window if the preceding text is centered with the `<center>` tag or `<div align=center>`, or right-aligned by being in a right-aligned table cell (see the `align` attribute options below). [`<p>`, 4.1.2] [`<th>` and `<td>`, 11.2.3]

The only content allowed within the `<table>` tag besides the optional `<caption>` tag is one or more `<tr>` tags, which define each row of table contents.

11.2.1.1 The align attribute

Like images, tables are rectangular objects that float in the browser display, aligned according to the current text flow: Normally, the browser left-justifies a table, abutting its left edge to the left margin of the display window. Or the table may be centered if under the influence of the `<center>` tag, centered paragraph, or centered division. Unlike images, however, tables are normally not inline objects. Text content normally flows above and below a table, not beside it. You change that display behavior with the `align` attribute for the `<table>` tag.

The `align` attribute accepts a value of either `left` or `right`, indicating that the table should be placed flush against the left or right margin of the text flow, with the text flowing around the table. This alignment style corresponds to the left and right alignment of images with text wrapping around the image.

\<table\>

Function:

Define a table

Attributes:

ALIGN
BACKGROUND **O**
BGCOLOR **N** **O**
BORDER
BORDERCOLOR **O**
BORDERCOLORLIGHT **O**
BORDERCOLORDARK **O**
CELLPADDING
CELLSPACING
CLASS **N** **O**
COLS **N** **O**
FRAME **O**
HEIGHT **N**
HSPACE **N** **O**
NOWRAP **O**
STYLE **N** **O**
RULES **O**
VALIGN **O**
VSPACE **N** **O**
WIDTH

End tag:

\</table\>; never omitted

Contains:

table_content

Used in:

block

You use the `align` attribute within the `<table>` tag differently than within the `<tr>`, `<td>`, and `<th>` tags. In those tags, the attribute controls text alignment within the table cells, not alignment of the table within the containing text flow.

11.2.1.2 The bgcolor and background attributes

You may make the background of a table a different color than the document's background with the `bgcolor` attribute for the `<table>` tag. The color value for the `bgcolor` attribute must be set to either an RGB color value or a standard color name. Both the syntax of color values and the acceptable color names are provided in Appendix F, *Color Names and Values.*

The extended browsers give every cell in the table (including the caption) this background color. You may also set individual row and cell colors by providing the `bgcolor` attribute or a style attribute for those rows or cells.

The `background` attribute, supported only by Internet Explorer, supplies the URL of an image that is tiled to fill the background of the table. The image will be clipped if the table is smaller than the image. By using this attribute with a border-less table, you can put text over an image contained within a document.

11.2.1.3 The bordercolor, bordercolorlight, and bordercolordark attributes

Supported by Internet Explorer only, these attributes set the color of the table borders, if displayed. Their values can be either an RGB hexadecimal color value or a standard color name, both of which are described fully in Appendix F, *Color Names and Values*.

Netscape and Internet Explorer normally draw a table border with three colors. Netscape uses light and dark variations on the document's background color. Internet Explorer does, too, unless you set those colors with special attributes: the `bordercolorlight` and `bordercolordark` colors shade the edges of the border to give it a 3D appearance, while `bordercolor` shades the central body of the border.

The effectiveness of the 3D effect is tied directly to the relationship of these three colors. In general, the light color should be about 25 percent brighter than the border color, and the dark color should be about 25 percent darker.

11.2.1.4 The border, frame, and rules attributes

The optional `border` attribute for the `<table>` tag tells the browser to draw lines around the table and the rows and cells within it. The default is no borders or cell rule lines at all. With Netscape, `border` is all or nothing, affecting the appearance and spacing both of the frame around the table and the rule lines between data cells. Internet Explorer, on the other hand, lets you individually modify the various line segments that make up the borders around the table (`frame`), as well as around the data cells (`rules`).

You may specify a value for `border`, but you don't have to. Alone, the attribute simply enables borders and a set of default characteristics. Netscape and Internet Explorer let you supply an integer value for `border` equal to the pixel width of the chiseled-edge lines that make the table appear to be embossed onto the page.

The Internet Explorer `frame` attribute modifies `border`'s effects for the lines that surround the table. The default value—what you get if you don't use `frame` at all—is `box`, which tells the browser to draw all four lines around the table. The value `void` removes all four of the `frame` segments. The `frame` values `above`, `below`, `lhs`, and `rhs` draw the various border segments on the top, bottom, left, or right side, respectively, of the table. The value `hsides` draws borders on the top and bottom (horizontal) sides of the table; `vsides` draws borders on the left and right (vertical) sides of the table.

With Internet Explorer, you also may control the thickness of a table's internal cell borders via the `rules` attribute. The default behavior, represented by the misleading value of `none`,[*] is to draw cell rule lines matching the size and specifications of the border attribute. Specifying `groups` places thicker borders between row and column groups defined by the `<thead>`, `<tbody>`, `<tfoot>`, and `<colgroup>` tags. Using `rows` or `cols` places thicker borders between every row or column, respectively, while using `all` places thicker borders around every cell in the table. [Internet Explorer table extensions, 11.3]

11.2.1.5 The cellspacing attribute

The `cellspacing` attribute controls the amount of space placed between adjacent cells in a table and along the outer edges of cells along the edges of a table.

Browsers normally puts two pixels of space between cells and along the outer edges of the table. If you include a `border` attribute in the `<table>` tag, the cell spacing between interior cells grows by two more pixels (four total) to make space for the chiseled edge on the interior border. The outer edges of edge cells grow by the value of the `border` attribute.

By including the `cellspacing` attribute you can widen or reduce the interior cell borders. For instance, to make the thinnest possible interior cell borders, include the `border` and `cellspacing=0` attributes in the table's tag.

11.2.1.6 The cellpadding attribute

The `cellpadding` attribute controls the amount of space between the edge of a cell and its contents, which by default is one pixel. You may make all the cell contents in a table touch their respective cell borders by including `cellpadding=0` in the table tag. You may also increase the `cellpadding` space by setting its value greater than 1.

11.2.1.7 Combining border, cellspacing, and cellpadding attributes

The interactions between the `border`, `cellpadding`, and `cellspacing` attributes of the `<table>` tag combine in ways that can be confusing. Figure 11-2 summarizes how these attributes interact to create interior and exterior borders of various widths.

---

[*] The value "none" is misleading because you can't remove the table's cell rule lines when the border attribute is in effect.

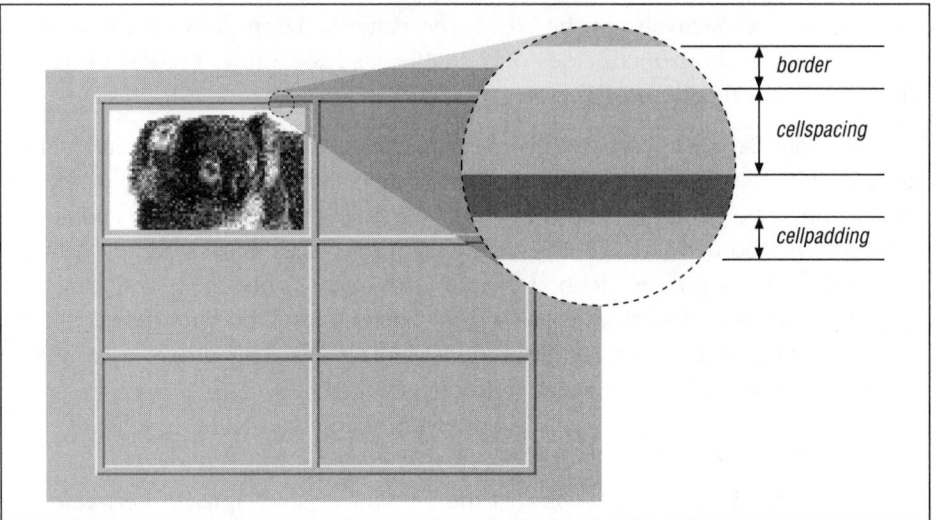

Figure 11-2. The border, cellspacing, and cellpadding attributes of a table

While all sorts of combinations of the `border` and `cellspacing` attributes are possible, these are the most common:

- `border=1` and `cellspacing=0` produces the narrowest possible interior and exterior borders: two pixels wide.

- `border=n` and `cellspacing=0` makes the narrowest possible interior borders (two pixels wide), with an external border that is n plus one pixels wide.

- `border=1` and `cellspacing=n` tables have equal-width exterior and interior borders, all with chiseled edges just one pixel wide. All borders will be n plus two pixels wide.

11.2.1.8 The cols attribute

To format a table, the browser must first read the entire table contents, determining the number and width of each column in the table. This can be a lengthy process for long tables, forcing users to wait to see your pages. The `cols` attribute tells the browser, in advance, how many columns to expect in the table. The value of this attribute is an integer value defining the number of columns in the table.

This attribute provides only advice to the browser. If you define a different number of columns, the browser is free to ignore the `cols` attribute in order to render the table correctly. In general, it is good form to include this attribute with your `<table>` tag, if only to help the browser do a better job of formatting your tables.

11.2.1.9 The hspace and vspace attributes

Just as with inline images, the `hspace` and `vspace` attributes tell Internet Explorer and Netscape to add some extra room on the left and right sides (for `hspace`) and the top and bottom (for `vspace`) of a table, thereby setting it off from the window edge and surrounding content. The attribute value is the integer number of pixels for that padding; a value of 0 is the default.

Figure 11-3 illustrates the effect of the `hspace` and `vspace` attribute spacing around a left-justified table with wraparound text.

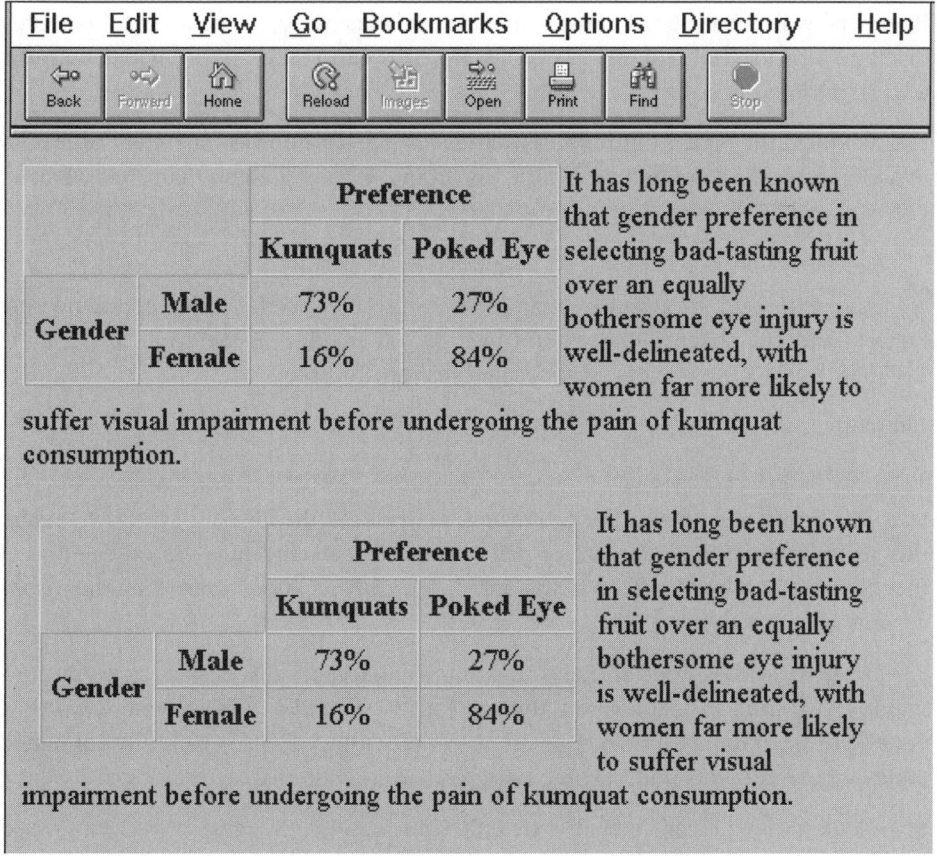

Figure 11-3. The hspace and vspace attributes give a table some breathing room

11.2.1.10 The style and class attributes

The `style` attribute for the `<table>` tag creates an inline style for the tag, over-riding any other style rule in effect. The `class` attribute lets you apply a predefined set of properties for this particular `<table>` tag; its value is the name of that class. [`style` attribute, 9.1.1] [`class` attribute, 9.2.4]

11.2.1.11 *The valign attribute*

The `valign` attribute for the `<table>` tag currently is supported only by Internet Explorer. It sets the default vertical alignment of data in their cells for the entire table. You achieve similar effects in Netscape by including a `valign` attribute within the individual `<tr>`, `<td>`, and `<th>` tags.

Acceptable values for the `valign` attribute in `<table>` are `top` or `bottom`; the default vertical position is the center of the cell.

11.2.1.12 *The width and height attributes*

Browsers will automatically make a table only as wide as needed to correctly display all of the cell contents. If necessary, you can make a table wider with the `width` attribute.

The value of the `width` attribute is either an integer number of pixels or a relative percentage of the screen width, including values greater than 100 percent. For example,

```
<table width=400>
```

tells the extended browser to make the table 400 pixels wide, including any borders and cell spacing that extend into the outer edge of the table. If the table is wider than 400 pixels, the browser ignores the attribute.

Alternatively,

```
<table width="50%">
```

tells the browser to make the table half as wide as the display window. Again, this width includes any borders or cell spacing that extend into the outer edge of the table, and has no effect if the table normally is more than half the user's current screen width.

Use relative widths for tables you want to automatically resize to the user's window; for instance, tables you always want to extend across the entire window (`<table width="100%">`). Use an absolute width value for carefully formatted tables whose contents will become hard to read in wide display windows.

For Netscape, you can use the `height` attribute to suggest a recommended height for the table. The browser will make the table no shorter than this height, but may make the table taller if needed to contain the table's contents. This attribute is useful when trying to stretch tables to fit in a frame or some specific area of a document, but is of little use otherwise.

11.2.2 The <tr> Tag

Every row in a table is created with a `<tr>` tag. Within the `<tr>` tag are one or more cells containing headers, each defined with the `<th>` tag, and data, each defined with the `<td>` tag (see below).

<tr>

Function:
   Define a row within a table

Attributes:
   ALIGN
   BGCOLOR **N** **O**
   BORDERCOLOR **O**
   BORDERCOLORLIGHT **O**
   BORDERCOLORDARK **O**
   CLASS **N** **O**
   NOWRAP
   STYLE **N** **O**
   VALIGN

End tag:
   </tr>; may be omitted

Contains:
   tr_content

Used in:
   table_content

Every row in a table has the same number of cells as the longest row; the browser automatically creates empty cells to pad rows with fewer defined cells.

11.2.2.1 The align attribute

The extended browsers automatically align cell contents inside their respective cells. The `align` attribute for the `<tr>` tag lets you change the default horizontal alignment of all the cells in a row. The attribute affects all the cells within the current row, but not subsequent rows.

An `align` attribute value of `left`, `right`, or `center` causes the extended browser to align the contents of each cell in the row against the left or right edge, or in the center of the cell, respectively. In addition, Internet Explorer supports a value of `justify` so that each line of text fills the cell. You also may change the alignment for individual cells within a row, overriding the value of the `align` attribute in the `<tr>` tag with the `align` attribute for the `<th>` and `<td>` tags, as described below. Accordingly, use the `align` attribute in the `<tr>` tag to specify the most common cell content justification for the row (if not the default), and use a different `align` attribute for those individual cells that deviate from that common alignment.

Table 11-1 displays the horizontal (`align`) and vertical (`valign`) table cell-content attribute values and options. Values in parentheses are the defaults.

Table 11-1. Horizontal and vertical table cell-content attribute values and options

Attribute	Netscape and Internet Explorer		Mosaic	
	Headers	Data	Headers	Data
align	Left	(Left)	(Left)	(Left)
	(Center)	Center	Center	Center
	Right	Right	Right	Right
valign[1]	Top	Top	(Top)	(Top)
	(Center)	(Center)	N/A[2]	N/A
	Bottom	Bottom	N/A	N/A
	Baseline	Baseline	N/A	N/A

[1] Internet Explorer also supports a universal `valign` attribute for the `<table>` tag

[2] N/A = Not available

11.2.2.2 *The bgcolor attribute*

Like its relative for the `<table>` tag, the `bgcolor` attribute for the `<tr>` tag sets the background color of the entire row.* Its value is either an RGB color value or a standard color name. Both the syntax of color values and the acceptable color names are provided in Appendix F, *Color Names and Values.*

Every cell in the row will be given this background color. Individual cell colors can be changed by providing the `bgcolor` attribute for those cells.

11.2.2.3 *The bordercolor, bordercolorlight, and bordercolordark attributes*

Like their brethren for the `<table>` tag, Internet Explorer lets you use these attributes to set the color of the borders within the current row.

Their values override any values set by the corresponding attribute in the containing `<table>` tag. See the corresponding description of these extensions in 11.2.1.3 for details. Color values can be either an RGB color value or a standard color name, both of which are described fully in Appendix F, *Color Names and Values.*

---

* Unlike `<table>` with Internet Explorer though, `<tr>` does not support a background image.

11.2.2.4 The nowrap attribute

Browsers treat each table cell as though it's a browser window unto itself, flowing contents inside the cell as they would common body contents (although subject to special table-cell alignment properties). Accordingly, the browsers automatically wrap text lines to fill the allotted table cell space. The `nowrap` attribute, when included in a table row, stops that normal word wrapping in all cells in that row. With `nowrap`, the browser assembles the contents of the cell onto a single line, unless you insert a `<br>` or `<p>` tag, which then forces a break so that the contents continue on a new line inside the table cell.

11.2.2.5 The style and class attributes

The `style` attribute for the `<tr>` tag creates an inline style for the table row, overriding any other style rule in effect. The `class` attribute lets you apply a predefined set of properties for this particular `<tr>` tag; its value is the name of that class. Note that to set `<tr>` style properties at the document level or in an external style sheet, you must use the contextual selector `TABLE TR`.

Not all style properties may apply. For instance, you cannot place a background image behind an individual table row as you can behind the entire table. However, you can set the text contents colors and font styles, for example. [`style` attribute, 9.1.1] [`class` attribute, 9.2.4]

11.2.2.6 The valign attribute

You may change the default vertical alignment for the contents of data cells contained within a table row. Normally, the browsers render cell contents centered vertically. By including the `valign` attribute in the `<tr>` tag with a value of `top` or `bottom`, you tell the extended browsers to place the table row's contents flush against the top or bottom of their cells or aligned to the baseline of the top line of text in other cells in the row (Figure 11-4). The value `center`, although acceptable, has no real effect since it simply reiterates the default vertical alignment.

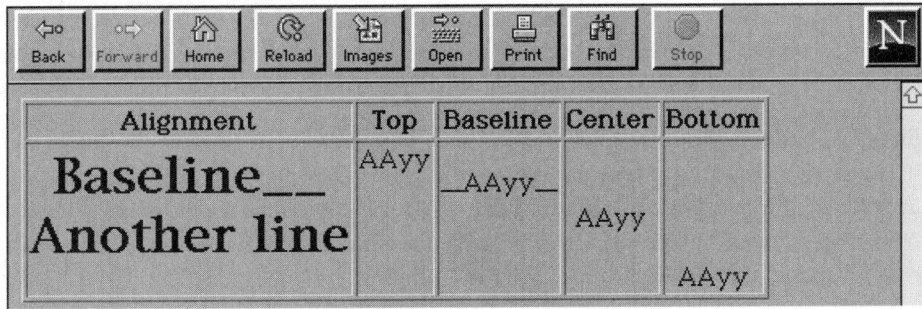

Figure 11-4. Effects of the valign attribute on table cell content alignment

```
<table border>
  <tr>
    <th>Alignment</th>
    <th>Top</th>
    <th>Baseline</th>
    <th>Center</th>
    <th>Bottom</th>
  </tr>
  <tr align=center>
    <th><h1>Baseline....<br>Line 2</h1></th>
    <td valign=top>AAyy</td>
    <td valign=baseline>_AAyy_</td>
    <td valign=center>AAyy</td>
    <td valign=bottom>AAyy</td>
  </tr>
</table>
```

11.2.3 *The <th> and <td> Tags*

The `<th>` and `<td>` tags go inside the `<tr>` tags of an HTML table to create the cells and contents within the row. The tags operate similarly; the only real differences are that the browsers render header text—meant to entitle or otherwise describe table data—in boldface font style and that the default alignment of their respective contents may be different (Table 11-1).

Like those available for the table row (`<tr>`) tag, the table cell tags support a rich set of style and content-alignment attributes you may apply to a single data or header cell. These attributes override the default values for the current row. There are also special attributes that control the number of columns or rows a cell may span in the table.

The contents of the `<th>` and `<td>` tags can be anything you might put in the body of an HTML document, including text, images, forms, and so on—even another table. And, as described earlier, the browser automatically creates a table large enough, both vertically and horizontally, to display all the contents of any and all the cells.

If a particular row has fewer header or data items than other rows, the browser adds empty cells at the end to fill the row. If you need to make an empty cell before the end of a row, for instance, to indicate a missing data point, create a header or data cell with no content.

Empty cells look different than those containing data or headers if the table has borders: the empty cell will not be seemingly embossed onto the window, but instead is simply left blank. If you want to create an empty cell that has incised borders like all the other cells in your table, be sure to place a minimal amount of content in the cell: a single `<br>` tag, for instance.

<th> and <td>

Function:

Define table data and header cells

Attributes:

ALIGN
BACKGROUND **❶**
BGCOLOR **Ⓝ** **❶**
BORDERCOLOR **❶**
BORDERCOLORLIGHT **❶**
BORDERCOLORDARK **❶**
CLASS
COLSPAN
HEIGHT
NOWRAP
ROWSPAN
STYLE
VALIGN
WIDTH

End tag:

</th> or </td>; may be omitted

Contains:

body_content

Used in:

tr_content

11.2.3.1 The align and valign attributes

The `align` and `valign` attributes are identical to those of the same name for the table row tag (`<tr>`; see previous), except that when used with a `<th>` or `<td>` tag, they control the horizontal or vertical alignment of content in just the current cell. Their value overrides any alignment established by the respective `align` or `valign` attribute of the `<tr>` tag, but does not affect the alignment of subsequent cells. See Table 11-1 for alignment details.

You may set the `align` attribute's value to `left`, `right`, or `center`, causing the browsers to align the cell contents against the left or right edge, or in the center of the cell, respectively. In addition, Internet Explorer supports a value of `justify` to fill each line of text so that it is flush to both sides of the cell. The `valign` attribute may have a value of `top`, `bottom`, `center`, or `baseline`, telling the browser to align the cell's contents to the top or bottom edge, or in the center of the cell, or (Netscape only) to the baseline of the first line of text in other cells in the row.

11.2.3.2 *The width attribute*

Like its twin in the `<table>` tag that lets you widen a table, the `width` attribute for table cell tags lets you widen an individual cell and, hence, the entire column it occupies. You set the `width` to an integer number of pixels, or a percentage indicating the cell's width as a fraction of the table as a whole.

For example,

```
<th width=400>
```

sets the current header cell's width, and hence the entire column of cells, to 400 pixels wide. Alternatively,

```
<td width="40%">
```

creates a data cell whose column will occupy 40 percent of the entire table's width.

Since the extended browsers make all cells in a column the same width, you should place a `width` attribute in only one cell within a column, preferably the first instance of the cell in the first row, for source readability. If two or more cells in the same column happen to have `width` attributes, the widest one is honored. You can't make a column thinner than the width the browser automatically determines is the minimum needed to display all of any cell contents in the column. So, if the browser determines that the column of cells needs to be at least 150 pixels wide to accommodate all the cells' contents, it will completely ignore a width attribute in one of the column's cell tags that attempts to make the cell only 100 pixels wide.

11.2.3.3 *The height attribute*

This attribute specifies a minimum height, in pixels, for the current cell. Since all cells in a row have the same height, this attribute need only be specified on one cell in the row, preferably the first. If some other cell in the row needs to be taller to accommodate its contents, this attribute is ignored and all the cells in the row will be set to the larger size.

By default, all the cells in a row are the height of the largest cell in the row that just accommodates its contents.

11.2.3.4 *The colspan attribute*

It's common to have a table header that describes several columns beneath it, like the headers we use in Table 11-1. Use the `colspan` attribute in a table header or data tag to extend an HTML table cell across two or more columns in its row. Set the value of the `colspan` attribute to an integer value equal to the number of columns you want the header or data cell to span. For example,

```
<td colspan=3>
```

tells the browser to make the cell occupy the same horizontal space as three cells in rows above or below it. The browser flows the contents of the cell to occupy the entire space.

What happens if there aren't enough extra cells on the right? The browser just extends the cell over as many columns as exist to the right; it doesn't add extra empty cells to each row to accommodate an over-extended `colspan` value. You may defeat that limitation by adding the needed extra, but content-less, cells to a single row. (Give them a single `<br>` tag as their contents if you want Netscape's embossed border around them.)

11.2.3.5 The rowspan attribute

Just as the `colspan` attribute layers a table cell across several columns, the `rowspan` attribute stretches a cell down two or more rows in the table.

You include the `rowspan` attribute in the `<th>` or `<td>` tag of the uppermost row of the table where you want the cell to begin and set its value equal to the number of rows you want it to span. The cell then occupies the same space as the current row and an appropriate number of cells below that row. The browser flows the contents of the cell to occupy the entire extended space. For example,

```
<td rowspan=3>
```

creates a cell that occupies the current row plus two more rows below that.

Like the `colspan` attribute, the browser ignores over-extended `rowspan` attributes and will only extend the current cell down rows you've explicitly defined by other `<tr>` tags following the current row. The browsers will not add empty rows to a table to fill a rowspan below the last defined row in a table.

11.2.3.6 Combining colspan and rowspan

You may extend a single cell both across several columns and down several rows by including both the `colspan` and `rowspan` attributes in its table header or data tag. For example,

```
<th colspan=3 rowspan=4>
```

creates a header cell that, as you might expect, spans across three columns and down four rows, including the current cell and extending two more cells to the right and three more cells down. The browser flows the contents of the cell to occupy the entire space, aligned inside according to the current row's alignment specifications or to those you may explicitly include in the same tag, as described earlier.

11.2.3.7 *The nowrap attribute*

Browsers treat each table cell as though it's a browser window unto itself, flowing contents inside the cell as they would common body contents (although subject to special table-cell alignment properties). Accordingly, the browsers automatically wrap text lines to fill the allotted table cell space. The `nowrap` attribute, when included in a table header or data tag, stops that normal word wrapping. With `nowrap`, the browser assembles the contents of the cell onto a single line, unless you insert a `<br>` or `<p>` tag, which then forces a break so that the contents continue on a new line inside the table cell.

11.2.3.8 *The bgcolor and background attributes*

Yet again, you can change the background color—this time for an individual data cell. This attribute's value is either an RGB hexadecimal color value or a standard color name. Both the syntax of color values and the acceptable color names are provided in Appendix F, *Color Names and Values.*

The `background` attribute, supported only by Internet Explorer, supplies the URL of an image that is tiled to fill the background of the cell. The image will be clipped if the cell is smaller than the image.

Neither `background` nor `bgcolor` will override a related style sheet property.

11.2.3.9 *The bordercolor, bordercolorlight, and bordercolordark attributes*

Internet Explorer lets you alter the colors that make up an individual cell's border—if table borders are turned on with the `border` attribute, of course. See the respective attributes' descriptions under the `<table>` tag in 11.2.1.3 for details.

The values for these three attributes override any values set for the containing `<table>` or `<tr>` tag. Their values can be either an RGB color value or a standard color name, both of which are described fully in Appendix F, *Color Names and Values.*

11.2.3.10 *The style and class attributes*

The `style` attribute for the `<td>` and `<th>` tags creates an inline style for the table cell, overriding any other style rule or related attribute in effect. The `class` attribute lets you apply a predefined set of properties for the particular tag; its value is the name of that class. For instance, you can set the text contents, colors and font styles. Unlike with the `<tr>` tag, but like `<table>`, you can place an image behind an individual data cell's contents.

To set <td> or <th> style properties at the document level or in an external style sheet, you must use their contextual selector: **TABLE TD** or **TABLE TH**. [style attribute, 9.1.1] [class attribute, 9.2.4].

11.2.4 The <caption> Tag

A table commonly needs a caption to explain its contents, so the extended browsers provide a table-caption tag. Authors typically place the <caption> tag and its contents immediately after the <table> tag, but it can be placed nearly anywhere inside the table and between the row tags. The caption may contain any body content, much like a cell within a table.

<caption>

Function:
    Define a table caption

Attributes:
    ALIGN
    CLASS **N** **O**
    STYLE **N** **O**
    VALIGN **O**

End tag:
    </caption>; never omitted

Contains:
    body_content

Used in:
    table_content

Unfortunately for document authors, Netscape Navigator implements one method of caption alignment and positioning, while Internet Explorer provides a conflicting set of attributes for the same purpose. By default, the browsers center the caption with respect to the table, including word wrapping when necessary.

11.2.4.1 The align and valign attributes

By default, browsers place the caption's contents centered above the table. You may place it below the table with the **align** attribute set to the value **bottom** (the value **top**, of course, is equivalent to the default).

Internet Explorer uses the align attribute to control the horizontal position of the caption and provides the **valign** attribute to change the caption's vertical position. With Internet Explorer, set the **align** attribute to **left**, **center** (the default), or `right` to position the caption to the respective location relative to the table. Use the `valign` attribute to place a caption at the `top` or `bottom` of the table. The other browsers ignore Internet Explorer's different caption-align values and attributes.

11.2.4.2 The style and class attributes

Like the `<td>` and `<th>` table tags, the `style` attribute for the `<caption>` tag creates an inline style for the table caption, overriding any other style rule in effect. The `class` attribute lets you apply a predefined set of properties for the particular tag; its value is the name of that class. Be sure to use the contextual selector `TABLE CAPTION` when referring to caption styles at the document level or in external style sheets. [`style` attribute, 9.1.1] [`class` attribute, 9.2.4].

11.3 Internet Explorer Table Extensions

While it is possible to build a simple table quickly, complex HTML tables with varying border styles, running headers and footers, and column-based layout are not easily constructed from the HTML 3.2 table model. Microsoft has rectified this inadequacy somewhat by adding a number of table layout controls to their Internet Explorer browser (Version 3.0 and later). These controls provide row-based grouping and running headers and footers, along with column-based layout controls.

There is good news and bad news about these table extensions, of course. They provide a nice way to make your tables more attractive and presentable, but they only work within Internet Explorer, which, at the time this book is written, is not the most popular browser. If you choose to use these extensions, make sure your tables stand up with the other browsers, too, without the additional layout and grouping features available with Internet Explorer. Otherwise, you will lose a significant chunk of your audience.

11.3.1 Defining Table Sections

Within HTML 3.2 tables, all rows are created equal. In real tables, some rows are more equal than others. And most tables have header and footer rows that repeat from page to page. In large tables, adjacent rows are grouped and delineated with different rules to make the table easier to read and understand. Internet Explorer supports all of these features with the `<thead>`, `<tfoot>`, and `<tbody>` tags.

11.3.1.1 The <thead> tag

Use the `<thead>` tag to define a set of table header rows.

The `<thead>` tag may appear once within a `<table>` tag, at the beginning. Within the `<thead>` tag, you may place one or more `<tr>` tags, defining the

---

\<thead\> ❶

Function:
Define a table header

Attributes:
ALIGN
CLASS
STYLE
VALIGN

End tag:
\</thead\>; may be omitted

Contains:
table_content

Used in:
table_content

---

rows within the table header. If given the opportunity, Internet Explorer will replicate these heading rows when the table is printed or displayed in multiple sections. Thereafter, Internet Explorer will repeat these headings on each printed page if the table appears on more than one page.

The ending \</thead\> tag is optional and may be omitted. Since the \<thead\> tag only appears in tables where, presumably, other rows will be designated as the table body or footer, the \<thead\> tag is automatically closed when the browser encounters a \<tbody\> or \<tfoot\> tag or when the table ends.

The attributes of the \<thead\> tag—align, class, style, and valign—operate identically, take the same values, and affect all the enclosed \<tr\> contents as if you had specified them individually for each \<tr\> entry. The align attribute accepts values of left, right, center, or justify, controlling the horizontal alignment of text in the heading rows. Similarly, the valign attribute accepts values of top, middle, or bottom and behaves just like the valign attribute in the \<tr\> tag, dictating the vertical alignment of text in the heading rows. The by-now-familiar attributes for setting the content style properties are style and class.

If you don't specify any alignments or style attribute, Internet Explorer centers the heading text vertically and horizontally within their respective cells, equivalent to specifying align=center and valign=middle for each. Of course, individual row and cell or style sheet specifications may override these attributes.

11.3.1.2 The <tfoot> tag

Use the `<tfoot>` tag to define a footer for Internet Explorer tables.

<tfoot> ❶

Function:
>   Define a table footer

Attributes:
>   None

End tag:
>   </tfoot>; may be omitted

Contains:
>   *table_content*

Used in:
>   *table_content*

The `<tfoot>` tag may appear only once just before the end of a table. Like `<thead>`, it may contain one or more `<tr>` tags that let you define those rows that Internet Explorer uses as the table footer. Thereafter, the browser repeats these rows if the table is broken across multiple physical or virtual pages. Most often, Internet Explorer repeats the table footer at the bottom of each portion of a table printed on multiple pages.

The closing `</tfoot>` tag is optional, since the footer ends when the table ends. There are no attributes for the `<tfoot>` tag. If you have special alignment attributes for your table footer, you'll need to specify them for each row within the `<tfoot>` tag.

11.3.1.3 The <tbody> tag

Use the `<tbody>` tag to divide your Internet Explorer table into discrete sections.

The `<tbody>` tag collects one or more rows into a group within a table. It is perfectly acceptable to have no `<tbody>` tags within a table, although where you might include one, you probably will have two or more `<tbody>` tags within a table. So identified, you can give each `<tbody>` group different rule line sizes above and below the section. Within a `<tbody>` tag, only table rows may be defined using the `<tr>` tag.

The closing `</tbody>` tag is optional, since the section ends at the next `<tbody>` or `<tfoot>` tag, or when the table ends. There are no attributes for

---

<tbody> ❶

Function:
   Define a section within a table

Attributes:
   None

End tag:
   </tbody>; may be omitted

Contains:
   table_content

Used in:
   table_content

---

the <tbody> tag. If you have special alignment attributes for this section, you'll
need to specify them for each row within the <tbody> tag.

11.3.1.4 Using table sections

From a presentation standpoint, the most important thing you can do with the
<thead>, <tfoot>, and <tbody> tags is divide your table into logical sections
that are delimited by different borders. By default, Internet Explorer does not do
anything special with the borders around the headers, footers, and sections within
your table. By adding the rules attribute to the <table> tag, however, you can
draw thicker rule lines between your <thead>, one or more <tbody>, and
<tfoot> table sections, helping readers better understand your table's
organization. [<table> rules, 11.2.1.4]

For example, here is the simple table you saw earlier in this chapter augmented
with a header and footer. Notice that we've omitted many of the unnecessary
closing tags for brevity and readability:

```
<table border cellspacing=0 cellpadding=5 rules=groups>
  <caption align=bottom>Kumquat versus a poked eye, by gender</caption>
  <thead>
    <tr>
      <td colspan=2 rowspan=2>
      <th colspan=2 align=center>Preference
    </tr>
    <tr>
      <th>Eating Kumquats
      <th>Poke In The Eye
    </tr>
  </thead>
  <tbody>
    <tr align=center>
```

```
        <th rowspan=2>Gender
        <th>Male
        <td>73%
        <td>27%
      </tr>
      <tr align=center>
        <th>Female
        <td>16%
        <td>84%
      </tr>
    </tbody>
    <tfoot>
      <tr>
        <td colspan=4 align=center>
          Note: eye pokes did not result in permanent injury
  </table>
```

The resulting HTML table as rendered by Internet Explorer is shown in Figure 11-5. Notice how the rules after the table header and before the footer are thinner than the borders around the other table rows? This happened because we included the special `rules=groups` attribute to the `<table>` tag. Similar effects may be obtained by specifying `rules=rows` or `rules=all` (see below).

Figure 11-5. Use Internet Explorer's extensions to specially section your tables

Long tables often benefit from thicker rules every few rows, making it easier to read the table. Do this by grouping the rules in your table with several `<tbody>` tags. Each set of rows contained in a single `<tbody>` tag will have thicker rules before and after it.

Here is an expanded version of our table example, with additional sections set off as separate groups.

```
<table border cellspacing=0 cellpadding=5 rules=groups>
  <caption align=bottom>Kumquat versus a poked eye, by gender</caption>
```

```
    <thead>
      <tr>
        <td colspan=2 rowspan=2>
        <th colspan=2 align=center>Preference
      <tr>
        <th>Eating Kumquats
        <th>Poke In The Eye
    <tbody>
      <tr align=center>
        <th rowspan=4>Gender
        <th>Males under 18
        <td>94%
        <td>6%
      <tr align=center>
        <th>Males over 18
        <td>73%
        <td>27%
    <tbody>
      <tr align=center>
        <th>Females under 18
        <td>34%
        <td>66%
      <tr align=center>
        <th>Females over 18
        <td>16%
        <td>84%
    <tfoot>
      <tr>
        <td colspan=4 align=center>
          Note: eye pokes did not result in permanent injury
  </table>
```

The result is shown in Figure 11-6.

In this case, we wind up with four rows in the table, separated into two groups by a thicker rule between them. Any number of groups could be created within the table by adding more <tbody> tags.

11.3.2 Defining Column Groups

The HTML table model is row-centric, defining tables as a collection of cells organized into rows. Sometimes, though, it is easier to deal with your table as a collection of columns. Using the <colgroup> and <col> tags, Internet Explorer helps you turn the tables and think in columns.

Unlike the sectioning tags we describe above, which are interspersed with the rows of a table to define headers, footers, and sections within the table, the column-related tags cannot be intermingled with the content of a table. Instead, you must place them at the very beginning of a table, before the content. They define the model by which Internet Explorer renders the columns.

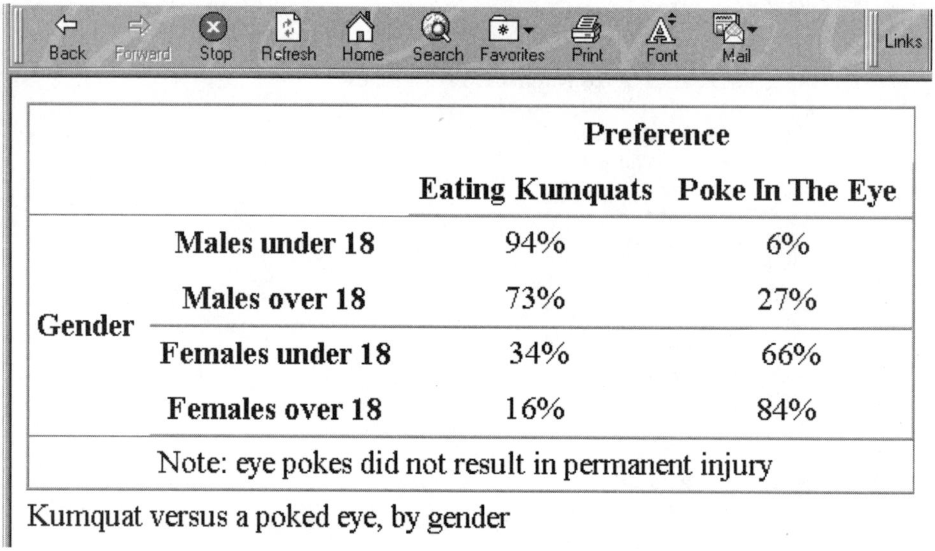
Back
Forward
Stop
Refresh
Home
Search
Favorites
Print
Font
Mail
Links
Preference
Eating Kumquats
Poke In The Eye
Gender
Males under 18
94%
6%
Males over 18
73%
27%
Females under 18
34%
66%
Females over 18
16%
84%
Note: eye pokes did not result in permanent injury
Kumquat versus a poked eye, by gender

Figure 11-6. Multiple <tbody> segments further divide a table

11.3.2.1 The <colgroup> tag

The <colgroup> tag defines a column group.

You can use the `<colgroup>` tag in two ways: as a single definition of several identical columns or as a container for several dissimilar columns. The `<colgroup>` tag may only appear within a `<table>` tag, but you may define one or more column groups within a table. The ending `</colgroup>` tag is rarely used; instead, the `<colgroup>` ends at the next `<colgroup>`, `<thead>`, `<tbody>`, `<tfoot>`, or `<tr>` tag.

Use the `span` attribute with the `<colgroup>` tag to achieve the first type of column grouping. The value of the span attribute is the integer number of columns affected by the `<colgroup>` tag. For example, a table with six columns—four in the first group and two in the other—would appear in the source code as:

```
<colgroup span=4>
<colgroup span=2>
```

When Internet Explorer collects the table cells into columns by the example definition, it groups the first four cells in each row as the first column group and the next two cells into a second column group. Any other attributes of the individual `<colgroup>` tags then are applied to the columns contained within that group.

To use the `<colgroup>` tag as a container for dissimilar columns, leave out the span attribute, but include within each `<colgroup>` tag an individual `<col>` tag for each column within the group. For instance:

```
<colgroup>
  <col>
  <col>
  <col>
  <col>
<colgroup>
  <col>
  <col>
```

This method creates the same number of columns in each group as we had with the `span` attribute, but lets you specify column attributes individually. You can still supply attributes for all the columns via the `<colgroup>` tag, but they will be overridden by the attributes in the `<col>` tags, as appropriate.

<colgroup> ❶

Function:
> Define a column group within a table

Attributes:
> ALIGN
> CLASS
> SPAN
> STYLE
> VALIGN
> WIDTH

End tag:
> </colgroup>; usually omitted

Contains:
> *column_content*

Used in:
> *table_content*

The `align`, `valign`, `width`, `class`, and `style` attributes control the familiar aspects of each columns in the `<colgroup>`-encapsulated column group. These attributes accept the same values and behave exactly like the equivalent attributes for the `<td>` tag. [<th> and <td>, 11.2.3]

For instance, suppose we want our first example group of four columns to each occupy 20 percent of the table, with the remaining two columns taking up 10 percent each of the total table width. That's easy with the span attribute:

```
<colgroup span=4 width="20%">
<colgroup span=2 width="10%">
```

The structure also can be done with individually specified columns:

```
<colgroup width="20%">
  <col>
  <col>
  <col>
  <col>
<colgroup width="10%">
  <col>
  <col>
```

There is no reason not to use both methods in the same table. For instance, we could specify our example column groupings, complete with `width` attributes:

```
<colgroup span=4 width="20%" align=right>
<colgroup width="10%">
  <col align=left>
  <col align=right>
```

Notice that this lets us align the contents of the two columns of the second group individually (the default alignment is centered).

11.3.2.2 The <col> tag

Use the `<col>` tag to control the appearance of one or more columns within a column group.

<col> ❶

Function:
   Define a column within a column group

Attributes:
   ALIGN
   SPAN

End tag:
   None

Contains:
   Nothing

Used in:
   column_content

The `<col>` tag may appear only within a `<colgroup>` tag within a table. It has no content, and thus has no ending tag. Rather, it represents one or more columns within a `<colgroup>` to which Internet Explorer (not Netscape) applies the `<col>` tag's attributes.

The `align` attribute affects the placement of content within the columns. This attribute accepts the same values and behaves exactly like the equivalent attribute for the `<td>` tag. [`<th>` and `<td>`, 11.2.3]

The `span` attribute for the `<col>` tag, like the `<colgroup>` tag, lets you specify how many successive columns are affected by this `<col>` tag. By default, only one is affected. For example, let's create a `<colgroup>` that has five columns. We align the first and last columns to the left and right, respectively, while the middle three are centered:

```
<colgroup>
  <col align=left>
  <col align=center span=3>
  <col align=right>
```

The `<col>` tag should only be used within `<colgroup>` tags that do not themselves use the `span` attribute. Otherwise, Internet Explorer ignores the individual `<col>` tags and their attributes.

11.3.2.3 Using column groups

Column groups are easier to use than they first appear. Think of them as a template of how to format your table columns. Their main purpose is to create groups that can be separated by thicker rules within your table, and to streamline the process of applying formatting attributes to all the cells in one or more columns.

Returning to our original table example, we can place a thicker rule between the column labels and the data cells by placing the column labels in one column group and the data cells in another:

```
<table border cellspacing=0 cellpadding=5 rules=groups>
  <caption align=bottom>Kumquat versus a poked eye, by gender</caption>
  <colgroup span=2>
  <colgroup span=2>
  <thead>
    <tr>
      <td colspan=2 rowspan=2>
      <th colspan=2 align=center>Preference
    <tr>
      <th>Eating Kumquats
      <th>Poke In The Eye
  <tbody>
    <tr align=center>
      <th rowspan=4>Gender
      <th>Males under 18
      <td>94%
      <td>6%
    <tr align=center>
      <th>Males over 18
```

```
        <td>73%
        <td>27%
    <tbody>
      <tr align=center>
        <th>Females under 18
        <td>34%</td>
        <td>66%</td>
      <tr align=center>
        <th>Females over 18
        <td>16%
        <td>84%
    <tfoot>
      <tr>
        <td colspan=4 align=center>
          Note: eye pokes did not result in permanent injury
  </table>
```

The results are shown in Figure 11-7. All we added were the two `<colgroup>` tags; the additional borders were drawn by the `rules=groups` attribute in the `<table>` tag. For borders between column groups to be drawn, the rules attribute must be set to either `groups`, `cols`, or `all`. 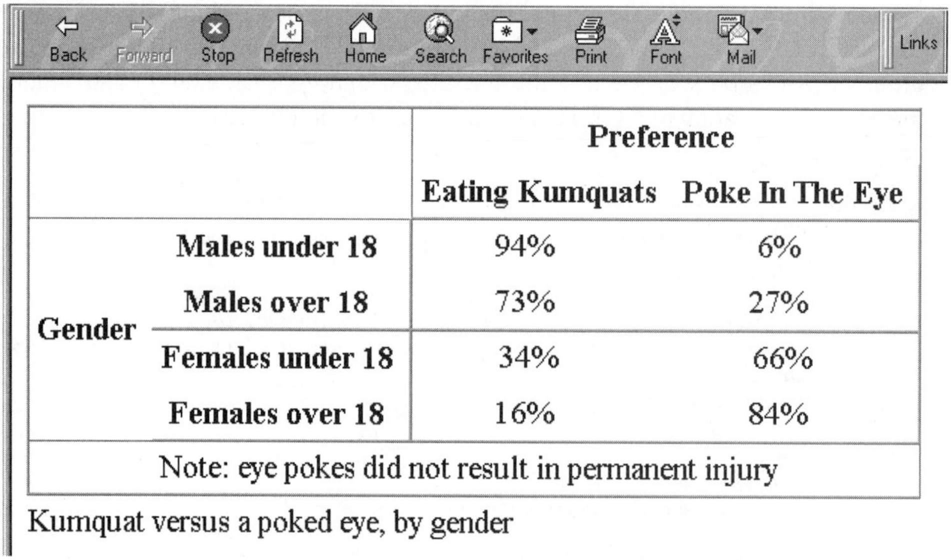

| | | Preference | |
		Eating Kumquats	Poke In The Eye
Gender	**Males under 18**	94%	6%
	Males over 18	73%	27%
	Females under 18	34%	66%
	Females over 18	16%	84%
Note: eye pokes did not result in permanent injury			

Kumquat versus a poked eye, by gender

Figure 11-7. Example integrates the various Internet Explorer table extensions

11.4 Beyond Ordinary Tables

On the face of it, HTML tables are ordinary: just a way for academics and other like-minded data crunchers to format items into columns and rows for easy comparison. Scratch below the surface, though, and you will see that tables are really extraordinary. Besides `<pre>`, the `<table>` tag and related attributes provide the only way for you to easily control the *layout* of your document in HTML. The content inside a `<pre>` tag, of course, is very limited. Tables, on the other hand, may contain nearly anything allowed in normal body content, including multimedia and forms. And the table structure lets you explicitly control where those elements appear in the users' browser window. With the right combinations of attributes, tables provide a way for you to create multicolumn text, and side and straddle heads in HTML. They also enable you to make your forms easier to read, understand, and fill out. That's just for starters.

We don't know that we can recommend you get too caught up with page layout— tables or beyond. Remember, HTML is not about looks but about content. But…

It's easy to argue that at least tables of information benefit from some controlled layout, and that HTML forms follow a close second. Tables provide the only way to create predictable, browser-independent layouts for your web pages. Used in moderation and filled with quality content, tables are a tool that every HTML author should be able to wield.

And now that we've whetted your appetite for page layout with tables, don't despair that we've let you down by ending this chapter without examples—we have several in Chapter 15, *Tips, Tricks, and Hacks*.

12

Frames

Beginning with Netscape Navigator 2.0, HTML authors have been able to divide the browser's main display window into independent window *frames*, each simultaneously displaying a different document—something like a wall of monitors in a TV control room. Instantly popular, frames were soon adopted (and extended) by Microsoft for Internet Explorer, although they have not been incorporated into the HTML 3.2 standard.

Since everything discussed in this chapter is an extension to HTML 3.2, we'll dispense with our normal "extension" notation and denote only those attributes and tags that are unique to Netscape or Internet Explorer. Otherwise, be aware that all tags and attributes discussed herein, although supported by both browsers, nonetheless are extensions and not standard components of HTML.

12.1 An Overview of Frames

Figure 12-1 is a simple example of a frame display. It shows how the document window may be divided into columns and rows of individual frames separated by rules and scroll bars. Although it is not immediately apparent in the example, each frame in the window is displaying an independent document. We use different HTML documents in the example, but the individual documents may contain any valid content the browser is capable of displaying, including multimedia. If the frame's contents include a hyperlink the user selects, the new document's contents, even another frame document, may replace that same frame, another frame's content, or the entire browser window.

You enable frames with a special frame document. Its contents do not get displayed. Rather, the frame document contains extension HTML tags that tell the browser how to divide its main display window into discrete frames, and what documents go inside the frames.

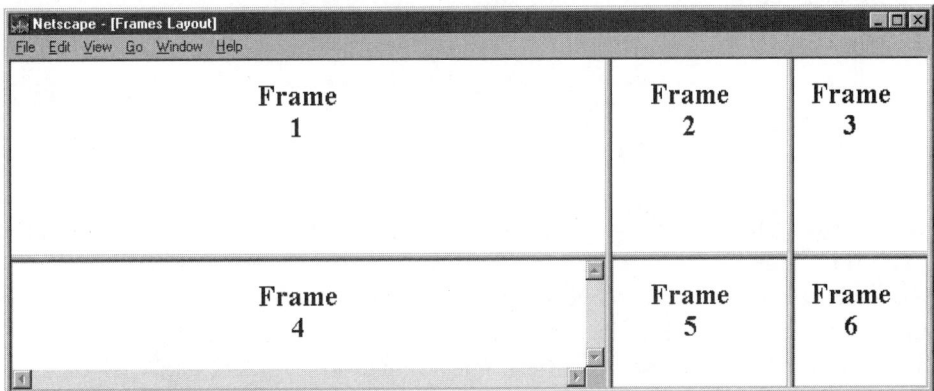

Figure 12-1. A simple six-panel frame layout for Netscape

The individual documents referenced and displayed in the frame document window act independently, to a degree; the frame document controls the entire window. You can, however, direct one frame's document to load new content into another frame. That's done by attaching a name to a frame and targeting the named frame with a special attribute for the hyperlink <a> tag.

12.2 *Frame Tags*

There are three new HTML tags used by both Netscape and Internet Explorer to create a frame document: <frameset>, <frame>, and <noframes>. In addition, Internet Explorer provides the <iframe> tag, which you may use to create inline, or *floating*, frames.

A *frameset* is simply the collection of frames that make up the browser's window. Column- and row-definition attributes for the <frameset> tag let you define the number and initial sizes for the columns and rows of frames. The <frame> tag defines which document—HTML or otherwise—initially goes into the frames within those framesets, and is where you may give the frame a name to use for document hypertext links.

Here is the HTML source that was used to generate Figure 12-1:

```
<html>
<head>
<title>Frames Layout</title>
</head>
<frameset rows="60%,*" cols="65%,20%,*">
  <frame src="frame1.html">
  <frame src="frame2.html">
  <frame src="frame3.html" name="fill_me">
  <frame scrolling=yes src="frame4.html">
  <frame src="frame5.html">
  <frame src="frame6.html">
```

```
    <noframes>
      Sorry, this document can be viewed only with a
      frames-capable browser.
      <a href = "frame1.html">Take this link</a>
      to the first HTML document in the set.
    </noframes>
  </frameset>
  </html>
```

Notice a few things in the simple frame example and its rendered image (Figure 12-1). First, the order in which the browser fills the frames in a frameset goes across each row. Second, frame 4 sports a scrollbar because we told it to, even though the contents may otherwise fit without scrolling. (Scrollbars automatically appear if the contents overflow the frame's dimensions, unless explicitly disabled with the scrolling attribute in the **<frame>** tag.) [<frame>, 12.4.1]

Another item of interest is the **name** attribute in one of the frame tags. Once named, you can reference a particular frame as the location in which to display a hypertext-linked document. To do that, you add a special **target** attribute to the anchor (<a>) tag of the source hypertext link. For instance, to link a document called **new.html** for display in frame 3, which we've named "fill_me", the anchor looks like this:

```
    <a href="new.html" target="fill_me">
```

If the user chooses the link, say in frame 1, the **new.html** document will replace the original **frame3.html** contents in frame 3. [target for <a>, 12.7]

Finally, although Netscape and Internet Explorer both support frames, it is possible that some other browser users will try and view your frame documents. That's why each of your key frame documents should provide a back door to your HTML document collection with the **<noframes>** tag. Frame-compatible browsers display your frames; non-compatible browsers display the alternative **<noframes>** content.

12.2.1 What's in a Frame?

Anyone who has opened more than one window on their desktop display to compare contents or operate interrelated applications knows instinctively the power of frames.

One simple use for frames is to put content that is common in a collection, such as copyright notices, introductory material, and navigational aids, into one frame, with all other document content in an adjacent frame. As the user visits new pages, each loads into the scrolling frame, while the fixed-frame content persists.

A richer frame document-enabled environment provides navigational tools for your document collections. For instance, assign one frame to hold a table of contents and various searching tools for the collection. Have another frame hold the user-selected document contents. As users visit your pages in the content frame, they never lose sight of the navigational aids in the other frame.

Another beneficial use of frame documents is to compare a returned HTML form with its original for verification of the content by the submitting user. By placing the form in one frame and its submitted result in another, you let the user quickly verify that the result corresponds to the data entered in the form. If the results are incorrect, the form is readily available to be filled out again.

12.3   Frame Layout

Frame layout is similar to table layout. Using the `<frameset>` tag, you arrange frames into rows and columns while defining their relative or absolute sizes.

12.3.1   The *<frameset>* Tag

The `<frameset>` tag lets you define a collection of frames and control their spacing and borders.

<frameset>

Function:
    Define a collection of frames

Attributes:
    BORDER **N**
    BORDERCOLOR **N**
    COLS
    FRAMEBORDER
    FRAMESPACING **❶**
    ONBLUR
    ONFOCUS
    ONLOAD
    ONUNLOAD
    ROWS

End tag:
    </frameset>; never omitted

Contains:
    frameset_content

Used in:
    html_content

Use the `<frameset>` tag to define a collection of frames and other framesets. Framesets also may be nested, allowing for a richer set of layout capabilities.

Use the `<frameset>` tag in lieu of a `<body>` tag in the frame document. You may not include any other content except valid `<head>` and `<frameset>` content in a frame document. Combining frames with a conventional document containing `<body>` may result in unpredictable browser behavior.

12.3.1.1 *The rows and cols attributes*

The `<frameset>` tag has one required attribute: either `cols` or `rows`—your choice. They define the size and number of columns (`cols`) or `rows` of either frames or nested framesets for the document window. Both attributes accept a quote-enclosed, comma-separated list of values that specify either the absolute (pixels) or relative (percentage or remaining space) width (for columns) or height (for rows) for the frames. The number of attribute values determines how many rows or columns of frames the browser will display in the document window.

As with tables, the browser will match the size you give a frameset as closely as possible. The browser will not, however, extend the boundaries of the main document window to accommodate framesets that would otherwise exceed those boundaries or fill the window with empty space if the specified frames don't fill the window. Rather, the browsers allocate space to a particular frame relative to all other frames in the row and column and resolutely fills the entire document window. (Did you notice a frame document window does not have scroll bars?)

For example,

```
<frameset rows="150,300,150">
```

creates three rows of frames, each extending across the entire document window. The first and last frames are set to 150 pixels tall, the second to 300 pixels. In reality, unless the browser window is exactly 600 pixels tall, the browser automatically and proportionately stretches or compresses the first and last frames so that each occupies one quarter of the window space. The center row occupies the remaining half of the window space.

Frame row and column size values expressed as a percentage of the window dimensions are more sensible. For instance, the following example is effectively identical to the previous one:

```
<frameset rows="25%,50%,25%">
```

Of course, if the percentages don't add up to 100 percent, the browser automatically and proportionally resizes each row to make up the difference.

If you are like us, making things add up is not a strength. Perhaps some of the frame designers suffer the same difficulty, which would explain why they included the very nifty asterisk option for `<frameset>` `rows` and `cols` values. It tells the browser to size the respective column or row to whatever space is left over after putting adjacent frames into the frameset.

For example, when the browser encounters the frame tag:

```
<frameset cols="100,*">
```

it makes a fixed-sized column 100 pixels wide, and then creates another frame column that occupies all of the remaining space in the frameset.

Here's a fancier layout example:

```
<frameset cols="10,*,10">
```

This one creates two very thin columns down the edges of the frameset and gives the remaining center portion to the middle column.

You may also use the asterisk for more than one row- or column-attribute value. In that case, the corresponding rows or columns equally divide the available space. For example,

```
<frameset rows="*,100,*">
```

creates a 100-pixel tall row in the middle of the frameset and equal-sized rows above and below it.

If you precede the asterisk with an integer value, the corresponding row or column gets proportionally more of the available space. For example,

```
<frameset cols="10%,3*,*,*">
```

creates four columns: the first column occupies 10 percent of the overall width of the frameset. The browser then gives the second three-fifths of the remaining space, and the third and the fourth are each given one-fifth of the remaining space.

Using asterisks (especially with the numeric prefix) makes it easy to divide up the remaining space in a frameset.

Be aware, too, that unless you explicitly tell it not to, the browser lets users manually resize the individual frame document's columns and rows, and hence change the relative proportions each frame occupies in their frames display. To prevent this, see the `noresize` attribute for the `<frame>` tag. [`<frame>`, 12.4.1]

12.3.1.2 Controlling frame borders and spacing

The lack of standards has given rise to a number of potentially conflicting attributes that you may use to define and change the borders surrounding the frames in a frameset.

Both Internet Explorer and Netscape use the `frameborder` attribute to disable or explicitly enable frame borders. (By default, every frame in a frameset as well as the frameset window itself is rendered with a 3D border; see Figure 12-1.) The two browsers' documentation disagree about the particular values for the `frameborder` attribute, but both acknowledge the other's conventions. Hence, setting the value of `frameborder` to 0 or `no` turns borders off (see Figure 12-2); 1 or `yes` turns borders on.

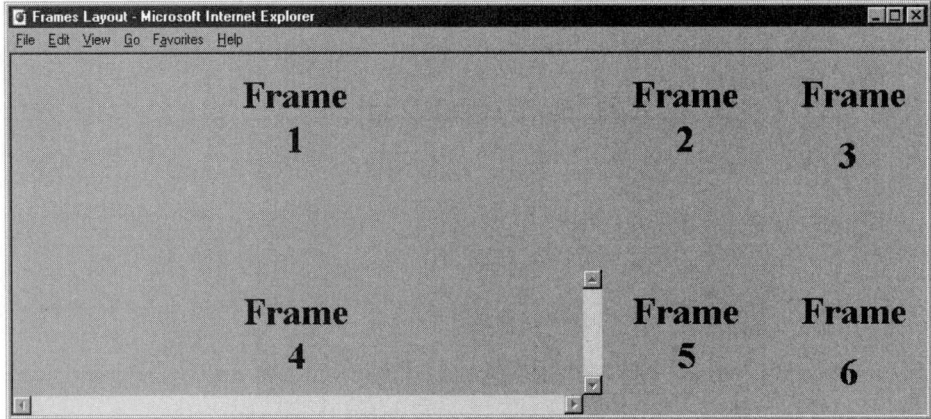

Figure 12-2. The frameborder attribute lets you remove the spacing between frames

Internet Explorer and Netscape do disagree, however, as to how you may control the thickness of the borders. Internet Explorer supports the `framespacing` attribute, whose value is the number of pixels you want between frames (see Figure 12-2). The attribute affects all frames and framesets nested within the current frameset as displayed by Internet Explorer. In practice, you should set it once on the outermost `<frameset>` to create a consistent border appearance for all of the frames in a single page.

Netscape only accepts the `border` attribute to define the border width, with an integer value in pixels. Like Internet Explorer, Netscape allows you to include the `frameborder` attribute with any `<frameset>` tag, affecting all nested frames and framesets, but unlike Internet Explorer, Netscape restricts the `border` attribute to the outermost `<frameset>`, ensuring that all frame borders are the same width within that `<frameset>`.

Since browsers ignore unsupported attributes, it is possible to define frame borders so that both browsers do the right thing. Just make sure to use the same `framespacing` and `border` values.

Finally, with Netscape you can control the color of the frame borders using the `bordercolor` attribute (Figure 12-3). It accepts a color name or hexadecimal triple as its value. A complete list of color names and values can be found in Appendix F, *Color Names and Values.*

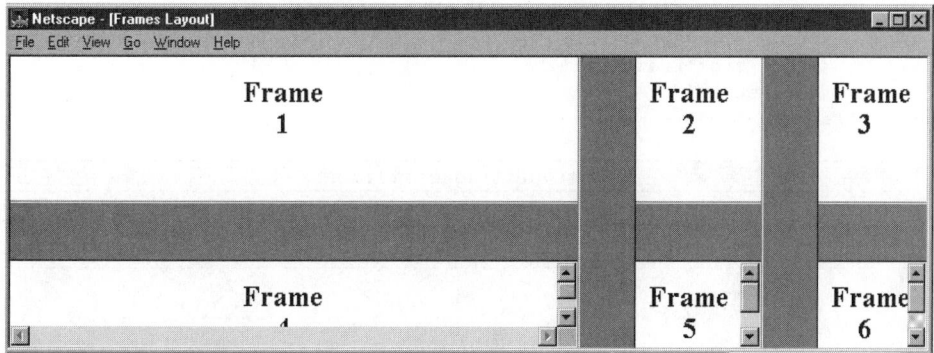

Figure 12-3. Netscape accepts border and bordercolor to control the color and spacing between frames

12.3.1.3 Frames and JavaScript

Internet Explorer and Netscape support JavaScript-related event handlers that let your frame documents react when they are first loaded and when the frame window gets resized (onLoad); unloaded from the browser by the user (onUn-load); when the window containing the frameset loses focus, such as when the user selects another window (onBlur); or when the frameset becomes the active window (onFocus). Included as <frameset> attributes, these event handlers take quote-enclosed lists of JavaScript commands and function calls as their value. For example, you might notify the user when all the contents have been loaded into their respective frames of a lengthy frameset:

```
<frameset onLoad="window.alert('Everything is loaded. You may now
continue.')">
```

These four attributes may also be used with the <body> tag. We cover JavaScript in more detail in 13.3.3.

12.3.2 Nesting <frameset> Tags

You can create some elaborate browser displays with a single <frameset>, but the frame layout is unimaginative. Instead, create staggered frames and other more complex layouts with multiple <frameset> tags nested within a top-level <frameset> in the frame document.

For example, create a layout of two columns, the first with two rows and the second with three rows (Figure 12-4), by nesting two <frameset> tags with row specifications within a top-level <frameset> that specifies the columns:

```
<frameset cols="50%,*">
  <frameset rows="50%,*">
```

```
      <frame src="frame1.html">
      <frame src="frame2.html">
   </frameset>
   <frameset rows ="33%,33%,*">
      <frame src="frame3.html">
      <frame src="frame4.html">
      <frame src="frame5.html">
   </frameset>
</frameset>
```

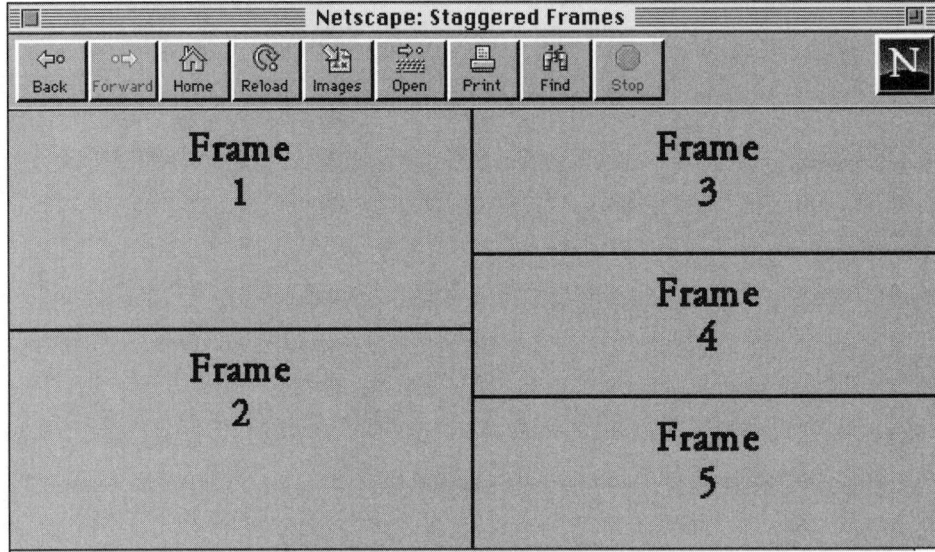

Figure 12-4. Staggered frame layouts use nested <frameset> tags

12.4 Frame Contents

A frame document contains no displayable content, except perhaps a message for non–frame-enabled browsers (see `<noframes>` later in this chapter). Instead, `<frame>` tags inside the one or more `<frameset>` tags, which encapsulate the contents of a frame document, provide URL references to the individual documents that occupy each frame. [`<noframes>`, 12.5]

12.4.1 The <frame> Tag

The `<frame>` tag appears only within a `<frameset>`. Use it to set, via its associated `src` attribute, the URL of the document content that initially gets displayed inside the respective frame.

Frames are placed into a frameset column by column, from left to right, and then row by row, from top to bottom, so the sequence and number of `<frame>` tags inside the `<frameset>` tag are important.

<frame>

Function:
> Define a single frame in a <frameset>

Attributes:
> BORDERCOLOR ▉
> FRAMEBORDER
> MARGINHEIGHT
> MARGINWIDTH
> NAME
> NORESIZE
> SCROLLING
> SRC

End tag:
> </frame>; rarely included

Contains:
> Nothing

Used in:
> *frameset_content*

The browser displays empty frames for <frame> tags that do not have a src attribute. It also displays empty frames if the <frameset> tag calls for more frames than the corresponding <frame> tags define. Such orphans remain empty; you cannot put content into them later, even if they have a target "name" for display redirection (see 12.4.1.2).

12.4.1.1 The src attribute

The value of the src attribute for the <frame> tag is a URL of the document that is to be displayed in the frame. There is no other way to provide content for a frame. You shouldn't, for instance, include any <body> content within the frame document; the browser will ignore the frame tags and display just the contents of a <body> tag if it comes first, or vice versa.

The document referenced by the src attribute may be any valid HTML document or displayable object, including images and multimedia. In particular, the referenced document may itself be composed of one or more frames. The frames are displayed within the referencing frame, providing yet another way of achieving complex layouts using nested frames.

Since the source may be a complete HTML document, all the features of HTML apply within a frame, including backgrounds and colors, tables, fonts, and the like. Unfortunately, this also means that multiple frames in a single browser window may conflict with each other. Specifically, if each nested frame document (not a regular HTML document) has a different `<title>` tag, the title of the overall browser window will be the title of the most recently loaded frame document. The easiest way to avoid this problem is to ensure that all related frame documents use the same title.

12.4.1.2 The name attribute

The optional `name` attribute for the `<frame>` tag labels that frame for later reference by the `target` attribute for the hypertext link anchor `<a>` tag and the `<form>` tag. This way, you can alter the contents of a frame using a link in another frame. Otherwise, like normal browser windows, hypertext-linked documents replace the contents of the source frame. We discuss names and targets in greater length later in this chapter. [target for `<a>`, 12.7]

The value of the `name` attribute is a text string enclosed in quotation marks.

12.4.1.3 The noresize attribute

Even though you may explicitly set their dimensions with attributes in the `<frameset>` tag, users can manually alter the size of a column or row of frames. To suppress this behavior, add the `noresize` attribute to the frame tags in the row or column whose relative dimensions you do not want users fiddling with. For a two-by-two frame document, a `noresize` attribute in any one of the four associated frame tags will effectively freeze the relative proportions of all the frames, for example.

The `noresize` attribute is especially useful for frames that contain fixed images serving as advertisements, a button bar, or a logo. By fixing the size of the frame to contain just the image and setting the `noresize` attribute, you guarantee that the image will be displayed in the intended manner and that the remainder of the browser window will always be given over to the other frames in the document.

12.4.1.4 The scrolling attribute

The browser will display vertical and horizontal scrollbars with frames whose contents are larger than the allotted window space. If there is sufficient room for the content, the scrollbars disappear. The `scrolling` attribute for the `<frame>` tag gives you explicit control over whether the scroll bars appear or disappear.

With `scrolling="yes"`, the browser adds scroll bars to the designated frame even if there is nothing to scroll. If you set the `scrolling` attribute value to `no`, scrollbars will never be added to the frame, even if the frame contents are larger than the frame itself. The value `auto`, supported only by Netscape, works as if you didn't include the `scrolling` attribute in the tag; Netscape adds scrollbars as needed. To achieve `auto` behavior in Internet Explorer, simply omit the `scrolling` attribute altogether.

12.4.1.5 The marginheight and marginwidth attributes

The browser normally places a small amount of space between the edge of a frame and its contents. You can change those margins with the `marginheight` and `marginwidth` attributes, each including a value for the exact number of pixels to place around the frame contents.

You cannot make a margin less than one pixel, or make it so large there is no room for the frame contents. That's because these attributes, like most other HTML ones, advise; they do not dictate to the browser. If your desired margin values cannot be accommodated, the browser ignores them and renders the frame as best it can.

12.4.1.6 The frameborder and bordercolor attributes

You may add or remove borders from a single frame with the `frameborder` attribute. Values of `yes` or `1` and `no` or `0` respectively enable or disable borders for the frame and override the value of the `frameborder` attribute for any frameset containing the frame.

Note that the browsers do react somewhat differently to border specifications. Netscape, for instance, removes an individual border only if adjacent frames sharing that border have borders turned off. Internet Explorer, in the other hand, will remove those adjacent borders, but only if they are not explicitly turned on in those adjacent frames. Our advice is to explicitly control the borders for each frame if you want to consistently control the borders for all frames across both browsers.

With Netscape only, you also can change the color of the individual frame's borders with the `bordercolor` attribute. Use a color name or hexadecimal triple as its value. If two adjacent frames have different `bordercolor` attributes, the resulting border color is undefined. A complete list of color names and values can be found in Appendix F, *Color Names and Values*.

12.5 The <noframes> Tag

A frame document has no `<body>`. In fact, it must not, since the browser will ignore any frame tags if it finds any `<body>` content before it encounters the first `<frameset>` tag. A frame document, therefore, is all but invisible to any non-frame capable browser. The `<noframes>` tag gives some relief to the frame-disabled.

<noframes>

Function:
Supply content for nonframe-compatible browsers

Attributes:
None

End tag:
</noframes>; sometimes omitted

Contains:
body_content

Used in:
frameset_content

Use the <noframes> tag only within the outermost <frameset> tag of a frame document. The content inside the <noframes> tag and its required end tag (</noframes>) is not displayed by any frame-capable browser, but is displayed in lieu of other contents in the frame document by browsers that do not handle frames. The contents of the <noframes> tag can be any normal HTML body content, including the <body> tag itself.

Although this tag is optional, experienced HTML authors typically include the <noframes> tag in their frame documents with content that warns a frame-incompatible browser user that they're missing the show. And smart authors will give those users a way out, if not direct access to the individual documents that make up the frame document contents. Remember our first frame example in this chapter? Figure 12-5 shows what happens when that frame document gets loaded into an old version of Mosaic.

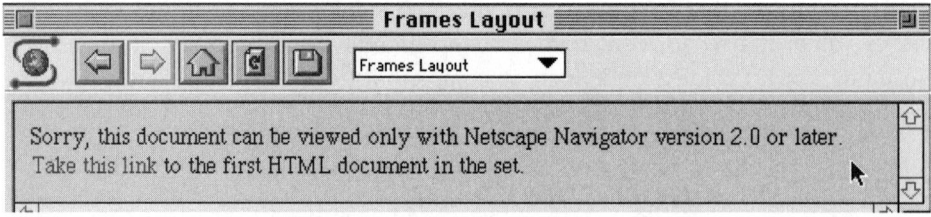

Figure 12-5. A <noframes> message in a nonframe-capable browser

```
<noframes>
  Sorry, this document can be viewed only with Netscape
  Navigator version 1.2 or later.
  <a href="frame1.html">Take this link</a>
  to the first HTML document in the set.
</noframes>
```

The reason <noframes> works is that most browsers are extremely tolerant of erroneous tags and incorrect documents. A nonframe browser simply ignores the frame tags. What's left, then, is the content of the <noframes> tag, which the browser dutifully displays.

If your browser strictly enforces some version of HTML that does not support frames, it may simply display an error message and refuse to display the document, even if it contains a <noframes> tag.

12.6 Inline Frames

To this point, our discussion has centered around frames that are defined as part of a frameset. A frameset, in turn, replaces the conventional <body> of a document and supplies content to the user via its contained frames.

Internet Explorer let you do things a bit differently: You also can define a frame that exists within a conventional document, displayed as part of that document's text flow. These frames behave a lot like inline images, which is why they are known as inline frames.

12.6.1 The <iframe> Tag

Define an inline frame with the <iframe> tag.

The <iframe> tag is *not* used within a <frameset> tag. Instead, it appears anywhere in your document that an <img> tag could appear. The tag defines a rectangular region within the document in which the browser displays a separate HTML document, including scrollbars and borders.

Most of the attributes for the <iframe> tag, including the frameborder, marginheight, marginwidth, name, scrolling, and src attributes, behave exactly as the corresponding attributes for the <frame> tag. For further information on these attributes, see 12.4.1.

Use the content of the <iframe> tag to provide information to users of browsers other than Internet Explorer. Internet Explorer ignores these contents whereas all other browsers ignore the <iframe> tag and therefore display its contents as if it were regular body content. For instance, use the <iframe> content to explain to non–Internet Explorer users what they are missing:

```
...other document content
<iframe src="sidebar.html" width=75 height=200 align=right>
Your browser does not support inline frames.  To view this
<a href="sidebar.html">document</a> correctly, you'll need
a copy of Internet Explorer.
</iframe>
...subsequent document content
```

<iframe> ❶

Function:
> Define an inline frame within a text flow

Attributes:
> ALIGN
> FRAMEBORDER
> HEIGHT
> MARGINHEIGHT
> MARGINWIDTH
> NAME
> SCROLLING
> SRC
> WIDTH

End tag:
> </iframe>; never omitted

Contains:
> *body_content*

Used in:
> *text*

In this example, we let the user know that they were accessing an unsupported feature, and provided a link to the missing content.

12.6.1.1 The align attribute

Like the `align` attribute for the `<img>` tag, this inline frame attribute lets you control where the frame gets placed inline with the adjacent text or moved to the edge of the document, allowing text to flow around the frame. [image alignment, 5.2.6.4]

For inline alignment, use `top`, `middle`, or `bottom` as the value of this attribute. The frame will be aligned with the top, middle, or bottom of the adjacent text, respectively.

To allow text to flow around the inline frame, use the `left` or `right` values for this attribute. The frame will be moved to the left or right edge of the text flow, respectively, and the remaining content of the document will be flowed around the frame. This behavior is exactly like that of images whose `align` attribute has been set to `left` or `right`.

12.6.1.2 The height and width attributes

Internet Explorer puts the contents of an inline frame into a predefined, 150 pixel-tall, 300 pixel-wide box. Use the `height` and `width` attributes with values as the number of pixels to change those dimensions.

12.6.2 Using Inline Frames

Although you probably will shy away from inline frames for most of your web pages, they can be useful, particularly for providing information related to the current document being viewed, similar to the sidebar articles you'd find in a conventional printed publication. Unfortunately, a large component of your audience will not be able to view the inline frames, so make sure you include appropriate alternative content within the `<iframe>` and `</iframe>` tags to help those less fortunate viewers find the frame contents.

Except for their location within conventional document content, inline frames are treated exactly like regular frames. You can load other documents into the inline frame using its name (see following section) and link to other documents from within the inline frame.

12.7 Named Frame or Window Targets

As we discussed in the `<frame>` tag description section, you can label a frame by adding the `name` attribute to its `<frame>` tag. Once named, the frame may become the destination display window for a hypertext-linked document selected within a document displayed in some other frame. You accomplish this redirection by adding the special `target` attribute to the anchor that references the document.

12.7.1 The target Attribute for the <a> Tag

If you include a `target` attribute within an `<a>` tag, the browser will load and display the document named in the tag's `href` attribute in a frame or window whose name matches the target. If the named frame or window doesn't exist, the browser will open a new window, give it the specified name, and load the new document into that window. Thereafter, hypertext-linked documents that target that name will load into the new window.

Targeted hypertext links makes it easy to create effective navigational tools. A simple table of contents document, for example, might redirect documents into a separate window:

```
<h3>Table of Contents</h3>
<ul>
  <li><a href="pref.html" target="view_window">Preface</a>
```

```
    <li><a href="chap1.html" target="view_window">Chapter 1</a>
    <li><a href="chap2.html" target="view_window">Chapter 2</a>
    <li><a href="chap3.html" target="view_window">Chapter 3</a>
  </ul>
```

The first time the user clicks one of the table of contents hypertext links, the browser will open a new window, name it "view_window," and display the desired document's contents inside it. If the user selects another link from the example table of contents and the "view_window" is still open, the browser will again load the selected document into that window, replacing the previous document.

Throughout the whole process, the window containing the table of contents is accessible to the user. By clicking on a link in one window, the user causes the contents of the other window to change.

Similarly, you can place the table of contents into one frame of a two-frame document and use the adjacent frame for display of the selected documents:

```
    <frameset cols="150,*">
      <frame src="toc.html">
      <frame src="pref.html" name="view_frame">
    </frameset>
```

When the browser initially displays the two frames, the left frame contains the table of contents, and the right frame contains the preface (see Figure 12-6).

Figure 12-6. Table of contents frame controls content of adjacent frame

When a user selects a link from the table of contents in the left frame (for example, Chapter 1), the browser loads and displays the associated document into the "view_frame" frame on the right side (Figure 12-7). As other links are selected, the right frame's contents change, while the left frame continuously makes the table of contents available to the user.

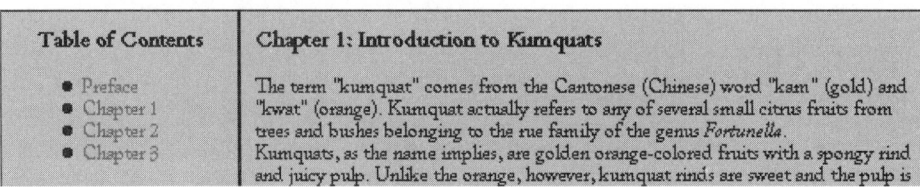

Figure 12-7. Chapter 1's contents are displayed in the adjacent frame

12.7.2 Special Targets

There are four reserved target names for special document redirection actions:

`_blank`

> The browser always loads a `target="_blank"` linked document into a newly opened, unnamed window.

`_self`

> This target value is the default for all `<a>` tags that do not specify a target, causing the target document to be loaded and displayed in the same frame or window as the source document. This target is redundant and unnecessary unless used in combination with the `target` attribute in the `<base>` tag in a document's head (see below).

`_parent`

> The `_parent` target causes the document to be loaded into the parent window or frameset containing the frame containing the hypertext reference. If the reference is in a window or top-level frame, it is equivalent to the target `_self`.

> A brief example may help clarify how this link works. Consider a link in a frame that is part of a three-column frameset. This frameset, in turn, is a row in the top-level frameset being displayed in the browser window. This arrangement is shown in Figure 12-6.

> If no target is specified for the hypertext link, it is loaded into the containing frame. If a target of `_parent` is specified, the document is loaded into the area occupied by the three-column frameset containing the frame that contains the link.

`_top`

> This target causes the document to be loaded into the window containing the hypertext link, replacing any frames currently displayed in the window.

> Continuing with the frame hierarchy shown in Figure 12-8, using a target of `_top` would remove all the contained frames and load the document into the entire browser window.

All four of these names begin with the underscore character. Any other window or target name beginning with an underscore is ignored by the browser. Don't use the underscore as the first character of the name of any frame you define in your documents.

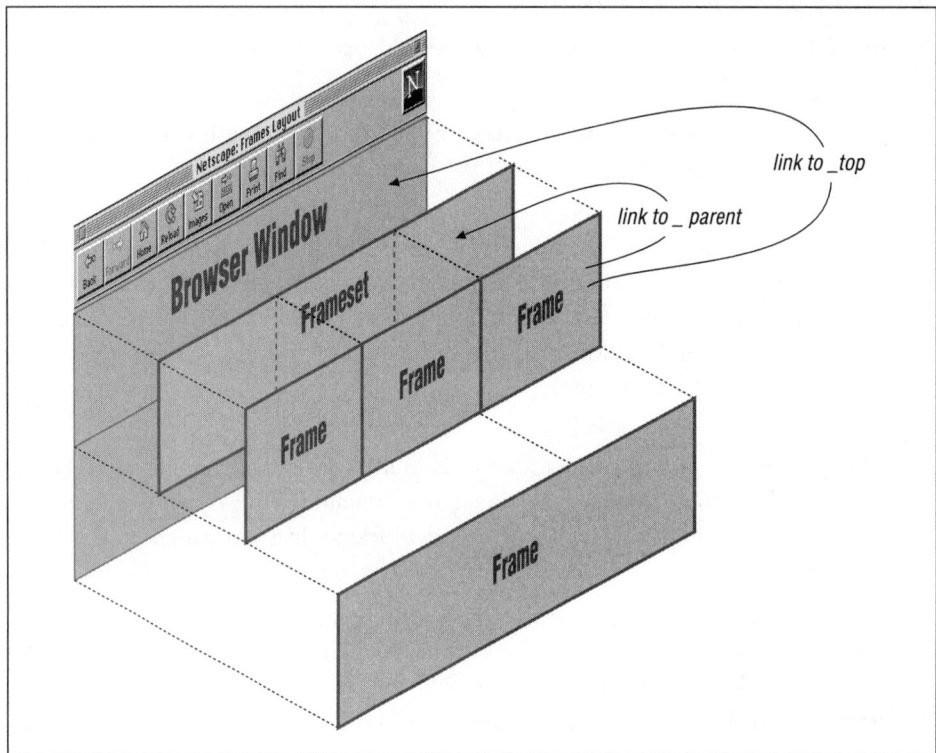

Figure 12-8. Using special hypertext targets in nested frames and framesets

12.7.3 The <base> Default Target

It can be tedious to specify a target for every hypertext link in your documents, especially when most are targeted at the same window or frame. To alleviate this problem, you can add a **target** attribute to the **<base>** tag. [<base>, 7.7.1]

The **target** attribute in the **<base>** tag sets the default target for every hypertext link in the current document that does not contain an explicit **target** attribute. For example, in our example table of contents document, almost every link causes the document to be displayed in another window named "view_frame." Rather than include that target in each hypertext link, you should place the common target in the table of contents' **<base>** tag within its **<head>**:

```
<html>
<head>
<title>Table of Contents</title>
<base target="view_frame">
</head>
<body>
<h3>Table of Contents</h3>
```

```
<ul>
  <li><a href="pref.html">Preface</a>
  <li><a href="chap1.html">Chapter 1</a>
  <li><a href="chap2.html" >Chapter 2</a>
  <li><a href="chap3.html">Chapter 3</a>
</ul>
</body>
</html>
```

Notice that we don't include any other target references in the list of hyperlinks, because the browser will load and display all the respective documents in the base target "view_frame."

12.7.3.1 Traditional link behavior

Before the onset of frames, each time you clicked on a hyperlink, the corresponding document replaced the contents of the browser window. With frames, this behavior is modified so that the corresponding document replaces the content of the referencing frame. This is often not the desired behavior and can be disconcerting to people browsing your documents.

For example, suppose you have arranged all of the documents on your site to present themselves in three frames: a navigational frame at the top of the browser window, a scrolling content frame in the middle, and a feedback form at the bottom. You named the content frame with the `name` attribute of the `<frame>` tag in the top-level document for your collection and used the `target` attribute of the `<base>` tag in every document on your site to ensure that all links will be loaded into the center content frame.

This arrangement works perfectly for all the documents on your site, but what happens when a user selects a link that takes them to a different site? The referenced document will still be loaded into the center content frame. Now the user is confronted by a document from some other site, surrounded by your navigation and feedback frames!

The solution is to make sure that every hypertext link that references a remote document has a `target` of `_top`. This way, when someone selects a link that takes them away from your site, the remote document will replace the contents of the entire browser window, including your navigation and feedback frames. If the majority of the links in your documents are to other sites, you might consider adding `target="_top"` to a `<base>` tag in your document, and using explicit `target` attributes in the links to your local documents.

13

In this chapter:
- *Applets*
- *Embedded Content*
- *JavaScript*
- *JavaScript Style Sheets*

Executable Content

Truth be told, pure HTML is like a comic book in a world full of Saturday morning cartoons. Save for the occasional animated GIF image, a pure HTML page, although attractive, is a static presentation of text and images. HTML documents need not be limited like the print medium. The Web is a digital dynamo of animation and processing activity, spread over the worldwide Internet. And, with recent innovations, HTML can shimmy, too.

To spice up those otherwise dull pages, a number of HTML tags exist solely to inject dynamic content into your pages. Commonly known as an *applet* or *script*, and embedded into the HTML document, these programs get delivered to your browser and executed in any of several different ways. During execution, the applets and scripts may generate dynamic HTML content, interact with the user, validate form data, or even create windows and run entire applications independent of your HTML pages. The possibilities are endless, and go far beyond the document model originally envisioned for HTML.

In this chapter, we describe how dynamic content can augment your HTML documents. We'll show you, with simple examples, how to embed and include executable content—scripts and applets—in your HTML documents. We won't, however, even begin to pretend to teach you how to write and debug your own applet programs. This is a book about HTML, after all. Rather, get an expert opinion: turn to any of the many excellent texts from O'Reilly, including *Java-Script: The Definitive Guide*, *Java in a Nutshell*, and *Exploring Java*.

13.1 Applets

One of the most exciting recent developments in web technologies is the ability to deliver applications directly to the user's browser, where they are executed on the client machine. These applications are typically small tools—hence the term "applet"—that perform simple tasks on the client computer, including a variety of HTML page display enhancements.

Applets, like client-side image maps, represent a shift in the basic model of web communications. Until recently, servers performed most of the computational work on the Web; client browsers being not much more than glorified terminals. With applets and client-side image maps, Web technology is shifting toward the client, distributing some or all of the computational load from the server to the client and browser.

Applets also represent a way of extending a browser's features without forcing users to purchase or otherwise acquire a new browser, as is the case when developers implement new tag and attribute extensions to HTML. Nor do users have to acquire and install a special application, as is required for helper or plugin applications. This means that once users have a browser that supports applets, you can deliver browser extensions immediately, including HTML display and multimedia innovations.

13.1.1 The Applet Model

Applets are like other accessory parts of an HTML document. The browser first loads the HTML page, examines it for special tags that identify applets, which, like other Web resources you identified with a URL, and retrieves the applet via the normal HTTP protocol.

Once downloaded, the browser provides a portion of the document display space for the applet to use as its own display space. You may control the size and position of this display area; the applet controls what is presented inside.

During execution, the applet has access to a restricted environment within the user's computer. For instance, applets have access to the mouse and keyboard, and may receive input from the user. They can initiate network connections and retrieve data from other servers on the Internet. In sum, applets are full-fledged programs, complete with a variety of input and output mechanisms, along with a full suite of network services.

Several applets may be placed in a single document; they all execute in parallel and may communicate with each other. While the browser may limit their access to its computer system, applets have complete control of their virtual environment within the browser.

13.1.2 The Applet Advantage

There are several advantages of applets, not the least of which is providing more compelling user interfaces within a web page. For instance, an applet might create a unique set of menus, choices, text fields, and similar user-input tools different from those available through the browser. When the user clicks a button within the applet's interaction/display region, the applet might respond by displaying results within the region, signaling another applet, or even by loading a completely new page into the browser.

We don't mean to imply that the only use of applets is to enhance the user interface. An applet is a full-fledged program that can perform any number of computational and user-interactive tasks on the client computer. An applet might implement a real-time video display, or perform circuit simulation, or engage the user in a game, and so on.

13.1.3 Using Applets Correctly

An applet is nothing more than another tool you may use to produce compelling and useful web pages. Keep in mind that an applet uses computational resources on the client to run and therefore places a load on the user's computer. It can degrade system performance.

Similarly, if an applet uses a lot of network bandwidth to accomplish its task (a real-time video feed, for example), it may make other network communication unbearably slow. While such applications are fun, they do little more than annoy your target audience.

To use an applet correctly, balance the load between the browser and the server. For each page, decide which tasks are best left to the server (forms processing, index searches, and the like) and which tasks are better suited for local processing (user interface enhancements, real-time data presentation, small animations, input validation, and so on). Divide the processing accordingly. Remember that many users have slower network connections and computers than you do and design your applets to satisfy the majority of your audience.

Used the right way, applets seamlessly enhance your pages and provide a satisfying experience for your audience. Used improperly, applets are just another annoying bandwidth waster, alienating your users and hurting your pages.

13.1.4 Writing Applets

Creating applets is a programming task, not usually a job for the HTML author, and certainly way beyond the scope of this book. For details, we recommend you consult any of the many applet programming texts that have recently appeared on bookshelves everywhere, including those from O'Reilly & Associates.

Today, one language dominates the applet programming world: Java. Developed by Sun Microsystems of Mountain View, California, Java supports an object-oriented programming style wherein classes of applets can be used and reused to build complex applications.

By invention, applets built from the same language should run with any browser that supports them. In reality, certain Microsoft implementation decisions have caused some valid Java applets to fail when running on Internet Explorer. Hopefully, Microsoft will fix these problems and Java will remain a universal programming language for the Web. In any case, the conscientious Java programmer should keep abreast of the latest technology and create applets that are certifiably 100% pure Java. Microsoft, in particular, is trying to get programmers to use proprietary extensions to Java that will work on only Microsoft platforms. We recommend avoiding any vendor extensions to Java that deviate from the standard Java 1.1 version currently in widespread use.

We should take this opportunity to also mention ActiveX, an alternative applet programming technology available only from Microsoft. ActiveX is proprietary, closely coupled to various versions of Microsoft Windows, and is only fully functional when used with Internet Explorer. ActiveX applets will run on versions of Internet Explorer targeted to various versions of Windows, but a single ActiveX applet will not run on these different versions without recompilation. This is in contrast with Java applets, where a single Java applet can be written and compiled once and immediately run on a broad range of browsers and operating systems.

ActiveX also presents an unacceptably high security risk to any user whose browser supports ActiveX technology. It is ridiculously easy to penetrate and damage a computer running a browser that allows ActiveX applets to be executed. For this reason, we cannot recommend ActiveX as a viable applet implementation technology and we go so far as to recommend that users disable ActiveX capability within their browser—specifically, Internet Explorer.

13.1.5 The <applet> Tag

Use the <applet> tag within your HTML document to name the applet that the browser should download and execute. Also, use the tag to define a region within the document display for the applet's display area. You may also supply alternative content within the <applet> tag for display by browsers that do not support applets.

Function:

Insert an application into the current text flow

Attributes:

ALIGN
ALT
ARCHIVE **N**
CODE
CODEBASE
HEIGHT
HSPACE
MAYSCRIPT
NAME
TITLE **❶**
VSPACE
WIDTH

End tag:

</applet>; never omitted

Contains:

applet_content

Used in:

text

`Code` is the only required attribute. It identifies the class name of the Java program.

The browser inserts the applet display region into the containing text flow exactly like an inline image: without line breaks and as a single large entity. The browser downloads and executes the applet just after download and display of the HTML document, and continues execution until the code terminates itself or when the user stops viewing the page containing the applet.

Most applets require one or more parameters that you supply in the HTML document to control their execution. Put these parameters between the `<applet>` tag and its corresponding `</applet>` end tag using the `<param>` tag. The browser passes the document-specific parameters to the applet at time of execution. [`<param>`, 13.1.6]

13.1.5.1 The align attribute

Like an image, you may control the alignment of an applet's display region with respect to its surrounding text. In fact, the `<applet>` tag's `align` attribute honors all the alignment values used by the `<img>` tag, including `top`, `texttop`,

middle, absmiddle, baseline, bottom, and absbottom, as well as left
and right alignments for wrap-around content. [image alignment, 5.2.6.4]

13.1.5.2 The alt attribute

The alt attribute gives you a way to tell users gracefully that something is
missing if, for some reason, the applet cannot or will not execute on their
computer. Its value is a quote-enclosed message string that, like the alt attribute
for images, gets displayed in lieu of the applet itself.

The alt message is only for browsers that support applets. See 13.1.5.11 to find
out how to inform users of applet-incapable browsers why they can't view an
applet.

13.1.5.3 The archive attribute

Supported only by Netscape, the archive attribute lets you collect common Java
classes into a single library that is cached on the user's local disk. Once cached,
the browser doesn't need to use the network to access an applet; it retrieves the
software from the local cache, thereby reducing the inherent delays of additional
network activity to load the class.

The value of the archive attribute is a URL identifying the archive file. The
suffix of the archive filename may be either *.zip* or *.jar*. *.zip* files are in the
familiar ZIP archive format, generated by PKZIP and many other utilities. *.jar* files
are in the new Java archive format; currently, support for *.jar* files is spotty at
best, but they will become more widespread. *.jar* files support compression and
some advanced features like digital signatures.

You may use the archive attribute with any <applet> tag, even if the class
referenced by the tag's code attribute does not exist in the archive. If the class is
not found in the archive, the browser simply attempts to retrieve the class relative
to the document URL or the codebase URL, if specified.

13.1.5.4 The code attribute

The code attribute is required. Use it to specify the filename of the Java class to
be executed by the browser. Note that this is *not* a URL; the browser assumes the
applet file is in the same directory as the host HTML document. To make the
search relative to another storage location, use the codebase attribute described
in 13.1.5.5 or an archive, as described above. Also, the extension suffix of the filename should be *.class*. If you don't include the suffix, some browsers
automatically will append *.class* when searching for the applet.

For example, to execute a clock Java applet contained in a file named *clock.class*,
you might include in your HTML document the code:

```
<applet code=clock.class>
</applet>
```

The browser will locate the code for the applet using the current document's base URL. Hence, if the current document's URL is:

```
http://www.kumquat.com/harvest_time.html
```

the browser will retrieve the applet code for our `clock` class example above as:

```
http://www.kumquat.com/clock.class
```

13.1.5.5 The codebase attribute

Use the `codebase` attribute to provide an alternative base URL from which the browser will retrieve an applet file. The value of this attribute is a URL pointing to a directory containing the class defined by the `code` attribute. The `codebase` URL overrides, but does not permanently replace, the document's base URL, which is the default if you don't use `codebase`. [URLs, 7.2]

Continuing with our previous examples, suppose your document came from *http://www.kumquat.com*, but the `clock` applet is kept in a separate directory named `classes`. You cannot retrieve the applet by specifying `code=classes/clock.class`. Rather, include the `codebase` attribute and new base URL:

```
<applet code=clock.class codebase="http://www.kumquat.com/classes/">
</applet>
```

which resolves to the URL:

```
http://www.kumquat.com/classes/clock.class
```

Although we used an absolute URL in this example, you also can use a relative URL. For instance, in most cases the applets are stored on the same server as the host HTML documents, so we'd usually be better off, for relocation's sake, specifying a relative URL for the codebase, such as:

```
<applet code=clock.class codebase="/classes/">
</applet>
```

13.1.5.6 The name attribute

The `name` attribute lets you supply a unique name for this instance of the code class—the copy of the applet that runs on the individual user's computer. Like other named elements in your HTML document, providing a name for the applet lets other parts of your HTML document, including other applets, reference and interact with this one, such as sharing computed results.

For example, suppose you have two clock applets in your document, along with two applets the user operates to set those clocks. Provide unique names for the clock applets using the **name** attribute, then pass those names to the setting applets using the **<param>** tag, which we discuss later in this chapter:

```
<applet code=clock.class name=clock1>
</applet>
<applet code=clock.class name=clock2>
</applet>
<applet code=setter.class>
  <param name=clockToSet value=clock1>
</applet>
<applet code=setter.class>
  <param name=clockToSet value=clock2>
</applet>
```

Since we have no need to distinguish between the Setter applets, we choose not to name their instances.

13.1.5.7 The height and width attributes

Identical to the counterparts for the <img> tag, the **height** and **width** attributes define the size of the applet's display region in the document. They both accept values indicating the size of the region in pixels. [<img> height and width, 5.2.6.9]

The display region's dimensions often must match some other applet requirement, so be careful to check these values with the applet programmer. Sometimes, the applet may scale its display output to match your specified region.

For example, suppose our example clock applet should grow or shrink to fit nearly any size display region. Hence, we might create a square clock 100 pixels wide by 100 pixels tall:

```
<applet code=clock.class height=100 width=100>
</applet>
```

13.1.5.8 The hspace and vspace attributes

As with a floating or inline image, surrounding text tightly abuts an applet's display region. The **hspace** and **vspace** attributes let you interpose some empty space around the applet region to set it off from the text. Both attributes accept a value that indicates pixels of space, with the **hspace** attribute creating a space to the left and right of the region; the **vspace** attribute adds space above and below the region.

For instance, to give our example clock some breathing room on the page, we might place an additional five pixels of space around it:

```
<applet code=clock.class height=100 width=100 hspace=5 vspace=5>
</applet>
```

13.1.5.9 The mayscript attribute

The `mayscript` attribute, supported only by Netscape, indicates that the Java applet will be accessing JavaScript features within the browser. Normally, Java applets attempting to access JavaScript cause a browser error. If your applets access JavaScript, you must specify `mayscript` in the `<applet>` tag.

13.1.5.10 The title attribute

The value of this attribute is a quoted string, which is used by Internet Explorer to provide a title, if necessary, for the applet. This attribute is not supported by Netscape.

13.1.5.11 Supporting incompatible browsers

Since some browsers may not support applets or the `<applet>` tag, sometimes you may need to tell readers what they are missing. You do this by including HTML body content between the `<applet>` and `</applet>` tags.

Browsers that support the `<applet>` tags ignore the HTML content inside. (Use the `alt` attribute to notify applet-enabled browser users when the applet doesn't display for some reason.) Of course, browsers that don't support applets don't recognize the `<applet>` tags. Being generally tolerant of apparent HTML mistakes, they will usually ignore the unrecognized tag and blithely go on to display whatever content may appear inside. It's as simple as that. The following fragment tells applet-incapable browser users they won't see our clock example:

```
<applet code=clock.class>
  If your browser were capable of handling applets, you'd see
  a nifty clock right here!
</applet>
```

Remember that this contained text is different from the text supplied by the `alt` attribute of the `<applet>` tag. The `alt` text is displayed by browsers that support the `<applet>` tag but cannot execute or display the specified applet. The contained text is displayed by browsers that do not support the `<applet>` tag at all. In order to accommodate both classes of browsers, the considerate author supplies both for each `<applet>` tag:

```
<applet code=clockclass height=100 width=100
  alt="[ Clock applet not available ]">
  <param name=style value=analog>
  If your browser were capable of handling applets, you'd see
  a nifty analog clock right here!
</applet>
```

13.1.6 The <param> Tag

The <param> tag supplies parameters for a containing <applet> or <object> tag. [<object>, 13.2.3]

<param>

Function:
    Supply a parameter to an <applet>

Attributes:
    NAME
    TYPE ❶
    VALUE
    VALUETYPE ❶

End tag:
    None

Contains:
    Nothing

Used in:
    applet_content

The <param> tag has no content and no end tag. It appears, perhaps with other <param> tags, only between an <applet> or <object> tag and its end tag. Use the <param> tag to pass parameters to the applet program or embedded object as required for it to function correctly.

13.1.6.1 The name and value attributes

The <param> tag has two required attributes: **name** and **value**. Both attributes accept strings as their value and together define a name/value pair that the browser passes to the applet.

For instance, our Clock applet example might let users specify the time zone by which it sets its hour hand. To pass the parameter named "timezone" with the value "EST" to our example applet, you would specify the parameters as:

```
<applet code=clock.class>
  <param name=timezone value=EST>
</applet>
```

Since both attributes had simple strings for values, we did not enclose the values in quotation marks. For values with embedded punctuation and spaces, be sure to delimit the strings accordingly.

The browser will pass the name/value pairs to the applet, but that is no guarantee that the applet is expecting the parameters, that the names and values are correct, or that the applet will even use the parameters. Correct parameter names, including capitalization, and acceptable values are determined by the applet author. The wise HTML document author will work closely with the applet author or have detailed documentation to ensure that the applet parameters are named correctly and assigned valid values.

13.1.6.2 *The type and valuetype attributes*

The `type` and `valuetype` attributes are supported only by Internet Explorer. Use them to define the type of the parameter the browser passes to the embedded object and how that object is to interpret the value. Used only with `<param>` tags contained within an `<object>` tag (see 13.2), these attributes have no use with parameters being passed to Java applets.

The `valuetype` attribute can have one of three values: `data`, `ref`, or `object`. The value `data` indicates that the parameter value is a simple string. This is the default value. Using `ref` indicates that the value is a URL of some other resource on the web. Finally, `object` indicates that the value is the name of another embedded object in the current document. This may be needed to support inter-object communication within an HTML document.

The value of the `type` attribute is the MIME media type of the value of the parameter. This is usually of no significance when the parameter value is a simple string, but can be important when the value is actually a URL pointing to some other object on the Web. In those cases, the embedded object may need to know the MIME type of the object in order to use it correctly. For example, this parameter tells the embedded object that the parameter is actually the URL of a Microsoft Word document:

```
<param name=document value=http://kumquats.com/quat.doc
   type=application/msword valuetype=url>
```

13.2 Embedded Content

The `<applet>` tag lets you insert programs, usually Java applets, into your HTML pages. As an extension to this concept, the popular browsers also let you insert data "objects" in your pages. These objects are grist for special applications, known as *plug-ins*, which are created by third-party vendors and are usually distributed over the Web to interested users. If the user owns a copy of the plug-in, the embedded object in your HTML document automatically causes the browser to execute the application, which in turn uses the object's information for processing and display.

Initially, plug-ins addressed the dearth of multimedia content available on the Web. The first plug-ins supported video and audio feeds, for example, and other nifty content like animation that was just not possible with plain HTML. As programmers grew more sophisticated, plug-ins evolved to include applications like games, database interfaces, and graphical interface elements.

In this section, we cover two tags that support embedded content. The `<embed>` tag lets you include an object whose MIME type references the plug-in needed to process and possibly display that object. The `<object>` tag is a hybrid of the `<embed>` and `<applet>` tags, supporting both embedded objects and applets.

13.2.1 The *<embed>* Tag

<embed> **N** **O**

Function:
    Embed an object in a document

Attributes:
    ALIGN **N**
    BORDER **N**
    HEIGHT
    HIDDEN
    HSPACE **N**
    NAME
    PALETTE
    PLUGINSPAGE **N**
    SRC
    TYPE **N**
    UNITS
    VSPACE **N**
    WIDTH

End tag:
    None

Contains:
    Nothing

Used in:
    text

Use the `<embed>` tag to include a reference in your HTML document to some special plug-in application and perhaps data for that application. Reference the data object via the `src` attribute and URL value for download by the browser. The browser uses the MIME type of the `src`'d object to determine the plug-in required to process the object. Alternatively, you may also use the `type` attribute to specify a MIME type without an object, and thereby initiate execution of a plug-in application, if it exists on the user's computer.

Like all other tags, the `<embed>` tag has a set of predefined attributes that define parameters and modify the tag's behavior. Unlike most other tags, however, the browsers let you include plug-in-specific name/value attribute pairs in `<embed>` that, instead of altering the action of the tag itself, get passed to the plug-in application for further processing.

For example, this tag:

```
<embed src=movie.avi width=320 height=200 autostart=true loop=3>
```

has attributes that are processed by the `<embed>` tag (`src`, `width`, and `height`) and two that are not recognized, but rather passed to the plug-in associated with AVI video clips: `autostart` and `loop`.

It is not possible to document all the possible attributes that the many different plug-ins might need with their associated `<embed>` tag. Instead, you must turn to the plug-in developer to learn about all their required and optional attributes for each particular plug-in you plan to use in your pages.

13.2.1.1 The align, border, height, width, hspace, and vspace attributes

The browser invariably displays embedded objects to the user in a region set aside within the document window. The `<embed>` tag's `align`, `border`, `height`, `width`, `hspace`, and `vspace` attributes let you control the appearance of that region exactly as they do for the `<img>` tag, so we won't belabor them here. [`<img>`, 5.2.6]

Briefly, the `height` and `width` attributes control the size of the viewing region. Normally, you should specify the height and width in pixels, but you may also use some other units of measure if you also specify the `units` attribute (see 13.2.1.8). The `hspace` and `vspace` attributes define a margin, in pixels, around the viewing region. The `align` attribute determines how the browser aligns the region within surrounding text, while the `border` attribute determines the width of the border surrounding the viewing region.

Only Netscape supports the `align`, `border`, `hspace`, and `vspace` attributes for the `<embed>` tag.

13.2.1.2 The hidden attribute

The `hidden` attribute makes an object invisible to the user, forcing it to have a height and width of zero. Note that setting `hidden` does not cause the browser to display an empty region within the document, but rather completely remove the object from the containing text flow.

This attribute is useful for audio streams placed within HTML documents. The HTML entry:

```
<embed src=music.wav hidden autostart=true loop=true>
```

embeds an audio object in the page. The browser does not show anything to the user, but rather plays background music for the page. By contrast, the plug-in associated with:

```
<embed src=music.wav>
```

might present an audio control panel to users so that they might start and stop the audio playback, adjust the volume, and so forth.

13.2.1.3 The name attribute

Like other **name** attributes, this one also lets your label the embedded object for later reference by other elements in your document, including other objects. The value of the attribute is a character string.

13.2.1.4 The palette attribute

The **palette** attribute is supported by both Netscape and Internet Explorer, but in completely different ways. With Netscape, the value of the palette attribute is either **foreground** or **background**, indicating which palette of window system colors the plug-in uses for its display.

With Internet Explorer, the value of **palette** is instead a pair of hexadecimal color values, separated by a vertical bar. The first value determines the foreground color used by the plug-in; the second sets the background color. Thus, specifying this **palette**:

```
palette=#ff0000|#00ff00
```

causes the plug-in to use red as its foreground color and green as its background color. For a complete description of hexadecimal color values, see Appendix F, *Color Names and Values.*

13.2.1.5 The pluginspage attribute

The **pluginspage** attribute, supported only by Netscape, specifies the URL of a web page that provides instruction on where to obtain and how to install the plug-in associated with the embedded object.

13.2.1.6 The src attribute

Like its document-referencing counterparts for a myriad of other tags, the `src` attribute supplies the URL of the data object that you embed in the HTML document. The server providing the object must be configured so that it notifies the browser of the correct MIME type of the object. If not, the browser will use the suffix of the last element of the `src` value—the object's filename in the URL path—to determine the type of the object. The browser uses this MIME type to determine which plug-in it will execute to process the object.

If you don't include a `src` attribute with the `<embed>` tag, you've got to include a `type` attribute to explicitly reference the MIME type and, hence, the plug-in application.

13.2.1.7 The type attribute

Use the `type` attribute in addition to or in lieu of the `src` attribute. Its value explicitly indicates the MIME type of the embedded object, which in turn determines which plug-in the browser will invoked to process the object. This attribute is not required if you include the `src` attribute and the browser can determine the object type from the object's URL or server. You must supply a `type` attribute if you don't include the `src` attribute.

It may seem odd to use an `<embed>` tag without a `src` attribute reference to some object, but this is common if the plug-in requires no data or retrieves its data dynamically after it is started. In these cases, the `type` attribute is required so that the browser knows which plug-in to invoke.

13.2.1.8 The units attribute

The default units of measure for the `height` and `width` attributes that control the `<embed>` display space is pixels. The `units` attribute lets you explicitly state that absolute measure of `pixels`, or change it to the relative `en`, which measure is one-half the current point size of text in the document. With the `en` units, you tailor the object's viewing area (viewport) to be proportional to its immediately surrounding content, the size of which is varied by the user.

For example,

```
<embed src=movie.avi height=200 width=320 units=pixels>
```

creates a view port for the window 200 by 320 pixels. By changing `units` to `en`, that same view port, when included within a flow of 12-point text, will become 1200 by 1920 pixels.

13.2.2 The <noembed> Tag

Some browsers do not support the `<embed>` tag. The `<noembed>` tag makes it easy to supply alternative content that tells users what they are missing.

<noembed> ◼ ❶

Function:
> Supply content to <embed>-incompatible browsers

Attributes:
> None

End tag:
> None

Contains:
> Nothing

Used in:
> *text*

The popular browsers ignore the contents of the `<noembed>` tag, whereas browsers that do not support the `<embed>` tag will display the contents of the `<noembed>` tag. Normally, use the contents of the `<noembed>` tag to display some sort of message placating users of inadequate browsers:

```
<embed src=cool.mov autostart=true loop=true>
<noembed>To view the cool movie, you need to upgrade to a browser
that supports the &lt;embed&gt; tag!</noembed>
```

We recommend using a `<noembed>` message only in those cases where the object is crucial for the user to comprehend and use your HTML document. And, in those cases, provide a link to a document that can stand alone without the embedded object, or nicely explain the difficulty.

13.2.3 The <object> Tag

The `<object>` tag provides the functionality of both the `<applet>` and `<embed>` tags. Use it to insert Java and other applets into a document, along with their parameters, or to embed objects in a document, causing the browser to invoke their associated plug-ins.

The `<object>` tag was originally implemented by Microsoft to support the insertion of ActiveX applets into documents. Microsoft later added limited support for the `<embed>` and `<applet>` tags and added `<embed>`-like capabilities to `<object>`, along with the ability to handle Java applets. In a similar manner,

Netscape initially supported the `<embed>` and `<applet>` tags and later provided limited support for the `<object>` tag.

All this jostling for position by the browser giants makes us nervous. We just can't predict what extension will be supported today, and in what form, versus what will or won't be available tomorrow. Accordingly, we don't recommend that you use the `<object>` tag. Rather, use the individual `<embed>` and `<applet>` tags for their intended purposes.

\<object\> Ⓝ ➊

Function:
  Embed an object or applet in a document

Attributes:
  ALIGN
  BORDER ➊
  CLASSID
  CODEBASE
  CODETYPE ➊
  DATA
  DECLARE ➊
  HEIGHT
  HSPACE ➊
  ID Ⓝ
  NAME ➊
  NOTAB ➊
  SHAPES ➊
  STANDBY ➊
  TABINDEX ➊
  TITLE ➊
  TYPE
  USEMAP ➊
  VSPACE ➊
  WIDTH

End tag:
  `</object>`; never omitted

Contains:
  object_content

Used in:
  text

Most of the various attributes for the `<object>` tag are identical to those supported by their `<embed>` and `<applet>` counterparts.

The contents of the <object> tag may be any valid HTML content, along with <param> tags that pass parameters to an applet. If the browser can retrieve the requested object and successfully process it, either as an applet or via a plug-in, the contents of the <object> tag, except for the <param> tags, are ignored. If any problem occurs during the retrieval and processing of the object, the browser won't insert the object into the document, but instead displays the contents of the <object> tag, except for the <param> tags. In short, you should use the contents of the <object> tag to provide alternative content for browsers that cannot handle the <object> tag or if the object cannot be successfully loaded.

13.2.3.1 The align, border, height, width, hspace, and vspace attributes

These attributes control the appearance of the <object> display region exactly like the corresponding attributes of the <img> tag. The height and width attributes control the size of the viewing region. The hspace and vspace attributes define a margin, in pixels, around the viewing region. The align attribute determines how the browser aligns the region in context with the surrounding text, while the border attribute determines the width of the border surrounding the viewing region. [<img>, 5.2.6]

The border, hspace, and vspace attributes are supported only by Internet Explorer.

13.2.3.2 The classid attribute

Use the classid attribute and URL value to reference the object that the browser is to include in the document. The classid attribute is similar to the code attribute of the <applet> tag, providing the name of the file containing the object, and is used in conjunction with the codebase attribute to determine the full URL of the object to be retrieved and placed in the document.

13.2.3.3 The codebase attribute

Use the codebase attribute to reference applet or object data files that are not located in the same directory as the host HTML document. The value of this attribute is a URL that is used, along with the value of the classid attribute, to locate and download the desired object. The codebase URL value may be absolute or relative; if relative, it is assumed to be relative to the containing document's URL.

13.2.3.4 The codetype attribute

The codetype attribute is for Internet Explorer only and specifies the MIME type of the object. This attribute is only required if the browser cannot determine the code type from the `classid` and `codebase` attributes, or if the server does not deliver the correct MIME type when downloading the object.

13.2.3.5 The data attribute

The `data` attribute lets you associate a separate data file, if any, that is to be processed by the object. The data attribute's value is the URL of the file, either absolute or relative to the document's base URL or that which you provide with the codebase attribute. The browser determines the data type by the type of object that is being inserted in the document. This attribute is similar to the `src` attribute of the `<embed>` tag in that it downloads data to be processed by the included object. The difference between the `<embed>` and `<object>` tags is that the `<embed>` tag infers the processing application based upon the data type, while the `<object>` tag expects you to explicitly specify the application by the `classid` and `codebase` attributes.

13.2.3.6 The declare attribute

The `declare` attribute lets you define an object, but restrains the browser from actually downloading and processing it. Used in conjunction with the name attribute, this facility is similar to a forward declaration in a more conventional programming language which lets you defer download of an object until it actually gets used in the document.

This attribute is supported only by Internet Explorer.

13.2.3.7 The id and name attributes

Use the `id` and `name` attributes to label an object for later reference by other elements of your HTML document, including other objects. Unfortunately, only Netscape supports the `id` attribute, while only Internet Explorer supports the `name` attribute. To be safe, you should name your objects with both attributes, since the browsers will ignore attributes they do not support.

13.2.3.8 The notab attribute

For Internet Explorer with ActiveX objects only, the `notab` attribute excludes the object from the document tabbing order.

13.2.3.9 The shapes and usemap attributes

For use with Internet Explorer only, the `shapes` attribute, informs the browser that the object is mouse-sensitive and contains shaped hyperlinks, much like a client-side image map. In fact, with `shapes` you must also provide the `usemap` attribute with its URL for the map that defines the hyperlink hot spots within the object's display area. A complete discussion of client-side image maps can be found in 7.5.2.

13.2.3.10 The standby attribute

The `standby` attribute lets you have Internet Explorer only display a message— the attribute's value text string—during the time the browser is downloading the object data. If your objects are large or you expect slow network response, add this attribute as a courtesy to your users.

13.2.3.11 The tabindex attribute

The value of the `tabindex` attribute is an integer that defines the position of the object in the document's tabbing sequence. Browsers place interactive objects, along with form elements, in the tabbing sequence in the order they appear in the document. To change this sequence with Internet Explorer only, use the `tabindex` attribute.

13.2.3.12 The title attribute

Internet Explorer only lets you specially entitle your objects with the `title` attribute. It takes a text string as its value. The browser may choose to display this title to the user or may use it in some other manner while rendering the document.

13.2.3.13 The type attribute

The `type` attribute lets you explicitly define the MIME type of the data that appear in the file you declare with the `data` attribute. If you don't provide data, or if the MIME type of the data is apparent from the URL or is provided by the server, you may omit this attribute. We recommend you include it anyway, to ensure that your data is handled correctly by the browser and the included object.

13.3 JavaScript

Whether `<applet>`, `<object>`, or `<embed>`, all the executable content we've talked about so far have had one common trait: they are separate from the browser and the HTML document—separate data, separate execution engine.

JavaScript is different. It is a scripting language that taps the native functionality of the browser. You may sprinkle JavaScript statements throughout your documents, either as blocks of code or single statements attached to individual tags. The Java-Script-enabled browsers, including both Netscape and Internet Explorer, interpret and act upon the JavaScript statements you provide to do such things as alter the appearance of the document, control the display, validate and manipulate form elements, and perform general computational tasks.

Like with Java, we will not pretend to teach JavaScript programming in this book. We'll show you how to embed and execute JavaScript within your documents, and ask that you turn to books like *JavaScript: The Definitive Guide*, from O'Reilly, for a complete definition of the JavaScript language.

13.3.1 The <script> Tag

One way to place JavaScript code in your document is via the `<script>` tag.

<script>

Function:
> Define an executable script within a document

Attributes:
> LANGUAGE **N** **O**
> SRC **N** **O**

End tag:
> </script>; never omitted

Contains:
> *scripts*

Used in:
> *head_content, body_content*

Everything between the `<script>` and `</script>` tags is processed by the browser as executable JavaScript statements and data. You cannot place HTML within this tag; it will flagged as an error by the browser.

Browsers that do not support the `<script>` tag will process contents of the tag as regular HTML, to the confusion of the user. For this reason, and as with the new `<style>` tag, we recommend that you include the contents of the `<script>` tag inside HTML comments:

```
<script language="JavaScript">
<!--
    JavaScript statements go here
// -->
</script>
```

For browsers that ignore the `<script>` tag, the contents are masked by the HTML comments delimiters `<!--` and `-->`. JavaScript-enabled browsers, on the other hand, automatically recognize and interpret the JavaScript statements delimited by the comment tags. By using this skeleton for all your `<script>` tags, you can be sure that all browsers will handle your document gracefully, if not completely.

You may include more than one `<script>` tag in a document, located in either the `<head>` or the `<body>`. The JavaScript-enabled browser executes the statements in order as they occur. Variables and functions defined within one `<script>` tag may be referenced by JavaScript statements in other `<script>` tags. In fact, one common JavaScript programming style is to use a single `<script>` in the document `<head>` to define common functions and global variables for the document, and then to call those functions and reference their variables in other JavaScript statements sprinkled throughout the document.

13.3.1.1 The language attribute

Use the `language` attribute in the `<script>` tag to declare the scripting language you used to compose the contents of the tag. If you are using Java-Script—by far the most common HTML scripting language on the Web—set this attribute's value to `JavaScript`. You may occasionally see the `language` value `VBScript`, indicating that the enclosed code is written in Microsoft's Visual Basic Script.

With JavaScript, you may also use the value `"JavaScript 1.1"`, indicating that the enclosed script is to be processed only by Netscape 3.0 or later. Netscape 2.0, which supports JavaScript 1.0, will not process scripts identified as `"Java-Script 1.1"`.

13.3.1.2 The src attribute

For particularly large JavaScript programs, you might want to store the code in a separate file. In these cases, have the browser load that separate file through the `src` attribute. The value of the `src` attribute is the URL of the file containing the JavaScript program. The stored file should have a MIME type of `application/x-javascript`; but will also be properly handled automatically by the server if the filename suffix is *.js*.

For example,

```
<script language=JavaScript src="http://www.kumquat.com/quatscript.js">
</script>
```

tells the `<script>`-able browser to load a JavaScript program called *quatscript.js* from the server. Even though there are no `<script>` contents, the ending `</script>` is still required.

13.3.2 The <noscript> Tag

So that you can tell users of browsers that do not support the `<script>` tag that they are missing something, Netscape supports the `<noscript>` tag.

<noscript> Ⓝ

Function:

Supply content to <script>-challenged browsers

Attributes:

None

End tag:

</noscript>; never omitted

Contains:

body_content

Used in:

text

Unfortunately, only Netscape 3.0 and later versions ignore the contents of the `<noscript>` tag. So even `<script>`-able browsers like Internet Explorer and Netscape 2.0 will display the contents of the `<noscript>` tag, to the confusion of their users.

So, in reality, the `<noscript>` tag has limited usefulness due to its inconsistent support among browsers. There are other ways to detect and handle `<script>`-challenged browsers, detailed in any good JavaScript book.

13.3.3 JavaScript Event Handlers

One of the most important features provided by JavaScript is the ability to detect and react to events that occur while a document is loaded, rendered, and used. The JavaScript code that handles these events may be placed within the `<script>` tag, but more commonly it is associated with a specific tag via one or more special tag attributes.

For example, you might want to invoke a JavaScript functions when the user passes the mouse over a hyperlink in a document. The JavaScript-aware browsers support a special "mouse over" event-handler attribute for the `<a>` tag called `onMouseOver` to do just that:

```
<a href=doc.html onMouseOver="document.status='Click me!'; return
true">
```

When the mouse passes over this example link, the browser executes the Java-Script statements. (Notice that the two JavaScript statements are enclosed in quotes and separated by a semi-colon, and that single quotes surround the text-message portion of the first statement.)

While a complete explanation of this code is beyond our scope, the net result is that the browser places the message "Click me!" in the status bar of the browser window. Commonly, HTML authors use this simple JavaScript function to display a more descriptive explanation of a hyperlink, in place of the often cryptic URL which the browser traditionally displays in the status window.

The value of any of the JavaScript event handler attributes is a quoted string containing one or more JavaScript statements, separated by semicolons. Extremely long statements can be broken across several lines, if needed. Care should also be taken in using entities for embedded double quotes in the statements, to avoid a syntax error when processing the attribute value.

We list the various JavaScript event handlers and their associated tags in Table 13-1, along with the section of this book that describes them in more detail.

Table 13-1. JavaScript event handlers and their supporting HTML tags

Event Handlers	HTML Tags	See section
onAbort	`<img>`	5.2.6.14
onBlur	`<body>`	12.3.1.3
	`<frameset>`	12.3.1.3
	`<input>`	10.2.9
	`<select>`	10.4.1.3
	`<textarea>`	10.3.3
onChange	`<input>`	10.2.9
	`<select>`	10.4.1.3
	`<textarea>`	10.3.3
onClick	`<a>`	7.3.1.4
	`<input>`	10.2.9
	`<select>`	10.4.1.3
onError	`<img>`	5.2.6.14
onFocus	`<body>`	12.3.1.3
	`<frameset>`	12.3.1.3
	`<input>`	10.2.9
	`<select>`	10.4.1.3
	`<textarea>`	10.3.3
onLoad	`<body>`	12.3.1.3
	`<frameset>`	12.3.1.3
	`<img>`	5.2.6.14
onMouseOut	`<a>`	7.3.1.4
	`<area>`	7.5.4.6

Table 13-1. JavaScript event handlers and their supporting HTML tags (continued)

Event Handlers	HTML Tags	See section
onMouseOver	`<a>`	7.3.1.4
	`<area>`	7.5.4.6
onReset	`<form>`	10.1.1.9
onSelect	`<input>`	10.2.9
	`<textarea>`	10.3.3
onSubmit	`<form>`	10.1.1.9
onUnload	`<body>`	12.3.1.3
	`<frameset>`	12.3.1.3

13.3.4 JavaScript URLs

You can replace any conventional URL reference in a document with one or more JavaScript statements. The browser then executes the JavaScript code, rather than download another document, whenever the browser references the URL. The result of the last statement is taken to be the "document" referenced by the URL and is displayed by the browser accordingly. The result of the last statement is *not* the URL of a document; it is the actual content to be displayed by the browser.

To create a JavaScript URL, use `javascript` as the URL's protocol:

```
<a href="javascript:generate_document()">
```

In the example, the JavaScript function `generate_document()` gets executed whenever the hyperlink gets selected by the user. The value returned by the function, presumably a valid HTML document, is rendered and displayed by the browser.

It may be that the executed statement returns no value. In these cases, the current document is left unchanged. For example, this JavaScript URL:

```
<a href="javascript:alert('Error!')">
```

pops up an alert dialog box, and does nothing else. The document containing the hyperlink would still be visible after the dialog box gets displayed and is dismissed by the user.

13.3.5 JavaScript Entities

Character entities in HTML consist of an ampersand, an entity name or number, and a closing semicolon. They are used to insert special or reserved characters into documents.

Similarly, JavaScript entities consist of an ampersand, one or more JavaScript statements enclosed in curly braces, and a closing semicolon. For example:

```
&{document.fgColor};
```

More than one statement must be separated by semicolons within the curly
braces. The value of the last (or only) statement is converted to a string and
replaces the entity in the document.

Normally, HTML entities can appear anywhere in a document. JavaScript entities
are restricted to being values of tag attributes. This lets you write "dynamic tags"
whose attributes are not known until the document is loaded and the JavaScript
executed. For example,

```
<body text=&{favorite_color()};>
```

will set the text color of the document to the color value returned by the individual's `favorite_color()` function.

13.3.6 The <server> Tag

The `<server>` tag is a strange beast. It is processed by the web server, and
never seen by the browser. So what you can do with this tag depends on the
server you are using, not the reader's browser. The Netscape server uses the
`<server>` tag to let you to place JavaScript statements within an HTML document that get processed by the server. The result of executing these statements is
inserted into the document, replacing the `<server>` tag. A complete discussion
of this so-called "server-side" JavaScript is completely beyond this book; we
include this brief reference only to document the `<server>` tag.

<server> ◨

Function:
   Define server-side JavaScript

Attributes:
   None

End tag:
   </server>; never omitted

Contains:
   JavaScript

Used in:
   head_content

Like the `<script>` tag, the `<server>` tag contains JavaScript code. However,
the latter tag and content code must appear inside the document `<head>`, not
elsewhere. It is extracted from the document and executed by the server when
the document is requested for download.

Obviously, server-side JavaScript is tightly coupled to your server. To fully exploit this tag and the benefits of server-side JavaScript or other server-side programming languages, consult your web server's documentation for complete details.

13.4 JavaScript Style Sheets

Much of a browser's work is manipulating the display, and much of their display code already had been exposed for JavaScripting. So it seemed only natural, perhaps even relatively easy, for the developers at Netscape to implement JavaScript Style Sheets. Based on the W3C recommended Cascading Style Sheet model (CSS; see Chapter 9, *Cascading Style Sheets*), this alternative document style technology lets you prescribe display properties for all the various HTML elements, either inline as tag attributes, at the document level, or for an entire document collection.

JavaScript Style Sheets (JSS) are a Netscape invention. In fact, for a short time in the fall of 1996, Netscape appeared ready to eschew the CSS methodology, which Internet Explorer already had implemented, and use JSS exclusively for HTML document designers with their new browser, Netscape Navigator 4.0. Fortunately, the new version now supports both JSS and CSS technologies.

We are strong proponents of reasonable standards. The CSS model is a good one, and it is good that Netscape has decided to support it. Whether Internet Explorer will someday support JSS is not known, but it is clear that Microsoft intends continued support for the CSS standard and the promised HTML 4.0 standard (they haven't had good results bucking web standards in the past).

But standards aren't the whole story. We can't imagine that the HTML author, let alone the page layout designer, is going to abide the rigid programming syntax of JavaScript, starting with the importance of letter case in property names. Very unHTML. Nonetheless, there are some advantages to JSS that some authors will find useful, even though it restricts their document's full potential to the select Netscape 4 user.

We believe style sheets are an important innovation for HTML, and JSS is a very powerful way to provide them. Nonetheless, we recommend using CSS for reasons of consistency and ease—unless you specifically need some feature of JSS.

We thoroughly discuss the concepts and ideas behind HTML style sheets—specifically, Cascading Style Sheets—in Chapter 9, so we won't repeat ourselves here. Rather, we address only how to create and manipulate styles with JavaScript. Before forging ahead in this section, we recommend that you first absorb the information in Chapter 9.

13.4.1 *JavaScript Style Sheet Syntax*

Netscape 4 implements JSS by extending several existing HTML tags and defining a few new objects that store your document's styles.

13.4.1.1 *External, document-level, and inline JSS*

As with CSS, you may reference and load external JSS files with the `<link>` tag. For example:

```
<link href="styles.js" rel=stylesheet type=text/JavaScript>
```

The only real difference between this one and the one for a CSS external style sheet is that the type attribute of the `<link>` tag is set to `text/JavaScript` instead of `text/CSS`. The referenced file, *styles.js*, contains JavaScript statements that define styles and classes that Netscape will then use to control display of the current document.

You define document-level JSS within a `<style>` tag in the `<head>` of the document, just like CSS. Again, there is only one real difference in that you set the `type` attribute of the `<style>` tag to `text/JavaScript` instead of `text/CSS`.

The contents of the `<style>` tag for JSS are quite different from those for CSS, however. For example:

```
<style type=text/JavaScript>
<!--
    tags.BODY.marginLeft = "20px";
    tags.P.fontWeight = "bold";
  // -->
</style>
```

First, notice that we use the standard JavaScript and HTML comments to surround our JSS definitions, preventing non-compliant browsers from processing them as HTML content. Also notice that the syntax of the style definition is that of JavaScript, where letter case *does* make a difference, amongst other things.

You associate inline JavaScript-based style rules with a specific tag using the `style` attribute, just like CSS inline styles. The value of the attribute is a list of JSS assignments, separated by semicolons. For example,

```
<p style="color = 'green'; fontWeight = 'bold'">
```

creates a green, bold-faced text paragraph. Notice first that you need to enclose inline style values within single quotation marks, not double quotation marks as you might use for document-level and in external JSS styles. This is reasonable, since the style attribute value itself must be enclosed in double quotation marks.

Also note that inline JSS definitions use only the property name, not the containing tag object that owns the property. This makes sense, since inline JSS styles affect only the current tag, not all instances of the tag.

13.4.1.2 JSS values

In general, all of the values you may use for CSS may also be used in JSS definitions. For keyword, length, and percentage values, simply enclose the value in quotes and use it as you would any string value in JavaScript. Thus, the CSS value `bold` becomes `"bold"` or `'bold'` for JSS document-level or inline styles, respectively; `12pt` in CSS becomes `'12pt'` or `"12pt"` in JSS.

Specify color values as the color name or a hexadecimal color value, enclosed in single or double quotes. The CSS decimal rgb notation is not supported in JSS.

JSS URL values are strings containing the desired URL. Thus, the CSS URL value `url(http://www.kumquat.com)` becomes `'http://www.kumquat.com'` for a JSS inline style; or `"http://www.kumquat.com"` at the document level.

One unique power of JSS is that any value can be computed dynamically when the document is processed by the browser. Instead of statically specifying the font size, for example, you can compute it on the fly:

```
tags.P.fontSize = favorite_font_size();
```

We assume that the JavaScript function `favorite_font_size()` somehow determines the desired font size and returns a string value containing that size. This, in turn, is assigned to the `fontSize` property for the `<p>` tag, defining the font size for all paragraphs in the document.

13.4.1.3 Defining styles for tags

JavaScript defines a new document property, `tags`, that contains the style properties for all HTML tags. To define a style for a tag, you simply set the appropriate property of the desired style property within the `tag` property of the `document` object. For example:

```
document.tags.P.fontSize = '12pt';
document.tags.H2.color = 'blue';
```

These two JSS definitions set the font size for the `<p>` tag to 12 points and render all `<h2>` tags in blue. The equivalent CSS definitions are:

```
P {font-size : 12pt}
H2 {color : blue}
```

Since the `tags` property always refers to the current document, you may omit `document` from any JSS tag style definition. We could have written the previous two styles as:

```
tags.P.fontSize = '12pt';
tags.H2.color = 'blue';
```

Moreover, as we mention above, you may omit the tag name, as well as the `document` and `tags` properties for inline JSS using the style attribute.

Capitalization and case are significant in JSS. The tag names within the `tags` property must always be fully capitalized. The embedded capital letters within the tag properties are significant: any deviation from the exact lettering produces an error, and Netscape won't honor your JSS declaration. All of the following JSS definitions are invalid, though the reason is not overly apparent:

```
tags.p.fontsize = '12pt';
tags.Body.Color = 'blue';
tags.P.COLOR = 'red';
```

The correct versions are:

```
tags.P.fontSize = '12pt';
tags.BODY.color = 'blue';
tags.P.color = 'red';
```

It can be very tedious to specify a number of properties for a single tag, so you can take advantage of the JavaScript `with` statement to reduce your typing burden. These styles:

```
tags.P.fontSize = '14pt';
tags.P.color = 'blue';
tags.P.fontWeight = 'bold';
tags.P.leftMargin = '20%';
```

can be more easily written as:

```
with (tags.P) {
  fontSize = '14pt';
  color = 'blue';
  fontWeight = 'bold';
  leftMargin = '20%';
  }
```

You can apply similar styles to diverse tags just as easily:

```
with (tags.P, tags.LI, tags.H1) {
  fontSize = '14pt';
  color = 'blue';
  fontWeight = 'bold';
  leftMargin = '20%';
  }
```

13.4.1.4 Defining style classes

Like CSS, JSS lets you target styles for specific ways in which a tag may be used in your document. JSS uses the `classes` property to define separate styles for the same tag. There are no predefined properties within the `classes` property;

instead, any property you reference is defined as a class to be used by the current document. For example:

```
classes.bold.P.fontWeight = 'bold';
with (classes.abstract.P) {
    leftMargin = '20pt';
    rightMargin = '20pt';
    fontStyle = 'italic';
    textAlign = 'justify';
    }
```

The first style defines a class of the `<p>` tag named `bold` whose font weight is set to bold. The next style uses the `with` statement to create a class of the `<p>` tag named `abstract` with the specified properties. The equivalent CSS rules would be:

```
P.bold {font-weight : bold}
P.abstract {left-margin : 20pt;
            right-margin : 20pt;
            font-style : italic;
            text-align : justify
            }
```

Once defined, use a JSS class just like any CSS class: with the `class` attribute and the class name.

Like CSS, JSS also lets you define a class without defining the tag that will use the class. This lets you define generic classes that you can later apply to any tag. To create a generic style class in JSS, use the special tag property `all`:

```
classes.green.all.color = "green";
```

You can then add `class="green"` to any tag to have Netscape render its contents in green. The equivalent CSS is:

```
.green {color : green}
```

13.4.1.5 Using contextual styles

One of the most powerful aspects of CSS is its contextual style capability, wherein the browser applies a style to tags only if they appear in the document in a certain nesting. JSS supports contextual styles as well, through the special `contextual()` method within the `tags` property. The parameters to this method are the tags and classes that define the context in which Netscape will apply the style. For example,

```
tags.contextual(tags.UL, tags.UL, tags.LI).listStyleType = 'disc';
```

defines a context wherein the elements (`tags.LI`) of an unordered list nested within another unordered list (`tags.UL, tags.UL`) use the disc as their bullet symbol. The CSS equivalent is:

```
UL UL LI {list-style-type : disc}
```

You can mix tags and classes in the `contextual()` method. For instance:

```
tags.contextual(classes.abstract.P, tags.EM).color = 'red';
```

tells the browser to display in red <em> tags that appear within paragraphs that are of the `abstract` class. The CSS equivalent is:

```
P.abstract EM {color : red}
```

Since the `tags` object is unambiguously included within the `contextual()` method, you may omit them from the definition. Hence, our nested list example may be rewritten as:

```
tags.contextual(UL, UL, LI).listStyleType = 'disc';
```

13.4.2 JavaScript Style Sheet Properties

A subset of the CSS style properties are supported in JSS. The JSS style properties, their CSS equivalents, and the sections in which those properties are fully documented are shown in Table 13-2.

Table 13-2. JavaScript Style Sheet properties and their Cascading Style Sheet equivalents

JSS Property	CSS Property	See section
`align`	`float`	9.3.6.8
`backgroundImage`	`background-image`	9.3.4.3
`backgroundColor`	`background-color`	9.3.4.2
`borderBottomWidth`	`border-bottom-width`	9.3.6.4
`borderLeftWidth`	`border-left-width`	9.3.6.4
`borderRightWidth`	`border-right-width`	9.3.6.4
`borderStyle`	`border-style`	9.3.6.5
`borderTopWidth`	`border-top-width`	9.3.6.4
`clear`	`clear`	9.3.6.7
`display`	`display`	9.3.8.1
`fontSize`	`font-size`	9.3.3.2
`fontStyle`	`font-style`	9.3.3.3
`height`	`height`	9.3.6.9
`lineHeight`	`line-height`	9.3.5.2
`listStyleType`	`list-style-type`	9.3.7.3
`marginBottom`	`margin-bottom`	9.3.6.10
`marginLeft`	`margin-left`	9.3.6.10
`marginRight`	`margin-right`	9.3.6.10
`marginTop`	`margin-top`	9.3.6.10
`paddingBottom`	`padding-bottom`	9.3.6.11

*Table 13-2. JavaScript Style Sheet properties and their Cascading Style Sheet
        equivalents (continued)*

JSS Property	CSS Property	See section
paddingLeft	padding-left	9.3.6.11
paddingRight	padding-right	9.3.6.11
paddingTop	padding-top	9.3.6.11
textDecoration	text-decoration	9.3.5.4
textTransform	text-transform	9.3.5.6
textAlign	text-align	9.3.5.3
textIndent	text-indent	9.3.5.5
verticalAlign	vertical-align	9.3.5.7
whiteSpace	white-space	9.3.8.2
width	width	9.3.6.12

JSS also defines three methods that allow you to define margins, padding, and border widths within a single style property. The three methods, `margins()`, `paddings()`, and `borderWidths()`, accept four parameters, corresponding to the top, right, bottom, and left margin, padding or border width, respectively. Unlike their CSS counterparts (`margin`, 9.3.6.10, `padding`, 9.3.6.11, and `border-width`, 9.3.6.4), these JSS methods require that you always specify all four parameters. There is no shorthand way in JSS to set multiple margins, paddings, or border widths with a single value.

14

Dynamic Documents

The standard HTML document model is a static one. Once displayed on the browser, a document does not change unless the user initiates some activity like selecting a hyperlink with the mouse. The developers at Netscape Communications found that limitation unacceptable and built in some special features to their Navigator browser that let you change HTML document content dynamically. In fact, they provide for two different mechanisms for dynamic documents, which we describe in detail in this chapter. Internet Explorer supports some of these mechanisms, which we'll discuss as well.

We should mention that many people believe dynamic documents will be obsolete in a very short time, displaced by plug-in browser accessories and, in particular, applets. Nonetheless, Netscape and Internet Explorer continue to support dynamic documents, and we believe the technology has virtues you should be aware of, if not take advantage of, in your HTML documents. [applets, 13.1]

14.1 An Overview of Dynamic Documents

If you remember from our discussion in Chapter 1, *HTML and the World Wide Web*, the client browser initiates data flow on the Web by contacting a server with a document request. The server honors the request by downloading the document. The client subsequently displays the document's contents to the user. For normal web documents, a single transaction initiated from the client side is all that is needed to collect and display the document. Once displayed, however, it does not change.

Dynamic documents, on the other hand, are the result of multiple transactions initiated from either or both the server side and the client side. A *client-pull* document is one that initiates multiple transactions from the client side. When the server is the instigator, the dynamic document is known as a *server-push* document.

In a client-pull document, special HTML codes tell the client to periodically request and download another document from one or more servers on the network, dynamically updating the display.

Server-push documents also advance the way servers communicate with clients. Normally over the Web, the client stays connected with a server for only as long as it takes to retrieve a single document.* With server-push documents, the connection remains open and the server continues to send data periodically to the client, adding to or replacing the previous contents.

Netscape is currently the only browser able to handle server-push dynamic HTML documents correctly; both Internet Explorer and Netscape support client-pull documents. With other browsers, you might see only part of the dynamic document at best. At worst, the browser will completely reject the document. Unfortunately, because dynamic documents are client-server processes, they don't work without an HTTP server. That means you can't develop and test your dynamic HTML documents stored as local files, unless you have a server running locally, as well.

14.1.1 Another Word of Caution

As always, we tell you exactly how to use these exciting but nonstandard features, and we admonish you not to use them unless you have a compelling and overriding reason to do so. We are particularly strident with that admonition for dynamic documents, not only because they aren't part of the HTML standard, but because dynamic documents can hog the network. They require larger, longer downloads than their static counterparts. And they require many more (in the case of client-pull) or longer-term (for server-push) client-server connections. Multiple connections on a single server are limited to a few of the vast millions of Web users at a time. We'd hate to see your readers miss out because you've created a jiggling image in a dynamic HTML document that would otherwise have been an effective and readily accessible static document more people could enjoy.

---

* One connection per document is true even for inline images browsers may automatically download from the server. If you don't believe us, just watch the status line at the bottom of your browser while you download an HTML document with several images. You should see many "Contacting the server" and "Reading the file…" or similar messages.

14.2   Client-Pull Documents

Client-pull documents are relatively easy to prepare. All you need to do is embed a <meta> tag in the header of your HTML document. The special tag tells the client Netscape browser to display the current document for a specified period of time, and then load and display an entirely new one just as if the user had selected the new document from a hyperlink. (Note that currently there is no way to dynamically change just a portion of an HTML document using client-pull.) [<meta>, 7.8.1]

14.2.1   Uniquely Refreshing

Client-pull dynamic documents work with Netscape and Internet Explorer because the browsers respond to a special HTTP header field called "Refresh."

You may recall from previous discussions that whenever an HTTP server sends a document to the client browser, it precedes the document's data with one or more header fields. One header field, for instance, contains a description of the document's content type, used by the browser to decide how to display the document's contents. For example, the server precedes HTML documents with the header "Content-type: text/html," whose meaning should be fairly obvious.

As we discussed at length in Chapter 7, *Links and Webs*, you may add your own special fields to an HTML document's HTTP header by inserting a <meta> tag into its <head>. [<meta>, 7.8.1]

The HTTP Refresh field implements client-pull dynamic HTML documents, enabled by the <meta> tag format:

```
<meta http-equiv="Refresh" content="field value">
```

The tag's http-equiv attribute tells the HTTP server to include the Refresh field, with a value specified by the content attribute (if any, carefully enclosed in quotation marks), in the string of headers it sends to the client browser just before it sends the rest of the document's content. The browser recognizes the Refresh header as the mark of a dynamic HTML document and responds accordingly, as we discuss next.

14.2.2   The Refresh Header Contents

The value of the content attribute in the special <meta> Refresh tag determines when and how the browser updates the current document. Set it to an integer, and the browser will delay that many seconds before automatically loading another document. You may set the content field value to zero, meaning no delay at all. In that case, the browser loads the next document immediately after it finishes rendering the current one, by which you may achieve some very crude animation effects. [content, 7.8.1.2]

14.2.2.1 Refreshing the same document

If the Refresh field's content value is the number of seconds alone, the browser reloads that same document over and over again, delaying the specified time between each cycle, until the user goes to another document or shuts down the browser.

For example, the browser will reload the following client-pull HTML document every 15 seconds:

```
<html>
<head>
<meta http-equiv="Refresh" content="15">
<title>Kumquat Market Prices</title>
</head>
<body>
<h3> Kumquat Market Prices</h3>
Kumquats are currently trading at $1.96 per pound.
</body>
</html>
```

The financial wizards among you may have noticed that with some special software tricks on the server side, you can update the price of kumquats in the HTML document so that it acts like a ticker-tape machine: the latest kumquat commodity price updated every 15 seconds.

14.2.2.2 Refreshing with a different document

Rather than reload the same document repeatedly, you can tell the browser to dynamically load a different document. You do so by adding that document's absolute URL after the delay time and an intervening semicolon in the `<meta>` tag's `content` attribute. For example,

```
<meta http-equiv="Refresh"
  content="15; URL=http://www.kumquat.com/next.html">
```

would cause the browser to retrieve the *next.html* document from the *www.kumquat.com* web server after having displayed the current document for 15 seconds.

The URL must be an absolute one, including server type and full pathname; relative URLs don't work.

14.2.2.3 Cycling among documents

Keep in mind that the effects of the Refresh `<meta>` tag only apply to the document in which it appears. Hence, to cycle among several documents, you must include a Refresh `<meta>` tag in each one. The `content` value for each document in the cycle must contain an absolute URL that points to the next document, with the last document pointing back to the first one to complete the cycle.

For example, the following are the `<meta>` tags for the headers of each in a three HTML-document cycle:

In the document *first.html*:

```
<meta http-equiv="Refresh"
  content="30; URL=http://www.kumquat.com/second.html">
```

The document *second.html* contains:

```
<meta http-equiv="Refresh"
  content="30; URL=http://www.kumquat.com/third.html">
```

And the *third.html* document has in its `<head>` (besides other crazy ideas):

```
<meta http-equiv="Refresh"
  content="30; URL=http://www.kumquat.com/first.html">
```

Left alone, the browser will endlessly loop among the three documents at 30-second intervals.

Cycling documents make excellent attractors, catching the attention of passers-by to a web-driven kiosk, for example. Users may then navigate through the wider collection of kiosk documents by clicking hyperlinks in one of the kiosk's attractor pages and subsequent ones.[*]

To return to the cycling set of attractors, each document in the rest of the collection should have their own Refresh fields that eventually point back to the attractor. You should specify a fairly long delay period for the nonattractor pages—120 to 300 seconds or more—so that the kiosk doesn't automatically reset while a user is reading the current document. However, the delay period should be short enough so that the kiosk resets to the attractor mode in a reasonable period of time after the user finishes.

14.2.3 Pulling Non-HTML Content

Netscape's and Internet Explorer's client-pull feature is not restricted to HTML documents, although it is certainly easiest to create dynamic documents with HTML. With a bit of server-side programming, you can add a Refresh field to the HTTP header of any sort of document from audio files to images to video clips.

---

[*] This brings up a good point: the user may override the Refresh dynamic action at any time; for instance, by clicking a hyperlink before the client-pull timeout expires. The browser always ignores the Refresh action in lieu of user interaction.

For example, create a real-time video feed by adding a Refresh header field in each of a sequence of images grabbed and digitized from a camera. Include a delay of zero with the URL that points to the next image, so that as quickly as the browser displays one image, it retrieves the next. Assuming that the network keeps up, the result is a crude (really crude) TV.

Since the browser clears the window before presenting each subsequent image, the resulting flicker and flash make it almost impossible to present a coherent sequence of images. This technique is more effective when presenting a series of images designed to be viewed as a slide show, where the user expects some sort of display activity between each of the images.

Perhaps a better use of the client-pull feature is with long-playing multimedia documents for which Netscape and Internet Explorer use special helper applications to display. On a multitasking computer, such as one running UNIX or Windows 95, the browser downloads one document, while a helper application plays another. Combine the client-pull capabilities with that multitasking to improve multimedia document performance. Rather than wait for a single, large document like a movie or audio file to download before playing, break it into smaller segments, each automatically downloaded by the previous segment via the Refresh header. The browser will play the first segment while downloading the second, then third, then fourth, and so on.

14.2.4 Combining Refresh with Other HTTP Header Fields

You can have your client-pull dynamic HTML documents perform some neat tricks by combining the effects of the Refresh field with other HTTP header fields. One combination in particular, is most useful: Refresh with a "Redirect" field.

The Redirect field lets the server tell the browser to retrieve the requested document elsewhere at the field's accompanying URL value. The client browser automatically redirects its request to the new URL and gets the document from the new location, usually without telling the user. We retrieve redirected documents all the time and may never notice.

The most common cause for redirection is when someone moves their HTML document collection to a new directory or to a new server. As a courtesy, the webmaster programs the original host server to send an HTTP header field containing the Redirect field and new URL (without a document body) to any and all browsers that request the document from the original location. That way, the new document location is transparent to users, and they won't have to reset their browser bookmarks.

But sometimes you want the user to reset their bookmarks to the new location because the old one won't be redirecting browsers forever, perhaps because it's being taken out of service. One way to notify users of the new location is to have the redirection URL point to some HTML document other than the home page of the new collection that contains a message about the new location. Once noted, users then take a "Continue" hyperlink to the new home page location and set their bookmarks accordingly.

By combining the Redirect and Refresh fields, you can make that notification screen automatically move to the new home page. If the browser receives an HTTP header with both fields, it will honor both; it immediately fetches the redirected URL and displays it, and it sets the refresh timer and replacement URL, if specified. When the time expires, the browser retrieves the next URL—your new home page location—automatically.

14.2.4.1 A random URL generator

Another application for the combination of Redirect and Refresh HTTP header fields is a perpetual, random URL generator. You'll need some programming skills to create a server-side application that selects a random URL from a prepared list and outputs a Redirect field that references that URL along with a Refresh field that reinvokes the random-URL application after some delay.

When Netscape or Internet Explorer receives the complete header, it immediately loads and displays the randomly selected document specified in the Redirect field's URL. After the delay specified in the Refresh field, the browser reruns the random-URL generator on the server (as specified in the Refresh URL), and the cycle starts over. The result is an endless cycle of random URLs displayed at regular intervals.

14.2.5 Performance Considerations

Client-pull documents consume extra network resources, especially when the refresh delay is small, since each refresh involves a completely new connection to a server. It may take a browser several seconds to contact the server and begin retrieving the document. As a result, rapid updates generally are not feasible, especially over slow network connections.

Use client-pull dynamic documents for low-frequency updates of entire documents, or for cycling among documents without user intervention.

14.3 Server-Push Documents

Server-push dynamic documents are driven from the server side. The client-server connection remains open after an initial transfer of data, and the server periodically sends new data to the client, updating the document's display. Server-push is made possible by some special programming, not special HTML embedded tags, on the server side, and is enabled by the multipart mixed-media type feature of Multipurpose Internet Mail Extensions (MIME), the computer industry's standard for multimedia document transmission over the Internet.

Server-push documents currently are not supported by Internet Explorer.

14.3.1 The Multipart/Mixed-Media Type

As we mentioned earlier in this chapter in the discussion of client-pull dynamic documents, the HTTP server sends a two-part transmission to the client browser: a header describing the document followed by the document itself. The document's MIME type is part of the HTTP header field. Normally, the server includes `Content-type: text/html` in an HTML document's header before sending its actual contents. By changing that content type to multipart/mixed-media, you can send an HTML document or several documents in several pieces, rather than in a single chunk. Only Netscape, though, understands and responds to the multipart header field; the other browsers either ignore additional parts or refuse the document altogether.

The general form of the MIME multipart mixed-media content type header looks like this:

```
Content-type: multipart/mixed;boundary="SomeRandomString"
```

This HTTP header component tells the Netscape client to expect the document to follow in several parts and to look for **SomeRandomString**, which separates the parts. That boundary string should be unique and not appear anywhere in any of the individual parts. The content of the server-to-client transmission looks like this:

```
--SomeRandomString
Content-type: text/plain

Data for the first part
--SomeRandomString
Content-type: text/plain

Data for the second part

--SomeRandomString--
```

The above example has two document parts, both plain text. The server sends each part preceded by our **SomeRandomString** document-boundary delimiter preceded by two dashes, followed by the `Content-type` field, and then the data for each part. The last transmission from server to client is a single reference to the boundary string followed by two more dashes indicating that this was the last part of the document.

Upon receipt of each part, the Netscape browser automatically adds the incoming data to the current document display.

You've got to write a special HTTP server application to enable this type of server-push dynamic document; one that creates the special HTTP MIME multipart/mixed header and sends the various documents separated by the boundary delimiter.

14.3.2 Multipart Mixed-Replace-Media Type

Server-push dynamic document authors also may use an experimental variant of the MIME multipart mixed-media content known as *multipart mixed-replace-media*. The difference between this special content-type and its predecessor is that, rather than simply adding content to the current display, the "replace" version has each subsequent part replace the preceding one.

The format of the mixed-replace HTTP header is very similar to its multipart mixed counterpart; the only difference is in the `Content-type`:

```
multipart/x-mixed-replace;boundary=SomeRandomString
```

All other rules regarding the format of the multipart content are the same, including the boundary string used to separate the parts and the individual `Content-type` fields for each part of the content.

14.3.3 Exploiting Multipart Documents

It is easy to see how you can use the two special MIME multipart content types to create server-push dynamic documents. By delaying the time between parts, you might create an automatically scrolling message in the Netscape browser window. Or by replacing portions of the document through the x-mixed-replace MIME type, you might include a dynamic billboard in your document, perhaps even animation.

Note in particular that server-push multipart documents need not apply only to HTML or other plain text documents. Images, too, are a MIME-encoded content type, so you can have the HTTP server transmit several images in sequence as parts of a multipart transmission. Since you may also have each new image replace the previous one, the result is crude animation. Done correctly over a network of sufficient bandwidth, the effect can be quite satisfying.

14.3.3.1 Efficiency considerations

Server-push documents keep a connection open between the client and server for the duration of the dynamic document's activity. For some servers, this may consume extra network resources and may also require that several processes remain active, servicing the open connection. Make sure the server-push process (and, hence, the client-server connection) expire upon completion or after some idle period. Otherwise, someone will inadvertently camp on an endlessly cycling server-push document and choke off other users' access to the server.

Before choosing to implement server-push documents, make sure that your server can support the added processing and networking load. Keep in mind that many simultaneous server-push documents may be active, multiplying the impact on the server and seriously affecting overall server performance.

14.3.4 Creating a Server-Push Document

You create a special application that runs with the HTTP server to enable server-push dynamic documents. The application must create the special MIME Content-type header field that notifies the Netscape browser that the following document comes in several parts—added to or replacing a portion of the current document. The application must also create the appropriate boundary delimiter and send the Content-type header and data for each part, perhaps also delaying transmission of each part by some period of time. You will need to consult your server's documentation to learn how to create a server-side application that can be invoked by accessing a specific URL on the server. With some servers this may be as simple as placing the application in a certain directory on the server. With others, you may have to bend over backwards and howl at the moon on certain days.

14.3.4.1 Server-push example application for NCSA and Apache httpd

The NCSA and Apache *httpd* servers run on most UNIX systems. Administrators usually configure the server to run server-side applications stored in a directory named *cgi-bin*.

The following is a simple UNIX shell script that illustrates how to send a multipart document to a Netscape client via NCSA or Apache *httpd:*[*]

```
#!/bin/sh
#
# Let the client know we are sending a multipart document
```

---

[*] It is an idiosyncrasy of NCSA *httpd* that no spaces are allowed in the Content-type field that precedes your multipart document. Some authors like to place a space after the semicolon and before the boundary keyword. Don't do this with NCSA *httpd*; run the whole Content-type together without spaces to get the server to recognize the correct multipart content type.

```
# with a boundary string of "NEXT"
#
echo "HTTP/1.0 200"
echo "Content-type: multipart/x-mixed-replace;boundary=NEXT"
echo ""
echo "--NEXT"
while true
do
#
# Send the next part, followed by a boundary string
# Then sleep five seconds before repeating
#
 echo "Content-type: text/html"
 echo ""
 echo "<html>"
 echo "<head>"
 echo "<title>Processes On This Server</title>"
 echo "</head>"
 echo "<body>"
 echo "<h3> Processes On This Server</h3>"
 echo "Date:"
 date
 echo "<p>"
 echo "<pre>"
 ps -el
 echo "</pre>"
 echo "</body>"
 echo "</html>"
 echo "--NEXT"
 sleep 5
done
```

In a nutshell, this example script updates a list of the processes running on the server machine every five seconds. The update continues until the browser breaks the connection by moving on to another document, or after completing 60 cycles (about five minutes).

We offer this shell script example to illustrate the basic logic behind any server-push document generator. In reality, you should create your server-side applications using a more conventional programming language like Perl or C. The applications run more efficiently and can better detect when the client has severed the connection to the server.

15

Tips, Tricks, and Hacks

We've sprinkled a number of tips, tricks, and hacks throughout this book, along with style guidelines, examples, and instructions. So why have a special chapter on tips, tricks, and hacks of HTML? Because it's where many readers will leaf when they pick up this book for the first time. HTML is the language, albeit constrained, that makes the World Wide Web on the Internet the exciting place that it is. And interested readers want to know, "How do I do the cool stuff?"

15.1 Top of the Tips

The most important tip for even veteran HTML authors is to surf for yourself. We can show and explain a few neat tricks to get you started, but there are thousands of HTML authors out there combining and recombining HTML tags and juggling content to create compelling and useful documents.

Get a bona fide Internet account; get a copy of Netscape, Internet Explorer, and whatever other browser you feel comfortable operating; get connected; and get cruising. Collect web site URLs from friends, business associates, and the traditional media. Even local TV and radio stations have taken to announcing some of their sponsors' web site URLs. And consult the many different Internet web directories like Yahoo and AltaVista for new and up-to-date addresses for the web sites that suit your lifestyle or business niche.

Examine (don't steal) their pages for eye-catching and effective pages and use them to guide your own creations. Capture and examine the source HTML documents for the juicy bits. Get a feel of the more effective web collections. How are their documents organized? How large is each document? And so on.

We all learn from experience, so go get it.

15.1.1 Design for Your Audience

We continuously argue throughout the book that, with HTML documents, content matters most, not look. That doesn't mean that presentation doesn't matter.

Effective HTML documents match your target audience's expectations, giving them a familiar environment in which to explore and gather information. Serious academicians expect a treatise on the physiology of the kumquat to appear journal-like: long on meaningful words, figures, and diagrams and short on frivolous trappings like cute bullets and font abuse. Don't insult the reader's eye, except when exercising artistic license to jar or attack your reader's sensibilities.

By anticipating your audience and by designing your documents to appeal to their tastes, you also subtly deflect unwanted surfers from your pages. Undesirables, such as penniless college students surfing your commercial site, may hog your server's resources and prevent the buying audience you desire from ready access to your pages.

For example, you can use subtle colors and muted text transitions between sections for a classical art museum's collection to mimic the hushed environment of a real classical art museum. The typical rock-n-roll crazed web surfer maniac probably won't spend more than a glance at your site, but the millionaire arts patron might.

Also, use effective layout to gently guide your readers' eyes to areas of interest in your documents. Do that by adhering to the basic rules of document layout and design, such as placing figures and diagrams nearby—if not inline—with their content reference. Nothing's worse than having to scroll up and down the browser window in a desperate search for a picture that can explain everything.

We won't lie and suggest that we're design experts. We aren't, but they're not hard to find. So, another tip for the serious web page author: seek professional help. The best situation is to have design experience yourself. Next best is to have a pro looking over your shoulder, or at least somewhere within earshot.

Make a trip to your local library and do some reading on your own, too. Even better yet, browse the various online HTML guides. Check out *Designing for the Web* by O'Reilly & Associates. Your readers will be glad you did. [design tools, 1.6]

15.1.2 Boilerplate HTML Documents

The next best tip we can give you is to reuse your documents. Don't start from scratch each time. Rather, develop a consistent framework, even to the point of a content outline into which you add the detail and character for each page. You might even endevour to create style sheets, so that the look and feel of you documents remain consistent.

Here's our contribution to help start your boilerplate HTML document collection. The following source contains what the HTML standard currently tells us is the minimum content that should appear in every HTML document (regardless of what the browsers might let you get away with) and then some added for document clarity. Use it as a skeleton for your own HTML documents:

```
<html>
<head>
<title>Required--replace this title with your own</title>
</head>
<body>
<h3>Reiterate the title here</h3>
...Insert your document's contents here...
<address>Include your name and contact information
usually at the end of the document</address>
</body>
</html>
```

15.2 Trivial or Abusive?

There is perhaps no more abused or abusive HTML document device than the `<blink>` tag extension for text content currently supported by, thank heaven, only the Netscape browser.[*]

It works by alternating the color of the text enclosed between the `<blink>` tag and its end tag (`</blink>`)—incessantly! It's not only ugly (reminiscent of the very bad video-text displays on a hotel TV), but it's excruciatingly annoying. The reader can't turn it off except to scroll beyond that portion of the document or hyperlink out of the document altogether. [physical styles, 4.5]

Okay, so it grabs readers' attention to make an important point. Just make sure it's a *very* important point. And here's a tip: Make it easy for the reader to get by the blinking segment in your document. Surround it with empty space or with pleasant, but vacuous content that they don't have to read.

15.3 Custom Bullets

One common use of the definition list has nothing to do with definitions, but instead deals with adding custom bullets to an otherwise unordered list. In this trick, leave the `<dt>` tag empty, and add an `<img>` tag that references the

---

[*] Few web surfers use Internet Explorer, so you rarely and thankfully won't find many HTML documents using the browser's equally tacky `<marquee>` feature.

desired bullet image at the beginning of each `<dd>` tag. [`<dl>`, 8.7.1] For example:

```
<dl>
   <dt><dd><img src="fancy_bullet.gif"> Pickled Kumquats
   <dt><dd><img src="fancy_bullet.gif"> 'Quats and 'Kraut
   <dt><dd><img src="fancy_bullet.gif"> 'Quatshakes
   <dt><dd><img src="fancy_bullet.gif"> Liver with Fried 'Quats
</dl>
```

The fancier list is shown in Figure 15-1.

Figure 15-1. Custom bullets for unordered lists

Keep in mind that this trick works well only if your list items are short enough to not wrap within the browser window. If the item does wrap, the next line will start aligned with the left edge of the bullet, not the left edge of the text, as you might hope.

15.4 *Tricks with Tables*

Enough with the cheap tricks. On to some really good ones: tricks with the HTML `<table>` tag and attributes that add some attractive features to your documents.

By design, HTML tables let authors create appealing, accessible tables of information. But the HTML table tags also can be exploited to create innovative, attractive page designs that are otherwise unobtainable in standard HTML.

15.4.1 *Multicolumn Pages*

One very common and popular page-layout element missing from HTML until recently is multiple columns of text. Although Netscape now supports the `<multicol>` extension, for a more universal solution (at least until the majority of your audience gets the latest version of Netscape), place your document content inside a table of one row with two or more columns. [`<multicol>`, 6.2.1]

15.4.1.1 Basic multicolumn layout

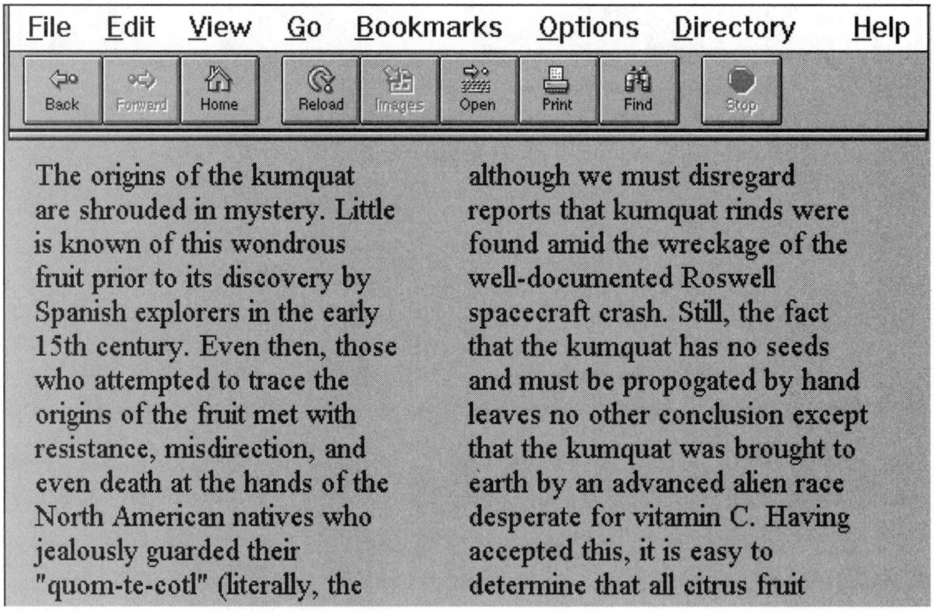

The basic two-column layout using `<table>` has a single table row with three data cells: one each for the columns of text and an intervening empty cell to more attractively separate the two columns. We've also added a large `cellspacing` attribute value to create additional intervening space between the columns.

The following example table is an excellent template for a simple two-column text layout:

```
<table border=0 cellspacing=7>
  <tr>
    <td>Copy for column 1...
    <td><br>
    <td>Copy for column 2...
  </table>
```

See Figure 15-2 for the results.

Figure 15-2. A simple two-column layout

The one thing the browsers won't do is automatically balance the text in the columns, resulting in adjacent columns of approximately the same length. You'll have to experiment with your document, manually shifting text from one column to another until you achieve a nicely balanced page.

Keep in mind, though, that users may resize their display windows and the columns' contents will shift accordingly. So don't spend a lot of time getting the last sentences of each column to line up exactly; they're bound to be skewed in other browser window widths.

Of course, you can easily convert the example layout to three or more columns by dividing the text among more cells in the table. But keep in mind that pages with more than three columns may prove difficult to read on small displays where the actual column width might be quite small.

15.4.1.2 Straddle heads

The basic multicolumn format is just the start. By adding cells that span across the columns, you create headlines. Similarly, you can make figures span across more than one column: simply add the `colspan` attribute to the cell containing the headline or figure. Figure 15-3 shows an attractive three-column layout with straddle heads and a spanning figure, created from the following HTML source with table tags:

```
<table border=0 cellspacing=7>
  <tr>
    <th colspan=5><h2>The History of the Kumquat</h2>
  <tr valign=top>
    <td rowspan=2>Copy for column 1...
    <td rowspan=2 width=24><br>
    <td >Copy for column 2...
    <td width=24><br>
    <td >Copy for column 3...
  <tr>
    <td colspan=3 align=center><img src="pics/fruit.gif">
    <p>
    <i>The Noble Fruit</i>
</table>
```

To achieve this nice layout, we used the `colspan` attribute on the cell in the first row to span all five table columns (three with copy and the two intercolumn spaces). We use the `rowspan` attribute on the first column and its adjacent column spacer to extend the columns down beside the figure. The figure's cell has a `colspan` attribute so that the contents span the other two columns and intervening spaces.

15.4.2 Side Heads

The only text-heading features available in HTML are the `<h1>` through `<h6>` tags. These tags are always embedded in the text flow, separating adjacent paragraphs of text. Through multiple columns, you can achieve an alternative style that places headings into a separate side column, running vertically alongside the document text.

Figure 15-4 shows you a fairly fancy pair of side heads, the result of the following bit of source HTML table code:

File	Edit	View	Go	Bookmarks	Options	Directory	Help

Back	Forward	Home	Reload	Images	Open	Print	Find	Stop

The History of the Kumquat

The origins of the kumquat are shrouded in mystery. Little is known of this wondrous fruit prior to its discovery by Spanish explorers in the early 15th century. Even then, those who attempted to trace the origins of the fruit met with resistance, misdirection, and even death at the hands of the North American natives who jealously guarded their "quom-te-cotl" (literally, the *fruit of life*).

although we must disregard reports that kumquat rinds were found amid the wreckage of the well-documented Roswell spacecraft crash. Still,

the fact that the kumquat has no seeds and must be propogated by hand leaves no other conclusion except that the

The Noble Fruit

Figure 15-3. Fancy straddle heads and spanning figures with HTML table tags

```
<table>
  <tr>
  <th width="30%" align=right>
    <h3>Section 1</h3>
  <td>
  <td>
    Copy for section 1 goes on and on a bit
    so that it will take up more than one line in the
    table cell window...
  <tr>
  <th align=right>
    <h3>Section 2</h3>
  <td>
  <td>
    Copy for section 2 goes on and on a bit
    so that it will take up more than one line in the
    table cell window...
  </table>
```

Notice how we create reasonably attractive side heads set off from the left margin of the browser window by adjusting the first header cell's width and right-justifying the cell contents.

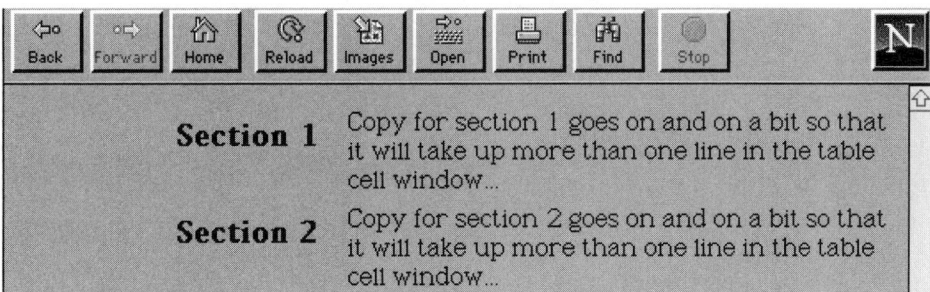

Figure 15-4. Table tags created these side heads

Just as in our multicolumn layout, the example side-head layout uses an empty column to create a space between the narrow left column containing the heading and the wider right column containing the text associated with that heading. It's best to specify that column's width as a percentage of the table width, rather than explicitly in numbers of pixels to make sure that the heading column scales to fit both wide and narrow display windows.

15.4.2.1 When tables aren't implemented

One of the dangers of being overly dependent on tables is that your documents are usually unreadable when viewed with browsers that don't support tables. In the case of side heads, though, your document will come out just fine on a "table-challenged" browser.

Most browsers follow one of the Internet's basic tenets: be liberal in what you accept and strict in what you create. This usually means the browser will ignore tags that don't make sense, including all of the markup that creates a table.

In the case of our side-head layout, the browsers that can't do tables ignore the table tags and only see this part of the document:

```
<h3>Section 1</h3>
   Copy for section 1 goes on and on a bit
   so that it will take up more than one line in the
   table cell window...
<h3>Section 2</h3>
   Copy for section 2 goes on and on a bit
   so that it will take up more than one line in the
   table cell window...
```

Of course, this is a perfectly valid sequence of HTML that generates a conventional document with sections divided by <h3> headers. Your document will look fine, regardless of the browser, table-capable or not.

15.4.3 Better Forms Layout

Of all the features in HTML, it's forms that cry out for better layout control. Unlike other structured elements in HTML, forms look best when rendered in a fixed layout with precise margins and vertical alignment of elements. However, except for carefully planned <pre> formatted form segments, the common language just doesn't give us any special tools to better control forms layout.

15.4.3.1 Basic form layout

Your forms will almost always look better and be easier for your readers to follow if you use a table to structure and align the form's elements. For example, you might use a vertical alignment to your forms, with field labels to the left and their respective form elements aligned to an adjacent vertical margin on the right. Don't try that with just standard HTML.

Rather, prepare a form that contains a two-column table. The following HTML source does just that, as shown in Figure 15-5:

```
<form method=post action="http:/cgi-bin/process">
  <table>
    <tr>
      <th align=right>Name:
      <td><input type=text size=32>
    <tr>
      <th align=right>Address:
      <td><input type=text size=32>
    <tr>
      <th align=right>Phone:
      <td><input type=text size=12>
    <tr>
      <td colspan=2 align=center>
      <input type=submit value="Register">
  </table>
</form>
```

Of course, more complex form layouts can be managed with tables. We recommend you first sketch the form layout on paper and then plan how various combinations of table elements, including row- and column-straddled table cells might be used to effect the layout.

15.4.3.2 Building forms with nested tables

As we mentioned earlier, you may place a table inside the cell of another table. While this alone can lead to some elaborate table designs, nested tables also are

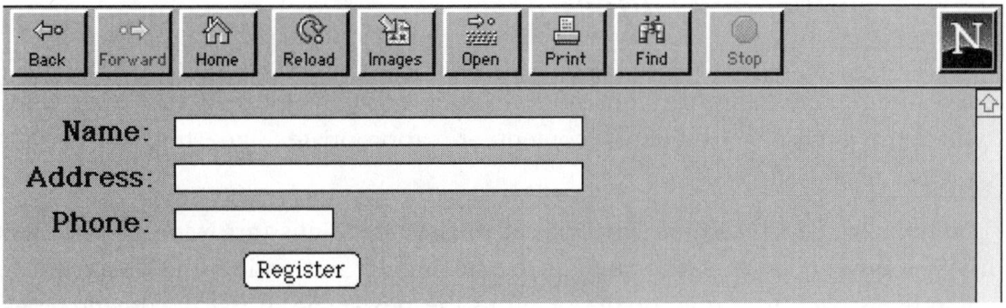

Figure 15-5. Align your forms nicely with tables

useful for managing a subset of form elements within the larger table containing
the entire form. The best application for using a nested table in a form is for
laying out checkboxes and radio buttons.

For example, insert the following row containing a table into the form table in the
previous example. It creates a checkbox with four choices:

```
<tr>
  <th align=right valign=top>Preferences:
  <td>
  <table>
    <tr>
    <td><input type=checkbox name=pref>Lemons
    <td><input type=checkbox name=pref>Limes
    <tr>
    <td><input type=checkbox name=pref>Oranges
    <td><input type=checkbox name=pref>Kumquats
  </table>
```

Figure 15-6 shows you how this nested table attractively formats the checkboxes,
which browsers would otherwise render on a single line and not well aligned.

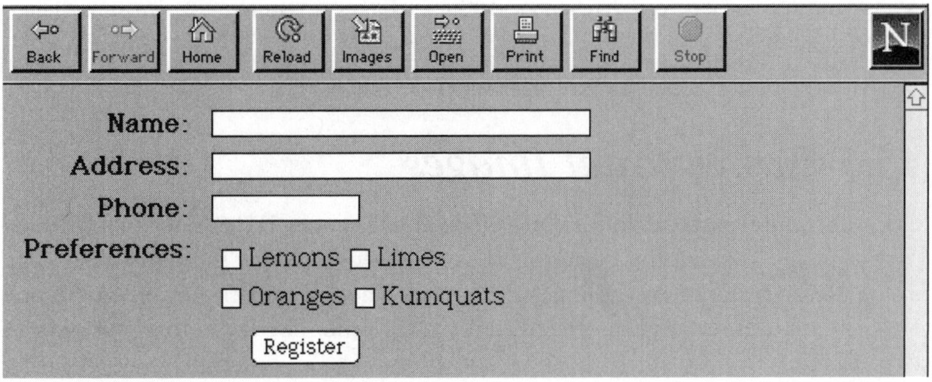

Figure 15-6. Nesting tables to format elements of a form

15.4.4 Embedded Guides

We generally argue for subtlety when you include hyperlinks in your documents, embedding them within the content and within context. But there are times when prominent guides to additional content are appropriate, like street signs in a crowded neighborhood.

Traditionally, HTML authors have placed their street signs (arrow icons with text labels) between major sections or at the beginning and end of the document to guide users back to a home page or on to the next page in the document series. Using `<table>` and its align attribute, you also can embed those guideposts within the document flow, but distinct from the content. And tables help you align the signpost elements for a more pleasing and concise presentation.

The following HTML segment, for example, uses a two-column table to set a hyperlink guide apart from the document content. The technique also nicely aligns the guide's graphical and textual elements, thereby giving the reader a clear and distinct option to jump to another section of the document, as shown in Figure 15-7:

```
The role of the kumquats in earthly and cosmic affairs has been well
documented.
Nearly from the moment that humankind began recording history — even as
oral tradition — historians have reported the extraordinary and
omnipresent influences of kumquats.
<p>
<table align=right>
  <tr>
   <td><a href="#arts"><img src="pics/d_arrow.gif" border=0></a>
   <td><a href="#arts"><h6>Kumquat influence<br>in the Arts</h6></a>
  </tr>
</table>
Early in the history of man, the kumquat played a vital role in the
formation of religious beliefs.  Central to annual harvest
celebrations was the day upon which kumquats ripened.  Likened to the
sun (<i>sol</i>), the golden fruit was taken (<i>stisus</i>) from the
trees on the day the sun stood highest in the sky.  We carry this day
forward even today, as our summer <i>solstice</i>.
```

15.5 Transparent Images

One of the most popular tricks you'll find on everyone's HTML pages is the transparent image. They let the background show through, giving the remainder of the image the appearance of floating on the page. The effect is clever and is the only way to put nonrectangular images in your HTML document displays. [image formats, 5.2.1]

Creating a transparent image is easy, once you understand how the process works and which images are candidates for transparency.

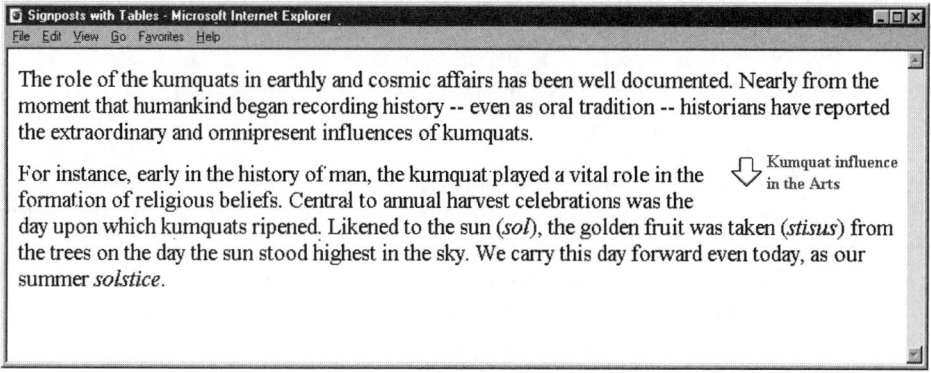

Figure 15-7. Tables let you embed signposts in your content flow

15.5.1 Colors, Maps, and Indexes

Images represent their colors in one of two ways: directly, or through a *colormap*.

In the direct method, each pixel in the image contains the actual RGB values that define the color of that pixel. Such images are often called *true color* images, since the number of distinct colors in the image is generally quite large. It is often the case that very few pixels in a true color image share the same color, with many pixels having subtly different variations of the same color. The most popular image format using this representation method is the JPEG format.

Colormap-based images keep all the different colors used in the image in a table known as the colormap. Each pixel in the image contains an index into the table of that pixel's color. In general, the table is fairly small, usually less than 256 colors. This means that many pixels share the same color, and that whole groups of pixels can have their color changed by simply altering the appropriate entry in the colormap. The most common image format using colormaps is the GIF format.

Image transparency is only possible with images containing a colormap, and is currently defined only for images using the GIF89a format. In this format, one entry in the colormap is tagged as the transparent color. All pixels containing the index of that entry will be made transparent when the image is displayed.

For example, consider an image containing eight colors. The colormap is eight entries long, with indices numbered zero through seven. Each pixel in the image contains a value from zero to seven, corresponding to its color in the colormap. If you indicate that the second entry in the color map, whose index is one, will be transparent, all pixels with the value one will be made transparent when the image is rendered.

15.5.2 *Creating a Potentially Transparent Image*

The cookbook way to create a transparent image is easy: take a conventional image, determine the color to be made transparent, and convert the image to GIF89a format, marking that color as transparent.

The most difficult part for most people is finding a conventional image that is suitable for conversion. To make the background of an image transparent, the *entire* background must be one color. Unfortunately, many images do not meet this simple criteria. Scanned images, for example, usually have backgrounds that are a mix of several slightly different shades of one color. Since only one color can be made transparent, the result is a mottled background, part transparent and part opaque.

Many image-editing tools use a process known as *dithering* to create certain colors in an image. Dithered colors are not pure, but are a mix of several other colors. This mixture is not amenable to transparency. You'll often find dithering used on systems with small colormaps, like conventional 16-color VGA displays on some PCs.

Finally, some images have a pure background color, but that color is also used in parts of the image you want to keep opaque. Since every pixel having the appropriate colormap index is made transparent, these portions of the image become transparent as well.

In all cases, the problem can be solved by loading the image into an image editor, turning off dithering, and painting the background areas, usually by hand, to be a single color not used anywhere else in the image. Make sure you save the result as a GIF image, so that the colormap and pixel indexes will be retained.

15.5.3 *Converting the Image*

Once you have an acceptable image, and you've determined the color you wish to make transparent, you'll need to convert the image to GIF89a format.

For PC and UNIX users, a public-domain utility called *giftrans* does the job nicely. To convert an image, use this command:

```
giftrans -t index original.gif > new.gif
```

Replace *index* with the numeric index of the color to be made transparent. *Original.gif* and *new.gif* are the original nontransparent image and the resulting transparent image.

Apple Macintosh users have the advantage, though: they can use a single tool named *Transparency* to accomplish the conversion. It was written by Aaron Giles at Cornell University, who generously makes it available at no charge over the Internet. Check Yahoo or your favorite Archie resource to locate it on a server near you.

These tools can do far more than simply convert transparent images. For a complete discussion of transparency and image conversion, including links to the actual tools, visit:

http://members.aol.com/htmlguru/transparent_images.html

15.6 Creating New Windows

For the vast majority of links in your documents, you'll want the newly loaded document displayed in the same window, replacing the previous one. That makes sense, since your users usually follow a sequential path through your collection.

But sometimes it makes sense to open a document in a new window, so that the new document and the old document are both directly accessible on the user's screen. If the new document is related to the original, for instance, it makes sense to have both in view. More commonly, the new document starts the user down a new web of documents, and you want them to see and remember where they came from.

Regardless of the reason, it is easy to open a new browser window from your HTML document. All you need to do is add the `target` attribute in the appropriate hyperlink (`<a>`) tag.

We normally use the `target` attribute to load a document into a specific frame that you've named in a frameset. It also serves to create a new window by one of two methods:

- Reference a new name. If you haven't previously defined a name and then use that new name as the value for the `target` attribute of a hyperlink, Netscape and Internet Explorer automatically create a new window with that name and load the referenced document into that window. This is the preferred way to create new windows, since you can subsequently use the name to load other documents into the same window. Using this technique, you can control which document gets loaded where.

- Create an unnamed window. Some browsers like Netscape and Internet Explorer support a special target named `_blank`[*] that lets you create a new window. The `_blank` window has limited use, though, because it is nameless—you cannot direct any other documents into that window. (New documents loaded via hyperlinks selected by the user within the window get displayed in that same window, of course.)

---

[*] Some browsers also accept the name `_new`. If you can't get `_blank` to work with your browser, try `_new`.

15.7 Multiple Frames in One Link

Loading a new document from a hyperlink is a snap, even if you put the new document into an alternative frame or window from its hyperlink parent. Occasionally, though, you'll want to load documents into two frames when the user clicks just one link. With a bit of trickery you can load two or more frames at one time, provided they are arranged a certain way in the browser window.

Consider this frame layout:

```
<frameset rows=2>
  <frameset cols=2>
    <frame name=A>
    <frame name=B>
  </frameset>
  <frameset>
    <frame name=C>
    <frame name=D>
  </frameset>
</frameset>
```

If someone clicks a link in frame A, the only thing you can do is update one of the four frames. Suppose you wanted to update frames B and D at the same time?

The trick is to replace frames B and D with a single frame, like this:

```
<frameset cols=2>
  <frameset rows=2>
    <frame name=A>
    <frame name=C>
  </frameset>
  <frame name=BD>
</frameset>
```

Ahah! Now you have a single target in which to load a single document, frame BD. The document you load should contain the original frames B and D in one column, like this:

```
<frameset cols=2>
  <frame name=B>
  <frame name=D>
</frameset>
```

The two frames will fill frame BD. When you update frame BD, both frames will be replaced, giving the appearance of two frames being updated at one time.

The drawback to this is that the frames must be adjacent and able to be grouped into a single document. For most pages, though, this solution works fairly well.

We've only scratched the surface of HTML tips and tricks here. Our advice: keep hacking!

HTML Grammar

For the most part, the exact syntax of an HTML document is not rigidly enforced by a browser. This gives authors wide latitude in creating documents and gives rise to documents that work on most browsers, but are actually incompatible with the standard. Stick to the standards unless your documents are fly-by-night affairs.

The HTML standard explicitly defines the ordering and nesting of tags and document elements. This syntax is embedded within the HTML Document Type Definition and is not readily understood by those not versed in SGML (see Appendix D, *The HTML 3.2 DTD*). Accordingly, we provide an alternate definition of the allowable HTML syntax, using a fairly common tool called a "grammar."

Grammar, whether it defines English sentences or HTML documents, is just a set of rules that indicate the order of language elements. These language elements can be divided into two sets: *terminal* (the actual words of the language) and *nonterminal* (all other grammatical rules). In HTML, the words correspond to the embedded markup tags and text in a document.

To use the grammar to create a valid HTML document, follow the order of the rules to see where the tags and text may be placed to create a valid HTML document.

A.1 Grammatical Conventions

We use a number of typographic and punctuation conventions to make our grammar easy to understand.

A.1.1 Typographic and Naming Conventions

For our HTML grammar, we denote the terminals with a bold, monospaced Courier typeface. The nonterminals appear in italicized text.

We also use a simple naming convention for the majority of our nonterminals: if one defines the syntax of a specific HTML tag, its name will be the tag name followed by "_*tag*." If a nonterminal defines the various language elements that may be nested within a certain tag, its name will be the tag name followed by "_*content*."

For example, if you are wondering exactly which elements are allowed within an `<a>` tag, you can look for the *a_content* rule within the grammar. Similarly, to determine the correct syntax of a definition list created with the `<dl>` tag, look for the *dl_tag* rule.

A.1.2 Punctuation Conventions

Each rule in the grammar starts with the rule's name, followed by the replacement symbol (::=) and the rule's value. We've intentionally kept the grammar simple, but we do use three punctuation elements to denote alternation, repetition, and optional elements in the grammar.

A.1.2.1 Alternation

Alternation indicates that a rule may actually have several different values, and you must choose exactly one of them. Vertical bars (|) separate the alternatives for the rule.

For example, the *heading* rule is equivalent to any one of six HTML heading tags, and so appears in the table as:

heading	::=	*h1_tag*
	|	*h2_tag*
	|	*h3_tag*
	|	*h4_tag*
	|	*h5_tag*
	|	*h6_tag*

The *heading* rule tells us that wherever the *heading* nonterminal appears in a rule, you can replace it with exactly one of the actual heading tags.

A.1.2.2 Repetition

Repetition indicates that an element within a rule may be repeated some number of times. Repeated elements are enclosed in curly braces ({...}). The closing brace has a subscripted number other than one if the element must be repeated a minimum number of times.

For example, the `<ul>` tag may only contain `<li>` tags, or it may actually be empty. The rule, therefore, is:

> *ul_tag*   ::=   `<ul>`
>
>   {*li_tag*}$_0$
>
>   `</ul>`

The rule says that the syntax of the `<ul>` tag requires the `<ul>` tag, zero or more `<li>` tags, followed by a closing `</ul>` tag.

We spread this rule across several lines and indented some of the elements to make it more readable only; it does not imply that your documents must actually be formatted this way.

A.1.2.3 Optional elements

Some elements may appear in a document, but are not required. Optional elements are enclosed in square brackets ([and]).

The `<table>` tag, for example, has an optional caption:

> *table_tag*   ::=   `<table>`
>
>   [*caption_tag*]
>
>   {*tr_tag*}$_0$
>
>   `</table>`

In addition, the rule says that a table begins with the `<table>` tag, followed by an optional caption, zero or more table-row tags, and ends with the `</table>` tag.

A.1.3 More Details

Our grammar stops at the tag level; it does not delve further to show the syntax of each tag, including tag attributes. For these details, refer to the HTML Quick Reference card included with this book.

A.1.4 Predefined Nonterminals

The HTML standard defines a few specific kinds of content that correspond to various types of text. We use these content types throughout the grammar. They are:

literal_text

> Text is interpreted exactly as specified; no character entities or style tags are recognized.

plain_text

> Regular characters in the document character encoding, along with character entities denoted by the ampersand character.

style_text

> Like *plain_text*, with physical- and content-based style tags allowed.

A.2 The Grammar

The grammar is a composite of the HTML 2.0 standard tags and special extensions to the language as enabled by the latest versions of NCSA Mosaic, Netscape Communication's Netscape Navigator, and Microsoft's Internet Explorer.

The rules are in alphabetical order. The starting rule for an entire document is named *html_document.*

a_tag	::=	`<a>`
		$\{a\_content\}_0$
		`</a>`
*a_content**	::=	*heading*
		| *text*
address_tag	::=	`<address>`
		$\{address\_content\}_0$
		`</address>`
address_content	::=	*p_tag*
		| *text*
applet_content	::=	$\{$`<param>`$\}_0$
		body_content
applet_tag	::=	`<applet>`
		applet_content
		`</applet>`

---

* *a_content* may not contain *a_tags*; you may not nest `<a>` tags within other `<a>` tags.

b_tag	::=	`<b>` *text* `</b>`
basefont_tag	::=	`<basefont>`
		body_content
		`</basefont>`
big_tag	::=	`<big>` *text* `</big>`
blink_tag	::=	`<blink>` *text* `</blink>`
block	::=	{*block_content*}$_0$
block_content	::=	`<isindex>`
	|	*basefont_tag*
	|	*blockquote_tag*
	|	*center_tag*
	|	*dir_tag*
	|	*div_tag*
	|	*dl_tag*
	|	*form_tag*
	|	*listing_tag*
	|	*menu_tag*
	|	*multicol_tag*
	|	*nobr_tag*
	|	*ol_tag*
	|	*p_tag*
	|	*pre_tag*
	|	*table_tag*
	|	*ul_tag*
	|	*xmp_tag*
blockquote_tag	::=	`<blockquote>`
		body_content
		`</blockquote>`
body_content	::=	`<bgsound>`
	|	`<hr>`
	|	*address_tag*
	|	*block*
	|	*heading*
	|	*layer_tag*
	|	*map_tag*
	|	*marquee_tag*
	|	*text*

body_tag	::=	`<body>`
		{*body_content*}$_0$
		`</body>`
caption_tag	::=	`<caption>`
		body_content
		`</caption>`
center_tag	::=	`<center>`
		body_content
		`</center>`
cite_tag	::=	`<cite>` *text* `</cite>`
code_tag	::=	`<code>` *text* `</code>`
colgroup_content	::=	{`<col>`}$_0$
colgroup_tag	::=	`<colgroup>`
		colgroup_content
content_style	::=	*cite_tag*
	|	*code_tag*
	|	*dfn_tag*
	|	*em_tag*
	|	*kbd_tag*
	|	*samp_tag*
	|	*strong_tag*
	|	*var_tag*
dd_tag	::=	`<dd>`
		flow
		`</dd>`
dfn_tag	::=	`<dfn>` *text* `</dfn>`
dir_tag[*]	::=	`<dir>`
		{*li_tag*}
		`</dir>`
div_tag	::=	`<div>`
		body_content
		`</div>`
dl_content	::=	*dt_tag dd_tag*

---

[*] The *li_tag* within the *dir_tag* may not contain any element found in a *block*.

dl_tag	::=	`<dl>`
		{*dl_content*}
		`</dl>`
dt_tag	::=	`<dt>`
		text
		`</dt>`
em_tag	::=	`<em>` *text* `</em>`
flow	::=	{*flow_content*}$_0$
flow_content	::=	*block*
	|	*text*
font_tag	::=	`<font>` *style_text* `</font>`
*form_content**	::=	`<input>`
	|	`<keygen>`
	|	*body_content*
	|	*select_tag*
	|	*textarea_tag*
form_tag	::=	`<form>`
		{*form_content*}$_0$
		`</form>`
frameset_content	::=	`<frame>`
	|	*noframes_tag*
frameset_tag	::=	`<frameset>`
		{*frameset_content*}$_0$
		`</frameset>`
h1_tag	::=	`<h1>` *text* `</h1>`
h2_tag	::=	`<h2>` *text* `</h2>`
h3_tag	::=	`<h3>` *text* `</h3>`
h4_tag	::=	`<h4>` *text* `</h4>`
h5_tag	::=	`<h5>` *text* `</h5>`
h6_tag	::=	`<h6>` *text* `</h6>`
head_content	::=	`<base>`
	|	`<isindex>`
	|	`<link>`
	|	`<meta>`
	|	`<nextid>`

---

* *form_content* may not contain *form_tags*; you may not nest one `<form>` within another `<form>`.

		|	*style_tag*
		|	*title_tag*
head_tag	::=	`<head>`	
		{*head_content*}$_0$	
		`</head>`	
heading	::=	*h1_tag*	
		|	*h2_tag*
		|	*h3_tag*
		|	*h4_tag*
		|	*h5_tag*
		|	*h6_tag*
html_content	::=	*head_tag body_tag*	
		|	*head_tag frameset_tag*
html_document	::=	*html_tag*	
html_tag	::=	`<html>`	
		html_content	
		`</html>`	
i_tag	::=	`<i>` *text* `</i>`	
ilayer_tag	::=	`<ilayer>`	
		body_content	
		`</ilayer>`	
kbd_tag	::=	`<kbd>` *text* `</kbd>`	
layer_tag	::=	`<layer>`	
		body_content	
		`</layer>`	
li_tag	::=	`<li>`	
		flow	
		`</li>`	
listing_tag	::=	`<listing>`	
		literal_text	
		`</listing>`	
map_content	::=	{`<area>`}$_0$	
map_tag	::=	`<map>`	
		map_content	
		`</map>`	
marquee_tag	::=	`<marquee>`	
		style_text	
		`</marquee>`	

menu_tag[*]	::=	`<menu>`
		$\{li\_tag\}_0$
		`</menu>`
multicol_tag	::=	`<multicol>`
		body_content
		`</multicol>`
nobr_tag	::=	`<nobr>` *text* `</nobr>`
noembed_tag	::=	`<noembed>` *text* `</noembed>`
noframes_tag	::=	`<noframes>`
		$\{body\_content\}_0$
		`</noframes>`
noscript_tag	::=	`<noscript>` *text* `</noscript>`
object_content	::=	$\{$`<param>`$\}_0$
		body_content
object_tag	::=	`<object>`
		object_content
		`</object>`
ol_tag	::=	`<ol>`
		$\{li\_tag\}$
		`</ol>`
option_tag	::=	`<option>`
		plain_text
		`</option>`
p_tag	::=	`<p>`
		text
		`</p>`
physical_style	::=	*b_tag*
		big_tag
		blink_tag
		font_tag
		i_tag
		s_tag
		small_tag
		span_tag

---

[*] The *li_tag* within the *menu_tag* may not contain any element found in a *block*.

		|	*strike_tag*
		|	*sub_tag*
		|	*sup_tag*
		|	*tt_tag*
		|	*u_tag*
pre_content	::=		` `
		|	`<hr>`
		|	*a_tag*
		|	*style_text*
pre_tag	::=		`<pre>`
			$\{pre\_content\}_0$
			`</pre>`
s_tag	::=		`<s>` *text* `</s>`
samp_tag	::=		`<samp>` *text* `</samp>`
script_tag[*]	::=		`<script>` *plain_text* `</script>`
select_tag	::=		`<select>`
			$\{option\_tag\}$
			`</select>`
server_tag[†]	::=		`<server>` *plain_text* `</server>`
small_tag	::=		`<small>` *text* `</small>`
span_tag	::=		`<span>` *text* `</span>`
strike_tag	::=		`<strike>` *text* `</strike>`
strong_tag	::=		`<strong>` *text* `</strong>`
style_tag	::=		`<style>` *plain_text* `</style>`
sub_tag	::=		`<sub>` *text* `</sub>`
sup_tag	::=		`<sup>` *text* `</sup>`
table_cell	::=		*td_tag*
		|	*th_tag*
table_content	::=		`<tbody>`
		|	`<tfoot>`
		|	`<thead>`
		|	*tr_tag*

---

[*] A *script_tag* may be placed anywhere within an HTML document, without regard to syntactic rules.

[†] A *server_tag* may be placed anywhere within an HTML document, without regard to syntactic rules.

table_tag	::=	`<table>`
		[*caption_tag*]
		{*colgroup_tag*}$_0$
		{*table_content*}$_0$
		`</table>`
td_tag	::=	`<td>`
		body_content
		`</td>`
text	::=	{*text_content*}$_0$
text_content	::=	` `
	|	`<embed>`
	|	`<iframe>`
	|	`<img>`
	|	`<spacer>`
	|	`<wbr>`
	|	*a_tag*
	|	*applet_tag*
	|	*content_style*
	|	*ilayer_tag*
	|	*noembed_tag*
	|	*noscript_tag*
	|	*object_tag*
	|	*plain_text*
	|	*physical_style*
textarea_tag	::=	`<textarea>` *plain_text* `</textarea>`
th_tag	::=	`<th>`
		body_content
		`</th>`
title_tag	::=	`<title>` *plain_text* `</title>`
tr_tag	::=	`<tr>`
		{*table_cell*}$_0$
		`</tr>`
tt_tag	::=	`<tt>` *text* `</tt>`
u_tag	::=	`<u>` *text* `</u>`
ul_tag	::=	`<ul>`
		{*li_tag*}
		`</ul>`

var_tag	::=	`<var>` *text* `</var>`
xmp_tag	::=	`<xmp>`
		literal_text
		`</xmp>`

B

HTML Tag Quick Reference

In the following table, we list in alphabetical order all the known and some undocumented HTML tags and attributes currently supported by one or more of today's browsers.

As with the other sections of this book, we use the Netscape and Microsoft icons to the far right of each item to show which browser supports that tag or attribute. If no icon is shown, the tag or attribute is part of the HTML 3.2 standard and is supported by both browsers.

We include each tag's possible attributes (some required) indented below their respective tags. In the description, we give possible attribute values as either a range of integer numbers or a definitive list of options, where possible.

`<a> ... </a>`	Create a hyperlink anchor (`href` attribute) or fragment identifier (`name` attribute)	
`class=name`	Specify a style class controlling the appearance of this tag	**N O**
`href=url`	Specify the URL of a hyperlink target (required if not a name anchor)	
`name=name`	Specify the name of a fragment identifier (required if not a hypertext reference anchor)	
`onclick=applet`	Specify an applet to run when user clicks on the image	**N O**
`onmouseout=applet`	Specify an applet to run when the mouse leaves the image	**N**
`onmouseover=applet`	Specify an applet to run when the mouse enters the image	**N O**

rel=*relationship*	Indicate the *relationship* from this document to the target	
rev=*relationship*	Indicate the reverse *relationship* of the target to this document	
style=*style*	Specify an inline style for this tag	**N O**
target=*name*	Define the name of the frame or window to receive the referenced document	**N O**
title=*string*	Provide a title for the target document	
<address> ... </address>	The enclosed text is an address	
<applet> ... </applet>	Define an executable applet within a text flow	
align=*position*	Align the <applet> region to either the top, middle, bottom (default), left, right, absmiddle, baseline, or absbottom of the text in the line	
alt=*string*	Specify alternative text to replace the <applet> region within browsers that support the <applet> tag, but cannot execute the application	
archive=*url*	Specify a class archive to be downloaded to the browser and then searched for code class	**N**
code=*class*	Specify the class name of the code to be executed (required)	
codebase=*url*	URL from which the code is retrieved	
height=*n*	Specify the height, in pixels, of the <applet> region	
hspace=*n*	Specify additional space, in pixels, to allow to the left and right of the <applet> region	
mayscript	If present, allows the applet to access JavaScript within the page	**N**
name=*name*	Specify the name of this particular instance of the <applet>	
title=*string*	Provide a title for the applet	**O**
vspace=*n*	Specify additional space, in pixels, to allow above and below the <applet> region	
width=*n*	Specify the width, in pixels, of the <applet> region	
<area>	Define a mouse-sensitive area in a client-side image map	
alt=*string*	Provide alternative text to be displayed by nongraphical browsers	

`coords=`*list*	Specify a comma-separated *list* of *shape*-dependent coordinates that define the edge of this area	
`href=`*url*	Specify the URL of a hyperlink target associated with this area	
`nohref`	Indicate that no document is associated with this area; clicking in the area has no effect	
`notab`	Do not include this area in the tabbing order	**O**
`onmouseout=`*applet*	Specify an applet to be run when the mouse leaves this area	**N**
`onmouseover=`*applet*	Specify an applet to be run when the mouse enters this area	**N**
`shape=`*shape*	Define the region's shape to be `circ`, `circle`, `poly`, `polygon`, `rect`, or `rectangle`	
`taborder=`*n*	Specify this area's position in the tabbing order	**O**
`target=`*name*	Specify the frame or window to receive the document linked by this area	**N**
`title=`*string*	Provide a title for this area	**O**
`<b>` ... `</b>`	Format the enclosed text using a bold typeface	
`class=`*name*	Specify a style class controlling the appearance of this tag	**N O**
`style=`*style*	Specify an inline style for this tag	**N O**
`<base>`	Specify the base URL for all relative URLs in this document	
`href=`*url*	Specify the base URL (required)	
`target=`*name*	Define the default target of all `<a>` links in the document	**N O**
`<basefont>`	Specify the font size for subsequent text	
`color=`*color*	Specify the base font's color	**O**
`name=`*name*	Specify local font to be used for the base font	**O**
`size=`*value*	Set the basefont size of 1 to 7 (required; default is 3)	
`<bgsound>`	Define background audio for the document	**O**
`loop=`*value*	Set the number of times to play the audio; *value* may be an integer or the value `infinite`	**O**
`src=`*url*	Provide the URL of the audio file to be played	**O**

`<big>` ... `</big>`	Format the enclosed text using a bigger typeface	
`class=`*name*	Specify a style class controlling the appearance of this tag	**N** **O**
`style=`*style*	Specify an inline style for this tag	**N** **O**
`<blink>` ... `</blink>`	Cause the enclosed content to blink	**N**
`<blockquote>` ... `</blockquote>`	The enclosed text is a block quotation	
`<body>` ... `</body>`	Delimit the beginning and end of the document body	
`alink=`*color*	Set the color of active hypertext links in the document	
`background=`*url*	Specify the URL of an image to be tiled in the document background	
`bgcolor=`*color*	Set the background color of the document	
`bgproperties=`*value*	With *value* set to `fixed`, prevent the background image from scrolling with the document content	**O**
`class=`*name*	Specify a style class controlling the appearance of this tag	**N** **O**
`leftmargin=`*value*	Set the size, in pixels, of the document's left margin	**O**
`link=`*color*	Set the color of unvisited hypertext links in the document	
`onblur=`*applet*	Specify an applet to be run when the mouse leaves the document window	**N** **O**
`onfocus=`*applet*	Specify an applet to be run when the mouse enters the document window	**N** **O**
`onload=`*applet*	Specify an applet to be run when the document is loaded	**N** **O**
`onunload=`*applet*	Specify an applet to be run when the document is unloaded	**N** **O**
`style=`*style*	Specify an inline style for this tag	**N** **O**
`text=`*color*	Set the color of regular text in the document	
`topmargin=`*value*	Set the size, in pixels, of the document's top margin	**O**
`vlink=`*color*	Set the color of visited links in the document	
` `	Break the current text flow, resuming at the beginning of the next line	
`clear=`*margin*	Break the flow and move downward until the desired *margin*, either `left`, `right`, `none`, or `all`, is clear	

`<caption> ... </caption>`	Define a caption for a table		
`align=`*position*	For Netscape, set the vertical position of the caption to either `top` or `bottom`. For Internet Explorer, set the horizontal alignment of the caption to either `left`, `center`, or `right`.		
`class=`*name*	Specify a style class controlling the appearance of this tag	**N**	**O**
`style=`*style*	Specify an inline style for this tag	**N**	**O**
`valign=`*position*	Set the vertical position of the caption to either `top` or `bottom`		**O**
`<center> ... </center>`	Center the enclosed text		
`<cite> ... </cite>`	The enclosed text is a citation		
`class=`*name*	Specify a style class controlling the appearance of this tag	**N**	**O**
`style=`*style*	Specify an inline style for this tag	**N**	**O**
`<code> ... </code>`	The enclosed text is a code sample		
`class=`*name*	Specify a style class controlling the appearance of this tag	**N**	**O**
`style=`*style*	Specify an inline style for this tag	**N**	**O**
`<col>`	Define a column within a `<colgroup>`		**O**
`align=`*position*	Set the column alignment to `left`, `center`, or `right`		**O**
`span=`*n*	Define the number of columns affected by this `<col>` tag		**O**
`<colgroup>`	Define a column group within a table		**O**
`align=`*position*	Set the horizontal alignment of text within the columns to either `left`, `center`, or `right`		**O**
`class=`*name*	Specify a style class controlling the appearance of this tag		**O**
`span=`*n*	Define the number of columns in the group		**O**
`style=`*style*	Specify an inline style for this tag		**O**
`valign=`*position*	Set the vertical alignment of text within the columns to either `top`, `middle`, or `bottom`		**O**
`width=`*n*	Set the width, in pixels or as a percentage, of each column in the group		**O**
`<comment> ... </comment>`	Place a comment in the document. Comments will be visible in all other browsers.		**O**

`<dd> ... </dd>`	Define the definition portion of an element in a definition list	
class=*name*	Specify a style class controlling the appearance of this tag	🅽 🄾
style=*style*	Specify an inline style for this tag	🅽 🄾
`<dfn> ... </dfn>`	Format the enclosed text as a definition	
class=*name*	Specify a style class controlling the appearance of this tag	🅽 🄾
style=*style*	Specify an inline style for this tag	🅽 🄾
`<dir> ... </dir>`	Create a directory list containing `<li>` tags	
class=*name*	Specify a style class controlling the appearance of this tag	🅽 🄾
compact	Make the list more compact if possible	
style=*style*	Specify an inline style for this tag	🅽 🄾
type=*bullet*	Set the bullet style for this list to either `circle`, `disc` (default), or `square`	🅽 🄾
`<div> ... </div>`	Create a division within a document	
align=*type*	Align the text within the division to `left`, `center`, or `right`	
class=*name*	Specify a style class controlling the appearance of this tag	🅽 🄾
lang=*name*	Specify the language used for this division	🄾
nowrap	Suppress word wrapping within this division	🄾
style=*style*	Specify an inline style for this tag	🅽 🄾
`<dl> ... </dl>`	Create a definition list containing `<dt>` and `<dd>` tags	
class=*name*	Specify a style class controlling the appearance of this tag	🅽 🄾
compact	Make the list more compact if possible	
style=*style*	Specify an inline style for this tag	🅽 🄾
`<dt> ... </dt>`	Define the definition term portion of an element in a definition list	
class=*name*	Specify a style class controlling the appearance of this tag	🅽 🄾
style=*style*	Specify an inline style for this tag	🅽 🄾
`<em> ... </em>`	Format the enclosed text with additional emphasis	
class=*name*	Specify a style class controlling the appearance of this tag	🅽 🄾
style=*style*	Specify an inline style for this tag	🅽 🄾

`<embed>`	Embed an application in a document	**N** **O**
`align=position`	Align the applet area to either the `top` or `bottom` of the adjacent text, or to the `left` or `right` margin of the page, with subsequent text flowing around the applet	**N**
`border=n`	Specify the size, in pixels, of the border around the applet	**N**
`height=n`	Specify the height, in pixels, of the applet	**N** **O**
`hidden`	If present, hide the applet on the page	**N** **O**
`hspace=n`	Define, in pixels, additional space to be placed to the left and right of the applet	**N**
`name=name`	Provide a name for the applet	**N** **O**
`palette=value`	In Netscape, a value of `foreground` causes the applet to use the foreground palette in Windows only; `background` uses the background palette. In Internet Explorer, provides the foreground and background colors for the applet, specified as two color values separated by a vertical bar (|)	**N** **O**
`pluginspage=url`	Provides the URL of the page containing instructions for installing the plug-in associated with the applet	**N**
`src=url`	Supplies the URL of the data to be fed to the applet	**N** **O**
`type=type`	Specifies the MIME type of the plug-in to be used	**N**
`units=type`	Set the units for the height and width attributes to either `pixels` (the default) or `en` (half the text point size)	**N** **O**
`vspace=n`	Define, in pixels, additional space to be placed above and below the applet	**N**
`width=n`	Specify the width, in pixels, of the applet	**N** **O**
`<font> ... </font>`	Set the size or color of the enclosed text	
`color=color`	Set the color of the enclosed text to the desired `color`	
`face=list`	Set the typeface of the enclosed text to the first available font in the comma-separated `list` of font names	**N** **O**
`size=value`	Set the size to absolute size 1 to 7, or relative to the `<basefont>` size using `+n` or `-n` (required)	

`<form> ... </form>`	Delimit a form	
`action=`*url*	Specify the URL of the application that will process the form (required)	
`class=`*name*	Specify a style class controlling the appearance of this tag	🅽 🅞
`enctype=`*encoding*	Specify how the form element values will be encoded	
`method=`*style*	Specify the parameter-passing *style*, either `get` or `post` (required)	
`name=`*name*	Supply a name for this form for use by JavaScript	🅽
`onreset=`*applet*	Specify an applet to be run when the form is reset	🅽
`onsubmit=`*applet*	Specify an applet to be run when the form is submitted	🅽 🅞
`style=`*style*	Specify an inline style for this tag	🅽 🅞
`target=`*name*	Specify the name of the frame or window to receive the results of the form after submission	🅽 🅞
`<frame> ... </frame>`	Define a frame within a frameset	🅽 🅞
`bordercolor=`*color*	Set the color of the frame's border to *color*	🅽
`frameborder=`*n*	If *value* is `yes` (Netscape only) or `1` (Netscape and Internet Explorer), enable frame borders. If *value* is `no` (Netscape only) or `0` (Netscape and Internet Explorer), disable frame borders.	🅽 🅞
`marginheight=`*n*	Place *n* pixels of space above and below the frame contents	🅽 🅞
`marginwidth=`*n*	Place *n* pixels of space to the left and right of the frame contents	🅽 🅞
`name=`*name*	Define the name of the frame	🅽 🅞
`noresize`	Disable user resizing of the frame	🅽 🅞
`scrolling=`*type*	Always add scrollbars (`yes`), never add scrollbars (`no`), or for Netscape only, add scrollbars when needed (`auto`)	🅽 🅞
`src=`*url*	Define the URL of the source document for this frame	🅽 🅞
`<frameset> ... </frameset>`	Define a collection of frames or other framesets	🅽 🅞
`border=`*n*	Set the thickness of the frame borders in this frameset	🅽
`bordercolor=`*color*	Define the color of the borders in this frameset	🅽

`cols=`*list*	Specify the number and width of frames within a frameset	**N** **O**
`frameborder=`*value*	If *value* is `yes` (Netscape only) or `1` (Netscape and Internet Explorer), enable frame borders. If *value* is `no` (Netscape only) or `0` (Netscape and Internet Explorer), disable frame borders.	**N** **O**
`framespacing=`*n*	Define the thickness of the frame borders in this frameset	**O**
`onblur=`*applet*	Define an applet to be run when the mouse leaves this frameset	**N**
`onfocus=`*applet*	Define an applet to be run when the mouse enters this frameset	**N**
`onload=`*applet*	Define an applet to be run when this frameset is loaded	**N**
`onunload=`*applet*	Define an applet to be run when this frameset is removed from the display	**N**
`rows=`*list*	Specify the number and height of frames within a frameset	**N** **O**
`<h`*n*`>` ... `</h`*n*`>`	The enclosed text is a level *n* header; for level *n* from 1 to 6	
`align=`*type*	Specify the heading alignment as either `left` (default), `center`, or `right`	
`class=`*name*	Specify a style class controlling the appearance of the heading	**N** **O**
`style=`*style*	Specify an inline style for this tag	**N** **O**
`<head>` ... `</head>`	Delimit the beginning and end of the document head	
`<hr>`	Break the current text flow and insert a horizontal rule	
`align=`*type*	Specify the rule alignment as either `left`, `center` (default), or `right`	
`class=`*name*	Specify a style class controlling the appearance of the rule	**N** **O**
`color=`*color*	Define the color of the rule	**O**
`noshade`	Do not use 3D shading to render the rule	
`size=`*pixels*	Set the thickness of the rule to an integer number of `pixels`	
`style=`*style*	Specify an inline style for this tag	**N** **O**
`width=`*value* or *%*	Set the width of the rule to either an integer number of pixels or a percentage of the page width	

`<html> ... </html>`	Delimit the beginning and end of the entire HyperText Markup Language document	
`version=`*string*	Indicate the HTML version used to create this document	
`<i> ... </i>`	Format the enclosed text in an *italic* typeface	
`class=`*name*	Specify a style class controlling the appearance of this tag	**N** **O**
`style=`*style*	Specify an inline style for this tag	**N** **O**
`<iframe> ... </iframe>`	Define an inline frame	**O**
`align=`*position*	Set the position of the frame aligned to the **top**, **center**, or **bottom** of the surrounding text, or flush against the **left** or **right** margins with subsequent text flowing around the frame	**O**
`frameborder=`*value*	If *value* is **1**, enable frame borders. If *value* is **0**, disable frame borders.	**O**
`height=`*n*	Set the height, in pixels, of the frame	**O**
`marginheight=`*n*	Place *n* pixels of space above and below the frame contents	**O**
`marginwidth=`*n*	Place *n* pixels of space to the left and right of the frame contents	**O**
`name=`*name*	Define the name of the frame	**O**
`scrolling=`*type*	Always add scrollbars (**yes**) or never add scrollbars (**no**)	**O**
`src=`*url*	Define the URL of the source document for this frame	**O**
`width=`*n*	Set the width, in pixels, of the frame	**O**
`<ilayer> ... </ilayer>`	Define an inline layer	**N**
`above=`*name*	Place this layer above the named layer	**N**
`background=`*url*	Specify a background image for the layer	**N**
`below=`*name*	Place this layer below the named layer	**N**
`bgcolor=`*color*	Specify the background color for the layer	**N**
`class=`*name*	Specify a style class controlling the appearance of this tag	**N**
`clip=`*edge*	Define the layer's clipping region, in pixels. If *left* and *top* are 0, they may be omitted	**N**
`left=`*n*	Define, in pixels, the position of the layer's left edge from the containing line of text	**N**
`name=`*name*	Provide a name for the layer	**N**

src=*url*	Supply the content of the layer from another document	**N**
style=*style*	Specify an inline style for this tag	**N**
top=*n*	Define, in pixels, the position of the layer's top edge from the containing line of text	**N**
visibility=*value*	Determine whether to show the layer, hide the layer, or inherit the visibility attribute from a containing layer	**N**
width=*n*	Define the width, in pixels, of the layer	**N**
z-index=*n*	Specify the layer's position in the stacking order	**N**
<img>	Insert an image into the current text flow	
align=*type*	Align the image to either the top, middle, bottom (default), left, or right of the text in the line. For Netscape Navigator, additionally to the absmiddle, baseline, or absbottom of the text.	
alt=*text*	Provide alternative text for non-image-capable browsers	
border=*n*	Set the pixel thickness of the border around images contained within hyperlinks	
class=*name*	Specify a style class controlling the appearance of this tag	**N** **O**
controls	Add playback controls for embedded video clips	**O**
dynsrc=*url*	Specify the URL of a video clip to be displayed	**O**
height=*n*	Specify the height of the image in scan lines	
hspace=*n*	Specify the space, in pixels, to be added to the left and right of the image	
ismap	Indicate that the image is mouse-selectable when used within an <a> tag	
loop=*value*	Set the number of times to play the video; *value* may be an integer or the value infinite	**O**
lowsrc=*url*	Specify a low-resolution image to be loaded by the browser first, followed by the image specified by the src attribute	**N**
name=*name*	Provide a name for the image for use by JavaScript	**N**
onabort=*applet*	Provide an applet to be run if the loading of the image is aborted	**N**

onerror=*applet*	Provide an applet to be run if the loading of the image is unsuccessful	**N**
onload=*applet*	Provide an applet to be run if the loading of the image is successful	**N**
src=*url*	Specify the source URL of the image to be displayed (required)	
start=*start*	Specify when to play the video clip, either `fileopen` or `mouseover`	**O**
style=*style*	Specify an inline style for this tag	**N O**
usemap=*url*	Specify the map of coordinates and links that define the hypertext links within this image	
vspace=*n*	Specify the vertical space, in pixels, added at the top and bottom of the image	
width=*n*	Specify the width of the image in pixels	
<input type=button>	Create a checkbox input element within a <form>	**N O**
name=*name*	Specify the name of the parameter to be passed to the form-processing application if the input element is selected (required)	**N O**
notab	Specifies that this element is not part of the tabbing order	**O**
onclick=*applet*	Specify an applet to be run if the user clicks this element	**N O**
taborder=*n*	Specifies this element's position in the tabbing order	**O**
value=*string*	Specify the value of the parameter sent to the form-processing application if this form element is selected (required)	**N O**
<input type=checkbox>	Create a checkbox input element within a <form>	
checked	Mark the element as initially selected	
name=*string*	Specify the name of the parameter to be passed to the form-processing application if the input element is selected (required)	
notab	Specifies that this element is not part of the tabbing order	**O**
onclick=*applet*	Specify an applet to be run if the user clicks this element	**N O**
taborder=*n*	Specifies this element's position in the tabbing order	**O**

`value=`*string*	Specify the value of the parameter sent to the form-processing application if this form element is selected (required)
`<input type=file>`	Create a file-selection element within a `<form>`
`maxlength=`*n*	Specify the maximum number of characters to accept for this element
`name=`*name*	Specify the name of the parameter that is passed to the form-processing application for this input element (required)
`notab`	Specifies that this element is not part of the tabbing order ⓞ
`size=`*n*	Specify the number of characters to display for this element
`taborder=`*n*	Specifies this element's position in the tabbing order ⓞ
`<input type=hidden>`	Create a hidden element within a `<form>`
`name=`*name*	Specify the name of the parameter that is passed to the form-processing application for this input element (required)
`value=`*string*	Specify the value of this element that is passed to the form-processing application
`<input type=image>`	Create an image input element within a `<form>`
`align=`*type*	Align the image to either the `top`, `middle`, or `bottom` of the form element's text
`border=`*n*	Set the pixel thickness of the border of the image
`onclick=`*applet*	Specify an applet to be run if the user clicks this element Ⓝ ⓞ
`name=`*name*	Specify the name of the parameter to be passed to the form-processing application for this input element (required)
`notab`	Specifies that this element is not part of the tabbing order ⓞ
`src=`*url*	Specify the source URL of the image (required)
`taborder=`*n*	Specifies this element's position in the tabbing order ⓞ
`<input type=password>`	Create a content-protected text-input element within a `<form>`
`maxlength=`*n*	Specify the maximum number of characters to accept for this element

name=*name*	Specify the name of the parameter to be passed to the form-processing application for this input element (required)	
notab	Specifies that this element is not part of the tabbing order	○
onblur=*applet*	Specify an applet to be run when the mouse leaves this element	🅽 ○
onchange=*applet*	Specify an applet to be run when the user changes the value of this element	🅽 ○
onfocus=*applet*	Specify an applet to be run when the mouse enters this element	🅽 ○
onselect=*applet*	Specify an applet to be run if the user clicks this element	🅽 ○
size=*n*	Specify the number of characters to display for this element	
taborder=*n*	Specifies this element's position in the tabbing order	○
value=*string*	Specify the initial value for this element	
<input type=radio>	Create a radio-button input element within a <form>	
checked	Mark the element as initially selected	
name=*name*	Specify the name of the parameter that is passed to the form-processing application if this input element is selected (required)	
notab	Specifies that this element is not part of the tabbing order	○
onclick=*applet*	Specify an applet to be run if the user clicks this element	🅽 ○
taborder=*n*	Specifies this element's position in the tabbing order	○
value=*string*	Specify the value of the parameter that is passed to the form-processing application if this element is selected (required)	
<input type=reset>	Create a reset button within a <form>	
notab	Specifies that this element is not part of the tabbing order	○
onclick=*applet*	Specify an applet to be run if the user clicks this element	🅽 ○
taborder=*n*	Specifies this element's position in the tabbing order	○
value=*string*	Specify an alternate label for the reset button (default is "Reset")	

`<input type=submit>`	Create a submit button within a `<form>`	
`name=`*name*	Specify the name of the parameter that is passed to the form-processing application for this input element (required)	
`notab`	Specifies that this element is not part of the tabbing order	**O**
`onclick=`*applet*	Specify an applet to be run if the user clicks this element	**N** **O**
`taborder=`*n*	Specifies this element's position in the tabbing order	**O**
`value=`*string*	Specify an alternate label for the submit button, as well as the value passed to the form-processing application for this parameter if this button is clicked	
`<input type=text>`	Create a text input element within a `<form>`	
`maxlength=`*n*	Specify the maximum number of characters to accept for this element	
`name=`*name*	Specify the name of the parameter that is passed to the form-processing application for this input element (required)	
`notab`	Specify that this element is not part of the tabbing order	**O**
`onblur=`*applet*	Specify an applet to be run when the mouse leaves this element	**N** **O**
`onchange=`*applet*	Specify an applet to be run when the user changes the value of this element	**N** **O**
`onfocus=`*applet*	Specify an applet to be run when the mouse enters this element	**N** **O**
`onselect=`*applet*	Specify an applet to be run if the user clicks this element	**N** **O**
`size=`*n*	Specify the number of characters to display for this element	
`taborder=`*n*	Specify this element's position in the tabbing order	**O**
`value=`*string*	Specify the initial value for this element	
`<isindex>`	Create a "searchable" HTML document	
`action=`*url*	PFor Internet Explorer only, provide the URL of the program that will perform the searching action	**O**
`prompt=`*string*	Provide an alternate prompt for the input field	

`<kbd> ... </kbd>`	The enclosed text is keyboard-like input	
`class=`*name*	Specify a style class controlling the appearance of this tag	**N** **O**
`style=`*style*	Specify an inline style for this tag	**N** **O**
`<keygen>`	Generate key information in a form	**N**
`challenge=`*string*	Provide a challenge string to be packaged with the key	**N**
`name=`*name*	Provide a name for the key	**N**
`<layer> ... </layer>`	Define a layer	**N**
`above=`*name*	Place this layer above the named layer	**N**
`background=`*url*	Specify a background image for the layer	**N**
`below=`*name*	Place this layer below the named layer	**N**
`bgcolor=`*color*	Specify the background color for the layer	**N**
`class=`*name*	Specify a style class controlling the appearance of this tag	**N**
`clip=`*edge*	Define the layer's clipping region, in pixels. If *left* and *top* are 0, they may be omitted	**N**
`left=`*n*	Define, in pixels, the position of the layer's left edge from the containing document or layer	**N**
`name=`*name*	Provide a name for the layer	**N**
`src=`*url*	Supply the content of the layer from another document	**N**
`style=`*style*	Specify an inline style for this tag	**N**
`top=`*n*	Define, in pixels, the position of the layer's top edge from the containing document or layer	**N**
`visibility=`*value*	Determine whether to `show` the layer, `hide` the layer, or `inherit` the visibility attribute from a containing layer	**N**
`width=`*n*	Define the width, in pixels, of the layer	**N**
`z-index=`*n*	Specify the layer's position in the stacking order	**N**
`<li> ... </li>`	Delimit a list item in an ordered (`<ol>`) or unordered (`<ul>`) list	
`class=`*name*	Specify a style class controlling the appearance of this tag	**N** **O**
`style=`*style*	Specify an inline style for this tag	**N** **O**

type=*format*	Set the type of this list element to the desired *format*. For <li> within <ol>: A (capital letters), a (lowercase letters), I (capital Roman numerals), i (lowercase Roman numerals), or 1 (Arabic numerals; default). For <li> within <ul>: circle, disc (default), or square.
value=*n*	Set the number for this list item to *n*
<link>	Define a link between this document and another document in the document <head>
href=*url*	Specify the hypertext reference URL of the target document
rel=*relation*	Indicate the relationship from this document to the target
rev=*relation*	Indicate the reverse relationship from the target to this document
title=*string*	Provide a title for the target document
type=*string*	Specify the MIME type for the linked document. Usually used in conjunction with links to stylesheets, when the type is set to text/css

The type=*string* row is marked with **N** **O**.

<listing> ... </listing>	Same as <pre width=132> ... </pre>; deprecated, do not use
<map> ... </map>	Define a map containing hotspots in a client-side image map
name=*name*	Define the name of this map (required)
<marquee> ... </marquee>	Create a scrolling-text marquee (Internet Explorer only) **O**
align=*position*	Align the marquee to the top, middle, or bottom of the surrounding text **O**
behavior=*style*	Define marquee style to be scroll, slide, or alternate **O**
bgcolor=*color*	Set the background color of the marquee **O**
class=*name*	Specify a style class controlling the appearance of this tag **O**
direction=*dir*	Define the direction, left or right, the text is to scroll **O**
height=*n*	Define the height, in pixels, of the marquee area **O**
hspace=*n*	Define the space, in pixels, to be inserted left and right of the marquee **O**
loop=*value*	Set the number of times to animate the marquee; *value* is an integer or infinite **O**

`scrollamount=`*value*	Set the number of pixels to move the text for each scroll movement	**O**
`scrolldelay=`*value*	Specify the delay, in milliseconds, between successive movements of the marquee text	**O**
`style=`*style*	Specify an inline style for this tag	**O**
`vspace=`*n*	Define the space, in pixels, to be inserted above and below of the marquee	**O**
`width=`*n*	Define the width, in pixels, of the marquee area	**O**
`<menu> ... </menu>`	Define a menu list containing `<li>` tags	
`class=`*name*	Specify a style class controlling the appearance of this tag	**N** **O**
`compact`	Make the list more compact if possible	
`style=`*style*	Specify an inline style for this tag	**N** **O**
`type=`*bullet*	Set the bullet style for this list to either `circle`, `disc` (default), or `square`	**N** **O**
`<meta>`	Provides additional information about a document	
`charset=`*name*	Specify the character set to be used with this document	**O**
`content=`*string*	Specify the value for the meta-information (required)	
`http-equiv=`*string*	Specify the HTTP equivalent name for the meta-information and cause the server to include the name and content in the HTTP header for this document when it is transmitted to the client	
`name=`*string*	Specify the name of the meta-information	
`<multicol> ...` `</multicol>`	Define a multi-column text flow	**N**
`class=`*name*	Specify a style class controlling the appearance of this tag	**N**
`cols=`*n*	Specify the number of columns	**N**
`gutter=`*n*	Define the spacing, in pixels, between columns	**N**
`style=`*style*	Specify an inline style for this tag	**N**
`width=n`	Define the width of the entire column group	**N**
`<nobr> ... </nobr>`	No breaks allowed in the enclosed text	**N** **O**
`<noembed> ... </noembed>`	Define content to be presented by browsers that do not support the `<embed>` tag	**N**

`<noframes>` ... `</noframes>`	Define content to be presented by browsers that do not support frames	**N** **O**
`<noscript>` ... `</noscript>`	Define content to be presented by browsers that do not support the `<script>` tag	**N**
`<object>`	Insert an object into a document	**O**
`align=`*position*	Align the object with the surrounding text (`texttop`, `middle`, `text-middle`, `baseline`, `textbottom`, and `center`) or against the margin with subsequent text flowing around the applet (`left` and `right`)	**N** **O**
`border=`*n*	Define, in pixels, the object's border width	**O**
`classid=`*url*	Supply the URL of the object	**N** **O**
`codebase=`*url*	Supply the URL of the object's code base	**N** **O**
`codetype=`*type*	Specify the MIME type of the code base	**O**
`data=`*url*	Supply data for the object	**N** **O**
`declare`	Declare this object without instantiating it	**O**
`height=`*n*	Define, in pixels, the height of the object	**N** **O**
`hspace=`*n*	Provide extra space, in pixels, to the right and left of the object	**O**
`id=`*name*	Define the name of this object	**N**
`name=`*name*	Define the name of this object	**O**
`notab`	Do not make this object part of the tabbing order	**O**
`shapes`	Specify that this object has shaped hyperlinks	**O**
`standby=`*string*	Define a message to display while the object loads	**O**
`tabindex=`*n*	Specify this object's position in the document tab order	**O**
`title=`*string*	Provide a title for this object	**O**
`type=`*type*	Specify the MIME type for the object data	**N** **O**
`usemap=`*url*	Defines an image map for use with this object	**O**
`vspace=`*n*	Provide extra space, in pixels, above and below of the object	**O**
`width=`*n*	Define, in pixels, the width of the object	**N** **O**

`<ol> ... </ol>`	Define an ordered list containing numbered (ascending) `<li>` elements	
`class=`*name*	Specify a style class controlling the appearance of this tag	**N O**
`compact`	Present the list in a more compact manner	
`start=`*n*	Start numbering the list at *n*, instead of 1	
`style=`*style*	Specify an inline style for this tag	**N O**
`type=`*format*	Set the numbering *format* for this list to either `A` (capital letters), `a` (lowercase letters), `I` (capital Roman numerals), `i` (lowercase Roman numerals), or `1` (Ararbic numerals; default)	
`<option> ... </option>`	Define an option within a `<select>` item in a `<form>`	
`class=`*name*	Specify a style class controlling the appearance of this tag	**N O**
`selected`	Make this item initially selected	
`style=`*style*	Specify an inline style for this tag	**N O**
`value=`*string*	Return the specified value to the form-processing application instead of the `<option>` contents	
`<p> ... </p>`	Start and end a paragraph	
`align=`*type*	Align the text within the paragraph to `left`, `center`, or `right`	
`class=`*name*	Specify a style class controlling the appearance of this tag	**N O**
`style=`*style*	Specify an inline style for this tag	**N O**
`<param> ... </param>`	Supply a parameter to a containing `<applet>`	
`name=`*name*	Define the name of the parameter	
`type=`*type*	Specify the MIME type of the parameter	**O**
`value=`*string*	Define the value of the parameter	
`valuetype=`*type*	Define the type of the value attribute, either as `data`, `ref` (the value is a URL pointing to the data), or `object` (the value is the name of an object in this document)	**O**
`<plaintext>`	Render the remainder of the document as preformatted plain text	

`<pre> ... </pre>`	Render the enclosed text in its original, preformatted style, honoring line breaks and spacing verbatim	
`width=`*n*	Size the text, if possible, so that *n* characters fit across the display window	
`<s> ... </s>`	Same as `<strike>`. The enclosed text is struck through with a horizontal line	**N O**
`class=`*name*	Specify a style class controlling the appearance of this tag	**N O**
`style=`*style*	Specify an inline style for this tag	**N O**
`<samp> ... </samp>`	The enclosed text is a sample	
`class=`*name*	Specify a style class controlling the appearance of this tag	**N O**
`style=`*style*	Specify an inline style for this tag	**N O**
`<script> ... </script>`	Define a script within a document	**N O**
`language=`*name*	Specify the script language as either `vbscript` or `javascript`	**N O**
`src=`*url*	Provide the URL of the document containing the scripts	**N O**
`<select> ... </select>`	Define a multiple-choice menu or scrolling list within a `<form>`, containing one or more `<option>` tags	
`class=`*name*	Specify a style class controlling the appearance of this tag	**N O**
`multiple`	Allow user to select more than one `<option>` within the `<select>`	
`name=`*name*	Define the name for the selected `<option>` values that, if selected, are passed to the form-processing application (required)	
`onblur=`*applet*	Specify an applet to be run when the mouse leaves this element	**N**
`onchange=`*applet*	Specify an applet to be run when the user changes the value of this element	**N**
`onclick=`*applet*	Specify an applet to be run if the user clicks this element	**N**
`onfocus=`*applet*	Specify an applet to be run when the mouse enters this element	**N**
`size=`*n*	Display *n* items using a pulldown menu for `size=1` (without `multiple` specified) and a scrolling list of *n* items otherwise	
`style=`*style*	Specify an inline style for this tag	**N O**
`<server> ... </server>`	Define a LiveWire script	**N**

`<small> ... </small>`	Format the enclosed text using a smaller typeface	
`class=`*name*	Specify a style class controlling the appearance of this tag	**N O**
`style=`*style*	Specify an inline style for this tag	**N O**
`<spacer>`	Create blank space in a document	**N**
`align=`*position*	Align a block spacer with either the surrounding text (`top`, `texttop`, `middle`, `absmiddle`, `baseline`, `bottom`, `absbottom`) or against a margin with subsequent text flowing around the spacer (`left` and `right`)	**N**
`height=`*n*	Define the height, in pixels, of a block spacer	**N**
`size=`*n*	Define the length, in pixels, of a horizontal or vertical spacer	**N**
`type=`*type*	Set spacer type to one of `block`, `horizontal`, or `vertical`	**N**
`width=`*value*	Define the width, in pixels, of a block spacer	**N**
`<span> ... </span>`	Define a span of text for style application	**N O**
`class=`*name*	Specify a style class controlling the appearance of this tag	**N O**
`style=`*style*	Specify an inline style for this tag	**N O**
`<strike> ... </strike>`	The enclosed text is struck through with a horizontal line	
`class=`*name*	Specify a style class controlling the appearance of this tag	**N O**
`style=`*style*	Specify an inline style for this tag	**N O**
`<strong> ... </strong>`	Strongly emphasize the enclosed text	
`class=`*name*	Specify a style class controlling the appearance of this tag	**N O**
`style=`*style*	Specify an inline style for this tag	**N O**
`<style> ... </style>`	Define one or more document level styles	**N O**
`type=`*type*	Define the format of the styles (always `text/css`)	**N O**
`<sub> ... </sub>`	Format the enclosed text as subscript	
`class=`*name*	Specify a style class controlling the appearance of this tag	**N O**
`style=`*style*	Specify an inline style for this tag	**N O**

`<sup> ... </sup>`	Format the enclosed text as superscript		
`class=`*name*	Specify a style class controlling the appearance of this tag	**N**	**O**
`style=`*style*	Specify an inline style for this tag	**N**	**O**
`<table> ... </table>`	Define a table		
`align=`*position*	Align the table either `left` or `right` and flow the subsequent text around the table		
`background=`*url*	Define a background image for the table		**O**
`bgcolor=`*color*	Define the background color for the entire table	**N**	**O**
`border=`*n*	Create a border *n* pixels wide		
`bordercolor=`*color*	Define the border color for the entire table		**O**
`bordercolordark=`*color*	Define the dark border-highlighting color for the entire table		**O**
`bordercolorlight=`*color*	Define the light border-highlighting color for the entire table		**O**
`cellpadding=`*n*	Place *n* pixels of padding around each cell's contents		
`cellspacing=`*n*	Place *n* pixels of spacing between cells		
`class=`*name*	Specify a style class controlling the appearance of this tag	**N**	**O**
`cols=`*n*	Specify the number of columns in this table	**N**	**O**
`frame=`*type*	Define where table borders are displayed, either `border` (default), `void`, `above`, `below`, `hsides`, `lhs`, `rhs`, `vsides`, or `box`		**O**
`height=`*n*	Define the height of the table in pixels	**N**	
`hspace=`*n*	Specify the horizontal space, in pixels, added at the left and right of the table	**N**	
`nowrap`	Supress text wrapping in table cells		**O**
`rules=`*edges*	Determine where inner dividers are drawn, either `none` (default), `groups` (only around row and column groups), `rows`, `cols`, or `all`.		**O**
`style=`*style*	Specify an inline style for this tag	**N**	**O**
`valign=`*position*	Align text in the table to either the `top`, `center`, `bottom`, or `baseline`		**O**
`vspace=`*n*	Specify the vertical space, in pixels, added at the top and bottom of the table	**N**	
`width=`*n*	Set the width of the table to *n* pixels or a percentage of the window width		

`<tbody>...</tbody>`	Create a row group within a table	**O**
`<td> ... </td>`	Define a table data cell	
`align=`*position*	Align the cell contents to the `left`, `center`, or `right`	
`background=`*url*	Define a background image for this cell	**O**
`bgcolor=`*color*	Define the background color for the cell	**N** **O**
`bordercolor=`*color*	Define the border color for the cell	**O**
`bordercolordark=`*color*	Define the dark border highlighting color for the cell	**O**
`bordercolorlight=`*color*	Define the light border highlighting color for the cell	**O**
`class=`*name*	Specify a style class controlling the appearance of this tag	**N** **O**
`colspan=`*n*	Have this cell straddle *n* adjacent columns	
`height=`*n*	Define the height, in pixels, for this cell	
`nowrap`	Do not automatically wrap and fill text in this cell	
`rowspan=`*n*	Have this cell straddle n adjacent rows	
`style=`*style*	Specify an inline style for this tag	**N** **O**
`valign=`*position*	Vertically align this cell's contents to the `top`, `center`, `bottom`, or `baseline` of the cell	
`width=`*n*	Set the width of this cell to *n* pixels or a percentage of the table width	
`<textarea> ...` `</textarea>`	Define a multiline text input area within a `<form>`; content of the `<textarea>` tag is the initial, default value	
`class=`*name*	Specify a style class controlling the appearance of this tag	**N** **O**
`cols=`*n*	Display *n* columns (characters) of text within the text area	
`name=`*string*	Define the name for the text-area value that is passed to the form-processing application (required)	
`onblur=`*applet*	Specify an applet to be run when the mouse leaves this element	**N**
`onchange=`*applet*	Specify an applet to be run when the user changes the value of this element	**N**
`onfocus=`*applet*	Specify an applet to be run when the mouse enters this element	**N**
`onselect=`*applet*	Specify an applet to be run if the user clicks this element	**N**

`rows=`*n*	Display *n* rows of text within the text area	
`style=`*style*	Specify an inline style for this tag	**N** **O**
`wrap=`*style*	Set word wrapping within the text area to `off`, `virtual` (display wrap, but do not transmit to server), or `physical` (display and transmit wrap)	**N**
`<tfoot> ... </tfoot>`	Define a table footer	**O**
`<th> ... </th>`	Define a table header cell	
`align=`*position*	Align the cell contents to the `left`, `center`, or `right`	
`background=`*url*	Define a background image for this cell	**O**
`bgcolor=`*color*	Define the background color for the cell	**N** **O**
`bordercolor=`*color*	Define the border color for the cell	**O**
`bordercolordark=`*color*	Define the dark border highlighting color for the cell	**O**
`bordercolorlight=`*color*	Define the light border highlighting color for the cell	**O**
`class=`*name*	Specify a style class controlling the appearance of this tag	**N** **O**
`colspan=`*n*	Have this cell straddle *n* adjacent columns	
`height=`*n*	Define the height, in pixels, of this cell	
`nowrap`	Do not automatically wrap and fill text in this cell	
`rowspan=`*n*	Have this cell straddle *n* adjacent rows	
`style=`*style*	Specify an inline style for this tag	**N** **O**
`valign=`*position*	Vertically align this cell's contents to the `top`, `center`, `bottom`, or `baseline` of the cell	
`width=`*n*	Set the width of this cell to *n* pixels or a percentage of the table width	
`<thead> ... </thead>`	Define a table heading	**O**
`align=`*position*	Define the horizontal text alignment in the heading, either `left`, `center`, `right`, or `justify`	**O**
`class=`*name*	Specify a style class controlling the appearance of this tag	**O**
`style=`*style*	Specify an inline style for this tag	**O**
`valign=`*position*	Define the vertical text alignment in the heading, either `left`, `center`, `right`, or `justify`	**O**
`<title> ... </title>`	Define the HTML document's title	

`<tr> ... </tr>`	Define a row of cells within a table	
`align=type`	Align the cell contents in this row to the `left`, `center`, or `right`	
`bgcolor=color`	Define the background color for this row	N O
`bordercolor=color`	For Internet Explorer, define the border color for this row	O
`bordercolordark=color`	For Internet Explorer, define the dark border-highlighting color for this row	O
`bordercolorlight=color`	For Internet Explorer, define the light border-highlighting color for this row	O
`class=name`	Specify a style class controlling the appearance of this tag	N O
`nowrap`	Disable word wrap for all cells in this row	O
`style=style`	Specify an inline style for this tag	N O
`valign=position`	Vertically align the cell contents in this row to the `top`, `center`, `bottom`, or `baseline` of the cell	
`<tt> ... </tt>`	Format the enclosed text in teletype-style (monospaced) font	
`class=name`	Specify a style class controlling the appearance of this tag	N O
`style=style`	Specify an inline style for this tag	N O
`<u> ... </u>`	The enclosed text is underlined	
`class=name`	Specify a style class controlling the appearance of this tag	N O
`style=style`	Specify an inline style for this tag	N O
`<ul> ... </ul>`	Define an unordered list of bulleted `<li>` elements	
`class=name`	Specify a style class controlling the appearance of this tag	N O
`compact`	Display the list in a more compact manner	
`style=style`	Specify an inline style for this tag	N O
`type=bullet`	Set the bullet style for this list to either `circle`, `disc` (default), or `square`	
`<var> ... </var>`	The enclosed text is a variable's name	
`class=name`	Specify a style class controlling the appearance of this tag	N O
`style=style`	Specify an inline style for this tag	N O
`<wbr>`	Indicate a potential word break point within a `<nobr>` section	N O
`<xmp> ... </xmp>`	Same as `<pre width=80> ... </pre>`; deprecated, do not use	

C

Cascading Style Sheet Properties Quick Reference

In the following table, we list in alphabetical order all the properties defined in the World Wide Web Consortium's Recommended Specification for Cascading Style Sheets, Level 1 (*http://www.w3.org/pub/WWW/TR/REC-CSS1*).

NOTE   We know that browser support of style sheets will change faster than we can reprint this book, so we have created a separate "compliance document" that you can use to determine how style sheets are implemented by the latest releases of the browsers. You can find this document at *http://www.ora.com/info/html/*. Whenever that document and this appendix differ, the document should be considered more accurate.

As in other sections of this book, we use the Netscape and Microsoft icons to the far right of each property to show which browser supports that property. Properties with no icons are not currently supported by any browser.

We also include the number of the section in this book that fully defines the property.

We include each property's possible values, defined as either an explicit keyword (shown in `constant width`) or as one of these values:

color
> Either a color name or hexadecimal RGB value, as defined in Appendix F, *Color Names and Values*, or an RGB triple of the form
>
>   rgb(red, green, blue)
>
> where `red`, `green`, and `blue` are either numbers in the range 0 to 255 or percentage values indicating the brightness of that color component. Values

of 255 or 100% indicate that the corresponding color component is at its brightest; values of 0 or 0% indicate that the corresponding color component is turned completely off. For example,

```
rgb(27, 119, 207)
rgb(50%, 75%, 0%)
```

are both valid color specifications.

length

An optional sign (either + or –) immediately followed by a number (with or without a decimal point) immediately followed by a two-character unit identifier. For values of zero, the unit identifier may be omitted.

The unit identifiers em and ex refer to the overall height of the font and to the height of the letter "x", respectively. The unit identifier px is equal to a single pixel on the display device. The unit identifiers in, cm, mm, pt, and pc refer to inches, centimeters, millimeters, points, and picas, respectively. There are 72.27 points per inch, and 12 points in a pica.

number

An optional sign, immediately followed by a number (with or without a decimal point).

percent

An optional sign, immediately followed by a number (with or without a decimal point), immediately followed by a percent sign. The actual value is computed as a percentage of some other element property, usually the element's size.

url

The keyword url, immediately followed (no spaces) by a left parenthesis, followed by a URL optionally enclosed in single or double quotes, followed by a matching right parenthesis. For example,

```
url("http://members.aol.com/htmlguru")
```

is a valid URL value.

Finally, some values are lists of other values and are described as a "list of" some other value. In these cases, a list consists of one or more of the allowed values, separated by commas.

If there are several different values allowed for a property, these alternative choices are separated by vertical bars (|).

If the standard defines a default value for the property, that value is <u>underlined</u>.

background		Composite property for the `back-ground-attach-ment`, `background-color`, `back-ground-image`, `background-position`, and `background-repeat` properties; value is any of these properties' values, in any order	9.3.4.6	**N** **O**
background-attachment	`scroll` | `fixed`	Determines if the background image is fixed in the window or scrolls as the document scrolls	9.3.4.1	**N**
background-color	*color* | `transparent`	Sets the background color of an element	9.3.4.2	**N**
background-image	*url* | `none`	Sets the background image of an element	9.3.4.3	**N**
background-position	*percent* | *length* | `top` | `center` | `bottom` | `left` | `right`	Sets the initial position of the element's background image, if specified; values are normally paired to provide x, y positions. Default position is `0% 0%`	9.3.4.4	**N**
background-repeat	`repeat` | `repeat-x` | `repeat-y` | `no-repeat`	Determines how the background image is repeated (tiled) across an element	9.3.4.5	**N**
border		Sets all four borders on an element; value is one or more of a *color*, a value for `border-width`, and a value for `border-style`	9.3.6.6	
border-bottom		Sets the bottom border on an element; value is one or more of a *color*, a value for `border-bottom-width`, and a value for `border-style`	9.3.6.6	

border-bottom-width	*length* | `thin` | `medium` | `thick`	Sets the thickness of an element's bottom border	9.3.6.4
border-color	*color*	Sets the color of all four of an element's borders; default is the color of the element	9.3.6.3
border-left		Sets the left border on an element; value is one or more of a *color*, a value for `border-left-width`, and a value for `border-style`	9.3.6.6
border-left-width	*length* | `thin` | `medium` | `thick`	Sets the thickness of an element's left border	9.3.6.4
border-right		Sets the right border on an element; value is one or more of a *color*, a value for `border-right-width`, and a value for `border-style`	9.3.6.6
border-right-width	*length* | `thin` | `medium` | `thick`	Sets the thickness of an element's right border	9.3.6.4
border-style	`dashed` | `dotted` | `double` | `groove` | `inset` | `none` | `outset` | `ridge` | `solid`	Sets the style of all four of an element's borders	9.3.6.5
border-top		Sets the top border on an element; value is one or more of a *color*, a value for `border-top-width`, and a value for `border-style`	9.3.6.6
border-top-width	*length* | `thin` | `medium` | `thick`	Sets the thickness of an element's top border	9.3.6.4
border-width	*length* | `thin` | `medium` | `thick`	Sets the thickness of all four of an element's borders	9.3.6.4

clear	both	left	none	right	Sets which margins of an element must not be adjacent to a floating element; the element will be moved down until that margin is clear	9.3.6.7	**N**
color	*color*	Sets the color of an element	9.3.4.7	**N O**
display	block	inline	list-item	none	Controls how an element is displayed	9.3.8.1	
float	left	none	right	Determines if an element will float to the left or right, allowing text to wrap around it, or be displayed inline (using none)	9.3.6.8	**N**
font		Sets all the font attributes for an element; value is any of the values for font-style, font-variant, font-weight, font-size, line-height, and font-family, in that order	9.3.3.6	**N O**
font-family	list of font names	Define the font for an element, either as a specific font or as one of the generic fonts serif, sans-serif, cursive, fantasy, and monospace	9.3.3.1	**N O**
font-size	xx-small	x-small	small	medium	large	x-large	xx-large	larger	smaller	*length*	*percent*	Define the font size	9.3.3.2	**N O**
font-style	normal	italic	oblique	Define the style of the face, either normal or some type of slanted style	9.3.3.3	**N O**

font-variant	`normal` | `small-caps`	Define a font to be in SMALL CAPS	9.3.3.4	
font-weight	`normal` | `bold` | `bolder` | `lighter` | *number*	Define the font weight. If a *number* is used, it must be a multiple of 100 between 100 and 900; 400 is normal, 700 is the same as the keyword `bold`.	9.3.3.5	**N** **O**
height	*length* | `auto`	Define the height of an element	9.3.6.9	**N**
letter-spacing	*length* | `normal`	Inserts additional space between text characters	9.3.5.1	
line-height	*length* | *number* | *percent* | `normal`	Sets the distance between adjacent text baselines	9.3.5.2	**N** **O**
list-style		Defines list-related styles using any of the values for `list-style-image`, `list-style-position`, and `list-style-type`	9.3.7.4	
list-style-image	*url* | `none`	Define an image to be used as a list item's marker, in lieu of the value for `list-style-type`	9.3.7.1	
list-style-position	`inside` | `outside`	Indents or extends (default) a list item's marker with respect to the item's content	9.3.7.2	
list-style-type	`circle` | `disc` | `square` | `decimal` | `lower-alpha` | `lower-roman` | `none` | `upper-alpha` | `upper-roman`	Define a list item's marker for either unordered lists (`circle`, `disc`, or `square`) or for ordered lists (`decimal`, `lower-alpha`, `lower-roman`, `none`, `upper-alpha`, or `upper-roman`)	9.3.7.3	
margin	*length* | *percent* | `auto`	Define all four of an element's margins	9.3.6.10	**N** **O**

margin-bottom	*length* | *percent* | `auto`	Define the bottom margin of an element; default value is 0	9.3.6.10	**N**
margin-left	*length* | *percent* | `auto`	Define the left margin of an element; default value is 0	9.3.6.10	**N** **O**
margin-right	*length* | *percent* | `auto`	Define the right margin of an element; default value is 0	9.3.6.10	**N** **O**
margin-top	*length* | *percent* | `auto`	Define the top margin of an element; default value is 0	9.3.6.10	**N** **O**
padding		Define all four padding amounts around an element	9.3.6.4	
padding-bottom	*length* | *percent*	Define the bottom padding of an element; default value is 0	9.3.6.4	**N**
padding-left	*length* | *percent*	Define the left padding of an element; default value is 0	9.3.6.4	**N**
padding-right	*length* | *percent*	Define the right padding of an element; default value is 0	9.3.6.4	**N**
padding-top	*length* | *percent*	Define the top padding of an element; default value is 0	9.3.6.4	**N**
text-align	`center` | `justify` | `left` | `right`	Set the text alignment style for an element	9.3.5.3	**N** **O**
text-decoration	`blink` | `line-through` | `none` | `overline` | `underline`	Define any decoration for the text; values may be combined	9.3.5.4	**N** **O**
text-indent	*length* | *percent*	Define the indentation of the first line of text in an element; default value is 0	9.3.5.5	**N** **O**

text-transform	capitalize | lowercase | none | upper-case	Transform the text in the element accordingly	9.3.5.6	**N**
vertical-align	*percent* | base-line | bottom | middle | sub | super | text-bottom | text-top | top	Set the vertical positioning of an element	9.3.5.7	
word-spacing	*length* | normal	Insert additional space between words	9.3.5.8	
white-space	normal | nowrap | pre	Define how whitespace within an element is handled	9.3.8.2	
width	*length* | *percent* | auto	Define the width of an element	9.3.6.12	**N**

D

The HTML 3.2 DTD

The HTML 3.2 standard is formally defined as an SGML Document Type Definition (DTD). It is from this DTD that the standard is documented, and upon which this book is based. Note that we have reprinted this DTD verbatim and have not attempted to add extensions to it. Where our description and the DTD deviate, assume the DTD is correct.

```
<!--
        W3C Document Type Definition for the HyperText Markup Language
        version 3.2 as ratified by a vote of W3C member companies.
        For more information on W3C look at URL http://www.w3.org/

        Date: Tuesday January 14th 1997

        Author: Dave Raggett <dsr@w3.org>

        HTML 3.2 aims to capture recommended practice as of early '96
        and as such to be used as a replacement for HTML 2.0 (RFC 1866).
        Widely deployed rendering attributes are included where they
        have been shown to be interoperable. SCRIPT and STYLE are
        included to smooth the introduction of client-side scripts
        and style sheets. Browsers must avoid showing the contents
        of these element Otherwise support for them is not required.
        ID, CLASS and STYLE attributes are not included in this version
        of HTML.
-->

<!ENTITY % HTML.Version
        "-//W3C//DTD HTML 3.2 Final//EN"

        -- Typical usage:

            <!DOCTYPE HTML PUBLIC "-//W3C//DTD HTML 3.2 Final//EN">
            <html>
            ...
            </html>
        --
        >
```

```
<!--================== Deprecated Features Switch =========================-->

<!ENTITY % HTML.Deprecated "INCLUDE">

<!--================== Imported Names =====================================-->

<!ENTITY % Content-Type "CDATA"
        -- meaning a MIME content type, as per RFC1521
        -->

<!ENTITY % HTTP-Method "GET | POST"
        -- as per HTTP specification
        -->

<!ENTITY % URL "CDATA"
        -- The term URL means a CDATA attribute
           whose value is a Uniform Resource Locator,
           See RFC1808 (June 95) and RFC1738 (Dec 94).
        -->

<!-- Parameter Entities -->

<!ENTITY % head.misc "SCRIPT|STYLE|META|LINK" -- repeatable head elements -->

<!ENTITY % heading "H1|H2|H3|H4|H5|H6">

<!ENTITY % list "UL | OL |  DIR | MENU">

    <!ENTITY % preformatted "PRE | XMP | LISTING">
]]>

<!ENTITY % preformatted "PRE">

<!--================= Character mnemonic entities =========================-->

<!ENTITY % ISOlat1 PUBLIC
       "ISO 8879-1986//ENTITIES Added Latin 1//EN//HTML">
%ISOlat1;

<!--================= Entities for special symbols =========================-->
<!-- &trade and &cbsp are not widely deployed and so not included here -->

<!ENTITY amp     CDATA "&#38;"   -- ampersand         -->
<!ENTITY gt      CDATA "&#62;"   -- greater than      -->
<!ENTITY lt      CDATA "&#60;"   -- less than         -->

<!--================== Text Markup =========================================-->

<!ENTITY % font "TT | I | B  | U | STRIKE | BIG | SMALL | SUB | SUP">

<!ENTITY % phrase "EM | STRONG | DFN | CODE | SAMP | KBD | VAR | CITE">

<!ENTITY % special "A | IMG | APPLET | FONT | BASEFONT | BR | SCRIPT | MAP">

<!ENTITY % form "INPUT | SELECT | TEXTAREA">

<!ENTITY % text "#PCDATA | %font | %phrase | %special | %form">

<!ELEMENT (%font|%phrase) - - (%text)*>

<!-- there are also 16 widely known color names although
  the resulting colors are implementation dependent:

    aqua, black, blue, fuchsia, gray, green, lime, maroon,
    navy, olive, purple, red, silver, teal, white, and yellow
```

```
    These colors were originally picked as being the standard
    16 colors supported with the Windows VGA palette.
    -->

<!ELEMENT FONT - - (%text)*      -- local change to font -->
<!ATTLIST FONT
    size    CDATA    #IMPLIED     -- [+]nn e.g. size="+1", size=4 --
    color   CDATA    #IMPLIED     -- #RRGGBB in hex, e.g. red: color="#FF0000" --
    >

<!ELEMENT BASEFONT - O EMPTY     -- base font size (1 to 7)-->
<!ATTLIST BASEFONT
    size    CDATA    #IMPLIED     -- e.g. size=3 --
    >

<!ELEMENT BR    - O EMPTY     -- forced line break -->
<!ATTLIST BR
        clear (left|all|right|none) none -- control of text flow --
        >

<!--================= HTML content models ===============================-->
<!--
    HTML has three basic content models:

        %text       character level elements and text strings
        %flow       block-like elements e.g. paragraphs and lists
        %bodytext   as %flow plus headers H1-H6 and ADDRESS
-->

<!ENTITY % block
    "P | %list | %preformatted | DL | DIV | CENTER |
     BLOCKQUOTE | FORM | ISINDEX | HR | TABLE">

<!-- %flow is used for DD and LI -->

<!ENTITY % flow "(%text | %block)*">

<!--================= Document Body ======================================-->

<!ENTITY % body.content "(%heading | %text | %block | ADDRESS)*">

<!ENTITY % color "CDATA" -- a color specification: #HHHHHH @@ details? -->

<!ENTITY % body-color-attrs "
        bgcolor %color #IMPLIED
        text %color #IMPLIED
        link %color #IMPLIED
        vlink %color #IMPLIED
        alink %color #IMPLIED
        ">

<!ELEMENT BODY O O  %body.content>
<!ATTLIST BODY
        background %URL #IMPLIED  -- texture tile for document background --
        %body-color-attrs;  -- bgcolor, text, link, vlink, alink --
        >

<!ENTITY % address.content "((%text;) | P)*">

<!ELEMENT ADDRESS - - %address.content>

<!ELEMENT DIV - - %body.content>
<!ATTLIST DIV
        align   (left|center|right) #IMPLIED -- alignment of following text --
        >

<!-- CENTER is a shorthand for DIV with ALIGN=CENTER -->
<!ELEMENT center - - %body.content>
```

```
<!--================== The Anchor Element ==================================-->

<!ELEMENT A - - (%text)* -(A)>
<!ATTLIST A
        name     CDATA    #IMPLIED    -- named link end --
        href     %URL     #IMPLIED    -- URL for linked resource --
        rel      CDATA    #IMPLIED    -- forward link types --
        rev      CDATA    #IMPLIED    -- reverse link types --
        title    CDATA    #IMPLIED    -- advisory title string --
        >

<!--================== Client-side image maps ============================-->

<!-- These can be placed in the same document or grouped in a
     separate document although this isn't yet widely supported -->

<!ENTITY % SHAPE "(rect|circle|poly)">
<!ENTITY % COORDS "CDATA" -- comma separated list of numbers -->

<!ELEMENT MAP - - (AREA)*>
<!ATTLIST MAP
    name    CDATA    #IMPLIED
    >

<!ELEMENT AREA - O EMPTY>
<!ATTLIST AREA
    shape    %SHAPE    rect
    coords   %COORDS  #IMPLIED  -- defines coordinates for shape --
    href     %URL     #IMPLIED  -- this region acts as hypertext link --
    nohref   (nohref) #IMPLIED  -- this region has no action --
    alt      CDATA    #REQUIRED -- needed for non-graphical user agents --
    >

<!--================== The LINK Element ==================================-->

<!ENTITY % Types "CDATA"
        -- See Internet Draft: draft-ietf-html-relrev-00.txt
           LINK has been part of HTML since the early days
           although few browsers as yet take advantage of it.

           Relationship values can be used in principle:

               a) for document specific toolbars/menus when used
                  with the LINK element in the document head:
               b) to link to a separate style sheet
               c) to make a link to a script
               d) by stylesheets to control how collections of
                  html nodes are rendered into printed documents
               e) to make a link to a printable version of this document
                  e.g. a postscript or pdf version
-->

<!ELEMENT LINK - O EMPTY>
<!ATTLIST LINK
        href     %URL     #IMPLIED    -- URL for linked resource --
        rel      %Types   #IMPLIED    -- forward link types --
        rev      %Types   #IMPLIED    -- reverse link types --
        title    CDATA    #IMPLIED    -- advisory title string --
        >

<!--================== Images ============================================-->

<!ENTITY % Length "CDATA"   -- nn for pixels or nn% for percentage length -->
<!ENTITY % Pixels "NUMBER"  -- integer representing length in pixels -->

<!-- Suggested widths are used for negotiating image size
     with the module responsible for painting the image.
     align=left or right cause image to float to margin
     and for subsequent text to wrap around image -->
```

```
<!ENTITY % IAlign "(top|middle|bottom|left|right)">

<!ELEMENT IMG     - O EMPTY --  Embedded image -->
<!ATTLIST IMG
         src       %URL      #REQUIRED  -- URL of image to embed --
         alt       CDATA     #IMPLIED   -- for display in place of image --
         align     %IAlign   #IMPLIED   -- vertical or horizontal alignment --
         height    %Pixels   #IMPLIED   -- suggested height in pixels --
         width     %Pixels   #IMPLIED   -- suggested width in pixels --
         border    %Pixels   #IMPLIED   -- suggested link border width --
         hspace    %Pixels   #IMPLIED   -- suggested horizontal gutter --
         vspace    %Pixels   #IMPLIED   -- suggested vertical gutter --
         usemap    %URL      #IMPLIED   -- use client-side image map --
         ismap     (ismap)   #IMPLIED   -- use server image map --
         >

<!-- USEMAP points to a MAP element which may be in this document
   or an external document, although the latter is not widely supported -->

<!--=================== Java APPLET tag ======================================-->
<!--
   This tag is supported by all Java enabled browsers. Applet resources
   (including their classes) are normally loaded relative to the document
   URL (or <BASE> element if it is defined). The CODEBASE attribute is used
   to change this default behavior. If the CODEBASE attribute is defined then
   it specifies a different location to find applet resources. The value
   can be an absolute URL or a relative URL. The absolute URL is used as is
   without modification and is not effected by the documents <BASE> element.
   When the codebase attribute is relative, then it is relative to the
   document URL (or <BASE> tag if defined).
-->
<!ELEMENT APPLET - - (PARAM | %text)*>
<!ATTLIST APPLET
        codebase %URL      #IMPLIED   -- code base --
        code     CDATA     #REQUIRED  -- class file --
        alt      CDATA     #IMPLIED   -- for display in place of applet --
        name     CDATA     #IMPLIED   -- applet name --
        width    %Pixels   #REQUIRED  -- suggested width in pixels --
        height   %Pixels   #REQUIRED  -- suggested height in pixels --
        align    %IAlign   #IMPLIED   -- vertical or horizontal alignment --
        hspace   %Pixels   #IMPLIED   -- suggested horizontal gutter --
        vspace   %Pixels   #IMPLIED   -- suggested vertical gutter --
        >

<!ELEMENT PARAM - O EMPTY>
<!ATTLIST PARAM
         name    NMTOKEN   #REQUIRED  -- The name of the parameter --
         value   CDATA     #IMPLIED   -- The value of the parameter --
         >

<!--
Here is an example:

    <applet codebase="applets/NervousText"
        code=NervousText.class
        width=300
        height=50>
    <param name=text value="Java is Cool!">
    <img src=sorry.gif alt="This looks better with Java support">
    </applet>
-->

<!--=================== Horizontal Rule ======================================-->

<!ELEMENT HR     - O EMPTY>
<!ATTLIST HR
        align (left|right|center) #IMPLIED
        noshade (noshade) #IMPLIED
```

```
          size  %Pixels #IMPLIED
          width %Length #IMPLIED
          >
<!--================== Paragraphs==============================-->

<!ELEMENT P     - O (%text)*>
<!ATTLIST P
        align (left|center|right) #IMPLIED
        >

<!--================== Headings ==============================-->

<!--
  There are six levels of headers from H1 (the most important)
  to H6 (the least important).
-->

<!ELEMENT ( %heading )  - -  (%text;)*>
<!ATTLIST ( %heading )
        align (left|center|right) #IMPLIED
        >

<!--================== Preformatted Text ===================-->

<!-- excludes images and changes in font size -->

<!ENTITY % pre.exclusion "IMG|BIG|SMALL|SUB|SUP|FONT">

<!ELEMENT PRE - - (%text)* -(%pre.exclusion)>
<!ATTLIST PRE
        width NUMBER #implied -- is this widely supported? --
        >

<![ %HTML.Deprecated [

<!ENTITY % literal "CDATA"
        -- historical, non-conforming parsing mode where
           the only markup signal is the end tag
           in full
        -->

<!ELEMENT (XMP|LISTING) - - %literal>
<!ELEMENT PLAINTEXT - O %literal>

]]>

<!--================== Block-like Quotes ===================-->

<!ELEMENT BLOCKQUOTE - - %body.content>

<!--================== Lists ==============================-->

<!--
    HTML 3.2 allows you to control the sequence number for ordered lists.
    You can set the sequence number with the START and VALUE attributes.
    The TYPE attribute may be used to specify the rendering of ordered
    and unordered lists.
-->

<!-- definition lists - DT for term, DD for its definition -->

<!ELEMENT DL    - -  (DT|DD)+>
<!ATTLIST DL
        compact (compact) #IMPLIED -- more compact style --
        >

<!ELEMENT DT - O  (%text)*>
```

```
<!ELEMENT DD - O  %flow;>

<!-- Ordered lists OL, and unordered lists UL -->
<!ELEMENT (OL|UL) - -  (LI)+>

<!--
      Numbering style
   1    arablic numbers     1, 2, 3, ...
   a    lower alpha         a, b, c, ...
   A    upper alpha         A, B, C, ...
   i    lower roman         i, ii, iii, ...
   I    upper roman         I, II, III, ...

   The style is applied to the sequence number which by default
   is reset to 1 for the first list item in an ordered list.

   This can't be expressed directly in SGML due to case folding.
-->

<!ENTITY % OLStyle "CDATA" -- constrained to: [1|a|A|i|I] -->

<!ATTLIST OL -- ordered lists --
         type      %OLStyle    #IMPLIED    -- numbering style --
         start     NUMBER      #IMPLIED    -- starting sequence number --
         compact  (compact)    #IMPLIED    -- reduced interitem spacing --
         >

<!-- bullet styles -->

<!ENTITY % ULStyle "disc|square|circle">

<!ATTLIST UL -- unordered lists --
         type     (%ULStyle)   #IMPLIED    -- bullet style --
         compact (compact)     #IMPLIED    -- reduced interitem spacing --
         >

<!ELEMENT (DIR|MENU) - -  (LI)+ -(%block)>
<!ATTLIST DIR
         compact (compact) #IMPLIED
         >
<!ATTLIST MENU
         compact (compact) #IMPLIED
         >

<!-- <DIR>            Directory list               -->
<!-- <DIR COMPACT>    Compact list style           -->
<!-- <MENU>           Menu list                    -->
<!-- <MENU COMPACT>   Compact list style           -->

<!-- The type attribute can be used to change the bullet style
     in unordered lists and the numbering style in ordered lists -->

<!ENTITY % LIStyle "CDATA" -- constrained to: "(%ULStyle|%OLStyle)" -->

<!ELEMENT LI - O %flow -- list item -->
<!ATTLIST LI
         type     %LIStyle     #IMPLIED    -- list item style --
         value    NUMBER       #IMPLIED    -- reset sequence number --
         >

<!--=============== Forms =================================================-->

<!ELEMENT FORM - - %body.content -(FORM)>
<!ATTLIST FORM
         action %URL #IMPLIED  -- server-side form handler --
         method (%HTTP-Method) GET -- see HTTP specification --
         enctype %Content-Type; "application/x-www-form-urlencoded"
         >
```

```
<!ENTITY % InputType
        "(TEXT | PASSWORD | CHECKBOX | RADIO | SUBMIT
            | RESET | FILE | HIDDEN | IMAGE)">

<!ELEMENT INPUT - O EMPTY>
<!ATTLIST INPUT
        type %InputType TEXT     -- what kind of widget is needed --
        name  CDATA    #IMPLIED  -- required for all but submit and reset --
        value CDATA    #IMPLIED  -- required for radio and checkboxes --
        checked (checked) #IMPLIED -- for radio buttons and check boxes --
        size CDATA     #IMPLIED  -- specific to each type of field --
        maxlength NUMBER #IMPLIED -- max chars allowed in text fields --
        src   %URL     #IMPLIED  -- for fields with background images --
        align %IAlign #IMPLIED   -- vertical or horizontal alignment --
        >

<!ELEMENT SELECT - - (OPTION+)>
<!ATTLIST SELECT
        name CDATA #REQUIRED
        size NUMBER #IMPLIED
        multiple (multiple) #IMPLIED
        >

<!ELEMENT OPTION - O (#PCDATA)*>
<!ATTLIST OPTION
        selected (selected) #IMPLIED
        value  CDATA  #IMPLIED -- defaults to element content --
        >

<!-- Multi-line text input field. -->

<!ELEMENT TEXTAREA - - (#PCDATA)*>
<!ATTLIST TEXTAREA
        name CDATA #REQUIRED
        rows NUMBER #REQUIRED
        cols NUMBER #REQUIRED
        >

<!--======================= Tables =========================================-->

<!-- Widely deployed subset of the full table standard, see RFC 1942
     e.g. at http://www.ics.uci.edu/pub/ietf/html/rfc1942.txt -->

<!-- horizontal placement of table relative to window -->
<!ENTITY % Where "(left|center|right)">

<!-- horizontal alignment attributes for cell contents -->
<!ENTITY % cell.halign
        "align  (left|center|right) #IMPLIED"
        >

<!-- vertical alignment attributes for cell contents -->
<!ENTITY % cell.valign
        "valign  (top|middle|bottom)  #IMPLIED"
        >

<!ELEMENT table - - (caption?, tr+)>
<!ELEMENT tr - O (th|td)*>
<!ELEMENT (th|td) - O %body.content>

<!ATTLIST table                         -- table element --
        align      %Where;  #IMPLIED -- table position relative to window --
        width      %Length  #IMPLIED -- table width relative to window --
        border     %Pixels  #IMPLIED -- controls frame width around table --
        cellspacing %Pixels #IMPLIED -- spacing between cells --
        cellpadding %Pixels #IMPLIED -- spacing within cells --
        >
```

```
<!ELEMENT CAPTION - - (%text;)* -- table or figure caption -->
<!ATTLIST CAPTION
        align (top|bottom) #IMPLIED
        >


<!ATTLIST tr                      -- table row --
        %cell.halign;             -- horizontal alignment in cells --
        %cell.valign;             -- vertical alignment in cells --
        >


<!ATTLIST (th|td)                 -- header or data cell --
        nowrap (nowrap)  #IMPLIED -- suppress word wrap --
        rowspan NUMBER   1        -- number of rows spanned by cell --
        colspan NUMBER   1        -- number of cols spanned by cell --
        %cell.halign;             -- horizontal alignment in cell --
        %cell.valign;             -- vertical alignment in cell --
        width   %Pixels  #IMPLIED -- suggested width for cell --
        height  %Pixels  #IMPLIED -- suggested height for cell --
        >


<!--================= Document Head ========================================-->

<!-- %head.misc defined earlier on as "SCRIPT|STYLE|META|LINK" -->

<!ENTITY % head.content "TITLE & ISINDEX? & BASE?">

<!ELEMENT HEAD O O  (%head.content) +(%head.misc)>

<!ELEMENT TITLE - - (#PCDATA)* -(%head.misc)
            -- The TITLE element is not considered part of the flow of text.
               It should be displayed, for example as the page header or
               window title.
            -->

<!ELEMENT ISINDEX - O EMPTY>
<!ATTLIST ISINDEX
        prompt CDATA #IMPLIED -- prompt message -->

<!--
    The BASE element gives an absolute URL for dereferencing relative
    URLs, e.g.

         <BASE href="http://foo.com/index.html">
         ...
         <IMG SRC="images/bar.gif">

    The image is deferenced to

         http://foo.com/images/bar.gif


    In the absence of a BASE element the document URL should be used.
    Note that this is not necessarily the same as the URL used to
    request the document, as the base URL may be overridden by an HTTP
    header accompanying the document.
-->

<!ELEMENT BASE - O EMPTY>
<!ATTLIST BASE
        href %URL  #REQUIRED
        >

<!ELEMENT META - O EMPTY -- Generic Metainformation -->
<!ATTLIST META
        http-equiv  NAME     #IMPLIED  -- HTTP response header name  --
        name        NAME     #IMPLIED  -- metainformation name       --
        content     CDATA    #REQUIRED -- associated information      --
        >
```

```
<!-- SCRIPT/STYLE are place holders for transition to next version of HTML -->

<!ELEMENT STYLE  - - CDATA -- placeholder for style info -->
<!ELEMENT SCRIPT - - CDATA -- placeholder for script statements -->

<!-- ELEMENT STYLE  - - (#PCDATA)*  -(%head.misc) -- style info -->
<!-- ELEMENT SCRIPT - - (#PCDATA)*  -(%head.misc) -- script statements -->

<!--================ Document Structure =====================================-->

<!ENTITY % version.attr "VERSION CDATA #FIXED '%HTML.Version;'.>

<![ %HTML.Deprecated [
    <!ENTITY % html.content "HEAD, BODY, PLAINTEXT?">
]]>

<!ENTITY % html.content "HEAD, BODY">

<!ELEMENT HTML O O  (%html.content)>
<!ATTLIST HTML
        %version.attr; >
```

E

Character Entities

The following table collects the defined standard, proposed, and several nonstandard, but generally supported, character entities for HTML.

Entity names, if defined, appear for their respective characters and can be used in the HTML character-entity sequence &name; to define any character for display by the browser. Otherwise, or alternatively for named characters, use the character's three-digit numeral value in the sequence &#nnn; to specially define an HTML character entity. Actual characters, however, may or may not be displayed by the browser depending on the computer platform and user-selected font for display.

Not all 256 characters in the ISO character set appear in the table. Missing ones are not recognized by the browser as either named or numeric entities.

To be sure that your documents are fully compliant with the HTML 3.2 standard, use only those named character entities whose conformance column is blank. Characters whose conformance column contains a "P" (Proposed) are generally supported by the current browsers, although not part of the HTML standard. Defy compliance by using the nonstandard "N" entities.

Numeric Entity	Named Entity	Symbol	Description	Conformance
&#009;			Horizontal tab	
&#010;			Line feed	
&#013;			Carriage return	
&#032;			Space	
&#033;		!	Exclamation point	
&#034;	&quot;	"	Quotation mark	
&#035;		#	Hash mark	

Numeric Entity	Named Entity	Symbol	Description	Conformance
&#036;		$	Dollar sign	
&#037;		%	Percent sign	
&#038;	&amp;	&	Ampersand	
&#039;		'	Apostrophe	
&#040;		(	Left parenthesis	
&#041;		)	Right parenthesis	
&#042;		*	Asterisk	
&#043;		+	Plus sign	
&#044;		,	Comma	
&#045;		-	Hyphen	
&#046;		.	Period	
&#047;		/	Slash	
0 – 9		0–9	Digits 0–9	
&#058;		:	Colon	
&#059;		;	Semicolon	
&#060;	&lt;	<	Less than	
&#061;		=	Equals sign	
&#062;	&gt;	>	Greater than	
&#063;		?	Question mark	
&#064;		@	Commercial at sign	
A – Z		A–Z	Letters A–Z	
&#091;		[	Left square bracket	
&#092;		\	Backslash	
&#093;		]	Right square bracket	
&#094;		^	Caret	
&#095;		_	Underscore	
&#096;		`	Gravè accent	
a – z		a–z	Letters a–z	
&#123;		{	Left curly brace	
|		|	Vertical bar	
&#125;		}	Right curly brace	
&#126;		~	Tilde	
&#130;		‚		N
&#131;		ƒ	Florin	N
&#132;		„	Right double quote	N

Numeric Entity	Named Entity	Symbol	Description	Conformance
&#133;		…	Ellipsis	N
&#134;		†	Dagger	N
&#135;		‡	Double dagger	N
&#136;		^	Circumflex	N
&#137;		‰	Permil	N
&#138;		–		N
&#139;		<	Less than sign	N
&#140;		Œ	Capital OE ligature	N
&#145;		'	Left single quote	N
&#146;		'	Right single quote	N
&#147;		"	Left double quote	N
&#148;		"	Right double quote	N
&#149;		•	Bullet	N
&#150;		–	En dash	N
&#151;		—	Em dash	N
&#152;		~	Tilde	N
&#153;		™	Trademark	N
&#154;		–		N
&#155;		>	Greater than sign	N
&#156;		œ	Small oe ligature	N
&#159;		Ÿ	Capital Y, umlaut	N
			Nonbreaking space	P
&#161;	&iexcl;	¡	Inverted exclamation point	P
&#162;	&cent;	¢	Cent sign	P
&#163;	&pound;	£	Pound sign	P
&#164;	&curren;	¤	General currency sign	P
&#165;	&yen;	¥	Yen sign	P
&#166;	&brvbar;	¦	Broken vertical bar	P
&#167;	&sect;	§	Section sign	P
&#168;	&uml;	¨	Umlaut	P
&#169;	&copy;	©	Copyright	P
&#170;	&ordf;	ª	Feminine ordinal	P
&#171;	&laquo;	«	Left angle quote	P
&#172;	&not;	¬	Not sign	P
&#173;	&shy;	—	Soft hyphen	P

Numeric Entity	Named Entity	Symbol	Description	Conformance
&#174;	&reg;	®	Registered trademark	P
&#175;	&macr;	¯	Macron accent	P
&#176;	&deg;	°	Degree sign	P
&#177;	&plusmn;	±	Plus or minus	P
&#178;	&sup2;	^{2}	Superscript 2	P
&#179;	&sup3;	^{3}	Superscript 3	P
&#180;	&acute;	´	Acute accent	P
&#181;	&micro;	µ	Micro sign (Greek mu)	P
&#182;	&para;	¶	Paragraph sign	P
&#183;	&middot;	·	Middle dot	P
&#184;	&cedil;	¸	Cedilla	P
&#185;	&sup1;	^{1}	Superscript 1	P
&#186;	&ordm;	º	Masculine ordinal	P
&#187;	&raquo;	»	Right angle quote	P
&#188;	&frac14;	¼	Fraction one-fourth	P
&#189;	&frac12;	½	Fraction one-half	P
&#190;	&frac34;	¾	Fraction three-fourths	P
&#191;	&iquest;	¿	Inverted question mark	P
&#192;	&Agrave;	À	Capital A, grave accent	
&#193;	&Aacute;	Á	Capital A, acute accent	
&#194;	&Acirc;	Â	Capital A, circumflex accent	
&#195;	&Atilde;	Ã	Capital A, tilde	
&#196;	&Auml;	Ä	Capital A, umlaut	
&#197;	&Aring;	Å	Capital A, ring	
&#198;	&AElig;	Æ	Capital AE ligature	
&#199;	&Ccedil;	Ç	Capital C, cedilla	
&#200;	&Egrave;	È	Capital E, grave accent	
&#201;	&Eacute;	É	Capital E, acute accent	
&#202;	&Ecirc;	Ê	Capital E, circumflex accent	
&#203;	&Euml;	Ë	Capital E, umlaut	
&#204;	&Igrave;	Ì	Capital I, grave accent	
&#205;	&Iacute;	Í	Capital I, acute accent	
&#206;	&Icirc;	Î	Capital I, circumflex accent	
&#207;	&Iuml;	Ï	Capital I, umlaut	

Numeric Entity	Named Entity	Symbol	Description	Conformance
&#208;	&ETH;	Ð	Capital eth, Icelandic	
&#209;	&Ntilde;	Ñ	Capital N, tilde	
&#210;	&Ograve;	Ò	Capital O, grave accent	
&#211;	&Oacute;	Ó	Capital O, acute accent	
&#212;	&Ocirc;	Ô	Capital O, circumflex accent	
&#213;	&Otilde;	Õ	Capital O, tilde	
&#214;	&Ouml;	Ö	Capital O, umlaut	
&#215;	&times;	×	Multiply sign	P
&#216;	&Oslash;	Ø	Capital O, slash	
&#217;	&Ugrave;	Ù	Capital U, grave accent	
&#218;	&Uacute;	Ú	Capital U, acute accent	
&#219;	&Ucirc;	Û	Capital U, circumflex accent	
&#220;	&Uuml;	Ü	Capital U, umlaut	
&#221;	&Yacute;	Y	Capital Y, acute accent	
&#222;	&THORN;	Þ	Capital thorn, Icelandic	
&#223;	&szlig;	ß	Small sz ligature, German	
&#224;	&agrave;	à	Small a, grave accent	
&#225;	&aacute;	á	Small a, acute accent	
&#226;	&acirc;	â	Small a, circumflex accent	
&#227;	&atilde;	ã	Small a, tilde	
&#228;	&auml;	ä	Small a, umlaut	
&#229;	&aring;	å	Small a, ring	
&#230;	&aelig;	æ	Small ae ligature	
&#231;	&ccedil;	ç	Small c, cedilla	
&#232;	&egrave;	è	Small e, grave accent	
&#233;	&eacute;	é	Small e, acute accent	
&#234;	&ecirc;	ê	Small e, circumflex accent	
&#235;	&euml;	ë	Small e, umlaut	
&#236;	&igrave;	ì	Small i, grave accent	
&#237;	&iacute;	í	Small i, acute accent	
&#238;	&icirc;	î	Small i, circumflex accent	
&#239;	&iuml;	ï	Small i, umlaut	
&#240;	&eth;	∂	Small eth, Icelandic	

Numeric Entity	Named Entity	Symbol	Description	Conformance
&#241;	&ntilde;	ñ	Small n, tilde	
&#242;	&ograve;	ò	Small o, grave accent	
&#243;	&oacute;	ó	Small o, acute accent	
&#244;	&ocirc;	ô	Small o, circumflex accent	
&#245;	&otilde;	õ	Small o, tilde	
&#246;	&ouml;	ö	Small o, umlaut	
&#247;	&divide;	÷	Division sign	P
&#248;	&oslash;	ø	Small o, slash	
&#249;	&ugrave;	ù	Small u, grave accent	
&#250;	&uacute;	ú	Small u, acute accent	
&#251;	&ucirc;	û	Small u, circumflex accent	
&#252;	&uuml;	ü	Small u, umlaut	
&#253;	&yacute;	y	Small y, acute accent	
&#254;	&thorn;	þ	Small thorn, Icelandic	
&#255;	&yuml;	ÿ	Small y, umlaut	

F

Color Names and Values

Within Netscape Navigator and Internet Explorer, you can change the color of various elements of your document, including these elements (partial list; see main text for all occasions).

Element	Associated Tag and Attribute
Document background	`<body bgcolor=color>`
All document text	`<body text=color>`
Active hyperlinks	`<body alink=color>`
Visited hyperlinks	`<body vlink=color>`
Regular hyperlinks	`<body link=color>`
Small portion of text	`<font color=color>`

Table cells	`<table=color>`
	`<tr bgcolor=color>`
	`<td bgcolor=color>`
	`<th bgcolor=color>`

F.1 Color Values

In all cases, you may specify the color value as a six-digit hexadecimal number that represents the red, green, and blue (RGB) components of the color. The first two digits correspond to the red component of the color, the next two the green component, and the last two the blue component. A value of 00 corresponds to the component being completely off; a value of FF (255) corresponds to the component being completely on. Thus, bright red is FF0000, bright green is 00FF00, and bright blue is 0000FF. Other primary colors are mixtures of two components, such as yellow (FFFF00), magenta (FF00FF), and cyan (00FFFF). White (FFFFFF) and black (000000) are also easy to figure out.

You use these values in a tag by replacing the color with the RGB triple, preceded by a pound sign (#). Thus, to make all visited links display as magenta, use this body tag:

```
<body vlink="#FF00FF">
```

F.2 Color Names

Unfortunately, determining the hexadecimal value for more esoteric colors like "papaya whip" or "navajo white" is very difficult. You can go crazy trying to adjust the RGB triple for a color to get the shade just right, especially when each adjustment requires loading a document into your browser to view the result.

To make life easier, the HTML 3.2 standard defines sixteen standard color names that can be used anywhere a numeric color value can be used. For example, you can make all visited links in the display magenta with the following attribute and value for the body tag:

```
<body vlink="magenta">
```

The color names and RGB values defined in the HTML 3.2 standard are:

aqua (#00FFFF)	gray (#808080)	navy (#000080)	silver (#C0C0C0)
black (#000000)	green (#008000)	olive (#808000)	teal (#008080)
blue (#0000FF)	lime (#00FF00)	purple (#800080)	yellow (#FFFF00)
fuchsia (#FF00FF)	maroon (#800000)	red (#FF0000)	white (#FFFFFF)

Netscape goes well beyond the HTML 3.2 standard and supports the several hundred color names defined for use in the X Window System. Note that these color names may contain no spaces; also, the word "gray" may be spelled "grey" in any color name.

Those colors marked with an asterisk (*) actually represent a family of colors numbered one through four. Thus, there are actually four variants of blue, named "blue1," "blue2," "blue3," and "blue4," along with plain old "blue." Blue1 is the lightest of the four; blue4 the darkest. The unnumbered color name is the same color as the first; thus, blue and blue1 are identical.

Finally, if all that isn't enough, there are one hundred variants of gray (and grey) numbered 1 through 100. "Gray1" is the darkest, "gray100" is the lightest, and "gray" is very close to "gray75."

The Netscape-supported colors are:

aliceblue	darkturquoise	lightseagreen	palevioletred*
antiquewhite*	darkviolet	lightskyblue*	papayawhip
aquamarine*	deeppink*	lightslateblue	peachpuff*

azure*	deepskyblue*	lightslategray	peru
beige	dimgray	lightsteelblue*	pink*
bisque*	dodgerblue*	lightyellow*	plum*
black	firebrick*	limegreen	powderblue
blanchedalmond	floralwhite	linen	purple*
blue*	forestgreen	magenta*	red*
blueviolet	gainsboro	maroon*	rosybrown*
brown*	ghostwhite	mediumaquamarine	royalblue*
burlywood*	gold*	mediumblue	saddlebrown
cadetblue*	goldenrod*	mediumorchid*	salmon*
chartreuse*	gray	mediumpurple*	sandybrown
chocolate*	green*	mediumseagreen	seagreen*
coral*	greenyellow	mediumslateblue	seashell*
cornflowerblue	honeydew*	mediumspringgreen	sienna*
cornsilk*	hotpink*	mediumturquoise	skyblue*
cyan*	indianred*	mediumvioletred	slateblue*
darkblue	ivory*	midnightblue	slategray*
darkcyan	khaki*	mintcream	snow*
darkgoldenrod*	lavender	mistyrose*	springgreen*
darkgray	lavenderblush*	moccasin	steelblue*
darkgreen	lawngreen	navajowhite*	tan*
darkkhaki	lemonchiffon*	navy	thistle*
darkmagenta	lightblue*	navyblue	tomato*
darkolivegreen*	lightcoral	oldlace	turquoise*
darkorange*	lightcyan*	olivedrab*	violet
darkorchid*	lightgoldenrod*	orange*	violetred*
darkred	lightgoldenrodyellow	orangered*	wheat*
darksalmon	lightgray	orchid*	white
darkseagreen*	lightgreen	palegoldenrod	whitesmoke
darkslateblue	lightpink*	palegreen*	yellow*
darkslategray*	lightsalmon*	paleturquoise*	yellowgreen

F.3   The Standard Color Map

Supporting hundreds of color names and millions of RGB triples is nice, but the reality is that the majority of users can only display 256 colors on their system. When confronted with a color not defined in this set of 256, the browser has two choices: convert the color to one of the existing colors, or dither the color using the available colors in the color map.

Conversion is easy; the color is compared to all the other colors in the color map and is replaced by the closest color found. Dithering is more difficult. Using two or more colors in the color map, the errant color is approximated by mixing different ratios of the available colors. Viewed up close, you'll see a pattern of alternating pixels using the available colors. At a distance, the pixels blend to form a color close to the original color.

In general, your images will look best if you can avoid both conversion and dithering. Conversion will make your colors appear "off"; dithering makes them look fuzzy. How to avoid these problems? Easy: use colors in the standard color map when creating your images.

The standard color map actually has 216 values in it. There are six variants of red, six of green, and six of blue that are combined in all possible ways to create these 216 (6 × 6 × 6) colors. These variants have decimal brightness values of 0, 51, 102, 153, 204, and 255, corresponding to hexadecimal values of 00, 33, 66, 99, CC, and FF. Colors like 003333 (dark cyan) and 999999 (medium gray) exist directly in the color map and won't be converted or dithered.

Keep in mind that many of Netscape's extended color names are not in the standard color map and will be converted or dithered to a (hopefully) similar color. Using color names, while convenient, does not guarantee that the desired color will be used by the browser.

When creating images, try to use colors in the standard color map. When selecting colors for text, links, or backgrounds, make sure you select colors in the standard color map. Your pages will look better and will be more consistent when viewed with different browsers.

Index

Symbols

& (ampersand) for entities, 416, 23, 45
, (comma) in styles, 260
= (equal sign) for tag attributes, 41
< (less-than sign), 23
<!-- --> tags, 20, 45
% (percent sign) for character
        encoding, 181
(pound sign)
    for entities, 23
    for name anchors, 28, 204
    in URLs, 185
? (question mark) in URLs, 181, 186
" (quotation mark)
    for attribute values, 41
    in URLs, 181
/ (slash)
    in ending tags, 19
    in URLs, 181, 185
~ (tilde) in URLs, 185

A

<a> tags, 27, 151, 197–203
above attribute (<layer>), 170–173
absbottom alignment, 124
absmiddle alignment, 124
absolute
    font size, 82–83
    URLs, 26, 195
accept attribute (<input>), 315

action attribute
    <form>, 301
    <isindex>, 222
action buttons, 318–322
ActiveX technology, 395
<address> tags, 99–100
addresses, 99–100
    IP addresses, 183
Advanced Research Projects Agency
        (ARPA), 2
align attribute
    <applet>, 396
    <caption>, 359
    <col>, 369
    <div>, 56
    <embed>, 404
    <h#>, 63
    <hr>, 107
    <iframe>, 386
    <img>, 29, 121–125
    <marquee>, 147
    <object>, 409
    <p>, 59
    <spacer>, 159
    <table>, 344–345
    <th> and <td>, 355
    <tr>, 351–352
alignment
    columns (see column layout)
    forms and, 333
    frames, 386

About the Authors

Chuck Musciano (*CMusciano@aol.com*) grew up on the East Coast, having spent time in Maryland, Georgia, and New Jersey before acquiring a B.S. in computer science from Georgia Tech in 1982. He spent the next 15 years in the employ of Harris Corporation in Melbourne, Florida, first as a compiler writer and crafter of tools and later as a member of Harris' Advanced Technology Group. His focus on UNIX-based technology led to a position within Harris' Corporate Data Center, managing UNIX systems. Along the way, he grew to know and love the Internet, having contributed a number of publicly available tools to the Net and started the still-running *Internet Movie Ratings Report*. The Web was a natural next step, and he has been running various web sites for several years. Most recently, he has taken a position with the American Kennel Club in Raleigh, North Carolina, managing their mainframe and UNIX-based database environment. Chuck has written on UNIX-related topics in the trade press for the past decade, most visibly as the "Webmaster" columnist for *Sunworld* (*http://www.sun.com/sunworldonline*) and the "HTML Q&A" columnist for *Netscapeworld* (*http://www.netscapeworld.com*). In his spare time he enjoys life in North Carolina with his wife Cindy, daughter Courtney, and son Cole.

Bill Kennedy (*wkennedy@activmedia.com*) is currently president and chief technology officer for *Activ*Media, Inc., a high-tech marketing and market-research firm based in cyberspace (*http://www.activmedia.com*). Among other ventures, he is actively involved in the development and sales of mobile robotics platforms used primarily in artificial intelligence and fuzzy logic research, and for training. In past lives, Bill acquired a Ph.D. and performed basic research for 12 years in the fields of biochemistry and biophysics; developed educational software with Kinemation; was editor-in-chief of *A+ Publishing*; and was a technical, then senior editor for *SunWorld/Advanced Systems* magazine.

Colophon

Our look is the result of reader comments, our own experimentation, and distribution channels. Distinctive covers complement our distinctive approach to technical topics, breathing personality and life into potentially dry subjects. UNIX and its attendant programs can be unruly beasts. Nutshell Handbooks help you tame them.

The animal featured on the cover of *HTML: The Definitive Guide* is a koala. The koala is an Australian marsupial, the only member of the Phascolarctidae family. This cuddly looking animal was the original model for teddy bears, although it actually is not related to bears.

Koalas use their extremely sharp claws for climbing eucalyptus trees. They subsist almost exclusively on eucalyptus leaves and bark. They are picky eaters, eating only about 20 of the approximately 350 species of eucalyptus in Australia. Since eucalyptus leaves contain the precursors to hydrocyanic acid, or cyanide, koalas also occasionally eat soil, which helps detoxify their food. Koalas in the wild rarely, if ever, drink water. Eucalyptus leaves contain approximately 67% water, and that is enough for the koala diet.

Koalas are tiny, approximately one half of a gram, when they are born. Twin births are very unusual, but a mother koala will adopt an abandoned baby if she finds one. The young koala stays in its mother's pouch for approximately seven months. Unlike most marsupials, the koala's pouch opens towards the rear, not towards the head. At the end of the seven month period, the mother begins to wean the baby off of a purely milk diet by introducing it to predigested eucalyptus leaves. After leaving the pouch, the young koala is carried on its mother's back until it is a year old. Koalas leave their mother's home range at 18 months. While trying to establish their own home range, koalas have a very high mortality rate.

Koalas were once plentiful in Australia, but as a result of epidemics in 1887–1889 and 1900–1903 and unrestrained hunting throughout the 20th century, koalas came close to extinction. They are a protected species and are rebuilding their population, but at present they survive only in eastern Australia.

Edie Freedman designed the cover of this book, using a 19th-century engraving from the Dover Pictorial Archive. The cover layout was produced with Quark XPress 3.3 using the ITC Garamond font. Whenever possible, our books use RepKover™, a durable and flexible lay-flat binding. If the page count exceeds RepKover's limit, perfect binding is used.

The inside layout was designed Jennifer Niederst and Nancy Priest. Text was prepared in FrameMaker 5.0 and implemented by Mike Sierra. The text and heading fonts are ITC Garamond Light and Garamond Book. The illustrations that appear in the book were created in Macromedia Freehand 5.0 by Chris Reilley. This colophon was written by Clairemarie Fisher O'Leary.

 # More Titles from O'Reilly

Developing Web Content

Building Your Own WebSite

By Susan B. Peck & Stephen Arrants
1st Edition July 1996
514 pages, ISBN 1-56592-232-8

This is a hands-on reference for Windows® 95 and Windows NT™ desktop users who want to host their own site on the Web or on a corporate intranet. You'll also learn how to connect your web to information in other Windows applications, such as word processing documents and databases. Packed with examples and tutorials on every aspect of Web management. Includes the highly acclaimed WebSite™ 1.1 on CD-ROM.

Web Client Programming with Perl

By Clinton Wong
1st Edition March 1997
250 pages, ISBN 1-56592-214-X

Web Client Programming with Perl teaches you how to extend scripting skills to the Web. This book teaches you the basics of how browsers communicate with servers and how to write your own customized Web clients to automate common tasks. It is intended for those who are motivated to develop software that offers a more flexible and dynamic response than a standard Web browser.

JavaScript: The Definitive Guide, Regular Edition

By David Flanagan
2nd Edition January 1997
672 pages, ISBN 1-56592-234-4

In this second edition, the author of the best-selling, *Java in a Nutshell* describes the server-side JavaScript application, LiveWire, developed by Netscape and Sun Microsystems.

The book describes the version of JavaScript shipped with Navigator 2.0, 2.0.1, and 2.0.2, and also the much-changed version of JavaScript shipped with Navigator 3.0. LiveConnect, used for communication between JavaScript and Java applets, and addresses commonly encountered bugs on JavaScript objects.

HTML: The Definitive Guide, Second Edition

By Chuck Musciano & Bill Kennedy
2nd Edition April 1997
520 pages, ISBN 1-56592-235-2

The second edition covers the most up-to-date version of the HTML standard (the proposed HTML version 3.2), Netscape 4.0 and Internet Explorer 3.0, plus all the common extensions, especially Netscape extensions. The authors address all the current version's elements, explaining how they work and interact with each other. Includes a style guide that helps you to use HTML to accomplish a variety of tasks, from simple online documentation to complex marketing and sales presentations.

Designing for the Web:
Getting Started in a New Medium

By Jennifer Niederst with Edie Freedman
1st Edition April 1996
180 pages, ISBN 1-56592-165-8

Designing for the Web gives you the basics you need to hit the ground running. Although geared toward designers, it covers information and techniques useful to anyone who wants to put graphics online. It explains how to work with HTML documents from a designer's point of view, outlines special problems with presenting information online, and walks through incorporating images into Web pages, with emphasis on resolution and improving efficiency.

WebMaster in a Nutshell

By Stephen Spainhour & Valerie Quercia
1st Edition October 1996
378 pages, ISBN 1-56592-229-8

Web content providers and administrators have many sources of information, both in print and online. *WebMaster in a Nutshell* pulls it all together into one slim volume – for easy desktop access. This quick-reference covers HTML, CGI, Perl, HTTP, server configuration, and tools for Web administration.

O'REILLY™

TO ORDER: **800-998-9938** • **order@ora.com** • **http://www.ora.com/**
OUR PRODUCTS ARE AVAILABLE AT A BOOKSTORE OR SOFTWARE STORE NEAR YOU.
FOR INFORMATION: **800-998-9938** • **707-829-0515** • **info@ora.com**

Perl

Programming Perl, Second Edition

By Larry Wall, Tom Christiansen,
& Randal L. Schwartz
2nd Edition September 1996
676 pages, ISBN 1-56592-149-6

Programming Perl, Second Edition, is
coauthored by Larry Wall, the creator of
Perl. Perl is a language for easily manipulating text, files, and processes. It provides
a more concise and readable way to do
many jobs that were formerly accomplished (with difficulty) by
programming with C or one of the shells. This heavily revised
second edition contains a full explanation of Perl version 5.003.

Learning Perl, Second Edition

By Randal L. Schwartz
Foreword by Larry Wall
2nd Edition July 1997
400 pages, ISBN 1-56592-284-0

This second edition of *Learning Perl*,
with a foreword by Perl author Larry Wall,
fully covers Perl, Version 5. In this new
edition, program examples and exercise
answers have been radically updated to
reflect typical usage under Perl 5, and
numerous details have been added or modified. In addition,
you'll find new sections introducing Perl references and CGI programming.

Learning Perl, Second Edition is ideal for system administrators, programmers, and anyone else wanting a down-to-earth
introduction to this useful language. Written by a Perl trainer, its
aim is to make a competent, hands-on Perl programmer out of
the reader as quickly as possible. The book takes a tutorial
approach and includes hundreds of short code examples, along
with some lengthy ones. The relatively inexperienced programmer will find *Learning Perl* easily accessible. For a comprehensive and detailed guide to advanced programming with Perl, read
O'Reilly's companion book, *Programming Perl, Second Edition*.

CGI Programming on the World Wide Web

By Shishir Gundavaram
1st Edition March 1996
450 pages, ISBN 1-56592-168-2

This book offers a comprehensive explanation of CGI and related techniques for
people who hold on to the dream of providing their own information servers on
the Web. It starts at the beginning,
explaining the value of CGI and how it
works, then moves swiftly into the subtle details of programming.

Perl 5 Desktop Reference

By Johan Vromans
1st Edition February 1996
44 pages, ISBN 1-56592-187-9

This is the standard quick-reference guide for
the Perl programming language. It provides a
complete overview of the language, from variables to input and output, from flow control to
regular expressions, from functions to document formats—all packed into a convenient,
carry-around booklet. Updated to cover Perl version 5.003.

Mastering Regular Expressions

By Jeffrey E. F. Friedl
1st Edition January 1997
368 pages, ISBN 1-56592-257-3

Regular expressions, a powerful tool for
manipulating text and data, are found in
scripting languages, editors, programming
environments, and specialized tools. In
this book, author Jeffrey Friedl leads you
through the steps of crafting a regular
expression that gets the job done. He examines a variety of tools
and uses them in an extensive array of examples, dedicating an
entire chapter to Perl.

O'REILLY™

TO ORDER: **800-998-9938** • *order@ora.com* • *http://www.ora.com/*
OUR PRODUCTS ARE AVAILABLE AT A BOOKSTORE OR SOFTWARE STORE NEAR YOU.
FOR INFORMATION: **800-998-9938** • **707-829-0515** • *info@ora.com*

Java Programming

Exploring Java, Second Edition

By Patrick Niemeyer & Joshua Peck
2nd Edition June 1997 (est.)
500 pages (est.), ISBN 1-56592-271-9

The second edition of *Exploring Java*, fully revised to cover Version 1.1 of the JDK, introduces the basics of Java, the object-oriented programming language for networked applications. The ability to create animated World Wide Web pages sparked the rush to Java. But what also makes this language so important is that it's truly portable. The code runs on any machine that provides a Java interpreter, whether Windows 95, Windows NT, the Macintosh, or any flavor of UNIX.

Java in a Nutshell, Second Edition

By David Flanagan
2nd Edition May 1997
650 pages, ISBN 1-56592-262-X

The bestselling Java book just got better. Java programmers migrating to 1.1 find this second edition of Java in a Nutshell contains everything they need to get up to speed.

Newcomers find it still has all of the features that have made it the Java book most often recommended on the Internet. This complete quick reference contains descriptions of all of the classes in the core Java 1.1 API, making it the only quick reference that a Java programmer needs.

Java Virtual Machine

By Troy Downing & Jon Meyer
1st Edition March 1997
440 pages, ISBN 1-56592-194-1

This book is a comprehensive programming guide for the Java Virtual Machine (JVM). It gives readers a strong overview and reference of the JVM so that they may create their own implementations of the JVM or write their own compilers that create Java object code. A Java assembler is provided with the book, so the examples can all be compiled and executed.

Java Language Reference, Second Edition

By Mark Grand
2nd Edition July 1997 (est.)
448 pages, ISBN 1-56592-326-X

The second edition of the *Java Language Reference* is an invaluable tool for Java programmers, especially those who have migrated to Java 1.1. Part of O'Reilly's Java documentation series, this complete reference describes all aspects of the Java language plus new features in Version 1.1, such as inner classes, final local variables and method parameters, anonymous arrays, class literals, and instance initializers.

Java Fundamental Classes Reference

By Mark Grand
1st Edition May 1997
1152 pages , ISBN 1-56592-241-7

The *Java Fundamental Classes Reference* provides complete reference documentation for the Java fundamental classes.

This book takes you beyond what you'd expect from a standard reference manual. Classes and methods are, of course, described in detail. It offers tutorial-style explanations of the important classes in the Java Core API and includes lots of sample code to help you learn by example.

Java AWT Reference

By John Zukowski
1st Edition March 1997
1100 pages, ISBN 1-56592-240-9

With AWT, you can create windows, draw, work with images, and use components like buttons, scrollbars, and pulldown menus. *Java AWT Reference* covers the classes that comprise the java.awt, java.awt.image, and java.applet packages. These classes provide the functionality that allows a Java application to provide user interaction in a graphical environment. It offers a comprehensive explanation of how AWT components fit together with easy-to-use reference material on every AWT class and lots of sample code to help you learn by example.

O'REILLY™

TO ORDER: **800-998-9938** • **order@ora.com** • **http://www.ora.com/**
OUR PRODUCTS ARE AVAILABLE AT A BOOKSTORE OR SOFTWARE STORE NEAR YOU.
FOR INFORMATION: **800-998-9938** • **707-829-0515** • **info@ora.com**

Java Programming *continued*

Java Threads

By Scott Oaks and Henry Wong
1st Edition January 1997
252 pages, ISBN 1-56592-216-6

Java Threads is a comprehensive guide to the intricacies of threaded programming in Java, covering everything from the most basic synchronization techniques to advanced topics like writing your own thread scheduler.

Java Threads uncovers the one tricky but essential aspect of Java programming and provides techniques for avoiding deadlock, lock starvation, and other topics.

Java Network Programming

By Elliotte Rusty Harold
1st Edition February 1997
448 pages, ISBN 1-56592-227-1

Java Network Programming is a complete introduction to developing network programs, both applets and applications, using Java; covering everything from networking fundamentals to remote method invocation (RMI).

It also covers what you can do without explicitly writing network code, how you can accomplish your goals using URLs and the basic capabilities of applets.

Developing Java Beans

By Rob Englander
1st Edition June 1997 (est.)
300 pages (est.), ISBN 1-56592-289-1

With *Developing Java Beans,* you'll learn how to create components that can be manipulated by tools like Borland's Latte or Symantec's Visual Cafe, enabling others to build entire applications by using and reusing these building blocks. Beyond the basics, *Developing Java Beans* teaches you how to create Beans that can be saved and restored properly; how to take advantage of introspection to provide more information about a Bean's capabilities; how to provide property editors and customizers that manipulate a Bean in sophisticated ways; and how to integrate Java Beans into ActiveX projects.

Java in a Nutshell, DELUXE EDITION

By various authors
1st Edition June1997 (est.)
ISBN 1-56592-304-9
includes CD-ROM and books.

Java in a Nutshell, Deluxe Edition, is a Java programmer's dream come true in one small package. The heart of this Deluxe Edition is the Java reference library on CD-ROM, which brings together five indispensable volumes for Java developers and programmers, linking related info across books. It includes: *Exploring Java 2nd Edition*, *Java Language Reference, 2nd Edition*, *Java Fundamental Classes Reference*, *Java AWT Reference*, and *Java in a Nutshell, 2nd Edition*, included both on the CD-ROM and in a companion desktop edition. This deluxe library gives you everything you need to do serious programming with Java 1.1.

Database Programming with JDBC and Java

By George Reese
1st Edition July 1997 (est.)
300 pages (est.), ISBN 1-56592-270-0

Java and databases make a powerful combination. Getting the two sides to work together, however, takes some effort—largely because Java deals in objects while most databases do not.

This book describes the standard Java interfaces that make portable,object-oriented access to relational databases possible, and offers a robust model for writing applications that are easy to maintain. It introduces the JDBC and RMI packages and uses them to develop three-tier applications (applications divided into a user interface, an object-oriented logic component, and an information store). Covers Java 1.1.

How to stay in touch with O'Reilly

1. Visit Our Award-Winning Web Site

http://www.ora.com/

★ "Top 100 Sites on the Web" —*PC Magazine*
★ "Top 5% Web sites" —*Point Communications*
★ "3-Star site" —*The McKinley Group*

Our web site contains a library of comprehensiveproduct information (including book excerpts and tables of contents), downloadable software, background articles, interviews with technology leaders, links to relevant sites, book cover art, and more. File us in your Bookmarks or Hotlist!

2. Join Our Email Mailing Lists

New Product Releases

To receive automatic email with brief descriptions of all new O'Reilly products as they are released, send email to: **listproc@online.ora.com**
Put the following information in the first line of your message (*not* in the Subject field):
subscribe ora-news "Your Name" of "Your Organization" (for example: subscribe ora-news Kris Webber of Fine Enterprises)

O'Reilly Events

If you'd also like us to send information about trade show events, special promotions, and other O'Reilly events, send email to: **listproc@online.ora.com**
Put the following information in the first line of your message (*not* in the Subject field):
subscribe ora-events "Your Name" of "Your Organization"

3. Get Examples from Our Books via FTP

There are two ways to access an archive of example files from our books:

Regular FTP

- ftp to:
  ftp.ora.com
  (login: anonymous
  password: your email address)
- Point your web browser to:
  ftp://ftp.ora.com/

FTPMAIL

- Send an email message to:
  ftpmail@online.ora.com
  (Write "help" in the message body)

4. Visit Our Gopher Site

- Connect your gopher to:
  gopher.ora.com

- Point your web browser to:
  gopher://gopher.ora.com/

- Telnet to:
  gopher.ora.com
  login: gopher

5. Contact Us via Email

order@ora.com
To place a book or software order online. Good for North American and international customers.

subscriptions@ora.com
To place an order for any of our newsletters or periodicals.

books@ora.com
General questions about any of our books.

software@ora.com
For general questions and product information about our software. Check out O'Reilly Software Online at **http://software.ora.com/** for software and technical support information. Registered O'Reilly software users send your questions to: **website-support@ora.com**

cs@ora.com
For answers to problems regarding your order or our products.

booktech@ora.com
For book content technical questions or corrections.

proposals@ora.com
To submit new book or software proposals to our editors and product managers.

international@ora.com
For information about our international distributors or translation queries. For a list of our distributors outside of North America check out:
http://www.ora.com/www/order/country.html

O'Reilly & Associates, Inc.
101 Morris Street, Sebastopol, CA 95472 USA
TEL   707-829-0515 or 800-998-9938
        (6am to 5pm PST)
FAX   707-829-0104

O'REILLY™

TO ORDER: **800-998-9938** • **order@ora.com** • **http://www.ora.com/**
OUR PRODUCTS ARE AVAILABLE AT A BOOKSTORE OR SOFTWARE STORE NEAR YOU.
FOR INFORMATION: **800-998-9938** • **707-829-0515** • **info@ora.com**

International Distributors

UK, Europe, Middle East and Northern Africa (except France, Germany, Switzerland, & Austria)

INQUIRIES

International Thomson Publishing Europe
Berkshire House
168-173 High Holborn
London WC1V 7AA, United Kingdom
Telephone: 44-171-497-1422
Fax: 44-171-497-1426
Email: itpint@itps.co.uk

ORDERS

International Thomson Publishing Services, Ltd.
Cheriton House, North Way
Andover, Hampshire SP10 5BE, United Kingdom
Telephone: 44-264-342-832
 (UK orders)
Telephone: 44-264-342-806
 (outside UK)
Fax: 44-264-364418 (UK orders)
Fax: 44-264-342761 (outside UK)
UK & Eire orders: itpuk@itps.co.uk
International orders: itpint@itps.co.uk

France

Editions Eyrolles
61 bd Saint-Germain
75240 Paris Cedex 05
France
Fax: 33-01-44-41-11-44

FRENCH LANGUAGE BOOKS

All countries except Canada
Phone: 33-01-44-41-46-16
Email: geodif@eyrolles.com

ENGLISH LANGUAGE BOOKS

Phone: 33-01-44-41-11-87
Email: distribution@eyrolles.com

Australia

WoodsLane Pty. Ltd.
7/5 Vuko Place, Warriewood NSW 2102
P.O. Box 935, Mona Vale NSW 2103
Australia
Telephone: 61-2-9970-5111
Fax: 61-2-9970-5002
Email: info@woodslane.com.au

Germany, Switzerland, and Austria

INQUIRIES

O'Reilly Verlag
Balthasarstr. 81
D-50670 Köln
Germany
Telephone: 49-221-97-31-60-0
Fax: 49-221-97-31-60-8
Email: anfragen@oreilly.de

ORDERS

International Thomson Publishing
Königswinterer Straße 418
53227 Bonn, Germany
Telephone: 49-228-97024 0
Fax: 49-228-441342
Email: order@oreilly.de

Asia (except Japan & India)

INQUIRIES

International Thomson Publishing Asia
60 Albert Street #15-01
Albert Complex
Singapore 189969
Telephone: 65-336-6411
Fax: 65-336-7411

ORDERS

Telephone: 65-336-6411
Fax: 65-334-1617
thomson@signet.com.sg

New Zealand

WoodsLane New Zealand Ltd.
21 Cooks Street (P.O. Box 575)
Wanganui, New Zealand
Telephone: 64-6-347-6543
Fax: 64-6-345-4840
Email: info@woodslane.com.au

Japan

O'Reilly Japan, Inc.
Kiyoshige Building 2F
12-Banchi, Sanei-cho
Shinjuku-ku
Tokyo 160 Japan
Telephone: 81-3-3356-5227
Fax: 81-3-3356-5261
Email: kenji@ora.com

India

Computer Bookshop (India) PVT. LTD.
190 Dr. D.N. Road, Fort
Bombay 400 001
India
Telephone: 91-22-207-0989
Fax: 91-22-262-3551
Email: cbsbom@giasbm01.vsnl.net.in

The Americas

O'Reilly & Associates, Inc.
101 Morris Street
Sebastopol, CA 95472 U.S.A.
Telephone: 707-829-0515
Telephone: 800-998-9938 (U.S. & Canada)
Fax: 707-829-0104
Email: order@ora.com

Southern Africa

International Thomson Publishing
Southern Africa
Building 18, Constantia Park
138 Sixteenth Road
P.O. Box 2459
Halfway House, 1685 South Africa
Telephone: 27-11-805-4819
Fax: 27-11-805-3648